Peterson's CULINARY SCHOOLS & PROGRAMS

12th Edition

PETERSON'S
A nelnet COMPANY

PETERSON'S

A nelnet COMPANY

About Peterson's

To succeed on your lifelong educational journey, you will need accurate, dependable, and practical tools and resources. That is why Peterson's is everywhere education happens. Because whenever and however you need education content delivered, you can rely on Peterson's to provide the information, know-how, and guidance to help you reach your goals. Tools to match the right students with the right school. It's here. Personalized resources and expert guidance. It's here. Comprehensive and dependable education content—delivered whenever and however you need it. It's all here.

For more information, contact Peterson's, 2000 Lenox Drive, Lawrenceville, NJ 08648; 800-338-3282; or find us on the World Wide Web at www.petersons.com/about.

Stephen Clemente, President; Fern A. Oram, Content Director; Bernadette Webster, Operations Director; Roger S. Williams, Sales and Marketing; Laura J. Paul, Editor; Mark D. Snider, Production Editor; Steve Sauermelch, Research Project Manager; Phyllis Johnson, Programmer; Ray Golaszewski, Manufacturing Manager; Linda M. Williams, Composition Manager; Janet Garwo, Mimi Kaufman, Karen Mount, Danielle Vreeland, Client Relations Representatives

ISBN-13: 978-0-7689-2548-7
ISBN-10: 0-7689-2548-7

Printed in the United States of America

10 9 8 7 6 5 4 3 2 1 11 10 09

Twelfth Edition

CONTENTS

A NOTE FROM THE PETERSON'S EDITORS

For more than ten years, Peterson's has given students and parents the most comprehensive, up-to-date information on culinary institutions in the United States and abroad. *Peterson's Culinary Schools & Programs* features advice and tips on the culinary school search and selection process, such as how to choose and pay for a cooking school and how to then make the most of your culinary career.

Opportunities abound for culinary students, and this guide can help you find what you want in a number of ways:

- For advice and guidance in the culinary school search and selection process, just turn the page to our **So You Want a Career in the Culinary Arts** section. Providing insight into how to know which school is right for you and why, "Get Cooking!" explains the increasingly important role a cooking school education has in a cooking career. Wondering how you'll pay? "Paying for Your Culinary Education" has all the tips and answers so that you'll wonder no more! "Charting a Successful Culinary Career" answers that burning question: What can I do with a cooking degree besides open a restaurant? Finally, "Culinary Apprenticeships" outlines the benefits of this exciting training option.
- You'll then want to read through "How to Use This Guide," which explains the information presented in the individual culinary school profiles, lists culinary degree and certificate acronyms, and defines how we collect our data.
- Up next is the **Quick-Reference Chart**, where programs are listed geographically, and you can see, at a glance, the areas of specialization (culinary arts, baking and pastry, management) and the credentials they offer. You can also see if programs offer apprenticeships.
- Following that are the **Profiles of Professional Programs** and **Profiles of Apprenticeship Programs.** Here you'll find our unparaleled culinary program descriptions, arranged

alphabetically by state and by country. They provide a complete picture of need-to-know information about culinary schools and apprenticeship programs, including program affiliation, areas of study, facilities, student and faculty profiles, expenses, and financial aid and housing availability. All the information you need to apply is placed together at the conclusion of each profile.

- If you already have specifics in mind, turn to the **Indexes.** Here you can search for a culinary school based on the certificate, diploma, or degree programs it offers. If you already have schools in mind that pique your interest, you can use the Alphabetical Listing of Schools and Programs index to search for these schools.

Peterson's publishes a full line of resources to help guide you through the culinary school admissions process. Peterson's publications can be found at your local bookstore or library and at your high school guidance office; you can access us online at www.petersons.com.

We welcome any comments or suggestions you may have about this publication and invite you to complete our online survey at www.petersons.com/booksurvey. Your feedback will help us make your educational dreams possible.

Schools will be pleased to know that Peterson's helped you in your selection. Admissions staff members are more than happy to answer questions, address specific problems, and help in any way they can. The editors at Peterson's wish you great success in your culinary school search!

SO YOU WANT A CAREER IN THE CULINARY ARTS

GET COOKING!

What You Need to Know About Your Culinary Education

Selecting the finest ingredients. Combining them into a symphony of flavor. Presenting a culinary masterpiece. When preparing a meal feels less like work and more like a labor of love, you've found your calling.

And so have millions of like-minded culinary artists in the foodservice industry. According to the National Restaurant Association, foodservice employs 12.8 million people, making it the second-largest employer in the United States, behind the U.S. Government. That number is projected to grow to 14.8 million by 2017. Given its size, the industry can offer a substantial number of jobs, including a variety of positions in food preparation. But only the crème de la crème can snag the most coveted slots.

So how can you rise to the top?

It takes more than just talent and passion to make a good chef great. Much like stock forms the base of any good soup, a formal culinary education provides a solid foundation of knowledge on which to build your career. You'll find that what you learn in cooking school you can use throughout your life, whether you graduated fifteen years, fifteen months, or 15 minutes ago.

Lots of successful chefs have built culinary empires without the help of institutional training. But even the most seasoned professionals who didn't attend cooking school recommend that aspiring chefs enroll in a culinary program. And if you're already a foodservice professional, a culinary education will complement your experience in the industry.

In an increasingly competitive field, you need all the advantages you can get and culinary education provides the knowledge that experience alone doesn't give you. With the rigors of daily restaurant life, you'll have little time to learn a lot on the job. When you enroll in a cooking school, however, you can tailor your curriculum to a narrow focus, so you can spend your time gaining expertise in the area where your interests lie.

Culinary school exposes you to a wide variety of relevant information, such as theory, international cuisine, and techniques. You'll get to apply what you learn in the classroom to what you do in the kitchen, working with experienced chefs and state-of-the-art equipment. You'll repeat basic and advanced cooking skills until you've mastered them, an opportunity that the real world can't always offer you. Then, you'll get to use your skills in professional kitchens;

most cooking-school programs require hands-on training, usually in partnership with local restaurants.

Just by completing a program, you show potential employers that you're dedicated and hard working. Best of all, you'll get to spend time doing what you love to do—namely, expressing your creative culinary self.

FINDING THE RIGHT FIT

Some institutes offer programs leading to associate or bachelor's degrees in such fields as culinary arts, pastry and baking arts, and culinary management, to name a few. Completing a degree program normally takes between two and four years. Although it can be an investment in both time and money, you do earn college-level credit in a degree program. Other institutions offer certificates and diplomas, which take less time to finish, usually between two and ten months, but do not grant you college credit.

Discovering your options and narrowing the field are essential to getting into the program that's best for you. First, figure out what you want to do. Is baking your calling, or do you prefer contemporary French cuisine? Find schools that offer your specialty. A great place to start your search is by asking chefs in your area for recommendations. The Internet also provides an easy way to gather copious amounts of information on programs that fit your needs.

Once you've compiled your list of schools, gather as much information as you can from their Web sites, brochures, viewbooks, and other materials. Talk to faculty members and students at each institution to see whether you'd be a good fit with the program. If you can, spend a day—and even sit in on a class or two—at your top prospective schools.

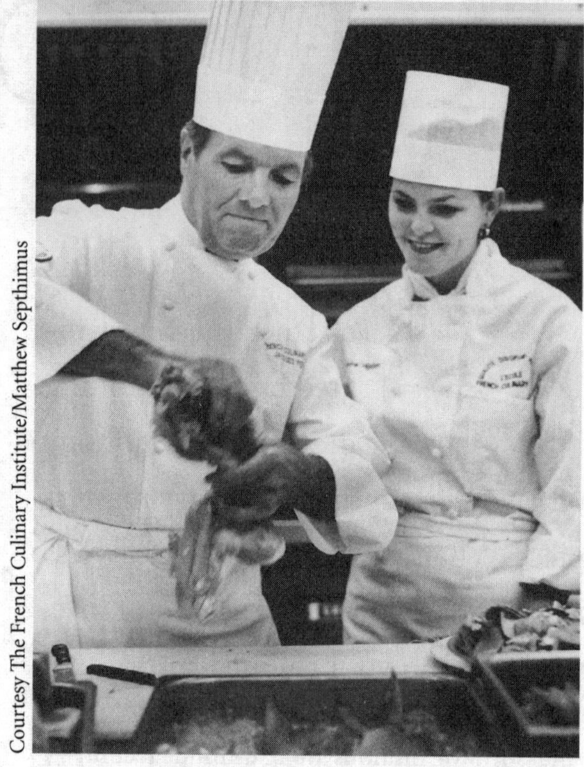

Courtesy The French Culinary Institute/Matthew Septhimus

Now that you've got your short list of programs, how do you choose? It's important to keep these factors in mind:

- Is the school accredited? By whom?
- Where is it located?
- Does the program suit your interests?
- What are the curriculum's requirements? What kind of classes will you take?
- When are classes held? Are there flexible scheduling options?
- Must students get practical experience, for example, in an externship? If so, do students earn credit for it?
- Are study-abroad opportunities offered?
- What facilities—classrooms, libraries, computers, and, most important, kitchen equipment—are available for student use?
- What are the current students like?

- How big are the classes? What is the student-faculty ratio?
- Are there job-placement and other career services available?
- Where do the program's alumni work? Are they successful?
- How much does the program cost?

Culinary programs can range between $15,000 and $30,000, depending on the school and type of program. The total cost, however, includes more than just tuition; you'll have to figure in fees, room and board, books and other supplies, and travel expenses. But don't be intimidated by the price tag—need- and merit-based financial aid can help you manage the cost. If you're willing to do a little digging, you can find several culinary scholarship opportunities online and through schools, businesses, and charitable foundations, among other places. As with most scholarships, it's best to apply for them as soon as possible. Contact the financial aid departments at your prospective schools to find out what aid opportunities are available to you and how and when to apply.

ENTRÉE

Admission requirements vary widely, depending on the program. Some schools simply ask you to fill out an application form and pay a fee, while others will also require you to have an interview and submit high school and/or college transcripts, test scores, essays, a resume, letters of recommendation, and a work sample. Typically, degree programs have more demanding application requirements than certificate or diploma programs.

Application questions might try to determine your background; whether you've traveled and, if so, where; what research you've conducted on the industry (e.g., through attending lectures or reading literature); why you're interested in the culinary arts; and, perhaps most revealing, why you've chosen to apply to a particular school. Be sure to answer honestly yet succinctly and show that you've done your homework. This is your chance to demonstrate your commitment to the program.

If you're interested in a competitive school, remember that not everyone gets in, so find ways to set yourself apart. Stick closely to application requirements, especially the deadlines. Get some work experience before you apply, even if it's just a summer stint at a neighborhood cafe. Play up your experience in other fields as well, since it can show that you're ready for the demands of education.

Don't forget that having some work experience before applying to any school can never hurt; it can be helpful in finding out whether this is truly what you want to do—and whether you're cut out for it.

As with financial aid opportunities, it is imperative to apply to any program as early as possible. A timely application can't hurt your chances of getting in.

EARNING YOUR TOQUE BLANCHE

Your hard work may have paid off once your acceptance letter finally arrives, but you've only really just started. School can be rigorous and rewarding. You'll quickly learn that the glamorous image of the chef so often portrayed in pop culture isn't entirely accurate—if your work experience hasn't already showed you this reality. After all, only those who have actually sweated, served, and survived in an actual kitchen know just how intense it can be. Yet you'll find that your sacrifices are worth it if you get to do what you love every day.

Take advantage of every opportunity you come across at school. Read as much as you can so you can stay up-to-date with the latest industry trends. Ask many questions, not just of faculty members, but of your peers as well. Learn as much as possible, especially outside the classroom. Volunteer whenever you can. And get to know your instructors; you can make lasting connections that can help you throughout your professional life.

It's likely you won't have the time—or the energy—to work full-time while you're enrolled in a program, but you should complement your education with more work experience. There are several reasons for this:

- You'll reinforce classroom lessons and apply them in real-world settings.
- You'll retain more of what you're learning.
- You'll see what you're not learning.
- You can pursue other related interests as you discover them.

You don't have to work at the most prestigious place to learn the best lessons. As is true of most anything, what you get out of your experience depends on what you make of it.

Many culinary programs require students to complete an externship, in which they work in a restaurant for a short time to get practical experience. Like internships, externships may be paid or unpaid. Unlike internships, they are much shorter, often only a few weeks. An externship student might do less actual work and more shadowing.

Apply the same research skills you used in your culinary program search to obtain an externship. Scout out several externship possibilities; you can generate leads by speaking to your professors and to chefs. To get the experience you want, offer to work for free if you can afford to do so. Although any work experience is valuable, land an externship at the best place you can. Not only will you gain indispensable

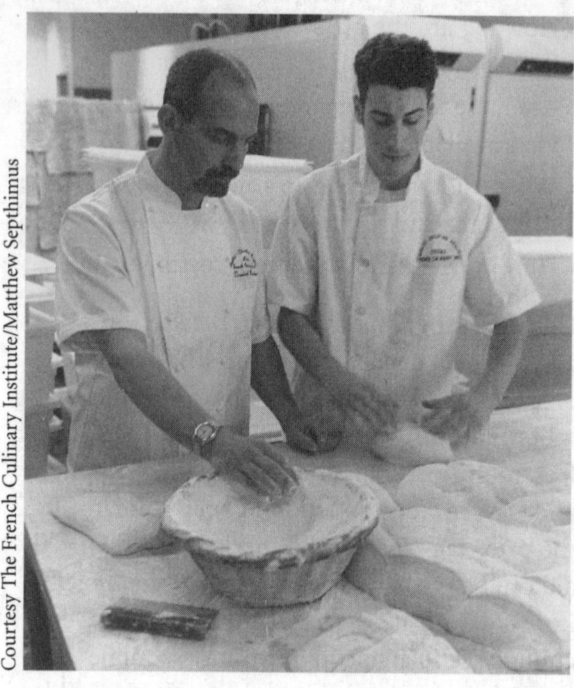

Courtesy The French Culinary Institute/Matthew Septhimus

knowledge, but also you'll have an addition to your resume that can help you nab a great job after graduation. Be sure to demonstrate your solid work ethic while you're on the job—come in early, stay late, get along with your coworkers, and take direction well from your boss. Even if your externship doesn't immediately lead to a post-graduation position, you could still earn glowing recommendations to help you in your job search.

CONTINUALLY REFINING YOUR PALATE

You may find that you discover the most important lessons outside the classroom. And working in foodservice means you'll never stop learning. Graduation is only the beginning. To stay ahead of the curve, you'll need to be proactive about continuing your culinary education, whether with more schooling, more work experience, or both.

For busy adults, many institutions offer for-credit and noncredit continuing education classes; a few culinary schools have continuing education programs for the working chef. In addition, seminars, lectures, and the like—many given by world-renown chefs—can be found everywhere, even in your neighborhood. Check out places like local libraries and schools for more information. Some national associations, such as the American Culinary Federation, have local chapters that can point you in the right direction. If you still can't find anything in your neck of the woods, online education is always an option. Some culinary artists have online tutorials to help you refine your skills, or you can take a formal class through distance learning.

Some culinary experts say, to get the most from your education, don't take a chef position right after graduation—although it's highly unlikely that you'll land such a prestigious position as a newly minted graduate. You'll still have a lot to learn, and your time will be better spent working your way up in the best places possible. Try to work for chefs you admire. Absorb all the information you can. And remember that, even though you don't (and won't) know everything, your talent, passion, and culinary education will blend together nicely in the recipe for your continuing success.

Paying for Your Culinary Education

Madge Griswold

Finding and Applying for Scholarships

Culinary training can be expensive—nearly as expensive as attending a private university and sometimes more expensive than attending a public university. Few prospective students can simply pay the bills from their own savings. Some depend on their parents' generosity to fund their studies. Fortunately, help is available through loans and other financial aid programs and also in the form of scholarships.

Once you have decided which schools are most appealing to you, contact the financial aid office at each to determine exactly what kind of assistance is available. Some schools even have work-study arrangements that allow students to work part-time and study as well.

Financial aid offices at culinary schools administer financial aid programs of various kinds and also provide basic advice about securing education loans. You should consider this advice to be an integral part of your overall career planning. Financing your degree should be viewed as a long-term investment in your professional career. You should understand how this complex system works to be sure you are getting the best deal possible.

You may be eligible for grant assistance if financial need is proved. A grant is an outright award of money, whereas a loan must be paid back. Financial aid officers are more than happy to counsel you about these options.

Scholarship awards are usually based on talent and potential. Financial need may or may not be considered when a scholarship is awarded. Requirements for scholarship candidates are established by the donors of specific scholarships. Scholarships are awarded by culinary schools themselves and also by a number of professional culinary associations. A serious applicant in need of substantial financial assistance should explore all of these avenues. Additional information is provided later in this article, but you should also do your own research using the Web. A good place to start is at Peterson's (www.petersons.com) or at www.finaid.org.

When you plan for your culinary education, you'll want to find the best mix of grants, scholarships, loans, and work-study opportunities. In many cases, loans for education can be used to support a student's whole educational experience, including tuition, room and board, books, tools, and transportation. The financial aid office will put together the best aid "package" to meet your needs. If you feel this aid "package" is not sufficient, you should meet with the aid office either to reexamine your current situation or investigate other alternatives.

Many local community colleges have established fine culinary programs that are considerably cheaper than traditional programs at private institutions. You may want to consider programs at some of the community schools described in this guide. Many schools have excellent reputations locally and offer generous financial aid packages and scholarship assistance. And remember, culinary education is only part of preparing for a career in the culinary field. The rest is *you*—your knowledge, your talents, your creativity, and your overall work experience.

Financial Assistance at a Glance

Grants—*outright awards based on financial need. Ask the financial aid advisers at the schools you are interested in for details.*

Scholarships—*awards for culinary study based on talent or potential for excellence in the culinary field. Scholarships are awarded by both schools and organizations related to the culinary field. If you are interested in applying for culinary scholarships, ask about them when discussing options with the financial aid advisers.*

Loans—*available to persons who qualify for them. Loans, unlike grants and scholarships, must be paid back once you graduate. Ask the financial aid advisers at the schools you are interested in for details or ask about student loans at your local bank.*

Work-Study Programs—*programs that allow students to work while studying. Ask the financial aid advisers at the schools you are interested in whether such programs exist at their institutions and how you can be considered for these worthwhile programs.*

APPLYING FOR SCHOLARSHIPS

Almost all culinary schools award scholarships to truly promising students, so remember to ask for information about each school's requirements. In addition, many organizations associated with the culinary field award scholarships. You will want to begin addressing the scholarship application process even before you send in your admission application because the scholarship process can take longer than the admission process.

Each organization that provides scholarship aid has its own criteria for making awards, its own application process, and its own time frame. Many of these organizations evaluate applications only once a year. Some do it two or three times a year. Some organizations offer scholarships only for specialized kinds of study or to students with specific talents and characteristics. Others administer a broad range of scholarships.

Scholarships awarded by organizations (other than schools) are of two kinds:

1. **Awards for specific schools.** These awards are usually for tuition credit, although occasionally some aid is given for room and board, books, uniforms, or tools.
2. **Awards of a specific cash value that can be used at a variety of institutions.** Awards like these are usually designated by the donors to be applied only against tuition. They cannot be used to help pay for room and board, books, tools, uniforms, or getting to and from school. Cash-value awards generally are paid by the awarding organization directly to the chosen institution. Rarely, if ever, is money paid directly to a student to use as he or she wishes.

Since decisions about scholarship aid are based on the promise of achievement in the culinary field and not just financial need, it's a good idea to think through what kind of impression you want to make on the person or committee who will be evaluating your application. Here are some pointers from an experienced scholarship committee judge:

- Check your spelling carefully. If you are unsure of how to spell a word, look it up in a dictionary. Spelling errors detract from the message you are trying to communicate.
- Fill in all the information and submit all materials requested. You could be disqualified for not following directions.
- Be sure that all materials requested to be sent separately *are* sent separately. Frequently, letters of recommendation are requested separately to give some privacy to the referees and to ensure that they actually are the authors of the letters.
- List all work experience in the culinary field. Culinary work often demands long hours and considerable physical and mental effort. The fact that you have worked in the culinary field and understand the demands of your chosen career is important to judges. If you have done volunteer work in the culinary field, be sure to list that as well.
- Throughout the evaluation process, be prepared to explain your goals in life and your plans for the next few years. Lofty ambitions may be lauded but unrealistic plans are not.
- If you are asked to write an essay, write it yourself. This should be obvious; it's cheating if someone else writes your essay. A reviewer who suspects that you have not written your own essay may disqualify your entire application. Don't try to impress reviewers with flowery language or French culinary terms unless you actually have worked in a French kitchen and need to describe a station or task in French because of it. Don't list impossible or outrageous goals. If you are 18, it's unlikely that in five years you will be the executive chef in a prominent hotel or own your own restaurant. Remember that the readers of your application are food professionals who are well aware of how long it takes to achieve a position in the field and how much it costs to start a restaurant.
- Make your essay original. If you have had unique experiences that have influenced you to become involved in the culinary profession, by all means include them, but don't say that ever since you were a little child you have wanted to

go into the culinary field. It may be true, but it's trite. Tell the reader what is unique and special about you, why you deserve the scholarship, and what it will enable you to do with your life.

THE SCHOLARSHIP INTERVIEW

These interviews can be fun because you may find that you and your interviewer have many experiences and ideas in common. Your interviewer will probably put you at ease quickly. Your interviewer is interested in learning how well you speak and how well you present yourself. Conversation with you will convey to the interviewer how committed you are to your culinary goals and something about yourself other than your culinary side. You might be asked "What do you do when you are not cooking?" Your interviewer will also try to make sure you really understand just what the scholarship can and cannot do for you. Often interviewers act as advisers to candidates, pointing out opportunities they may have overlooked. An interview can be an excellent opportunity for you to present what is unique about you and why you deserve to be given a specific award. Look forward to this opportunity.

SCHOLARSHIP OPPORTUNITIES

In addition to the schools themselves, a number of organizations award scholarships for culinary education. Some organizations give scholarships only for very specific purposes. Others give scholarships only for management training or for graduate work.

American Culinary Federation (ACF)

This long-established association of professional cooks has a membership of more than 19,000 and more than 230 chapters in many cities. In addition to its apprenticeship program, which provides an excellent alternate approach to culinary training, the ACF awards some scholarships on the national level. Contacts at the local level will be able to provide information about any scholarships awarded by a local chapter. For information about a local chapter, contact the ACF at 800-624-9458 Ext. 102. Information about scholarships at the national level may be obtained by calling this number or by writing to:

The American Academy of Chefs
180 Center Place Way
St. Augustine, FL 32095
Phone: 904-824-4468 or
800-624-9458 Ext. 102 (toll-free)
Fax: 904-825-4758
E-mail: academy@acfchefs.net
Web site: www.acfchefs.org

American Dietetic Association (ADA)

This organization is made up of more than 67,000 members, 75 percent of whom are registered dietitians. It only awards scholarships for registered dietitians working toward master's degrees. If you think you are eligible, contact them at:

American Dietetic Association
120 South Riverside Plaza, Suite 2000
Chicago, IL 60606-6995
Phone: 800-877-1600 Ext. 5400 (toll-free)
E-mail: education@eatright.org
Web site: www.eatright.org

The American Institute of Wine & Food (AIWF)

A nonprofit organization created to promote appreciation of wine and food and encourage scholarly education in gastronomy, this more than 4,000-member organization has twenty-five chapters in U.S. cities. Only certain chapters of the AIWF give scholarships for culinary education. Some are administered by the individual chapters; others are administered through the facilities of the International Association of Culinary Professionals (IACP) Foundation scholarship committee. You can reach AIWF at:

The American Institute of Wine & Food
213–37 39th Avenue
Box 216
Bayside, NY 11361
Phone: 800-274-2493 (toll-free)
Fax: 718-522-0204
E-mail: info@aiwf.org
Web site: www.aiwf.org

Careers through Culinary Arts Program, Inc. (C-CAP)

A school-to-work program, established in a number of major metropolitan areas, C-CAP integrates culinary training at the high school level with work and business experience. C-CAP provides awards and scholarships ranging from $1000 to full tuition and assists students in making college and career choices. If you are a high school student, ask your guidance counselor if there is a C-CAP program in your area and how you might participate.

Careers through Culinary Arts Program, Inc.
250 West 57th Street, Suite 2015
New York, NY 10107
Phone: 212-974-7111
Fax: 212-974-7117
E-mail: info@ccapinc.org
Web site: www.ccapinc.org

Confrérie de la Chaîne des Rôtisseurs

A long-established organization for promoting appreciation of fine food and wine, this society has members in more than seventy countries and has granted more than $2 million in scholarships to more than sixty qualifying schools since 1996. Scholarships are established directly with culinary schools. Interested candidates should ask financial aid officers at specific schools about these awards.

Confrérie de la Chaîne des Rôtisseurs
Chaîne House at Fairleigh Dickinson University
285 Madison Avenue
Madison, NJ 07940-1099
Phone: 973-360-9200
Fax: 973-360-9330
E-mail: chaine@chaineus.org
Web site: www.chaineus.org

The Culinary Trust

This charitable and educational affiliate of the International Association of Culinary Professionals has, as one of its functions, the administration of scholarships that provide either tuition-credit assistance at specific institutions or financial assistance that can be applied to a variety of institutions. The Culinary Trust scholarship committee awards scholarships on an annual cycle, with an application deadline of December 15 for scholarships beginning the following July 1. Interested applicants should consult The Culinary Trust office, since deadlines sometimes change. Contact them at:

The Culinary Trust
P.O. Box 273
New York, NY 10013
Phone: 646-224-6989 or 888-345-4666 (toll-free)
E-mail: info@theculinarytrust.com/
Web site: www.theculinarytrust.com

International Foodservice Editorial Council (IFEC)

Dedicated to the improvement of media communications quality in the food field, this small organization of food service magazine editors and public relations executives awards between four and six scholarships annually to persons seeking careers that combine food service and communications.

IFEC
P.O. Box 491
Hyde Park, NY 12538
Phone: 845-229-6973
Fax: 845-229-6993
E-mail: ifec@ifeconline.com
Web site: www.ifeconline.com

International Food Service Executives Association (IFSEA)

A long-established educational and community service association, this group provides some scholarships of its own and also provides information about scholarships offered by other organizations.

IFSEA
8155 Briar Cliff Drive
Castle Pines North, CO 80108-8215
Phone: 720-733-8001 or
800-893-5499 (toll-free)
Fax: 720-733-8999
Web site: www.ifsea.com

The James Beard Foundation

This prominent organization of food professionals, devoted to the ideals and principles of legendary American cook and writer James Beard, awards a number of substantial scholarships each year. The application deadline is usually in May.

Educational and Community
Programming
The James Beard Foundation
6 West 18th Street, 10th Floor
New York, NY 10011
Phone: 212-627-1128
Fax: 212-627-1064
E-mail: scholarships@jamesbeard.org
Web site: www.jamesbeard.org

Les Dames d'Escoffier International (LDEI)

This association has chapters in many major cities. One of its major purposes is the creation and awarding of scholarships to assist women with culinary training. These scholarships are awarded directly by the chapters. Women who are interested in applying for such scholarships should contact LDEI's executive director, Greg Jewell, at ldei@aecmanagement.com, or visit their Web site at www.ldei.org.

National Restaurant Association Educational Foundation

An educational organization that produces a variety of courses, video training sessions, seminars, and other educational opportunities for persons in the hospitality industry, this group also offers scholarships.

National Restaurant Association
Educational Foundation
175 West Jackson Boulevard, Suite 1500
Chicago, IL 60604-2702
Phone: 312-715-1010 (Chicagoland) or
800-765-2122 (toll-free)
E-mail: info@restaurant.org/
Web site: www.nraef.org

Women Chefs & Restaurateurs (WCR)

An association specifically designed to promote the education and advancement of women in the culinary profession and to promote the industry overall, the WCR distributes more than $100,000 to its members for professional development. For further information, contact them at:

Women Chefs & Restaurateurs
455 South Fourth Street, Suite 650
Louisville, KY 40202
Phone: 502-581-0300 or
877-927-7787 (toll-free)
Fax: 502-589-3602
E-mail: wcr@hqtrs.com
Web site: www.womenchefs.org

Madge Griswold, CCP, is an author and culinary historian, past Chairman of the Board of Trustees of the International Association of Culinary Professionals Foundation, founding Chairman of the American Institute of Wine & Food's Baja Arizona chapter, and a member of the James Beard Foundation. Among her publications are two sections of Culinaria: The United States, A Culinary Discovery, *Cologne: Könemann. She is a member of the editorial advisory board of the journal* Gastronomica.

CHARTING A SUCCESSFUL CULINARY CAREER

Barbara Sims-Bell

What Can You Do with a Cooking Degree (besides open a restaurant)?

You love to cook; garlic essence smells better to you than an expensive French perfume; your friends and family say you should have a restaurant (well, maybe not your family); and right now you're seriously studying the choice of the best culinary training you can afford to allow you to live your dream. But it is never too early to contemplate the future, to think about opportunities that will come along after culinary training.

Chef, caterer, pastry cook, and restaurant cook are merely the most familiar four; there are hundreds of jobs in the food industry. You may want to consider preparing for positions in management as executive chef, or sales as catering director, or administration in food and beverage management. Maybe you'll want to explore developing specialty products—a line of sauces, dressings, or convenience foods, for example—for retail or wholesale markets. There are also teaching opportunities in professional cooking schools (possibly even the one you choose to attend). Others set out to become a restaurant consultant to entrepreneurs who want to start a restaurant or improve the one they own. Still another option is food writing and editing for magazines and books devoted to food and cooking.

For any of these career directions, you'll find the best and the broadest preparation in an accredited school program. You will come out with a certificate or a degree, and forever after when you are asked, "Where did you get your training?" you can refer to an accepted and respected credential in professional cooking. This training provides you with a lifelong basis for understanding quality raw ingredients, creating balance and pleasure in combined flavors, and presenting a beautiful plate to the diner.

Yes, you keep learning, but culinary school gives you a base of knowledge to test and compare to new trends, new ingredients, and your own creativity.

WHERE CAN I GO FROM HERE?

When most culinary students start their training, they believe they have found the work they want to do for the rest of their lives—and many are right. But some are surprised when they find so much routine and boredom and repetitive tasks. You haven't seen appetizers until you've assembled 3,000 identical stuffed puffs for a hotel reception. House salad? You'll clean and prep cases of the same greens and garnishes day after day. And the signature white chocolate mousse and meringue dacquoise layers you always wanted to perfect? You'll be preparing untold orders for it every evening. You have to love it.

If managerial positions are more to your liking, you'll need more than cooking skills. Managers create the working environment for the staff, often developing a sixth sense to recognize problems before they erupt. They are the motivational force that drives the staff. They must understand finance and business reports and their implications. They must have highly sensitive character judgment and the ability to manage people from hiring to mentoring to firing.

If your interests take you into catering and sales, think about these skills: You'll need to be able to research a product and explore your market. You'll need to really enjoy being with people. You'll need to draw on strong self-esteem to hear "no" and not take it personally. You'll need internal discipline to keep the work flowing. You'll need communication skills to persuade people that your product is best. And you'll need to be strongly motivated to make a sale.

WHERE DO I FIT?

To choose a career path that seems right for you, you'll need to define your own personality profile, whether it gives you the skills you need if you want to move higher or take a detour and move sideways. Or do you need to add some skills that you haven't yet developed?

One approach is to see a qualified career counselor for an evaluation of your strengths and weaknesses. Even if you reject or overrule the findings, you may gain an understanding of yourself that you didn't have before. Career testing extracts from us an inventory of our preferences.

Professional career counselors have the training, experience, and credentials to help you explore some of the possible choices that tempt you. They use finely tuned tests, such as Myers-Briggs, Holland, and Strong Interest. Then they interpret the test reports to give you additional guidance, either to follow your obvious bent or to stretch yourself into other areas with training and exploration. As in everything, there are quacks and there are bona fide wizards. The best course is to check the credentials of anyone you're considering.

Whether or not you seek outside career guidance, you should do some soul-searching on your own. Take stock of who you are. What are your best skills? Break them down into culinary, service, finance, research, communication, and management. Some of the categories will be longer than others; that tells you where you've placed your learning emphasis and where you'll have to work a bit harder. Think about your lifestyle and workplace values. Is independence something you seek, or do routine and stability matter more? Are you aiming for wealth or is leisure time now more important? Another significant list is what leisure activities you enjoy the most, then rating them by cost, whether they are solitary or social activities, and whether you've been able to fit them into your life lately. Are you a risk taker or do you proceed with caution? Even the most cautious of us can be successful entrepreneurs, but your own slant between these two types is important for you to know.

GETTING THE WHOLE CULINARY PICTURE

An easy and enjoyable way to learn about the spectrum of food-related jobs is by joining one or more professional organizations. Among the largest are the American Culinary Federation (ACF) and the International Association of Culinary Professionals (IACP). There are regional culinary groups—guilds, societies, alliances—in many large urban areas, and if the school you choose doesn't have the information, someone at IACP headquarters will be able to give you a current name and address near you to contact. Even if you are not yet a bona fide culinarian, as soon as you are enrolled in a professional program, you can usually join in the student-member category—at a lower annual dues rate. Most organizations allow guests to come to their meetings and programs—a good way to get connected and see if you feel comfortable in the group before joining.

Among the rewards of joining a local culinary group are developing friendships; meeting potential mentors; learning from varied guest speakers; finding job leads; getting customer referrals when another member is too booked to take the work; learning unrelated skills when you volunteer to work on program, membership, and communication committees; contributing to the community when you volunteer to work on a food-related benefit; and cultivating the lifelong asset of connections.

Take an inventory of people you know who you can call for culinary guidance. Culinary groups provide a wealth of leads and good food and wine to enjoy. Get the name and phone number, call to find out when and where the next meeting will be, and ask if they welcome guests. When you get there tell the greeter "I'm new here; who can I talk to about (baking, catering kitchens, ethnic ingredient stores, this organization, volunteering)"—pick a topic and start listening. Bring your business cards (not having them is unforgivable), give them out, and be sure to take cards from members you meet. Write the date of the meeting and what you talked about on the back before you go to sleep that night. Thus begins the building of a personal network, the invaluable channel to your peers.

The first time I met a friend of mine she was working as a waitress at a sort-of-Italian café where our Roundtable for Women in Foodservice chapter was having a program titled "Networking." I was moderating the panel, and the waitress was mesmerized by the dynamic group of professional women who were the audience. I noticed her enthusiasm, talked to her a bit, and encouraged her to join our chapter. With a university degree in soils science, she was working as a server, she said, "because that is what I like to do more than anything else"—and her people skills were what I continued to notice as she joined the chapter, came to meetings, and changed jobs a few times. Within a year, she was hired by the oldest established winery in our region as Tasting Room

Stephanie Hersh

Stephanie Hersh defined her career goal of being a pastry chef at the age of 6 with the gift of a Betty Crocker Easy-Bake Oven. It was simplistic cause and effect: She produced the sweet offerings from batters, and everyone fluttered around telling her she was "terrific." She figured this could last her whole lifetime if she just kept on making cake. Her granny lived nearby and regularly let the diminutive yet determined youngster bake alongside her, making family desserts and good, sweet stuff.

Her parents were harder nuts to crack, insisting on scholastic accomplishment, first in her private high school, then in a four-year college. Looking back, she thinks it was the best for her because she "needed to grow up before going to culinary school." She worked part-time in restaurants, both front of the house and back, making some headway in the cooking hierarchy as she became more experienced. The work was everything she dreamed: It gave her pleasure, satisfaction, self-esteem, and self-confidence. Her personality drove her to "always be the best," and she knew that to be the best she had to have professional training. The restaurant business was changing at that time, and she knew it would no longer be possible to work up in kitchens from dishwasher to executive chef. Restaurant owners were hiring the applicants with the best culinary education. In 1985, Stephanie graduated from The Culinary Institute of America in Hyde Park, New York.

Her first professional job as a hotel pastry chef in Boston was a rude awakening. For the first time, pastries became work to do and get done, and it wasn't fun. She still had her pastry shop dream, and to feed her savings faster she devised a dual plan, based on her new goals—"I just wanted to cook and enjoy it and make money." Stephanie took a job as a private chef, live-in, for a small family with 2 professional working parents and 2 children. With her daytimes freed up, she enrolled at Katharine Gibbs School, figuring she could still be a private chef and work days as a secretary, with almost no living expenses. Then something happened.

Julia Child phoned the school asking if they had a graduate to recommend, commenting that it would be nice if the person knew something about cooking. When they described Stephanie's culinary background, she turned her down, saying that she really wanted a secretary, not a chef. Stephanie was in the school office when it happened and asked permission to call Julia back so she could press her case for herself. There was serious persuasion involved on Stephanie's part, but the statement was repeated: "I just want a secretary; I don't need anyone to work in my kitchen." Stephanie agreed that she just wanted to be a secretary. The next morning, minutes after arriving at the Cambridge house, Stephanie was in the kitchen prepping three recipes for demonstration stages and cooking aromatic fish stew for serving. Julia had forgotten she had agreed to a television taping/interview and greeted Stephanie with a fistful of recipe copies and almost no instruction except "just wiggle a finger at me when you've got it all ready," while she went back to the camera crew.

Suddenly Stephanie Hersh was an administrator, a facilitator, an essential sidekick, and accepted—smack, dab, in the center of the high-profile food industry. She loved her job. Her schooling continued, and, with Julia's encouragement, Stephanie was the first graduate in Boston University's master's program in gastronomy. She later ran her own business, Chef Steph, through which she sold cakes and pastries and organized cooking parties for children. An active member of International Association of Culinary Professionals (IACP), Hersh lives and works in New Zealand.

Manager and then became its local Sales Manager. Her education in soils and geology gave her a head start in understanding wine production for her job. "Who you know" only opens the door, but "what you know" gets you the job.

TRAVEL STAGES FOR A CAREER

If you have already identified some role models in the food industry and have learned a little about their lives and careers, you know that a long stretch of steady, hard work is the story of their success. We can divide that stretch into sections, though, and understand ways that your own success can be realized.

Beginner

Focus on a career plan for yourself as early as you can. You will make changes, take detours, and acquire unrelated skills that you want to use, but having a predetermined route tells you whether you're lost or just on a scenic loop. Use the professional network you are gathering right away. At first that may be primarily your fellow students and your teachers, but they are an important network for you to maintain. How do you use them? As questions arise in your mind, ask "Whom do I know who might answer this?" Make contact with the person, ask your questions, strengthen your bond. Ask your teachers and your mentors about industry conferences and trade shows you can attend, and make an effort to go. The more you know what is going on in the food industry, the better you can steer yourself to success. Donate your time and skills to publicized events—does your school or your restaurant put on fund-raisers for community projects? Volunteer to assist, to cook, to serve, or to do whatever is needed and talk to your peers

Courtesy The French Culinary Institute/Matthew Septhimus

at the event. Remember, always take your business cards and give them out as you are collecting new ones. Write on the backs! As soon as you become a "head chef"—whether in your own restaurant or as an employee—create some public appearance opportunities for yourself. Participate in community benefits that feature a group of local chefs providing the food. If you are developing a product through the restaurant or on your own, find opportunities to have guests taste it at local events. If you author a cookbook, offer to do book signings at local bookstores. Work closely with your culinary peers, participate in public events as much as possible, and barter your services for product. Keep your name out there, and it will become your billboard.

Intermediate

This is the stage to position yourself for publicity. The first step is to run your business (whether self-owned or profit-sharing status) so well you can be absent on tour. Go to Beard House dinners in New York City, and talk to them about scheduling you to cook one. Contact the nearest chapter of the American Institute of Wine & Food and ask if it will set up a program using you as a guest chef. Develop your public speaking skills; if you need help with public speaking, contact your local adult education program for workshops and local coaches. The better you can hold your audience's attention while you speak (and this includes table side in your restaurant), the more you will promote your success. As soon as you are confident speaking to medium-size groups (50 to 200 people) and have something to talk about, offer to be a speaker at professional conferences: the American Culinary Federation, the International Association of Culinary Professionals, and regional culinary organizations. After a few more experiences, and when word of your entertainment value gets around, you will be paid travel and lodging expenses to be a speaker (and in time you'll be paid an honorarium, as well). At this midcareer stage, you can search out ways to market your name, and offers will come to you unsolicited: consider allowing your name to be used on aprons or chef's clothing labels (this can be either your own merchandise line or the use of your name). Newcomers to the restaurant business looking for help and advice may turn to you, and you can decide whether to give it freely or charge as a consultant (probably a little of both, depending on the circumstances). By now, you recognize the need for a support network to help you manage some of these outside activities: a lawyer, an accountant, a marketing assistant, and possibly a booking agent. Don't sit back thinking that when you need them they will be there. As with everything, you have to look ahead and look out for yourself.

Advanced

If you're doing it right, now is the stage to get paid for having fun. If you still want to cook, you'll be doing it, probably with one or two trained cooks behind you so you can take care of the peripheral business you've created. Here are some ways you'll find to stimulate your creative juices and make money at the same time: You'll be paid an honorarium and expenses as a speaker. You'll be recruited to head business development teams for other culinary start-ups. You'll be paid for product and service endorsements. You may spin off your name or your label on merchandise for royalties. You'll attract potential investors and/or buyers for expansion or retirement from your own restaurant or company. If this is fun for you, you'll find the time to do it.

Graduate

This is the time to be a mentor and a philanthropist within your culinary community. When you were a beginner in professional training, your school probably brought in the best local chefs to inspire you. You may have received a culinary scholarship from one of the professional organizations. Now it's your turn to be on the giving side. You'll still get requests to speak and be paid well for most of the gigs, but consider giving some time to smaller groups of the next generation of chefs. The appearances you'll get paid for will be keynoter, industry spokesperson, and expert; consider being on a panel or a roundtable to answer questions one-on-one. You will be offered an investment position in food companies solely as an adviser. The fee you get for endorsements will be higher than ever. To truly be a graduate in this career field, you will consciously find, promote, and mentor promising individuals who can advance the industry in the future. Well done!

KEEPING YOUR OPTIONS OPEN

The future of any career, say, ten or twenty years ahead, is excruciatingly difficult to focus in on. Whether you look through a camera's viewer or through eyeglasses customized to your needs, you make physical adjustments to bring a faraway object into focus.

Once you have chosen a culinary school for your training and started instruction, it's already time to start asking about future opportunities. Bombard your chefs at school with questions about what you need to know for jobs that sound enticing to you. You may not act on that information for several years, but you've started to adjust your focus whenever you gather more knowledge about future opportunities.

The speck on the horizon that is your future career is barely visible now, but as you move toward it or look for it through a magnifier, you will develop your own vision, and it will become excitingly clear to you. Good luck to every one of you.

Barbara Sims-Bell was the founder of and primary instructor at the Santa Barbara Cooking School from 1979 to 1985. She is the author of two books about careers and jobs in the culinary field, Career Opportunities in the Food and Beverage Industry, *New York: Facts on File, 1995, and* FoodWork—Jobs in the Food Industry and How to Get Them, *Santa Barbara, California: Advocacy Press, 1994.*

CULINARY APPRENTICESHIPS

American Culinary Federation

Culinary apprenticeships are on-the-job training programs reinforced by related instruction from educational institutions. Many successful apprenticeship programs offer an associate degree. Apprentices receive years of documented work experience while also receiving an education that is specific to the industry, and apprentice graduates can confidently accept a job based on the experience received during their apprenticeship program. These graduates also receive Certified Cook status through the American Culinary Federation (ACF) National Certification Program. The ultimate designation of Chef comes through additional experience and education.

Experience and Education

The success of apprenticeship comes from the commitment made by the industry chef and management, the education institution, and the American Culinary Federation (local and national). Each of these entities is responsible for maintaining high-quality standards.

Employers of apprentices enjoy the benefit of committed and loyal culinarians who enhance the enthusiasm and positive attitudes of the entire staff. Apprentices enter a kitchen starting at the beginning, giving the supervising chef the unique opportunity to develop a mentorship relationship with the apprentice. The *Training Log* cultivates this relationship by requiring a weekly entry by the apprentice. The supervising chef periodically reviews these entries.

The ACF Apprenticeship Program offers a unique connection between industry and education. The standard curriculum and competencies are delivered by the supervising chef in tandem with the educational institution. An apprenticeship can strengthen many ACF chapters by providing chefs with a purpose: to share their culinary knowledge and expertise.

The ACF Apprenticeship Program began in 1976 with a grant from the United States government. Today, it is one of two programs remaining from that training initiative and is the seventh-largest apprenticeship program in the United States.

Reprinted with the permission of the American Culinary Federation.

HOW TO USE THIS GUIDE

Find the Right Culinary School for You

Peterson's Culinary Schools & Programs is a comprehensive guide to culinary schools in the United States and abroad. The guide provides detailed descriptions of hundreds of professional degree and apprenticeship programs.

QUICK-REFERENCE CHART

The **Quick-Reference Chart** lists programs by state and country, indicates what degrees or awards are offered, shows if apprenticeships are available, and notes if the program offers degree specializations in the areas of culinary arts, baking and pastry, or management. Please be aware that there are other degree specializations, and you will have to refer to individual profiles to discover what an individual program may offer beyond these popular ones.

PROFILES OF PROFESSIONAL PROGRAMS

Peterson's Culinary Schools & Programs profiles are organized into two main sections, each arranged alphabetically by state within the United States and by country. The first section includes profiles of professional programs and the second, profiles of apprenticeship programs.

Professional programs offer formalized instruction in a class setting. A diploma, degree, or certificate is awarded to the student at the end of successful completion of a predetermined curriculum of courses and a minimum number of credit hours. Workplace training in the form of an externship or work-study program may be an option but is not usually required. An apprenticeship is essentially an on-the-job training program. Typical apprenticeship programs entail completion of a specific term of full-time employment for wages in a food service kitchen under a qualified chef. Classroom culinary instruction is usually required in addition to the scheduled work, and a certificate may be awarded.

General Information. Indicates private or public institution, coeducational or single-sex, type of institution, and the campus setting. The founding year of the institution is also listed, as is institutional accreditation information.

Program Information. Indicates the year the program started offering classes, program accreditation, the program calendar (semester, quarter, etc.), the type of degrees and awards offered, degree and award specializations, and the length of time needed to complete the degree or award.

Program Affiliation. Lists those organizations to which the school or program belongs.

Areas of Study. Includes the courses available.

Facilities. Lists the number and types of facilities available to students.

(Typical) Student Profile. Provides the total number of students enrolled in the program and the number who are full-time and part-time and the age range of students.

Faculty. Provides the total number of faculty members, the number who are full-time and part-time, and the number who are culinary accredited, industry professionals, master bakers, or master chefs. The names of prominent faculty members and their degree or certificate level are listed if provided. The faculty-student ratio is also listed.

Prominent Alumni and Current Affiliation. Provides information on notable alumni and the restaurant/hotel/facility with which they are affiliated.

Special Programs. Notes special educational opportunities offered by the program.

Typical Expenses. Includes information on full-time, part-time, in-state, and out-of-state tuition costs; special program-related fees; and application fees. Dollar signs without further notation refer to U.S. currency.

Financial Aid. Provides information on the number and amount of program-specific loans and scholarships awarded during the 2005–06, 2006–07, or 2007–08 academic year and unique financial aid opportunities available to students. (This section covers only culinary-related financial aid and does not include types of financial aid that are open to all students, such as Pell Grants and Stafford Loans.)

Housing. Indicates the type of on-campus housing available, as well as the typical cost of off-campus housing in the area.

Application Information. Provides information on application deadlines, the number of students who applied for admission to the program, and the number of students accepted to the program for the 2005–06, 2006–07, or 2007–08 academic year, and application materials that are required.

Contact. Includes the name, address, telephone and fax numbers, and e-mail address (if provided) of the contact person for the program and the Web address of the program or institution.

PROFILES OF APPRENTICESHIP PROGRAMS

Program Information. Indicates if the apprenticeship program is directly sponsored by a college, university, or culinary institute; if the program is approved by the American Culinary Federation; if an apprentice is eligible to receive a degree from a college or university upon successful completion of the program; and if any special apprenticeships are available.

Placement Information. Provides the number and types of locations where apprentices may be placed and lists the most popular placement locations of participants.

(Typical) Apprentice Profile. Indicates the number of participants, the age range of participants, and the application materials a prospective apprentice must submit.

Typical Expenses. Provides information on the basic costs of participating in the program as well as the application fee and special program-related fees.

Entry-Level Compensation. Indicates the typical salary for an apprentice at the beginning of the apprenticeship program.

Contact. Includes the name, address, telephone and fax numbers, and e-mail address (if provided) of the contact person for the apprenticeship program and the Web address of the program or institution.

INDEXES

Two indexes are available at the end of the book. The first index, Certificate, Diploma, and Degree Programs, lists programs by whether they offer a certificate or diploma or a degree (associate, bachelor's, master's, or doctoral). The second index, Alphabetical Listing of Schools and Programs, is an alphabetical list by name of the program or institution.

CULINARY DEGREES AND CERTIFICATES

Below is a list of degrees and certificates common to the culinary and hospitality industries. You'll often see these acronyms following the names of faculty members to indicate their level of education and certification.

AA	Associate of Arts
AAC	American Academy of Chefs
AAS	Associate of Applied Science
BA	Bachelor of Arts
BS	Bachelor of Science
CAGS	Certificate of Advanced Graduate Study
CC	Certified Culinarian
CCC	Certified Chef de Cuisine
CCE	Certified Culinary Educator
CCM	Certified Club Manager
CCP	Certified Culinary Professional
CDM	Certified Dietary Manager
CDN	Certified Dietetics Nutritionist
CEC	Certified Executive Chef
CEPC	Certified Executive Pastry Chef
CFBE	Certified Food and Beverage Executive
CFBM	Certified Food and Beverage Manager
CFE	Certified Food Executive
CFSC	Certified Food Service Consultant
CFSM	Certified Food Service Manager
CHA	Certified Hotel Administrator
CHAE	Certified Hospitality Accounting Executive
CHE	Certified Hospitality Educator
CHM	Certified Hospitality Manager
CMB	Certified Master Baker
CMC	Certified Master Chef
CMPC	Certified Master Pastry Chef
CPC	Certified Pastry Culinarian
CPCE	Certified Professional Catering Executive
CRDE	Certified Rooms Division Executive
CSC	Certified Sous Chef
CWC	Certified Working Chef
CWPC	Certified Working Pastry Chef
DFS	Doctor of Food Service
DTR	Dietetic Technician, Registered
EdD	Doctor of Education
EPC	Executive Pastry Chef
FADA	Fellow of the American Dietetic Association
FMP	Food Service Management Professional
FCSI	Foodservice Consultants Society International
HRTA	Hotel, Restaurant, and Travel Administration
LD	Licensed Dietitian

LRD	Licensed Registered Dietician
MA	Master of Arts
MBA	Master of Business Administration
MEd	Master of Education
MHRIM	Master of Hotel, Restaurant, and Institutional Management
MOF	Meilleur Ouvrier de France
MPC	Master Pastry Chef
MPH	Master of Public Health
MPS	Master of Professional Studies
MS	Master of Science
MSA	Master of Science in Administration
MSEd	Master of Science in Education
PhD	Doctor of Philosophy
RD	Registered Dietitian
REHS	Registered Environmental Health Specialist

DATA COLLECTION PROCEDURES

Information in this book was collected between summer 2005 and summer 2008 using *Peterson's Survey of Culinary Programs.* Changes may occur after publication, so be sure to contact the institutions directly for the most current information on their programs.

QUICK-REFERENCE CHART

State/School	Credentials Offered	Culinary Arts	Baking and Pastry	Management	Apprenticeship Programs
Alabama					
ACF Greater Montgomery Chapter					■
Alabama Agricultural and Mechanical University	B, M			■	
CULINARD, The Culinary Institute of Virginia College	D	■			
The Gulf Coast Culinary Institute	C, A	■	■	■	
Tuskegee University	B			■	
The University of Alabama	C, B			■	
Alaska					
Alaska Vocational Technical Center/Alaska Culinary Academy	C	■	■		
University of Alaska Anchorage	A, B	■		■	
University of Alaska Fairbanks	C, A	■	■		
Arizona					
Arizona Culinary Institute	D	■	■	■	
Arizona Western College	C, A	■		■	
Central Arizona College	C, A	■		■	
Chefs Association of Southern Arizona, Tucson					■
The International Culinary School at The Art Institute of Phoenix	A, B	■	■		
The International Culinary School at The Art Institute of Tucson	A, B	■	■		

Credentials: ***C*** *= Certificate;* ***D*** *= Diploma;* ***A*** *= Associate Degree;* ***B*** *= Bachelor's Degree;* ***M*** *= Master's Degree;* ***Ph.D.*** *= Doctorate*

State/School	Credentials Offered	Culinary Arts	Baking and Pastry	Management	Apprenticeship Programs
Maricopa Skill Center	C				
Northern Arizona University	C, B	■		■	
Pima Community College	C, A	■			
Scottsdale Community College	C, A	■		■	
Scottsdale Culinary Institute	C, A, B	■	■	■	
Arkansas					
Ozarka College	C, A	■			
Pulaski Technical College Arkansas Culinary School	C, A	■	■		
University of Arkansas at Pine Bluff	B			■	
California					
American River College	C, A	■	■	■	
Barona Valley Ranch Resort & Casino					■
Bauman College: Holistic Nutrition & Culinary Arts–Berkeley	C				
Bauman College: Holistic Nutrition & Culinary Arts–Penngrove	C				
Bauman College: Holistic Nutrition & Culinary Arts–Santa Cruz	C				
California Culinary Academy	C, A	■	■	■	
California School of Culinary Arts	D, A	■	■	■	
California State Polytechnic University, Pomona	B			■	
Chef Eric's Culinary Classroom	C	■	■		

State/School	Credentials Offered	Culinary Arts	Baking and Pastry	Management	Apprenticeship Programs
California *(continued)*					
Chef Is Chef Culinary School	C				
City College of San Francisco	A	■		■	
College of the Canyons	A			■	
Contra Costa College	C, A	■	■		
The Culinary Institute of America	C, A	■	■		
Epicurean School of Culinary Arts	C		■		
Institute of Technology	C, D	■	■		
Institute of Technology–Modesto	C, D	■	■		
Institute of Technology–Roseville	C, D	■	■		
The International Culinary School at The Art Institute of California–Inland Empire	A, B	■		■	
The International Culinary School at The Art Institute of California–Los Angeles	D, A, B	■	■	■	
The International Culinary School at The Art Institute of California–Orange County	D, A, B	■	■	■	
The International Culinary School at The Art Institute of California–Sacramento	D, A, B	■	■	■	
The International Culinary School at The Art Institute of California–San Diego	A, B	■	■	■	
The International Culinary School at The Art Institute of California–San Francisco	A, B	■		■	
The International Culinary School at The Art Institute of California–Sunnyvale	A, B	■		■	
JobTrain	C	■			
Kitchen Academy	D	■			

Credentials: ***C*** *= Certificate;* ***D*** *= Diploma;* ***A*** *= Associate Degree;* ***B*** *= Bachelor's Degree;* ***M*** *= Master's Degree;* ***Ph.D.*** *= Doctorate*

State/School	Credentials Offered	Culinary Arts	Baking and Pastry	Management	Apprenticeship Programs
Kitchen Academy–Sacramento	D	■			
Lake Tahoe Community College	C, A	■	■		
Long Beach City College	C, A	■	■	■	
Mission College	C, A			■	
Modesto Junior College	C, A	■			
Monterey Peninsula College	C, A		■	■	
Mt. San Antonio College	C, A			■	
Napa Valley College	C	■			
National Culinary and Bakery School	C	■	■		
The New School of Cooking	D	■	■		
Orange Coast College	C, A	■		■	
Oxnard College	C, A	■		■	
Professional Culinary Institute	D, A	■	■	■	
Quality College of Culinary Careers	C, A	■	■		
Richardson Researches, Inc.	D				
Riverside Community College	C, A	■			
San Diego Mesa College	C, A	■		■	
San Francisco Culinary/Pastry Program					■
Santa Barbara City College	C, A	■		■	
Tante Marie's Cooking School	C	■	■		
University of San Francisco	B			■	

State/School	Credentials Offered	Culinary Arts	Baking and Pastry	Management	Apprenticeship Programs
California *(continued)*					
Westlake Culinary Institute	C	■	■		
Colorado					
ACF Colorado Chefs Association					■
Colorado Mountain College	C, A	■			
Colorado Mountain College					■
Cook Street School of Fine Cooking	D	■			
Culinary School of the Rockies	D	■	■		
Front Range Community College	C, A	■		■	
The International Culinary School at The Art Institute of Colorado	D, A, B	■	■	■	
Johnson & Wales University–Denver Campus	A, B	■	■	■	
Mesa State College	C, A	■			
Metropolitan State College of Denver	C, B	■		■	
Pikes Peak Community College	C, A	■	■	■	
School of Natural Cookery	C				
Connecticut					
Briarwood College	A			■	
Center for Culinary Arts	D	■			
Center for Culinary Arts	D	■			
Clemens College	C, A	■		■	
Connecticut Culinary Institute	D	■	■		

Credentials: ***C*** *= Certificate;* ***D*** *= Diploma;* ***A*** *= Associate Degree;* ***B*** *= Bachelor's Degree;* ***M*** *= Master's Degree;* ***Ph.D.*** *= Doctorate*

State/School	Credentials Offered	Culinary Arts	Baking and Pastry	Management	Apprenticeship Programs
Connecticut Culinary Institute–Suffield	D	■	■		
Gateway Community College	C, A	■		■	
Naugatuck Valley Community College	C, A	■		■	
Delaware					
Delaware State University	B			■	
Delaware Technical and Community College	A	■			
Delaware Technical and Community College	D, A	■		■	
University of Delaware	B, M			■	
District of Columbia					
Howard University	B			■	
Florida					
ACF Treasure Coast Chapter					■
Atlantic Technical Center	C	■			
Bethune-Cookman University	B			■	
Charlotte Technical Center	C	■			
First Coast Technical College	C	■	■		
Florida Culinary Institute A Division of Lincoln College of Technology	D, A, B	■	■	■	
Fort Lauderdale ACF Inc.					■
Gulf Coast Community College	A	■		■	
Hillsborough Community College	C, A	■		■	

State/School	Credentials Offered	Culinary Arts	Baking and Pastry	Management	Apprenticeship Programs
Florida ***(continued)***					
Indian River Community College	C, A	■		■	
Indian River Community College					■
The International Culinary School at The Art Institute of Fort Lauderdale	D, A, B	■	■	■	
The International Culinary School at The Art Institute of Jacksonville	D, A, B	■		■	
The International Culinary School at The Art Institute of Tampa	D, A, B	■	■	■	
Johnson & Wales University–North Miami	A, B	■	■	■	
Keiser University	A	■			
Keiser University	A	■			
Keiser University	A	■	■		
Le Cordon Bleu College of Culinary Arts, Miami	D, A	■	■		
Manatee Technical Institute	C	■			
Northwood University, Florida Campus	A, B			■	
Notter School of Pastry Arts	C, D		■		
Orlando Culinary Academy	D, A	■	■	■	
Palm Beach Community College	A			■	
Pensacola Junior College	A	■		■	
Pinellas Technical Education Center–Clearwater Campus	C	■			
St. Thomas University	B			■	

Credentials: ***C*** *= Certificate;* ***D*** *= Diploma;* ***A*** *= Associate Degree;* ***B*** *= Bachelor's Degree;* ***M*** *= Master's Degree;* ***Ph.D.*** *= Doctorate*

State/School	Credentials Offered	Culinary Arts	Baking and Pastry	Management	Apprenticeship Programs
University of Central Florida	B, M, Ph.D.			■	
Valencia Community College	C, A	■	■	■	
Webber International University	A, B			■	
Georgia					
Augusta Technical College	D	■			
Chattahoochee Technical College	D, A	■			
Coastal Georgia Community College	C	■			
Georgia Southern University	B			■	
Georgia State University	C, B, M			■	
The International Culinary School at The Art Institute of Atlanta	D, A, B	■	■	■	
Le Cordon Bleu College of Culinary Arts, Atlanta	C, A	■	■		
North Georgia Technical College	C, D, A	■			
North Georgia Technical College, Blairsville Campus	C, D, A	■			
Ogeechee Technical College	C, D, A	■			
Savannah Technical College	D, A	■			
West Georgia Technical College	C, D	■			
Hawaii					
Leeward Community College	C, A		■	■	
Maui Community College	C, A	■	■	■	

State/School	Credentials Offered	Culinary Arts	Baking and Pastry	Management	Apprenticeship Programs
Hawaii *(continued)*					
Travel Institute of the Pacific	D	■	■		
University of Hawaii–Kapiolani Community College	C, A	■	■		
Idaho					
Boise State University	C, A	■			
Idaho State University	C, A	■		■	
Illinois					
Black Hawk College	A	■			
College of DuPage	C, A	■	■	■	
College of Lake County	C, A	■		■	
The Cooking and Hospitality Institute of Chicago	C, A	■	■		
Elgin Community College	C, A	■	■	■	
The International Culinary School at The Illinois Institute of Art–Chicago	C, A, B	■	■	■	
Joliet Junior College	C, A	■	■	■	
Kendall College	C, A, B	■	■	■	
Lexington College	A, B			■	
Lincoln Land Community College	C, A	■	■	■	
Parkland College	C, A			■	
Robert Morris College	A, B	■		■	
Southwestern Illinois College	C, A	■		■	

Credentials: ***C*** *= Certificate;* ***D*** *= Diploma;* ***A*** *= Associate Degree;* ***B*** *= Bachelor's Degree;* ***M*** *= Master's Degree;* ***Ph.D.*** *= Doctorate*

State/School	Credentials Offered	Culinary Arts	Baking and Pastry	Management	Apprenticeship Programs
Triton College	C, A	■	■	■	
University of Illinois at Urbana–Champaign	B			■	
Washburne Culinary Institute	C, A	■	■		
Indiana					
Ball State University	A, B			■	
The Chef's Academy at Indiana Business College	A, B	■	■	■	
Indiana University–Purdue University Fort Wayne	A, B			■	
The International Culinary School at The Art Institute of Indianapolis	C, A, B	■	■	■	
Ivy Tech Community College–Central Indiana	C, A	■	■	■	
Ivy Tech Community College–North Central	A	■	■	■	
Ivy Tech Community College–Northeast	A	■	■		
Ivy Tech Community College–Northwest	C, A	■	■	■	
Iowa					
Des Moines Area Community College	A	■		■	
Iowa Lakes Community College	D, A			■	
Iowa State University of Science and Technology	B, M, Ph.D.			■	
Kirkwood Community College	C, D, A	■	■	■	
Kansas					
American Institute of Baking	C		■		

State/School	Credentials Offered	Culinary Arts	Baking and Pastry	Management	Apprenticeship Programs
Kansas ***(continued)***					
The International Culinary School at The Art Institute of International–Kansas City	A, B	■			
Johnson County Community College	C, A		■	■	
Johnson County Community College					■
Kansas City Kansas Area Technical School	C			■	
Kentucky					
Elizabethtown Community and Technical College	C, D	■		■	
Sullivan University	D, A, B	■		■	
Sullivan University	D, A, B	■	■	■	
Western Kentucky University	B			■	
Louisiana					
Delgado Community College	C, A	■	■	■	
Delgado Community College					■
Grambling State University	B			■	
Louisiana Culinary Institute, LLC	D, A	■			
Louisiana Technical College–Baton Rouge Campus	C, D	■			
Nicholls State University	A, B	■			
Sclafani Cooking School, Inc.	C				
Southern University at Shreveport	C, A			■	
University of Louisiana at Lafayette	B			■	

Credentials: ***C*** *= Certificate;* ***D*** *= Diploma;* ***A*** *= Associate Degree;* ***B*** *= Bachelor's Degree;* ***M*** *= Master's Degree;* ***Ph.D.*** *= Doctorate*

State/School	Credentials Offered	Culinary Arts	Baking and Pastry	Management	Apprenticeship Programs
Maine					
Eastern Maine Community College	C, A	■		■	
Southern Maine Community College	A	■			
York County Community College	C, A	■		■	
Maryland					
Allegany College of Maryland	A	■	■		
Anne Arundel Community College	C, A	■	■	■	
Baltimore International College	C, A, B, M	■	■	■	
L'Academie de Cuisine	C	■	■		
Lincoln Tech	D	■			
Wor-Wic Community College	C, A	■		■	
Massachusetts					
Branford Hall Career Institute	C	■			
Bristol Community College	A	■	■		
Bunker Hill Community College	C, A	■			
The Cambridge School of Culinary Arts	C, D	■	■		
Endicott College	B			■	
International Institute of Culinary Arts	C, D	■	■	■	
Massasoit Community College	C, A	■			
Middlesex Community College	C, A	■		■	
Newbury College	C, A, B	■	■	■	

State/School	Credentials Offered	Culinary Arts	Baking and Pastry	Management	Apprenticeship Programs
Massachusetts *(continued)*					
University of Massachusetts Amherst	C, B, M			■	
Michigan					
ACF Blue Water Chefs Association					■
ACF Michigan Chefs de Cuisine Association					■
Baker College of Muskegon	C, A, B	■	■	■	
Central Michigan University	B			■	
Grand Rapids Community College	C, A	■	■	■	
Grand Valley State University	B			■	
Great Lakes Culinary Institute at Northwestern Michigan College	C, A	■			
Henry Ford Community College	C, A	■	■	■	
The International Culinary School at The Art Institute of Michigan	C, A, B	■	■	■	
Lake Michigan College	C, A			■	
Macomb Community College	C, A	■	■	■	
Michigan State University	B, M			■	
Mott Community College	A	■	■	■	
Northern Michigan University	A, B			■	
Northwood University	A, B			■	
Oakland Community College	C, A	■	■	■	
Schoolcraft College	C, A	■	■		

*Credentials: **C** = Certificate; **D** = Diploma; **A** = Associate Degree; **B** = Bachelor's Degree; **M** = Master's Degree; **Ph.D.** = Doctorate*

State/School	Credentials Offered	Culinary Arts	Baking and Pastry	Management	Apprenticeship Programs
Washtenaw Community College	C, A	■	■	■	
Minnesota					
Hennepin Technical College	C, D, A	■			
Hibbing Community College	D, A	■		■	
The International Culinary School at The Art Institutes International Minnesota	C, A, B	■	■	■	
Le Cordon Bleu Minneapolis/St. Paul	C, A	■	■		
South Central College	D, A	■		■	
Mississippi					
Coahoma Community College	C, A	■		■	
Meridian Community College	A			■	
Mississippi Gulf Coast Community College	D			■	
Mississippi University for Women	B	■			
Missouri					
Chefs de Cuisine of St. Louis Association					■
College of the Ozarks	B			■	
Columbia Missouri Chapter ACF					■
Jefferson College	C, A	■			
Penn Valley Community College	A				
St. Louis Community College	C, A	■	■	■	
University of Missouri–Columbia	B, M			■	

State/School	Credentials Offered	Culinary Arts	Baking and Pastry	Management	Apprenticeship Programs
Montana					
Flathead Valley Community College	A	■			
The University of Montana–Missoula	C, A	■		■	
Nebraska					
ACF Professional Chefs and Culinarians of the Heartland					■
Central Community College–Hastings Campus	D, A	■		■	
Metropolitan Community College	A	■	■	■	
Southeast Community College, Lincoln Campus	A	■		■	
Nevada					
The International Culinary School at The Art Institute of Las Vegas	A, B	■	■	■	
Le Cordon Bleu College of Culinary Arts, Las Vegas	C, A	■	■		
University of Nevada, Las Vegas	B	■		■	
New Hampshire					
New Hampshire Community Technical College	C, D, A	■	■		
Southern New Hampshire University	C, A, B, M	■	■	■	
University of New Hampshire	A			■	
New Jersey					
Atlantic Cape Community College	C, A	■	■	■	
Bergen Community College	C, A	■		■	
Brookdale Community College	C, A	■		■	

Credentials: ***C*** *= Certificate;* ***D*** *= Diploma;* ***A*** *= Associate Degree;* ***B*** *= Bachelor's Degree;* ***M*** *= Master's Degree;* ***Ph.D.*** *= Doctorate*

State/School	Credentials Offered	Culinary Arts	Baking and Pastry	Management	Apprenticeship Programs
Burlington County College	C, A	■	■	■	
Hudson County Community College	C, A	■	■	■	
Mercer County Community College	C, A	■	■	■	
Middlesex County College	C, A	■		■	
Technical Institute of Camden County	D	■			
Thomas Edison State College	B			■	
Union County College	A			■	
New Mexico					
Culinary Business Academy	C				
Luna Community College	C, A	■			
New Mexico State University	B			■	
The Roswell Job Corps Center	C	■			
New York					
Broome Community College	A			■	
Career Academy of New York	C	■	■	■	
Culinary Academy of Long Island	C	■	■	■	
The Culinary Institute of America	C, A, B	■	■	■	
Erie Community College, City Campus	C, A	■	■		
Erie Community College, North Campus	A	■		■	
The French Culinary Institute at The International Culinary Center	C	■	■	■	

State/School	Credentials Offered	Culinary Arts	Baking and Pastry	Management	Apprenticeship Programs
New York ***(continued)***					
Genesee Community College	C, A			■	
The Institute of Culinary Education	D	■	■	■	
Julie Sahni's School of Indian Cooking	D	■			
Mohawk Valley Community College	C, A	■		■	
Monroe College	A, B	■	■	■	
Monroe Community College	C, A	■		■	
Nassau Community College	C, A			■	
The Natural Gourmet Institute for Health and Culinary Arts	D	■			
New York City College of Technology of the City University of New York	A, B			■	
New York Institute of Technology	C, A, B	■	■	■	
New York University	B, M, Ph.D.			■	
Niagara County Community College	C, A	■	■	■	
Niagara University	B			■	
Onondaga Community College	C, A	■		■	
Paul Smith's College	C, A, B	■	■	■	
Plattsburgh State University of New York	B			■	
Rochester Institute of Technology	B, M			■	
St. John's University	B			■	
State University of New York College at Cobleskill	C, A, B	■		■	

Credentials: ***C*** *= Certificate;* ***D*** *= Diploma;* ***A*** *= Associate Degree;* ***B*** *= Bachelor's Degree;* ***M*** *= Master's Degree;* ***Ph.D.*** *= Doctorate*

State/School	Credentials Offered	Culinary Arts	Baking and Pastry	Management	Apprenticeship Programs
State University of New York College at Oneonta	B			■	
State University of New York College of Agriculture and Technology at Morrisville	A, B			■	
State University of New York College of Technology at Alfred	A	■	■		
State University of New York College of Technology at Delhi	A, B	■		■	
Sullivan County Community College	C, A	■	■	■	
Syracuse University	B			■	
Tompkins Cortland Community College	A			■	
Westchester Community College	A	■		■	
Wilson Technological Center	C	■			
North Carolina					
Asheville-Buncombe Technical Community College	A	■	■	■	
Central Piedmont Community College	C, D, A	■	■	■	
East Carolina University	B, M			■	
The International Culinary School at The Art Institute of Charlotte	A, B	■		■	
The International Culinary School at The Art Institute of Raleigh–Durham	A, B	■		■	
Johnson & Wales University–Charlotte	A, B	■	■	■	
Southwestern Community College	C, A	■			
The University of North Carolina at Greensboro	B, M, Ph.D.			■	

State/School	Credentials Offered	Culinary Arts	Baking and Pastry	Management	Apprenticeship Programs
North Carolina *(continued)*					
Wake Technical Community College	C, A	■	■	■	
Wilkes Community College	C, A	■	■		
North Dakota					
North Dakota State College of Science	D, A			■	
Ohio					
ACF Columbus Chapter					■
Ashland University	B			■	
Cincinnati State Technical and Community College	C, A	■		■	
Columbus State Community College	C, A		■	■	
Cuyahoga Community College, Metropolitan Campus	C, A	■		■	
The International Culinary Arts & Sciences Institute (ICASI)	C, D	■	■		
The International Culinary School at The Art Institute of Ohio–Cincinnati	D, A	■	■		
Owens Community College	C, A	■		■	
Sinclair Community College	C, A	■		■	
The University of Akron	C, A	■		■	
Zane State College	C, A	■			
Oklahoma					
Metro Area Vocational Technical School District 22	C			■	
Oklahoma State University, Okmulgee	A	■			

Credentials: ***C*** *= Certificate;* ***D*** *= Diploma;* ***A*** *= Associate Degree;* ***B*** *= Bachelor's Degree;* ***M*** *= Master's Degree;* ***Ph.D.*** *= Doctorate*

State/School	Credentials Offered	Culinary Arts	Baking and Pastry	Management	Apprenticeship Programs
Oregon					
Central Oregon Community College	C, A	■		■	
Chemeketa Community College	C, A			■	
Culinary Awakenings	C	■			
International School of Baking	C		■		
Lane Community College	C, A	■		■	
Linn-Benton Community College	A			■	
Oregon Coast Culinary Institute	A	■	■		
Oregon Culinary Institute	C, D, A	■	■		
Southern Oregon University	B			■	
Western Culinary Institute	D, A	■	■	■	
Pennsylvania					
ACF Laurel Highlands Chapter					■
Bucks County Community College	C, A	■	■	■	
Bucks County Community College					■
Butler County Community College	C, A			■	
Cheyney University of Pennsylvania	B			■	
Commonwealth Technical Institute	D, A	■			
Delaware Valley College	A, B	■		■	
Drexel University	B	■		■	
East Stroudsburg University of Pennsylvania	B			■	

State/School	Credentials Offered	Culinary Arts	Baking and Pastry	Management	Apprenticeship Programs
Pennsylvania ***(continued)***					
Greater Altoona Career and Technology Center	D	■	■		
Harrisburg Area Community College	C, D, A	■	■	■	
Indiana University of Pennsylvania	C, B	■	■	■	
The International Culinary School at The Art Institute of Philadelphia	D, A, B	■	■	■	
The International Culinary School at The Art Institute of Pittsburgh	D, A, B	■		■	
The International Culinary School at The Art Institute of Pittsburgh—Online Division	B	■		■	
JNA Institute of Culinary Arts	D, A	■		■	
Keystone Technical Institute		■			
Lehigh Carbon Community College	A			■	
Mercyhurst College	A, B	■		■	
Northampton County Area Community College	D, A	■		■	
Pennsylvania College of Technology	A, B	■	■	■	
Pennsylvania Culinary Institute	D, A	■	■	■	
The Pennsylvania State University–University Park Campus	A, B, M, Ph.D.			■	
The Restaurant School at Walnut Hill College	A, B	■	■	■	
Seton Hill University	B			■	
Westmoreland County Community College	C, A	■	■	■	
Widener University	B, M			■	

Credentials: ***C*** *= Certificate;* ***D*** *= Diploma;* ***A*** *= Associate Degree;* ***B*** *= Bachelor's Degree;* ***M*** *= Master's Degree;* ***Ph.D.*** *= Doctorate*

State/School	Credentials Offered	Culinary Arts	Baking and Pastry	Management	Apprenticeship Programs
Winner Institute of Arts & Sciences Culinary Education	A	■			
Yorktowne Business Institute	C, D, A	■	■	■	
YTI Career Institute	D, A	■	■	■	
Rhode Island					
Johnson & Wales University	A, B	■	■	■	
South Carolina					
The Culinary Institute of Charleston	C, A	■	■	■	
Greenville Technical College	C, A	■	■	■	
Horry-Georgetown Technical College	C, A	■	■		
The International Culinary School at The Art Institute of Charleston	C, A, B	■	■	■	
South Dakota					
Mitchell Technical Institute	D, A	■			
South Dakota State University	B, M, Ph.D.			■	
Tennessee					
The International Culinary School at The Art Institute of Tennessee–Nashville	D, A, B	■	■	■	
Nashville State Technical Community College	C, A	■			
Pellissippi State Technical Community College	C, A			■	
Walters State Community College	C, A	■		■	

State/School	Credentials Offered	Culinary Arts	Baking and Pastry	Management	Apprenticeship Programs
Texas					
Aims Academy	D	■			
AIMS Academy School of Culinary Arts	D	■			
Austin Community College	C, A	■		■	
Central Texas College	C, A	■		■	
Culinary Academy of Austin, Inc.	D	■	■		
Culinary Institute Alain and Marie LeNôtre	D, A	■	■		
Del Mar College	C, A	■	■	■	
El Paso Community College	C, A	■	■	■	
Galveston College	C, A	■		■	
Houston Community College System	C, A	■	■	■	
The International Culinary School at The Art Institute of Dallas	C, A, B	■		■	
The International Culinary School at The Art Institute of Houston	D, A, B	■	■	■	
Lamar University	C, B, M	■		■	
Le Cordon Bleu Institute of Culinary Arts	D	■			
Northwood University, Texas Campus	A, B			■	
Remington College–Dallas Campus	A	■			
San Jacinto College–Central Campus	C, A	■		■	
Texas Culinary Academy	C, A	■	■		
University of Houston	B, M			■	

Credentials: ***C*** *= Certificate;* ***D*** *= Diploma;* ***A*** *= Associate Degree;* ***B*** *= Bachelor's Degree;* ***M*** *= Master's Degree;* ***Ph.D.*** *= Doctorate*

State/School	Credentials Offered	Culinary Arts	Baking and Pastry	Management	Apprenticeship Programs
University of North Texas	B, M			■	
Utah					
The International Culinary School at The Art Institute of Salt Lake City	D, A, B	■	■	■	
Utah Valley State College	A	■			
Vermont					
Champlain College	C, B			■	
Johnson State College	B			■	
New England Culinary Institute	C, A, B	■	■	■	
Virginia					
The International Culinary School at The Art Institute of Washington	D, A, B	■	■	■	
James Madison University	B			■	
J. Sargeant Reynolds Community College	C, A	■	■	■	
Northern Virginia Community College	C, A	■		■	
Stratford University	D, A, B	■	■	■	
Tidewater Community College	C, A	■		■	
Virginia State University	B			■	
Washington					
Bellingham Technical College	C, A	■	■		
The International Culinary School at The Art Institute of Seattle	D, A, B	■	■	■	

State/School	Credentials Offered	Culinary Arts	Baking and Pastry	Management	Apprenticeship Programs
Washington *(continued)*					
Olympic College	C, A			■	
Seattle Central Community College	C, A	■			
South Puget Sound Community College	C, A	■			
West Virginia					
West Virginia Northern Community College	C, A	■			
Wisconsin					
Blackhawk Technical College	C, A	■	■		
Chefs of Milwaukee					■
Fox Valley Technical College	C, D, A	■	■	■	
Madison Area Technical College	D, A	■	■	■	
Milwaukee Area Technical College	D, A	■	■	■	
Moraine Park Technical College	C, D, A	■	■	■	
Nicolet Area Technical College	C, D, A	■	■	■	
Southwest Wisconsin Technical College	D, A	■		■	
University of Wisconsin–Stout	B, M			■	
Wyoming					
Sheridan College	C, A	■		■	
U.S. Territory - Virgin Islands					
University of the Virgin Islands	A			■	

Credentials: ***C*** *= Certificate;* ***D*** *= Diploma;* ***A*** *= Associate Degree;* ***B*** *= Bachelor's Degree;* ***M*** *= Master's Degree;* ***Ph.D.*** *= Doctorate*

■ CULINARY PROGRAMS AT-A-GLANCE—CANADA ■

School	Credentials Offered	Culinary Arts	Baking and Pastry	Management	Apprenticeship Programs
Canadore College of Applied Arts & Technology	C, D	■		■	
Culinary Institute of Vancouver Island at Vancouver Island University	C, D	■	■	■	
George Brown College	C, D	■	■	■	
Georgian College of Applied Arts and Technology	D	■			
Holland College	C, D	■	■	■	
Humber Institute of Technology and Advanced Learning	C, D	■		■	
The International Culinary School at The Art Institute of Vancouver	C, D	■	■	■	
Le Cordon Bleu, Ottawa Culinary Arts Institute	C, D	■	■		
Liaison College	D			■	
Mount Saint Vincent University	C, D, B			■	
Niagara College Canada	C, D, B	■		■	
Northern Alberta Institute of Technology	C, D	■	■	■	
Northwest Culinary Academy of Vancouver	D	■	■		
Pacific Institute of Culinary Arts	C, D	■	■	■	
St. Clair College of Applied Arts and Technology	C, D	■		■	
SAIT-Polytechnic School of Hospitality and Tourism	C, D	■	■	■	
Stratford Chefs School	D	■			

Credentials: ***C*** *= Certificate;* ***D*** *= Diploma;* ***A*** *= Associate Degree;* ***B*** *= Bachelor's Degree;* ***M*** *= Master's Degree;* ***Ph.D.*** *= Doctorate*

School	Credentials Offered	Culinary Arts	Baking and Pastry	Management	Apprenticeship Programs
Canada *(continued)*					
University of Guelph	B, M			■	
University of New Brunswick, Saint John Campus	B			■	

Credentials: ***C*** *= Certificate;* ***D*** *= Diploma;* ***A*** *= Associate Degree;* ***B*** *= Bachelor's Degree;* ***M*** *= Master's Degree;* ***Ph.D.*** *= Doctorate*

■ CULINARY PROGRAMS AT-A-GLANCE—INTERNATIONAL ■

Country/School	Credentials Offered	Culinary Arts	Baking and Pastry	Management	Apprenticeship Programs
Australia					
Le Cordon Bleu Australia	C, D, B, M	■	■	■	
Le Cordon Bleu Sydney Culinary Arts Institute	D	■	■	■	
Finland					
Haaga-Helia University of Applied Sciences	B, M			■	
France					
Ecole des Arts Culinaires et de l'Hôtellerie de Lyon	C, D, B, M	■		■	
Ecole Supérieure de Cuisine Française Groupe Ferrandi	C	■	■		
Le Cordon Bleu	C, D	■	■		
Ritz–Escoffier Paris	C, D, M	■	■	■	
Italy					
APICIUS International School of Hospitality	C	■	■	■	
The International Cooking School of Italian Food and Wine	C	■			
Italian Culinary Institute for Foreigners–USA	C, D	■			
Italian Food Artisans, LLC	C	■			
Italian Institute for Advanced Culinary and Pastry Arts	C	■			
Japan					
Le Cordon Bleu Japan	C	■	■	■	

*Credentials: **C** = Certificate; **D** = Diploma; **A** = Associate Degree; **B** = Bachelor's Degree; **M** = Master's Degree; **Ph.D.** = Doctorate*

Country/School	Credentials Offered	Culinary Arts	Baking and Pastry	Management	Apprenticeship Programs
Japan ***(continued)***					
Le Cordon Bleu Kobe	C	■	■		
Lebanon					
Le Cordon Bleu Liban					
Mexico					
Le Cordon Bleu Mexico	C, D	■	■		
Le Cordon Bleu Mexico					
Netherlands					
Le Cordon Bleu Amsterdam					
New Zealand					
New Zealand School of Food and Wine	C	■		■	
Peru					
Le Cordon Bleu Peru	C	■	■	■	
Philippines					
Center for Culinary Arts, Manila	C, D	■	■	■	
Republic of Korea					
Le Cordon Bleu Korea	C, D, B, M	■		■	
Singapore					
At-Sunrice GlobalChef Academy	C, D	■	■		
South Africa					
Christina Martin School of Food and Wine	C, D	■			

Credentials: ***C*** *= Certificate;* ***D*** *= Diploma;* ***A*** *= Associate Degree;* ***B*** *= Bachelor's Degree;* ***M*** *= Master's Degree;* ***Ph.D.*** *= Doctorate*

Country/School	Credentials Offered	Culinary Arts	Baking and Pastry	Management	Apprenticeship Programs
Spain					
Le Cordon Bleu Madrid					
Switzerland					
DCT Hotel and Culinary Arts School, Switzerland	C, D	■	■	■	
IMI University Centre	B	■		■	
Thailand					
Le Cordon Bleu Dusit Culinary School	C, D	■	■	■	
United Kingdom					
Cookery at the Grange	C	■			
Le Cordon Bleu–London Culinary Institute	C, D	■	■		
Leith's School of Food and Wine	C, D	■			
Rosie Davies	C	■			
Tante Marie School of Cookery	C, D	■			

PROFILES OF PROFESSIONAL PROGRAMS

Alabama

Alabama Agricultural and Mechanical University

Nutrition and Hospitality Management

Normal, Alabama

General Information
Public, coeducational, university. Urban campus. Founded in 1875. Accredited by Southern Association of Colleges and Schools.

Program Information
Offered since 1985. Accredited by American Dietetic Association. Program calendar is divided into semesters. 2-year master's degree in nutrition and hospitality management. 4-year bachelor's degree in hospitality management. 4-year bachelor's degree in general dietetics.

Program Affiliation
American Dietetic Association.

Areas of Study
Hospitality management; nutrition.

Facilities
Catering service; 2 laboratories; 2 lecture rooms; student lounge; teaching kitchen; delicatessen; kiosk breakfast.

Typical Student Profile
46 total: 43 full-time; 3 part-time.

Financial Aid
In 2006, 1 scholarship was awarded (award was $750). Employment placement assistance is available. Employment opportunities within the program are available.

Housing
Apartment-style and single-sex housing available.

Application Information
Students may begin participation in January, June, and August. Application deadline for fall is July 15. Application deadline for spring is December 1. Application deadline for summer is May 15. In 2006, 5 applied; 5 were accepted. Applicants must have high school diploma.

Contact
Director of Admissions, Nutrition and Hospitality Management, PO Box 232, Normal, AL 35762. Telephone: 256-858-4103. Fax: 256-858-5433. World Wide Web: http://www.aamu.edu/.

CULINARD, The Culinary Institute of Virginia College

Culinary Arts

Birmingham, Alabama

General Information
Private, coeducational, culinary institute. Urban campus. Founded in 2000. Accredited by Accrediting Council for Independent Colleges and Schools.

Program Information
Offered since 2000. Accredited by American Culinary Federation Accrediting Commission. Program calendar is divided into quarters. 36-week diploma in culinary arts.

Program Affiliation
American Culinary Federation; National Restaurant Association; The Bread Bakers Guild of America.

Areas of Study
Culinary skill development; food preparation; garde-manger; international cuisine; introduction to food service; kitchen management; meal planning; meat cutting; meat fabrication; menu and facilities design; patisserie; sanitation; saucier; soup, stock, sauce, and starch production.

Facilities
Bake shop; 10 classrooms; 5 computer laboratories; demonstration laboratory; food production kitchen; learning resource center; 10 lecture rooms; library; public restaurant; student lounge; 10 teaching kitchens.

Student Profile
186 full-time. 105 are under 25 years old; 62 are between 25 and 44 years old; 19 are over 44 years old.

Faculty
13 total: 12 full-time; 1 part-time. 12 are industry professionals; 1 is a master chef; 5 are certified sanitarians; 1 registered dietitian. Prominent faculty: Chef Antony Osborne (European Master Pastry Chef); Chef Mike Buttles, BA, MSEd, CCe, C/F; Chef Bernie Kazenske, CEPC, ACE; Melinda Rice, REHS/RS. Faculty-student ratio: 1:16.

CULINARD, The Culinary Institute of Virginia College *(continued)*

Prominent Alumni and Current Affiliation
Steven Vallejo, Princess Cruise Lines; Jeffrey Bowie, Commanders Palace, New Orleans; Jonathan Smith (Executive Chef), Morrisons Management Brookwood Hospital.

Special Programs
Student hot food competitions, real world experiences in the industry (externship), community events/dinners with local celebrity chefs.

Typical Expenses
Application fee: $100. Tuition: $19,050. Program-related fee includes $750 for chefs kit.

Financial Aid
Program-specific awards include work study programs (3 positions available), career loan program. Employment placement assistance is available. Employment opportunities within the program are available.

Application Information
Students may begin participation in January, February, April, June, and October. Applications are accepted continuously. In 2007, 223 applied; 186 were accepted. Applicants must interview; submit a formal application and Wonderlic test.

Contact
Mr. Tom Jackson, Manager of Admissions, Culinary Arts, 436 Palisades Boulevard, Birmingham, AL 35209. Telephone: 205-943-2136. Fax: 205-943-2111. E-mail: tom.jackson@culinard.com. World Wide Web: http://www.culinard.com/.

See display on page 65.

The Gulf Coast Culinary Institute

Gulf Shores, Alabama

General Information
Public, coeducational, two-year college. Urban campus. Founded in 1965. Accredited by Southern Association of Colleges and Schools.

Program Information
Offered since 1994. Accredited by American Culinary Federation Accrediting Commission, American Dietetic Association, Council on Hotel, Restaurant and Institutional Education. Program calendar is divided into semesters. 1-year certificate in pastry/baking. 1-year certificate in hotel/restaurant management. 1-year certificate in dietary management. 1-year certificate in culinary arts. 1-year certificate in condominium/resort management. 2-year associate degree in pastry/baking. 2-year associate degree in hotel/restaurant management. 2-year associate degree in food service management. 2-year associate degree in dietary management. 2-year associate degree in culinary arts. 2-year associate degree in condominium/resort management. 3-year associate degree in pastry/baking apprenticeship. 3-year associate degree in culinary arts apprenticeship.

Program Affiliation
American Culinary Federation; American Institute of Baking; American Wine Society; Confrerie de la Chaine des Rotisseurs; Council on Hotel, Restaurant, and Institutional Education; National Restaurant Association; National Restaurant Association Educational Foundation; Retailer's Bakery Association; Society of Wine Educators.

Areas of Study
Baking; beverage management; cake decorating; confectionery show pieces; controlling costs in food service; culinary French; culinary skill development; food preparation; food purchasing; food service math; garde-manger; international cuisine; introduction to food service; management and human resources; meal planning; meat cutting; meat fabrication; menu and facilities design; nutrition; patisserie; sanitation; saucier; seafood processing; soup, stock, sauce, and starch production; spices and aromatics; wines and spirits.

Facilities
Bakery; 4 classrooms; computer laboratory; 2 demonstration laboratories; food production kitchen; garden; gourmet dining room; 2 laboratories; learning resource center; 2 lecture rooms; library; 2 student lounges; teaching kitchen.

Student Profile
235 total: 200 full-time; 35 part-time. 95 are under 25 years old; 55 are between 25 and 44 years old; 85 are over 44 years old.

Faculty
12 total: 3 full-time; 9 part-time. 7 are industry professionals; 5 are culinary-certified teachers. Prominent faculty: Ron Koetter, CEC, CCE, AAC; Jim Hurtubise, CWPC; Edward Bushaw, CHA, CFBE; Eduard Douglas, CPC. Faculty-student ratio: 1:25.

Prominent Alumni and Current Affiliation
Chef Jack Baker, CEC, Cosmo's Restaurant/Cobalt Restaurant; Chef Lenny Hust, CEC, Greenbrier Resort; Mr. Brandon Wikes, Director of Sales-Renaissance Hotel, Houston, TX.

Special Programs
Culinary competitions, 2-year paid internship.

The Gulf Coast Culinary Institute *(continued)*

Typical Expenses

In-state tuition: $93 per semester hour full-time (in district), $93 per semester hour part-time. Out-of-state tuition: $186 per semester hour full-time, $186 per semester hour part-time. Program-related fees include $200 for cutlery; $80 for uniform.

Financial Aid

In 2007, 6 scholarships were awarded (average award was $1000). Program-specific awards include American Culinary Federation scholarship $5000, Alabama Hospitality Association $5000. Employment placement assistance is available. Employment opportunities within the program are available.

Housing

Coed housing available. Average on-campus housing cost per month: $380. Average off-campus housing cost per month: $600.

Application Information

Students may begin participation in January, May, and August. Applications are accepted continuously. In 2007, 75 applied; 75 were accepted. Applicants must submit a formal application.

Contact

Edward Bushaw, Division Chair-Hospitality Administration, 3301 Gulf Shores Parkway, Gulf Shores, AL 36542. Telephone: 251-968-3103. Fax: 251-968-3120. E-mail: ebushaw@faulknerstate.edu. World Wide Web: http://www.gulfcoastculinaryinstitute.com/.

See display on page 67.

Tuskegee University

Tuskegee, Alabama

General Information

Private, coeducational, comprehensive institution. Small-town setting. Founded in 1881. Accredited by Southern Association of Colleges and Schools.

Program Information

Accredited by American Dietetic Association. Program calendar is divided into semesters. 4-year bachelor's degree in hospitality management.

Program Affiliation

American Dietetic Association.

Areas of Study

Nutrition.

Facilities

Bake shop; bakery; cafeteria; catering service; classroom; coffee shop; computer laboratory; demonstration laboratory; food production kitchen; garden; gourmet dining room; laboratory; learning resource center; lecture room; library; public restaurant; snack shop; student lounge; teaching kitchen; vineyard.

Typical Student Profile

20 full-time.

Financial Aid

Employment placement assistance is available.

Housing

Apartment-style and single-sex housing available.

Application Information

Students may begin participation in January, June, and August. Applications are accepted continuously. Applicants must interview; submit a formal application and an essay.

Contact

Director of Admissions, Old Administration Building, Suite 101, Tuskegee, AL 36088-1920. Telephone: 334-727-8500. Fax: 334-727-4402. World Wide Web: http://www.tuskegee.edu/.

The University of Alabama

Restaurant, Hotel and Meetings Management

Tuscaloosa, Alabama

General Information

Public, coeducational, university. Suburban campus. Founded in 1831. Accredited by Southern Association of Colleges and Schools.

Program Information

Offered since 1986. Accredited by American Association of Family and Consumer Sciences. National Restaurant Association Educational Foundation ManageFirst certificates available. Program calendar is divided into semesters. 1-semester certificate in ServSafe certification. 4-year bachelor's degree in restaurant and hospitality management. 4-year certificate in American Hotel & Lodging Association operations.

Program Affiliation

American Dietetic Association; American Hotel and Lodging Association; Council on Hotel, Restaurant, and Institutional Education; National Restaurant Association; National Restaurant Association Educational Foundation.

Areas of Study
Baking; beverage management; buffet catering; controlling costs in food service; convenience cookery; food preparation; food purchasing; food service communication; food service math; introduction to food service; kitchen management; management and human resources; meal planning; menu and facilities design; nutrition and food service; restaurant opportunities; sanitation; soup, stock, sauce, and starch production; wines and spirits.

Facilities
2 classrooms; computer laboratory; learning resource center; food science laboratory; 2 multimedia rooms.

Special Programs
Practicum in hospitality management (1,000 hours) or internship in hospitality management (400–600 hours).

Financial Aid
In 2006, 15 scholarships were awarded (average award was $2000). Employment placement assistance is available.

Housing
Coed, apartment-style, and single-sex housing available.

Application Information
Students may begin participation in January and August. Applications are accepted continuously. Applicants must submit a formal application.

Contact
Director of Admissions, Restaurant, Hotel and Meetings Management, Box 870158, Tuscaloosa, AL 35487. Telephone: 205-348-9147. Fax: 205-348-3789. World Wide Web: http://www.ches.ua.edu/RHM/.

Alaska

Alaska Vocational Technical Center/Alaska Culinary Academy

Culinary Arts and Sciences Department

Seward, Alaska

General Information
Public, coeducational, culinary institute. Rural campus. Founded in 1969. Accredited by Council on Occupational Education.

Program Information
Offered since 1972. Accredited by American Culinary Federation Accrediting Commission. Program calendar is continuous. 212-training day certificate in professional cooking. 212-training day certificate in professional baking. 302-training day certificate in professional cooking and baking.

Program Affiliation
American Culinary Federation; National Restaurant Association; National Restaurant Association Educational Foundation.

Areas of Study
Baking; beverage management; buffet catering; confectionery show pieces; controlling costs in food service; culinary skill development; food preparation; food purchasing; food service math; garde-manger; international cuisine; introduction to food service; kitchen management; management and human resources; meal planning; meat cutting; meat fabrication; menu and facilities design; nutrition; nutrition and food service; patisserie; sanitation; saucier; soup, stock, sauce, and starch production; wines and spirits.

Facilities
Bakery; cafeteria; classroom; computer laboratory; food production kitchen; gourmet dining room; learning resource center; library; public restaurant; snack shop; student lounge; teaching kitchen.

Typical Student Profile
30 full-time.

Financial Aid
In 2006, 2 scholarships were awarded (average award was $700). Employment placement assistance is available. Employment opportunities within the program are available.

Housing
Coed and apartment-style housing available.

Application Information
Students may begin participation in January, August, and October. Applications are accepted continuously. Applicants must have high school diploma or GED, be 18 years of age, and meet physical requirements for program.

Contact
Director of Admissions, Culinary Arts and Sciences Department, PO Box 889, 518 3rd Avenue, Seward, AK 99664. Telephone: 800-478-5389. Fax: 907-224-4143. World Wide Web: http://avtec.labor.state.ak.us/.

University of Alaska Anchorage

Culinary Arts and Hospitality

Anchorage, Alaska

General Information

Public, coeducational, comprehensive institution. Suburban campus. Founded in 1954. Accredited by Northwest Commission on Colleges and Universities.

Program Information

Offered since 1972. Accredited by American Dietetic Association. Program calendar is divided into semesters. 2-year associate degree in culinary arts. 4-year bachelor's degree in hospitality and restaurant management.

Program Affiliation

American Culinary Federation; American Dietetic Association; Council on Hotel, Restaurant, and Institutional Education; Dietary Managers Association; Foodservice Educators Network International; Institute of Food Technologists; International Association of Culinary Professionals; National Association of Catering Executives; National Restaurant Association; National Restaurant Association Educational Foundation.

Areas of Study

Baking; beverage management; buffet catering; controlling costs in food service; culinary skill development; food preparation; food purchasing; food service math; garde-manger; international cuisine; kitchen management; management and human resources; meal planning; meat cutting; meat fabrication; menu and facilities design; nutrition; patisserie; restaurant opportunities; sanitation; saucier; seafood processing; soup, stock, sauce, and starch production; wines and spirits.

Facilities

Bake shop; 3 classrooms; demonstration laboratory; 2 food production kitchens; garden; gourmet dining room; learning resource center; lecture room; library; public restaurant; 2 teaching kitchens.

Student Profile

210 total: 140 full-time; 70 part-time.

Faculty

13 total: 6 full-time; 7 part-time. 4 are industry professionals; 2 are culinary-certified teachers; 5 are registered dietitians. Prominent faculty: Timothy Doebler, CCE; Dr. Anne Bridges, RD; Carrie King, RD, LD; Naomi Everett. Faculty-student ratio: 1:18 average.

PROMINENT ALUMNI AND CURRENT AFFILIATION
Don Ellis, Executive Chef, Anchorage Hilton; Evan Hall, Assistant Manager, Denai'na Convention Center; Kathleen Davis, Kathy's Creative Catering.

SPECIAL PROGRAMS
2 semesters of study at either University of Nevada, Las Vegas or Northern Arizona University for students in bachelor's program (required), 1 semester study abroad program at the Italian Culinary Institute-Florence, Italy (APICIUS).

TYPICAL EXPENSES
Application fee: $40. In-state tuition: $134 per credit. Out-of-state tuition: $427 per credit. Program-related fees include $350 for cutlery, uniforms/kitchen; $300 for tools, utensils/bakery; $110 for grocery items.

FINANCIAL AID
In 2007, 5 scholarships were awarded (average award was $2000). Program-specific awards include in-house scholarship opportunities. Employment placement assistance is available. Employment opportunities within the program are available.

HOUSING
Coed, apartment-style, and single-sex housing available. Average on-campus housing cost per month: $750. Average off-campus housing cost per month: $900.

APPLICATION INFORMATION
Students may begin participation in January and August. Application deadline for fall is June 1. Application deadline for spring is September 1. In 2007, 68 applied; 68 were accepted. Applicants must submit a formal application and have high school diploma or GED.

CONTACT
Timothy Doebler, Director, Culinary Arts and Hospitality, 3211 Providence Drive, Cuddy Hall, Anchorage, AK 99508. Telephone: 907-786-4728. Fax: 907-786-1402. E-mail: aftwd@uaa.alaska.edu. World Wide Web: http://www.uaa.alaska.edu/.

UNIVERSITY OF ALASKA FAIRBANKS

Culinary Arts

Fairbanks, Alaska

GENERAL INFORMATION
Public, coeducational, university. Suburban campus. Founded in 1917. Accredited by Northwest Commission on Colleges and Universities.

PROGRAM INFORMATION
Offered since 1986. Accredited by Northwest Commission on Colleges and Universities. National Restaurant Association Educational Foundation ManageFirst certificates available. Program calendar is divided into semesters. 1-year certificate in culinary arts. 1-year certificate in cooking. 1-year certificate in baking. 2-year associate degree in culinary arts.

PROGRAM AFFILIATION
American Culinary Federation; American Institute of Wine & Food; International Association of Culinary Professionals; International Food Service Executives Association; National Restaurant Association; National Restaurant Association Educational Foundation; The Bread Bakers Guild of America.

AREAS OF STUDY
Baking; buffet catering; confectionery show pieces; controlling costs in food service; convenience cookery; culinary French; culinary skill development; food preparation; food purchasing; food service math; garde-manger; international cuisine; introduction to food service; kitchen management; meal planning; meat cutting; meat fabrication; nutrition; patisserie; sanitation; saucier; seafood processing; soup, stock, sauce, and starch production; wines and spirits.

FACILITIES
Bake shop; bakery; cafeteria; catering service; 2 classrooms; computer laboratory; demonstration laboratory; food production kitchen; learning resource center; lecture room; library; student lounge; teaching kitchen.

TYPICAL STUDENT PROFILE
158 total: 18 full-time; 140 part-time.

FINANCIAL AID
In 2006, 3 scholarships were awarded (average award was $500). Employment placement assistance is available. Employment opportunities within the program are available.

HOUSING
Coed housing available.

APPLICATION INFORMATION
Students may begin participation in January and September. Applications are accepted continuously. In 2006, 36 applied; 22 were accepted. Applicants must submit a formal application.

CONTACT
Director of Admissions, Culinary Arts, 604 Barnette Street, Fairbanks, AK 99701. Telephone: 907-455-2809. Fax: 907-455-2828. World Wide Web: http://www.tvc.uaf.edu/.

ARIZONA

ARIZONA CULINARY INSTITUTE

Scottsdale, Arizona

GENERAL INFORMATION

Private, coeducational, culinary institute. Suburban campus. Founded in 2001. Accredited by Accrediting Commission of Career Schools and Colleges of Technology.

PROGRAM INFORMATION

Offered since 2001. Program calendar is continuous. 9-month diploma in culinary arts, baking, and restaurant management.

PROGRAM AFFILIATION

American Culinary Federation; American Institute of Wine & Food; International Association of Culinary Professionals; National Association of Catering Executives; National Restaurant Association; National Restaurant Association Educational Foundation; Society of Wine Educators.

AREAS OF STUDY

Baking; beverage management; confectionery show pieces; controlling costs in food service; culinary French; culinary skill development; food preparation; food purchasing; food service math; garde-manger; international cuisine; introduction to food service; kitchen management; management and human resources; meat cutting; meat fabrication; menu and facilities design; nutrition; patisserie; restaurant opportunities; sanitation; saucier; soup, stock, sauce, and starch production; wines and spirits.

FACILITIES

2 bakeries; 3 classrooms; computer laboratory; 3 food production kitchens; gourmet dining room; learning resource center; 2 lecture rooms; library; public restaurant; student lounge; 5 teaching kitchens.

STUDENT PROFILE

175 full-time. 92 are under 25 years old; 73 are between 25 and 44 years old; 10 are over 44 years old.

FACULTY

12 total: 11 full-time; 1 part-time. 10 are industry professionals; 2 are culinary-certified teachers. Prominent faculty: Jennifer Sedig; Glenn Humphrey, CEC, CCE; Michael Dudley; Matthew Mattox. Faculty-student ratio: 1:16.

SPECIAL PROGRAMS

3-month paid internship.

TYPICAL EXPENSES

Application fee: $25. Tuition: $24,990 per diploma. Program-related fee includes $1805 for knives, books, uniforms, supplies.

FINANCIAL AID

In 2007, 15 scholarships were awarded (average award was $500); 155 loans were granted (average loan was $25,000). Employment placement assistance is available. Employment opportunities within the program are available.

HOUSING

Average off-campus housing cost per month: $400–$700.

APPLICATION INFORMATION

Students may begin participation in January, February, April, May, July, August, September, and November. Applications are accepted continuously. In 2007, 468 applied; 440 were accepted. Applicants must submit a formal application and high school diploma/GED.

CONTACT

Admissions Director, 10585 North 114th Street, Suite 401, Scottsdale, AZ 85259. Telephone: 480-603-1066. Fax: 480-603-1067. E-mail: info@azculinary.com. World Wide Web: http://www.azculinary.com/.

See display on page 73.

ARIZONA WESTERN COLLEGE

Culinary Arts/Dietary Management/Hotel and Restaurant Management

Yuma, Arizona

GENERAL INFORMATION

Public, coeducational, two-year college. Rural campus. Founded in 1962. Accredited by North Central Association of Colleges and Schools.

PROGRAM INFORMATION

Offered since 1996. Accredited by Dietary Manager Program accredited by Dietary Managers Association. Program calendar is divided into semesters. 2-semester certificate in dietary manager. 2-semester certificate in culinary arts. 2-year associate degree in hotel/restaurant management.

PROGRAM AFFILIATION

Dietary Managers Association.

AREAS OF STUDY

Baking; food preparation; food purchasing; garde-manger; international cuisine; management and human resources; meal planning; nutrition; restaurant opportunities; sanitation; soup, stock, sauce, and starch production.

Arizona Western College *(continued)*

Facilities
Classroom; computer laboratory; food production kitchen; gourmet dining room; learning resource center; lecture room; library.

Typical Student Profile
17 total: 12 full-time; 5 part-time. 12 are under 25 years old; 3 are between 25 and 44 years old; 2 are over 44 years old.

Special Programs
Placement in local restaurants for field experience, placement in local extended-care facilities for institutional food experience.

Financial Aid
Employment placement assistance is available.

Housing
Coed housing available.

Application Information
Students may begin participation in January and August. Application deadline for spring is January 15. Application deadline for fall is August 15. In 2006, 17 applied; 17 were accepted. Applicants must submit a formal application.

Contact
Director of Admissions, Culinary Arts/Dietary Management/Hotel and Restaurant Management, PO Box 929, Yuma, AZ 85366. Telephone: 928-344-7779. Fax: 928-317-6119. World Wide Web: http://www.azwestern.edu/.

Central Arizona College

Hotel and Restaurant Management/Culinary Arts/Nutrition and Dietetics

Coolidge, Arizona

General Information
Public, coeducational, two-year college. Rural campus. Founded in 1970. Accredited by North Central Association of Colleges and Schools.

Program Information
Offered since 1990. Accredited by American Culinary Federation Accrediting Commission, Council on Hotel, Restaurant and Institutional Education. Program calendar is divided into semesters. 1-year certificate in dietary manager. 17-credit certificate in restaurant management. 17- to 19-credit certificate in cook's level I. 18-credit certificate in hotel/lodging management. 2-year associate degree in hotel and restaurant management. 2-year associate degree in dietetic technician. 2-year associate degree in cook level 2-culinary apprenticeship.

Program Affiliation
American Culinary Federation; American Dietetic Association; Council on Hotel, Restaurant, and Institutional Education; National Restaurant Association; National Restaurant Association Educational Foundation.

Areas of Study
Baking; beverage management; controlling costs in food service; culinary skill development; food preparation; food purchasing; food service math; garde-manger; hotel management; introduction to food service; management and human resources; nutrition; nutrition and food service; restaurant management; sanitation.

Typical Student Profile
60 total: 40 full-time; 20 part-time. 40 are under 25 years old; 20 are between 25 and 44 years old.

Special Programs
Apprenticeship program (ACF Resort and Country Club Chefs).

Financial Aid
Employment opportunities within the program are available.

Housing
Coed housing available.

Application Information
Students may begin participation in January and August. Applications are accepted continuously. Applicants must submit a formal application, letters of reference, and an essay.

Contact
Director of Admissions, Hotel and Restaurant Management/Culinary Arts/Nutrition and Dietetics, 8470 North Overfield Road, Coolidge, AZ 85228. Telephone: 520-426-4403. Fax: 520-426-4259. World Wide Web: http://www.centralaz.edu/.

The International Culinary School at The Art Institute of Phoenix

Phoenix, Arizona

General Information
Private, coeducational institution.

Program Information
Accredited by American Culinary Federation (Associate in Culinary Arts program). Associate degree in Culinary Arts. Associate degree in Baking and Pastry Arts. Bachelor's degree in Culinary Arts.

Contact
Office of Admissions, 2233 West Dunlap Avenue, Phoenix, AZ 85021-2859. Telephone: 602-331-7500. World Wide Web: http://www.artinstitutes.edu/phoenix/.

See color display following page 332.

The International Culinary School at The Art Institute of Tucson

Tucson, Arizona

General Information
Private, coeducational institution.

Program Information
Associate degree in Culinary Arts. Associate degree in Baking and Pastry. Bachelor's degree in Culinary Arts.

Contact
Office of Admissions, 5099 E. Grant Road, Suite 100, Tucson, AZ 85712. Telephone: 520-318-2700. World Wide Web: http://www.artinstitutes.edu/tucson.

See color display following page 332.

Maricopa Skill Center

Food Preparation Program

Phoenix, Arizona

General Information
Public, coeducational, adult vocational school. Urban campus. Founded in 1962. Accredited by North Central Association of Colleges and Schools.

Program Information
Offered since 1977. Program calendar is year-round, year-round. 14-week certificate in pantry goods maker (salad maker). 18-week certificate in kitchen helper. 18-week certificate in baker's helper. 27-week certificate in cook's apprentice.

Program Affiliation
National Restaurant Association; National Restaurant Association Educational Foundation.

Areas of Study
Baking; food preparation; food service math; introduction to food service; meat cutting; restaurant opportunities; soup, stock, sauce, and starch production.

Facilities
Cafeteria; catering service; classroom; demonstration laboratory; food production kitchen; learning resource center; lecture room; public restaurant; student lounge; teaching kitchen.

Typical Student Profile
40 full-time.

Financial Aid
Employment placement assistance is available.

Application Information
Students may begin participation year-round. Applications are accepted continuously. Applicants must submit student information form and make financial arrangements, complete TABE assessment.

Contact
Director of Admissions, Food Preparation Program, 1245 East Buckeye Road, Phoenix, AZ 85034. Telephone: 602-238-4331. Fax: 602-238-4307. World Wide Web: http://www.maricopaskillcenter.com/.

Northern Arizona University

School of Hotel and Restaurant Management

Flagstaff, Arizona

General Information
Public, coeducational, university. Small-town setting. Founded in 1899. Accredited by North Central Association of Colleges and Schools.

Program Information
Offered since 1987. Accredited by Council on Hotel, Restaurant and Institutional Education, Accreditation Commission for Programs in Hospitality Administration. Program calendar is divided into semesters. Certificate in managing customer service. 15-credit hour certificate in restaurant management. 15-credit hour certificate in international tourism management. 15-week certificate in culinary arts for management. 4-year bachelor's degree in international hospitality management. 4-year bachelor's degree in hotel and restaurant management.

Program Affiliation
American Hotel and Lodging Association; Council on Hotel, Restaurant, and Institutional Education; International Food Service Executives Association; National Restaurant Association; National Restaurant Association Educational Foundation.

Northern Arizona University *(continued)*

Areas of Study
Beverage management; controlling costs in food service; event planning; food preparation; food purchasing; introduction to food service; management and human resources; restaurant opportunities; sanitation; wines and spirits.

Facilities
Classroom; coffee shop; computer laboratory; demonstration laboratory; food production kitchen; gourmet dining room; learning resource center; lecture room; public restaurant; student lounge; teaching kitchen.

Typical Student Profile
877 total: 777 full-time; 100 part-time.

Special Programs
Paid internships, summer program in Europe, International Student Exchange program.

Financial Aid
In 2006, 110 scholarships were awarded (average award was $1200). Employment placement assistance is available. Employment opportunities within the program are available.

Housing
Coed, apartment-style, and single-sex housing available.

Application Information
Students may begin participation in January, May, and August. Application deadline for fall is March 1. Application deadline for spring is December 1. In 2006, 900 applied. Applicants must submit a formal application and ACT or SAT scores, high school diploma.

Contact
Director of Admissions, School of Hotel and Restaurant Management, NAU Box 5638, Building 33A, Flagstaff, AZ 86011-5638. Telephone: 928-523-9050. Fax: 928-523-1711. World Wide Web: http://www.nau.edu/hrm.

Pima Community College

Culinary Arts Program

Tucson, Arizona

General Information
Public, coeducational, two-year college. Urban campus. Founded in 1966. Accredited by North Central Association of Colleges and Schools.

Program Information
Offered since 1970. Program calendar is divided into semesters. 1-year certificate in culinary arts. 2-year associate degree in culinary arts.

Program Affiliation
Chefs Association of Southern Arizona; Slow Food International.

Areas of Study
Baking; beverage management; controlling costs in food service; culinary skill development; food preparation; food service math; garde-manger; international cuisine; management and human resources; meal planning; meat cutting; meat fabrication; menu and facilities design; nutrition; nutrition and food service; sanitation; saucier; seafood processing; soup, stock, sauce, and starch production; wines and spirits.

Facilities
Cafeteria; catering service; 4 classrooms; computer laboratory; demonstration laboratory; food production kitchen; learning resource center; library; public restaurant; teaching kitchen.

Typical Student Profile
72 full-time. 15 are under 25 years old; 45 are between 25 and 44 years old; 12 are over 44 years old.

Special Programs
Culinary Club, culinary team, apprenticeship (2 or 3 years).

Financial Aid
Program-specific awards include Culinary Club Scholarship, Chef's Association Scholarship. Employment placement assistance is available. Employment opportunities within the program are available.

Application Information
Students may begin participation in January and August. Applications are accepted continuously. In 2006, 220 applied; 72 were accepted. Applicants must interview; and submit an application, placement test scores, or academic transcripts.

Contact
Director of Admissions, Culinary Arts Program, 5901 South Calle Santa Cruz, Tucson, AZ 85709-6080. Telephone: 520-206-5164. Fax: 520-206-5143. World Wide Web: http://www.pima.edu/.

Scottsdale Community College

Culinary Arts Program

Scottsdale, Arizona

General Information

Public, coeducational, two-year college. Suburban campus. Founded in 1969. Accredited by North Central Association of Colleges and Schools.

Program Information

Offered since 1984. Accredited by American Culinary Federation Accrediting Commission. Program calendar is divided into semesters. 1-semester certificate in culinary fundamentals. 2-semester certificate in professional culinary arts. 2-semester certificate in culinary arts. 2-year associate degree in professional culinary arts. 2-year associate degree in hospitality management. 2-year associate degree in culinary fundamentals. 2-year associate degree in culinary arts.

Program Affiliation

American Culinary Federation; National Restaurant Association; Women Chefs and Restaurateurs.

Areas of Study

Baking; beverage management; buffet catering; controlling costs in food service; culinary skill development; dining room service; food preparation; food purchasing; food service communication; food service math; garde-manger; international cuisine; introduction to food service; kitchen management; management and human resources; meal planning; meat cutting; meat fabrication; menu and facilities design; nutrition; nutrition and food service; patisserie; restaurant opportunities; sanitation; saucier; seafood processing; soup, stock, sauce, and starch production.

Facilities

Bake shop; 3 classrooms; computer laboratory; demonstration laboratory; 2 food production kitchens; gourmet dining room; learning resource center; lecture room; library; 2 public restaurants; student lounge; teaching kitchen.

Typical Student Profile

72 full-time. 29 are under 25 years old; 36 are between 25 and 44 years old; 7 are over 44 years old.

Special Programs

Culinary competitions.

Financial Aid

In 2006, 5 scholarships were awarded (average award was $1000); 25 loans were granted (average loan was $2000). Employment placement assistance is available.

Application Information

Students may begin participation in January and August. Applications are accepted continuously. In 2006, 300 applied; 72 were accepted. Applicants must interview; and submit a formal application and placement scores in English, reading and math.

Contact

Director of Admissions, Culinary Arts Program, 9000 East Chaparral Road, Scottsdale, AZ 85256. Telephone: 480-423-6241. Fax: 480-423-6091. World Wide Web: http://www.scottsdalecc.edu/culinary.

Scottsdale Culinary Institute

Le Cordon Bleu

Scottsdale, Arizona

General Information

Private, coeducational, culinary institute. Suburban campus. Founded in 1986. Accredited by Accrediting Commission of Career Schools and Colleges of Technology.

Program Information

Offered since 1986. Accredited by American Culinary Federation Accrediting Commission. Program calendar is divided into six-week cycles. 15-month associate degree in Le Cordon Bleu Patisserie and Baking. 15-month associate degree in Le Cordon Bleu Hospitality and Restaurant Management. 15-month associate degree in Le Cordon Bleu Culinary Arts. 29-month bachelor's degree in Le Cordon Bleu Hospitality and Restaurant Management. 30-month bachelor's degree in Le Cordon Bleu Culinary Management. 8-month certificate in Le Cordon Bleu Culinary Arts. 9-month certificate in Le Cordon Bleu Patisserie and Baking.

Program Affiliation

American Culinary Federation; American Institute of Wine & Food; Council on Hotel, Restaurant, and Institutional Education; International Association of Culinary Professionals; International Wine & Food Society; James Beard Foundation, Inc.; National Restaurant Association; Phoenix Restaurant Association; Women Chefs and Restaurateurs.

Areas of Study

Baking; beverage management; buffet catering; confectionery show pieces; controlling costs in food service; culinary skill development; food preparation; food purchasing; food service communication; food service math; garde-manger; international cuisine; introduction to food service; management and human resources; meal planning; meat cutting; meat fabrication; menu and facilities design; nutrition; nutrition and food

Scottsdale Culinary Institute *(continued)*

service; patisserie; restaurant opportunities; sanitation; saucier; seafood processing; soup, stock, sauce, and starch production; wines and spirits.

Facilities

2 bake shops; 2 catering services; 5 classrooms; computer laboratory; demonstration laboratory; 2 food production kitchens; garden; 2 gourmet dining rooms; learning resource center; 3 lecture rooms; library; 2 public restaurants; snack shop; student lounge; 10 teaching kitchens.

Typical Student Profile

1200 full-time.

Special Programs

Paid externships, culinary competitions, participation in community and resort events.

Financial Aid

In 2006, 30 scholarships were awarded (average award was $2000); 250 loans were granted (average loan was $2611). Employment placement assistance is available. Employment opportunities within the program are available.

Application Information

Students may begin participation in January, February, March, April, May, July, August, September, October, November, and December. Applications are accepted continuously. Applicants must submit a formal application, essay, academic transcripts, and have a high school diploma or GED.

Contact

Director of Admissions, Le Cordon Bleu, 8100 East Camelback Road, Suite 1001, Scottsdale, AZ 85251. Telephone: 800-848-2433. Fax: 480-990-0351. World Wide Web: http://www.chefs.com/.

Arkansas

Ozarka College

Culinary Arts

Melbourne, Arkansas

General Information

Public, coeducational, two-year college. Small-town setting. Founded in 1973. Accredited by North Central Association of Colleges and Schools.

Program Information

Offered since 1973. Accredited by Arkansas Hospitality Association. Program calendar is divided into semesters. 2-semester certificate in culinary arts. 4-semester associate degree in general technology (culinary arts emphasis).

Program Affiliation

American Culinary Federation; American Dietetic Association; National Restaurant Association; National Restaurant Association Educational Foundation.

Areas of Study

Baking; buffet catering; controlling costs in food service; culinary skill development; food preparation; food purchasing; food service math; garde-manger; international cuisine; introduction to food service; kitchen management; management and human resources; meal planning; nutrition; nutrition and food service; patisserie; sanitation; saucier; seafood processing; soup, stock, sauce, and starch production.

Facilities

Catering service; classroom; computer laboratory; demonstration laboratory; food production kitchen; gourmet dining room; laboratory; learning resource center; lecture room; library; public restaurant; student lounge; teaching kitchen.

Typical Student Profile

16 total: 15 full-time; 1 part-time. 7 are under 25 years old; 4 are between 25 and 44 years old; 5 are over 44 years old.

Special Programs

Skills USA culinary competitions, Disney World intern opportunities, student participation in corporate food shows.

Financial Aid

In 2006, 2 scholarships were awarded (average award was $1000). Program-specific awards include off-campus catering opportunities. Employment placement assistance is available. Employment opportunities within the program are available.

Application Information

Students may begin participation in August. Application deadline for fall is May 31. In 2006, 25 applied; 15 were accepted. Applicants must interview; submit a formal application, letters of reference, and an essay.

Contact

Director of Admissions, Culinary Arts, PO Box 10, Melbourne, AR 72556. Telephone: 870-368-7371. Fax: 870-368-2091. World Wide Web: http://www.ozarka.edu/.

Pulaski Technical College Arkansas Culinary School

Little Rock, Arkansas

General Information

Public, coeducational, two-year college. Urban campus. Founded in 1995. Accredited by North Central Association of Colleges and Schools.

Program Information

Offered since 1995. Accredited by Arkansas State Department of Higher Education. National Restaurant Association Educational Foundation ManageFirst certificates available. Program calendar is divided into semesters. 1-year certificate in culinary arts. 1-year certificate in baking and pastry arts. 2-year associate degree in culinary arts.

Program Affiliation

American Culinary Federation; National Restaurant Association; National Restaurant Association Educational Foundation.

Areas of Study

Baking; beverage management; buffet catering; confectionery show pieces; controlling costs in food service; convenience cookery; culinary French; culinary skill development; food preparation; food purchasing; food service communication; food service math; garde-manger; international cuisine; introduction to food service; kitchen management; management and human resources; meal planning; meat cutting; meat fabrication; menu and facilities design; nutrition; nutrition and food service; patisserie; restaurant opportunities; sanitation; saucier; seafood processing; soup, stock, sauce, and starch production; wines and spirits.

Facilities

Bakery; 4 classrooms; computer laboratory; demonstration laboratory; food production kitchen; laboratory; learning resource center; library; student lounge; teaching kitchen.

Typical Student Profile

93 total: 83 full-time; 10 part-time. 30 are under 25 years old; 40 are between 25 and 44 years old; 23 are over 44 years old.

Special Programs

Culinary competitions, culinary anthropology, summer credit in Italy, practicum.

Financial Aid

In 2006, 20 scholarships were awarded.

Application Information

Students may begin participation in January, June, and August. Applications are accepted continuously. In 2006, 100 applied; 85 were accepted. Applicants must interview; submit a formal application, letters of reference, an essay, transcripts, GRE/high school diploma.

Contact

Director of Admissions, 4901 Asher Avenue, Little Rock, AR 72204. Telephone: 866-804-CHEF(2433). Fax: 501-570-4095. World Wide Web: http://www.pulaskitech.edu/programs_of_study/culinary/default.asp.

University of Arkansas at Pine Bluff

Food Service Restaurant Management

Pine Bluff, Arkansas

General Information

Public, coeducational, comprehensive institution. Urban campus. Founded in 1873. Accredited by North Central Association of Colleges and Schools.

Program Information

Offered since 1957. Accredited by American Dietetic Association. Program calendar is divided into semesters. 4-year bachelor's degree in food service and restaurant management. 4-year bachelor's degree in dietetics and nutrition.

Program Affiliation

American Dietetic Association; Council on Hotel, Restaurant, and Institutional Education.

Areas of Study

Food service management; nutrition; nutrition and food service; restaurant management.

Facilities

Cafeteria; 2 computer laboratories; food production kitchen; 3 laboratories; learning resource center; 2 lecture rooms; 3 libraries; student lounge; teaching kitchen.

Typical Student Profile

16 full-time. 16 are under 25 years old.

Financial Aid

Employment placement assistance is available.

Housing

Single-sex housing available.

University of Arkansas at Pine Bluff *(continued)*

Application Information
Students may begin participation in January and August. Applications are accepted continuously. In 2006, 6 applied; 6 were accepted. Applicants must submit a formal application.

Contact
Director of Admissions, Food Service Restaurant Management, Department of Human Sciences, 1200 North University Drive, Mail Slot 4971, Pine Bluff, AR 71601. Telephone: 870-575-8807. Fax: 870-575-4684. World Wide Web: http://www.uapb.edu/.

California

American River College

Hospitality Management Program

Sacramento, California

General Information
Public, coeducational, two-year college. Suburban campus. Founded in 1955. Accredited by Western Association of Schools and Colleges.

Program Information
Offered since 1975. Program calendar is divided into semesters. 1-year certificate in introductory baking. 1.5-year certificate in restaurant management. 1.5-year certificate in culinary arts. 2-year associate degree in culinary arts.

Program Affiliation
American Culinary Federation; National Restaurant Association.

Areas of Study
Baking; dining room management; food preparation; kitchen management; restaurant management.

Facilities
Bake shop; classroom; gourmet dining room; laboratory; lecture room.

Typical Student Profile
330 total: 220 full-time; 110 part-time.

Special Programs
Culinary competitions, student-run fine dining restaurant open to public.

Application Information
Students may begin participation in January, June, and August. Applications are accepted continuously.

Contact
Director of Admissions, Hospitality Management Program, 4700 College Oak Drive, Sacramento, CA 95841-4286. Telephone: 916-484-8656. Fax: 916-484-8880. World Wide Web: http://www.arc.losrios.edu/chef.

Bauman College: Holistic Nutrition & Culinary Arts–Berkeley

Natural Chef Training Program

Berkeley, California

General Information
Private, coeducational, culinary institute. Founded in 1984.

Program Information
Offered since 1997. Program calendar is divided into semesters. 5-month certificate in natural chef.

Program Affiliation
Sonoma County Culinary Guild; World Association of Chefs and Cooks.

Areas of Study
Baking; buffet catering; controlling costs in food service; culinary French; culinary skill development; ethnic cuisine; food preparation; food purchasing; food service math; healthy professional cooking; international cuisine; kitchen management; meal planning; menu and facilities design; nutrition; nutrition and food service; organic gardening; sanitation; saucier; soup, stock, sauce, and starch production; therapeutic cooking; vegetarian cooking.

Facilities
Classroom; computer laboratory; demonstration laboratory; food production kitchen; learning resource center; lecture room; library; teaching kitchen.

Typical Student Profile
125 full-time. 50 are under 25 years old; 50 are between 25 and 44 years old; 25 are over 44 years old.

Special Programs
French intensive organic gardening, classes in herbal remedies and cooking for a variety of health problems, personal chef focus.

Financial Aid
Employment placement assistance is available. Employment opportunities within the program are available.

Application Information
Students may begin participation in March and September. Applications are accepted continuously. In 2006, 125 applied; 125 were accepted. Applicants must interview; submit a formal application, letters of reference, an essay, resume, photo.

Contact
Director of Admissions, Natural Chef Training Program, PO Box 940, Penngrove, CA 94951. Telephone: 800-987-7530. Fax: 707-795-3375. World Wide Web: http://www.iet.org/cai.html.

Bauman College: Holistic Nutrition & Culinary Arts–Penngrove

Natural Chef Training Program

Penngrove, California

General Information
Private, coeducational, culinary institute. Small-town setting.

Program Information
Program calendar is divided into semesters. 5-month certificate in natural chef.

Program Affiliation
Sonoma County Culinary Guild; World Association of Chefs and Cooks.

Areas of Study
Baking; buffet catering; controlling costs in food service; culinary French; culinary skill development; ethnic cuisine; food preparation; food purchasing; food service math; healthy professional cooking; international cuisine; kitchen management; meal planning; menu and facilities design; nutrition; nutrition and food service; organic gardening; sanitation; saucier; soup, stock, sauce, and starch production; therapeutic cooking; vegetarian cooking.

Facilities
Classroom; computer laboratory; demonstration laboratory; food production kitchen; learning resource center; lecture room; library; teaching kitchen.

Typical Student Profile
125 full-time. 50 are under 25 years old; 50 are between 25 and 44 years old; 25 are over 44 years old.

Special Programs
French intensive organic gardening, classes in herbal remedies and cooking for a variety of health problems, personal chef focus.

Financial Aid
Employment placement assistance is available. Employment opportunities within the program are available.

Application Information
Students may begin participation in March and September. Applications are accepted continuously. In 2006, 125 applied; 125 were accepted. Applicants must interview; submit a formal application, letters of reference, an essay, resume, photo.

Contact
Director of Admissions, Natural Chef Training Program, PO Box 940, Penngrove, CA 94951. Telephone: 800-987-7530. Fax: 707-795-3375. World Wide Web: http://www.baumancollege.org.

Bauman College: Holistic Nutrition & Culinary Arts–Santa Cruz

Natural Chef Training Program

Santa Cruz, California

General Information
Private, coeducational, culinary institute. Small-town setting.

Program Information
Program calendar is divided into semesters. 5-month certificate in natural chef.

Program Affiliation
Sonoma County Culinary Guild; World Association of Chefs and Cooks.

Areas of Study
Baking; buffet catering; controlling costs in food service; culinary French; culinary skill development; ethnic cuisine; food preparation; food purchasing; food service math; healthy professional cooking; international cuisine; kitchen management; meal planning; menu and facilities design; nutrition; nutrition and food service; organic gardening; sanitation; saucier; soup, stock, sauce, and starch production; therapeutic cooking; vegetarian cooking.

Bauman College: Holistic Nutrition & Culinary Arts–Santa Cruz *(continued)*

Facilities
Classroom; computer laboratory; demonstration laboratory; food production kitchen; learning resource center; lecture room; library; teaching kitchen.

Typical Student Profile
125 full-time. 50 are under 25 years old; 50 are between 25 and 44 years old; 25 are over 44 years old.

Special Programs
French intensive organic gardening, classes in herbal remedies and cooking for a variety of health problems, personal chef focus.

Financial Aid
Employment placement assistance is available. Employment opportunities within the program are available.

Application Information
Students may begin participation in March and September. Applications are accepted continuously. In 2006, 125 applied; 125 were accepted. Applicants must interview; submit a formal application, letters of reference, an essay, resume, photo.

Contact
Director of Admissions, Natural Chef Training Program, PO Box 940, Penngrove, CA 94951. Telephone: 800-987-7530. Fax: 707-795-3375. World Wide Web: http://www.baumancollege.org.

California Culinary Academy

San Francisco, California

General Information
Private, coeducational, culinary institute. Urban campus. Founded in 1977. Accredited by Accrediting Commission of Career Schools and Colleges of Technology.

Program Information
Offered since 1977. Accredited by American Culinary Federation Accrediting Commission. Program calendar is continuous. 30-week certificate in baking and pastry arts. 45-week associate degree in Le Cordon Bleu Hospitality and Restaurant Management. 60-week associate degree in Le Cordon Bleu culinary arts.

Program Affiliation
American Culinary Federation; American Institute of Wine & Food; California Restaurant Association; International Association of Culinary Professionals; National Restaurant Association.

Areas of Study
Baking; beverage management; buffet catering; casino and gaming; confectionery show pieces; controlling costs in food service; culinary French; culinary skill development; food preparation; food purchasing; food service math; garde-manger; global cuisine; international cuisine; introduction to food service; kitchen management; management and human resources; meat cutting; meat fabrication; menu and facilities design; nutrition; nutrition and food service; patisserie; restaurant opportunities; sanitation; saucier; seafood processing; soup, stock, sauce, and starch production; wines and spirits.

Facilities
Bake shop; 6 bakeries; cafeteria; 10 classrooms; coffee shop; 2 computer laboratories; 6 demonstration laboratories; 8 food production kitchens; gourmet dining room; 5 laboratories; learning resource center; library; 2 public restaurants; snack shop; student lounge; 3 teaching kitchens; retail shop; mixology laboratory; casino.

Typical Student Profile
950 full-time.

Special Programs
Externships for all programs (as of January 2008), culinary competitions, 3 Le Cordon Bleu certified programs (as of January 2008).

Financial Aid
In 2006, 25 scholarships were awarded (average award was $1775); 56 loans were granted (average loan was $14,120). Program-specific awards include Career Education Scholarship Fund, Future Chef of America high school competitions. Employment placement assistance is available. Employment opportunities within the program are available.

Housing
Coed housing available.

Application Information
Students may begin participation in January, February, April, May, July, August, September, and November. Applications are accepted continuously. Applicants must interview; submit a formal application and application fee, entrance exam, and have proof of high school graduation or GED.

Contact
Director of Admissions, 625 Polk Street, San Francisco, CA 94102. Telephone: 800-229-2433. Fax: 415-771-2194. World Wide Web: http://www.baychef.com/.

California School of Culinary Arts

Le Cordon Bleu Programs

Pasadena, California

General Information

Private, coeducational, culinary institute. Urban campus. Founded in 1994. Accredited by Accrediting Council for Independent Colleges and Schools.

Program Information

Offered since 1994. 1-year diploma in Le Cordon Bleu Patisserie and Baking. 15-month associate degree in Le Cordon Bleu Culinary Arts. 42-week diploma in Le Cordon Bleu Patisserie and Baking (weeknight and Saturday classes). 60-week associate degree in Le Cordon Bleu Hospitality and Restaurant Management.

Program Affiliation

American Culinary Federation.

Financial Aid

Employment placement assistance is available. Employment opportunities within the program are available.

Application Information

Applications are accepted continuously. Applicants must interview; submit a formal application and pre-enrollment exam, high school diploma or equivalent.

Contact

Director of Admissions, Le Cordon Bleu Programs, 521 East Green Street, Pasadena, CA 91101. Telephone: 866-230-9450. World Wide Web: http://www.csca.edu/.

California State Polytechnic University, Pomona

The Collins School of Hospitality Management

Pomona, California

General Information

Public, coeducational, comprehensive institution. Suburban campus. Founded in 1938. Accredited by Western Association of Schools and Colleges.

Program Information

Offered since 1973. Accredited by Council on Hotel, Restaurant and Institutional Education. Program calendar is divided into quarters. 4-year bachelor's degree in hotel and restaurant management.

Program Affiliation

American Culinary Federation; Council on Hotel, Restaurant, and Institutional Education; International Association of Culinary Professionals; National Restaurant Association; National Restaurant Association Educational Foundation; Society of Wine Educators.

Areas of Study

Beverage management; beverage marketing; club management; controlling costs in food service; culinary product development; food preparation; food purchasing; food service math; hotel management; introduction to food service; kitchen management; management and human resources; meal planning; menu and facilities design; restaurant management; restaurant opportunities; sanitation; soup, stock, sauce, and starch production; wines and spirits.

Facilities

10 classrooms; computer laboratory; food production kitchen; gourmet dining room; laboratory; 5 lecture rooms; library; public restaurant; student lounge; 2 demonstration auditoriums.

Special Programs

Participation at national trade shows.

Financial Aid

In 2006, 23 scholarships were awarded (average award was $1500).

Housing

Coed housing available.

Application Information

Students may begin participation in January, March, June, and September. Application deadline for spring is August 31. Application deadline for summer is February 28. Application deadline for fall is November 30. Application deadline for winter is June 30. In 2006, 496 applied; 262 were accepted. Applicants must submit a formal application.

Contact

Director of Admissions, The Collins School of Hospitality Management, 3801 West Temple Avenue, Pomona, CA 91768-2557. Telephone: 909-869-2275. Fax: 909-869-4805. World Wide Web: http://www.csupomona.edu/~cshm/collins_school/index.shtml.

Chef Eric's Culinary Classroom

Professional and Recreational Cooking School

Los Angeles, California

General Information

Private, coeducational, culinary institute. Urban campus. Founded in 2003.

Program Information

Offered since 2003. Program calendar is continuous. 10-week certificate in International cuisines of the world. 10-week certificate in comprehensive baking I. 10-week certificate in baking II—advanced. 10-week certificate in advanced meal preparation/presentation. 20-week certificate in comprehensive culinary arts program.

Areas of Study

Baking; buffet catering; controlling costs in food service; convenience cookery; culinary French; culinary skill development; food preparation; food purchasing; food service communication; food service math; garde-manger; international cuisine; introduction to food service; meal planning; meat cutting; meat fabrication; nutrition; nutrition and food service; plating and presentation; restaurant opportunities; sanitation; seafood processing; soup, stock, sauce, and starch production; special events management.

Facilities

Classroom; demonstration laboratory; food production kitchen; gourmet dining room; lecture room; library; student lounge; teaching kitchen; special event room.

Typical Student Profile

750 total: 150 full-time; 600 part-time. 100 are under 25 years old; 400 are between 25 and 44 years old; 250 are over 44 years old.

Special Programs

Over 40 special recreational classes (3 hours each on nights and weekends), Children's Culinary Academy 1,2,3 (summers only), 4-week introduction to culinary arts program.

Financial Aid

In 2006, 2 scholarships were awarded (average award was $2200). Program-specific awards include available payment plans. Employment placement assistance is available.

Application Information

Students may begin participation year-round. Applications are accepted continuously.

Contact

Director of Admissions, Professional and Recreational Cooking School, 2366 Pelham Avenue, Los Angeles, CA 90064. Telephone: 310-470-2640. Fax: 310-470-2642. World Wide Web: http://www.culinaryclassroom.com/.

Chef Is Chef Culinary School

North Hollywood, California

General Information

Private, coeducational, culinary institute. Urban campus. Founded in 2007.

Program Information

Offered since 2007. Program calendar is continuous. Certificate in Certified Professional Food Manager. 36-week certificate in Professional Chef.

Program Affiliation

American Culinary Federation; Green Restaurant Association.

Areas of Study

Baking; beverage management; controlling costs in food service; culinary French; culinary skill development; food preparation; food purchasing; food service math; garde-manger; international cuisine; kitchen management; meat cutting; meat fabrication; patisserie; sanitation; saucier; seafood processing; soup, stock, sauce, and starch production; wines and spirits.

Facilities

Bake shop; classroom; food production kitchen; gourmet dining room.

Faculty

11 total: 5 full-time; 6 part-time. 11 are culinary-certified teachers. Prominent faculty: Soerke Peters Executive Chef. Faculty-student ratio: 1:1.

Special Programs

One-on-one training in Italian restaurant setting (only 12 students per 9 months program); ice carving class in San Diego for 2 days including hotel; tea seminar; wine seminar and cheese seminar; field trips including farmers market, meat plant, fish plant, bakery, and farm.

Typical Expenses

Application fee: $50. Tuition: $8295 per 9 months. Program-related fee includes tuition includes knife set, uniforms and books.

Financial Aid

Program-specific awards include student loan assistance, 50% at enrollment and $500 a month. Employment placement assistance is available.

Chef Is Chef Culinary School *(continued)*

Housing

Average off-campus housing cost per month: $600–$1000.

Application Information

Students may begin participation in January, February, March, April, May, June, September, October, November, and December. Applications are accepted continuously. In 2007, 60 applied; 2 were accepted. Applicants must interview; submit a formal application and 250 word essay describing your reasons for wishing to pursue a career in the culinary industry and proof of high school graduation or equivalent; hands-on working interview 1 day.

Contact

Soerke Peters, Office of Admissions, 4100 Cahuenga Boulevard, North Hollywood, CA 91602. Telephone: 800-708-9512. Fax: 800-708-9521. E-mail: info@chefischef.com. World Wide Web: http://www.chefischef.com.

See display on page 85.

City College of San Francisco

Culinary Arts and Hospitality Studies Department

San Francisco, California

General Information

Public, coeducational, two-year college. Urban campus. Founded in 1935. Accredited by Western Association of Schools and Colleges.

Program Information

Offered since 1936. Accredited by American Culinary Federation Accrediting Commission. Program calendar is divided into semesters. 4-semester associate degree in hotel management. 4-semester associate degree in food service management. 4-semester associate degree in culinary arts.

Program Affiliation

American Culinary Federation; American Institute of Wine & Food; California Hotel and Motel Association; California Restaurant Association; Council on Hotel, Restaurant, and Institutional Education; Gastronomic Club; National Restaurant Association; National Restaurant Association Educational Foundation; Women Chefs and Restaurateurs.

Areas of Study

Baking; beverage management; buffet catering; confectionery show pieces; controlling costs in food service; culinary French; culinary skill development; food preparation; food purchasing; food service communication; food service math; garde-manger; hospitality accounting; hospitality law; hospitality marketing; international cuisine; introduction to food service; kitchen management; management and human resources; meat cutting; meat fabrication; menu and facilities design; nutrition; nutrition and food service; orientation to hospitality; patisserie; restaurant opportunities; sanitation; saucier; seafood processing; soup, stock, sauce, and starch production; wines and spirits.

Facilities

Bake shop; cafeteria; catering service; 3 classrooms; computer laboratory; demonstration laboratory; 3 food production kitchens; gourmet dining room; 3 lecture rooms; library; public restaurant; snack shop; 5 teaching kitchens.

Student Profile

250 total: 220 full-time; 30 part-time. 50 are under 25 years old; 150 are between 25 and 44 years old; 50 are over 44 years old.

Faculty

19 total: 11 full-time; 8 part-time. 11 are industry professionals. Faculty-student ratio: 1:15.

Prominent Alumni and Current Affiliation

Sean O'Brien, Chef/Owner, Myth Restaurant; Belinda Leong, Restaurant Gary Danko, Pastry Chef; Maggie Pond, Cesar, Chef/Partner.

Special Programs

240-hour internship at one of 100 hotels/restaurants in Bay Area.

Typical Expenses

In-state tuition: $300 per semester (15 units). Out-of-state tuition: $2550 per semester (15 units). Tuition for international students: $2850 per semester (15 units). Program-related fees include $150 for uniforms; $240 for kitchen tools; $250 for books (per semester).

Financial Aid

In 2007, 40 scholarships were awarded (average award was $1000). Program-specific awards include Hotel and Restaurant Foundation scholarships. Employment placement assistance is available. Employment opportunities within the program are available.

Housing

Average off-campus housing cost per month: $1000.

Application Information

Students may begin participation in January and August. Application deadline for spring is November 13. Application deadline for fall is April 10. In 2007, 200 applied; 180 were accepted. Applicants must submit a formal application, an essay; international students must submit TOEFL scores (minimum 475).

City College of San Francisco *(continued)*

Contact

Lynda Hirose, Program Advisor, Culinary Arts and Hospitality Studies Department, 50 Phelan Avenue, SW156, San Francisco, CA 94112-1821. Telephone: 415-239-3152. Fax: 415-239-3913. E-mail: cahs@ccsf.edu. World Wide Web: http://www.ccsf.edu/cahs.

See display on page 87.

College of the Canyons

Hotel and Restaurant Management

Santa Clarita, California

General Information

Public, coeducational, two-year college. Suburban campus. Founded in 1969. Accredited by Western Association of Schools and Colleges.

Program Information

Offered since 1990. Program calendar is divided into semesters. 2-year associate degree in restaurant management. 2-year associate degree in hotel management. 2-year associate degree in combined hotel and restaurant management.

Areas of Study

Beverage management; controlling costs in food service; hospitality law; hotel operations; kitchen management; management and human resources; nutrition and food service; restaurant opportunities; sales/marketing; sanitation.

Facilities

Classroom; computer laboratory; learning resource center; library.

Typical Student Profile

100 full-time.

Special Programs

Internships, wine tasting appreciation class.

Financial Aid

In 2006, 2 scholarships were awarded (average award was $500). Employment placement assistance is available.

Application Information

Students may begin participation in January, June, and August. Applications are accepted continuously. In 2006, 54 applied; 54 were accepted. Applicants must submit a formal application.

Contact

Director of Admissions, Hotel and Restaurant Management, 26455 Rockwell Canyon Road, Santa Clarita, CA 91355. Telephone: 661-362-3712. Fax: 661-259-8302. World Wide Web: http://www.coc.cc.ca.us/.

Contra Costa College

Culinary Arts

San Pablo, California

General Information

Public, coeducational, two-year college. Urban campus. Founded in 1948. Accredited by Western Association of Schools and Colleges.

Program Information

Offered since 1964. Program calendar is divided into semesters. 2-year certificate in cooking. 2-year certificate in baking. 3-year associate degree in culinary arts.

Program Affiliation

National Restaurant Association.

Areas of Study

Baking; buffet catering; confectionery show pieces; controlling costs in food service; culinary French; culinary skill development; food preparation; food purchasing; food service communication; food service math; garde-manger; international cuisine; introduction to food service; kitchen management; management and human resources; meal planning; meat cutting; meat fabrication; menu and facilities design; nutrition; patisserie; sanitation; saucier; seafood processing; soup, stock, sauce, and starch production; wines and spirits.

Facilities

Bakery; cafeteria; 2 classrooms; 4 computer laboratories; gourmet dining room; 2 laboratories; library; public restaurant; 2 teaching kitchens.

Typical Student Profile

180 total: 100 full-time; 80 part-time.

Special Programs

Related internships, culinary competitions.

Financial Aid

In 2006, 3 scholarships were awarded (average award was $500). Program-specific awards include California Restaurant Association scholarships. Employment placement assistance is available. Employment opportunities within the program are available.

Application Information
Students may begin participation in January and August. Applications are accepted continuously. In 2006, 100 applied; 100 were accepted. Applicants must submit a formal application.

Contact
Director of Admissions, Culinary Arts, 2600 Mission Bell Drive, San Pablo, CA 94806-3195. Telephone: 510-235-7800 Ext. 4409. Fax: 510-236-6768. World Wide Web: http://www.contracosta.cc.ca.us.

The Culinary Institute of America

The Culinary Institute of America at Greystone

St. Helena, California

General Information
Private, coeducational, culinary institute. Rural campus. Founded in 1946. Accredited by Accrediting Commission of Career Schools and Colleges of Technology, Middle States Association of Colleges and Schools.

Program Information
Offered since 1946. Program calendar is divided into semesters. 21-month associate degree in culinary arts. 30-week certificate in baking and pastry arts. 30-week certificate in accelerated culinary arts.

Program Affiliation
American Culinary Federation; American Dietetic Association; American Institute of Baking; American Institute of Wine & Food; Confrerie de la Chaine des Rotisseurs; Council on Hotel, Restaurant, and Institutional Education; International Association of Culinary Professionals; International Foodservice Editorial Council; James Beard Foundation, Inc.; Napa Valley Wine Library Association; National Association for the Specialty Food Trade, Inc.; National Restaurant Association; Oldways Preservation and Exchange Trust; Society of Wine Educators; Sommelier Society of America; The Bread Bakers Guild of America; Women Chefs and Restaurateurs.

Areas of Study
Baking; beverage management; buffet catering; confectionery show pieces; controlling costs in food service; culinary skill development; food preparation; food service math; garde-manger; international cuisine; introduction to food service; management and human resources; meat cutting; meat fabrication; menu and facilities design; nutrition; nutrition and food service; patisserie; restaurant opportunities; sanitation; saucier; seafood processing; soup, stock, sauce, and starch production; wines and spirits.

Facilities
2 bake shops; cafeteria; 7 classrooms; computer laboratory; 2 demonstration laboratories; garden; library; public restaurant; student lounge; 6 teaching kitchens; amphitheater.

Typical Student Profile
125 full-time. 105 are under 25 years old; 20 are between 25 and 44 years old.

Special Programs
21-week paid externship (associate's only).

Financial Aid
Program-specific awards include ACAP Dean's Scholarship ($2000), Classic Residences by Hyatt Scholarship ($5,000). Employment placement assistance is available. Employment opportunities within the program are available.

Housing
Coed housing available.

Application Information
Students may begin participation in January, March, April, July, September, and October. Applications are accepted continuously. Applicants must interview; submit a formal application, letters of reference, an essay, academic transcripts; and pass math and writing competency exams.

Contact
Director of Admissions, The Culinary Institute of America at Greystone, Admissions Officer, 1946 Campus Drive, Hyde Park, NY 12538. Telephone: 800-CULINARY. World Wide Web: http://www.prochef.com/.

See display on page 221.

Epicurean School of Culinary Arts

Los Angeles, California

General Information
Private, coeducational, culinary institute. Urban campus. Founded in 1985.

Program Information
Offered since 1985. Program calendar is continuous. Certificate in baking II. Certificate in baking I. 10-session certificate in baking III. 10-week certificate in professional chef II. 25-week certificate in professional chef I.

Epicurean School of Culinary Arts *(continued)*

Financial Aid
Employment placement assistance is available.

Application Information
Students may begin participation year-round. Applications are accepted continuously. Applicants must submit an informal application.

Contact
Director of Admissions, 8500 Melrose Avenue, Los Angeles, CA 90069. Telephone: 310-659-5990. Fax: 310-659-0302. World Wide Web: http://EpicureanSchool.com/.

Institute of Technology

Clovis, California

General Information
Private institution.

Program Information
Certificate in culinary arts specialist. Certificate in baking and pastry specialist. Diploma in culinary arts professional.

Contact
Director of Admissions, 731 W. Shaw, Clovis, CA 93612. Telephone: 800-696-6146. World Wide Web: http://www.it-colleges.edu/.

Institute of Technology–Modesto

Modesto, California

General Information
Coeducational institution.

Program Information
Certificate in culinary arts professional. Certificate in baking and pastry specialist. Diploma in culinary arts professional.

Application Information
Applications are accepted continuously.

Contact
Director of Admissions, 5737 Stoddard Road, Modesto, CA 95356. Telephone: 800-696-6146. World Wide Web: http://www.it-colleges.edu/modesto.php.

Institute of Technology–Roseville

Roseville, California

General Information
Coeducational institution.

Program Information
Certificate in culinary arts professional. Certificate in baking and pastry specialist. Diploma in culinary arts professional.

Application Information
Applications are accepted continuously.

Contact
Director of Admissions, 333 Sunrise Avenue, Suite 400, Roseville, CA 95661. Telephone: 800-696-6146. World Wide Web: http://www.it-colleges.edu/roseville.php.

The International Culinary School at The Art Institute of California–Inland Empire

San Bernardino, California

General Information
Private, coeducational institution.

Program Information
Associate degree in Culinary Arts. Bachelor's degree in Culinary Management.

Contact
Office of Admissions, 630 East Brier Drive, San Bernardino, CA 92408. Telephone: 909-915-2100. World Wide Web: http://www.artinstitutes.edu/inlandempire/.

See color display following page 332.

The International Culinary School at The Art Institute of California–Los Angeles

Santa Monica, California

General Information
Private, coeducational institution.

Program Information
Associate degree in Culinary Arts. Associate degree in Baking and Pastry. Bachelor's degree in Culinary Management. Diploma in The Art of Cooking. Diploma in Baking and Pastry.

Contact
Office of Admissions, 2900 31st Street, Santa Monica, CA 90405. Telephone: 310-752-4700. World Wide Web: http://www.artinstitutes.edu/losangeles/.

See color display following page 332.

The International Culinary School at The Art Institute of California–Orange County

Santa Ana, California

General Information
Private, coeducational institution.

Program Information
Associate degree in Culinary Arts. Associate degree in Baking and Pastry. Bachelor's degree in Culinary Management. Diploma in Baking and Pastry. Diploma in Art of Cooking.

Contact
Office of Admissions, 3601 West Sunflower Avenue, Santa Ana, CA 92704. Telephone: 714-830-0200. World Wide Web: http://www.artinstitutes.edu/orangecounty/.

See color display following page 332.

The International Culinary School at The Art Institute of California–Sacramento

Sacramento, California

General Information
Private, coeducational institution.

Program Information
Associate degree in Culinary Arts. Bachelor's degree in Culinary Management. Diploma in Baking and Pastry. Diploma in Art of Cooking.

Contact
Office of Admissions, 2850 Gateway Oaks Drive, Suite 100, Sacramento, CA 95833. Telephone: 916-830-6320. World Wide Web: http://www.artinstitutes.edu/sacramento/.

See color display following page 332.

The International Culinary School at The Art Institute of California–San Diego

San Diego, California

General Information
Private, coeducational institution.

Program Information
Associate degree in Culinary Arts. Associate degree in Baking and Pastry. Bachelor's degree in Culinary Management.

Contact
Office of Admissions, 7650 Mission Valley Road, San Diego, CA 92108. Telephone: 858-598-1200. World Wide Web: http://www.artinstitutes.edu/sandiego/.

See color display following page 332.

The International Culinary School at The Art Institute of California–San Francisco

San Francisco, California

General Information
Private, coeducational institution.

Program Information
Associate degree in Culinary Arts. Bachelor's degree in Culinary Management.

Contact
Office of Admissions, 1170 Market Street, San Francisco, CA 94102. Telephone: 415-865-0198. World Wide Web: http://www.artinstitutes.edu/sanfrancisco/.

See color display following page 332.

The International Culinary School at The Art Institute of California–Sunnyvale

Sunnyvale, California

General Information
Private, coeducational institution.

Program Information
Associate degree in Culinary Arts. Bachelor's degree in Culinary Management.

Contact
Office of Admissions, 1120 Kifer Road, Sunnyvale, CA 94086. Telephone: 408-962-6400. World Wide Web: http://www.artinstitutes.edu/sunnyvale/.

See color display following page 332.

JobTrain

Culinary Arts Program

Redwood City, California

General Information
Private, coeducational, adult vocational school. Suburban campus. Founded in 1965. Accredited by Western Association of Schools and Colleges.

Program Information
Offered since 1965. Accredited by Western Association of Schools and Colleges. Program calendar is continuous, year-round. 3-month certificate in culinary arts.

Program Affiliation
National Restaurant Association; National Restaurant Association Educational Foundation.

Areas of Study
Baking; buffet catering; controlling costs in food service; culinary French; culinary skill development; food preparation; food purchasing; food service communication; food service math; garde-manger; international cuisine; introduction to food service; kitchen management; management and human resources; meal planning; meat cutting; menu and facilities design; nutrition; nutrition and food service; patisserie; restaurant opportunities; sanitation; saucier; seafood processing; soup, stock, sauce, and starch production; wines and spirits.

Facilities
Catering service; classroom; food production kitchen; learning resource center; lecture room; library; public restaurant.

Typical Student Profile
70 total: 45 full-time; 25 part-time.

Special Programs
Two-week externship (unpaid).

Financial Aid
Program-specific awards include opportunity to work with caterers. Employment placement assistance is available. Employment opportunities within the program are available.

Application Information
Students may begin participation year-round. Applications are accepted continuously. Applicants must submit a formal application.

Contact
Director of Admissions, Culinary Arts Program, 1200 O'Brien Drive, Menlo Park, CA 94025. Telephone: 650-330-6429. Fax: 650-324-3419. World Wide Web: http://www.jobtrainworks.org/jobtrain/index.html.

Kitchen Academy

Hollywood, California

General Information
Coeducational, culinary institute. Urban campus.

Program Information
30-week diploma in professional culinary arts.

Financial Aid
Employment placement assistance is available.

Application Information
Applications are accepted continuously. Applicants must interview; submit a formal application and Wonderlic Exam.

Contact
Director of Admissions, 6370 West Sunset Boulevard, Hollywood, CA 90028. Telephone: 888-807-7222. World Wide Web: http://www.kitchenacademy.com/.

Kitchen Academy–Sacramento

Sacramento, California

General Information
Coeducational, culinary institute. Urban campus.

Program Information
30-week diploma in professional culinary arts.

Financial Aid
Employment placement assistance is available.

Application Information
Applications are accepted continuously. Applicants must interview; submit a formal application and Wonderlic Exam.

Contact
Director of Admissions, 2450 Del Paso Road, Sacramento, CA 95834. Telephone: 888-807-7222. World Wide Web: http://www.kitchenacademy.com/.

Lake Tahoe Community College

Culinary Arts Department

South Lake Tahoe, California

General Information
Public, coeducational, two-year college. Small-town setting. Founded in 1975. Accredited by Western Association of Schools and Colleges.

Program Information
Offered since 2000. Program calendar is divided into quarters. Certificate of specialization in cooking. 1-year certificate of achievement in culinary arts. 1-year certificate of specialization in wine. 1-year certificate of specialization in whole life foods. 1-year certificate of specialization in global cuisine. 1-year certificate of specialization in baking and pastry. 1- to 2-year advanced certificate in culinary arts. 2-quarter certificate in culinary arts. 2- to 3-year associate degree in culinary arts.

Program Affiliation
American Center for Wine, Food and the Arts; American Culinary Federation; Chefs Collaborative 2000; Copia; National Restaurant Association Educational Foundation; Oldways Preservation and Exchange Trust.

Areas of Study
Baking; beverage management; buffet catering; controlling costs in food service; culinary skill development; food preparation; food purchasing; food service math; garde-manger; history of food and cooking; ice carving; international cuisine; introduction to food service; kitchen management; management and human resources; nutrition; patisserie; restaurant opportunities; sanitation; soup, stock, sauce, and starch production; wines and spirits.

Facilities
Bake shop; cafeteria; catering service; classroom; computer laboratory; demonstration laboratory; food production kitchen; garden; gourmet dining room; lecture room; public restaurant; teaching kitchen.

Typical Student Profile
450 total: 50 full-time; 400 part-time. 80 are under 25 years old; 200 are between 25 and 44 years old; 170 are over 44 years old.

Special Programs
Field trips and classes in Napa Valley and San Francisco Bay area, paid externships in Lake Tahoe and regional restaurants and resorts, membership in Tahoe Epicurean Club.

Financial Aid
In 2006, 1 scholarship was awarded (award was $1000). Program-specific awards include Foundation Scholarship for advanced classes at CIA Greystone, Lenore Fahey Memorial Scholarship. Employment placement assistance is available. Employment opportunities within the program are available.

Application Information
Students may begin participation in January, April, July, and September. Applications are accepted continuously. Applicants must submit a formal application.

Contact
Director of Admissions, Culinary Arts Department, One College Drive, South Lake Tahoe, CA 96150. Telephone: 530-541-4660 Ext. 334. Fax: 530-541-7852. World Wide Web: http://www.ltcc.edu/.

Long Beach City College

Culinary Arts

Long Beach, California

General Information
Public, coeducational, two-year college. Urban campus. Founded in 1927. Accredited by Western Association of Schools and Colleges.

Program Information
Offered since 1949. Accredited by American Dietetic Association. Program calendar is divided into semesters. 0.5-year certificate in food handlers certification. 1-year certificate in dietetic service supervisor. 1.5-year associate degree in restaurant management. 1.5-year associate degree in hotel/restaurant management. 1.5-year associate degree in commercial baking and pastry. 1.5-year associate degree in catering management. 1.5-year certificate in restaurant management. 1.5-year certificate in dietetic technician. 1.5-year certificate in culinary arts. 1.5-year certificate in commercial baking and pastry. 1.5-year certificate in catering management. 2-year associate degree in dietetic technician. 2-year associate degree in dietetic service supervisor. 2-year associate degree in culinary arts.

Long Beach City College *(continued)*

Program Affiliation

Academic Culinaire Paris; American Culinary Federation; American Dietetic Association; American Institute of Baking; Confrerie de la Chaine des Rotisseurs; French Chefs Association of California; National Restaurant Association; National Restaurant Association Educational Foundation; Société Culinaire Philanthropique; The Bread Bakers Guild of America; Toques Blanches.

Areas of Study

Baking; beverage management; buffet catering; controlling costs in food service; culinary French; culinary skill development; food preparation; food purchasing; food service communication; food service math; garde-manger; international cuisine; introduction to food service; kitchen management; meal planning; meat cutting; meat fabrication; menu and facilities design; nutrition; nutrition and food service; patisserie; restaurant opportunities; sanitation; saucier; seafood processing; soup, stock, sauce, and starch production; wines and spirits.

Facilities

2 bake shops; 2 cafeterias; 2 catering services; 4 classrooms; coffee shop; 2 computer laboratories; 4 demonstration laboratories; 4 food production kitchens; garden; gourmet dining room; 2 learning resource centers; 4 lecture rooms; 2 libraries; 2 public restaurants; 2 snack shops; 2 student lounges; 3 teaching kitchens.

Typical Student Profile

155 total: 37 full-time; 118 part-time. 63 are under 25 years old; 64 are between 25 and 44 years old; 28 are over 44 years old.

Special Programs

Culinary set competitions, food expositions and field trips (produce, meat, and seafood processing companies).

Financial Aid

Program-specific awards include home economics and dietetics scholarships.

Application Information

Students may begin participation in January, June, and August. Applications are accepted continuously. Applicants must submit a formal application.

Contact

Director of Admissions, Culinary Arts, 4901 East Carson Street, Long Beach, CA 90808. Telephone: 562-938-4502. Fax: 562-938-4334. World Wide Web: http://www.lbcc.edu/.

Mission College

Hospitality Management Program

Santa Clara, California

General Information

Public, coeducational, two-year college. Urban campus. Founded in 1967. Accredited by Western Association of Schools and Colleges.

Program Information

Offered since 1967. Accredited by American Culinary Federation Accrediting Commission, Council on Hotel, Restaurant and Institutional Education. National Restaurant Association Educational Foundation ManageFirst certificates available. Program calendar is divided into semesters. 2-semester certificate in food service fundamentals. 3-semester certificate in food service. 4-semester associate degree in food service management.

Program Affiliation

American Culinary Federation; California Restaurant Association; Council on Hotel, Restaurant, and Institutional Education; Hospitality Sales and Marketing Association International; National Association of Catering Executives; National Association of College and University Food Service; National Restaurant Association; National Restaurant Association Educational Foundation; The Bread Bakers Guild of America.

Areas of Study

Baking; beverage management; buffet catering; controlling costs in food service; culinary skill development; food preparation; food purchasing; food service math; international cuisine; introduction to food service; kitchen management; management and human resources; meal planning; meat cutting; meat fabrication; menu and facilities design; nutrition; nutrition and food service; restaurant operation; restaurant opportunities; sanitation; saucier; seafood processing; soup, stock, sauce, and starch production; wines and spirits.

Facilities

Catering service; 3 classrooms; computer laboratory; demonstration laboratory; food production kitchen; garden; gourmet dining room; laboratory; 2 lecture rooms; 2 public restaurants; teaching kitchen.

Typical Student Profile

275 total: 175 full-time; 100 part-time.

Special Programs

Attendance at national conferences and NRA show, culinary competitions, on-site visits to industry segments, one-day wine tours, hands-on catering opportunities.

Financial Aid
In 2006, 4 scholarships were awarded (average award was $250). Program-specific awards include industry-sponsored awards. Employment placement assistance is available. Employment opportunities within the program are available.

Application Information
Students may begin participation in January, May, and August. Application deadline for fall is September 4. Application deadline for spring is February 4. Application deadline for summer is June 7. Applicants must submit a formal application and have high school diploma or GED.

Contact
Director of Admissions, Hospitality Management Program, 3000 Mission College Boulevard, Santa Clara, CA 95050. Telephone: 408-855-5252. Fax: 408-855-5452. World Wide Web: http://www.missioncollege.org/.

Modesto Junior College

Culinary Arts

Modesto, California

General Information
Public, coeducational, two-year college. Urban campus. Founded in 1921. Accredited by Western Association of Schools and Colleges.

Program Information
Offered since 1998. Program calendar is divided into semesters. 1-year certificate in culinary arts. 2-year associate degree in culinary arts.

Areas of Study
Baking; beverage management; buffet catering; controlling costs in food service; culinary French; culinary skill development; food preparation; food purchasing; food service communication; food service math; garde-manger; international cuisine; introduction to food service; kitchen management; management and human resources; meal planning; meat cutting; meat fabrication; menu and facilities design; nutrition; nutrition and food service; patisserie; restaurant opportunities; sanitation; saucier; soup, stock, sauce, and starch production; wines and spirits.

Facilities
Bake shop; catering service; classroom; 3 computer laboratories; demonstration laboratory; food production kitchen; 2 learning resource centers; lecture room; library.

Typical Student Profile
30 full-time.

Financial Aid
In 2006, 8 scholarships were awarded (average award was $125). Employment placement assistance is available. Employment opportunities within the program are available.

Application Information
Students may begin participation in August. Applications are accepted continuously. In 2006, 30 were accepted. Applicants must go through a regular community college application/registration process.

Contact
Director of Admissions, Culinary Arts, 435 College Avenue, Modesto, CA 95350-5800. Telephone: 209-575-6975. Fax: 209-575-6989. World Wide Web: http://mjc.yosemite.cc.ca.us/.

Monterey Peninsula College

Hospitality Program

Monterey, California

General Information
Public, coeducational, two-year college. Small-town setting. Founded in 1947. Accredited by Western Association of Schools and Colleges.

Program Information
Offered since 1975. Program calendar is divided into semesters. 1-year certificate in hospitality operations. 2-semester certificate of completion in line cook. 2-semester certificate of completion in food service management. 2-semester certificate of completion in baking and pastry arts. 2-year associate degree in restaurant management.

Program Affiliation
American Hotel and Lodging Association; Council on Hotel, Restaurant, and Institutional Education; Monterey County Hospitality Association.

Areas of Study
Baking; beverage management; culinary skill development; food purchasing; garde-manger; nutrition; sanitation; special events management.

Facilities
2 classrooms; laboratory; teaching kitchen.

Typical Student Profile
70 total: 40 full-time; 30 part-time.

Financial Aid
Program-specific awards include local scholarships provided by Hospitality Association.

Monterey Peninsula College *(continued)*

Application Information

Students may begin participation in January and August. Applications are accepted continuously. Applicants must submit a formal application and application prior to start date.

Contact

Director of Admissions, Hospitality Program, 980 Fremont Street, Monterey, CA 93940. Telephone: 831-646-4134. Fax: 831-759-9675. World Wide Web: http://www.mpchospitalityprogram.com/.

Mt. San Antonio College

Hospitality and Restaurant Management

Walnut, California

General Information

Public, coeducational, two-year college. Suburban campus. Founded in 1946. Accredited by Western Association of Schools and Colleges.

Program Information

Offered since 1946. Program calendar is divided into semesters. 1-year certificate in hospitality: restaurant management: Level II. 1-year certificate in hospitality: restaurant management: Level I. 1-year certificate in hospitality management: Level II. 1-year certificate in hospitality management: Level I. 1-year certificate in food services. 1-year certificate in catering. 2-year associate degree in hospitality and restaurant management.

Program Affiliation

National Restaurant Association.

Areas of Study

Accounting; controlling costs in food service; food preparation; food service math; garde-manger; introduction to food service; management and human resources; menu and facilities design; nutrition; nutrition and food service; patisserie; restaurant opportunities; sanitation; saucier; seafood processing; soup, stock, sauce, and starch production.

Facilities

Classroom; computer laboratory; demonstration laboratory; food production kitchen; lecture room; teaching kitchen.

Typical Student Profile

175 total: 67 full-time; 108 part-time. 125 are under 25 years old; 44 are between 25 and 44 years old; 6 are over 44 years old.

Special Programs

Job internships (paid/unpaid).

Financial Aid

Employment placement assistance is available. Employment opportunities within the program are available.

Application Information

Students may begin participation in January, February, June, and August. Applications are accepted continuously. Applicants must submit a formal application.

Contact

Director of Admissions, Hospitality and Restaurant Management, 1100 North Grand Avenue, Walnut, CA 91789-1399. Telephone: 909-594-5611 Ext. 4139. Fax: 909-468-3936. World Wide Web: http://www.mtsac.edu/.

Napa Valley College

Napa Valley Cooking School

St. Helena, California

General Information

Public, coeducational, culinary institute. Suburban campus. Founded in 1996. Accredited by Western Association of Schools and Colleges.

Program Information

Offered since 1996. Program calendar is divided into semesters. 14-month certificate in culinary arts.

Program Affiliation

American Culinary Federation.

Areas of Study

Baking; buffet catering; controlling costs in food service; culinary French; culinary skill development; food preparation; food purchasing; food service math; garde-manger; international cuisine; introduction to food service; kitchen management; meat cutting; meat fabrication; menu and facilities design; nutrition; nutrition and food service; patisserie; restaurant opportunities; sanitation; saucier; seafood processing; soup, stock, sauce, and starch production; vegetarian cookery; wine and food; wines and spirits.

Facilities

Classroom; computer laboratory; food production kitchen; garden; lecture room; library; student lounge; teaching kitchen; vineyard.

Typical Student Profile

18 full-time. 3 are under 25 years old; 14 are between 25 and 44 years old; 1 is over 44 years old.

Special Programs
Tours of wineries and local farms, 5-month externship.

Financial Aid
Program-specific awards include 2 Culinary Institute of America scholarships ($1000), various culinary association scholarships ($1000–$5000). Employment placement assistance is available.

Application Information
Students may begin participation in August. Applications are accepted continuously. Applicants must interview; submit a formal application, letters of reference, high school diploma/GED, academic transcripts, and 200-word essay describing career interest.

Contact
Director of Admissions, Napa Valley Cooking School, 1088 College Avenue, St. Helena, CA 94574. Telephone: 707-967-2930. Fax: 707-967-2909. World Wide Web: http://www.napavalley.edu/apps/comm.asp?Q=29.

National Culinary and Bakery School

La Mesa, California

General Information
Private, coeducational, culinary institute. Suburban campus. Founded in 1993.

Program Information
Offered since 1993. Program calendar is continuous. 10-week certificate in pastry. 10-week certificate in bakery. 4-month certificate in culinary arts.

Program Affiliation
American Culinary Federation; National Restaurant Association; National Restaurant Association Educational Foundation.

Areas of Study
Baking; confectionery show pieces; controlling costs in food service; culinary French; culinary skill development; food preparation; food purchasing; food service math; garde-manger; international cuisine; introduction to food service; kitchen management; meal planning; meat cutting; meat fabrication; menu and facilities design; nutrition; patisserie; restaurant opportunities; sanitation; saucier; seafood processing; soup, stock, sauce, and starch production.

Facilities
Bake shop; bakery; catering service; classroom; demonstration laboratory; food production kitchen; lecture room; library.

Typical Student Profile
75 full-time.

Special Programs
Field trips to places of work, catering events for internships, organic mushroom farms.

Financial Aid
Program-specific awards include in-house private financing. Employment placement assistance is available.

Application Information
Applications are accepted continuously. Application deadline for for each session: 2 weeks prior to start. In 2006, 75 applied; 75 were accepted. Applicants must interview and demonstrate desire and passion to become professional chef.

Contact
Director of Admissions, 8400 Center Drive, La Mesa, CA 91942. Telephone: 619-461-2800. Fax: 619-461-2881. World Wide Web: http://www.nationalschools.com/.

The New School of Cooking

Culver City, California

General Information
Private, coeducational institution. Urban campus. Founded in 1999.

Program Information
Offered since 1999. Program calendar is continuous. 10-week diploma in professional baking. 10-week diploma in culinary arts advanced. 20-week diploma in culinary arts.

Program Affiliation
American Culinary Federation; International Association of Culinary Professionals; James Beard Foundation, Inc.; Women Chefs and Restaurateurs.

Areas of Study
Baking; culinary French; culinary skill development; food preparation; meal planning; patisserie; sanitation; seafood processing; soup, stock, sauce, and starch production.

Facilities
Classroom; demonstration laboratory; food production kitchen; teaching kitchen.

Typical Student Profile
72 part-time. 5 are under 25 years old; 55 are between 25 and 44 years old; 12 are over 44 years old.

Special Programs
Regional ethnic series, vegetarian series and individual classes, wine education.

The New School of Cooking *(continued)*

Financial Aid
Employment placement assistance is available.

Application Information
Students may begin participation year-round. Applications are accepted continuously.

Contact
Director of Admissions, 8690 Washington Boulevard, Culver City, CA 90232. Telephone: 310-842-9702. World Wide Web: http://www.newschoolofcooking.com/.

Orange Coast College

Hospitality Department

Costa Mesa, California

General Information
Public, coeducational, two-year college. Suburban campus. Founded in 1947. Accredited by Western Association of Schools and Colleges.

Program Information
Offered since 1964. Accredited by American Culinary Federation Accrediting Commission. Program calendar is semester plus summer session. 1-year certificate in institutional dietetic service supervisor. 1-year certificate in fast food service. 1-year certificate in culinary arts. 1-year certificate in child nutrition programs. 1-year certificate in catering. 2-year associate degree in hotel management. 2-year associate degree in food service management. 2-year associate degree in culinary arts. 2-year certificate in restaurant supervision. 2-year certificate in institutional dietetic technician. 3-year certificate in cook apprentice. 30-month certificate in institutional dietetic service manager.

Program Affiliation
American Culinary Federation; American Dietetic Association; California Restaurant Association; Confrerie de la Chaine des Rotisseurs; International Food Service Executives Association; National Association of College and University Food Service; Retailer's Bakery Association.

Areas of Study
Baking; beverage management; buffet catering; controlling costs in food service; convenience cookery; culinary skill development; dining room management; food preparation; food purchasing; food service communication; food service math; garde-manger; hotel and restaurant law; international cuisine; introduction to food service; kitchen management; management and human resources; meal planning; meat cutting; meat fabrication; menu and facilities design; nutrition; nutrition and food service; patisserie; restaurant opportunities; sanitation; saucier; seafood processing; soup, stock, sauce, and starch production.

Facilities
Bake shop; bakery; cafeteria; catering service; 4 classrooms; computer laboratory; 2 food production kitchens; gourmet dining room; lecture room; library; public restaurant; student lounge.

Typical Student Profile
400 total: 200 full-time; 200 part-time. 90 are under 25 years old; 250 are between 25 and 44 years old; 60 are over 44 years old.

Special Programs
Food show seminar (3 three-hour sessions), student hot food team.

Financial Aid
In 2006, 30 scholarships were awarded. Employment placement assistance is available. Employment opportunities within the program are available.

Application Information
Students may begin participation in January and August. Applications are accepted continuously. Applicants must submit a formal application.

Contact
Director of Admissions, Hospitality Department, 2701 Fairview Road, PO Box 5005, Costa Mesa, CA 92628-5005. Telephone: 714-432-5835. Fax: 714-432-5609. World Wide Web: http://www.orangecoastcollege.com/.

Oxnard College

Hotel and Restaurant Management

Oxnard, California

General Information
Public, coeducational, two-year college. Suburban campus. Founded in 1975. Accredited by Western Association of Schools and Colleges.

Program Information
Offered since 1985. National Restaurant Association Educational Foundation ManageFirst certificates available. Program calendar is divided into semesters. 2-year associate degree in restaurant management. 2-year associate degree in culinary arts. 2-year certificate in restaurant management. 2-year certificate in culinary arts.

Program Affiliation
American Culinary Federation; Council on Hotel, Restaurant, and Institutional Education; National Restaurant Association Educational Foundation.

Areas of Study
Baking; beverage management; buffet catering; controlling costs in food service; convenience cookery; culinary French; culinary skill development; food preparation; food purchasing; food service communication; food service math; garde-manger; international cuisine; introduction to food service; kitchen management; management and human resources; meal planning; menu and facilities design; nutrition; nutrition and food service; restaurant opportunities; sanitation; saucier; soup, stock, sauce, and starch production; wines and spirits.

Facilities
Bake shop; cafeteria; catering service; 2 classrooms; computer laboratory; demonstration laboratory; 2 food production kitchens; gourmet dining room; laboratory; learning resource center; lecture room; library; public restaurant; teaching kitchen.

Typical Student Profile
140 total: 70 full-time; 70 part-time.

Special Programs
Sanitation certification (ServSafe Education Foundation NRA).

Financial Aid
In 2006, 13 scholarships were awarded (average award was $500); 10 loans were granted (average loan was $300). Program-specific awards include loan/voucher program for tools and uniforms. Employment placement assistance is available. Employment opportunities within the program are available.

Application Information
Students may begin participation in January, June, and August. Application deadline for fall is August 18. Application deadline for spring is January 5. Application deadline for summer is May 15. In 2006, 100 applied; 100 were accepted.

Contact
Director of Admissions, Hotel and Restaurant Management, 4000 South Rose Avenue, Oxnard, CA 93033. Telephone: 805-986-5869. Fax: 805-986-5806. World Wide Web: http://www.oxnardcollege.edu/programs/culinary/index.asp.

Professional Culinary Institute

Campbell, California

General Information
Private, coeducational, culinary institute. Suburban campus. Founded in 2004.

Program Information
Offered since 2005. Program calendar is continuous. 1-year associate degree in hospitality management. 11-week diploma in certified sommelier. 8-month diploma in culinary arts. 8-month diploma in baking and pastry arts.

Program Affiliation
American Culinary Federation; Court of Master Sommeliers; National Restaurant Association.

Areas of Study
Baking; beverage management; buffet catering; culinary French; culinary skill development; food preparation; garde-manger; international cuisine; introduction to food service; management and human resources; meat fabrication; menu and facilities design; nutrition; nutrition and food service; patisserie; sanitation; saucier; seafood processing; soup, stock, sauce, and starch production; wines and spirits.

Facilities
Bakery; catering service; 7 classrooms; 2 computer laboratories; 2 demonstration laboratories; library; 2 student lounges; 5 teaching kitchens.

Typical Student Profile
220 total: 120 full-time; 100 part-time. 30 are under 25 years old; 180 are between 25 and 44 years old; 10 are over 44 years old.

Special Programs
Graduate Enhancement program (1-4 day seminar per year for 2 years after graduation), tours of local vineyards and breweries, paid externships.

Financial Aid
In 2006, 2 scholarships were awarded (average award was $7500); 6 loans were granted (average loan was $15,000). Employment placement assistance is available.

Application Information
Students may begin participation in January, April, July, and October. Applications are accepted continuously. In 2006, 250 applied; 220 were accepted. Applicants must interview; submit a formal application, letters of reference, high school transcript and diploma or GED.

Contact
Director of Admissions, 700 West Hamilton Avenue, Suite 300, Campbell, CA 95008. Telephone: 408-370-9190. Fax: 408-370-9186. World Wide Web: http://www.pcichef.com/.

QUALITY COLLEGE OF CULINARY CAREERS

Fresno, California

GENERAL INFORMATION
Private, coeducational, culinary institute. Urban campus. Founded in 1994. Accredited by Accrediting Commission of Career Schools and Colleges of Technology.

PROGRAM INFORMATION
Program calendar is continuous. 14-week certificate in culinary arts. 2-year associate degree in professional cooking and culinary arts. 2-year associate degree in professional baking and pastry chef. 30-week certificate in culinary chef. 40-week certificate in food and beverage manager.

SPECIAL PROGRAMS
Culinary competitions.

APPLICATION INFORMATION
Applicants must interview; submit a formal application, letters of reference, and an essay.

CONTACT
Director of Admissions, 1776 North Fine Avenue, Fresno, CA 93726. Telephone: 559-497-5050.

RICHARDSON RESEARCHES, INC.

Davis, California

GENERAL INFORMATION
Private, coeducational, confectionery food consultancy company. Urban campus. Founded in 1972.

PROGRAM INFORMATION
Offered since 1977. 1-week diploma in confectionery technology. 1-week diploma in chocolate technology.

PROGRAM AFFILIATION
Institute of Food Technologists; National Confectioners Association of the US; Retail Confectioners International.

AREAS OF STUDY
Confectionery and chocolate technologies.

FACILITIES
Computer laboratory; demonstration laboratory; laboratory; lecture room.

TYPICAL STUDENT PROFILE
18 full-time.

APPLICATION INFORMATION
Applications are accepted continuously. Applicants must submit a formal application.

CONTACT
Director of Admissions, 5445 Hilltop Crescent, Oakland, CA 94618. Telephone: 510-653-4385. Fax: 510-653-4865. World Wide Web: http://www.richres.com/.

RIVERSIDE COMMUNITY COLLEGE

Culinary Academy

Riverside, California

GENERAL INFORMATION
Public, coeducational, two-year college. Suburban campus. Founded in 1916. Accredited by Western Association of Schools and Colleges.

PROGRAM INFORMATION
Offered since 1997. Program calendar is divided into semesters. 1-year certificate in culinary arts. 60-unit associate degree in culinary arts.

PROGRAM AFFILIATION
American Culinary Federation; California Restaurant Association.

AREAS OF STUDY
Baking; culinary skill development; food preparation; food purchasing; kitchen management; meal planning; restaurant opportunities; sanitation; saucier; soup, stock, sauce, and starch production.

FACILITIES
Bake shop; bakery; catering service; 2 classrooms; coffee shop; computer laboratory; 3 demonstration laboratories; food production kitchen; gourmet dining room; 3 laboratories; learning resource center; 2 lecture rooms; library; public restaurant; 3 teaching kitchens.

TYPICAL STUDENT PROFILE
146 total: 25 full-time; 121 part-time.

SPECIAL PROGRAMS
Field trips, food competitions, Skills USA/VICA Club.

FINANCIAL AID
In 2006, 3 scholarships were awarded. Employment placement assistance is available. Employment opportunities within the program are available.

APPLICATION INFORMATION
Students may begin participation in January and August. Application deadline for winter is October 3. Application deadline for fall is May 22. In 2006, 300 applied; 121 were accepted. Applicants must interview; submit a formal application and take aptitude test.

Contact
Director of Admissions, Culinary Academy, 1533 Spruce Street, Riverside, CA 92507. Telephone: 951-955-3311. Fax: 951-222-8095. World Wide Web: http://www.rcc.edu/academicprograms/culinary/index.cfm.

San Diego Mesa College

Hospitality Management

San Diego, California

General Information
Public, coeducational, two-year college. Urban campus. Founded in 1964. Accredited by Western Association of Schools and Colleges.

Program Information
Offered since 1964. Accredited by American Dietetic Association. Program calendar is divided into semesters. 1-year certificate in hotel management. 1-year certificate in dietetic supervision. 1-year certificate in destination and event management. 1-year certificate in culinary arts/culinary management. 2-year associate degree in hotel management. 2-year associate degree in destination and event management. 2-year associate degree in culinary arts/culinary management.

Program Affiliation
American Culinary Federation; American Dietetic Association.

Areas of Study
Baking; buffet catering; confectionery show pieces; controlling costs in food service; culinary French; culinary skill development; food preparation; food purchasing; garde-manger; introduction to food service; kitchen management; management and human resources; meal planning; meat cutting; meat fabrication; menu and facilities design; nutrition; nutrition and food service; restaurant opportunities; sanitation; saucier; seafood processing; soup, stock, sauce, and starch production.

Facilities
Bake shop; bakery; cafeteria; catering service; classroom; 2 computer laboratories; 2 demonstration laboratories; food production kitchen; garden; gourmet dining room; laboratory; learning resource center; lecture room; library; public restaurant; snack shop; student lounge; teaching kitchen.

Typical Student Profile
300 total: 200 full-time; 100 part-time.

Special Programs
Culinary competitions.

Financial Aid
In 2006, 8 scholarships were awarded (average award was $500). Employment opportunities within the program are available.

Application Information
Students may begin participation in January and August. Application deadline for fall is August 20. Application deadline for spring is January 15. In 2006, 150 applied; 150 were accepted. Applicants must have a high school diploma.

Contact
Director of Admissions, Hospitality Management, 7250 Mesa College Drive, San Diego, CA 92111. Telephone: 619-388-2240. Fax: 619-388-2677. World Wide Web: http://www.sdmesa.edu/.

Santa Barbara City College

Hotel, Restaurant, and Culinary Program

Santa Barbara, California

General Information
Public, coeducational, two-year college. Suburban campus. Founded in 1908. Accredited by Western Association of Schools and Colleges.

Program Information
Offered since 1970. Accredited by American Culinary Federation Accrediting Commission. Program calendar is divided into semesters. 4-semester certificate in restaurant management. 4-semester certificate in hotel management. 4-semester certificate in culinary arts. 5-semester associate degree in restaurant management. 5-semester associate degree in hotel management. 5-semester associate degree in culinary arts.

Program Affiliation
American Culinary Federation; American Institute of Wine & Food; California Restaurant Association; Confrerie de la Chaine des Rotisseurs; Council on Hotel, Restaurant, and Institutional Education; International Association of Culinary Professionals; National Restaurant Association; National Restaurant Association Educational Foundation; The Bread Bakers Guild of America.

Areas of Study
Baking; bartending; beverage management; buffet catering; confectionery show pieces; controlling costs in food service; convenience cookery; culinary French; culinary skill development; food preparation; food purchasing; food service communication; food service math; garde-manger; international cuisine; introduction to food service; kitchen management; management and

Santa Barbara City College ***(continued)***

human resources; meal planning; meat cutting; meat fabrication; menu and facilities design; nutrition and food service; patisserie; restaurant opportunities; restaurant ownership; sanitation; saucier; seafood processing; soup, stock, sauce, and starch production; wines and spirits.

Facilities

Bake shop; cafeteria; catering service; 3 classrooms; coffee shop; computer laboratory; demonstration laboratory; 5 food production kitchens; garden; gourmet dining room; laboratory; learning resource center; lecture room; library; 2 public restaurants; 2 snack shops; student lounge; 3 teaching kitchens; 2 food preparation laboratories.

Typical Student Profile

165 total: 150 full-time; 15 part-time. 116 are under 25 years old; 41 are between 25 and 44 years old; 8 are over 44 years old.

Special Programs

Student-run food operation, culinary competitions.

Financial Aid

In 2006, 60 scholarships were awarded (average award was $500). Program-specific awards include scholarships from private sources. Employment placement assistance is available. Employment opportunities within the program are available.

Application Information

Students may begin participation in January and August. Application deadline for spring is November 1. Application deadline for fall is June 1. In 2006, 120 applied; 100 were accepted. Applicants must interview; submit a formal application.

Contact

Director of Admissions, Hotel, Restaurant, and Culinary Program, 721 Cliff Drive, Santa Barbara, CA 93109-2394. Telephone: 805-965-0581 Ext. 2457. Fax: 805-962-0257. World Wide Web: http://www.sbcc.net/.

Tante Marie's Cooking School

San Francisco, California

General Information

Private, coeducational, culinary institute. Urban campus. Founded in 1979.

Program Information

Offered since 1979. 6-month certificate in professional pastry program. 6-month certificate in professional culinary program.

Program Affiliation

American Institute of Wine & Food; International Association of Culinary Professionals; James Beard Foundation, Inc.; San Francisco Professional Food Society; Women Chefs and Restaurateurs.

Areas of Study

Baking; culinary French; culinary skill development; food preparation; food purchasing; garde-manger; international cuisine; introduction to food service; meal planning; meat cutting; nutrition; patisserie; restaurant opportunities; sanitation; saucier; seafood processing; soup, stock, sauce, and starch production; wines and spirits.

Facilities

Demonstration laboratory; garden; 2 teaching kitchens.

Typical Student Profile

29 total: 15 full-time; 14 part-time.

Special Programs

1-month externship.

Financial Aid

Employment placement assistance is available. Employment opportunities within the program are available.

Application Information

Students may begin participation in April and October. Applications are accepted continuously. Applicants must submit a formal application and an essay.

Contact

Director of Admissions, 271 Francisco Street, San Francisco, CA 94133. Telephone: 415-788-6699. Fax: 415-788-8924. World Wide Web: http://www.tantemarie.com/.

University of San Francisco

Hospitality Management Program

San Francisco, California

General Information

Private, coeducational, university. Urban campus. Founded in 1855. Accredited by Western Association of Schools and Colleges.

Program Information

Offered since 1982. Accredited by The Association to Advance Collegiate Schools of Business (AACSB). Program calendar is divided into 4-1-4. 4-year bachelor's degree in hospitality industry management.

Program Affiliation
American Hotel and Lodging Association; California Restaurant Association; Golden Gate Restaurant Association; Hotel Council of San Francisco; International Foodservice Editorial Council; National Restaurant Association; National Restaurant Association Educational Foundation.

Areas of Study
Beverage management; controlling costs in food service; culinary skill development; events management; food preparation; food purchasing; food service communication; food service math; introduction to food service; kitchen management; management and human resources; meal planning; menu and facilities design; nutrition and food service; restaurant opportunities; sanitation; seafood processing; soup, stock, sauce, and starch production; wines and spirits.

Facilities
Classroom; demonstration laboratory; food production kitchen; gourmet dining room; lecture room; library; teaching kitchen.

Typical Student Profile
100 full-time. 97 are under 25 years old; 3 are between 25 and 44 years old.

Special Programs
San Francisco Educational Symposium, wine trip to Napa/Sonoma, 800-hour industry related work experience requirement, 200-hour mentorship program.

Financial Aid
In 2006, 10 scholarships were awarded (average award was $2100); 5 loans were granted (average loan was $8174). Program-specific awards include Joseph Drown Scholarship and Loan Fund, various endowed scholarships, partial tuition to full-tuition scholarships for transfer students. Employment placement assistance is available. Employment opportunities within the program are available.

Housing
Coed, apartment-style, and single-sex housing available.

Application Information
Students may begin participation in January and August. Application deadline for fall is February 1. Application deadline for spring is December 15. Application deadline for for fall early action is November 15. In 2006, 81 applied; 63 were accepted. Applicants must submit a formal application, letters of reference, an essay, SAT scores, high school and/or college transcripts.

Contact
Director of Admissions, Hospitality Management Program, 2130 Fulton Street, San Francicso, CA 94117-1046. Telephone: 415-422-6563. Fax: 415-422-2217. World Wide Web: http://www.usfca.edu/sobam/under/hosp/hospitality.html.

Westlake Culinary Institute

Let's Get Cookin'

Westlake Village, California

General Information
Private, coeducational, culinary institute. Founded in 1988.

Program Information
Offered since 1988. Certificate in catering, beginning course. 10-session certificate in baking. 24-session certificate in professional cooking.

Program Affiliation
International Association of Culinary Professionals.

Special Programs
Basic Techniques for Creative Cooking (twice a year).

Financial Aid
Employment placement assistance is available.

Application Information
Applicants must submit a formal application.

Contact
Director of Admissions, Let's Get Cookin', 4643 Lakeview Canyon Road, Westlake Village, CA 91361. Telephone: 818-991-3940. Fax: 805-495-2554. World Wide Web: http://www.letsgetcookin.com/.

Colorado

Colorado Mountain College

Culinary Institute

Keystone and Vail, Colorado

General Information
Public, coeducational, two-year college. Rural campus. Founded in 1967. Accredited by North Central Association of Colleges and Schools.

Colorado Mountain College ***(continued)***

Program Information

Offered since 1993. Accredited by American Culinary Federation Accrediting Commission. Program calendar is divided into semesters. 1-year certificate in garde manger. 1-year certificate in apprentice cook. 3-year associate degree in culinary arts (with apprenticeship).

Program Affiliation

American Culinary Federation.

Areas of Study

Baking; beverage management; buffet catering; controlling costs in food service; convenience cookery; culinary French; culinary skill development; food preparation; food purchasing; food service communication; food service math; garde-manger; international cuisine; introduction to food service; kitchen management; management and human resources; meal planning; meat cutting; meat fabrication; menu and facilities design; nutrition; nutrition and food service; patisserie; restaurant opportunities; sanitation; saucier; seafood processing; soup, stock, sauce, and starch production.

Facilities

Bake shop; bakery; 6 cafeterias; 4 catering services; 10 classrooms; coffee shop; 2 computer laboratories; 4 demonstration laboratories; 12 food production kitchens; 5 gourmet dining rooms; learning resource center; 12 lecture rooms; library; 12 public restaurants; snack shop; teaching kitchen.

Student Profile

75 full-time.

Faculty

12 total: 2 full-time; 10 part-time. 8 are industry professionals; 2 are culinary-certified teachers. Prominent faculty: Kevin Clarke, CC, JD; Todd Rymer, CEC. Faculty-student ratio: 1:15.

Special Programs

ACF apprenticeships at resorts in Keystone and Vail, culinary competitions.

Typical Expenses

In-state tuition: $1350 per year full-time (in district), $45 per credit hour part-time (in district), $2250 per year full-time (out-of-district), $75 per credit hour part-time (out-of-district). Out-of-state tuition: $7050 per year full-time, $235 per credit hour part-time. Program-related fee includes $850 for tools and texts.

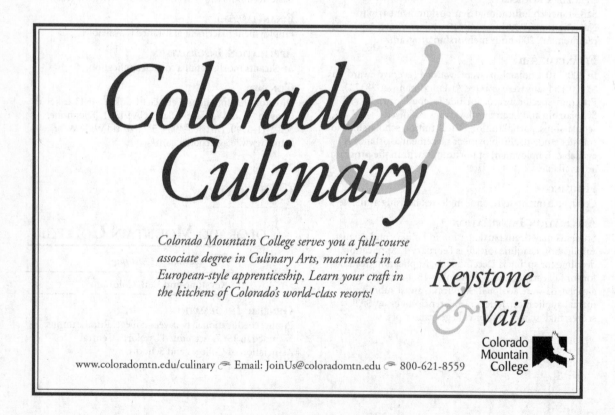

Financial Aid
In 2007, 6 scholarships were awarded (average award was $800). Employment placement assistance is available. Employment opportunities within the program are available.

Housing
Coed and apartment-style housing available. Average on-campus housing cost per month: $350–$450. Average off-campus housing cost per month: $1000.

Application Information
Students may begin participation in June and September. Application deadline for fall (Vail) is July 1. Application deadline for summer (Keystone) is January 15. In 2007, 100 applied; 30 were accepted. Applicants must interview; submit a formal application, letters of reference, an essay, academic transcripts, Accuplacer test scores or ACT/SAT scores.

Contact
Deborah Cutter, Central Admissions, Enrollment Specialist, Culinary Institute, 831 Grand Avenue, Glenwood Springs, CO 81601. Telephone: 800-621-8559. Fax: 970-947-8324. E-mail: dcutter@coloradomtn.edu. World Wide Web: http://www.coloradomtn.edu/.

Cook Street School of Fine Cooking

Professional Food and Wine Career Program

Denver, Colorado

General Information
Private, coeducational, culinary institute. Founded in 1999. Accredited by Accrediting Council for Continuing Education and Training.

Program Information
Offered since 1999. Accredited by State of Colorado Department of Higher Education, Veterans Administration. 18-week diploma in culinary arts.

Program Affiliation
American Culinary Federation; American Institute of Wine & Food; Chefs Collaborative; Colorado Chefs Association; Confrerie de la Chaine des Rotisseurs; Culinary Business Academy; International Association of Culinary Professionals; James Beard Foundation, Inc.; United States Personal Chef Association; Women Chefs and Restaurateurs.

Special Programs
3-week culinary education tour in France and Italy.

Financial Aid
Employment placement assistance is available. Employment opportunities within the program are available.

Application Information
Students may begin participation in January, April, July, and October. Applications are accepted continuously. Applicants must interview; submit a formal application, letters of reference, an essay, high school/college transcripts.

Contact
Director of Admissions, Professional Food and Wine Career Program, 1937 Market Street, Denver, CO 80202. Telephone: 303-308-9300. Fax: 303-308-9400. World Wide Web: http://www.cookstreet.com/.

Culinary School of the Rockies

Professional Culinary Arts Program

Boulder, Colorado

General Information
Private, coeducational, culinary institute. Urban campus. Founded in 1991. Accredited by Accrediting Council for Continuing Education and Training.

Program Information
Offered since 1996. Program calendar is divided into semesters. 15-week diploma in chef track. 5-week diploma in pastry arts. 6-month diploma in culinary arts.

Program Affiliation
American Culinary Federation; American Institute of Wine & Food; Chefs Collaborative; Chefs Cooperative; International Association of Culinary Professionals; James Beard Foundation, Inc.; National Restaurant Association; Slow Food International; Women Chefs and Restaurateurs.

Areas of Study
Baking; controlling costs in food service; culinary French; culinary skill development; food preparation; food purchasing; fundamentals of sensory awareness; garde-manger; international cuisine; kitchen management; meal planning; meat cutting; meat fabrication; menu and facilities design; nutrition and food service; palate development and education; patisserie; restaurant opportunities; sanitation; saucier; seafood processing; soup, stock, sauce, and starch production; wines and spirits.

Culinary School of the Rockies *(continued)*

Facilities
Classroom; computer laboratory; demonstration laboratory; food production kitchen; garden; learning resource center; lecture room; library; teaching kitchen.

Typical Student Profile
113 total: 65 full-time; 48 part-time.

Special Programs
1-month study in Avignon, France (includes work in a French restaurant), 5-week farm to table curriculum, Colorado Farms.

Financial Aid
In 2006, 1 scholarship was awarded (award was $8000); 75 loans were granted (average loan was $15,000). Program-specific awards include Sallie Mae Career Training Loans. Employment placement assistance is available. Employment opportunities within the program are available.

Application Information
Students may begin participation in January, February, May, July, and October. Applications are accepted continuously. In 2006, 150 applied; 112 were accepted. Applicants must interview; submit a formal application, letters of reference, an essay, copy of most recent school transcript.

Contact
Director of Admissions, Professional Culinary Arts Program, 637 South Broadway, Suite H, Boulder, CO 80305. Telephone: 303-494-7988. Fax: 303-494-7999. World Wide Web: http://www.culinaryschoolrockies.com/.

Front Range Community College

Hospitality/Food Management

Fort Collins, Colorado

General Information
Public, coeducational, two-year college. Suburban campus. Founded in 1968. Accredited by North Central Association of Colleges and Schools.

Program Information
Offered since 1998. Program calendar is divided into semesters. 10-credit certificate in beginning culinary arts. 2-year associate degree in hospitality/food management. 6-credit certificate in restaurant operations. 6-credit certificate in hotel operations. 8-credit certificate in advanced culinary arts. 9-credit certificate in hospitality supervision.

Program Affiliation
Colorado Restaurant Association; Council on Hotel, Restaurant, and Institutional Education; National Restaurant Association; National Restaurant Association Educational Foundation.

Areas of Study
Baking; controlling costs in food service; culinary skill development; food preparation; food purchasing; food service management; garde-manger; hospitality management; introduction to food service; kitchen management; management and human resources; meal planning; menu and facilities design; nutrition; nutrition and food service; patisserie; restaurant opportunities; sanitation.

Facilities
Bake shop; classroom; computer laboratory; demonstration laboratory; food production kitchen; laboratory; learning resource center; lecture room; library.

Typical Student Profile
45 total: 20 full-time; 25 part-time.

Special Programs
Culinary exhibitions, summer Rocky Mountain Resorts internships, three experiential internships.

Financial Aid
Employment placement assistance is available. Employment opportunities within the program are available.

Application Information
Students may begin participation in January and August. Applications are accepted continuously. In 2006, 40 applied; 40 were accepted. Applicants must submit a formal application.

Contact
Director of Admissions, Hospitality/Food Management, 4616 South Shields, Fort Collins, CO 80526. Telephone: 970-204-8196. Fax: 970-204-8440. World Wide Web: http://frontrange.edu/.

The International Culinary School at The Art Institute of Colorado

Denver, Colorado

General Information
Private, coeducational institution.

Program Information
Accredited by American Culinary Federation (Associate in Culinary Arts program). Associate degree in Culinary Arts. Associate degree in Baking and Pastry. Bachelor's degree in Culinary Management. Diploma in The Art of Cooking. Diploma in Baking and Pastry.

Contact
Office of Admissions, 1200 Lincoln Street, Denver, CO 80203-2172. Telephone: 303-837-0825. World Wide Web: http://www.artinstitutes.edu/denver/.

See color display following page 332.

Johnson & Wales University–Denver Campus

College of Culinary Arts

Denver, Colorado

General Information
Private, coeducational, four-year college. Urban campus. Founded in 2000. Accredited by New England Association of Schools and Colleges.

Program Information
Accredited by American Dietetic Association, CADE. Program calendar is divided into quarters. Associate degree in culinary arts. Associate degree in baking and pastry arts. Bachelor's degree in food service entrepreneurship. Bachelor's degree in culinary nutrition. Bachelor's degree in culinary arts and food service management. Bachelor's degree in baking & pastry arts and food service management.

Program Affiliation
American Culinary Federation; American Dietetic Association; American Institute of Baking; American Institute of Wine & Food; Confrerie de la Chaine des Rotisseurs; Council on Hotel, Restaurant, and Institutional Education; Institute of Food Technologists; International Association of Culinary Professionals; International Food Service Executives Association; James Beard Foundation, Inc.; National Restaurant Association; National Restaurant Association Educational Foundation; The Bread Bakers Guild of America.

Areas of Study
Baking; beverage management; buffet catering; food purchasing; garde-manger; management and human resources; meat cutting; nutrition; patisserie; sanitation.

Facilities
3 bake shops; bakery; cafeteria; catering service; 21 classrooms; 2 coffee shops; 5 computer laboratories; demonstration laboratory; 2 gourmet dining rooms; 8 laboratories; learning resource center; 6 lecture rooms; library; 2 public restaurants; snack shop; 5 student lounges; 7 teaching kitchens; storeroom; wine & beverage lab; University events center.

Student Profile
724 total: 701 full-time; 23 part-time. 619 are under 25 years old; 78 are between 25 and 44 years old; 4 are over 44 years old.

Faculty
20 total: 18 full-time; 2 part-time. 4 are industry professionals; 2 are culinary-certified teachers. Prominent faculty: John Johnson, CCC, CCE, AAC; Peter Henkel, CEC; Jerry Comar, CEPC; Carrie Stebbins, Certified Sommelier. Faculty-student ratio: 1:22.

Prominent Alumni and Current Affiliation
Anna Olson, Owner, Olson Foods and Bakery, TV Personality-Canadian Food Network; Lisa Herlinger, Owner, Ruby Jewel Ice Cream Treats, Inc..

Special Programs
Every culinary student gets a real-life, career-building work experience through internship or co-op, international study, ACF-certification and 1-year membership for all completing associates degree.

Typical Expenses
Tuition: $21,297 per year. Program-related fees include $1023 for general fee; $265 for orientation fee-first time Freshmen only; $300 for reservation deposit; $1026 for optional weekend meal plan.

Financial Aid
In 2007, 876 scholarships were awarded (average award was $4726). Employment placement assistance is available.

Housing
Coed housing available. Average on-campus housing cost per month: $1000.

Application Information
Students may begin participation in March, June, September, and December. Applications are accepted continuously. In 2007, 1,072 applied; 868 were accepted. Applicants must submit a formal application and official transcript from high school or college.

Contact
Kim Ostrowski, Director of Admissions, College of Culinary Arts, 7150 Montview Boulevard, Denver, CO 80220. Telephone: 877-598-3368. Fax: 303-256-9333. E-mail: admissions.den@jwu.edu. World Wide Web: http://culinary.jwu.edu/.

See color display following page 92.

Mesa State College

Colorado Culinary Academy

Grand Junction, Colorado

General Information
Public, coeducational, comprehensive institution. Urban campus. Founded in 1925. Accredited by North Central Association of Colleges and Schools.

Program Information
Offered since 1998. National Restaurant Association Educational Foundation ManageFirst certificates available. Program calendar is divided into semesters. 1-year certificate in culinary arts. 2-year associate degree in culinary arts.

Program Affiliation
American Culinary Federation; National Restaurant Association; National Restaurant Association Educational Foundation.

Areas of Study
Baking; beverage management; controlling costs in food service; culinary skill development; food preparation; food purchasing; food service math; food service supervision; garde-manger; international cuisine; introduction to food service; management and human resources; meat cutting; meat fabrication; menu and facilities design; nutrition and food service; sanitation; saucier; seafood processing; soup, stock, sauce, and starch production; wines and spirits.

Facilities
Bake shop; cafeteria; 4 classrooms; coffee shop; 2 computer laboratories; 2 demonstration laboratories; food production kitchen; gourmet dining room; learning resource center; library; public restaurant; teaching kitchen; baking kitchen.

Typical Student Profile
92 total: 80 full-time; 12 part-time. 74 are under 25 years old; 10 are between 25 and 44 years old; 8 are over 44 years old.

Special Programs
Culinary competitions, seven week paid internships, tours of Colorado wineries.

Financial Aid
In 2006, 3 scholarships were awarded (average award was $1500). Employment placement assistance is available. Employment opportunities within the program are available.

Housing
Coed, apartment-style, and single-sex housing available.

Application Information
Students may begin participation in January, June, and August. Application deadline for fall is August 23. Application deadline for spring is January 17. Applicants must interview; submit a formal application.

Contact
Director of Admissions, Colorado Culinary Academy, 2508 Blichmann Avenue, Grand Junction, CO 81505. Telephone: 970-255-2632. Fax: 970-255-2626. World Wide Web: http://www.mesastate.edu/.

Metropolitan State College of Denver

Hospitality, Meeting, and Travel Administration Department

Denver, Colorado

General Information
Public, coeducational, four-year college. Urban campus. Founded in 1963. Accredited by North Central Association of Colleges and Schools.

Program Information
Offered since 1963. Accredited by North Central Association of Colleges and Schools. Program calendar is divided into semesters. Certificate in Sommelier Diploma. 4-year bachelor's degree in restaurant administration. 4-year bachelor's degree in hotel administration. 4-year bachelor's degree in culinary arts administration.

Program Affiliation
American Culinary Federation; American Hotel and Lodging Association; Council on Hotel, Restaurant, and Institutional Education; International Food Service Executives Association; Les Amis d'Escoffier Society; National Restaurant Association; National Restaurant Association Educational Foundation; Slow Food International; Tasters Guild International.

Areas of Study
Beers; healthy professional cooking; kitchen management; nutrition; restaurant opportunities; wines and spirits.

Facilities
Bake shop; catering service; 4 classrooms; computer laboratory; demonstration laboratory; food production kitchen; gourmet dining room; learning resource center; 4 lecture rooms; library; public restaurant; 5 student lounges; teaching kitchen.

Typical Student Profile
475 total: 250 full-time; 225 part-time.

SPECIAL PROGRAMS
Swiss Hotel School exchange, international culinary and wine tours for college credit, Certified Cellar Manager Program, International Sommelier Guild Diploma, Tips Program, Bar-Code Certificate.

FINANCIAL AID
Program-specific awards include 2 Super Value Club Foods scholarships ($2000); 10 Southern Wine and Spirits Scholarship ($2000), Colorado Restaurant Association scholarship ($1000), International Sommelier Guild (10 at $75), 5 Culinary ProStart scholarships ($1000), CO Lodging Association (5 at $1000). Employment placement assistance is available. Employment opportunities within the program are available.

HOUSING
Apartment-style housing available.

APPLICATION INFORMATION
Students may begin participation in January and August. Application deadline for fall is August 15. Application deadline for spring is January 15. Applicants must submit a formal application.

CONTACT
Director of Admissions, Hospitality, Meeting, and Travel Administration Department, Campus Box 60, PO Box 173362, Osner, CO 80217. Telephone: 303-556-3152. Fax: 303-556-8046. World Wide Web: http://www.mscd.edu/.

PIKES PEAK COMMUNITY COLLEGE

Culinary Institute of Colorado Springs

Colorado Springs, Colorado

GENERAL INFORMATION
Public, coeducational, two-year college. Urban campus. Founded in 1968. Accredited by North Central Association of Colleges and Schools.

PROGRAM INFORMATION
Offered since 1986. Accredited by American Culinary Federation Accrediting Commission. National Restaurant Association Educational Foundation ManageFirst certificates available. Program calendar is divided into semesters. 1-year certificate in food service management. 1-year certificate in culinary arts. 1-year certificate in baking. 2-year associate degree in culinary arts. 2-year associate degree in baking pastry arts.

PROGRAM AFFILIATION
American Culinary Federation; National Restaurant Association; National Restaurant Association Educational Foundation.

AREAS OF STUDY
Baking; beverage management; buffet catering; confectionery show pieces; controlling costs in food service; convenience cookery; culinary French; culinary skill development; food preparation; food purchasing; food service communication; food service math; garde-manger; international cuisine; introduction to food service; kitchen management; management and human resources; meal planning; meat cutting; meat fabrication; menu and facilities design; nutrition; nutrition and food service; patisserie; restaurant opportunities; sanitation; saucier; seafood processing; soup, stock, sauce, and starch production; wines and spirits.

FACILITIES
Bake shop; bakery; catering service; classroom; coffee shop; 2 computer laboratories; demonstration laboratory; food production kitchen; laboratory; learning resource center; lecture room; library; 2 snack shops; student lounge; teaching kitchen.

TYPICAL STUDENT PROFILE
350 total: 150 full-time; 200 part-time. 150 are under 25 years old; 150 are between 25 and 44 years old; 50 are over 44 years old.

SPECIAL PROGRAMS
Culinary competitions, one-semester paid internship, guest speakers for local organizations.

FINANCIAL AID
In 2006, 15 scholarships were awarded (average award was $1500). Employment placement assistance is available. Employment opportunities within the program are available.

APPLICATION INFORMATION
Students may begin participation in January, June, and August. Applications are accepted continuously. In 2006, 150 applied. Applicants must interview; submit a formal application and take placement test.

CONTACT
Director of Admissions, Culinary Institute of Colorado Springs, 5675 South Academy Boulevard, Colorado Springs, CO 80906. Telephone: 719-502-3193. Fax: 719-502-3301. World Wide Web: http://www.ppcc.edu/.

SCHOOL OF NATURAL COOKERY

Boulder, Colorado

GENERAL INFORMATION
Private, coeducational, culinary institute. Small-town setting. Founded in 1983.

School of Natural Cookery *(continued)*

Program Information

Offered since 1983. Accredited by Colorado Department of Higher Education, Division of Private Occupational Schools. Program calendar is divided into semesters. 12-month certificate in teacher training. 4-month certificate in personal chef training.

Areas of Study

Baking; business plan development; controlling costs in food service; convenience cookery; culinary skill development; energetic nutrition; food preparation; food purchasing; food service communication; food service math; gardening; international cuisine; introduction to food service; kitchen management; management and human resources; meal planning; menu and facilities design; nutrition; nutrition and food service; performance dinners; personal chef repertoire; sanitation; soup, stock, sauce, and starch production; vegan gastronomy.

Facilities

Food production kitchen; garden; gourmet dining room; laboratory; library; student lounge; teaching kitchen.

Typical Student Profile

8 full-time. 2 are under 25 years old; 5 are between 25 and 44 years old; 1 is over 44 years old.

Special Programs

Internships for qualified graduates.

Financial Aid

Program-specific awards include financial aid loan program for qualified applicants, work-study assistance.

Application Information

Students may begin participation in January and July. Application deadline for fall is April 30. Application deadline for spring is October 30. In 2006, 20 applied; 8 were accepted. Applicants must interview, submit a formal application, an essay, and letters of reference.

Contact

Director of Admissions, PO Box 19466, Boulder, CO 80308. Telephone: 303-444-8068. World Wide Web: http://www.naturalcookery.com/.

Connecticut

Briarwood College

Southington, Connecticut

General Information

Private, coeducational, two-year college. Rural campus. Founded in 1966. Accredited by New England Association of Schools and Colleges.

Program Information

Offered since 1986. Program calendar is divided into semesters. 2-year associate degree in hotel/restaurant management.

Program Affiliation

Connecticut Restaurant Association; Council on Hotel, Restaurant, and Institutional Education; National Restaurant Association; National Restaurant Association Educational Foundation.

Areas of Study

Beverage management; food preparation; food purchasing; international cuisine; restaurant opportunities; sanitation.

Facilities

5 catering services; learning resource center; 4 lecture rooms; library; student lounge.

Typical Student Profile

13 total: 10 full-time; 3 part-time. 13 are under 25 years old.

Financial Aid

Employment placement assistance is available. Employment opportunities within the program are available.

Housing

Apartment-style housing available.

Application Information

Students may begin participation in January and September. Applications are accepted continuously. Applicants must submit a formal application.

Contact

Director of Admissions, 2279 Mount Vernon Road, Southington, CT 06489. Telephone: 860-628-4751. Fax: 860-628-6444. World Wide Web: http://www.briarwood.edu/.

Center for Culinary Arts

Culinary Arts

Cromwell, Connecticut

General Information

Private, coeducational, culinary institute. Founded in 1997. Accredited by Accrediting Commission of Career Schools and Colleges of Technology.

Program Information

Accredited by American Culinary Federation Accrediting Commission. 15-month diploma in culinary arts.

Program Affiliation

American Culinary Federation.

Facilities

3 teaching kitchens.

Application Information

Applicants must interview; submit a formal application.

Contact

Director of Admissions, Culinary Arts, 106 Sebethe Drive, Cromwell, CT 06416. Telephone: 860-613-3350. Fax: 860-613-3353. World Wide Web: http://www.lincolnedu.com/campus/cromwell-ct.

Center for Culinary Arts

Shelton, Connecticut

General Information

Accredited by Accrediting Commission of Career Schools and Colleges of Technology.

Program Information

Diploma in culinary arts.

Contact

Director of Admissions, 8 Progress Drive, Shelton, CT 06484. Telephone: 203-929-0592. World Wide Web: http://www.lincolnedu.com/campus/shelton-ct.

Clemens College

Suffield, Connecticut

General Information

Private, coeducational, two-year college. Small-town setting. Founded in 1992. Accredited by New England Association of Schools and Colleges.

Program Information

Offered since 1992. Program calendar is divided into quarters. 1-year certificate in hospitality management. 2-year associate degree in hospitality management. 2-year associate degree in culinary arts management.

Program Affiliation

Council on Hotel, Restaurant, and Institutional Education; International Food Service Executives Association; James Beard Foundation, Inc.; National Restaurant Association; National Restaurant Association Educational Foundation.

Areas of Study

Baking; beverage management; controlling costs in food service; culinary French; culinary skill development; food preparation; food purchasing; food service communication; food service math; garde-manger; hospitality management; international cuisine; introduction to food service; kitchen management; management and human resources; meal planning; meat fabrication; menu and facilities design; nutrition; nutrition and food service; patisserie; restaurant opportunities; sanitation; saucier; soup, stock, sauce, and starch production; travel and tourism; wines and spirits.

Facilities

Bake shop; cafeteria; classroom; computer laboratory; demonstration laboratory; food production kitchen; garden; gourmet dining room; laboratory; learning resource center; lecture room; library; snack shop; student lounge; teaching kitchen.

Typical Student Profile

50 full-time. 45 are under 25 years old; 5 are between 25 and 44 years old.

Special Programs

One 6-month paid internship, two career days per year attended by 4- and 5-star properties.

Financial Aid

In 2006, 40 scholarships were awarded. Program-specific awards include Presidential Scholarship ($2500). Employment placement assistance is available.

Housing

Coed housing available.

Application Information

Students may begin participation in February, April, August, and November. Applications are accepted continuously. Applicants must interview; submit a formal application, letters of reference, official high school transcript.

Contact

Director of Admissions, 1760 Mapleton Avenue, Suffield, CT 06078. Telephone: 860-668-3515. Fax: 860-668-7369. World Wide Web: http://www.clemenscollege.edu/.

Connecticut Culinary Institute

Hartford, Connecticut

General Information

Private, coeducational, culinary institute. Urban campus. Founded in 1987. Accredited by Accrediting Commission of Career Schools and Colleges of Technology.

Program Information

Offered since 1987. Accredited by American Culinary Federation Accrediting Commission. Program calendar is divided into quarters, year-round enrollments. 60-week diploma in pastry arts-full time. 60-week diploma in Italian culinary arts-full time. 60-week diploma in advanced culinary arts-full time. 90-week diploma in pastry arts-part time. 90-week diploma in culinary arts-part time.

Program Affiliation

American Culinary Federation; Connecticut Restaurant Association.

Areas of Study

Baking; controlling costs in food service; culinary skill development; culinary theory; food preparation; food purchasing; food service math; garde-manger; ice carving; international cuisine; introduction to food service; Italian Culinary; kitchen equipment; meal planning; meat cutting; meat fabrication; nutrition; nutrition and food service; restaurant opportunities; sanitation; seafood processing; soup, stock, sauce, and starch production; wines and spirits; world flavors.

Facilities

Cafeteria; 6 classrooms; 2 computer laboratories; demonstration laboratory; food production kitchen; 4 gourmet dining rooms; learning resource center; library; public restaurant; 10 student lounges; 6 teaching kitchens; courtyard; exercise facility; basketball court.

Student Profile

377 total: 292 full-time; 85 part-time.

Faculty

31 total: 29 full-time; 2 part-time. 1 is a National ACF gold medal winner. Prominent faculty: Chef Paul Montaito, CEC; Chef Barbara Howe; Chef Paul Zdanis, CEC. Faculty-student ratio: 1:15.

Special Programs

6-month paid externship (Culinary Arts), 10-week paid externship (Pastry Arts), culinary competitions, Italian program.

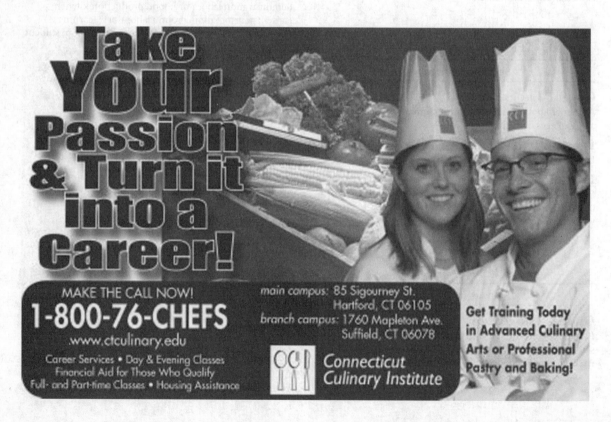

Typical Expenses
Application fee: $100. Tuition: $20,950 (Pastry Arts); $25,200 (Culinary Arts); $34,872 (Italian Culinary Arts). Program-related fees include $100 for insurance; $630 for tools; $460 for uniforms; $200 for technology; $65.40 for tax.

Financial Aid
In 2007, 20 scholarships were awarded (average award was $1000). Program-specific awards include James Beard Scholarships. Employment placement assistance is available. Employment opportunities within the program are available.

Housing
Coed and apartment-style housing available. Average on-campus housing cost per month: $700. Average off-campus housing cost per month: $900.

Application Information
Students may begin participation in January, March, July, and September. Applications are accepted continuously. Applicants must interview; submit a formal application and achieve satisfactory score in school's pre-enrollment test of verbal and quantitative skills.

Contact
Tina Merullo, Director of Admissions, 85 Sigourney Street, Hartford, CT 06105. Telephone: 800-762-4337. Fax: 860-895-6101. E-mail: admissions@ctculinary.com. World Wide Web: http://www.ctculinary.edu/.

Connecticut Culinary Institute–Suffield

Suffield, Connecticut

General Information
Private, coeducational, culinary institute. Rural campus. Founded in 1987. Accredited by Accrediting Commission of Career Schools and Colleges of Technology.

Program Information
Offered since 1987. Accredited by American Culinary Federation Accrediting Commission. Program calendar is divided into quarters, year-round enrollments. 60-week diploma in pastry arts-full time. 60-week diploma in Italian culinary arts-full time. 60-week diploma in culinary arts-full time. 90-week diploma in pastry arts-part time. 90-week diploma in culinary arts-part time.

Program Affiliation
American Culinary Federation.

Areas of Study
Baking; controlling costs in food service; culinary skill development; culinary theory; food preparation; food purchasing; food service math; garde-manger; ice carving; international cuisine; introduction to food service; Italian Culinary; kitchen equipment; meal planning; meat cutting; meat fabrication; nutrition; nutrition and food service; sanitation; seafood processing; soup, stock, sauce, and starch production; wines and spirits; world flavors.

Facilities
Bakery; cafeteria; 6 classrooms; computer laboratory; food production kitchen; lecture room; library; student lounge; 7 teaching kitchens; basketball court; game room; weight room.

Student Profile
111 total: 101 full-time; 10 part-time.

Faculty
8 total: 8 full-time. 1 is a National ACF gold medal winner. Prominent faculty: Paul J. Montaito, CEC; David McGurn, CEC; Joseph Mele, CEC. Faculty-student ratio: 1:15.

Special Programs
6-month paid externship (Culinary Arts), 10-week paid externship (Pastry Arts), culinary competitions, Italian program.

Typical Expenses
Application fee: $100. Tuition: $20,950 (Pastry Arts); $25,200 (Culinary Arts); $34,872 (Italian Culinary). Program-related fees include $100 for insurance; $630 for tools; $460 for uniforms; $200 for technology; $65.40 for tax.

Financial Aid
In 2007, 20 scholarships were awarded (average award was $1000). Program-specific awards include James Beard Scholarships. Employment placement assistance is available. Employment opportunities within the program are available.

Housing
Coed housing available. Average on-campus housing cost per month: $500. Average off-campus housing cost per month: $750.

Application Information
Students may begin participation in January, March, July, and September. Applications are accepted continuously. Applicants must interview; submit a formal application and entrance exam.

Contact
Tina Merullo, Director of Admissions, 85 Sigourney Street, Hartford, CT 06105. Telephone: 800-762-4337. Fax: 860-895-6101. E-mail: admissions@ctculinary.com. World Wide Web: http://www.ctculinary.edu/.

Gateway Community College

Hospitality Management

New Haven, Connecticut

General Information

Public, coeducational, two-year college. Urban campus. Founded in 1968. Accredited by New England Association of Schools and Colleges.

Program Information

Offered since 1985. Accredited by Council on Hotel, Restaurant and Institutional Education. Program calendar is divided into semesters. 1-year certificate in culinary arts. 2-year associate degree in hotel management. 2-year associate degree in foodservice management.

Program Affiliation

Council on Hotel, Restaurant, and Institutional Education; Hospitality Sales and Marketing Association International.

Areas of Study

Baking; beverage management; buffet catering; confectionery show pieces; controlling costs in food service; convenience cookery; culinary skill development; food preparation; food purchasing; food service math; international cuisine; introduction to food service; kitchen management; management and human resources; meal planning; nutrition; nutrition and food service; restaurant opportunities; sanitation; seafood processing; soup, stock, sauce, and starch production; wines and spirits.

Facilities

Bake shop; 2 cafeterias; 2 catering services; 4 computer laboratories; demonstration laboratory; 2 food production kitchens; gourmet dining room; laboratory; 2 libraries; public restaurant; 2 student lounges; teaching kitchen.

Typical Student Profile

160 total: 110 full-time; 50 part-time. 56 are under 25 years old; 56 are between 25 and 44 years old; 48 are over 44 years old.

Special Programs

One-day visit to the International Hotel/Restaurant show in New York City, internships.

Financial Aid

In 2006, individual scholarships were awarded at $500; individual loans were awarded at $1500. Employment placement assistance is available. Employment opportunities within the program are available.

Application Information

Students may begin participation in January and September. Application deadline for fall is September 6. Application deadline for spring is January 16. In 2006, 140 applied; 140 were accepted. Applicants must submit a formal application.

Contact

Director of Admissions, Hospitality Management, 60 Sargent Drive, New Haven, CT 06511-5918. Telephone: 203-285-2175. Fax: 203-285-2180. World Wide Web: http://www.gwctc.commnet.edu/.

Naugatuck Valley Community College

Hospitality Management Programs

Waterbury, Connecticut

General Information

Public, coeducational, two-year college. Urban campus. Founded in 1967. Accredited by New England Association of Schools and Colleges.

Program Information

Offered since 1982. Program calendar is divided into semesters. 1-semester certificate in dietary supervisor. 1-year certificate in culinary arts. 2-year associate degree in hotel management. 2-year associate degree in foodservice management.

Program Affiliation

American Wine Society; Council on Hotel, Restaurant, and Institutional Education; Institute of Food Technologists; National Restaurant Association; National Restaurant Association Educational Foundation.

Areas of Study

Buffet catering; controlling costs in food service; culinary skill development; food preparation; food purchasing; food service communication; food service math; garde-manger; international cuisine; introduction to food service; kitchen management; management and human resources; meal planning; menu and facilities design; nutrition; nutrition and food service; restaurant opportunities; sanitation; soup, stock, sauce, and starch production; wines and viniculture.

Facilities

Catering service; 2 classrooms; 6 computer laboratories; demonstration laboratory; food production kitchen; gourmet dining room; laboratory; learning resource center; library; student lounge; teaching kitchen; vineyard.

Typical Student Profile

115 total: 77 full-time; 38 part-time.

Special Programs
Cooperative education/work experience, international trips with student catering and sommelier clubs.

Financial Aid
Employment placement assistance is available. Employment opportunities within the program are available.

Application Information
Students may begin participation in January, May, and September. Applications are accepted continuously. Applicants must submit a formal application, high school transcript, immunization record.

Contact
Director of Admissions, Hospitality Management Programs, 750 Chase Parkway, Business Division, Waterbury, CT 06708. Telephone: 203-596-8739. Fax: 203-596-8767. World Wide Web: http://www.nvctc.commnet.edu/.

Delaware

Delaware State University

Dover, Delaware

General Information
Public, coeducational, comprehensive institution. Suburban campus. Founded in 1891. Accredited by Middle States Association of Colleges and Schools.

Program Information
Offered since 1982. Accredited by Accreditation Commission for Programs in Hospitality Administration (ACPHA). National Restaurant Association Educational Foundation ManageFirst certificates available. Program calendar is divided into semesters. 4-year bachelor's degree in hospitality and tourism management.

Program Affiliation
Council on Hotel, Restaurant, and Institutional Education; National Restaurant Association; National Restaurant Association Educational Foundation; National Society for Minorities in Hospitality.

Facilities
Classroom; laboratory; public restaurant.

Typical Student Profile
56 total: 52 full-time; 4 part-time.

Special Programs
Paid internships, networking opportunities with hospitality/tourism industry.

Financial Aid
In 2006, individual scholarships were awarded at $1000. Program-specific awards include American Hotel and Lodging Association Award ($1000), NSMH award ($1500), Hyatt, Delaware Lodging Association award ($1000). Employment placement assistance is available. Employment opportunities within the program are available.

Housing
Coed and apartment-style housing available.

Application Information
Students may begin participation in January and September. Application deadline for fall is June 1. Application deadline for spring is December 1. In 2006, 20 applied; 8 were accepted. Applicants must submit a formal application.

Contact
Director of Admissions, 1200 North Dupont Highway, Dover, DE 19901. Telephone: 302-887-7992. Fax: 302-857-6983. World Wide Web: http://www.desu.edu/som/hospitalityandtourism.php.

Delaware Technical and Community College

Culinary Arts Technology

Dover, Delaware

General Information
Public, coeducational, two-year college. Suburban campus. Founded in 1967. Accredited by Middle States Association of Colleges and Schools.

Program Information
Offered since 1993. Program calendar is divided into semesters. 2-year associate degree in culinary arts.

Program Affiliation
American Culinary Federation; National Restaurant Association; National Restaurant Association Educational Foundation.

Facilities
Bake shop; cafeteria; catering service; classroom; computer laboratory; demonstration laboratory; food production kitchen; laboratory; library; teaching kitchen.

Financial Aid
In 2006, 2 scholarships were awarded (average award was $1000). Employment placement assistance is available. Employment opportunities within the program are available.

Delaware Technical and Community College *(continued)*

Application Information
Students may begin participation in January and August. Applications are accepted continuously.

Contact
Director of Admissions, Culinary Arts Technology, 100 Campus Drive, Dover, DE 19904. Telephone: 302-857-1706. Fax: 302-857-1798. World Wide Web: http://www.dtcc.edu/.

Delaware Technical and Community College

Culinary Arts/Food Service Management

Newark, Delaware

General Information
Public, coeducational, two-year college. Suburban campus. Founded in 1967. Accredited by Middle States Association of Colleges and Schools.

Program Information
Offered since 1993. Accredited by American Culinary Federation Accrediting Commission. National Restaurant Association Educational Foundation ManageFirst certificates available. Program calendar is divided into semesters. 1-year diploma in food service management. 2-year associate degree in food service management. 2-year associate degree in culinary arts.

Program Affiliation
American Culinary Federation; National Restaurant Association; National Restaurant Association Educational Foundation.

Areas of Study
Baking; beverage management; buffet catering; controlling costs in food service; convenience cookery; culinary skill development; food preparation; food purchasing; food service communication; food service math; garde-manger; international cuisine; introduction to food service; kitchen management; management and human resources; meal planning; meat cutting; meat fabrication; menu and facilities design; nutrition; nutrition and food service; patisserie; restaurant opportunities; sanitation; saucier; seafood processing; soup, stock, sauce, and starch production.

Facilities
Cafeteria; 10 classrooms; 20 computer laboratories; food production kitchen; gourmet dining room; learning resource center; lecture room; library; student lounge; teaching kitchen.

Typical Student Profile
125 total: 75 full-time; 50 part-time.

Financial Aid
In 2006, 3 scholarships were awarded. Employment placement assistance is available. Employment opportunities within the program are available.

Application Information
Students may begin participation in January, June, and August. Application deadline for fall is April 15. Application deadline for spring is November 15. In 2006, 53 applied; 24 were accepted. Applicants must submit a formal application and letters of reference.

Contact
Director of Admissions, Culinary Arts/Food Service Management, 400 Christiana-Stanton Road, Newark, DE 19713-2197. Telephone: 302-454-3954. Fax: 302-368-6620. World Wide Web: http://www.dtcc.edu/stanton-wilmington/.

University of Delaware

Hotel, Restaurant, and Institutional Management

Newark, Delaware

General Information
Public, coeducational, university. Urban campus. Founded in 1743. Accredited by Middle States Association of Colleges and Schools.

Program Information
Offered since 1988. Program calendar is divided into semesters. 2-year master's degree in hospitality information management. 4-year bachelor's degree in hotel, restaurant, and institutional management.

Program Affiliation
Council on Hotel, Restaurant, and Institutional Education.

Areas of Study
Beverage management; culinary skill development; food preparation; food purchasing; food service communication; introduction to food service; management and human resources; meal planning; menu and facilities design; restaurant opportunities.

Facilities
Gourmet dining room; public restaurant; hotel.

Typical Student Profile
400 full-time.

Financial Aid
Employment placement assistance is available. Employment opportunities within the program are available.

Housing
Coed and single-sex housing available.

Application Information
Students may begin participation in February and August. Application deadline for fall is January 15. Application deadline for spring is November 15. Applicants must submit a formal application.

Contact
Director of Admissions, Hotel, Restaurant, and Institutional Management, 14 West Main Street, Raub Hall, Newark, DE 19716. Telephone: 302-831-6077. Fax: 302-831-6395. World Wide Web: http://www.udel.edu/HRIM.

District of Columbia

Howard University

Center for Hospitality Management Education

Washington, District of Columbia

General Information
Private, coeducational, university. Urban campus. Founded in 1867. Accredited by Middle States Association of Colleges and Schools.

Program Information
Offered since 1970. Program calendar is divided into semesters. 4-year bachelor's degree in hospitality management.

Areas of Study
Bed & Breakfast; catering; food service; Individual Entrepreneur Options; lodging; meeting and event planning.

Facilities
Classroom; computer laboratory; learning resource center; lecture room; library; student lounge.

Typical Student Profile
50 total: 48 full-time; 2 part-time. 45 are under 25 years old; 5 are between 25 and 44 years old.

Special Programs
Internships, field trips, theoretical experiences.

Financial Aid
Program-specific awards include corporate support. Employment placement assistance is available. Employment opportunities within the program are available.

Housing
Coed and apartment-style housing available.

Application Information
Students may begin participation in January and August. Application deadline for fall is March 1. Application deadline for spring is November 1. Application deadline for summer session is April 1. Applicants must submit a formal application and letters of recommendation (helpful).

Contact
Director of Admissions, Center for Hospitality Management Education, 2400 Sixth Street, NW, Administration Building, Washington, DC 20059. Telephone: 202-806-1535. Fax: 202-806-4465. World Wide Web: http://www.bschool.howard.edu/Programs/undergradprograms/management/management.htm.

Florida

Atlantic Technical Center

Coconut Creek, Florida

General Information
Public, coeducational, technical institute. Suburban campus. Founded in 1970. Accredited by Council on Occupational Education.

Program Information
Offered since 1970. Accredited by American Culinary Federation Accrediting Commission. Program calendar is continuous. 1,500-hour certificate in commercial foods/culinary arts.

Program Affiliation
American Culinary Federation; National Restaurant Association.

Areas of Study
Baking; beverage management; convenience cookery; culinary skill development; food preparation; food purchasing; food service math; garde-manger; international cuisine; introduction to food service; kitchen management; management and human resources; meal planning; meat cutting; nutrition; patisserie; restaurant opportunities; sanitation; saucier; seafood processing; soup, stock, sauce, and starch production; wines and spirits.

Atlantic Technical Center *(continued)*

Facilities
Bakery; cafeteria; 3 classrooms; computer laboratory; demonstration laboratory; 2 food production kitchens; gourmet dining room; learning resource center; library; public restaurant.

Typical Student Profile
201 total: 96 full-time; 105 part-time.

Special Programs
Culinary competitions.

Financial Aid
Employment placement assistance is available. Employment opportunities within the program are available.

Application Information
Students may begin participation in January, April, June, August, and November. Applications are accepted continuously. Applicants must interview, and take Test of Adult Basic Education.

Contact
Director of Admissions, 4700 Coconut Creek Parkway, Coconut Creek, FL 33063. Telephone: 754-321-5100 Ext. 2046. Fax: 754-321-5134. World Wide Web: http://www.atlantictechcenter.com/.

Bethune-Cookman University

Hospitality Management Program

Daytona Beach, Florida

General Information
Private, coeducational, four-year college. Small-town setting. Founded in 1904. Accredited by Southern Association of Colleges and Schools.

Program Information
Offered since 1982. Accredited by Council on Hotel, Restaurant and Institutional Education, Accreditation Commission for Programs in Hospitality Administration. Program calendar is divided into semesters. 4-year bachelor's degree in hospitality management (travel and tourism concentration). 4-year bachelor's degree in hospitality management (lodging concentration). 4-year bachelor's degree in hospitality management (food and beverage concentration). 4-year bachelor's degree in hospitality management.

Program Affiliation
American Culinary Federation; Council on Hotel, Restaurant, and Institutional Education; Multicultural Food Service and Hospitality Alliance; National Restaurant Association; National Restaurant Association Educational Foundation.

Areas of Study
Beverage management; culinary skill development; food preparation; kitchen management; management and human resources; menu and facilities design; nutrition and food service; restaurant opportunities.

Facilities
Classroom; computer laboratory; food production kitchen; gourmet dining room; learning resource center; 2 lecture rooms; teaching kitchen.

Typical Student Profile
73 total: 68 full-time; 5 part-time.

Special Programs
National Society for Minorities in Hospitality (NSMH), summer internships, regional and national conferences.

Financial Aid
In 2006, 6 scholarships were awarded (average award was $1000). Program-specific awards include Ocean Waters, American Hotel and Lodging Association, Education Foundation, Marriott Scholarship Foundation. Employment placement assistance is available. Employment opportunities within the program are available.

Housing
Single-sex housing available.

Application Information
Students may begin participation in January, May, and August. Application deadline for fall is June 30. Application deadline for spring is November 30. Application deadline for summer is April 15. In 2006, 95 applied; 71 were accepted. Applicants must submit a formal application, letters of reference, high school transcript or GED, SAT or ACT scores.

Contact
Director of Admissions, Hospitality Management Program, 640 Dr. Mary McLeod Bethune Boulevard, Daytona Beach, FL 32114-3099. Telephone: 386-481-2871. Fax: 386-481-2980. World Wide Web: http://www.cookman.edu/.

Charlotte Technical Center

Culinary Arts Program

Port Charlotte, Florida

General Information

Public, coeducational, technical college. Urban campus. Founded in 1980. Accredited by Council on Occupational Education.

Program Information

Offered since 1980. Program calendar is divided into quarters. 1500-hour certificate in commercial foods and culinary arts.

Program Affiliation

American Culinary Federation; International Foodservice Editorial Council.

Areas of Study

Baking; buffet catering; controlling costs in food service; convenience cookery; culinary French; culinary skill development; food preparation; food purchasing; food service communication; food service math; garde-manger; ice sculpture; international cuisine; introduction to food service; kitchen management; management and human resources; meal planning; menu and facilities design; nutrition; patisserie; restaurant opportunities; safety and first aid; sanitation; saucier; seafood processing; soup, stock, sauce, and starch production; wines and spirits.

Facilities

Bake shop; cafeteria; catering service; classroom; computer laboratory; demonstration laboratory; food production kitchen; gourmet dining room; laboratory; learning resource center; library; public restaurant; snack shop; teaching kitchen.

Typical Student Profile

61 total: 21 full-time; 40 part-time. 40 are under 25 years old; 13 are between 25 and 44 years old; 8 are over 44 years old.

Special Programs

Annual tour and lecture at Ritz Carlton (Naples), culinary competitions.

Financial Aid

Program-specific awards include Florida Vocational Tuition Assistant, Charlotte Technical Center Scholarship. Employment placement assistance is available. Employment opportunities within the program are available.

Application Information

Students may begin participation in January, March, July, and October. Application deadline for summer term is July 30. Application deadline for fall term is September 30. Application deadline for winter term is December 30. Application deadline for spring term is March 30. Applicants must be at least 16 years of age and pass entrance exam.

Contact

Director of Admissions, Culinary Arts Program, 18150 Murdock Circle, Port Charlotte, FL 33948. Telephone: 941-255-7500 Ext. 115. Fax: 941-255-7509. World Wide Web: http://charlottetechcenter.ccps.k12.fl.us/CulinaryArts.cfm.

First Coast Technical College

School of Culinary Arts

St. Augustine, Florida

General Information

Public, coeducational, two-year college. Small-town setting. Founded in 1969. Accredited by Council on Occupational Education, Southern Association of Colleges and Schools.

Program Information

Offered since 1969. Accredited by American Culinary Federation Accrediting Commission. National Restaurant Association Educational Foundation ManageFirst certificates available. Program calendar is divided into quarters. 18-month certificate in culinary arts. 6-month certificate in baking and pastry.

Program Affiliation

American Culinary Federation; Association of Dining Professionals; National Restaurant Association Educational Foundation.

Areas of Study

Baking; buffet catering; convenience cookery; food preparation; food purchasing; garde-manger; international cuisine; introduction to food service; kitchen management; management and human resources; meat cutting; meat fabrication; nutrition and food service; restaurant opportunities; sanitation; seafood processing.

Facilities

Bake shop; cafeteria; catering service; 6 classrooms; computer laboratory; demonstration laboratory; 3 food production kitchens; gourmet dining room; public restaurant.

Typical Student Profile

60 total: 50 full-time; 10 part-time.

Special Programs

Culinary competitions (team)—ACF, culinary competitions (individual)—Skills USA, Baking and Pastry Competition (Individual)—Skills USA.

First Coast Technical College *(continued)*

Financial Aid
Program-specific awards include scholarships from department (after 1 term in program). Employment placement assistance is available. Employment opportunities within the program are available.

Application Information
Students may begin participation in January, March, August, and October. Applications are accepted continuously. In 2006, 60 applied; 55 were accepted. Applicants must submit a formal application.

Contact
Director of Admissions, School of Culinary Arts, 2980 Collins Avenue, St. Augustine, FL 32084. Telephone: 904-829-1070. Fax: 904-829-1089. World Wide Web: http://www.fcti.org.

Florida Culinary Institute A Division of Lincoln College of Technology

West Palm Beach, Florida

General Information
Private, coeducational, culinary institute. Suburban campus. Founded in 1987. Accredited by Accrediting Council for Independent Colleges and Schools.

Program Information
Offered since 1987. Accredited by American Culinary Federation Accrediting Commission. Program calendar is divided into quarters. 12-month diploma in culinary essentials. 12-month diploma in baking and pastry essentials. 18-month associate degree in international baking and pastry. 18-month associate degree in food and beverage management. 18-month associate degree in culinary arts. 18-month diploma in international baking and pastry. 18-month diploma in food and beverage management. 18-month diploma in culinary arts. 36-month bachelor's degree in culinary management.

Program Affiliation
American Culinary Federation; Confrerie de la Chaine des Rotisseurs; Council on Hotel, Restaurant, and Institutional Education; International Association of Culinary Professionals; James Beard Foundation, Inc.; National Restaurant Association; National Restaurant Association Educational Foundation; Retailer's Bakery Association; U.S. Pastry Alliance.

Areas of Study
Baking; beverage management; buffet catering; confectionery show pieces; controlling costs in food service; convenience cookery; culinary French; culinary skill development; food preparation; food purchasing; food service communication; food service math; garde-manger; international cuisine; introduction to food service; kitchen management; management and human resources; meal planning; meat cutting; meat fabrication; menu and facilities design; nutrition; nutrition and food service; patisserie; restaurant opportunities; sanitation; saucier; seafood processing; soup, stock, sauce, and starch production; wines and spirits.

Facilities
2 bake shops; 9 classrooms; computer laboratory; garden; learning resource center; 2 lecture rooms; library; public restaurant; student lounge; 7 teaching kitchens.

Typical Student Profile
650 full-time.

Special Programs
Culinary competitions, field trips, junior chapter of ACF.

Financial Aid
In 2006, individual scholarships were awarded at $2000. Employment placement assistance is available.

Application Information
Students may begin participation in January, February, April, July, August, October, and November. Applications are accepted continuously. Applicants must submit a formal application, and either high school diploma/GED or take Test of Adult Basic Education.

Contact
Director of Admissions, 2410 Metrocentre Boulevard, West Palm Beach, FL 33407. Telephone: 561-842-8324. Fax: 561-842-9503. World Wide Web: http://www.floridaculinary.com/.

Gulf Coast Community College

Culinary Management

Panama City, Florida

General Information
Public, coeducational, two-year college. Small-town setting. Founded in 1957. Accredited by Southern Association of Colleges and Schools.

Program Information
Offered since 1987. Accredited by American Culinary Federation Accrediting Commission. Program calendar is divided into semesters. 2-year associate degree in culinary management.

Program Affiliation
American Culinary Federation; Confrerie de la Chaine des Rotisseurs; Florida Restaurant Association; National Restaurant Association; Retailer's Bakery Association; The Bread Bakers Guild of America.

Areas of Study
Baking; beverage management; buffet catering; confectionery show pieces; controlling costs in food service; convenience cookery; culinary French; culinary skill development; food preparation; food purchasing; food service communication; food service math; garde-manger; international cuisine; introduction to food service; kitchen management; management and human resources; meal planning; meat cutting; meat fabrication; menu and facilities design; nutrition; nutrition and food service; patisserie; restaurant opportunities; sanitation; saucier; seafood processing; soup, stock, sauce, and starch production; wines and spirits.

Facilities
2 bake shops; 2 classrooms; 3 demonstration laboratories; 2 food production kitchens; gourmet dining room; learning resource center; lecture room; library; public restaurant; teaching kitchen.

Typical Student Profile
139 total: 73 full-time; 66 part-time.

Special Programs
French exchange (8 weeks), American Culinary Federation competitions.

Financial Aid
In 2006, 8 scholarships were awarded (average award was $800). Employment placement assistance is available. Employment opportunities within the program are available.

Application Information
Students may begin participation in January and August. Applications are accepted continuously. Applicants must interview, submit a formal application, essay, academic transcripts, and take placement test.

Contact
Director of Admissions, Culinary Management, 5230 West Highway 98, Panama City, FL 32401. Telephone: 850-872-3839. Fax: 850-747-3259. World Wide Web: http://culinary.gulfcoast.edu/.

Hillsborough Community College

Hospitality Management

Tampa, Florida

General Information
Public, coeducational, two-year college. Urban campus. Founded in 1968. Accredited by Southern Association of Colleges and Schools.

Program Information
Offered since 1985. Accredited by American Culinary Federation Accrediting Commission. Program calendar is divided into semesters. 1-year certificate in food and beverage management. 2-year associate degree in restaurant management. 2-year associate degree in hotel management. 2-year associate degree in dietetic technician. 2-year associate degree in culinary arts.

Program Affiliation
American Culinary Federation; American Dietetic Association; International Food Service Executives Association; National Restaurant Association; National Restaurant Association Educational Foundation.

Areas of Study
Baking; beverage management; controlling costs in food service; culinary skill development; food preparation; food purchasing; food service math; garde-manger; international cuisine; introduction to food service; kitchen management; management and human resources; meal planning; menu and facilities design; nutrition; nutrition and food service; sanitation; saucier; seafood processing; wines and spirits.

Facilities
Bake shop; cafeteria; 2 classrooms; computer laboratory; demonstration laboratory; food production kitchen; laboratory; learning resource center; lecture room; library; public restaurant; snack shop; student lounge; teaching kitchen.

Typical Student Profile
147 full-time. 91 are under 25 years old; 43 are between 25 and 44 years old; 13 are over 44 years old.

Special Programs
2-year paid internship, culinary competitions.

Financial Aid
In 2006, 4 scholarships were awarded (average award was $500). Employment placement assistance is available. Employment opportunities within the program are available.

Housing
Apartment-style housing available.

Hillsborough Community College *(continued)*

Application Information
Students may begin participation in January, May, and August. Applications are accepted continuously. In 2006, 204 applied. Applicants must submit a formal application and high school diploma or GED.

Contact
Director of Admissions, Hospitality Management, PO Box 30030, Tampa, FL 33630. Telephone: 813-253-7358. Fax: 813-253-7400. World Wide Web: http://www.hccfl.edu/.

Indian River Community College

Culinary Institute of the Treasure Coast

Fort Pierce, Florida

General Information
Public, coeducational, two-year college. Small-town setting. Founded in 1960. Accredited by Southern Association of Colleges and Schools.

Program Information
Offered since 1994. Accredited by American Culinary Federation Accrediting Commission. Program calendar is divided into semesters. 2-year associate degree in restaurant management and culinary arts. 3-year certificate in commercial foods and culinary arts apprenticeship.

Program Affiliation
American Culinary Federation.

Areas of Study
Baking; buffet catering; controlling costs in food service; culinary French; food preparation; food purchasing; food service communication; food service math; garde-manger; introduction to food service; kitchen management; management and human resources; meal planning; meat cutting; meat fabrication; menu and facilities design; nutrition and food service; sanitation; saucier; seafood processing; soup, stock, sauce, and starch production.

Facilities
3 bake shops; 4 classrooms; 3 demonstration laboratories; 3 food production kitchens; 3 laboratories; learning resource center; 2 teaching kitchens.

Typical Student Profile
125 full-time. 62 are under 25 years old; 60 are between 25 and 44 years old; 3 are over 44 years old.

Special Programs
Tuition-free Apprenticeship Program, student trip to explore cultural cuisine.

Financial Aid
In 2006, 1 scholarship was awarded (award was $1000). Employment placement assistance is available. Employment opportunities within the program are available.

Housing
Apartment-style housing available.

Application Information
Students may begin participation in January, May, and August. Applications are accepted continuously. In 2006, 125 applied; 125 were accepted. Applicants must interview; submit a formal application, letters of reference, and an essay.

Contact
Director of Admissions, Culinary Institute of the Treasure Coast, 3209 Virginia Avenue, Fort Pierce, FL 34981. Telephone: 772-226-2511. Fax: 772-226-2520. World Wide Web: http://www.ircc.edu/.

The International Culinary School at The Art Institute of Fort Lauderdale

Fort Lauderdale, Florida

General Information
Private, coeducational institution.

Program Information
Accredited by American Culinary Federation (Associate in Culinary Arts program). Associate degree in Culinary Arts. Associate degree in Baking and Pastry. Bachelor's degree in Culinary Management. Diploma in Art of Cooking.

Contact
Office of Admissions, 1799 S.E. 17th Street, Fort Lauderdale, FL 33316. Telephone: 954-463-3000. World Wide Web: http://www.artinstitutes.edu/fortlauderdale/.

See color display following page 332.

The International Culinary School at The Art Institute of Jacksonville

A Branch of Miami International University of Art & Design

Jacksonville, Florida

General Information
Private, coeducational institution.

Program Information
Accredited by licensed by the Commission for Independent Education Florida Department of Education. Associate degree in Culinary Arts. Bachelor's degree in Culinary Management. Diploma in Culinary Arts: Skills.

Contact
Office of Admissions, A Branch of Miami International University of Art & Design, 8775 Baypine Road, Jacksonville, FL 32256-8528. Telephone: 904-486-3000. World Wide Web: http://www.artinstitutes.edu/jacksonville/.

See color display following page 332.

The International Culinary School at The Art Institute of Tampa

A Branch of Miami International University of Art & Design

Tampa, Florida

General Information
Private, coeducational institution.

Program Information
Associate degree in Wine, Spirits and Beverage Management. Associate degree in Culinary Arts. Bachelor's degree in Food and Beverage Management. Bachelor's degree in Culinary Management. Diploma in Baking and Pastry.

Application Information
Applicants must participation in the Wine, Spirits & Beverage Management program for those under 21 years of age will be conducted in accord with state law regarding the possession and consumption of alcoholic beverages.

Contact
Office of Admissions, A Branch of Miami International University of Art & Design, Parkside at Tampa Bay Park, 4401 North Himes Avenue, Suite 150, Tampa, FL 33614-7086. Telephone: 813-873-2112. World Wide Web: http://www.artinstitutes.edu/tampa/.

See color display following page 332.

Johnson & Wales University–North Miami

College of Culinary Arts

North Miami, Florida

General Information
Private, coeducational, four-year college. Urban campus. Founded in 1992. Accredited by New England Association of Schools and Colleges.

Program Information
Accredited by American Dietetic Association. Program calendar is divided into quarters. Associate degree in culinary arts. Associate degree in baking and pastry arts. Bachelor's degree in culinary arts and food service management. Bachelor's degree in baking & pastry and food service management.

Program Affiliation
American Culinary Federation; American Dietetic Association; American Institute of Baking; American Institute of Wine & Food; Confrerie de la Chaine des Rotisseurs; Council on Hotel, Restaurant, and Institutional Education; Institute of Food Technologists; International Association of Culinary Professionals; International Food Service Executives Association; International Foodservice Editorial Council; James Beard Foundation, Inc.; National Restaurant Association; National Restaurant Association Educational Foundation; Oldways Preservation and Exchange Trust; Sommelier Society of America; Tasters Guild International.

Areas of Study
Baking; beverage management; buffet catering; confectionery show pieces; controlling costs in food service; convenience cookery; culinary French; culinary skill development; food preparation; food purchasing; food service communication; food service math; garde-manger; international cuisine; introduction to food service; kitchen management; management and human resources; meat cutting; meat fabrication; menu and facilities design; nutrition; nutrition and food service; patisserie; restaurant opportunities; sanitation; saucier; seafood processing; soup, stock, sauce, and starch production.

Johnson & Wales University–North Miami *(continued)*

Facilities

Bake shop; cafeteria; 15 classrooms; 2 computer laboratories; 8 food production kitchens; 2 gourmet dining rooms; learning resource center; 6 lecture rooms; library; public restaurant; 2 student lounges; pastry shop; meatroom/butcher shop; beverage lab.

Student Profile

808 total: 757 full-time; 51 part-time. 685 are under 25 years old; 107 are between 25 and 44 years old; 16 are over 44 years old.

Faculty

22 total: 22 full-time. Prominent faculty: Drue Brandenburg, MS, CEC, CCE; Patricia Wilson, PhD; Felicia Pritchett; Todd Tonova, PhD. Faculty-student ratio: 1:20.

Prominent Alumni and Current Affiliation

Michelle Bernstein, Chef/Owner, Michu's Miami; Lorena Garcia, Chef/Owner, Elements Restaurant; Tom Condron, Corporate Executive Chef, Harpers Restaurant Group.

Special Programs

3-month internship (every culinary student gets a real life, career building work experience through internship/co-op), ACF certification and one year membership for all completing associate degrees.

Typical Expenses

Tuition: $21,297 per year. Program-related fees include $1023 for general fee; $265 for orientation fee; $1026 for optional weekend meal plan; $300 for room and board reservation deposit.

Financial Aid

In 2007, 974 scholarships were awarded (average award was $4127). Employment placement assistance is available. Employment opportunities within the program are available.

Housing

Coed and apartment-style housing available. Average on-campus housing cost per month: $1000. Average off-campus housing cost per month: $950.

Application Information

Students may begin participation in March, June, July, September, and December. Applications are accepted continuously. In 2007, 1,735 applied; 1,240 were accepted. Applicants must submit a formal application and official transcript from high school or college.

Contact

Jeff Greenip, Director of Admissions, College of Culinary Arts, 170 NE 127th Street, North Miami, FL 33181. Telephone: 800-BEA-CHEF. Fax: 305-892-7020. E-mail: admissions.nmia@jwu.edu. World Wide Web: http://culinary.jwu.edu/.

See color display following page 92.

Keiser University

Center for Culinary Arts

Melbourne, Florida

General Information

Private, coeducational, two-year college. Urban campus. Founded in 1989. Accredited by Southern Association of Colleges and Schools.

Program Information

Offered since 2004. Program calendar is 3 semesters per year. 20-month associate degree in culinary arts.

Areas of Study

Baking; food preparation; food purchasing; food service math; garde-manger; international cuisine; meal planning; meat cutting; meat fabrication; nutrition; sanitation; soup, stock, sauce, and starch production.

Facilities

Bake shop; 3 classrooms; 2 computer laboratories; 3 food production kitchens; gourmet dining room; learning resource center; library; student lounge; teaching kitchen.

Typical Student Profile

48 full-time. 15 are under 25 years old; 33 are between 25 and 44 years old.

Special Programs

ACF sanctioned culinary competitions.

Financial Aid

In 2006, 45 scholarships were awarded (average award was $1000); 51 loans were granted (average loan was $6228). Employment placement assistance is available.

Application Information

Students may begin participation in January, April, and August. In 2006, 20 applied; 10 were accepted.

Contact

Director of Admissions, Center for Culinary Arts, 900 South Babcock Street, Orlando, FL 32901. Telephone: 321-409-4800. Fax: 321-765-3766. World Wide Web: http://www.keiseruniversity.edu/culinary.

See display on page 125.

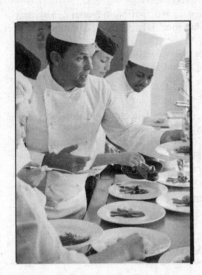

KEISER UNIVERSITY

Center for Culinary Arts

Sarasota, Florida

GENERAL INFORMATION

Private, coeducational, four-year college. Suburban campus. Founded in 1977. Accredited by Southern Association of Colleges and Schools.

PROGRAM INFORMATION

Offered since 2006. Program calendar is 3 semesters per year. 28-month associate degree in culinary arts.

PROGRAM AFFILIATION

American Culinary Federation; National Restaurant Association; National Restaurant Association Educational Foundation.

AREAS OF STUDY

Baking; controlling costs in food service; culinary French; culinary skill development; food preparation; food purchasing; garde-manger; international cuisine; introduction to food service; kitchen management; meal planning; meat cutting; meat fabrication; menu and facilities design; nutrition and food service; patisserie; sanitation; saucier; soup, stock, sauce, and starch production.

FACILITIES

Bake shop; 3 classrooms; 2 computer laboratories; 5 demonstration laboratories; 3 food production kitchens; gourmet dining room; 3 lecture rooms; library; student lounge.

STUDENT PROFILE

94 full-time. 54 are under 25 years old; 34 are between 25 and 44 years old; 6 are over 44 years old.

FACULTY

7 total: 6 full-time; 1 part-time. 6 are industry professionals. Prominent faculty: Chef Michael Moench, Program Director. Faculty-student ratio: 1:15.

SPECIAL PROGRAMS

4-month paid externship, culinary competitions.

TYPICAL EXPENSES

Application fee: $55. Program-related fee includes $145 for registration fee.

FINANCIAL AID

Employment placement assistance is available.

APPLICATION INFORMATION

Students may begin participation in January, February, March, April, May, June, July, August, September, October, and November. Applications are accepted continuously. Applicants must interview; submit a formal application and high school diploma or GED, entrance evaluation or SAT/ACT scores.

CONTACT

Michelle Miller, Associate Director of Admissions, Center for Culinary Arts, Admissions Department, 6151 Lake Osprey Drive, Sarasota, FL 34240. Telephone: 866-534-7372. Fax: 941-907-2016. E-mail: mimiller@keiseruniversity.edu. World Wide Web: http://www.keiseruniversity.edu/culinary.

See display on page 125.

KEISER UNIVERSITY

Center for Culinary Arts

Tallahassee, Florida

GENERAL INFORMATION

Private, coeducational institution. Urban campus. Founded in 1977. Accredited by Southern Association of Colleges and Schools.

PROGRAM INFORMATION

Offered since 1998. Accredited by American Culinary Federation Accrediting Commission. Program calendar is 3 semesters per year. 20-month associate degree in culinary arts. 20-month associate degree in baking and pastry arts.

PROGRAM AFFILIATION

American Culinary Federation; International Association of Culinary Professionals; National Restaurant Association; Women Chefs and Restaurateurs.

AREAS OF STUDY

Baking; confectionery show pieces; culinary French; culinary skill development; food preparation; food purchasing; food service communication; food service math; garde-manger; international cuisine; management and human resources; meat cutting; meat fabrication; menu and facilities design; nutrition; patisserie; sanitation; saucier; seafood processing; soup, stock, sauce, and starch production; wines and spirits.

FACILITIES

Bake shop; classroom; 3 food production kitchens; gourmet dining room.

STUDENT PROFILE

175 full-time.

Faculty
16 total: 11 full-time; 5 part-time. Prominent faculty: Kevin Keating, CEC, CCE; Harold Hilliard, CEC, CCE; Pam Manley, CC; Mark Cross, CMB. Faculty-student ratio: 1:14.

Prominent Alumni and Current Affiliation
Chris Windus, Blue Zoo, Walt Disney World Dolphin; David Stroffolino, Alberts Provence Restaurant; Matrell Hawkins.

Special Programs
4-month paid externship, culinary competitions.

Typical Expenses
Application fee: $55. Tuition: $6228 per semester. Program-related fees include $400 for cutlery set; $200 for uniforms.

Financial Aid
Employment placement assistance is available.

Application Information
Students may begin participation in January, March, May, July, September, and November. Applications are accepted continuously. Applicants must interview; submit a formal application and entrance evaluation.

Contact
Chef Kevin Keating, Dean of the Center for Culinary Arts, Center for Culinary Arts, 1700 Halstead Boulevard, Tallahassee, FL 32309. Telephone: 850-906-9494. Fax: 850-906-9497. E-mail: kevink@keiseruniversity.edu. World Wide Web: http://www.keiseruniversity.edu/culinary.

See display on page 125.

Le Cordon Bleu College of Culinary Arts, Miami

Le Cordon Bleu Culinary Program

Miramar, Florida

General Information
Coeducational, culinary institute.

Program Information
Associate degree in Le Cordon Bleu Culinary Arts. Diploma in Le Cordon Bleu Patisserie and Baking.

Special Programs
Externships.

Financial Aid
Employment placement assistance is available.

Application Information
Applications are accepted continuously. Applicants must interview; submit a formal application and high school diploma or equivalent.

Contact
Director of Admissions, Le Cordon Bleu Culinary Program, 3221 Enterprise Way, Miramar, FL 33025. Telephone: 888-569-3222. World Wide Web: http://www.miamiculinary.com/.

Manatee Technical Institute

Commercial Foods and Culinary Arts

Bradenton, Florida

General Information
Public, coeducational, technical institute. Suburban campus. Founded in 1961. Accredited by Council on Occupational Education, Southern Association of Colleges and Schools.

Program Information
Offered since 1981. Accredited by American Culinary Federation Accrediting Commission. National Restaurant Association Educational Foundation ManageFirst certificates available. Program calendar is divided into quarters. 1,440-hour certificate in commercial foods and culinary arts.

Program Affiliation
American Culinary Federation; National Restaurant Association; National Restaurant Association Educational Foundation; Retail Bakers of America.

Areas of Study
Baking; buffet catering; controlling costs in food service; convenience cookery; culinary French; culinary skill development; food preparation; food purchasing; food service communication; food service math; garde-manger; international cuisine; introduction to food service; kitchen management; meal planning; meat cutting; meat fabrication; menu and facilities design; nutrition; nutrition and food service; patisserie; restaurant opportunities; sanitation; saucier; seafood processing; soup, stock, sauce, and starch production.

Facilities
Bake shop; cafeteria; catering service; classroom; computer laboratory; demonstration laboratory; food production kitchen; learning resource center; 2 lecture rooms; library; 2 teaching kitchens.

Typical Student Profile
19 total: 17 full-time; 2 part-time.

Manatee Technical Institute *(continued)*

Special Programs

Culinary competition, Skills USA, ACF competitions, tours of various well-known kitchen operations, food irradiation facility.

Financial Aid

In 2006, 3 scholarships were awarded (average award was $300). Program-specific awards include Kiwanis scholarship, culinary scholarship. Employment placement assistance is available. Employment opportunities within the program are available.

Application Information

Students may begin participation in March, August, September, October, and December. In 2006, 30 applied; 25 were accepted. Applicants must interview, submit a formal application and take the Test of Adult Basic Education.

Contact

Director of Admissions, Commercial Foods and Culinary Arts, 5603 34th Street, West, Bradenton, FL 34210. Telephone: 941-751-7900. World Wide Web: http://www.manateetechnicalinstitute.org/programs/career/culinary_arts.html.

Northwood University, Florida Campus

Hotel, Restaurant, and Resort Management

West Palm Beach, Florida

General Information

Private, coeducational, four-year college. Urban campus. Founded in 1982. Accredited by North Central Association of Colleges and Schools.

Program Information

Offered since 1984. Program calendar is divided into quarters. 2-year associate degree in hotel, restaurant, resort management. 4-year bachelor's degree in hotel, restaurant, resort management.

Program Affiliation

Council on Hotel, Restaurant, and Institutional Education; National Restaurant Association; National Restaurant Association Educational Foundation; Palm Beach County Hotel and Lodging Association.

Areas of Study

Beverage management; food preparation; food purchasing; introduction to food service; management and human resources; menu and facilities design; restaurant opportunities; sanitation.

Facilities

Classroom; lecture room.

Typical Student Profile

47 full-time. 45 are under 25 years old; 2 are between 25 and 44 years old.

Special Programs

400-hour paid internship, attendance at National Restaurant Association trade show in Chicago, participation in Palm Beach County Hotel and Lodging Association trade show and job fair.

Financial Aid

In 2006, 8 scholarships were awarded (average award was $1000). Employment placement assistance is available. Employment opportunities within the program are available.

Housing

Single-sex housing available.

Application Information

Students may begin participation in March, June, September, and December. Applications are accepted continuously. In 2006, 110 applied; 75 were accepted. Applicants must submit a formal application and official transcripts, SAT or ACT results.

Contact

Director of Admissions, Hotel, Restaurant, and Resort Management, 2600 North Military Trail, West Palm Beach, FL 33409-2911. Telephone: 800-458-8325. Fax: 561-478-5500. World Wide Web: http://www.northwood.edu/.

Notter School of Pastry Arts

Orlando, Florida

General Information

Private, coeducational institution. Suburban campus. Founded in 1982.

Program Information

Offered since 1982. Accredited by American Culinary Federation Accrediting Commission. Program calendar is divided into weeks. 1-week certificate in wedding cake. 1-week certificate in sugar blowing and pulling showplace class. 1-week certificate in chocolate decoration. 1-week certificate in cakes and desserts. 1-week certificate in advanced sugar decoration. 1-week certificate in advanced chocolate decoration. 24-week diploma in European pastry and baking program.

Areas of Study

Confectionery show pieces; patisserie.

Facilities

Classroom; student lounge; teaching kitchen.

Financial Aid
Employment placement assistance is available. Employment opportunities within the program are available.

Application Information
Students may begin participation in January, February, March, April, May, June, July, August, September, October, and November.

Contact
Director of Admissions, 8204 Crystal Clear Lane #1600, Orlando, FL 32809. Telephone: 407-240-9057. Fax: 407-240-9056. World Wide Web: http://www.notterschool.com/.

Orlando Culinary Academy

Le Cordon Bleu Program

Orlando, Florida

General Information
Private, coeducational, culinary institute. Founded in 2002.

Program Information
Diploma in Le Cordon Bleu Patisserie and Baking. Diploma in Le Cordon Bleu Hospitality and Restaurant Management. 15-month associate degree in Le Cordon Bleu Culinary Arts.

Financial Aid
Employment placement assistance is available.

Application Information
Applications are accepted continuously. Applicants must interview and have high school diploma or GED.

Contact
Director of Admissions, Le Cordon Bleu Program, 8511 Commodity Circle, Suite 100, Orlando, FL 32819. Telephone: 888-793-3222. Fax: 407-888-4019. World Wide Web: http://www.orlandoculinary.com/.

Palm Beach Community College

Hospitality Management

Lake Worth, Florida

General Information
Public, coeducational, two-year college. Urban campus. Founded in 1933. Accredited by Southern Association of Colleges and Schools.

Program Information
Program calendar is divided into semesters. 2-year associate degree in hospitality and tourism management.

Program Affiliation
American Hotel and Lodging Association.

Areas of Study
Beverage management; meal planning; menu and facilities design.

Facilities
Demonstration laboratory; food production kitchen; gourmet dining room; teaching kitchen.

Typical Student Profile
42 part-time.

Application Information
Students may begin participation in January, May, and August. Applications are accepted continuously.

Contact
Director of Admissions, Hospitality Management, 4200 Congress Avenue, Lake Worth, FL 33461-4796. Telephone: 561-868-3377. Fax: 561-868-3584. World Wide Web: http://www.pbcc.edu/.

Pensacola Junior College

Hospitality and Tourism Management/Culinary Management

Pensacola, Florida

General Information
Public, coeducational, two-year college. Suburban campus. Founded in 1948. Accredited by Southern Association of Colleges and Schools.

Program Information
Offered since 1995. Accredited by American Culinary Federation Accrediting Commission. Program calendar is divided into semesters. 2-year associate degree in hospitality and tourism management. 2-year associate degree in culinary management.

Program Affiliation
American Culinary Federation; Council on Hotel, Restaurant, and Institutional Education.

Areas of Study
Baking; beverage management; buffet catering; confectionery show pieces; controlling costs in food service; culinary skill development; dining room management; food preparation; food purchasing; food service math; garde-manger; international cuisine; introduction to food service; kitchen management;

Pensacola Junior College *(continued)*

management and human resources; meal planning; menu and facilities design; nutrition; patisserie; sanitation; saucier; soup, stock, sauce, and starch production.

Facilities
Bake shop; classroom; computer laboratory; food production kitchen; gourmet dining room; learning resource center; public restaurant; student lounge; teaching kitchen.

Typical Student Profile
62 full-time.

Special Programs
Mystery box competitions.

Financial Aid
Program-specific awards include private scholarships. Employment placement assistance is available. Employment opportunities within the program are available.

Application Information
Students may begin participation in January, May, and August. Applications are accepted continuously. Applicants must submit a formal application.

Contact
Director of Admissions, Hospitality and Tourism Management/Culinary Management, 1000 College Boulevard, Pensacola, FL 32504-8998. Telephone: 850-484-2506. Fax: 850-484-1543. World Wide Web: http://www.pjc.edu/.

Pinellas Technical Education Center–Clearwater Campus

Culinary Arts/Commercial Food

Clearwater, Florida

General Information
Public, coeducational, two-year college. Urban campus. Founded in 1969. Accredited by Council on Occupational Education.

Program Information
Offered since 1969. Accredited by American Culinary Federation Accrediting Commission. Program calendar is divided into quarters. 1,500-hour certificate in culinary arts/commercial foods.

Program Affiliation
American Dietetic Association; Florida Restaurant Association; National Restaurant Association; National Restaurant Association Educational Foundation.

Areas of Study
Baking; buffet catering; convenience cookery; culinary skill development; food preparation; food purchasing; food service communication; food service math; garde-manger; international cuisine; introduction to food service; kitchen management; management and human resources; meal planning; meat fabrication; nutrition; nutrition and food service; sanitation; saucier; soup, stock, sauce, and starch production.

Facilities
Bake shop; bakery; cafeteria; catering service; 2 classrooms; computer laboratory; demonstration laboratory; 2 food production kitchens; gourmet dining room; 3 laboratories; learning resource center; lecture room; library; teaching kitchen.

Typical Student Profile
46 total: 28 full-time; 18 part-time.

Special Programs
Visits to industry, culinary competitions, field trips to food expositions.

Financial Aid
Program-specific awards include American Culinary Federation scholarships, Andrew's Scholarship, Florida Restaurant Association scholarship. Employment placement assistance is available.

Application Information
Students may begin participation in January, April, August, and October. Applications are accepted continuously. Applicants must interview, and submit a formal application.

Contact
Director of Admissions, Culinary Arts/Commercial Food, 6100 154th Avenue N, Clearwater, FL 33760. Telephone: 727-538-7167 Ext. 1140. Fax: 727-509-4246. World Wide Web: http://www.myptec.org/.

St. Thomas University

Tourism and Hospitality Management

Miami Gardens, Florida

General Information
Private, coeducational, university. Urban campus. Founded in 1961. Accredited by Southern Association of Colleges and Schools.

Program Information
Program calendar is divided into semesters. 4-year bachelor's degree in tourism and hospitality management.

Program Affiliation
American Hotel and Lodging Association; Council on Hotel, Restaurant, and Institutional Education; Florida Restaurant Association; Greater Miami Conventions and Visitors Bureau; International Food Service Executives Association; International Society of Travel and Tourism Educators; National Restaurant Association.

Areas of Study
Beverage management; controlling costs in food service; convention, trade show and destination management; food preparation; food purchasing; introduction to food service; kitchen management; management and human resources; meal planning; menu and facilities design; restaurant opportunities; sanitation; sport tourism.

Facilities
Classroom; computer laboratory; garden; learning resource center; lecture room; library.

Typical Student Profile
32 total: 30 full-time; 2 part-time. 27 are under 25 years old; 5 are between 25 and 44 years old.

Special Programs
Internships, experiential learning.

Financial Aid
In 2006, 2 scholarships were awarded (average award was $9000). Program-specific awards include donor scholarships, PIT employment. Employment opportunities within the program are available.

Housing
Single-sex housing available.

Application Information
Students may begin participation in January and August. Applications are accepted continuously. In 2006, 24 applied. Applicants must submit a formal application, letters of reference, and an essay.

Contact
Director of Admissions, Tourism and Hospitality Management, 16401 NW 37th Avenue, Miami Gardens, FL 33054. Telephone: 305-628-6712. Fax: 305-628-6591. World Wide Web: http://www.stu.edu/.

University of Central Florida

Rosen College of Hospitality Management

Orlando, Florida

General Information
Public, coeducational, university. Suburban campus. Founded in 1963. Accredited by Southern Association of Colleges and Schools.

Program Information
Offered since 1983. Accredited by Council on Hotel, Restaurant and Institutional Education. Program calendar is divided into semesters. 2-year master's degree in hospitality management. 3-year doctoral degree in hospitality education. 4-year bachelor's degree in restaurant management. 4-year bachelor's degree in event management. 4-year bachelor's degree in hospitality management.

Program Affiliation
American Culinary Federation; Council on Hotel, Restaurant, and Institutional Education; National Restaurant Association; National Restaurant Association Educational Foundation.

Areas of Study
Beverage management; controlling costs in food service; food preparation; food purchasing; food service management; management and human resources; restaurant operations; restaurant opportunities; wines and spirits.

Facilities
Cafeteria; catering service; 23 classrooms; coffee shop; 3 computer laboratories; demonstration laboratory; 2 food production kitchens; gourmet dining room; lecture room; library; student lounge; teaching kitchen.

Typical Student Profile
2,300 full-time. 2,100 are under 25 years old; 200 are between 25 and 44 years old.

Special Programs
Semester study abroad in France, 3 semester cooperative work experience, distinguished lectures series.

Financial Aid
In 2006, 100 scholarships were awarded (average award was $2500). Employment placement assistance is available. Employment opportunities within the program are available.

Housing
Coed and apartment-style housing available.

Application Information
Students may begin participation in January, May, June, and August. Application deadline for fall is May 1. Application deadline for spring is November 1. Application deadline for summer is March 1. Applicants must submit a formal application and SAT or ACT scores.

Contact
Director of Admissions, Rosen College of Hospitality Management, 9907 Universal Boulevard, Orlando, FL 32819. Telephone: 407-903-8166. Fax: 407-903-8104. World Wide Web: http://www.hospitality.ucf.edu/.

Valencia Community College

Culinary Management–Baking and Pastry Management

Orlando, Florida

General Information

Public, coeducational, two-year college. Urban campus. Founded in 1967. Accredited by Southern Association of Colleges and Schools.

Program Information

Offered since 1997. Program calendar is divided into semesters. 35-credit certificate in culinary arts. 35-credit certificate in baking and pastry arts. 64-credit associate degree in restaurant management. 64-credit associate degree in hospitality management. 64-credit associate degree in culinary management. 64-credit associate degree in baking and pastry management.

Program Affiliation

American Culinary Federation; Council on Hotel, Restaurant, and Institutional Education; Florida Restaurant Association; National Restaurant Association; National Restaurant Association Educational Foundation; The Bread Bakers Guild of America; Women Chefs and Restaurateurs.

Areas of Study

Baking; buffet catering; controlling costs in food service; convenience cookery; culinary French; culinary skill development; food preparation; food purchasing; food service communication; food service math; garde-manger; international cuisine; management and human resources; meal planning; meat cutting; meat fabrication; menu and facilities design; nutrition; nutrition and food service; patisserie; sanitation; saucier; seafood processing; soup, stock, sauce, and starch production; wines and spirits.

Facilities

Bakery; 6 classrooms; computer laboratory; 2 demonstration laboratories; food production kitchen; learning resource center; lecture room; library; teaching kitchen.

Typical Student Profile

530 total: 245 full-time; 285 part-time.

Special Programs

Participation in Florida Restaurant Association Southeast EXPO (assisting in culinary competitions), paid internship, participation in Walt Disney Food and Wine Festival at the Epcot Center.

Financial Aid

In 2006, 1 scholarship was awarded (award was $709). Employment placement assistance is available. Employment opportunities within the program are available.

Application Information

Students may begin participation in January, May, and August. Application deadline for fall is July 1. Application deadline for spring is November 1. Application deadline for summer is April 1. Applicants must submit a formal application and high school diploma or GED.

Contact

Director of Admissions, Culinary Management–Baking and Pastry Management, PO Box 3028, Orlando, FL 32802-3028. Telephone: 407-532-1880. Fax: 407-582-1900. World Wide Web: http://www.valencia.cc.fl.us.

Webber International University

Hospitality Business Management

Babson Park, Florida

General Information

Private, coeducational, comprehensive institution. Rural campus. Founded in 1927. Accredited by Southern Association of Colleges and Schools.

Program Information

Offered since 1972. Accredited by Council on Hotel, Restaurant and Institutional Education. National Restaurant Association Educational Foundation ManageFirst certificates available. Program calendar is divided into semesters. 2-year associate degree in hospitality business management. 4-year bachelor's degree in hospitality business management.

Program Affiliation

Council on Hotel, Restaurant, and Institutional Education; National Restaurant Association; National Restaurant Association Educational Foundation.

Areas of Study

Beverage management; controlling costs in food service; food purchasing; food service math; introduction to food service; kitchen management; management and human resources; meal planning; nutrition; restaurant opportunities.

Facilities

Cafeteria; 2 classrooms; 2 computer laboratories; food production kitchen; learning resource center; library; snack shop; student lounge.

Typical Student Profile
26 total: 25 full-time; 1 part-time. 25 are under 25 years old; 1 is between 25 and 44 years old.

Special Programs
2 internship opportunities worldwide, trip to International Hotel and Lodging Show (New York), trip to National Restaurant Association Food Service Show (Chicago), field trip to Las Vegas.

Financial Aid
Program-specific awards include Pro Start Scholarship-$2000 to graduate of high school culinary program who meets requirements, CFHLA Industry Scholarship-$1000. Employment placement assistance is available. Employment opportunities within the program are available.

Housing
Coed housing available.

Application Information
Students may begin participation in January, May, and September. Application deadline for fall is August 1. Application deadline for spring is December 1. Application deadline for summer is April 1. In 2006, 30 applied; 12 were accepted. Applicants must submit a formal application, letters of reference, an essay, SAT scores.

Contact
Director of Admissions, Hospitality Business Management, PO Box 96, Babson Park, FL 33827. Telephone: 800-741-1844. Fax: 863-638-1591. World Wide Web: http://webber.edu/.

Georgia

Augusta Technical College

Culinary Arts

Augusta, Georgia

General Information
Public, coeducational, two-year college. Suburban campus. Founded in 1961. Accredited by Southern Association of Colleges and Schools.

Program Information
Offered since 1984. Program calendar is divided into quarters. 6-quarter diploma in culinary arts.

Program Affiliation
American Culinary Federation.

Augusta Technical College ***(continued)***

Areas of Study
Baking; buffet catering; food preparation; food purchasing; garde-manger; menu and facilities design; nutrition and food service; sanitation; soup, stock, sauce, and starch production.

Facilities
Bake shop; cafeteria; catering service; 2 classrooms; demonstration laboratory; food production kitchen; gourmet dining room; laboratory; learning resource center; library; teaching kitchen.

Typical Student Profile
15 are under 25 years old; 25 are between 25 and 44 years old; 20 are over 44 years old.

Financial Aid
In 2006, 6 scholarships were awarded (average award was $800). Program-specific awards include ProMgmt. scholarship, American Culinary Federation scholarship. Employment placement assistance is available.

Application Information
Students may begin participation in March and September. Applications are accepted continuously. In 2006, 52 were accepted. Applicants must submit a formal application.

Contact
Director of Admissions, Culinary Arts, 3200 Augusta Tech Drive, Augusta, GA 30906. Telephone: 706-771-4084. Fax: 706-771-4016. World Wide Web: http://www.augusta.tec.ga.us.

Chattahoochee Technical College

Culinary Arts

Marietta, Georgia

General Information
Public, coeducational, two-year college. Suburban campus. Founded in 1961. Accredited by Southern Association of Colleges and Schools.

Program Information
Offered since 2001. Accredited by American Culinary Federation Accrediting Commission. Program calendar is divided into quarters. 12-month diploma in culinary arts. 24-month associate degree in culinary arts.

Program Affiliation
American Culinary Federation; International Association of Culinary Professionals; James Beard Foundation, Inc.; National Restaurant Association; National Restaurant Association Educational Foundation.

Areas of Study
Baking; beverage management; buffet catering; controlling costs in food service; culinary skill development; food preparation; food purchasing; food service math; garde-manger; international cuisine; introduction to food service; kitchen management; management and human resources; meat fabrication; menu and facilities design; nutrition and food service; sanitation; soup, stock, sauce, and starch production; wines and spirits.

Facilities
Bake shop; catering service; classroom; computer laboratory; demonstration laboratory; food production kitchen; gourmet dining room; 2 lecture rooms; library; public restaurant; student lounge; teaching kitchen.

Typical Student Profile
170 total: 150 full-time; 20 part-time.

Special Programs
Culinary competitions, twelve-day cooking tour of Italy.

Financial Aid
In 2006, 6 scholarships were awarded (average award was $500). Employment placement assistance is available. Employment opportunities within the program are available.

Application Information
Students may begin participation in January, March, July, and October. Applications are accepted continuously. In 2006, 100 applied; 75 were accepted. Applicants must interview; submit a formal application, letters of reference, an essay, official transcript from high school and/or college or original GED certificate.

Contact
Director of Admissions, Culinary Arts, 2680 Gordy Parkway, Marietta, GA 30066. Telephone: 770-509-6310. Fax: 770-509-6345. World Wide Web: http://www.chattcollege.com/.

Coastal Georgia Community College

Culinary Arts

Brunswick, Georgia

General Information

Public, coeducational, two-year college. Small-town setting. Founded in 1961. Accredited by Southern Association of Colleges and Schools.

Program Information

Offered since 1994. Accredited by American Culinary Federation Accrediting Commission. National Restaurant Association Educational Foundation ManageFirst certificates available. Program calendar is divided into semesters. 18-month technical certificate in culinary arts. 24-month certificate in culinary arts.

Program Affiliation

American Culinary Federation; American Hotel and Lodging Association; Council on Hotel, Restaurant, and Institutional Education.

Areas of Study

Baking; beverage management; buffet catering; business math; controlling costs in food service; culinary French; culinary skill development; food preparation; food purchasing; food service math; garde-manger; introduction to food service; kitchen management; management and human resources; meal planning; menu and facilities design; nutrition; nutrition and food service; sanitation; soup, stock, sauce, and starch production; wines and spirits.

Facilities

3 classrooms; computer laboratory; demonstration laboratory; food production kitchen; 2 learning resource centers; 2 libraries; student lounge; teaching kitchen.

Typical Student Profile

80 total: 5 full-time; 75 part-time.

Special Programs

Paid internships, culinary competitions.

Financial Aid

Employment placement assistance is available. Employment opportunities within the program are available.

Application Information

Students may begin participation in January, May, and August. Applications are accepted continuously. In 2006, 75 applied; 75 were accepted. Applicants must submit a formal application and take COMPASS test.

Contact

Director of Admissions, Culinary Arts, 3700 Altama Avenue, Brunswick, GA 31520. Telephone: 912-280-6899. Fax: 912-262-3283. World Wide Web: http://www.cgcc.edu/.

Georgia Southern University

Department of Family and Consumer Sciences

Statesboro, Georgia

General Information

Public, coeducational, comprehensive institution. Small-town setting. Founded in 1906. Accredited by Southern Association of Colleges and Schools.

Program Information

Offered since 1989. Accredited by American Dietetic Association. Program calendar is divided into semesters. 4-year bachelor's degree in nutrition and food science (dietetics). 4-year bachelor's degree in hotel and restaurant management.

Program Affiliation

American Culinary Federation; American Dietetic Association; Confrerie de la Chaine des Rotisseurs; Council on Hotel, Restaurant, and Institutional Education; National Restaurant Association; National Restaurant Association Educational Foundation.

Areas of Study

Beverage management; buffet catering; controlling costs in food service; convenience cookery; culinary French; culinary skill development; food preparation; food purchasing; food service communication; food service math; international cuisine; introduction to food service; kitchen management; management and human resources; meal planning; menu and facilities design; nutrition; nutrition and food service; restaurant opportunities; saucier; soup, stock, sauce, and starch production.

Facilities

6 classrooms; computer laboratory; demonstration laboratory; food production kitchen; gourmet dining room; laboratory; learning resource center; 6 lecture rooms; library; public restaurant; teaching kitchen.

Typical Student Profile

317 total: 276 full-time; 41 part-time. 289 are under 25 years old; 27 are between 25 and 44 years old; 1 is over 44 years old.

Special Programs

New York Hotel Show (fall), Georgia Hotel Tourism Convention (fall/spring).

Georgia Southern University *(continued)*

Financial Aid
In 2006, 4 scholarships were awarded (average award was $2500). Program-specific awards include Georgia Hospitality and Tourism Association Scholarship. Employment placement assistance is available.

Housing
Coed, apartment-style, and single-sex housing available.

Application Information
Students may begin participation in January and August. Application deadline for fall is August 1. Application deadline for spring is December 1. In 2006, 76 applied; 54 were accepted. Applicants must submit a formal application.

Contact
Director of Admissions, Department of Family and Consumer Sciences, PO Box 8024, Statesboro, GA 30460. Telephone: 912-681-5391. Fax: 912-486-7240. World Wide Web: http://chhs.georgiasouthern.edu/hospitality.

Georgia State University

Cecil B. Day School of Hospitality Administration

Atlanta, Georgia

General Information
Public, coeducational, university. Urban campus. Founded in 1913. Accredited by Southern Association of Colleges and Schools.

Program Information
Offered since 1973. Accredited by Council on Hotel, Restaurant and Institutional Education. Program calendar is divided into semesters. 1-year certificate in hospitality. 2-year master of business administration in hotel real estate. 4-year bachelor's degree in hospitality administration.

Program Affiliation
American Hotel and Lodging Association; Council on Hotel, Restaurant, and Institutional Education; National Restaurant Association; National Restaurant Association Educational Foundation.

Areas of Study
Controlling costs in food service; food preparation; food purchasing; food service communication; kitchen management; management and human resources; meal planning; menu and facilities design; restaurant opportunities; sanitation.

Facilities
Food production kitchen; dedicated classroom.

Typical Student Profile
320 total: 260 full-time; 60 part-time.

Special Programs
Student exchange program with European hospitality schools (semester), mentorship with industry executives (1 year), paid internships (semester).

Financial Aid
In 2006, 15–20 scholarships were awarded (average award was $1000). Program-specific awards include scholarships from American Lodging Association, Days Inns, and GSU Foundation. Employment opportunities within the program are available.

Housing
Coed and apartment-style housing available.

Application Information
Students may begin participation in January, June, and August. Application deadline for fall is June 1. Application deadline for spring is November 15. Application deadline for summer is April 1. Applicants must submit a formal application and high school transcripts, SAT or ACT scores.

Contact
Director of Admissions, Cecil B. Day School of Hospitality Administration, 35 Broad Street, Suite 220, Atlanta, GA 30303. Telephone: 404-413-7617. Fax: 404-413-7625. World Wide Web: http://robinson.gsu.edu/hospitality/index.htm.

The International Culinary School at The Art Institute of Atlanta

Atlanta, Georgia

General Information
Private, coeducational institution.

Program Information
Associate degree in Wines, Spirits and Beverage Management. Associate degree in Culinary Arts. Bachelor's degree in Food and Beverage Management. Bachelor's degree in Culinary Arts Management. Diploma in Culinary Arts–Culinary Skills. Diploma in Culinary Arts–Baking and Pastry.

Application Information
Applicants must participation in the Wines, Spirits & Beverage Management program for those under 21 years of age will be conducted in accord with state law regarding the possession and consumption of alcoholic beverages.

Contact
Office of Admissions, 6600 Peachtree Dunwoody Road, NE, 100 Embassy Row, Atlanta, GA 30328. Telephone: 770-394-8300. Fax: 770-394-0008. World Wide Web: http://www.artinstitutes.edu/atlanta/.

See color display following page 332.

Le Cordon Bleu College of Culinary Arts, Atlanta

Tucker, Georgia

General Information
Private, coeducational, two-year college. Suburban campus. Founded in 2003. Accredited by Accrediting Commission of Career Schools and Colleges of Technology.

Program Information
Offered since 2003. Accredited by American Culinary Federation Accrediting Commission. Program calendar is continuous. 10-month certificate in Le Cordon Bleu Patisserie and Baking. 15-month associate degree in Le Cordon Bleu Culinary Arts.

Program Affiliation
American Culinary Federation; The Bread Bakers Guild of America.

Areas of Study
Baking; culinary French; culinary skill development; patisserie.

Facilities
4 classrooms; computer laboratory; 5 food production kitchens; library; public restaurant; student lounge; 4 teaching kitchens.

Typical Student Profile
887 full-time.

Financial Aid
Employment placement assistance is available.

Application Information
Students may begin participation in January, February, April, May, July, August, October, and November. Applications are accepted continuously. Applicants must interview; submit a formal application.

Contact
Director of Admissions, Office of Admissions, 1927 Lakeside Parkway, Tucker, GA 30084. Telephone: 770-938-4711. Fax: 770-938-4571. World Wide Web: http://www.atlantaculinary.com/.

North Georgia Technical College

Culinary Arts

Toccoa, Georgia

General Information
Public, coeducational, two-year college. Rural campus. Founded in 1907. Accredited by Council on Occupational Education.

Program Information
Offered since 2005. Accredited by American Culinary Federation Accrediting Commission. National Restaurant Association Educational Foundation ManageFirst certificates available. Program calendar is divided into quarters. 2-quarter technical certificate in food production assistant. 5-quarter diploma in culinary arts. 7-quarter associate degree in culinary arts.

Program Affiliation
American Culinary Federation; National Restaurant Association; National Restaurant Association Educational Foundation.

Areas of Study
Baking; buffet catering; controlling costs in food service; culinary skill development; food preparation; food purchasing; food service communication; food service math; garde-manger; international cuisine; introduction to food service; kitchen management; meal planning; meat cutting; meat fabrication; menu and facilities design; nutrition; nutrition and food service; patisserie; restaurant opportunities; sanitation; saucier; seafood processing; soup, stock, sauce, and starch production.

Facilities
Library.

Typical Student Profile
46 total: 39 full-time; 7 part-time. 28 are under 25 years old; 11 are between 25 and 44 years old; 7 are over 44 years old.

Financial Aid
Program-specific awards include Hope scholarship program (Georgia residents). Employment placement assistance is available. Employment opportunities within the program are available.

North Georgia Technical College *(continued)*

Housing
Coed housing available.

Application Information
Students may begin participation in January, April, July, and October. Applications are accepted continuously. In 2006, 63 applied; 43 were accepted. Applicants must submit a formal application and health certification form.

Contact
Director of Admissions, Culinary Arts, 8989 Georgia Highway 17 South, Toccoa, GA 30577. Telephone: 706-779-8136. Fax: 706-779-8130. World Wide Web: http://www.northgatech.edu/.

North Georgia Technical College, Blairsville Campus

Culinary Arts

Blairsville, Georgia

General Information
Public, coeducational, two-year college. Rural campus. Founded in 1907. Accredited by Council on Occupational Education.

Program Information
Offered since 1998. Accredited by American Culinary Federation Accrediting Commission. National Restaurant Association Educational Foundation ManageFirst certificates available. Program calendar is divided into quarters. 2-quarter technical certificate in food production assistant. 3-quarter technical certificate in personal chef. 5-quarter diploma in culinary arts. 7-quarter technical associate degree in culinary arts.

Program Affiliation
American Culinary Federation; National Restaurant Association Educational Foundation; Research Chefs Association.

Areas of Study
Baking; buffet catering; controlling costs in food service; culinary skill development; food preparation; food purchasing; food service communication; food service math; garde-manger; international cuisine; introduction to food service; kitchen management; meal planning; meat cutting; meat fabrication; menu and facilities design; nutrition; nutrition and food service; patisserie; restaurant opportunities; sanitation; saucier; seafood processing; soup, stock, sauce, and starch production.

Facilities
Library; teaching kitchen.

Typical Student Profile
92 total: 55 full-time; 37 part-time. 31 are under 25 years old; 46 are between 25 and 44 years old; 15 are over 44 years old.

Financial Aid
Program-specific awards include Hope Scholarship program (Georgia residents). Employment placement assistance is available. Employment opportunities within the program are available.

Application Information
Students may begin participation in January, April, July, and October. Applications are accepted continuously. In 2006, 93 applied; 74 were accepted. Applicants must submit a formal application and health certification form.

Contact
Director of Admissions, Culinary Arts, 434 Meeks Avenue, Blairsville, GA 30512. Telephone: 706-439-6316. Fax: 706-439-6302. World Wide Web: http://www.northgatech.edu/.

Ogeechee Technical College

Culinary Arts Program

Statesboro, Georgia

General Information
Public, coeducational, two-year college. Small-town setting. Founded in 1986. Accredited by Council on Occupational Education.

Program Information
National Restaurant Association Educational Foundation ManageFirst certificates available. Program calendar is divided into quarters. 1-year diploma in culinary arts. 2-year associate degree in culinary arts. 9-month certificate in catering specialist.

Program Affiliation
National Restaurant Association Educational Foundation.

Areas of Study
Baking; buffet catering; confectionery show pieces; controlling costs in food service; culinary skill development; food preparation; food purchasing; food service communication; garde-manger; international cuisine; introduction to food service; kitchen management; management and human resources; meal planning; menu and facilities design; nutrition and food service; patisserie; sanitation.

Facilities
Classroom; computer laboratory; demonstration laboratory; food production kitchen; gourmet dining room; teaching kitchen.

Special Programs
Visits to food expos, culinary showcases, live work program.

Financial Aid
Program-specific awards include Stewart Scholarship. Employment placement assistance is available.

Application Information
Students may begin participation in January, April, July, and October. Applicants must submit a formal application.

Contact
Director of Admissions, Culinary Arts Program, 1 Joe Kennedy Boulevard, Statesboro, GA 30458. Telephone: 800-646-1316. Fax: 912-486-7704. World Wide Web: http://www.ogeecheetech.edu/.

Savannah Technical College

Culinary Institute of Savannah

Savannah, Georgia

General Information
Public, coeducational, two-year college. Urban campus. Founded in 1929. Accredited by Southern Association of Colleges and Schools.

Program Information
Offered since 1981. Accredited by American Culinary Federation Accrediting Commission. Program calendar is divided into quarters. 18-month associate degree in culinary arts. 18-month diploma in culinary arts.

Program Affiliation
American Culinary Federation; Savannah Tourism Leadership Council; Southeastern Retail Bakers Association.

Areas of Study
Baking; buffet catering; controlling costs in food service; culinary skill development; dining room/guest services; food preparation; food purchasing; food service math; garde-manger; international cuisine; introduction to food service; kitchen management; management and human resources; meal planning; meat fabrication; nutrition; restaurant opportunities; sanitation; saucier; soup, stock, sauce, and starch production.

Facilities
Bake shop; catering service; classroom; coffee shop; computer laboratory; demonstration laboratory; food production kitchen; garden; gourmet dining room; laboratory; learning resource center; lecture room; library; public restaurant; student lounge; teaching kitchen.

Typical Student Profile
135 total: 75 full-time; 60 part-time. 3 are under 25 years old; 132 are between 25 and 44 years old.

Special Programs
Field trips (restaurants, vendor warehouses, food processing plants), special food production presentations, culinary competitions.

Financial Aid
In 2006, 2 scholarships were awarded (average award was $1500). Program-specific awards include Hector Boiardi scholarship, Career Assistance Program, faculty and staff scholarships; Savannah Tourism Leadership Council Scholarships. Employment placement assistance is available.

Application Information
Students may begin participation in April and October. Applications are accepted continuously. Application deadline for all sessions: 30 days prior to start of each quarter. In 2006, 150 applied; 150 were accepted. Applicants must submit a formal application and have a high school diploma or GED and ASSET or SAT scores.

Contact
Director of Admissions, Culinary Institute of Savannah, 5717 White Bluff Road, Savannah, GA 31405-5521. Telephone: 912-443-5518. Fax: 912-303-1781. World Wide Web: http://www.savannahtech.edu/.

West Georgia Technical College

Culinary Arts

La Grange, Georgia

General Information
Public, coeducational, two-year college. Small-town setting. Founded in 1966. Accredited by Council on Occupational Education.

Program Information
Offered since 1996. Program calendar is divided into quarters. 18-month diploma in culinary arts. 6-month certificate in prep cook. 6-month certificate in food production worker I. 6-month certificate in basic culinary skills. 6-month certificate in assistant food purchasing agent.

Areas of Study
Beverage management; convenience cookery; food service communication; international cuisine; meat fabrication; menu and facilities design; nutrition; restaurant opportunities; wines and spirits.

West Georgia Technical College *(continued)*

Facilities
Classroom; library; student lounge; teaching kitchen.

Typical Student Profile
21 full-time. 10 are under 25 years old; 11 are between 25 and 44 years old.

Special Programs
NRA ServSafe certification, Culinary Food and Equipment Show of Atlanta, Sysco/US Food Service (local) Food and Equipment Show.

Financial Aid
Employment placement assistance is available.

Application Information
Students may begin participation in January, April, July, and October. Applications are accepted continuously. In 2006, 26 applied; 26 were accepted. Applicants must interview; submit a formal application.

Contact
Director of Admissions, Culinary Arts, 303 Fort Drive, La Grange, GA 30240. Telephone: 706-837-4246. Fax: 706-845-4340. World Wide Web: http://www.westgatech.edu/.

Hawaii

Leeward Community College

Culinary Institute of the Pacific

Pearl City, Hawaii

General Information
Public, coeducational, two-year college. Suburban campus. Founded in 1968. Accredited by Western Association of Schools and Colleges.

Program Information
Offered since 1972. Accredited by American Culinary Federation Accrediting Commission. Program calendar is divided into semesters. 1-semester certificate of completion in food service. 1-semester certificate in prep cook. 1.5-semester certificate in dining room service. 1.5-semester certificate in baking. 2-semester certificate of achievement in food service. 2-year associate degree in food service.

Program Affiliation
American Culinary Federation.

Areas of Study
Baking; beverage management; controlling costs in food service; culinary skill development; food preparation; food purchasing; food service math; garde-manger; international cuisine; introduction to food service; management and human resources; nutrition and food service; sanitation; soup, stock, sauce, and starch production.

Facilities
Bake shop; cafeteria; 3 classrooms; coffee shop; 3 food production kitchens; gourmet dining room.

Typical Student Profile
150 total: 100 full-time; 50 part-time.

Special Programs
Taste of the Stars, Japan study-abroad course in nutrition, networking opportunities with Hawaii's best chefs.

Financial Aid
Program-specific awards include Scholarship Branch Awards, industry scholarships. Employment placement assistance is available. Employment opportunities within the program are available.

Application Information
Students may begin participation in January and August. Application deadline for fall is July 15. Application deadline for spring is December 1. Applicants must submit a formal application.

Contact
Director of Admissions, Culinary Institute of the Pacific, 96-045 Ala Ike, Pearl City, HI 96782. Telephone: 808-455-0298. Fax: 808-455-0559. World Wide Web: http://www.lcc.hawaii.edu/.

Maui Community College

Food Service Program

Kahului, Hawaii

General Information
Public, coeducational, two-year college. Small-town setting. Founded in 1967. Accredited by Western Association of Schools and Colleges.

Program Information
Offered since 1977. Accredited by American Culinary Federation Accrediting Commission. Program calendar is divided into semesters. 1-year certificate in culinary arts. 2-year associate degree in food service-culinary arts specialty. 2-year associate degree in food service-baking specialty. 2-year associate degree in food service/restaurant supervision.

Passion. Meet Practical.
DISCOVER THE PERFECT MATCH AT KENDALL COLLEGE.
School of Culinary Arts
Les Roches School of Hospitality Management
School of Business
The acclaimed Schools of Kendall College deliver a unique combination of culinary and business coursework to prepare students with the right mix of book smarts and pure creativity to succeed in today's competitive service industries.
• Degree programs in Culinary Arts, Baking and Pastry, Hospitality Management and Business
• World-class Chicago campus
• A global network of internship and employment opportunities
• Multinational, accomplished faculty
• Financial aid available for those who qualify
877.588.8860
www.Kendall.edu
Kendall College
RIVERWORKS CAMPUS • CHICAGO
900 N. North Branch • Chicago, IL 60642

Sullivan University...

Experience The Difference!

The Sullivan University Advantage

Sullivan University has earned a reputation as one of the most successful culinary schools in America by offering students a unique opportunity to prepare for a rewarding career in today's professional hospitality world.

Sullivan University's National Center for Hospitality Studies has been listed among the ***top culinary schools in the nation.*** The Baking & Pastry Arts and Culinary Arts degree programs in Louisville are accredited by the American Culinary Federation Accrediting Commission. The University is regionally accredited by the Commission on Colleges of the Southern Association of Colleges and Schools to award associate, bachelor's, master's and doctoral degrees.

The main campus, located in Louisville, Kentucky, and the branch campus in Lexington, Kentucky, provide its students with access to more than 1,200 restaurants, as well as numerous other hospitality and travel related industries.

Modern, furnished apartments near each campus are available for non-resident students. Each apartment has access to laundry rooms, club house and the swimming pool. Daily transportation is provided by the University.

A Wide Range of Options

Sullivan offers students eight different undergraduate diplomas, associate degrees and bachelor's degree programs *(not all programs are offered at the Lexington campus)*.

- **Professional Baker**
- **Professional Cook**
- **Baking & Pastry Arts**
- **Culinary Arts**
- **Professional Catering**
- **Hotel/Restaurant Management**
- **BS in Hospitality Management (online)**
- **Travel, Tourism & Event Management**

A World Class Faculty

Sullivan's hospitality division has grown to more than 1100 students from 38 states and a number of foreign countries who choose to attend Sullivan for their career training. Our faculty includes ***International Culinary Olympic Gold-Medal winners*** and two chef-instructors are London Guild trained and one was Catering Chef to Great Britain's Royal household. The faculty bring over two hundred years of culinary, hospitality and hotel experience to their students.

Program Affiliation
American Culinary Federation; Confrerie de la Chaine des Rotisseurs; National Restaurant Association.

Areas of Study
Baking; beverage management; buffet catering; controlling costs in food service; culinary skill development; food preparation; food purchasing; food service communication; food service math; garde-manger; international cuisine; introduction to food service; management and human resources; menu and facilities design; nutrition; patisserie; restaurant opportunities; sanitation; soup, stock, sauce, and starch production; wines and spirits.

Facilities
Bake shop; cafeteria; catering service; classroom; computer laboratory; food production kitchen; garden; gourmet dining room; laboratory; lecture room; library; public restaurant; snack shop; teaching kitchen.

Typical Student Profile
155 total: 130 full-time; 25 part-time.

Special Programs
Culinary competitions, field experiences, fellowships.

Financial Aid
Employment placement assistance is available. Employment opportunities within the program are available.

Housing
Coed housing available.

Application Information
Students may begin participation in January, June, and August. Applications are accepted continuously. Applicants must submit a formal application.

Contact
Director of Admissions, Food Service Program, 310 Kaahumanu Avenue, Kahului, HI 96732. Telephone: 808-984-3225. Fax: 808-984-3314. World Wide Web: http://www.hawaii.edu/mcc/.

Travel Institute of the Pacific

Honolulu, Hawaii

General Information
Private, coeducational, culinary institute. Urban campus. Founded in 1974. Accredited by Accrediting Commission of Career Schools and Colleges of Technology.

Program Information
Offered since 1974. Program calendar is continuous. 1-year diploma in culinary arts. 1-year diploma in bakery/patisserie.

Program Affiliation
American Culinary Federation; Confrerie de la Chaine des Rotisseurs.

Areas of Study
Baking; culinary French; culinary skill development; garde-manger; patisserie; saucier; soup, stock, sauce, and starch production.

Facilities
Bake shop; bakery; 3 classrooms; computer laboratory; demonstration laboratory; 2 food production kitchens; gourmet dining room; 2 teaching kitchens.

Typical Student Profile
80 full-time. 16 are under 25 years old; 58 are between 25 and 44 years old; 6 are over 44 years old.

Application Information
Students may begin participation in January, April, July, and October. Applications are accepted continuously. In 2006, 110 applied; 92 were accepted. Applicants must interview; submit a formal application.

Contact
Director of Admissions, 1314 South King Street, Suite 1164, Honolulu, HI 96814. Telephone: 808-591-2708. Fax: 808-591-2709. World Wide Web: http://www.tiphawaii.com/.

University of Hawaii–Kapiolani Community College

Culinary Institute of the Pacific

Honolulu, Hawaii

General Information
Public, coeducational, two-year college. Urban campus. Founded in 1957. Accredited by Western Association of Schools and Colleges.

Program Information
Offered since 1965. Accredited by American Culinary Federation Accrediting Commission, Commission on Accreditation of Hospitality Management Programs (CAHM). Program calendar is divided into semesters. 18-month certificate in culinary arts. 2-year associate degree in patisserie. 2-year associate degree in culinary arts. 4-month certificate in patisserie. 4-month certificate in culinary arts.

Program Affiliation
American Culinary Federation; American Dietetic Association; Confrerie de la Chaine des Rotisseurs; Council on Hotel, Restaurant, and Institutional

University of Hawaii–Kapiolani Community College *(continued)*

Education; International Food Service Executives Association; National Restaurant Association; National Restaurant Association Educational Foundation.

Areas of Study
Asian Pacific cookery; baking; beverage management; confectionery show pieces; controlling costs in food service; food preparation; food service math; garde-manger; international cuisine; introduction to culinary arts; introduction to food service; management and human resources; meal planning; menu and facilities design; nutrition and food service; patisserie; sanitation; soup, stock, sauce, and starch production.

Facilities
2 bake shops; bakery; cafeteria; 12 classrooms; coffee shop; computer laboratory; demonstration laboratory; 4 food production kitchens; garden; 2 gourmet dining rooms; learning resource center; lecture room; library; 3 public restaurants; snack shop; student lounge; teaching kitchen.

Typical Student Profile
400 total: 200 full-time; 200 part-time. 150 are under 25 years old; 200 are between 25 and 44 years old; 50 are over 44 years old.

Special Programs
2-week (Christmas break) paid internships on neighbor islands, Walt Disney World College internship.

Financial Aid
In 2006, 45 scholarships were awarded (average award was $600); 250 loans were granted (average loan was $1200). Program-specific awards include Native Hawaiian student scholarships, culinary recipe scholarships. Employment placement assistance is available. Employment opportunities within the program are available.

Housing
Coed and apartment-style housing available.

Application Information
Students may begin participation in January, March, May, July, August, and October. Application deadline for fall is July 1. Application deadline for spring is November 15. Application deadline for summer is April 15. In 2006, 400 applied; 400 were accepted. Applicants must submit a formal application.

Contact
Director of Admissions, Culinary Institute of the Pacific, 4303 Diamond Head Road, Honolulu, HI 96816. Telephone: 808-734-9466. Fax: 808-734-9212. World Wide Web: http://www.kcc.hawaii.edu/.

Idaho

Boise State University

Culinary Arts Program

Boise, Idaho

General Information
Public, coeducational, comprehensive institution. Urban campus. Founded in 1932. Accredited by Northwest Commission on Colleges and Universities.

Program Information
Offered since 1979. Accredited by American Culinary Federation Accrediting Commission. Program calendar is divided into semesters. 12-month certificate in culinary arts. 18-month certificate in culinary arts. 2-year associate degree in culinary arts. 6-month certificate in culinary arts.

Program Affiliation
American Culinary Federation.

Areas of Study
Baking; beverage management; controlling costs in food service; culinary skill development; food preparation; food purchasing; food service math; garde-manger; international cuisine; kitchen management; meat fabrication; nutrition; patisserie; sanitation; soup, stock, sauce, and starch production; wines and spirits.

Facilities
Bake shop; bakery; catering service; 3 classrooms; 2 demonstration laboratories; food production kitchen; 3 laboratories; learning resource center; 3 lecture rooms; library; public restaurant; snack shop; student lounge; teaching kitchen.

Typical Student Profile
46 total: 40 full-time; 6 part-time.

Special Programs
One-semester paid internship.

Financial Aid
In 2006, 4 scholarships were awarded (average award was $300).

Housing
Coed, apartment-style, and single-sex housing available.

Application Information
Students may begin participation in January and August. Applications are accepted continuously. Applicants must submit a formal application and complete an entrance test.

Contact
Director of Admissions, Culinary Arts Program, 1910 University Drive, Boise, ID 83725-0399. Telephone: 208-426-1431. World Wide Web: http://www.idbsu.edu/.

Idaho State University

Culinary Arts Technology Program

Pocatello, Idaho

General Information
Public, coeducational, university. Rural campus. Founded in 1901. Accredited by Northwest Commission on Colleges and Universities.

Program Information
Offered since 1967. Accredited by American Culinary Federation Accrediting Commission. Program calendar is divided into semesters. 1-year certificate in culinary management. 1-year certificate in culinary arts. 2-year associate degree in restaurant management. 2-year associate degree in culinary management. 2-year associate degree in culinary arts.

Program Affiliation
American Culinary Federation; Council on Hotel, Restaurant, and Institutional Education.

Areas of Study
Baking; beverage management; buffet catering; controlling costs in food service; convenience cookery; culinary skill development; food preparation; food purchasing; food service math; garde-manger; international cuisine; introduction to food service; kitchen management; management and human resources; meal planning; meat cutting; menu and facilities design; nutrition and food service; patisserie; restaurant opportunities; sanitation; saucier; seafood processing; soup, stock, sauce, and starch production; wines and spirits.

Facilities
Bake shop; catering service; classroom; coffee shop; computer laboratory; food production kitchen; learning resource center; lecture room; library.

Typical Student Profile
27 total: 26 full-time; 1 part-time.

Special Programs
One-semester internship, culinary competitions.

Financial Aid
Employment placement assistance is available.

Housing
Coed housing available.

Application Information
Students may begin participation in January and August. Application deadline for fall is August 20. Application deadline for spring is January 10. Applicants must submit a formal application.

Contact
Director of Admissions, Culinary Arts Technology Program, Box 8380, Pocatello, ID 83209. Telephone: 208-282-3327. Fax: 208-282-2105. World Wide Web: http://www.isu.edu/.

Illinois

Black Hawk College

Culinary Arts

Moline, Illinois

General Information
Public, coeducational, two-year college. Founded in 1946. Accredited by North Central Association of Colleges and Schools.

Program Information
Program calendar is divided into semesters. 3-year associate degree in culinary arts.

Application Information
Students may begin participation in January and August. Applications are accepted continuously. Applicants must interview; submit a formal application.

Contact
Director of Admissions, Culinary Arts, 6600 34th Avenue, Moline, IL 61265-5899. Telephone: 309-796-5179. Fax: 309-792-5976. World Wide Web: http://www.bhc.edu/.

College of DuPage

Culinary Arts/Pastry Arts

Glen Ellyn, Illinois

General Information
Public, coeducational, two-year college. Suburban campus. Founded in 1967. Accredited by North Central Association of Colleges and Schools.

Program Information
Offered since 1967. Accredited by American Culinary Federation Accrediting Commission. Program calendar is divided into semesters. 1-year certificate in pastry. 1-year

College of DuPage *(continued)*

certificate in food service administration. 1-year certificate in culinary arts. 1-year certificate in beverage management. 2-year associate degree in food service administration. 2-year associate degree in culinary arts. 2-year associate degree in baking and pastry.

Program Affiliation

American Culinary Federation; American Institute of Baking; Council on Hotel, Restaurant, and Institutional Education; International Food Service Executives Association; National Restaurant Association; National Restaurant Association Educational Foundation; Retailer's Bakery Association.

Areas of Study

Asian cuisine; baking; beverage management; buffet catering; confectionery show pieces; controlling costs in food service; culinary skill development; food preparation; food purchasing; food service math; garde-manger; international cuisine; introduction to food service; kitchen management; management and human resources; menu and facilities design; nutrition; nutrition and food service; patisserie; sanitation; saucier; seafood processing; soup, stock, sauce, and starch production; wines and spirits.

Facilities

Bake shop; cafeteria; 2 classrooms; 3 computer laboratories; demonstration laboratory; food production kitchen; gourmet dining room; 2 laboratories; learning resource center; 2 lecture rooms; library; public restaurant; snack shop; student lounge; teaching kitchen.

Typical Student Profile

400 total: 160 full-time; 240 part-time. 160 are under 25 years old; 200 are between 25 and 44 years old; 40 are over 44 years old.

Special Programs

2-week culinary tour in Tuscany (Italy), one-week summer culinary tour in France, one-week wine and food tour of France.

Financial Aid

In 2006, 3 scholarships were awarded. Employment placement assistance is available. Employment opportunities within the program are available.

Application Information

Students may begin participation in January, May, and August. Applications are accepted continuously. In 2006, 200 applied; 200 were accepted. Applicants must submit a formal application.

Contact

Director of Admissions, Culinary Arts/Pastry Arts, College of DuPage, 425 Fawell Boulevard, Glen Ellyn, IL 60126. Telephone: 630-942-2315. Fax: 630-858-9399. World Wide Web: http://www.cod.edu/.

College of Lake County

Food Service Program

Grayslake, Illinois

General Information

Public, coeducational, two-year college. Suburban campus. Founded in 1967. Accredited by North Central Association of Colleges and Schools.

Program Information

Offered since 1987. National Restaurant Association Educational Foundation ManageFirst certificates available. Program calendar is divided into semesters. 1-semester certificate in cooking. 1-year certificate in food service management. 1-year certificate in culinary arts. 2-year associate degree in food service management.

Program Affiliation

American Culinary Federation; American Dietetic Association; Council on Hotel, Restaurant, and Institutional Education; National Restaurant Association; National Restaurant Association Educational Foundation.

Areas of Study

Baking; buffet catering; controlling costs in food service; convenience cookery; culinary skill development; food preparation; food purchasing; food service communication; food service math; garde-manger; international cuisine; introduction to food service; kitchen management; management and human resources; meal planning; menu and facilities design; nutrition; restaurant opportunities; sanitation; saucier; soup, stock, sauce, and starch production.

Facilities

Bake shop; cafeteria; catering service; 4 classrooms; 12 computer laboratories; 2 demonstration laboratories; 2 food production kitchens; learning resource center; library; 2 public restaurants; snack shop.

Typical Student Profile

175 total: 50 full-time; 125 part-time.

Special Programs

Applied Food Service Sanitation Refresher Course, Basset Course.

Financial Aid
In 2006, 2 scholarships were awarded (average award was $1000); 50 loans were granted (average loan was $500). Employment placement assistance is available. Employment opportunities within the program are available.

Application Information
Students may begin participation in January, June, and August. Applications are accepted continuously. In 2006, 50 applied; 50 were accepted. Applicants must submit a formal application.

Contact
Director of Admissions, Food Service Program, 19351 West Washington, Grayslake, IL 60030. Telephone: 847-543-2823. Fax: 847-223-7248. World Wide Web: http://www.clcillinois.edu/.

The Cooking and Hospitality Institute of Chicago

Le Cordon Bleu Program

Chicago, Illinois

General Information
Private, coeducational, culinary institute. Urban campus. Founded in 1983. Accredited by North Central Association of Colleges and Schools.

Program Information
Offered since 1991. Accredited by American Culinary Federation Accrediting Commission. Program calendar is continuous. 15-month associate degree in patisserie and baking. 15-month associate degree in culinary arts. 8-month certificate in culinary arts.

Program Affiliation
American Culinary Federation; American Institute of Wine & Food; International Association of Culinary Professionals; National Restaurant Association; National Restaurant Association Educational Foundation.

Areas of Study
Baking; beverage management; confectionery show pieces; controlling costs in food service; culinary French; culinary skill development; food preparation; food purchasing; food service math; garde-manger; international cuisine; introduction to food service; kitchen management; management and human resources; meal planning; meat cutting; meat fabrication; menu and facilities design; nutrition; patisserie; restaurant opportunities; sanitation; saucier; seafood processing; soup, stock, sauce, and starch production; wines and spirits.

Facilities
13 classrooms; 2 computer laboratories; 4 demonstration laboratories; 13 food production kitchens; learning resource center; library; public restaurant; student lounge.

Typical Student Profile
898 total: 721 full-time; 177 part-time. 574 are under 25 years old; 272 are between 25 and 44 years old; 52 are over 44 years old.

Special Programs
Graduates with AAS receive Le Cordon Bleu Diplôme.

Financial Aid
In 2006, 56 scholarships were awarded (average award was $580); 230 loans were granted (average loan was $9855). Program-specific awards include Alternative Educational Loans. Employment placement assistance is available. Employment opportunities within the program are available.

Application Information
Students may begin participation in January, February, April, May, July, August, September, and November. Applications are accepted continuously. Applicants must submit a formal application.

Contact
Director of Admissions, Le Cordon Bleu Program, 361 West Chestnut, Chicago, IL 60610-3050. Telephone: 312-873-2064. Fax: 312-798-2903. World Wide Web: http://www.chic.edu/.

Elgin Community College

Culinary Arts and Hospitality Institute of Elgin

Elgin, Illinois

General Information
Public, coeducational, two-year college. Suburban campus. Founded in 1949. Accredited by North Central Association of Colleges and Schools.

Program Information
Offered since 1971. Accredited by American Culinary Federation Accrediting Commission. National Restaurant Association Educational Foundation ManageFirst certificates available. Program calendar is divided into semesters. 1-semester certificate in lead baker. 1-semester certificate in baking assistant. 1-year certificate in cook's helper. 2-semester certificate in prep cook. 2-semester certificate in hospitality. 2-year associate degree in restaurant management. 2-year associate degree in pastry chef. 2-year associate degree in hotel/motel management.

Elgin Community College ***(continued)***

2-year associate degree in culinary arts. 3-semester certificate in restaurant operations. 3-semester certificate in pastry chef assistant. 3-semester certificate in first cook.

Program Affiliation
American Culinary Federation; American Institute of Baking; Council on Hotel, Restaurant, and Institutional Education; National Restaurant Association; National Restaurant Association Educational Foundation.

Areas of Study
Baking; beverage management; controlling costs in food service; culinary French; culinary skill development; food preparation; food purchasing; food service math; garde-manger; introduction to food service; management and human resources; meat cutting; meat fabrication; menu and facilities design; nutrition; patisserie; restaurant opportunities; sanitation; saucier; seafood processing; soup, stock, sauce, and starch production.

Facilities
2 bakeries; cafeteria; catering service; 4 classrooms; 4 demonstration laboratories; 5 food production kitchens; gourmet dining room; 5 laboratories; learning resource center; 5 lecture rooms; library; public restaurant; snack shop; student lounge; business conference center.

Typical Student Profile
450 total: 300 full-time; 150 part-time.

Special Programs
International exchange with The Tourism School of Simmering Austria, internship opportunities, employment at BMW Championship Golf Tournament, culinary internships with Disney World.

Financial Aid
Program-specific awards include 5 National Restaurant Association scholarships per semester. Employment placement assistance is available. Employment opportunities within the program are available.

Application Information
Students may begin participation in January, May, and August. Applications are accepted continuously. In 2006, 300 applied. Applicants must submit a formal application and have a high school diploma or GED.

Contact
Director of Admissions, Culinary Arts and Hospitality Institute of Elgin, 1700 Spartan Drive, Room C AC 105A, Elgin, IL 60123. Telephone: 847-214-7461. Fax: 847-214-7510. World Wide Web: http://www.elgin.edu/.

The International Culinary School at The Illinois Institute of Art–Chicago

Chicago, Illinois

General Information
Private, coeducational institution.

Program Information
Accredited by American Culinary Federation (Associate in Culinary Arts program). Associate degree in Culinary Arts. Bachelor's degree in Culinary Management. Certificate in Professional Cooking. Certificate in Professional Baking and Pastry.

Contact
Office of Admissions, 350 N. Orleans Street, Chicago, IL 60654. Telephone: 312-280-3500. World Wide Web: http://www.artinstitutes.edu/chicago/.

See color display following page 332.

Joliet Junior College

Culinary Arts/Hospitality Management

Joliet, Illinois

General Information
Public, coeducational, two-year college. Suburban campus. Founded in 1901. Accredited by North Central Association of Colleges and Schools.

Program Information
Offered since 1970. Accredited by American Culinary Federation Accrediting Commission. Program calendar is divided into semesters. 1-year certificate in pastry arts. 1-year certificate in culinary arts. 1-year certificate in baking. 2-year associate degree in hospitality management. 2-year associate degree in culinary arts.

Program Affiliation
American Culinary Federation; American Institute of Wine & Food; Council on Hotel, Restaurant, and Institutional Education; International Association of Culinary Professionals; National Restaurant Association; National Restaurant Association Educational Foundation; Women Chefs and Restaurateurs.

Areas of Study
Baking; controlling costs in food service; culinary French; culinary skill development; food preparation; garde-manger; ice carving; management and human resources; sanitation; wines and spirits.

Facilities
3 bake shops; bakery; 2 cafeterias; 2 catering services; 10 classrooms; 2 coffee shops; computer laboratory; 2 demonstration laboratories; 3 food production kitchens; 2 gourmet dining rooms; learning resource center; 5 lecture rooms; 2 libraries; 2 public restaurants; snack shop; student lounge; 2 teaching kitchens; ice carving room.

Typical Student Profile
217 total: 118 full-time; 99 part-time. 144 are under 25 years old; 55 are between 25 and 44 years old; 18 are over 44 years old.

Special Programs
Culinary competitions, 1-year paid internships in U.S. and Germany, two-week trip to Europe to visit food and hotel venues.

Financial Aid
In 2006, 35 scholarships were awarded (average award was $996); 210 loans were granted (average loan was $2869). Employment placement assistance is available. Employment opportunities within the program are available.

Housing
Coed and apartment-style housing available.

Application Information
Students may begin participation in January, May, and August. Applications are accepted continuously. In 2006, 78 applied; 78 were accepted. Applicants must have a high school diploma or GED.

Contact
Director of Admissions, Culinary Arts/Hospitality Management, 1215 Houbolt Road, Joliet, IL 60431. Telephone: 815-280-2639. Fax: 815-280-2696. World Wide Web: http://www.jjc.edu/.

Kendall College

School of Culinary Arts and School of Hotel Management

Chicago, Illinois

General Information
Private, coeducational, four-year college. Urban campus. Founded in 1934. Accredited by North Central Association of Colleges and Schools.

Program Information
Offered since 1985. Accredited by American Culinary Federation Accrediting Commission, Higher Learning Commission of NCA. Program calendar is divided into quarters. 13-quarter bachelor's degree in culinary arts. 15-quarter bachelor's degree in hospitality management. 4-quarter certificate in personal chef. 4-quarter certificate in culinary arts/professional cookery. 4-quarter certificate in catering. 4-quarter certificate in baking and pastry arts. 5-quarter associate degree in culinary arts accelerated program. 6-quarter associate degree in baking and pastry arts. 7-quarter associate degree in culinary arts.

Program Affiliation
American Culinary Federation; American Institute of Baking; American Institute of Wine & Food; Council on Hotel, Restaurant, and Institutional Education; Hospitality Business Alliance; Illinois Restaurant Association; International Association of Culinary Professionals; National Restaurant Association; National Restaurant Association Educational Foundation; Northern Illinois Food Service Executives Association; Northern Illinois Hospitality Educators Association; The Bread Bakers Guild of America; Women Chefs and Restaurateurs.

Areas of Study
Baking; beverage management; buffet catering; confectionery show pieces; controlling costs in food service; convenience cookery; culinary French; culinary skill development; food preparation; food purchasing; food service communication; food service math; garde-manger; international cuisine; introduction to food service; kitchen management; management and human resources; meal planning; meat cutting; meat fabrication; menu and facilities design; nutrition; nutrition and food service; patisserie; restaurant opportunities; sanitation; saucier; seafood processing; soup, stock, sauce, and starch production; techniques of healthy cooking; wines and spirits.

Facilities
2 bake shops; cafeteria; catering service; 25 classrooms; coffee shop; 2 computer laboratories; 3 demonstration laboratories; 11 food production kitchens; garden; gourmet dining room; 4 laboratories; learning resource center; 25 lecture rooms; library; public restaurant; snack shop; student lounge; 11 teaching kitchens.

Typical Student Profile
1,448 total: 929 full-time; 519 part-time.

Special Programs
Internships (1–5 quarters), Culinary Competition Team, exchange programs in Marseille and Nice (France), Bluche (Switzerland), Montreal (Canada) and Tel Aviv (Israel).

Financial Aid
Program-specific awards include graduate assistant appointments, college work-study positions in Culinary Arts Department, Hospitality Department and others. Employment placement assistance is available. Employment opportunities within the program are available.

Kendall College *(continued)*

Housing
Apartment-style housing available.

Application Information
Students may begin participation in January, March, July, and September. Applications are accepted continuously. In 2006, 816 applied; 780 were accepted. Applicants must interview; submit a formal application, an essay, official transcripts, and ACT/SAT scores (freshmen).

Contact
Director of Admissions, School of Culinary Arts and School of Hotel Management, 900 N. North Branch Street, Chicago, IL 60622. Telephone: 877-588-8860. Fax: 312-752-2021. World Wide Web: http://www.kendall.edu/.

See color display following page 140.

Lexington College

Chicago, Illinois

General Information
Private, four-year college. Urban campus. Founded in 1977. Accredited by North Central Association of Colleges and Schools.

Program Information
Offered since 1977. Accredited by American Culinary Federation Accrediting Commission. Program calendar is divided into semesters. 2-year associate degree in hospitality management. 4-year bachelor's degree in hospitality management.

Program Affiliation
American Culinary Federation; Council on Hotel, Restaurant, and Institutional Education; Illinois Restaurant Association; National Restaurant Association; National Restaurant Association Educational Foundation; Women Chefs and Restaurateurs; Women's Foodservice Forum.

Areas of Study
Culinary skill development; events management; hotel and restaurant management; management and human resources.

Facilities
4 classrooms; computer laboratory; demonstration laboratory; library; student lounge; teaching kitchen.

Typical Student Profile
57 total: 48 full-time; 9 part-time. 41 are under 25 years old; 15 are between 25 and 44 years old; 1 is over 44 years old.

Special Programs
Summer internships (paid).

Financial Aid
In 2006, 14 scholarships were awarded (average award was $30,000); 50 loans were granted (average loan was $3000). Program-specific awards include Lexington Academic Grants. Employment placement assistance is available. Employment opportunities within the program are available.

Application Information
Students may begin participation in January and August. Applications are accepted continuously. In 2006, 48 applied; 46 were accepted. Applicants must submit a formal application, letters of reference, an essay, ACT or SAT scores.

Contact
Director of Admissions, 310 South Peoria Street, Chicago, IL 60607. Telephone: 312-226-6294 Ext. 226. Fax: 312-226-6405. World Wide Web: http://www.lexingtoncollege.edu/.

Lincoln Land Community College

Hospitality Management

Springfield, Illinois

General Information
Public, coeducational, two-year college. Urban campus. Founded in 1967. Accredited by North Central Association of Colleges and Schools.

Program Information
Offered since 1994. Accredited by Council on Hotel, Restaurant and Institutional Education. National Restaurant Association Educational Foundation ManageFirst certificates available. Program calendar is divided into semesters. 1-year certificate in pastry. 1-year certificate in lodging management. 1-year certificate in culinary arts. 1-year certificate in certified dietary manager. 2-year associate degree in hospitality management.

Program Affiliation
American Culinary Federation; American Dietetic Association; American Vegan Society; Confrerie de la Chaine des Rotisseurs; Council on Hotel, Restaurant, and Institutional Education; Dietary Managers Association; Illinois Restaurant Association; National Restaurant Association; National Restaurant Association Educational Foundation.

Areas of Study
Baking; buffet catering; controlling costs in food service; culinary French; culinary skill development; food preparation; food purchasing; food service communication; food service math; garde-manger; international cuisine; introduction to food service; kitchen management; management and human resources; meal planning; meat cutting; nutrition; nutrition and food service; patisserie; restaurant opportunities; sanitation; seafood processing; soup, stock, sauce, and starch production; wines and spirits.

Facilities
Bake shop; bakery; cafeteria; catering service; classroom; computer laboratory; demonstration laboratory; food production kitchen; garden; laboratory; learning resource center; lecture room; library; public restaurant; snack shop; student lounge; teaching kitchen.

Typical Student Profile
130 total: 30 full-time; 100 part-time. 45 are under 25 years old; 45 are between 25 and 44 years old; 40 are over 44 years old.

Special Programs
Paid internships, participation in culinary society events, membership in ACF chapter.

Financial Aid
In 2006, 6 scholarships were awarded (average award was $500); 10 loans were granted (average loan was $1000). Employment placement assistance is available. Employment opportunities within the program are available.

Application Information
Students may begin participation in January, June, and August. Applications are accepted continuously. Applicants must submit a formal application.

Contact
Director of Admissions, Hospitality Management, 5250 Shepherd Road, Springfield, IL 62794. Telephone: 217-786-2772. Fax: 217-786-2339. World Wide Web: http://www.llcc.edu/.

Parkland College

Hospitality Industry

Champaign, Illinois

General Information
Public, coeducational, two-year college. Small-town setting. Founded in 1967. Accredited by North Central Association of Colleges and Schools.

Program Information
Offered since 1981. Accredited by Council on Hotel, Restaurant and Institutional Education, Commission on Accreditation of Hospitality Management Programs. National Restaurant Association Educational Foundation ManageFirst certificates available. Program calendar is divided into semesters. 1-year certificate in hospitality industry: food service. 2-year associate degree in hospitality industry: restaurant management.

Program Affiliation
Council on Hotel, Restaurant, and Institutional Education; International Executive Food Association; International Food Service Executives Association; National Restaurant Association; National Restaurant Association Educational Foundation.

Areas of Study
Baking; beverage management; buffet catering; controlling costs in food service; convenience cookery; culinary skill development; food preparation; food purchasing; food service communication; food service math; international cuisine; introduction to food service; kitchen management; management and human resources; meal planning; meat fabrication; menu and facilities design; nutrition; nutrition and food service; restaurant opportunities; sanitation; soup, stock, sauce, and starch production; wines and spirits.

Facilities
Catering service; classroom; computer laboratory; demonstration laboratory; food production kitchen; learning resource center; lecture room; teaching kitchen.

Typical Student Profile
71 total: 34 full-time; 37 part-time. 41 are under 25 years old; 26 are between 25 and 44 years old; 4 are over 44 years old.

Special Programs
Food Service Sanitation Certification, semester or summer internships.

Financial Aid
In 2006, 5 scholarships were awarded (average award was $900). Program-specific awards include Arby's Foodservice/Restaurant Management Career Grant ($1000), William P. Myers Foundation Awards ($1000). Employment placement assistance is available. Employment opportunities within the program are available.

Application Information
Students may begin participation in January and August. Applications are accepted continuously. In 2006, 17 applied; 17 were accepted. Applicants must submit a formal application.

Parkland College *(continued)*

Contact
Director of Admissions, Hospitality Industry, 2400 West Bradley Avenue, Champaign, IL 61821-1806. Telephone: 217-351-2378. Fax: 217-373-3896. World Wide Web: http://www.parkland.edu/.

Robert Morris College

Institute of Culinary Arts

Aurora, Chicago, and Orland Park, Illinois

General Information
Private, coeducational, four-year college. Urban campus. Founded in 1913. Accredited by North Central Association of Colleges and Schools.

Program Information
Offered since 2003. National Restaurant Association Educational Foundation ManageFirst certificates available. Program calendar is divided into quarters, 5 ten-week academic sessions per year. 15-month associate degree in culinary arts. 3-year bachelor's degree in professional study in advanced culinary arts. 3-year bachelor's degree in hospitality management.

Program Affiliation
American Culinary Federation; American Dietetic Association; American Institute of Wine & Food; American Wine Society; Illinois Restaurant Association; International Association of Culinary Professionals; National Restaurant Association; National Restaurant Association Educational Foundation; Women Chefs and Restaurateurs.

Areas of Study
Baking; beverage management; buffet catering; controlling costs in food service; convenience cookery; culinary French; culinary skill development; food preparation; food purchasing; food service communication; food service math; garde-manger; international cuisine; introduction to food service; kitchen management; management and human resources; meal planning; meat cutting; meat fabrication; menu and facilities design; nutrition; restaurant opportunities; sanitation; saucier; seafood processing; soup, stock, sauce, and starch production; wines and spirits.

Facilities
32 computer laboratories; garden; 3 learning resource centers; 32 lecture rooms; 3 libraries; 2 snack shops; 4 student lounges; 7 teaching kitchens.

Student Profile
350 total: 325 full-time; 25 part-time.

Faculty
42 total: 6 full-time; 36 part-time. Prominent faculty: Brian Flower; Jennifer Bucko, MCFE; John Hudac; Scott Nitsche, CEC. Faculty-student ratio: 1:16.

Special Programs
Culinary explorations 1-week experience with Midwest agricultural sites, internships, international experience with Italian culinary schools.

Typical Expenses
Application fee: $30. Tuition: $6000 per quarter full-time, $4000 per quarter part-time. Program-related fees include $900 for lab fee (per session); $275 for knife kit; $180 for 3 uniforms.

Financial Aid
In 2007, 20 scholarships were awarded. Program-specific awards include 85% of students receive some type of financial aid. Employment placement assistance is available. Employment opportunities within the program are available.

Housing
Coed and apartment-style housing available. Average on-campus housing cost per month: $1000. Average off-campus housing cost per month: $1000.

Application Information
Students may begin participation in February and September. Applications are accepted continuously. In 2007, 600 applied; 450 were accepted. Applicants must interview; submit a formal application and proof of high school graduation or GED completion.

Contact
Nancy Rotunno, Executive Director, Institute of Culinary Arts, 401 South State Street, Chicago, IL 60605. Telephone: 312-935-6800. Fax: 312-935-6930. E-mail: nrotunno@robertmorris.edu. World Wide Web: http://www.robertmorris.edu/.

See display on page 151.

Southwestern Illinois College

Culinary Arts and Food Management

Granite City, Illinois

General Information
Public, coeducational, two-year college. Suburban campus. Founded in 1946. Accredited by North Central Association of Colleges and Schools.

Robert Morris College

rmc culinary

1913

Southwestern Illinois College *(continued)*

Program Information

Accredited by American Culinary Federation Accrediting Commission. Program calendar is divided into semesters. 1-semester certificate in culinary arts. 1-year certificate in food service and management. 2-year associate degree in culinary arts and food management.

Program Affiliation

American Culinary Federation; National Restaurant Association.

Areas of Study

Baking; beverage management; controlling costs in food service; culinary skill development; food preparation; food purchasing; food service math; garde-manger; international cuisine; introduction to food service; kitchen management; meal planning; meat cutting; nutrition; nutrition and food service; restaurant opportunities; sanitation; soup, stock, sauce, and starch production.

Facilities

2 bake shops; 2 bakeries; 2 cafeterias; 2 classrooms; coffee shop; 4 computer laboratories; 2 demonstration laboratories; 2 food production kitchens; 2 laboratories; 2 learning resource centers; 2 lecture rooms; 2 libraries; 2 student lounges; 2 teaching kitchens.

Typical Student Profile

150 total: 50 full-time; 100 part-time.

Special Programs

Semester internships, trip to National Restaurant Association show.

Financial Aid

In 2006, 2 scholarships were awarded (average award was $500). Program-specific awards include National Restaurant Association scholarships. Employment placement assistance is available. Employment opportunities within the program are available.

Application Information

Students may begin participation in January, June, and August. Applications are accepted continuously. Applicants must submit a formal application, have high school diploma or GED and food service sanitation license.

Contact

Director of Admissions, Culinary Arts and Food Management, 2500 Carlyle Road, Belleville, IL 62221. Telephone: 618-222-5436. Fax: 618-222-8964. World Wide Web: http://www.swic.edu/.

Triton College

Hospitality Industry Administration

River Grove, Illinois

General Information

Public, coeducational, two-year college. Urban campus. Founded in 1964. Accredited by North Central Association of Colleges and Schools.

Program Information

Offered since 1972. Accredited by American Culinary Federation Accrediting Commission. Program calendar is divided into semesters. 1-year certificate in restaurant management. 1-year certificate in hotel management. 1-year certificate in culinary arts. 1-year certificate in baking and pastry. 2-year associate degree in restaurant management. 2-year associate degree in hotel management. 2-year associate degree in culinary arts.

Program Affiliation

American Culinary Federation; American Institute of Baking; American Institute of Wine & Food; Council on Hotel, Restaurant, and Institutional Education; International Association of Culinary Professionals; National Restaurant Association; National Restaurant Association Educational Foundation.

Areas of Study

Baking; beverage management; food preparation; food purchasing; garde-manger; international cuisine; nutrition; sanitation; wines and spirits.

Facilities

Bake shop; bakery; cafeteria; catering service; 7 classrooms; coffee shop; computer laboratory; demonstration laboratory; food production kitchen; garden; gourmet dining room; learning resource center; 7 lecture rooms; 2 libraries; public restaurant; snack shop; student lounge; teaching kitchen; vineyard.

Typical Student Profile

250 total: 150 full-time; 100 part-time. 75 are under 25 years old; 100 are between 25 and 44 years old; 75 are over 44 years old.

Special Programs

Wine making class includes tours in southwest Michigan, culinary competition.

Financial Aid

In 2006, 8 scholarships were awarded (average award was $2000). Employment placement assistance is available. Employment opportunities within the program are available.

Application Information
Students may begin participation in January, June, and August. Applications are accepted continuously. In 2006, 150 applied; 150 were accepted. Applicants must submit a formal application.

Contact
Director of Admissions, Hospitality Industry Administration, 2000 Fifth Avenue, River Grove, IL 60171. Telephone: 708-456-0300 Ext. 3624. World Wide Web: http://www.triton.edu/.

University of Illinois at Urbana–Champaign

Hospitality Management/Department of Food Science and Human Nutrition

Urbana, Illinois

General Information
Public, coeducational, university. Urban campus. Founded in 1867. Accredited by North Central Association of Colleges and Schools.

Program Information
Offered since 1952. Accredited by American Dietetic Association. Program calendar is divided into semesters. 4-year bachelor's degree in hospitality management.

Program Affiliation
American Dietetic Association; Council on Hotel, Restaurant, and Institutional Education; Illinois Restaurant Association; Institute of Food Technologists.

Areas of Study
Buffet catering; controlling costs in food service; food preparation; food purchasing; food science; kitchen management; management and human resources; meat cutting; meat fabrication; nutrition; restaurant opportunities; sanitation.

Facilities
Cafeteria; catering service; classroom; computer laboratory; food production kitchen; gourmet dining room; laboratory; lecture room; student lounge; teaching kitchen.

Typical Student Profile
106 full-time. 106 are under 25 years old.

Special Programs
Practical work experience, professional work experience.

Financial Aid
Program-specific awards include two 4-year work-study scholarships ($2000 per year plus hourly wage). Employment placement assistance is available. Employment opportunities within the program are available.

Housing
Coed, apartment-style, and single-sex housing available.

Application Information
Students may begin participation in August. Application deadline for fall is January 1. Applicants must submit a formal application, an essay, ACT scores.

Contact
Director of Admissions, Hospitality Management/Department of Food Science and Human Nutrition, 901 West Illinois Street, Urbana, IL 61801. Telephone: 217-333-0302. World Wide Web: http://www.fshn.uiuc.edu/academics/undergraduate_programs/hospitality_management/.

Washburne Culinary Institute

Chicago, Illinois

General Information
Public, coeducational, culinary institute. Urban campus. Founded in 1937. Accredited by North Central Association of Colleges and Schools.

Program Information
Offered since 1937. Program calendar is divided into semesters, year-round. 48-week advanced certificate in culinary arts. 48-week advanced certificate in baking and pastry arts. 48-week advanced certificate in culinary arts. 48-week advanced certificate in baking and pastry arts. 64-week associate degree in baking and pastry arts. 80-week associate degree in culinary arts.

Program Affiliation
American Culinary Federation; International Food Service Executives Association; National Restaurant Association Educational Foundation.

Areas of Study
Baking; buffet catering; controlling costs in food service; culinary skill development; food preparation; food purchasing; food service math; garde-manger; international cuisine; introduction to food service; kitchen management; management and human resources; meal planning; meat cutting; meat fabrication; menu and facilities design; nutrition; nutrition and food service; patisserie; restaurant opportunities; sanitation; saucier; seafood processing; soup, stock, sauce, and starch production.

Washburne Culinary Institute *(continued)*

Facilities
3 bake shops; cafeteria; catering service; 8 classrooms; coffee shop; computer laboratory; demonstration laboratory; 9 food production kitchens; garden; 8 lecture rooms; library; 2 public restaurants; snack shop; 2 student lounges; 9 teaching kitchens.

Typical Student Profile
150 full-time. 25 are under 25 years old; 100 are between 25 and 44 years old; 25 are over 44 years old.

Special Programs
16-week experience in school's public restaurant, continuing education center at South Shore Cultural Center.

Financial Aid
In 2006, 25 scholarships were awarded (average award was $35,000). Employment placement assistance is available. Employment opportunities within the program are available.

Application Information
Students may begin participation in January, May, and August. Application deadline for fall is August 10. Application deadline for winter is January 10. Application deadline for summer is May 1. In 2006, 400 applied; 150 were accepted. Applicants must interview; submit a formal application.

Contact
Director of Admissions, 740 West 63rd Street, Chicago, IL 60620. Telephone: 773-281-8559. Fax: 773-602-5452. World Wide Web: http://kennedyking.ccc.edu/washburne/index.html.

Indiana

Ball State University

Department of Family and Consumer Sciences

Muncie, Indiana

General Information
Public, coeducational, university. Urban campus. Founded in 1918. Accredited by North Central Association of Colleges and Schools.

Program Information
Offered since 1975. Program calendar is divided into semesters. 2-year associate degree in hospitality and food management. 4-year bachelor's degree in hospitality and food management.

Program Affiliation
American Culinary Federation; Council on Hotel, Restaurant, and Institutional Education.

Areas of Study
Beverage management; buffet catering; controlling costs in food service; convenience cookery; culinary skill development; customer relations; food preparation; food purchasing; introduction to food service; kitchen management; management and human resources; meal planning; nutrition; nutrition and food service; restaurant opportunities; sanitation.

Facilities
5 classrooms; computer laboratory; food production kitchen; gourmet dining room; 3 laboratories; learning resource center; lecture room; library; public restaurant; student lounge; teaching kitchen.

Typical Student Profile
75 full-time. 65 are under 25 years old; 10 are between 25 and 44 years old.

Special Programs
Paid internships.

Financial Aid
Program-specific awards include 5 Moore Scholarships ($10,000). Employment placement assistance is available. Employment opportunities within the program are available.

Housing
Coed, apartment-style, and single-sex housing available.

Application Information
Students may begin participation in January, May, and August. Applications are accepted continuously. Applicants must submit a formal application and letters of reference.

Contact
Director of Admissions, Department of Family and Consumer Sciences, AT 150 D, Ball State University, Muncie, IN 47306. Telephone: 765-285-5956. Fax: 765-285-2314. World Wide Web: http://www.bsu.edu/fcs/article/0,1894,35151-4865-10251,00.html.

The Chef's Academy at Indiana Business College

Indianapolis, Indiana

General Information
Private, coeducational, culinary institute. Urban campus. Accredited by Accrediting Council for Independent Colleges and Schools.

Program Information
Offered since 2006. Program calendar is divided into quarters. 2-year associate degree in pastry arts. 2-year associate degree in culinary arts. 3-year bachelor's degree in hospitality and restaurant management.

Program Affiliation
American Culinary Federation; National Restaurant Association.

Facilities
Bake shop; bakery; 6 classrooms; 3 computer laboratories; 3 demonstration laboratories; 3 food production kitchens; gourmet dining room; learning resource center; 6 lecture rooms; library; student lounge; 3 teaching kitchens.

Student Profile
242 full-time.

Faculty
11 total: 9 full-time; 2 part-time. 11 are industry professionals. Prominent faculty: Chef Tony Hanslits; Chef Pierre Giacometti. Faculty-student ratio: 1:18.

Typical Expenses
Application fee: $50. Tuition: $265 per credit hour (for culinary arts; pastry arts; and hospitality & restaurant management programs). Program-related fee includes $100 for tuition deposit.

Financial Aid
In 2007, 4 scholarships were awarded (average award was $1000); 1 loan was granted (loan was $6000). Employment placement assistance is available.

Housing
Average off-campus housing cost per month: $489–$860.

Application Information
Students may begin participation in February, April, July, September, and November. Applications are accepted continuously. Applicants must interview and submit a high school diploma/GED.

Contact
Kathy Hodapp, Director of Admissions, 644 E. Washington Street, Indianapolis, IN 46204. Telephone: 317-656-4846. Fax: 317-264-7525. E-mail: kathy.hodapp@ibcschools.edu. World Wide Web: http://www.thechefsacademy.com.

See color display following page 140.

Indiana University–Purdue University Fort Wayne

Hospitality Management

Fort Wayne, Indiana

General Information
Public, coeducational, comprehensive institution. Suburban campus. Founded in 1917. Accredited by North Central Association of Colleges and Schools.

Program Information
Offered since 1976. Program calendar is divided into semesters. 2-year associate degree in hotel, restaurant, and tourism management. 4-year bachelor's degree in hospitality and tourism management.

Program Affiliation
Confrerie de la Chaine des Rotisseurs; Council on Hotel, Restaurant, and Institutional Education; National Restaurant Association Educational Foundation.

Areas of Study
Beverage management; buffet catering; controlling costs in food service; convenience cookery; culinary French; culinary skill development; food preparation; food purchasing; food service communication; food service math; introduction to food service; kitchen management; management and human resources; meal planning; menu and facilities design; nutrition; nutrition and food service; restaurant opportunities; sanitation; soup, stock, sauce, and starch production; tourism; wines and spirits.

Facilities
5 computer laboratories; demonstration laboratory; food production kitchen; learning resource center; library; 6 student lounges; ballroom.

Typical Student Profile
100 total: 80 full-time; 20 part-time.

Special Programs
Annual visits to New York, Las Vegas, Chicago, Walt Disney World, and international venues; opportunity for students to serve dining public in local hotels and restaurants.

Financial Aid
Employment placement assistance is available.

Housing
Apartment-style housing available.

Application Information
Students may begin participation in January and August. Applications are accepted continuously. Applicants must submit a formal application.

Indiana University–Purdue University Fort Wayne *(continued)*

Contact

Director of Admissions, Hospitality Management, Neff Hall, Room 330B, Fort Wayne, IN 46805-1499. Telephone: 260-481-6562. Fax: 260-481-5767. World Wide Web: http://www.ipfw.edu/cfs/undergrad/bshtm.shtml.

The International Culinary School at The Art Institute of Indianapolis

Indianapolis, Indiana

General Information

Private, coeducational institution.

Program Information

Accredited by licensed by the Indiana Commission on Proprietary Education. Associate degree in Culinary Arts. Bachelor's degree in Culinary Management. Certificate in Culinary Arts. Certificate in Baking and Pastry.

Contact

Office of Admissions, 3500 Depauw Boulevard, Suite 1010, Indianapolis, IN 46268. Telephone: 317-613-4800. World Wide Web: http://www.artinstitutes.edu/indianapolis/.

See color display following page 332.

Ivy Tech Community College–Central Indiana

Hospitality Administration Program

Indianapolis, Indiana

General Information

Public, coeducational, two-year college. Urban campus. Founded in 1963. Accredited by North Central Association of Colleges and Schools.

Program Information

Offered since 1981. Accredited by Council on Hotel, Restaurant and Institutional Education, Commission on Accreditation on Hospitality Management (CAHM). National Restaurant Association Educational Foundation ManageFirst certificates available. Program calendar is divided into semesters. 2-year associate degree in restaurant management. 2-year associate degree in hotel management specialty. 2-year associate degree in hospitality administration degree. 2-year associate degree in event management specialty. 2-year associate degree in culinary arts specialty. 2-year associate degree in baking and pastry arts specialty. 3-year associate degree in culinary arts (with apprenticeship). 8-month certificate in hospitality management. 8-month certificate in culinary arts. 8-month certificate in baking/pastry arts.

Program Affiliation

American Culinary Federation; Council on Hotel, Restaurant, and Institutional Education; International Wine & Food Society; National Restaurant Association; National Restaurant Association Educational Foundation; Retailer's Bakery Association; Society of Wine Educators; Women Chefs and Restaurateurs.

Areas of Study

Baking; beverage management; controlling costs in food service; culinary French; culinary skill development; food preparation; food purchasing; food service communication; food service math; garde-manger; international cuisine; introduction to food service; kitchen management; management and human resources; meat cutting; meat fabrication; menu and facilities design; nutrition; nutrition and food service; patisserie; restaurant opportunities; sanitation; saucier; seafood processing; soup, stock, sauce, and starch production; wines and spirits.

Facilities

Cafeteria; catering service; 20 classrooms; 3 computer laboratories; 2 food production kitchens; 2 laboratories; 3 lecture rooms; library; student lounge; 2 teaching kitchens.

Typical Student Profile

450 total: 180 full-time; 270 part-time.

Special Programs

2-week program at cooking school in Europe, culinary competitions, ACF student chapter-club.

Financial Aid

Employment placement assistance is available. Employment opportunities within the program are available.

Application Information

Students may begin participation in January, May, and August. Applications are accepted continuously. Applicants must submit a formal application and have a high school diploma, GED, or equivalent.

Contact

Director of Admissions, Hospitality Administration Program, 50 West Fall Creek Parkway, N. Drive, Indianapolis, IN 46208. Telephone: 317-921-4516. Fax: 317-921-4203. World Wide Web: http://www.ivytech.edu/indianapolis.

Ivy Tech Community College–North Central

South Bend, Indiana

General Information

Public, coeducational, two-year college. Urban campus. Founded in 1963. Accredited by North Central Association of Colleges and Schools.

Program Information

Offered since 2000. Accredited by American Culinary Federation Accrediting Commission. Program calendar is divided into semesters. 2-year associate degree in hospitality administration: restaurant management. 2-year associate degree in hospitality administration: culinary arts. 2-year associate degree in hospitality administration: baking and pastry.

Program Affiliation

American Culinary Federation.

Areas of Study

Baking.

Facilities

Bake shop; classroom; demonstration laboratory; food production kitchen; garden.

Typical Student Profile

180 total: 60 full-time; 120 part-time. 80 are under 25 years old; 80 are between 25 and 44 years old; 20 are over 44 years old.

Special Programs

Annual trip (different every year with some scholarships available).

Financial Aid

In 2006, 10 scholarships were awarded (average award was $500). Employment placement assistance is available.

Application Information

Students may begin participation in January and August. Applications are accepted continuously. In 2006, 60 applied; 60 were accepted. Applicants must submit a formal application and placement/assessment testing.

Contact

Director of Admissions, 220 Dean Johnson Boulevard, South Bend, IN 46601. Telephone: 574-289-7001 Ext. 5440. Fax: 574-245-7102. World Wide Web: http://www.ivytech.edu/.

Ivy Tech Community College–Northeast

Hospitality Administration

Fort Wayne, Indiana

General Information

Public, coeducational, two-year college. Suburban campus. Founded in 1969. Accredited by North Central Association of Colleges and Schools.

Program Information

Offered since 1969. Accredited by American Culinary Federation Accrediting Commission. Program calendar is divided into semesters. 2-year associate degree in culinary arts. 2-year associate degree in baking/pastry arts.

Program Affiliation

American Culinary Federation.

Areas of Study

Baking; confectionery show pieces; controlling costs in food service; food preparation; food purchasing; garde-manger; international cuisine; kitchen management; management and human resources; meat cutting; meat fabrication; nutrition; patisserie; sanitation; seafood processing; soup, stock, sauce, and starch production; wines and spirits.

Facilities

Bake shop; bakery; catering service; 4 classrooms; 2 computer laboratories; demonstration laboratory; food production kitchen; gourmet dining room; 3 laboratories; 3 lecture rooms; library; 2 student lounges; teaching kitchen.

Special Programs

10-day European culinary study tour.

Financial Aid

In 2006, 8 scholarships were awarded (average award was $2600). Program-specific awards include scholarships funded by Boiardi Endowment, Gordons Scholarship. Employment placement assistance is available.

Application Information

Students may begin participation in January, May, and August. Application deadline for fall is August 15. Application deadline for spring is December 15. Application deadline for summer is April 30. Applicants must submit a formal application.

Contact

Director of Admissions, Hospitality Administration, 3800 North Anthony Boulevard, Ft. Wayne, IN 46805. Telephone: 260-480-4240. Fax: 260-480-2051. World Wide Web: http://www.ivytech.edu/.

Ivy Tech Community College–Northwest

Hospitality Administration

Gary, Indiana

General Information
Public, coeducational, two-year college. Urban campus. Founded in 1963. Accredited by North Central Association of Colleges and Schools.

Program Information
Offered since 1985. Accredited by American Culinary Federation Accrediting Commission. Program calendar is divided into semesters. 1-year certificate in culinary arts. 2-year associate degree in restaurant management. 2-year associate degree in hotel/restaurant management. 2-year associate degree in culinary arts. 2-year associate degree in convention management. 2-year associate degree in bakery and pastry arts.

Program Affiliation
American Culinary Federation; National Restaurant Association; National Restaurant Association Educational Foundation; Women Chefs and Restaurateurs.

Areas of Study
Baking; buffet catering; controlling costs in food service; culinary French; culinary skill development; food preparation; food purchasing; garde-manger; international cuisine; introduction to food service; management and human resources; meal planning; meat cutting; meat fabrication; menu and facilities design; nutrition; patisserie; sanitation; saucier; seafood processing; soup, stock, sauce, and starch production; wines and spirits.

Facilities
Bake shop; 2 computer laboratories; 2 demonstration laboratories; gourmet dining room; learning resource center; library; student lounge; teaching kitchen.

Typical Student Profile
96 total: 75 full-time; 21 part-time.

Special Programs
National Restaurant Association shows, 2-week trip to France, National Convention for the American Culinary Education.

Financial Aid
In 2006, 8 scholarships were awarded (average award was $752). Employment placement assistance is available.

Application Information
Students may begin participation in January, May, and August. Applications are accepted continuously. Applicants must submit a formal application and have a high school diploma or GED.

Contact
Director of Admissions, Hospitality Administration, 3714 Franklin Street, Michigan City, IN 46360. Telephone: 219-981-1111 Ext. 4400. Fax: 219-981-4415. World Wide Web: http://www.ivytech.edu/.

Iowa

Des Moines Area Community College

Iowa Culinary Institute (ICI)

Ankeny, Iowa

General Information
Public, coeducational, two-year college. Urban campus. Founded in 1966. Accredited by North Central Association of Colleges and Schools.

Program Information
Offered since 1975. Accredited by American Culinary Federation Accrediting Commission. Program calendar is divided into semesters. 2-year associate degree in hotel/restaurant management. 2-year associate degree in culinary arts.

Program Affiliation
American Culinary Federation; National Restaurant Association.

Areas of Study
Baking; beverage management; buffet catering; culinary French; culinary skill development; food preparation; food purchasing; garde-manger; international cuisine; introduction to food service; menu and facilities design; nutrition; sanitation; soup, stock, sauce, and starch production; wines and spirits.

Facilities
Bake shop; cafeteria; 3 classrooms; computer laboratory; demonstration laboratory; 2 food production kitchens; gourmet dining room; learning resource center; lecture room; library.

Typical Student Profile
95 total: 90 full-time; 5 part-time. 48 are under 25 years old; 47 are between 25 and 44 years old.

Special Programs
French culinary exchange, field study tour of Chicago.

Financial Aid
Employment placement assistance is available.

Housing
Apartment-style housing available.

Application Information
Students may begin participation in January and September. Application deadline for spring is January 5. Application deadline for fall is August 1. In 2006, 120 applied; 90 were accepted. Applicants must submit a formal application.

Contact
Director of Admissions, Iowa Culinary Institute (ICI), 2006 South Ankeny Boulevard, Building #7, Ankeny, IA 50023. Telephone: 515-964-6532. Fax: 515-965-7129. World Wide Web: http://www.dmacc.edu/.

Iowa Lakes Community College

Hotel and Restaurant Management Program

Emmetsburg, Iowa

General Information
Public, coeducational, two-year college. Rural campus. Founded in 1967. Accredited by North Central Association of Colleges and Schools.

Program Information
Offered since 1973. Accredited by Council on Hotel, Restaurant and Institutional Education. Program calendar is divided into semesters. 1-year diploma in hospitality technology program. 2-year associate degree in hotel and restaurant management program. 2-year associate degree in dietary management program.

Program Affiliation
American Hotel and Lodging Association; Council on Hotel, Restaurant, and Institutional Education; Dietary Managers Association; Iowa Hospitality Association; Iowa Lodging Association; National Restaurant Association; National Restaurant Association Educational Foundation.

Areas of Study
Baking; beverage management; buffet catering; controlling costs in food service; convenience cookery; culinary skill development; food preparation; food purchasing; food service communication; food service math; garde-manger; hospitality law; international cuisine; introduction to food service; kitchen management; management and human resources; marketing; meal planning; menu and facilities design; nutrition; nutrition and food service; restaurant opportunities; sanitation; saucier; soup, stock, sauce, and starch production; wines and spirits.

Facilities
Bakery; 2 cafeterias; 3 catering services; 3 classrooms; coffee shop; 5 computer laboratories; demonstration laboratory; 2 food production kitchens; gourmet dining room; 2 laboratories; 3 learning resource centers; 2 lecture rooms; 3 libraries; public restaurant; snack shop; student lounge; teaching kitchen.

Typical Student Profile
45 total: 40 full-time; 5 part-time.

Special Programs
Iowa Hospitality Show in Des Moines, Midwest Hospitality Show in Minneapolis, Las Vegas Hospitality Show.

Financial Aid
In 2006, 5 scholarships were awarded (average award was $850); 35 loans were granted (average loan was $2600). Program-specific awards include National Restaurant Association scholarships, scholarships for freshmen and sophomores ($150), American Hotel and Lodging Association Scholarship. Employment placement assistance is available. Employment opportunities within the program are available.

Housing
Coed and apartment-style housing available.

Application Information
Students may begin participation in January, May, and August. Application deadline for fall is August 1. Application deadline for spring is January 1. Application deadline for summer is May 1. Applicants must interview; submit a formal application.

Contact
Director of Admissions, Hotel and Restaurant Management Program, 3200 College Drive, Emmetsburg, IA 50536-1098. Telephone: 712-852-5256. Fax: 712-852-2152. World Wide Web: http://www.iowalakes.edu/.

Iowa State University of Science and Technology

Hotel, Restaurant, and Institution Management

Ames, Iowa

General Information
Public, coeducational, university. Small-town setting. Founded in 1858. Accredited by North Central Association of Colleges and Schools.

Iowa State University of Science and Technology *(continued)*

Program Information

Offered since 1924. Accredited by Accreditation Commission for Programs in Hospitality Administration. National Restaurant Association Educational Foundation ManageFirst certificates available. Program calendar is divided into semesters. 2-year master's degree in hotel and restaurant management. 3-year doctoral degree in hotel and restaurant management. 4-year bachelor's degree in hotel and restaurant management.

Program Affiliation

American Dietetic Association; Council on Hotel, Restaurant, and Institutional Education; National Restaurant Association; National Restaurant Association Educational Foundation.

Areas of Study

Beverage management; controlling costs in food service; food preparation; food purchasing; introduction to food service; management and human resources; nutrition and food service; sanitation; wines and spirits.

Facilities

2 classrooms; computer laboratory; food production kitchen; laboratory; learning resource center; lecture room; library; public restaurant; student lounge; teaching kitchen.

Typical Student Profile

235 total: 225 full-time; 10 part-time.

Special Programs

Summer study abroad in Thailand, internships.

Financial Aid

In 2006, 27 scholarships were awarded (average award was $1000). Employment placement assistance is available. Employment opportunities within the program are available.

Housing

Coed, apartment-style, and single-sex housing available.

Application Information

Students may begin participation in January, June, and August. Applications are accepted continuously. In 2006, 65 applied; 50 were accepted. Applicants must submit a formal application, SAT or ACT scores, TOEFL scores (international applicants), and academic transcripts.

Contact

Director of Admissions, Hotel, Restaurant, and Institution Management, 31 Mackay Hall, Ames, IA 50011-1121. Telephone: 515-294-7474. Fax: 515-294-6364. World Wide Web: http://www.iastate.edu/.

Kirkwood Community College

Hospitality Programs

Cedar Rapids, Iowa

General Information

Public, coeducational, two-year college. Urban campus. Founded in 1966. Accredited by North Central Association of Colleges and Schools.

Program Information

Offered since 1968. Accredited by American Culinary Federation Accrediting Commission. Program calendar is divided into semesters. 1-year certificate in bakery. 1-year diploma in food service training. 2-year associate degree in restaurant management. 2-year associate degree in lodging management. 2-year associate degree in culinary arts.

Program Affiliation

National Restaurant Association; National Restaurant Association Educational Foundation.

Areas of Study

Baking; beverage management; buffet catering; controlling costs in food service; culinary competition; culinary skill development; food and culture; food preparation; food purchasing; food service communication; food service math; garde-manger; international cuisine; kitchen management; management and human resources; meal planning; meat fabrication; menu and facilities design; nutrition; sanitation; soup, stock, sauce, and starch production; wines and spirits.

Facilities

Bakery; catering service; 2 classrooms; computer laboratory; demonstration laboratory; food production kitchen; gourmet dining room; 2 laboratories; learning resource center; 2 lecture rooms; library; public restaurant.

Typical Student Profile

230 total: 165 full-time; 65 part-time.

Special Programs

Professional meetings and conventions (local, state, national), international study tours (offered periodically), culinary competition.

Financial Aid

Program-specific awards include study abroad travel scholarships. Employment opportunities within the program are available.

Application Information

Students may begin participation in January and August. Applications are accepted continuously. Applicants must submit a formal application, take placement tests, and attend a program conference.

Contact
Director of Admissions, Hospitality Programs, 6301 Kirkwood Boulevard SW, Cedar Rapids, IA 52403. Telephone: 319-398-4981. Fax: 319-398-1244. World Wide Web: http://www.kirkwood.edu/.

Kansas

American Institute of Baking

Baking Science and Technology

Manhattan, Kansas

General Information
Private, coeducational institution. Small-town setting. Founded in 1919. Accredited by North Central Association of Colleges and Schools.

Program Information
Offered since 1919. Program calendar is divided into semesters. 2.5-month certificate in maintenance engineering. 5-month certificate in baking science and technology.

Program Affiliation
American Institute of Baking.

Areas of Study
Baking; maintenance engineering.

Facilities
4 bake shops; bakery; 4 classrooms; computer laboratory; 4 demonstration laboratories; laboratory; library; student lounge; cookie-cracker production line.

Typical Student Profile
150 full-time.

Special Programs
Half-day tours of grain elevator, flour mill, and Kansas wheat farm, half-day tours of commercial wholesale bakeries, 50-lesson correspondence course in science of baking.

Financial Aid
In 2006, 25 scholarships were awarded (average award was $2500); 15 loans were granted (average loan was $2000). Program-specific awards include full-tuition scholarships for food science graduates. Employment placement assistance is available.

Housing
Coed housing available.

Application Information
Students may begin participation in February, July, August, and September. Applications are accepted continuously. Applicants must submit a formal application, letters of reference, an essay, and have a college degree, or 2 years of work experience, or completed a baking science course.

Contact
Director of Admissions, Baking Science and Technology, 1213 Bakers Way, Manhattan, KS 66502. Telephone: 800-633-5137. Fax: 785-537-1493. World Wide Web: http://www.aibonline.org.

The International Culinary School at The Art Institute of International–Kansas City

Lenexa, Kansas

General Information
Private, coeducational institution.

Program Information
Associate degree in Culinary Arts. Bachelor's degree in Culinary Arts.

Contact
Office of Admissions, 8208 Melrose Drive, Lenexa, KS 66214. Telephone: 913-217-4600. World Wide Web: http://www.artinstitutes.edu/kansascity/.

See color display following page 332.

Johnson County Community College

Hospitality Management Program

Overland Park, Kansas

General Information
Public, coeducational, two-year college. Suburban campus. Founded in 1967. Accredited by North Central Association of Colleges and Schools.

Program Information
Offered since 1975. Accredited by American Culinary Federation Accrediting Commission. Program calendar is divided into semesters. 1-year certificate in baking and pastry. 2-year associate degree in hotel management. 2-year associate degree in food and beverage management. 3-year associate degree in chef apprenticeship.

Johnson County Community College *(continued)*

Program Affiliation

American Culinary Federation; American Institute of Wine & Food; Council on Hotel, Restaurant, and Institutional Education; Hotel/Motel Association of Kansas City; Kansas Restaurant Hospitality Association; Missouri Restaurant Association; National Restaurant Association; National Restaurant Association Educational Foundation.

Areas of Study

Baking; beverage management; buffet catering; confectionery show pieces; controlling costs in food service; convenience cookery; culinary skill development; food preparation; food purchasing; food service math; garde-manger; international cuisine; introduction to food service; kitchen management; management and human resources; meal planning; menu and facilities design; nutrition; nutrition and food service; sanitation; saucier; seafood processing; soup, stock, sauce, and starch production; wines and spirits.

Facilities

Bake shop; 2 demonstration laboratories; food production kitchen; gourmet dining room; learning resource center; 4 lecture rooms; library; 2 teaching kitchens.

Typical Student Profile

473 total: 191 full-time; 282 part-time. 287 are under 25 years old; 35 are between 25 and 44 years old; 151 are over 44 years old.

Special Programs

National culinary competitions, ACF Knowledge Bowl competitions, trips to New York Hotel Show and NRA show in Chicago.

Financial Aid

In 2006, 20 scholarships were awarded (average award was $500). Program-specific awards include paid apprenticeship program. Employment placement assistance is available.

Application Information

Students may begin participation in January, June, and August. Application deadline for fall is August 15. Application deadline for spring is January 15. Application deadline for summer is May 1. In 2006, 144 applied; 144 were accepted. Applicants must submit a formal application.

Contact

Director of Admissions, Hospitality Management Program, 12345 College Boulevard, Overland Park, KS 66210. Telephone: 913-469-8500 Ext. 3250. Fax: 913-469-2560. World Wide Web: http://www.johnco.cc.ks.us/.

Kansas City Kansas Area Technical School

Professional Cooking

Kansas City, Kansas

General Information

Public, coeducational, adult vocational school. Urban campus. Founded in 1972. Accredited by North Central Association of Colleges and Schools.

Program Information

Offered since 1972. Program calendar is continuous, year-round. 6-month certificate in food service.

Areas of Study

Baking; catering; culinary skill development; dining room service; food preparation; food purchasing; food service management; garde-manger; introduction to food service; meal planning; patisserie; restaurant opportunities; sanitation; soup, stock, sauce, and starch production.

Facilities

Cafeteria; classroom; computer laboratory; food production kitchen; gourmet dining room; learning resource center; lecture room; library; snack shop.

Typical Student Profile

22 total: 10 full-time; 12 part-time.

Financial Aid

Employment placement assistance is available. Employment opportunities within the program are available.

Application Information

Students may begin participation in January, February, March, April, May, June, August, September, October, November, and December. Applications are accepted continuously. Applicants must have a high school diploma or GED.

Contact

Director of Admissions, Professional Cooking, 2220 North 59th Street, Kansas City, KS 66104. Telephone: 913-627-4100. World Wide Web: http://www.kckats.com/.

Kentucky

Elizabethtown Community and Technical College

Culinary Arts

Elizabethtown, Kentucky

General Information

Public, coeducational, two-year college. Small-town setting. Founded in 1966. Accredited by Southern Association of Colleges and Schools.

Program Information

Offered since 1975. Program calendar is divided into semesters. 12-month degree in food and beverage management. 12-month degree in culinary arts. 12-month degree in catering. 18-month diploma in food and beverage management. 18-month diploma in culinary arts. 18-month diploma in catering. 6- to 12-month certificate in professional development. 6- to 12-month certificate in culinary arts. 6- to 12-month certificate in catering.

Program Affiliation

International Association of Culinary Professionals; National Restaurant Association; National Restaurant Association Educational Foundation; Retailer's Bakery Association.

Areas of Study

Baking; beverage management; buffet catering; confectionery show pieces; controlling costs in food service; culinary skill development; food preparation; food purchasing; food service communication; food service math; garde-manger; international cuisine; introduction to food service; kitchen management; management and human resources; meal planning; menu and facilities design; nutrition; nutrition and food service; restaurant opportunities; sanitation; soup, stock, sauce, and starch production.

Facilities

Bake shop; cafeteria; catering service; classroom; computer laboratory; food production kitchen; learning resource center; library; teaching kitchen.

Typical Student Profile

38 total: 28 full-time; 10 part-time. 20 are under 25 years old; 18 are between 25 and 44 years old.

Special Programs

Field trips, public food demonstrations, culinary competitions.

Financial Aid

Program-specific awards include scholarships available through local organizations. Employment placement assistance is available. Employment opportunities within the program are available.

Application Information

Students may begin participation in January and August. Application deadline for fall is July 1. Application deadline for spring is November 30. Applicants must submit a formal application and academic transcripts; take the COMPASS Test.

Contact

Director of Admissions, Culinary Arts, 620 College Street Road, Elizabethtown, KY 42701. Telephone: 270-706-8732. Fax: 270-766-5131. World Wide Web: http://www.elizabethtown.kctcs.edu/index.cfm.

Sullivan University

National Center for Hospitality Studies

Lexington, Kentucky

General Information

Private, coeducational, four-year college. Suburban campus. Founded in 2005. Accredited by Southern Association of Colleges and Schools.

Program Information

Accredited by American Culinary Federation Accrediting Commission. Program calendar is divided into quarters. 12-month diploma in professional cook. 18-month associate degree in travel, tourism and event management. 18-month associate degree in culinary arts. 36-month bachelor's degree in hospitality management. 9-month diploma in travel and tourism.

Program Affiliation

American Culinary Federation; American Dietetic Association; American Institute of Wine & Food; Confrerie de la Chaine des Rotisseurs; Council on Hotel, Restaurant, and Institutional Education; International Association of Culinary Professionals; International Food Service Executives Association; James Beard Foundation, Inc.; National Restaurant Association; National Restaurant Association Educational Foundation; United States Personal Chef Association; Women Chefs and Restaurateurs.

Areas of Study

Baking; beverage management; buffet catering; confectionery show pieces; controlling costs in food service; culinary skill development; food preparation; food purchasing; food service communication; food service math; garde-manger; international cuisine;

Sullivan University *(continued)*

introduction to food service; kitchen management; management and human resources; meat cutting; meat fabrication; menu and facilities design; nutrition; nutrition and food service; patisserie; restaurant opportunities; sanitation; saucier; seafood processing; soup, stock, sauce, and starch production; wines and spirits.

Facilities

15 classrooms; 7 computer laboratories; 3 food production kitchens; garden; library; student lounge.

Student Profile

231 total: 190 full-time; 41 part-time. 99 are under 25 years old; 61 are between 25 and 44 years old; 30 are over 44 years old.

Faculty

8 total: 7 full-time; 1 part-time. 1 is an industry professional; 7 are culinary-certified teachers. Prominent faculty: John Fost, CHE, CEC, Associate Culinary Chair; William Hallman, CHE, CEC; Melissa Armstrong, CC; David G. Walls, CEC, CHE and Pamela Hamilton, CHE. Faculty-student ratio: 1:19.

Special Programs

3-month restaurant practicum, trip to Boston, MA and one-week cruise for travel and tourism majors.

Typical Expenses

Application fee: $100. Tuition: $32,370 per 18 months. Program-related fees include $1050 for comprehensive fee: uniforms, kitchen equipment for training, food product (per quarter); $50 for general fee (per class).

Financial Aid

In 2007, 6 scholarships were awarded (average award was $4000). Employment placement assistance is available. Employment opportunities within the program are available.

Housing

Apartment-style housing available. Average on-campus housing cost per month: $520.

Application Information

Students may begin participation in January, March, June, and September. Applications are accepted continuously. Application deadline for fall is September 15. Application deadline for winter is December 15. Application deadline for spring is March 15. Application deadline for summer is June 15. In 2007, 295 applied; 274 were accepted. Applicants must interview; submit a formal application and CPAT, SAT, or ACT scores and TOEFL score for international applicants.

Contact

Sue Michael, Director of Admissions, National Center for Hospitality Studies, 2355 Harrodsburg Road, Lexington, KY 40504. Telephone: 859-276-4357. Fax: 859-276-1153. E-mail: smichael@sullivan.edu. World Wide Web: http://www.sullivan.edu/.

See color display following page 140.

Sullivan University

National Center for Hospitality Studies

Louisville, Kentucky

General Information

Private, coeducational, comprehensive institution. Suburban campus. Founded in 1962. Accredited by Southern Association of Colleges and Schools.

Program Information

Offered since 1987. Accredited by American Culinary Federation Accrediting Commission. Program calendar is divided into quarters. 12-month diploma in professional cook. 18-month associate degree in travel and tourism. 18-month associate degree in professional catering. 18-month associate degree in hotel and restaurant management. 18-month associate degree in culinary arts. 18-month associate degree in baking and pastry arts. 36-month bachelor's degree in hospitality management. 9-month diploma in travel and tourism. 9-month diploma in professional baker.

Program Affiliation

American Culinary Federation; American Dietetic Association; American Institute of Wine & Food; Confrerie de la Chaine des Rotisseurs; Council on Hotel, Restaurant, and Institutional Education; International Association of Culinary Professionals; International Food Service Executives Association; James Beard Foundation, Inc.; Kentucky Restaurant Association; National Restaurant Association; National Restaurant Association Educational Foundation; Research Chefs Association; United States Personal Chef Association; Women Chefs and Restaurateurs.

Areas of Study

Baking; beverage management; buffet catering; confectionery show pieces; controlling costs in food service; culinary French; culinary skill development; food preparation; food purchasing; food service math; garde-manger; hotel restaurant management; international cuisine; introduction to food service; kitchen management; management and human resources; meat cutting; menu and facilities design; nutrition;

patisserie; professional catering; restaurant opportunities; sanitation; saucier; seafood processing; soup, stock, sauce, and starch production; travel and tourism; wines and spirits.

Facilities

5 bake shops; bakery; cafeteria; catering service; 41 classrooms; 7 computer laboratories; demonstration laboratory; 13 food production kitchens; garden; gourmet dining room; 3 laboratories; library; public restaurant; student lounge.

Student Profile

960 total: 850 full-time; 110 part-time. 375 are under 25 years old; 375 are between 25 and 44 years old; 210 are over 44 years old.

Faculty

33 total: 30 full-time; 3 part-time. 31 are industry professionals; 27 are culinary-certified teachers. Prominent faculty: Thomas Hickey, CEC, CCE, CFE, CHE; Derek Spendlove, CEPC, CCE, AAC; David H. Dodd, MBE, CEC, CCE. Faculty-student ratio: 1:19.

Prominent Alumni and Current Affiliation

Adam Hegadorn, Product Development Scientist, Sara Lee Foods; Lenny Scranton, Vice President Culinary and Vending Services, Morrison Health Care; Bret Syberg, Chef/Owner, Syberg Restaurants-St. Louis, MO.

Special Programs

Restaurant practicum (208 hours), culinary competitions, trip to Boston, MA and one-week cruise for hospitality (hotel-restaurant) majors.

Typical Expenses

Application fee: $90. Tuition: $32,370 per 18 months. Program-related fees include $50 for general fees per class; $1050 for comprehensive fee: uniforms, kitchen equipment for training, food product (per quarter).

Financial Aid

In 2007, 8 scholarships were awarded (average award was $6000). Employment placement assistance is available. Employment opportunities within the program are available.

Housing

Apartment-style housing available. Average on-campus housing cost per month: $440.

Application Information

Students may begin participation in January, March, June, and September. Applications are accepted continuously. Application deadline for fall is September 15. Application deadline for winter is December 15. Application deadline for spring is March 15. Application deadline for summer is June 15. In 2007, 940 applied; 860 were accepted. Applicants must interview; submit a formal application and CPAT, SAT, or ACT score and TOEFL score for international applicants.

Contact

Terri Thomas, Director of Admissions, National Center for Hospitality Studies, 3101 Bardstown Road, Louisville, KY 40205. Telephone: 502-456-6505. Fax: 502-456-0040. E-mail: admissions@sullivan.edu. World Wide Web: http://www.sullivan.edu/.

See color display following page 140.

Western Kentucky University

Hospitality Management and Dietetics

Bowling Green, Kentucky

General Information

Public, coeducational, comprehensive institution. Small-town setting. Founded in 1906. Accredited by Southern Association of Colleges and Schools.

Program Information

Offered since 1969. Accredited by American Dietetic Association. Program calendar is divided into semesters. 4-year bachelor's degree in hotel, restaurant, and tourism management.

Program Affiliation

American Dietetic Association; Council on Hotel, Restaurant, and Institutional Education; National Restaurant Association; National Restaurant Association Educational Foundation.

Areas of Study

Beverage management; buffet catering; controlling costs in food service; food preparation; food purchasing; international cuisine; introduction to food service; kitchen management; management and human resources; meal planning; nutrition; nutrition and food service; restaurant management; restaurant opportunities; sanitation.

Facilities

2 classrooms; computer laboratory; demonstration laboratory; food production kitchen; gourmet dining room; laboratory; learning resource center; 2 libraries; teaching kitchen.

Typical Student Profile

164 total: 153 full-time; 11 part-time. 144 are under 25 years old; 20 are between 25 and 44 years old.

Special Programs

2 semesters of paid internships.

Western Kentucky University *(continued)*

Financial Aid
In 2006, 3 scholarships were awarded (average award was $500). Program-specific awards include Rafferty Restaurant Scholarship, Kentucky Restaurant Association Scholarship, Bowling Green/Warren County Lodging Scholarship. Employment placement assistance is available. Employment opportunities within the program are available.

Housing
Coed and single-sex housing available.

Application Information
Students may begin participation in January and August. Application deadline for fall is August 1. Application deadline for spring is January 1. In 2006, 60 applied; 55 were accepted. Applicants must submit a formal application.

Contact
Director of Admissions, Hospitality Management and Dietetics, Department of Consumer and Family Sciences, 1906 College Heights Boulevard, #11037, Bowling Green, KY 42101-1037. Telephone: 270-745-4031. Fax: 270-745-3999. World Wide Web: http://www.wku.edu/hospitality.

Louisiana

Delgado Community College

Culinary Arts and Hospitality

New Orleans, Louisiana

General Information
Public, coeducational, two-year college. Urban campus. Accredited by Southern Association of Colleges and Schools.

Program Information
Offered since 1925. Accredited by American Culinary Federation Accrediting Commission. National Restaurant Association Educational Foundation ManageFirst certificates available. Program calendar is divided into semesters. 2-semester certificate in pastry arts. 3-semester certificate in hospitality management. 4-semester certificate in culinary arts. 6-semester associate degree in hospitality management. 6-semester associate degree in culinary arts. 6-semester associate degree in catering.

Program Affiliation
American Culinary Federation; American Institute of Wine & Food; Confrerie de la Chaine des Rotisseurs; International Association of Culinary Professionals; James Beard Foundation, Inc.; National Association of Catering Professionals; National Restaurant Association; National Restaurant Association Educational Foundation; Society of Wine Educators.

Areas of Study
Baking; buffet catering; confectionery show pieces; controlling costs in food service; food purchasing; garde-manger; management and human resources; nutrition; patisserie; sanitation; saucier; soup, stock, sauce, and starch production; wines and spirits.

Facilities
Bake shop; classroom; computer laboratory; garden; laboratory; lecture room; library; teaching kitchen.

Typical Student Profile
170 total: 120 full-time; 50 part-time.

Special Programs
4000-hour chef apprenticeship.

Financial Aid
Employment placement assistance is available.

Application Information
Students may begin participation in August. Application deadline for fall is May 30. In 2006, 100 applied; 60 were accepted. Applicants must submit a formal application, letters of reference, placement test.

Contact
Director of Admissions, Culinary Arts and Hospitality, 615 City Park Avenue, New Orleans, LA 70119. Telephone: 504-671-6199. Fax: 504-483-4893. World Wide Web: http://www.dcc.edu/.

Grambling State University

Hotel/Restaurant Management

Grambling, Louisiana

General Information
Public, coeducational, university. Rural campus. Founded in 1901. Accredited by Southern Association of Colleges and Schools.

Program Information
Offered since 1985. National Restaurant Association Educational Foundation ManageFirst certificates available. Program calendar is divided into semesters. 4-year bachelor's degree in hotel/restaurant management.

Program Affiliation
Council on Hotel, Restaurant, and Institutional Education; National Restaurant Association; National Restaurant Association Educational Foundation.

Areas of Study
Beverage management; food preparation; kitchen management; restaurant opportunities.

Facilities
Cafeteria; 2 catering services; 6 classrooms; computer laboratory; 4 demonstration laboratories; 3 food production kitchens; gourmet dining room; 4 laboratories; learning resource center; 2 lecture rooms; library; public restaurant; snack shop; student lounge; 2 teaching kitchens.

Typical Student Profile
62 total: 59 full-time; 3 part-time. 47 are under 25 years old; 9 are between 25 and 44 years old; 6 are over 44 years old.

Financial Aid
In 2006, individual scholarships were awarded at $500. Employment opportunities within the program are available.

Housing
Coed, apartment-style, and single-sex housing available.

Application Information
Students may begin participation in January, May, and August. In 2006, 33 applied; 22 were accepted.

Contact
Director of Admissions, Hotel/Restaurant Management, CSU Box 4200, Grambling, LA 71245. Telephone: 318-274-6183. Fax: 318-274-3292. World Wide Web: http://www.gram.edu/.

Louisiana Culinary Institute, LLC

Professional Cooking and Culinary Arts

Baton Rouge, Louisiana

General Information
Private, coeducational, culinary institute. Urban campus. Founded in 2002. Accredited by Council on Occupational Education.

Program Information
Offered since 2002. Accredited by Council on Occupational Education. National Restaurant Association Educational Foundation ManageFirst certificates available. Program calendar is 3 semesters. 12-month diploma in professional cooking and culinary arts. 16-month associate degree in occupational studies in culinary arts.

Program Affiliation
American Culinary Federation; International Association of Culinary Professionals; National Restaurant Association; National Restaurant Association Educational Foundation.

Areas of Study
Baking; beverage management; controlling costs in food service; convenience cookery; culinary French; culinary skill development; food preparation; food purchasing; food service communication; food service math; garde-manger; international cuisine; introduction to food service; kitchen management; management and human resources; meal planning; meat cutting; meat fabrication; menu and facilities design; nutrition; nutrition and food service; patisserie; sanitation; saucier; seafood processing; soup, stock, sauce, and starch production; wines and spirits.

Student Profile
120 full-time.

Faculty
6 are chef instructors which includes a Director and Dean of Education. Faculty-student ratio: 1:20.

Special Programs
2-day "stage" at Commander's Palace in New Orleans, externships in Hawaii, study abroad programs are just a few of the options in the special programs area, National competitions, The Home Plate Classic, tours of established historical companies, examples include McIlhenny's Tabasco plant, Tony Chechere's spice plant, and many others.

Typical Expenses
Tuition: $28,000 per associate degree; $21,000 for diploma program. Program-related fee includes $100 for one-time registration, meal plans, lab fees, uniforms, knives, and books.

Financial Aid
Program-specific awards include Internal Culinary Excellence Scholarships are available in value of $2500. External scholarships are also available from multiple areas, The National Restaurant Association (NRA) gave over 1.4 million dollars in culinary scholarships in 2008, these scholarships are available to all types of students and are strongly encouraged.

Application Information
Students may begin participation in April, August, and December. Applications are accepted continuously. Applicants must interview; submit a formal application, letters of reference, an essay, high school diploma or GED, and partake in state required skills test (if no college transcripts).

Producing World-Class Chefs

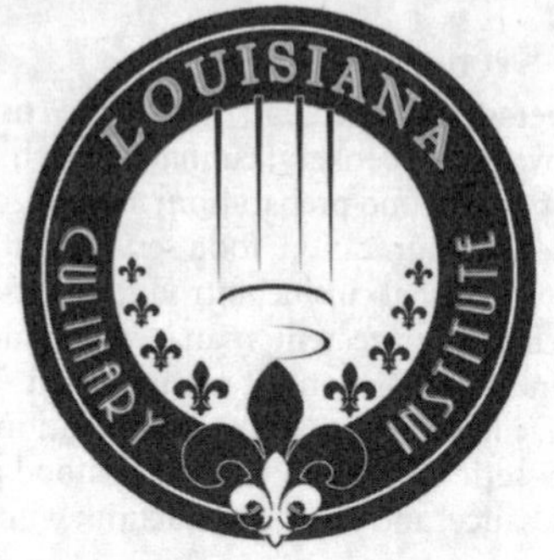

www.LouisianaCulinary.com

For an application please contact the Office of Admissions
TEL: (877) 769-8820
FAX: (225) 769-8792

5837 Essen Lane
Baton Rouge, LA 70810

LCI is an established culinary school that offers a great education and a professional experience which prepares students to excel in future employment.

LCI offers many educational choices, including an opportunity to earn an Associates Degree in Culinary Arts.

We are the preferred choice of the South when it comes to culinary schools.

In the Fall of 2008, LCI is relocating within Baton Rouge, LA and expanding into a brand new, state-of-the-art, approximately 30,000 sq. ft. facility.

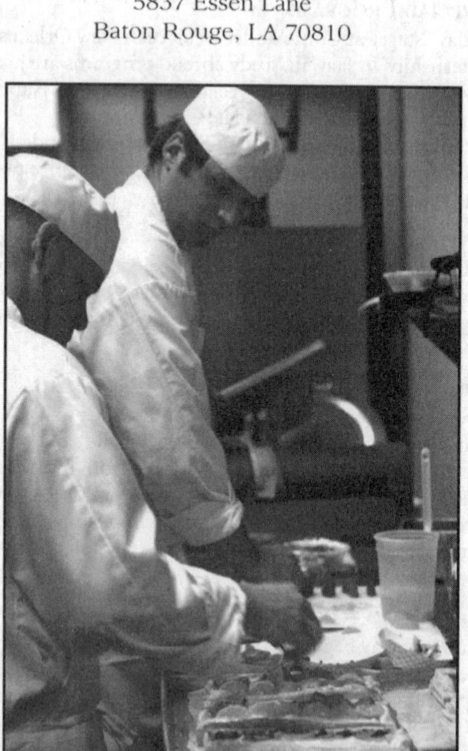

Louisiana Culinary Institute is a member of the International Assoiation of Culinary Professionals (IACP).

Contact
Admission Department, Professional Cooking and Culinary Arts, 5837 Essen Lane, Baton Rouge, LA 70810. Telephone: 877-769-8820. Fax: 225-769-8792. E-mail: admissions@louisianaculinary.com. World Wide Web: http://www.louisianaculinary.com/.

See display on page 168.

Louisiana Technical College–Baton Rouge Campus

Culinary Arts and Occupations

Baton Rouge, Louisiana

General Information
Public, coeducational, two-year college. Urban campus. Founded in 1974. Accredited by Southern Association of Colleges and Schools.

Program Information
Offered since 1974. Accredited by American Culinary Federation Accrediting Commission. Program calendar is divided into semesters. 18-month diploma in culinary arts and occupations. 3-month certificate in supervision. 3-month certificate in sanitation. 3-month certificate in nutrition.

Program Affiliation
American Culinary Federation; Louisiana Restaurant Association; National Restaurant Association Educational Foundation.

Areas of Study
Baking; controlling costs in food service; culinary skill development; food preparation; food purchasing; food service communication; food service math; garde-manger; kitchen management; management and human resources; meat fabrication; nutrition; nutrition and food service; sanitation; saucier; soup, stock, sauce, and starch production.

Facilities
Bake shop; 2 classrooms; computer laboratory; food production kitchen; garden; 2 public restaurants.

Typical Student Profile
45 total: 35 full-time; 10 part-time. 43 are under 25 years old; 2 are between 25 and 44 years old.

Special Programs
Culinary competitions.

Financial Aid
Employment placement assistance is available. Employment opportunities within the program are available.

Application Information
Students may begin participation in January and August. Applications are accepted continuously. Applicants must submit a formal application and complete an entrance test.

Contact
Director of Admissions, Culinary Arts and Occupations, 3250 North Acadian Thruway, East, Baton Rouge, LA 70805. Telephone: 225-359-9226. Fax: 225-359-9296. World Wide Web: http://www.region2.ltc.edu/.

Nicholls State University

Chef John Folse Culinary Institute

Thibodaux, Louisiana

General Information
Public, coeducational, comprehensive institution. Rural campus. Founded in 1948. Accredited by Southern Association of Colleges and Schools.

Program Information
Offered since 1994. Program calendar is divided into semesters. 2-year associate degree in culinary arts. 4-year bachelor's degree in culinary arts.

Program Affiliation
American Culinary Federation; Confrerie de la Chaine des Rotisseurs; Council on Hotel, Restaurant, and Institutional Education; Institut Paul Bocuse World Wide Alliance; National Restaurant Association; Research Chefs Association; Society for the Advancement of Food Service Research.

Areas of Study
Baking; beverage management; buffet catering; confectionery show pieces; controlling costs in food service; convenience cookery; culinary entrepreneurship; culinary French; culinary skill development; food preparation; food purchasing; garde-manger; international cuisine; introduction to food service; kitchen management; management and human resources; meal planning; meat cutting; meat fabrication; menu and facilities design; nutrition; nutrition and food service; patisserie; restaurant opportunities; sanitation; saucier; seafood processing; soup, stock, sauce, and starch production; wines and spirits.

Facilities
Bakery; cafeteria; catering service; 3 classrooms; 2 computer laboratories; demonstration laboratory; food production kitchen; gourmet dining room; 3 laboratories; 2 learning resource centers; 3 lecture rooms; library; public restaurant; snack shop; student lounge; 2 teaching kitchens.

Nicholls State University *(continued)*

Typical Student Profile
198 full-time. 169 are under 25 years old; 25 are between 25 and 44 years old; 4 are over 44 years old.

Special Programs
State and regional culinary competitions, summer study at Institut Paul Bocuse in Lyon, France.

Financial Aid
In 2006, 30 scholarships were awarded (average award was $800). Employment placement assistance is available.

Housing
Coed, apartment-style, and single-sex housing available.

Application Information
Students may begin participation in January and August. Application deadline for fall is July 15. Application deadline for spring is November 15. In 2006, 65 applied; 62 were accepted. Applicants must submit a formal application and high school transcript, minimum 2.5 high school GPA, ACT composite score of 20 or higher.

Contact
Director of Admissions, Chef John Folse Culinary Institute, PO Box 2099, Thibodaux, LA 70310. Telephone: 985-449-7091. Fax: 985-449-7089. World Wide Web: http://www.nicholls.edu/jfolse.

Sclafani Cooking School, Inc.

Commercial Cook/Baker Certificate

Metairie, Louisiana

General Information
Private, coeducational, culinary institute. Suburban campus. Founded in 1987.

Program Information
Offered since 1987. Accredited by Licensed by the Louisiana State Board of Regents as a Post Secondary Proprietary School. Program calendar is continuous, monthly. 4-week certificate in commercial cook/baker. 8-hour certificate in NRAEF ServSafe certificate.

Program Affiliation
American Culinary Federation; Foodservice Management Professionals; Louisiana Restaurant Association; National Restaurant Association; National Restaurant Association Educational Foundation.

Areas of Study
Baking; controlling costs in food service; culinary skill development; food preparation; food service math; garde-manger; introduction to food service; kitchen management; management and human resources; meal planning; restaurant opportunities; sanitation; saucier; soup, stock, sauce, and starch production.

Facilities
Bake shop; bakery; classroom; computer laboratory; demonstration laboratory; food production kitchen; lecture room; library; teaching kitchen; dining room.

Typical Student Profile
110 full-time.

Special Programs
Culinary SoftSkill Training (culinary interview, resume), Commercial Kitchen Management Systems.

Financial Aid
In 2006, 55 scholarships were awarded (average award was $4000). Program-specific awards include Workforce Investment Agency 100% Grants, Louisiana Department of Labor Incumbent Worker Training. Employment placement assistance is available.

Application Information
Students may begin participation year-round. Applications are accepted continuously. In 2006, 120 applied; 108 were accepted. Applicants must interview; submit a formal application and pass the Wonderlic aptitude test.

Contact
Director of Admissions, Commercial Cook/Baker Certificate, 107 Gennaro Place, Metairie, LA 70001. Telephone: 504-833-7861. Fax: 504-833-7872. World Wide Web: http://www.sclafanicookingschool.com/.

Southern University at Shreveport

Shreveport, Louisiana

General Information
Public, coeducational, two-year college. Urban campus. Founded in 1964. Accredited by Southern Association of Colleges and Schools.

Program Information
Offered since 1984. Accredited by Student can earn an industry certificate in hospitality from the Educational Institute of the American Hotel and Motel Association for each course in hospitality. Program calendar is divided into semesters. 1-year certificate in hospitality operation. 1-year certificate in food and beverage management. 2-year associate degree in hospitality.

Program Affiliation
Council on Hotel, Restaurant, and Institutional Education; Educational Institute American Hotel and Motel Association.

Areas of Study
Baking; beverage management; controlling costs in food service; convenience cookery; culinary French; food preparation; food purchasing; food service communication; food service math; international cuisine; kitchen management; management and human resources; meal planning; menu and facilities design; nutrition and food service; restaurant opportunities; sanitation.

Facilities
Catering service; classroom; computer laboratory; demonstration laboratory; gourmet dining room; laboratory; lecture room; library; snack shop; vineyard.

Typical Student Profile
16 full-time. 3 are under 25 years old; 9 are between 25 and 44 years old; 4 are over 44 years old.

Special Programs
Field trips to area food shows, internships with hospitality partners.

Financial Aid
Program-specific awards include industry scholarships. Employment placement assistance is available.

Application Information
Students may begin participation in January, June, and August. Application deadline for fall is August 30. Application deadline for spring is January 15. Application deadline for summer is June 6. Applicants must submit a formal application and high school transcript/diploma or equivalent.

Contact
Director of Admissions, Division of Business Studies, Shreveport, LA 71107. Telephone: 318-429-7236. Fax: 318-674-3313. World Wide Web: http://www.susla.edu/.

University of Louisiana at Lafayette

College of Applied Life Sciences

Lafayette, Louisiana

General Information
Public, coeducational, university. Urban campus. Founded in 1898. Accredited by Southern Association of Colleges and Schools.

Program Information
Offered since 1950. Accredited by American Dietetic Association. Program calendar is divided into semesters. 4-year bachelor's degree in hospitality management.

Program Affiliation
American Culinary Federation; American Dietetic Association; Confrerie de la Chaine des Rotisseurs; Council on Hotel, Restaurant, and Institutional Education; National Restaurant Association; National Restaurant Association Educational Foundation.

Areas of Study
Beverage management; controlling costs in food service; food purchasing; food service communication; hotel and restaurant management; kitchen management; management and human resources; meal planning; tourism management.

Facilities
Catering service; computer laboratory; food production kitchen; gourmet dining room; laboratory; library; public restaurant; teaching kitchen.

Typical Student Profile
95 total: 86 full-time; 9 part-time. 76 are under 25 years old; 18 are between 25 and 44 years old; 1 is over 44 years old.

Special Programs
Senior level 15-week internship, required 1,500 hours of work experience, trips to NRA and AMLA shows in New York, Chicago, and New Orleans.

Financial Aid
Employment placement assistance is available. Employment opportunities within the program are available.

Housing
Apartment-style and single-sex housing available.

Application Information
Students may begin participation in January, June, and August. Applications are accepted continuously. Applicants must submit a formal application and ACT or SAT scores.

Contact
Director of Admissions, College of Applied Life Sciences, PO Box 40399, Lafayette, LA 70504. Telephone: 337-482-5724. Fax: 337-482-5395. World Wide Web: http://www.louisiana.edu/.

MAINE

EASTERN MAINE COMMUNITY COLLEGE

Culinary Arts Department

Bangor, Maine

GENERAL INFORMATION
Public, coeducational, two-year college. Small-town setting. Founded in 1966. Accredited by New England Association of Schools and Colleges.

PROGRAM INFORMATION
Program calendar is divided into semesters. 1-year certificate in food service specialist. 2-year associate degree in culinary arts.

PROGRAM AFFILIATION
American Culinary Federation; International Association of Culinary Professionals; Maine Restaurant Association; National Restaurant Association; National Restaurant Association Educational Foundation.

FACILITIES
Bake shop; 2 bakeries; cafeteria; catering service; 2 classrooms; 5 computer laboratories; food production kitchen; garden; gourmet dining room; learning resource center; 2 lecture rooms; 2 libraries; public restaurant; snack shop; 3 student lounges; teaching kitchen.

TYPICAL STUDENT PROFILE
69 total: 64 full-time; 5 part-time.

SPECIAL PROGRAMS
Exchange program, culinary competitions, food shows.

FINANCIAL AID
In 2006, 2 scholarships were awarded (average award was $300). Employment placement assistance is available.

HOUSING
Coed housing available.

APPLICATION INFORMATION
Students may begin participation in January and August. Applications are accepted continuously. In 2006, 82 applied; 38 were accepted. Applicants must interview; submit a formal application and an essay.

CONTACT
Director of Admissions, Culinary Arts Department, 354 Hogan Road, Bangor, ME 04401. Telephone: 207-974-4680. Fax: 207-974-4683. World Wide Web: http://www.emcc.edu/.

SOUTHERN MAINE COMMUNITY COLLEGE

Culinary Arts

South Portland, Maine

GENERAL INFORMATION
Public, coeducational, two-year college. Suburban campus. Founded in 1946. Accredited by New England Association of Schools and Colleges.

PROGRAM INFORMATION
Offered since 1958. Program calendar is divided into semesters. 2-year associate degree in culinary arts/applied science.

PROGRAM AFFILIATION
American Culinary Federation; American Institute of Baking; Council on Hotel, Restaurant, and Institutional Education; Foodservice Educators Network International; International Association of Culinary Professionals; Maine Restaurant Association; National Restaurant Association; National Restaurant Association Educational Foundation.

AREAS OF STUDY
Baking; beverage management; buffet catering; confectionery show pieces; controlling costs in food service; culinary skill development; food preparation; food purchasing; food service communication; food service math; garde-manger; international cuisine; introduction to food service; kitchen management; management and human resources; meal planning; meat cutting; meat fabrication; menu and facilities design; nutrition; nutrition and food service; restaurant opportunities; sanitation; saucier; seafood processing; soup, stock, sauce, and starch production.

FACILITIES
Bake shop; bakery; 7 classrooms; computer laboratory; demonstration laboratory; 4 food production kitchens; gourmet dining room; 3 laboratories; learning resource center; lecture room; library; public restaurant; 2 teaching kitchens.

TYPICAL STUDENT PROFILE
150 total: 98 full-time; 52 part-time. 114 are under 25 years old; 34 are between 25 and 44 years old; 2 are over 44 years old.

SPECIAL PROGRAMS
Tours of food service establishments, guest lectures, study abroad program in Austria/Italy.

Financial Aid
In 2006, 8 scholarships were awarded (average award was $500). Employment placement assistance is available. Employment opportunities within the program are available.

Housing
Coed housing available.

Application Information
Students may begin participation in January and August. Applications are accepted continuously. In 2006, 151 applied; 89 were accepted. Applicants must submit a formal application.

Contact
Director of Admissions, Culinary Arts, Fort Road, South Portland, ME 04106. Telephone: 207-741-5500. Fax: 207-741-5760. World Wide Web: http://www.smccme.edu/.

York County Community College

Wells, Maine

General Information
Public, coeducational, two-year college. Small-town setting. Founded in 1994. Accredited by New England Association of Schools and Colleges.

Program Information
Offered since 1995. Program calendar is divided into semesters. 1-year certificate in food and beverage operations. 2-year associate degree in culinary arts.

Program Affiliation
Council on Hotel, Restaurant, and Institutional Education; National Restaurant Association; National Restaurant Association Educational Foundation.

Areas of Study
Baking; beverage management; controlling costs in food service; culinary skill development; food preparation; food purchasing; food service communication; food service math; garde-manger; international cuisine; kitchen management; management and human resources; meal planning; meat fabrication; menu and facilities design; nutrition and food service; sanitation; saucier; seafood processing; soup, stock, sauce, and starch production; wines and spirits.

Facilities
Bake shop; catering service; classroom; computer laboratory; demonstration laboratory; food production kitchen; learning resource center; library; student lounge; teaching kitchen.

Typical Student Profile
52 total: 26 full-time; 26 part-time.

Special Programs
Culinary competitions through the Maine Restaurant Association, Austria Exchange Program through Maine Community College System.

Financial Aid
In 2006, 3 scholarships were awarded (average award was $1200). Employment placement assistance is available.

Application Information
Students may begin participation in January, May, and September. Applications are accepted continuously. In 2006, 50 applied; 50 were accepted. Applicants must submit a formal application, an essay, high school transcript or GED, and take assessment test (administered by college).

Contact
Director of Admissions, 112 College Drive, Wells, ME 04090. Telephone: 207-646-9282. Fax: 207-641-0837. World Wide Web: http://www.yccc.edu/.

Maryland

Allegany College of Maryland

School of Hospitality, Tourism, and Culinary Arts

Cumberland, Maryland

General Information
Public, coeducational, two-year college. Suburban campus. Founded in 1961. Accredited by Middle States Association of Colleges and Schools.

Program Information
Offered since 1998. Program calendar is divided into semesters. 2-term/11 credit letter of recognition in culinary essential. 2-term/11 credit letter of recognition in baking essentials. 2-year associate degree in culinary arts.

Program Affiliation
American Dietetic Association.

Areas of Study
Baking; culinary skill development; kitchen management; restaurant opportunities; sanitation.

Facilities
Bake shop; 3 classrooms; 2 computer laboratories; food production kitchen; gourmet dining room; learning resource center; library; public restaurant; student lounge; teaching kitchen.

Allegany College of Maryland *(continued)*

Typical Student Profile
40 total: 16 full-time; 24 part-time. 34 are under 25 years old; 5 are between 25 and 44 years old; 1 is over 44 years old.

Special Programs
Responsibility for student-operated restaurant, ServSafe Certification with National Restaurant Association.

Financial Aid
In 2006, 1 scholarship was awarded (award was $1000). Program-specific awards include Culinary Arts is a statewide designated program. Employment placement assistance is available.

Housing
Apartment-style housing available.

Application Information
Students may begin participation in January and August. Applications are accepted continuously. In 2006, 77 applied; 74 were accepted. Applicants must interview; submit a formal application, an essay, separate culinary arts application.

Contact
Director of Admissions, School of Hospitality, Tourism, and Culinary Arts, 12401 Willowbrook Road, SE, Cumberland, MD 21502. Telephone: 301-784-5000. Fax: 301-784-5027. World Wide Web: http://www.allegany.edu/.

Anne Arundel Community College

Hospitality, Culinary Arts, and Tourism Institute

Arnold, Maryland

General Information
Public, coeducational, two-year college. Suburban campus. Founded in 1961. Accredited by Middle States Association of Colleges and Schools.

Program Information
Offered since 1988. Accredited by American Culinary Federation Accrediting Commission. Program calendar is divided into semesters. Associate degree in hotel/restaurant management-hospitality business management. Associate degree in hotel/restaurant management-culinary arts operations. Certificate in hotel/restaurant management-food service operations. Certificate in hotel/restaurant management-culinary arts operations. Certificate in hotel/lodging management. Certificate in catering operations. Certificate in baking and pastry arts operations.

Program Affiliation
American Culinary Federation; Council on Hotel, Restaurant, and Institutional Education; International Association of Culinary Professionals; International Food Service Executives Association; National Restaurant Association; National Restaurant Association Educational Foundation; Women Chefs and Restaurateurs.

Areas of Study
Baking; beverage management; buffet catering; confectionery show pieces; controlling costs in food service; convenience cookery; culinary French; culinary skill development; food preparation; food purchasing; food service math; garde-manger; international cuisine; introduction to food service; kitchen management; management and human resources; meal planning; meat fabrication; menu and facilities design; nutrition; nutrition and food service; patisserie; sanitation; saucier; soup, stock, sauce, and starch production; wines and spirits.

Facilities
Bake shop; 5 classrooms; computer laboratory; demonstration laboratory; 4 food production kitchens; learning resource center; student lounge.

Typical Student Profile
467 total: 169 full-time; 298 part-time. 282 are under 25 years old; 142 are between 25 and 44 years old; 43 are over 44 years old.

Special Programs
Student culinary team, international internship to Amalfi coast of Italy, internship in Hawaii, Student Chef's Club, ACF chef certification testing.

Financial Aid
In 2006, 9 scholarships were awarded. Employment placement assistance is available. Employment opportunities within the program are available.

Application Information
Students may begin participation in January, June, and September. Applications are accepted continuously. Applicants must submit a formal application.

Contact
Director of Admissions, Hospitality, Culinary Arts, and Tourism Institute, 101 College Parkway, CALT 129, Arnold, MD 21012. World Wide Web: http://www.aacc.edu/.

Baltimore International College

School of Culinary Arts

Baltimore, Maryland

General Information
Private, coeducational, four-year college. Urban campus. Founded in 1972. Accredited by Middle States Association of Colleges and Schools.

Program Information
Offered since 1972. Accredited by American Culinary Federation Accrediting Commission. Program calendar is divided into semesters. 12-month certificate in professional culinary arts. 2-year associate degree in professional cooking and baking. 2-year associate degree in professional cooking. 2-year associate degree in professional baking and pastry. 2-year master's degree in hospitality management. 22-month certificate in culinary arts-evening program. 4-year bachelor's degree in hospitality management with marketing concentration. 4-year bachelor's degree in hospitality management. 4-year bachelor's degree in culinary management.

Program Affiliation
American Culinary Federation; Council on Hotel, Restaurant, and Institutional Education; International Association of Culinary Professionals; National Restaurant Association.

Areas of Study
Baking; beverage management; buffet catering; classical cuisine; confectionery show pieces; controlling costs in food service; convenience cookery; culinary skill development; food preparation; food purchasing; food service communication; garde-manger; hotel operations; international cuisine; introduction to food service; kitchen management; management and human resources; marketing; meal planning; meat fabrication; menu and facilities design; nutrition; patisserie; restaurant operations; sanitation; saucier; seafood processing; soup, stock, sauce, and starch production; wines and spirits.

Facilities
21 classrooms; 2 computer laboratories; garden; gourmet dining room; learning resource center; library; public restaurant; snack shop; student lounge; 7 teaching kitchens; 2 public hotels; auditorium.

Typical Student Profile
800 full-time.

Special Programs
Externships, five-week course at campus in Ireland for associate and bachelor's students, accelerated programs.

Financial Aid
In 2006, 582 scholarships were awarded (average award was $3862). Program-specific awards include scholarships for alumni returning to complete bachelor's degree, Career Opportunity Grant, Leadership Grant. Employment placement assistance is available. Employment opportunities within the program are available.

Housing
Coed housing available.

Application Information
Students may begin participation in January, May, July, and September. Applications are accepted continuously. Applicants must submit a formal application and academic transcripts, SAT or ACT scores.

Contact
Director of Admissions, School of Culinary Arts, 17 Commerce Street, Baltimore, MD 21202. Telephone: 410-752-4710 Ext. 239. Fax: 410-752-3730. World Wide Web: http://www.bic.edu/.

L'Academie de Cuisine

Gaithersburg, Maryland

General Information
Private, coeducational, culinary institute. Suburban campus. Founded in 1976. Accredited by Accrediting Council for Continuing Education and Training.

Program Information
Offered since 1976. Program calendar is continuous, year-round. 34-week certificate in pastry arts. 48-week certificate in culinary arts.

Program Affiliation
American Institute of Wine & Food; Confrerie de la Chaine des Rotisseurs; International Association of Culinary Professionals; Les Dames d'Escoffier; National Restaurant Association; National Restaurant Association Educational Foundation; The Bread Bakers Guild of America; Women Chefs and Restaurateurs.

Areas of Study
Baking; buffet catering; controlling costs in food service; culinary French; culinary skill development; food preparation; food purchasing; food service math; garde-manger; international cuisine; kitchen management; meal planning; meat cutting; meat fabrication; menu and facilities design; nutrition; nutrition and food service; patisserie; sanitation; saucier; seafood processing; soup, stock, sauce, and starch production; wines and spirits.

L'Academie de Cuisine ***(continued)***

Facilities
2 demonstration laboratories; 4 food production kitchens; library; student lounge.

Typical Student Profile
130 full-time.

Special Programs
1-week culinary tour in Gascony, France.

Financial Aid
In 2006, 2 scholarships were awarded (average award was $4500). Employment placement assistance is available.

Application Information
Students may begin participation in January, April, July, and October. Applications are accepted continuously. In 2006, 160 applied; 140 were accepted. Applicants must interview; submit a formal application, letters of reference, an essay, resume, proof of high school graduation, and proof of age (18 or older).

Contact
Director of Admissions, 16006 Industrial Drive, Gaithersburg, MD 20877. Telephone: 301-670-8670. Fax: 301-670-0450. World Wide Web: http://www.lacademie.com/.

Lincoln Tech

Center for Culinary Arts

Columbia, Maryland

General Information
Private, coeducational institution. Accredited by Accrediting Commission of Career Schools and Colleges of Technology.

Program Information
Offered since 2007. Diploma in culinary arts.

Contact
Director of Admissions, Center for Culinary Arts, 9325 Snowden River Parkway, Columbia, MD 21046. Telephone: 410-290-7100.

Wor-Wic Community College

Hotel/Motel/Restaurant Management

Salisbury, Maryland

General Information
Public, coeducational, two-year college. Small-town setting. Founded in 1975. Accredited by Middle States Association of Colleges and Schools.

Program Information
Offered since 1976. Program calendar is divided into semesters. 1-year certificate in restaurant management. 1-year certificate in hotel/motel management. 1-year certificate in culinary arts. 2-year associate degree in hotel/motel/restaurant management. 2-year associate degree in culinary arts.

Program Affiliation
American Culinary Federation; Council on Hotel, Restaurant, and Institutional Education; National Restaurant Association; Ocean City Hotel-Motel-Restaurant Association.

Areas of Study
Baking; beverage management; controlling costs in food service; culinary French; culinary skill development; food preparation; food purchasing; garde-manger; international cuisine; introduction to food service; management and human resources; menu and facilities design; nutrition; patisserie; sanitation.

Facilities
Classroom; computer laboratory; gourmet dining room; teaching kitchen.

Typical Student Profile
49 total: 16 full-time; 33 part-time. 30 are under 25 years old; 17 are between 25 and 44 years old; 2 are over 44 years old.

Special Programs
Trade shows, guest chefs, access to many resort hotels in Ocean City and Salisbury for tours.

Financial Aid
In 2006, 3 scholarships were awarded (average award was $1000).

Application Information
Students may begin participation in January, May, July, and September. Applications are accepted continuously. In 2006, 101 applied; 101 were accepted. Applicants must submit a formal application.

Contact
Director of Admissions, Hotel/Motel/Restaurant Management, 32000 Campus Drive, Salisbury, MD 21804. Telephone: 410-334-2895. Fax: 410-334-2954. World Wide Web: http://www.worwic.edu/.

Massachusetts

Branford Hall Career Institute

Culinary Arts

Springfield, Massachusetts

General Information
Private institution. Accredited by Accrediting Council for Independent Colleges and Schools.

Program Information
Certificate in culinary arts.

Special Programs
Externships.

Contact
Director of Admissions, Culinary Arts, Technical Training Center, 189 Brookdale Drive, Springfield, MA 01104. Telephone: 800-959-7599. World Wide Web: http://www.branfordhall.com/.

Bristol Community College

Culinary Arts Department

Fall River, Massachusetts

General Information
Public, coeducational, two-year college. Suburban campus. Founded in 1965. Accredited by New England Association of Schools and Colleges.

Program Information
Offered since 1985. Program calendar is divided into semesters. 2-year associate degree in culinary arts. 2-year associate degree in baking/pastry arts.

Areas of Study
Baking; beverage management; buffet catering; confectionery show pieces; controlling costs in food service; culinary skill development; food preparation; food purchasing; food service math; garde-manger; international cuisine; introduction to food service; meal planning; nutrition; patisserie; sanitation; saucier; seafood processing; soup, stock, sauce, and starch production; wines and spirits.

Facilities
Bake shop; cafeteria; catering service; classroom; computer laboratory; food production kitchen; gourmet dining room; learning resource center; lecture room; library; teaching kitchen; bar/lounge.

Typical Student Profile
52 total: 50 full-time; 2 part-time. 40 are under 25 years old; 10 are between 25 and 44 years old; 2 are over 44 years old.

Special Programs
College-wide Honors Program, Skills USA.

Financial Aid
In 2006, 4 scholarships were awarded (average award was $500); 5 loans were granted (average loan was $150–$200). Program-specific awards include scholarships for second-year students. Employment placement assistance is available. Employment opportunities within the program are available.

Application Information
Students may begin participation in September. Applications are accepted continuously. In 2006, 82 applied; 65 were accepted. Applicants must interview; submit a formal application.

Contact
Director of Admissions, Culinary Arts Department, 777 Elsbree Street, Fall River, MA 02720. Telephone: 508-678-2811 Ext. 2111. Fax: 508-730-3290. World Wide Web: http://www.bristol.mass.edu/.

Bunker Hill Community College

Culinary Arts Program

Boston, Massachusetts

General Information
Public, coeducational, two-year college. Urban campus. Founded in 1973. Accredited by New England Association of Schools and Colleges.

Program Information
Offered since 1978. Program calendar is divided into semesters. 1-year certificate in culinary arts. 2-year associate degree in culinary arts.

Bunker Hill Community College *(continued)*

Program Affiliation

American Culinary Federation; Council on Hotel, Restaurant, and Institutional Education; Food Service Consultants International; National Restaurant Association; National Restaurant Association Educational Foundation.

Areas of Study

Baking; bar and beverage management; beverage management; buffet catering; café/bistro cuisine; controlling costs in food service; convenience cookery; culinary French; culinary skill development; dining room management; dining room service; food preparation; food purchasing; food service communication; food service math; garde-manger; hospitality law; international cuisine; introduction to food service; kitchen management; management and human resources; meal planning; meat cutting; menu and facilities design; nutrition; nutrition and food service; patisserie; sanitation; saucier; seafood processing; soup, stock, sauce, and starch production; wines and spirits.

Facilities

Bake shop; bakery; catering service; classroom; demonstration laboratory; food production kitchen; gourmet dining room; learning resource center; lecture room; library; public restaurant; teaching kitchen.

Typical Student Profile

280 total: 252 full-time; 28 part-time.

Special Programs

Culinary competitions.

Financial Aid

Employment placement assistance is available. Employment opportunities within the program are available.

Application Information

Students may begin participation in January and September. Applications are accepted continuously. Applicants must submit a formal application.

Contact

Director of Admissions, Culinary Arts Program, 250 New Rutherford Avenue, Boston, MA 02129. Telephone: 617-228-2171. Fax: 617-228-2052. World Wide Web: http://www.bhcc.mass.edu/.

The Cambridge School of Culinary Arts

Professional Chef's Program, Professional Pastry Program

Cambridge, Massachusetts

General Information

Private, coeducational, culinary institute. Urban campus. Founded in 1974. Accredited by Accrediting Commission of Career Schools and Colleges of Technology.

Program Information

Offered since 1974. Program calendar is divided into quarters. 16-week certificate in pastry arts training. 16-week certificate in culinary training. 37-week diploma in professional pastry training. 37-week diploma in professional chef training.

Program Affiliation

American Institute of Wine & Food; International Association of Culinary Professionals; James Beard Foundation, Inc.; National Restaurant Association; Oldways Preservation and Exchange Trust; Women Chefs and Restaurateurs.

Areas of Study

Baking; confectionery show pieces; controlling costs in food service; culinary French; culinary skill development; food preparation; food purchasing; garde-manger; international cuisine; kitchen management; meal planning; meat cutting; nutrition; nutrition and food service; patisserie; restaurant opportunities; sanitation; saucier; soup, stock, sauce, and starch production; wines and spirits.

Facilities

Learning resource center; 5 lecture rooms; library; student lounge; 5 teaching kitchens.

Student Profile

165 full-time. 36 are under 25 years old; 109 are between 25 and 44 years old; 20 are over 44 years old.

Faculty

30 total: 10 full-time; 20 part-time. 7 are industry professionals; 1 is a master chef; 1 is a master baker; 5 are culinary-certified teachers. Prominent faculty: Roberta Dowling, CCP; Jan Schiff, CCP; Stephan Viau, CCP; Delphin Gomes, Master Pastry Chef. Faculty-student ratio: 1:12.

Prominent Alumni and Current Affiliation

Craig "Andy" Beardslee, Hash House A Go Go, San Diego, CA; Steve DiFillippo, Davio's, Boston, MA; Lisa Raffael, Delicious Desserts, Falmouth, MA.

The Cambridge School of Culinary Arts *(continued)*

Special Programs
International culinary excursions, culinary competitions, externships and internships.

Typical Expenses
Application fee: $45. Tuition: $25,576 for diploma; $12,590 for certificate. Program-related fees include $290 for books; $480 for materials (diploma program); $245 for materials (certificate program); $950 for kitchen equipment and uniforms.

Financial Aid
In 2007, 5 scholarships were awarded (average award was $1000); 30 loans were granted (average loan was $15,000). Program-specific awards include The Anthony Spinazzola Foundation Awards, Future Chefs Scholarship. Employment placement assistance is available. Employment opportunities within the program are available.

Housing
Average off-campus housing cost per month: $1000.

Application Information
Students may begin participation in January, May, and September. Application deadline for fall is August 1. Application deadline for winter is December 1. Application deadline for spring (certificate) is April 1. In 2007, 178 applied; 168 were accepted. Applicants must interview; submit a formal application, letters of reference, an essay, resume, educational records.

Contact
Lilly Ascenzo, Admissions Representative, Professional Chef's Program, Professional Pastry Program, 2020 Massachusetts Avenue, Cambridge, MA 02140. Telephone: 617-354-2020. Fax: 617-576-1963. E-mail: info@cambridgeculinary.com. World Wide Web: http://www.cambridgeculinary.com/.

See display on page 179.

Endicott College

Hotel and Tourism Administration

Beverly, Massachusetts

General Information
Private, coeducational, comprehensive institution. Suburban campus. Founded in 1939. Accredited by New England Association of Schools and Colleges.

Program Information
Offered since 1994. Program calendar is divided into semesters. Bachelor's degree in spa and resort management. Bachelor's degree in senior community management. Bachelor's degree in events management. 4-year bachelor's degree in hospitality and tourism administration.

Program Affiliation
American Culinary Federation; American Hotel and Lodging Association; Club Managers Association of America; Council on Hotel, Restaurant, and Institutional Education; Massachusetts Restaurant Association; National Restaurant Association; National Restaurant Association Educational Foundation.

Areas of Study
Beverage management; buffet catering; controlling costs in food service; culinary French; culinary skill development; food preparation; food purchasing; food service communication; garde-manger; international cuisine; introduction to food service; kitchen management; management and human resources; meal planning; menu and facilities design; nutrition; restaurant opportunities; sanitation; soup, stock, sauce, and starch production; wines and spirits.

Facilities
Cafeteria; 3 classrooms; computer laboratory; food production kitchen; gourmet dining room; learning resource center; public restaurant; student lounge; teaching kitchen.

Typical Student Profile
155 full-time. 148 are under 25 years old; 7 are between 25 and 44 years old.

Special Programs
Community service activities, 1-semester internship, study abroad opportunities.

Financial Aid
In 2006, 4 scholarships were awarded (average award was $1500-$2000). Employment placement assistance is available.

Housing
Coed, apartment-style, and single-sex housing available.

Application Information
Students may begin participation in February and September. Applications are accepted continuously. In 2006, 213 applied; 120 were accepted. Applicants must submit a formal application, an essay, letters of reference, academic transcripts, and SAT scores.

Contact
Director of Admissions, Hotel and Tourism Administration, 376 Hale Street, Beverly, MA 01915-2096. Telephone: 978-921-1000. Fax: 978-232-2520. World Wide Web: http://www.endicott.edu/.

International Institute of Culinary Arts

Fall River, Massachusetts

General Information
Private, coeducational, culinary institute. Urban campus. Founded in 1997.

Program Information
Offered since 1997. Program calendar is divided into semesters. 1-year certificate in culinary. 1-year diploma in baking. 2-year grand diploma in culinary arts/restaurant hospitality. 2-year grand diploma in baking/pastry arts.

Program Affiliation
The Bread Bakers Guild of America.

Areas of Study
Baking; beverage management; buffet catering; confectionery show pieces; controlling costs in food service; convenience cookery; culinary French; culinary skill development; food preparation; food purchasing; food service communication; food service math; garde-manger; international cuisine; introduction to food service; kitchen management; management and human resources; meal planning; meat cutting; meat fabrication; menu and facilities design; nutrition; nutrition and food service; patisserie; restaurant opportunities; sanitation; saucier; seafood processing; soup, stock, sauce, and starch production; wines and spirits.

Facilities
Bake shop; 4 classrooms; computer laboratory; 6 food production kitchens; garden; 4 gourmet dining rooms; 5 lecture rooms; 2 libraries; 5 public restaurants; snack shop; student lounge.

Typical Student Profile
20 full-time. 18 are under 25 years old; 2 are over 44 years old.

Financial Aid
In 2006, 3 scholarships were awarded (average award was $11,500); 9 loans were granted (average loan was $11,000). Employment placement assistance is available. Employment opportunities within the program are available.

Application Information
Students may begin participation in January and September. Applications are accepted continuously. In 2006, 70 applied; 25 were accepted. Applicants must interview; submit letters of reference, an essay, formal application, and academic transcripts.

Contact
Director of Admissions, 100 Rock Street, Fall River, MA 02720. Telephone: 508-675-9305. Fax: 508-678-5214. World Wide Web: http://www.iicaculinary.com/.

Massasoit Community College

Culinary Arts Program

Brockton, Massachusetts

General Information
Public, coeducational, two-year college. Urban campus. Founded in 1966. Accredited by New England Association of Schools and Colleges.

Program Information
Offered since 1982. Program calendar is divided into semesters. 2-semester certificate in food production. 2-year associate degree in culinary arts.

Program Affiliation
National Restaurant Association; National Restaurant Association Educational Foundation.

Areas of Study
Baking; introduction to food service; soup, stock, sauce, and starch production; storeroom and inventory procedures.

Facilities
Bakery; classroom; computer laboratory; demonstration laboratory; food production kitchen; gourmet dining room; lecture room; library; student lounge; teaching kitchen.

Typical Student Profile
89 total: 54 full-time; 35 part-time.

Financial Aid
Employment placement assistance is available.

Application Information
Students may begin participation in January and September. Applications are accepted continuously. Applicants must submit a formal application.

Contact
Director of Admissions, Culinary Arts Program, One Massasoit Boulevard, Brockton, MA 02402-3996. Telephone: 508-588-9100 Ext. 1411. World Wide Web: http://www.massasoit.mass.edu/.

Middlesex Community College

Lowell, Massachusetts

General Information

Public, coeducational, two-year college. Urban campus. Founded in 1970. Accredited by New England Association of Schools and Colleges.

Program Information

Accredited by NEASC. Program calendar is divided into semesters. 1-year certificate in culinary arts. 2-year associate degree in hospitality management-culinary arts option.

Program Affiliation

Council on Hotel, Restaurant, and Institutional Education; National Restaurant Association; National Restaurant Association Educational Foundation.

Areas of Study

Baking; beverage management; buffet catering; confectionery show pieces; culinary skill development; food preparation; food purchasing; food service math; introduction to food service; kitchen management; management and human resources; menu and facilities design; nutrition and food service; patisserie; sanitation; soup, stock, sauce, and starch production; wines and spirits.

Facilities

Bake shop; bakery; classroom; computer laboratory; demonstration laboratory; food production kitchen; lecture room; library.

Typical Student Profile

25 total: 20 full-time; 5 part-time. 20 are under 25 years old; 5 are between 25 and 44 years old.

Financial Aid

Program-specific awards include local industry scholarships-through the Massachusetts Lodging Association. Employment placement assistance is available. Employment opportunities within the program are available.

Application Information

Students may begin participation in January and September. Application deadline for fall is September 6. Applicants must submit a formal application.

Contact

Director of Admissions, 33, Kearney Square, Lowell, MA 01852-1987. Telephone: 978-656-3170. Fax: 978-656-3150. World Wide Web: http://www.middlesex.mass.edu/.

Newbury College

Roger A. Saunders School of Hotel & Restaurant Management

Brookline, Massachusetts

General Information

Private, coeducational, four-year college. Suburban campus. Founded in 1962. Accredited by New England Association of Schools and Colleges.

Program Information

Offered since 1962. National Restaurant Association Educational Foundation ManageFirst certificates available. Program calendar is divided into semesters. 11-month certificate in pastry arts. 11-month certificate in meeting management. 11-month certificate in hotel and resort management. 11-month certificate in food service and restaurant management. 11-month certificate in buffet catering. 2-year associate degree in hotel and resort management. 2-year associate degree in food service and restaurant management. 2-year associate degree in culinary arts. 4-year bachelor's degree in hotel, restaurant, and service management/hotel administration concentration. 4-year bachelor's degree in hotel, restaurant, and service management/culinary management concentration.

Program Affiliation

National Restaurant Association Educational Foundation.

Student Profile

182 total: 142 full-time; 40 part-time.

Special Programs

Internships, operation of college's own restaurant.

Typical Expenses

Application fee: $50. Tuition: $35,000 per year full-time, $260 per credit part-time. Program-related fee includes $105 for credit hour (food, equipment, utilities and supplies).

Financial Aid

Employment placement assistance is available.

Housing

Coed housing available.

Application Information

Students may begin participation in January and September. Applications are accepted continuously. Application deadline for fall (early action) is December 1. Applicants must submit a formal application, letters of reference, an essay, transcripts.

Contact

Joseph Chillo, Vice President of Enrollment, Roger A. Saunders School of Hotel & Restaurant Management, 129 Fisher Avenue, Brookline, MA 02445. Telephone: 617-730-7007. Fax: 617-731-9618. E-mail: info@newbury.edu. World Wide Web: http://www.newbury.edu/.

University of Massachusetts Amherst

Hospitality and Tourism Management

Amherst, Massachusetts

General Information

Public, coeducational, university. Small-town setting. Founded in 1863. Accredited by New England Association of Schools and Colleges.

Program Information

Offered since 1938. Accredited by Council on Hotel, Restaurant and Institutional Education. National Restaurant Association Educational Foundation ManageFirst certificates available. Program calendar is divided into semesters. 2-year master's degree in hospitality and tourism management (MS/MBA joint degree). 2-year master's degree in hospitality and tourism management. 4-year bachelor's degree in hospitality and tourism management. 5-course certificate in event and tourism management. 5-course certificate in casino management.

Program Affiliation

Club Managers Association of America; Council on Hotel, Restaurant, and Institutional Education; National Restaurant Association; National Restaurant Association Educational Foundation.

Areas of Study

Beverage management; casino management; club management; events management; food service management; lodging; management and human resources; restaurant opportunities.

Facilities

Catering service; 5 classrooms; 3 coffee shops; computer laboratory; demonstration laboratory; food production kitchen; gourmet dining room; learning resource center; 3 lecture rooms; library; student lounge; teaching kitchen.

Typical Student Profile

639 full-time.

University of Massachusetts Amherst *(continued)*

Special Programs

600 hour work experience requirement, internships available, domestic, international and study abroad options.

Financial Aid

Employment placement assistance is available. Employment opportunities within the program are available.

Housing

Coed and apartment-style housing available.

Application Information

Students may begin participation in January and September. Applications are accepted continuously. Applicants must submit a formal application, letters of reference, and an essay.

Contact

Director of Admissions, Hospitality and Tourism Management, 101 Flint Lab, 90 Campus Center Way, Amherst, MA 01003. Telephone: 413-545-4049. World Wide Web: http://www.umass.edu/.

Michigan

Baker College of Muskegon

Culinary Arts and Food and Beverage Management

Muskegon, Michigan

General Information

Private, coeducational, four-year college. Suburban campus. Founded in 1888. Accredited by North Central Association of Colleges and Schools.

Program Information

Offered since 1997. Accredited by American Culinary Federation Accrediting Commission. Program calendar is divided into quarters. 1-year certificate in baking and pastry. 2-year associate degree in food and beverage management. 2-year associate degree in culinary arts. 4-year bachelor's degree in food and beverage management.

Program Affiliation

American Culinary Federation; Council on Hotel, Restaurant, and Institutional Education; National Restaurant Association; National Restaurant Association Educational Foundation; Tasters Guild International.

Areas of Study

Baking; beverage management; buffet catering; confectionery show pieces; controlling costs in food service; convenience cookery; culinary French; culinary skill development; food preparation; food purchasing; food service math; garde-manger; international cuisine; introduction to food service; kitchen management; management and human resources; meal planning; meat cutting; meat fabrication; menu and facilities design; nutrition; nutrition and food service; patisserie; restaurant opportunities; sanitation; saucier; seafood processing; soup, stock, sauce, and starch production; wines and spirits.

Facilities

Bake shop; catering service; 5 classrooms; 10 computer laboratories; demonstration laboratory; food production kitchen; garden; gourmet dining room; learning resource center; 105 lecture rooms; library; public restaurant; student lounge; teaching kitchen.

Typical Student Profile

330 full-time.

Special Programs

Culinary competitions, ice carving, international competitions and overseas excursions.

Financial Aid

Program-specific awards include National Restaurant Association scholarships ($2000), Warren A. Husid Memorial Scholarships ($2000). Employment placement assistance is available. Employment opportunities within the program are available.

Housing

Coed and apartment-style housing available.

Application Information

Students may begin participation in January, April, and September. Applications are accepted continuously. Applicants must submit a formal application and have high school diploma or GED.

Contact

Director of Admissions, Culinary Arts and Food and Beverage Management, 1903 Marquette Avenue, Muskegon, MT 49442. Telephone: 231-777-5207. Fax: 231-777-5256. World Wide Web: http://www.baker.edu/.

Central Michigan University

Foodservice Administration

Mount Pleasant, Michigan

General Information

Public, coeducational, university. Small-town setting. Founded in 1892. Accredited by North Central Association of Colleges and Schools.

Program Information

Accredited by American Dietetic Association. Program calendar is divided into semesters. 4-year bachelor's degree in food service administration. 4-year bachelor's degree in dietetics.

Program Affiliation

American Dietetic Association.

Areas of Study

Beverage management; culinary skill development; food preparation; food purchasing; menu and facilities design; nutrition and food service; sanitation.

Facilities

Demonstration laboratory.

Typical Student Profile

126 total: 111 full-time; 15 part-time. 111 are under 25 years old; 12 are between 25 and 44 years old; 3 are over 44 years old.

Special Programs

Food service internship.

Financial Aid

Program-specific awards include Rose J. Hogue Scholarship (junior or senior with 3.0 or higher GPA). Employment placement assistance is available. Employment opportunities within the program are available.

Housing

Coed housing available.

Application Information

Students may begin participation in January and August. Applications are accepted continuously. Applicants must submit a formal application.

Contact

Director of Admissions, Foodservice Administration, Wightman Hall 109, Mt. Pleasant, MI 48859. Telephone: 989-774-5591. World Wide Web: http://nutrition.cmich.edu/.

Grand Rapids Community College

Secchia Institute for Culinary Education

Grand Rapids, Michigan

General Information

Public, coeducational, two-year college. Urban campus. Founded in 1914. Accredited by North Central Association of Colleges and Schools.

Program Information

Offered since 1980. Accredited by American Culinary Federation Accrediting Commission. Program calendar is divided into semesters. 12-month certificate in baking and pastry arts. 21-month associate degree in culinary management. 21-month associate degree in culinary arts.

Program Affiliation

American Culinary Federation; American Institute of Baking; American Vegan Society; Confrerie de la Chaine des Rotisseurs; Council on Hotel, Restaurant, and Institutional Education; Foodservice Educators Network International; International Association of Culinary Professionals; International Food Service Executives Association; National Restaurant Association; National Restaurant Association Educational Foundation; North American Vegetarian Society; Retailer's Bakery Association; Society of Wine Educators; Tasters Guild International.

Areas of Study

Baking; beverage management; buffet catering; cake decorating; confectionery show pieces; controlling costs in food service; culinary skill development; deli-bakery operations; food preparation; food purchasing; food service math; garde-manger; ice carving; international cuisine; introduction to food service; kitchen management; management and human resources; meat fabrication; menu and facilities design; nutrition; nutrition and food service; patisserie; restaurant opportunities; sanitation; saucier; seafood processing; soup, stock, sauce, and starch production; table service; vegetarian and vegan cooking; wines and spirits.

Facilities

3 bake shops; cafeteria; catering service; 3 classrooms; coffee shop; computer laboratory; 2 demonstration laboratories; 3 food production kitchens; garden; 3 gourmet dining rooms; learning resource center; 3 lecture rooms; library; public restaurant; snack shop; student lounge; 6 teaching kitchens; 6 banquet rooms; beverage lab; wine education classroom.

Grand Rapids Community College
Secchia Institute for Culinary Education
the choice is yours...
Secchia Institute students choose from three programs:
Culinary Arts or Culinary Management
Our associate degree-granting programs in Applied Arts and Sciences can prepare you for an exciting career as a food and beverage director, executive chef, caterer or the proprietor of your own food service operation.
Baking and Pastry Arts
Our certificate-granting program can prepare you for a rewarding career as a baker, pastry chef, deli-bakery manager or the proprietor of your own bakery.
• See our listing in this edition of Peterson's Culinary Schools
• Visit our Web Site at www.grcc.edu/sice
• Contact us for more information at (616) 234-3690
• Visit our Center for Culinary Education, Grand Rapids, Michigan
Grand Rapids Community College
Secchia Institute for Culinary Education
Grand Rapids Community College
College is an equal opportunity institution. GRCC is a tobacco free campus effective 11/20/2008

Student Profile
495 total: 300 full-time; 195 part-time. 352 are under 25 years old; 118 are between 25 and 44 years old; 25 are over 44 years old.

Faculty
22 total: 12 full-time; 10 part-time. 17 are industry professionals; 2 are master chefs; 2 are culinary-certified teachers. Prominent faculty: Robert Garlough; Giles Renusson; Angus Campbell; Kevin Dunn. Faculty-student ratio: 1:18.

Special Programs
International exchange program, international culinary study tours, culinary competition.

Typical Expenses
Application fee: $20. In-state tuition: $82.50 per contact hour full-time (in district), $82.50 per contact hour part-time (in district), $173 per contact hour full-time (out-of-district), $173 per contact hour part-time (out-of-district). Out-of-state tuition: $253 per contact hour full-time, $253 per contact hour part-time. Program-related fees include $280 for knife kit; $350 for uniforms; $1000 for textbooks.

Financial Aid
In 2007, 19 scholarships were awarded (average award was $1000). Employment placement assistance is available. Employment opportunities within the program are available.

Housing
Average off-campus housing cost per month: $400.

Application Information
Students may begin participation in January and September. Applications are accepted continuously. In 2007, 170 applied; 160 were accepted. Applicants must submit a formal application and ACT scores or Accuplacer Test.

Contact
Mr. Randy Sahajdack, Program Director, Secchia Institute for Culinary Education, 143 Bostwick, NE, Grand Rapids, MI 49503. Telephone: 616-234-3690. Fax: 616-234-3698. E-mail: marp@grcc.edu. World Wide Web: http://www.grcc.edu/sice.

See display on page 186.

Grand Valley State University

Hospitality and Tourism Management

Allendale, Michigan

General Information
Public, coeducational, comprehensive institution. Suburban campus. Founded in 1960. Accredited by North Central Association of Colleges and Schools.

Program Information
Offered since 1977. Program calendar is divided into semesters. 4-year bachelor's degree in hospitality and tourism management.

Program Affiliation
American Dietetic Association; Council on Hotel, Restaurant, and Institutional Education; National Restaurant Association; Professional Convention Management Association.

Areas of Study
Beverage management; food and beverage service management; kitchen management; lodging; meeting and event planning; tourism.

Facilities
Classroom; computer laboratory; lecture room; library.

Typical Student Profile
407 total: 349 full-time; 58 part-time. 380 are under 25 years old; 25 are between 25 and 44 years old; 2 are over 44 years old.

Special Programs
4-week study abroad in Italy, semester abroad opportunities in Australia and New Zealand, 1,000 hours of coordinated internships.

Financial Aid
Employment placement assistance is available. Employment opportunities within the program are available.

Housing
Coed and apartment-style housing available.

Application Information
Students may begin participation in January, May, and September. Application deadline for fall is July 30. Application deadline for winter is November 30. Application deadline for summer is April 15. Applicants must submit a formal application and ACT score and minimum GPA.

Contact
Director of Admissions, Hospitality and Tourism Management, 1 Campus Drive, Allendale, MI 49401. Telephone: 616-895-2025. Fax: 616-895-2000. World Wide Web: http://gvsu.edu/.

Great Lakes Culinary Institute at Northwestern Michigan College

Great Lakes Culinary Institute

Traverse City, Michigan

General Information

Public, coeducational, culinary institute. Small-town setting. Founded in 1951. Accredited by North Central Association of Colleges and Schools.

Program Information

Offered since 1992. Accredited by American Culinary Federation Accrediting Commission. Program calendar is divided into semesters. 2-year associate degree in culinary arts. 2-year certificate in culinary arts.

Program Affiliation

American Culinary Federation; American Institute of Baking; Council on Hotel, Restaurant, and Institutional Education; National Restaurant Association; National Restaurant Association Educational Foundation; Tasters Guild International; The Bread Bakers Guild of America.

Areas of Study

Baking; buffet catering; controlling costs in food service; culinary skill development; food preparation; food purchasing; food service communication; food service math; garde-manger; international cuisine; introduction to food service; kitchen management; management and human resources; meal planning; nutrition; nutrition and food service; patisserie; restaurant opportunities; sanitation; soup, stock, sauce, and starch production.

Facilities

Bake shop; bakery; cafeteria; catering service; 3 classrooms; 2 computer laboratories; demonstration laboratory; food production kitchen; laboratory; 2 learning resource centers; 2 lecture rooms; library; public restaurant; student lounge; teaching kitchen; vineyard.

Typical Student Profile

190 total: 150 full-time; 40 part-time. 70 are under 25 years old; 110 are between 25 and 44 years old; 10 are over 44 years old.

Special Programs

6-month paid internship.

Financial Aid

In 2006, 8 scholarships were awarded (average award was $1500); 60 loans were granted (average loan was $2500). Program-specific awards include industry scholarships. Employment placement assistance is available. Employment opportunities within the program are available.

Housing

Coed, apartment-style, and single-sex housing available.

Application Information

Students may begin participation in January and August. Application deadline for fall is August 15. Application deadline for spring is December 15. In 2006, 160 applied; 120 were accepted. Applicants must submit a formal application.

Contact

Director of Admissions, Great Lakes Culinary Institute, 1701 East Front Street, Traverse City, MI 49686. Telephone: 800-748-0566 Ext. 51197. Fax: 231-995-1134. World Wide Web: http://www.nmc.edu/.

Henry Ford Community College

Hospitality Studies/Culinary Arts and Hotel Restaurant Management

Dearborn, Michigan

General Information

Public, coeducational, two-year college. Suburban campus. Founded in 1938. Accredited by North Central Association of Colleges and Schools.

Program Information

Offered since 1972. Accredited by American Culinary Federation Accrediting Commission. Program calendar is divided into semesters. 1-year certificate in hospitality service career. 1-year certificate in hospitality professional management. 1-year certificate in culinary/baking. 1-year certificate in culinary skills. 1-year certificate in culinary arts supervisor. 2-year associate degree in hotel/restaurant management. 2-year associate degree in culinary arts.

Program Affiliation

American Culinary Federation; American Institute of Baking; Council on Hotel, Restaurant, and Institutional Education; International Food Service Executives Association; Michigan Lodging and Tourism Association; Michigan Restaurant Association; National Restaurant Association; National Restaurant Association Educational Foundation.

Areas of Study

Baking; beverage management; confectionery show pieces; controlling costs in food service; culinary skill development; food preparation; food purchasing; food service communication; food service math; garde-manger; international cuisine; introduction to food service; kitchen management; management and human resources; meal planning; meat cutting; meat fabrication; menu and facilities design; nutrition; patisserie; sanitation; saucier; seafood processing; soup, stock, sauce, and starch production; wines and spirits.

Facilities
Bake shop; bakery; cafeteria; catering service; classroom; computer laboratory; 2 food production kitchens; gourmet dining room; laboratory; learning resource center; lecture room; library; public restaurant; snack shop; student lounge; teaching kitchen.

Typical Student Profile
225 full-time.

Special Programs
Culinary competitions, ice carving.

Financial Aid
Employment placement assistance is available. Employment opportunities within the program are available.

Application Information
Students may begin participation in January, May, July, and August. Applications are accepted continuously. Applicants must submit a formal application and have a high school diploma or GED.

Contact
Director of Admissions, Hospitality Studies/Culinary Arts and Hotel Restaurant Management, 5101 Evergreen Road, Dearborn, MI 48128-1495. Telephone: 313-845-6390. Fax: 313-845-9784. World Wide Web: http://www.hfcc.edu/.

The International Culinary School at The Art Institute of Michigan

Novi, Michigan

General Information
Private, coeducational institution.

Program Information
Accredited by Accrediting Commission of Career Schools and Colleges of Technology (ACCSCT) as a branch of the Illinois Institute of Art–Chicago. Associate degree in Culinary Arts. Bachelor's degree in Culinary Management. Certificate in Professional Baking and Pastry.

Contact
Office of Admissions, 28125 Cabot Drive, Suite 120, Novi, MI 48377. Telephone: 248-675-3800. World Wide Web: http://www.artinstitutes.edu/detroit.

See color display following page 332.

Lake Michigan College

Hospitality Management

Benton Harbor, Michigan

General Information
Public, coeducational, two-year college. Suburban campus. Founded in 1946. Accredited by North Central Association of Colleges and Schools.

Program Information
Offered since 1980. Accredited by Council on Hotel, Restaurant and Institutional Education. Program calendar is divided into semesters. 15-credit certificate in hospitality management. 30-credit certificate in hospitality management. 61-credit associate degree in hospitality management.

Program Affiliation
American Culinary Federation; American Institute of Wine & Food; American Wine Society; Council on Hotel, Restaurant, and Institutional Education; International Wine & Food Society; Napa Valley Wine Library Association; National Restaurant Association Educational Foundation; Society of Wine Educators; Sommelier Society of America; Tasters Guild International.

Areas of Study
Beverage management; controlling costs in food service; food purchasing; introduction to food service; menu and facilities design; nutrition; sanitation; wines and spirits.

Facilities
Classroom; food production kitchen; vineyard.

Typical Student Profile
70 total: 40 full-time; 30 part-time. 40 are under 25 years old; 25 are between 25 and 44 years old; 5 are over 44 years old.

Special Programs
Return to Learn, No Work Left Behind.

Financial Aid
In 2006, 2 scholarships were awarded (average award was $500). Program-specific awards include Rich Wohlfert Memorial scholarship. Employment placement assistance is available.

Application Information
Students may begin participation in January and August. Applications are accepted continuously. In 2006, 40 applied; 40 were accepted. Applicants must submit a formal application.

Lake Michigan College ***(continued)***

Contact

Director of Admissions, Hospitality Management, 2755 East Napier Avenue, Benton Harbor, MI 49022. Telephone: 616-927-8100 Ext. 5005. Fax: 616-927-8619. World Wide Web: http://www.lakemichigancollege.edu/.

Macomb Community College

Macomb Culinary Institute

Clinton Township, Michigan

General Information

Public, coeducational, two-year college. Suburban campus. Founded in 1954. Accredited by North Central Association of Colleges and Schools.

Program Information

Offered since 1969. Accredited by American Culinary Federation Accrediting Commission. National Restaurant Association Educational Foundation ManageFirst certificates available. Program calendar is divided into semesters. 1-year certificate in pastry arts. 1-year certificate in culinary management. 2-year associate degree in restaurant management. 2-year associate degree in pastry arts. 2-year associate degree in hospitality management. 2-year associate degree in culinary arts.

Program Affiliation

American Culinary Federation; Council on Hotel, Restaurant, and Institutional Education; Michigan Restaurant Association; National Restaurant Association; National Restaurant Association Educational Foundation.

Areas of Study

Baking; beverage management; buffet catering; confectionery show pieces; controlling costs in food service; culinary skill development; food preparation; food purchasing; food service communication; food service math; garde-manger; international cuisine; kitchen management; management and human resources; meal planning; meat cutting; meat fabrication; menu and facilities design; nutrition; nutrition and food service; patisserie; restaurant opportunities; sanitation; saucier; seafood processing; soup, stock, sauce, and starch production; wines and spirits.

Facilities

Bake shop; 4 classrooms; computer laboratory; demonstration laboratory; food production kitchen; gourmet dining room; learning resource center; lecture room; library; public restaurant; student lounge; 3 teaching kitchens.

Typical Student Profile

320 total: 160 full-time; 160 part-time.

Special Programs

Apprenticeship program with ACF Blue Water Chefs Association, IKA Culinary Olympics (every 4 years); Hot/Cold/Ice/Gingerbread/Skills USA competitions, culinary tour of France.

Financial Aid

In 2006, 3 scholarships were awarded (average award was $300). Employment placement assistance is available. Employment opportunities within the program are available.

Application Information

Students may begin participation in January and August. Applications are accepted continuously. Applicants must submit a formal application.

Contact

Director of Admissions, Macomb Culinary Institute, 44575 Garfield Road, Clinton Township, MI 48038. Telephone: 586-286-2088. Fax: 586-226-4725. World Wide Web: http://www.macomb.edu/.

Michigan State University

The School of Hospitality Business

East Lansing, Michigan

General Information

Public, coeducational, university. Suburban campus. Founded in 1855. Accredited by North Central Association of Colleges and Schools.

Program Information

Offered since 1927. Program calendar is divided into semesters. 1- to 2-year master's degree in hospitality business. 1- to 2-year master's degree in foodservice management. 2-year master of business administration in hospitality business. 4-year bachelor's degree in hospitality business.

Program Affiliation

American Culinary Federation; American Hotel and Lodging Association; Council on Hotel, Restaurant, and Institutional Education; National Restaurant Association; National Restaurant Association Educational Foundation; Society for Foodservice Management.

Areas of Study

Accounting; beverage management; controlling costs in food service; finance; food preparation; foodservice management; human resource management; introduction to food service; management and human resources; marketing; nutrition and food service; restaurant opportunities; sanitation; wines and spirits.

Facilities
6 classrooms; 4 computer laboratories; demonstration laboratory; 2 food production kitchens; gourmet dining room; learning resource center; lecture room; 2 libraries.

Typical Student Profile
800 full-time.

Special Programs
Paid internships, student club visits to program-related venues, leadership development in 10 clubs and 4 events.

Financial Aid
In 2006, 150 scholarships were awarded. Program-specific awards include industry-sponsored scholarships, need-based scholarships. Employment placement assistance is available. Employment opportunities within the program are available.

Housing
Coed, apartment-style, and single-sex housing available.

Application Information
Students may begin participation in January, May, and August. Applications are accepted continuously. Applicants must submit a formal application, an essay, letters of reference, and SAT, GRE, or GMAT scores.

Contact
Director of Admissions, The School of Hospitality Business, The School of Hospitality Business, MSU, 227 Eppley Center, East Lansing, MI 48824. Telephone: 517-353-9747. Fax: 517-432-1170. World Wide Web: http://www.bus.msu.edu/shb/.

Mott Community College

Culinary Arts Program

Flint, Michigan

General Information
Public, coeducational, two-year college. Urban campus. Founded in 1923. Accredited by North Central Association of Colleges and Schools.

Program Information
Offered since 1984. National Restaurant Association Educational Foundation ManageFirst certificates available. Program calendar is divided into semesters. 2-year associate degree in food service management. 2-year associate degree in culinary arts. 2-year associate degree in baking and pastry arts.

Program Affiliation
Flint/Saginaw Valley Chefs Association; National Restaurant Association; National Restaurant Association Educational Foundation.

Areas of Study
À la carte dining; baking; beverage management; buffet catering; confectionery show pieces; controlling costs in food service; culinary skill development; food preparation; food purchasing; food service math; garde-manger; international cuisine; introduction to food service; kitchen management; management and human resources; meal planning; meat cutting; meat fabrication; menu and facilities design; nutrition; patisserie; sanitation; specialty desserts.

Facilities
Bake shop; cafeteria; catering service; 5 classrooms; computer laboratory; demonstration laboratory; food production kitchen; gourmet dining room; laboratory; 2 public restaurants; 2 student lounges.

Typical Student Profile
207 total: 142 full-time; 65 part-time.

Special Programs
Internships, culinary competitions.

Financial Aid
In 2006, individual scholarships were awarded at $1000. Employment placement assistance is available. Employment opportunities within the program are available.

Application Information
Students may begin participation in January and September. Applications are accepted continuously. Applicants must submit a formal application.

Contact
Director of Admissions, Culinary Arts Program, 1401 East Court Street, Flint, MI 48501. Telephone: 810-232-7845. Fax: 810-232-6744. World Wide Web: http://www.mcc.edu/.

Northern Michigan University

Hospitality Management

Marquette, Michigan

General Information
Public, coeducational, comprehensive institution. Rural campus. Founded in 1899. Accredited by North Central Association of Colleges and Schools.

Northern Michigan University *(continued)*

PROGRAM INFORMATION

Offered since 1980. Program calendar is divided into semesters. 2-year associate degree in food service management. 4-year bachelor's degree in hospitality management.

PROGRAM AFFILIATION

American Culinary Federation; American Institute of Baking; Council on Hotel, Restaurant, and Institutional Education; National Restaurant Association; National Restaurant Association Educational Foundation.

AREAS OF STUDY

Hotel and restaurant management; kitchen management.

FACILITIES

Bake shop; cafeteria; catering service; 4 classrooms; computer laboratory; food production kitchen; garden; 3 laboratories; learning resource center; library; public restaurant; teaching kitchen.

TYPICAL STUDENT PROFILE

160 total: 140 full-time; 20 part-time. 120 are under 25 years old; 40 are between 25 and 44 years old.

SPECIAL PROGRAMS

Paid internships, international study.

FINANCIAL AID

In 2006, 6 scholarships were awarded (average award was $500). Program-specific awards include ProMgmt. Scholarships, ACF Upper Michigan Chapter scholarships, Thaddeus Bogdan scholarships. Employment placement assistance is available. Employment opportunities within the program are available.

HOUSING

Coed, apartment-style, and single-sex housing available.

APPLICATION INFORMATION

Students may begin participation in January and August. Application deadline for fall is July 1. Application deadline for spring is November 1. In 2006, 47 applied; 47 were accepted. Applicants must submit a formal application.

CONTACT

Director of Admissions, Hospitality Management, 1401 Presque Isle Avenue, Marquette, MI 49855-5366. Telephone: 906-227-2135. Fax: 906-227-1549. World Wide Web: http://www.nmu.edu/.

NORTHWOOD UNIVERSITY

Hotel, Restaurant, and Resort Management

Midland, Michigan

GENERAL INFORMATION

Private, coeducational, four-year college. Suburban campus. Founded in 1959. Accredited by North Central Association of Colleges and Schools.

PROGRAM INFORMATION

Offered since 1966. Program calendar is divided into quarters. 2-year associate degree in hotel/restaurant/resort management. 4-year bachelor's degree in hotel/restaurant/resort management.

PROGRAM AFFILIATION

Council on Hotel, Restaurant, and Institutional Education; Institute of Food Technologists; National Restaurant Association; National Restaurant Association Educational Foundation.

AREAS OF STUDY

Beverage management; controlling costs in food service; food preparation; food purchasing; introduction to food service; kitchen management; management and human resources; meal planning; menu and facilities design; nutrition; sanitation; wines and spirits.

FACILITIES

Classroom; demonstration laboratory; food production kitchen; gourmet dining room; lecture room; teaching kitchen.

TYPICAL STUDENT PROFILE

91 full-time. 89 are under 25 years old; 2 are between 25 and 44 years old.

SPECIAL PROGRAMS

3-month faculty-supervised internships, trips to AHLA show in New York and NRA show in Chicago, annual "live-in weekend" at Zehnders of Frankemuth.

FINANCIAL AID

In 2006, 34 scholarships were awarded (average award was $400). Employment placement assistance is available. Employment opportunities within the program are available.

HOUSING

Single-sex housing available.

APPLICATION INFORMATION

Students may begin participation in March, September, and December. Applications are accepted continuously. In 2006, 109 applied; 75 were accepted. Applicants must submit a formal application and an essay.

Contact
Director of Admissions, Hotel, Restaurant, and Resort Management, 4000 Whiting Drive, Midland, MI 48640. Telephone: 989-837-4273. Fax: 989-837-4490. World Wide Web: http://www.northwood.edu/.

Oakland Community College

Culinary Studies Institute

Farmington Hills, Michigan

General Information
Public, coeducational, two-year college. Suburban campus. Founded in 1964. Accredited by North Central Association of Colleges and Schools.

Program Information
Offered since 1965. Accredited by American Culinary Federation Accrediting Commission. Program calendar is divided into semesters. 1-year certificate in baking and pastry arts. 2-year associate degree in restaurant management. 2-year associate degree in hotel management. 2-year associate degree in culinary arts. 3-year certificate in culinary apprentice.

Program Affiliation
American Culinary Federation; American Dietetic Association; American Institute of Baking; Council on Hotel, Restaurant, and Institutional Education; National Restaurant Association; National Restaurant Association Educational Foundation; Tasters Guild International.

Areas of Study
Baking; beverage management; buffet catering; confectionery show pieces; controlling costs in food service; culinary skill development; food preparation; food purchasing; garde-manger; international cuisine; management and human resources; meat cutting; meat fabrication; menu and facilities design; nutrition; patisserie; sanitation; saucier; seafood processing; soup, stock, sauce, and starch production; wines and spirits.

Facilities
2 bake shops; cafeteria; catering service; 3 classrooms; computer laboratory; demonstration laboratory; 3 food production kitchens; 2 gourmet dining rooms; 4 laboratories; learning resource center; 2 lecture rooms; library; public restaurant; teaching kitchen; bakery retail center.

Typical Student Profile
225 total: 150 full-time; 75 part-time.

Special Programs
Ice carving/sugar artistry/culinary competitions.

Financial Aid
In 2006, 5 scholarships were awarded (average award was $500). Employment placement assistance is available. Employment opportunities within the program are available.

Application Information
Students may begin participation in January, May, and September. Application deadline for fall is July 15. Application deadline for winter is November 15. Application deadline for spring is April 15. Applicants must interview; submit a formal application.

Contact
Director of Admissions, Culinary Studies Institute, 27055 Orchard Lake Road, Farmington Hills, MI 48334. Telephone: 248-522-3700. Fax: 248-522-3706. World Wide Web: http://www.oaklandcc.edu/.

Schoolcraft College

Culinary Arts

Livonia, Michigan

General Information
Public, coeducational, two-year college. Suburban campus. Founded in 1961. Accredited by North Central Association of Colleges and Schools.

Program Information
Program calendar is divided into semesters. 1-year certificate in culinary arts. 2-year associate degree in culinary arts. 30-week certificate in baking and pastry.

Program Affiliation
American Culinary Federation.

Faculty
4 are master chefs; 2 are certified executive chefs. Faculty-student ratio: 1:16.

Special Programs
Salon competitions, local culinary competitions.

Typical Expenses
In-state tuition: $73 per credit hour (in district), $107 per credit hour (out-of-district). Out-of-state tuition: $160 per credit hour. Program-related fees include $1900 for lab fees for instruction; $225 for uniforms; $350 for knife set; $982 for books.

Financial Aid
Employment placement assistance is available. Employment opportunities within the program are available.

Application Information
Students may begin participation in January and August. Applications are accepted continuously. Applicants must submit a formal application, complete prerequisite course, transcripts, placement test or ACT.

Contact
Office of Admissions, Culinary Arts, 18600 Haggerty Road, Livonia, MI 48152-2696. Telephone: 734-462-4426. Fax: 734-462-4553. E-mail: admissions@schoolcraft.edu. World Wide Web: http://www.schoolcraft.edu/.

See display on page 194.

Washtenaw Community College

Culinary and Hospitality Management

Ann Arbor, Michigan

General Information
Public, coeducational, two-year college. Suburban campus. Founded in 1965. Accredited by North Central Association of Colleges and Schools.

Program Information
Offered since 1971. Accredited by American Culinary Federation Accrediting Commission. Program calendar is divided into semesters. 1-year certificate in hospitality management. 1-year certificate in culinary arts. 1-year certificate in baking and pastry. 2-year associate degree in culinary and hospitality management.

Program Affiliation
American Culinary Federation; Council on Hotel, Restaurant, and Institutional Education; National Restaurant Association; National Restaurant Association Educational Foundation.

Areas of Study
Baking; beverage management; buffet catering; controlling costs in food service; culinary skill development; food preparation; food purchasing; food service math; garde-manger; international cuisine; introduction to food service; kitchen management; management and human resources; meal planning; menu and facilities design; nutrition; nutrition and food service; patisserie; restaurant opportunities; sanitation; saucier; seafood processing; soup, stock, sauce, and starch production.

Facilities
Bake shop; cafeteria; catering service; 5 classrooms; coffee shop; 3 computer laboratories; 2 demonstration laboratories; food production kitchen; gourmet dining room; 3 laboratories; learning resource center; 5 lecture rooms; library; public restaurant; snack shop; 5 student lounges; 3 teaching kitchens.

Typical Student Profile
160 total: 110 full-time; 50 part-time.

Special Programs
Culinary competitions, paid internships.

Financial Aid
In 2006, 12 scholarships were awarded (average award was $500). Employment placement assistance is available.

Application Information
Students may begin participation in January, May, and September. Application deadline for fall is September 8. Application deadline for winter is January 6. Application deadline for spring/summer is May 5. Applicants must submit a formal application.

Contact
Director of Admissions, Culinary and Hospitality Management, 4800 East Huron River Drive, PO Box D-1, Ann Arbor, MI 48106. Telephone: 734-973-3531. Fax: 734-477-8523. World Wide Web: http://www.washtenaw.cc.mi.us/.

Minnesota

Hennepin Technical College

Culinary Arts Department

Brooklyn Park, Minnesota

General Information
Public, coeducational, two-year college. Suburban campus. Founded in 1972. Accredited by North Central Association of Colleges and Schools.

Program Information
Offered since 1972. Accredited by American Culinary Federation Accrediting Commission. National Restaurant Association Educational Foundation ManageFirst certificates available. Program calendar is divided into semesters. 1.5-year diploma in culinary arts. 15-month certificate in culinary arts. 2-year associate degree in culinary arts.

Program Affiliation
American Culinary Federation; American Institute of Baking.

Areas of Study
Baking; bar and beverage management; beverage management; buffet catering; confectionery show pieces; controlling costs in food service; convenience cookery; culinary French; culinary skill development; food preparation; food purchasing; food service communication; food service math; garde-manger;

Hennepin Technical College *(continued)*

hospitality law; hospitality marketing; international cuisine; introduction to food service; kitchen management; meal planning; meat cutting; meat fabrication; menu and facilities design; nutrition; nutrition and food service; restaurant opportunities; sanitation; saucier; seafood processing; soup, stock, sauce, and starch production; sugar work; wines and spirits.

Facilities

4 bake shops; 4 bakeries; 4 cafeterias; 4 catering services; 4 classrooms; coffee shop; 6 computer laboratories; 2 demonstration laboratories; 2 food production kitchens; 5 gourmet dining rooms; 4 laboratories; 20 learning resource centers; 25 lecture rooms; 20 libraries; 5 public restaurants; 4 snack shops; 2 student lounges; 20 teaching kitchens.

Typical Student Profile

120 full-time.

Special Programs

Specialized labs with individual students, culinary competitions, 1-year paid internships.

Financial Aid

In 2006, 5 scholarships were awarded (average award was $300); 4 loans were granted (average loan was $300). Program-specific awards include 3 Minneapolis ACF Scholarships ($500), Toby Landgraf Scholarships ($500). Employment placement assistance is available. Employment opportunities within the program are available.

Application Information

Students may begin participation in January and August. Application deadline for fall is October 1. Application deadline for spring is February 1. In 2006, 25 applied; 25 were accepted. Applicants must interview; submit a formal application.

Contact

Director of Admissions, Culinary Arts Department, 9000 Brooklyn Boulevard, Brooklyn Park, MN 55445. Telephone: 763-488-2412. Fax: 763-488-2938. World Wide Web: http://www.hennepintech.edu/.

Hibbing Community College

Culinary Arts

Hibbing, Minnesota

General Information

Public, coeducational, two-year college. Small-town setting. Founded in 1916. Accredited by North Central Association of Colleges and Schools.

Program Information

Offered since 1965. Program calendar is divided into semesters. 1-year diploma in culinary arts. 2-year diploma in food service and management. 5-semester associate degree in culinary arts.

Program Affiliation

National Restaurant Association.

Areas of Study

Baking; buffet catering; controlling costs in food service; culinary skill development; food preparation; food purchasing; food service management; food service math; international cuisine; introduction to food service; kitchen management; management and human resources; meal planning; meat cutting; meat fabrication; menu and facilities design; nutrition and food service; restaurant opportunities; sanitation; saucier; seafood processing; soup, stock, sauce, and starch production.

Facilities

Bake shop; bakery; cafeteria; 2 classrooms; coffee shop; 3 computer laboratories; demonstration laboratory; 2 food production kitchens; gourmet dining room; 2 laboratories; 3 learning resource centers; lecture room; 2 libraries; public restaurant; 3 student lounges; teaching kitchen.

Special Programs

Upper Midwest Hospitality Show, tours of food service distribution facilities (Sysco, Upper Lakes Foods, Fraboni Wholesalers).

Contact

Director of Admissions, Culinary Arts, 1515 East 25th Street, Hibbing, MN 55746. Telephone: 218-262-7228. World Wide Web: http://www.hibbing.edu/.

The International Culinary School at The Art Institutes International Minnesota

Minneapolis, Minnesota

General Information

Private, coeducational institution.

Program Information

Accredited by American Culinary Federation (Associate in Culinary Arts program). Associate degree in Culinary Arts. Associate degree in Baking and Pastry. Bachelor's degree in Hospitality Management. Bachelor's degree in Culinary Management. Certificate in The Art of Cooking. Certificate in Baking and Pastry.

Contact
Office of Admissions, 15 South 9th Street, Minneapolis, MN 55402. Telephone: 612-332-3361. World Wide Web: http://www.artinstitutes.edu/minneapolis/.

See color display following page 332.

Le Cordon Bleu Minneapolis/ St. Paul

Le Cordon Bleu Culinary Program

Mendota Heights, Minnesota

General Information
Private, coeducational, culinary institute. Suburban campus. Founded in 1999. Accredited by Accrediting Commission of Career Schools and Colleges of Technology.

Program Information
Offered since 1999. Accredited by American Culinary Federation. Program calendar is divided into quarters. 15-month associate degree in patisserie and baking. 15-month associate degree in Le Cordon Bleu culinary program. 6-month certificate in Le Cordon Bleu culinary.

Program Affiliation
American Culinary Federation.

Areas of Study
Baking; beverage management; controlling costs in food service; culinary French; culinary skill development; food preparation; food purchasing; food service math; garde-manger; international cuisine; introduction to food service; kitchen management; management and human resources; meal planning; meat cutting; meat fabrication; menu and facilities design; nutrition; patisserie; restaurant opportunities; sanitation; saucier; soup, stock, sauce, and starch production; wines and spirits.

Facilities
3 bakeries; cafeteria; 7 classrooms; 3 computer laboratories; 3 demonstration laboratories; 4 food production kitchens; gourmet dining room; learning resource center; 8 lecture rooms; library; public restaurant; 2 snack shops; student lounge; 6 teaching kitchens.

Typical Student Profile
710 full-time.

Special Programs
Culinary competitions, internship opportunities, clubs and organizations.

Financial Aid
In 2006, 25 scholarships were awarded (average award was $2000). Employment placement assistance is available. Employment opportunities within the program are available.

Application Information
Students may begin participation in January, February, April, June, July, August, October, and November. Applications are accepted continuously. Applicants must interview; submit a formal application.

Contact
Director of Admissions, Le Cordon Bleu Culinary Program, 1315 Mendota Heights Road, Mendota Heights, MN 55120. Telephone: 651-675-4700. Fax: 651-452-5282. World Wide Web: http://www.twincitiesculinary.com/.

South Central College

Culinary Arts

North Mankato, Minnesota

General Information
Public, coeducational, two-year college. Urban campus. Founded in 1947. Accredited by North Central Association of Colleges and Schools.

Program Information
Offered since 1968. Program calendar is divided into semesters. 16-month diploma in restaurant management. 16-month diploma in culinary arts. 24-month associate degree in restaurant management. 24-month associate degree in culinary arts.

Program Affiliation
American Institute of Baking; National Restaurant Association Educational Foundation.

Areas of Study
Baking; food preparation; kitchen management.

Facilities
Bake shop; cafeteria; catering service; 4 classrooms; coffee shop; demonstration laboratory; food production kitchen; garden; lecture room; library; student lounge.

Typical Student Profile
22 total: 18 full-time; 4 part-time. 10 are under 25 years old; 8 are between 25 and 44 years old; 4 are over 44 years old.

Special Programs
Culinary competitions, paid internships in restaurant management.

South Central College *(continued)*

Financial Aid
In 2006, 10 scholarships were awarded (average award was $500); 18 loans were granted (average loan was $5000). Program-specific awards include Toby-Landgraf Scholarship ($700). Employment placement assistance is available.

Application Information
Students may begin participation in January, May, and August. Applications are accepted continuously. In 2006, 25 applied; 25 were accepted. Applicants must submit a formal application.

Contact
Director of Admissions, Culinary Arts, 1920 Lee Boulevard, North Mankato, MN 56003. Telephone: 507-389-7229. Fax: 507-389-8950. World Wide Web: http://www.southcentral.edu/.

Mississippi

Coahoma Community College

Department of Culinary Arts

Clarksdale, Mississippi

General Information
Public, coeducational, two-year college. Rural campus. Founded in 1949. Accredited by Southern Association of Colleges and Schools.

Program Information
Offered since 2006. National Restaurant Association Educational Foundation ManageFirst certificates available. Program calendar is divided into semesters. 1-year certificate in culinary arts. 2-year associate degree in restaurant management. 2-year associate degree in culinary arts.

Areas of Study
Baking; buffet catering; culinary French; food preparation; garde-manger; international cuisine; management and human resources; menu and facilities design; restaurant opportunities; sanitation.

Facilities
Catering service; 2 classrooms; computer laboratory; food production kitchen; gourmet dining room; learning resource center; 2 lecture rooms; library; teaching kitchen.

Typical Student Profile
50 full-time. 20 are under 25 years old; 27 are between 25 and 44 years old; 3 are over 44 years old.

Special Programs
Regional culinary tours/dining tours (Louisiana, the Carolinas, etc.).

Financial Aid
Employment opportunities within the program are available.

Housing
Coed and single-sex housing available.

Application Information
Students may begin participation in January and August. Application deadline for fall is April 1. Application deadline for spring is October 1. In 2006, 50 applied; 50 were accepted. Applicants must submit a formal application and satisfactory scores on ACT and/or Accuplacer tests.

Contact
Director of Admissions, Department of Culinary Arts, 3240 Friars Point Road, Clarksdale, MS 38614. Telephone: 662-621-4205. Fax: 662-621-4297. World Wide Web: http://www.coahomacc.edu/.

Meridian Community College

Hotel and Restaurant Management Technology

Meridian, Mississippi

General Information
Public, coeducational, two-year college. Small-town setting. Founded in 1937. Accredited by Southern Association of Colleges and Schools.

Program Information
Offered since 1970. Program calendar is divided into semesters. 2-year associate degree in hotel and restaurant management.

Program Affiliation
American Hotel and Lodging Association; Mississippi Hotel and Motel Association; National Restaurant Association.

Areas of Study
Baking; beverage management; buffet catering; controlling costs in food service; convenience cookery; culinary skill development; food preparation; food purchasing; food service communication; food service math; garde-manger; international cuisine; introduction to food service; kitchen management; management and human resources; meal planning; meat cutting; meat fabrication; menu and facilities design; nutrition and food service; restaurant opportunities; sanitation; saucier; soup, stock, sauce, and starch production; wines and spirits.

Facilities
Classroom; computer laboratory; demonstration laboratory; food production kitchen; learning resource center; lecture room; teaching kitchen.

Typical Student Profile
33 full-time. 19 are under 25 years old; 12 are between 25 and 44 years old; 2 are over 44 years old.

Special Programs
Mississippi Hotel and Lodging Association Convention and Trade Show, DEX-DECA Management Skills Competition.

Financial Aid
In 2006, 1 scholarship was awarded (award was $1500). Employment placement assistance is available.

Housing
Coed, apartment-style, and single-sex housing available.

Application Information
Students may begin participation in January and August. Application deadline for fall is August 30. Application deadline for spring is January 12. In 2006, 28 applied; 28 were accepted. Applicants must submit a formal application.

Contact
Director of Admissions, Hotel and Restaurant Management Technology, 910 Highway 19 North, Meridan, MS 39307. Telephone: 601-484-8825. Fax: 601-484-8824. World Wide Web: http://www.mcc.cc.ms.us.

Mississippi Gulf Coast Community College

Culinary Arts and Related Food Technology

Perkinston, Mississippi

General Information
Public, coeducational, two-year college. Suburban campus. Founded in 1911. Accredited by Southern Association of Colleges and Schools.

Program Information
Program calendar is divided into semesters. 1-year diploma in food production and management technology.

Program Affiliation
American Culinary Federation.

Areas of Study
Baking; buffet catering; controlling costs in food service; fast foods; food preparation; food purchasing; food service math; meal planning; nutrition; quantity foods; sanitation.

Facilities
2 cafeterias; 2 classrooms; 2 food production kitchens.

Typical Student Profile
25 total: 23 full-time; 2 part-time.

Special Programs
Internship (up to 3 semesters).

Financial Aid
Employment placement assistance is available.

Housing
Single-sex housing available.

Application Information
Students may begin participation in January and August. Applications are accepted continuously. In 2006, 25 applied; 25 were accepted. Applicants must submit a formal application.

Contact
Director of Admissions, Culinary Arts and Related Food Technology, PO Box 609, Perkinston, MS 39573. Telephone: 601-928-6381. Fax: 601-928-6279. World Wide Web: http://www.mgccc.cc.ms.us.

Mississippi University for Women

Culinary Arts Institute

Columbus, Mississippi

General Information
Public, coeducational, comprehensive institution. Small-town setting. Founded in 1884. Accredited by Southern Association of Colleges and Schools.

Program Information
Offered since 1997. Program calendar is divided into semesters. 4-year bachelor's degree in culinary arts.

Program Affiliation
International Association of Culinary Professionals; National Restaurant Association; Research Chefs Association; Southern Foodways Alliance; Women Chefs and Restaurateurs.

Mississippi University for Women *(continued)*

Areas of Study

Baking; buffet catering; controlling costs in food service; culinary skill development; food for special diets; food preparation; food purchasing; food service communication; food service math; garde-manger; international cuisine; introduction to food service; kitchen management; meal planning; meat fabrication; nutrition; nutrition and food service; patisserie; sanitation; saucier; soup, stock, sauce, and starch production.

Facilities

Bake shop; cafeteria; classroom; computer laboratory; demonstration laboratory; 2 food production kitchens; garden; learning resource center; 10 lecture rooms; library; teaching kitchen; food photography kitchen.

Typical Student Profile

100 full-time. 70 are under 25 years old; 25 are between 25 and 44 years old; 5 are over 44 years old.

Special Programs

3-month paid internship, international internship.

Financial Aid

In 2006, 3 scholarships were awarded (average award was $500); 2 loans were granted (average loan was $500). Program-specific awards include internship grant stipend ($1000-2500). Employment placement assistance is available. Employment opportunities within the program are available.

Housing

Coed, apartment-style, and single-sex housing available.

Application Information

Students may begin participation in January, June, and August. Applications are accepted continuously. In 2006, 95 applied; 33 were accepted. Applicants must submit a formal application, SAT or ACT scores, and academic transcripts.

Contact

Director of Admissions, Culinary Arts Institute, 1100 College Street MUW 1639, Columbus, MS 39701-5800. Telephone: 662-241-7472. Fax: 662-241-7627. World Wide Web: http://www.muw.edu/culinary.

Missouri

College of the Ozarks

Hotel and Restaurant Management

Point Lookout, Missouri

General Information

Private, coeducational, four-year college. Small-town setting. Founded in 1906. Accredited by North Central Association of Colleges and Schools.

Program Information

Offered since 1993. Accredited by American Dietetic Association. National Restaurant Association Educational Foundation ManageFirst certificates available. Program calendar is divided into semesters. 4-year bachelor's degree in hotel and restaurant management: meeting and special event management emphasis. 4-year bachelor's degree in hotel and restaurant management: professional food service emphasis. 4-year bachelor's degree in hotel and restaurant management. 4-year bachelor's degree in food and nutrition. 4-year bachelor's degree in dietetics.

Program Affiliation

American Culinary Federation; American Dietetic Association; Council on Hotel, Restaurant, and Institutional Education; Missouri Hotel and Motel Association; National Restaurant Association; National Restaurant Association Educational Foundation.

Areas of Study

Baking; controlling costs in food service; culinary skill development; food preparation; food purchasing; garde-manger; international cuisine; introduction to food service; kitchen management; management and human resources; meal planning; menu and facilities design; nutrition; nutrition and food service; restaurant opportunities; sanitation; seafood processing; soup, stock, sauce, and starch production.

Facilities

Bake shop; cafeteria; catering service; 5 classrooms; computer laboratory; demonstration laboratory; food production kitchen; laboratory; learning resource center; lecture room; public restaurant; snack shop; student lounge; teaching kitchen.

Typical Student Profile

54 full-time. 52 are under 25 years old; 1 is between 25 and 44 years old; 1 is over 44 years old.

Special Programs

Paid internships, travel to regional program-related events and shows, leadership opportunities through student organizations.

Financial Aid
Employment placement assistance is available.

Housing
Single-sex housing available.

Application Information
Students may begin participation in August. Application deadline for fall is February 15. Application deadline for spring a year in advance is January 1. Applicants must interview; submit a formal application, letters of reference, an essay, ACT score, financial information (FAFSA form).

Contact
Director of Admissions, Hotel and Restaurant Management, PO Box 17, Point Lookout, MO 65726. Telephone: 417-239-1900 Ext. 119. Fax: 417-335-8140. World Wide Web: http://www.cofo.edu/.

Jefferson College

Culinary Arts

Hillsboro, Missouri

General Information
Public, coeducational, two-year college. Rural campus. Founded in 1963. Accredited by North Central Association of Colleges and Schools.

Program Information
Offered since 1999. Program calendar is divided into semesters. 1-semester certificate in NRA ServSafe certification. 2-year associate degree in culinary arts. 2-year certificate in culinary arts.

Program Affiliation
National Restaurant Association; National Restaurant Association Educational Foundation.

Areas of Study
Baking; beverage management; buffet catering; controlling costs in food service; culinary skill development; food preparation; food service communication; food service math; garde-manger; international cuisine; introduction to food service; kitchen management; management and human resources; meal planning; meat fabrication; menu and facilities design; nutrition; restaurant opportunities; sanitation; saucier; seafood processing; soup, stock, sauce, and starch production.

Facilities
Classroom; computer laboratory; demonstration laboratory; 2 food production kitchens; learning resource center; library; teaching kitchen.

Typical Student Profile
115 total: 75 full-time; 40 part-time. 40 are under 25 years old; 75 are between 25 and 44 years old.

Special Programs
Culinary competitions.

Housing
Apartment-style housing available.

Application Information
Students may begin participation in January and August. Applications are accepted continuously. In 2006, 210 applied; 105 were accepted. Applicants must submit a formal application.

Contact
Director of Admissions, Culinary Arts, 1000 Viking Drive, Hillsboro, MO 63050. Telephone: 636-797-3000. Fax: 636-789-3535. World Wide Web: http://www.jeffco.edu/.

Penn Valley Community College

Lodging and Food Service Department

Kansas City, Missouri

General Information
Public, coeducational, two-year college. Urban campus. Founded in 1975. Accredited by North Central Association of Colleges and Schools.

Program Information
Offered since 1975. Program calendar is divided into semesters. 4-semester associate degree in food and beverage. 6-semester associate degree in chef apprenticeship (both programs offered jointly with Johnson County Community College).

Typical Student Profile
9 total: 1 full-time; 8 part-time.

Application Information
Students may begin participation in January and August. Applications are accepted continuously. In 2006, 12 applied; 12 were accepted. Applicants must submit a formal application.

Contact
Director of Admissions, Lodging and Food Service Department, 12345 College Boulevard, Overland Park, KS 66210. Telephone: 913-469-8500. World Wide Web: http://www.mcckc.edu/.

St. Louis Community College

Hospitality Studies

St. Louis, Missouri

General Information
Public, coeducational, two-year college. Urban campus. Founded in 1964. Accredited by North Central Association of Colleges and Schools.

Program Information
Offered since 1964. Accredited by American Culinary Federation Accrediting Commission. National Restaurant Association Educational Foundation ManageFirst certificates available. Program calendar is divided into semesters. 1-year certificate in travel and tourism. 1-year certificate in restaurant management. 1-year certificate in hotel management. 1-year certificate in baking and pastry. 2-year associate degree in travel and tourism. 2-year associate degree in hospitality, baking and pastry. 2-year associate degree in hospitality management. 2-year associate degree in hospitality culinary.

Program Affiliation
American Culinary Federation; National Restaurant Association; National Restaurant Association Educational Foundation.

Areas of Study
Baking; culinary skill development.

Facilities
Bake shop; 3 classrooms; computer laboratory; demonstration laboratory; food production kitchen; garden; gourmet dining room; library.

Typical Student Profile
486 total: 227 full-time; 259 part-time.

Special Programs
Continuing education.

Financial Aid
Employment opportunities within the program are available.

Application Information
Students may begin participation in January, May, and August. Applications are accepted continuously.

Contact
Director of Admissions, Hospitality Studies, 5600 Oakland Avenue, St. Louis, MO 63110. Telephone: 314-644-9617. World Wide Web: http://www.stlcc.edu/.

University of Missouri–Columbia

Hotel and Restaurant Management

Columbia, Missouri

General Information
Public, coeducational, university. Small-town setting. Founded in 1839. Accredited by North Central Association of Colleges and Schools.

Program Information
Offered since 1971. Accredited by Council on Hotel, Restaurant and Institutional Education. Program calendar is divided into semesters. 2-Year master's degree in food science/hotel and restaurant management. 4-Year bachelor's degree in hotel and restaurant management.

Program Affiliation
Council on Hotel, Restaurant, and Institutional Education; Educational Institute-American Hotel and Motel Association; Institute of Food Technologists; National Restaurant Association; National Restaurant Association Educational Foundation.

Areas of Study
Beverage management; controlling costs in food service; food preparation; food purchasing; management and human resources; restaurant opportunities; sanitation.

Facilities
3 classrooms; 2 computer laboratories; 2 demonstration laboratories; 2 food production kitchens; lecture room; library; public restaurant; student lounge; 2 teaching kitchens.

Typical Student Profile
315 total: 290 full-time; 25 part-time. 300 are under 25 years old; 14 are between 25 and 44 years old; 1 is over 44 years old.

Special Programs
600-hour internship (paid by industry), self-designed internship.

Financial Aid
In 2006, 11 scholarships were awarded (average award was $1000). Employment placement assistance is available.

Housing
Coed, apartment-style, and single-sex housing available.

Application Information
Students may begin participation in January, June, and August. Applications are accepted continuously. Applicants must submit a formal application.

CONTACT
Director of Admissions, Hotel and Restaurant Management, 122 Eckles Hall, Columbia, MO 65211. Telephone: 573-884-7816. World Wide Web: http://hrm.missouri.edu/.

MONTANA

FLATHEAD VALLEY COMMUNITY COLLEGE

Culinary Arts

Kalispell, Montana

GENERAL INFORMATION
Public, coeducational, two-year college. Rural campus. Founded in 1967. Accredited by Northwest Commission on Colleges and Universities.

PROGRAM INFORMATION
Offered since 2005. Program calendar is divided into semesters. 2-year associate degree in culinary arts.

PROGRAM AFFILIATION
American Culinary Federation.

AREAS OF STUDY
Baking; beverage management; controlling costs in food service; culinary skill development; food preparation; food purchasing; food service communication; kitchen management; meal planning; meat cutting; meat fabrication; menu and facilities design; nutrition; nutrition and food service; patisserie; restaurant opportunities; sanitation; saucier; seafood processing; soup, stock, sauce, and starch production; wines and spirits.

FACILITIES
Classroom; 5 computer laboratories; demonstration laboratory; food production kitchen; laboratory; learning resource center; library; teaching kitchen.

TYPICAL STUDENT PROFILE
27 total: 22 full-time; 5 part-time. 22 are under 25 years old; 5 are between 25 and 44 years old.

SPECIAL PROGRAMS
140-hour internships (2), ten-day cooking tour of France and Italy (2nd year students).

FINANCIAL AID
In 2006, 3 scholarships were awarded (average award was $583). Employment placement assistance is available.

APPLICATION INFORMATION
Students may begin participation in January, June, and September. Applications are accepted continuously. Applicants must submit a formal application.

CONTACT
Director of Admissions, Culinary Arts, 777 Grandview Drive, Kalispell, MT 59901. Telephone: 406-756-3865. Fax: 406-756-3815. World Wide Web: http://www.fvcc.edu/.

THE UNIVERSITY OF MONTANA–MISSOULA

Culinary Arts Department/Food Service Management

Missoula, Montana

GENERAL INFORMATION
Public, coeducational, university. Suburban campus. Founded in 1893. Accredited by Northwest Commission on Colleges and Universities.

PROGRAM INFORMATION
Offered since 1974. Accredited by American Culinary Federation Accrediting Commission. Program calendar is divided into semesters. 1-year certificate in culinary arts. 2-year associate degree in food service management.

PROGRAM AFFILIATION
American Culinary Federation; Council on Hotel, Restaurant, and Institutional Education; International Food Service Executives Association; National Association of College and University Food Service; National Restaurant Association; National Restaurant Association Educational Foundation.

AREAS OF STUDY
Baking; beverage management; buffet catering; confectionery show pieces; controlling costs in food service; convenience cookery; culinary French; culinary skill development; food preparation; food purchasing; food service communication; food service math; garde-manger; international cuisine; introduction to food service; kitchen management; management and human resources; meal planning; meat fabrication; menu and facilities design; nutrition and food service; patisserie; restaurant opportunities; sanitation; saucier; seafood processing; soup, stock, sauce, and starch production; wines and spirits.

FACILITIES
Bake shop; cafeteria; 3 classrooms; 4 computer laboratories; food production kitchen; gourmet dining room; learning resource center; 4 lecture rooms; 2 libraries; student lounge.

The University of Montana–Missoula *(continued)*

Typical Student Profile

30 full-time. 20 are under 25 years old; 7 are between 25 and 44 years old; 3 are over 44 years old.

Special Programs

Specialized internships at local, regional, and national sites, individual culinary competitions (ACF), ACF Junior Team culinary competitions.

Financial Aid

In 2006, 2 scholarships were awarded (average award was $1500); 20 loans were granted (average loan was $6000). Employment placement assistance is available. Employment opportunities within the program are available.

Housing

Coed, apartment-style, and single-sex housing available.

Application Information

Students may begin participation in January and September. Applications are accepted continuously. In 2006, 50 applied; 30 were accepted. Applicants must submit a formal application.

Contact

Director of Admissions, Culinary Arts Department/Food Service Management, 909 South Avenue West, Missoula, MT 59801. Telephone: 406-243-7888. Fax: 406-243-7899. World Wide Web: http://www.cte.umt.edu/.

Nebraska

Central Community College–Hastings Campus

Hospitality Management and Culinary Arts

Hastings, Nebraska

General Information

Public, coeducational, two-year college. Small-town setting. Founded in 1966. Accredited by North Central Association of Colleges and Schools.

Program Information

Offered since 1970. Program calendar is semester plus summer session. 1-year diploma in hospitality services. 1-year diploma in culinary arts. 2-year associate degree in restaurant management. 2-year associate degree in hotel management. 2-year associate degree in culinary arts.

Program Affiliation

Council on Hotel, Restaurant, and Institutional Education; National Restaurant Association.

Areas of Study

Baking; beverage management; confectionery show pieces; controlling costs in food service; culinary skill development; food preparation; food purchasing; food service math; garde-manger; international cuisine; introduction to food service; kitchen management; management and human resources; meal planning; menu and facilities design; nutrition and food service; patisserie; sanitation; saucier; soup, stock, sauce, and starch production.

Facilities

Bake shop; cafeteria; catering service; 3 classrooms; 2 computer laboratories; food production kitchen; learning resource center; 2 lecture rooms; library; public restaurant; teaching kitchen.

Typical Student Profile

45 total: 30 full-time; 15 part-time. 30 are under 25 years old; 10 are between 25 and 44 years old; 5 are over 44 years old.

Special Programs

Annual field trip for club members (Las Vegas, Seattle, Chicago).

Financial Aid

In 2006, 3 scholarships were awarded (average award was $350). Employment placement assistance is available.

Housing

Coed, apartment-style, and single-sex housing available.

Application Information

Students may begin participation in January, February, March, April, May, June, August, September, October, November, and December. Applications are accepted continuously. In 2006, 25 applied; 25 were accepted. Applicants must submit a formal application.

Contact

Director of Admissions, Hospitality Management and Culinary Arts, Box 1024, Hastings, NE 68803. Telephone: 402-463-9811. Fax: 402-461-2506. World Wide Web: http://www.cccneb.edu/igsbase/igstemplate.cfm?SRC=DB&SRCN=&GnavID=134.

Metropolitan Community College

Institute for the Culinary Arts

Omaha, Nebraska

General Information

Public, coeducational, two-year college. Urban campus. Founded in 1974. Accredited by North Central Association of Colleges and Schools.

Program Information

Offered since 1974. Accredited by American Culinary Federation Accrediting Commission, Council on Hotel, Restaurant and Institutional Education. National Restaurant Association Educational Foundation ManageFirst certificates available. Program calendar is divided into quarters. 2-year associate degree in small business practices. 2-year associate degree in lodging transfer. 2-year associate degree in food and beverage management. 2-year associate degree in Culinology (TM). 2-year associate degree in culinary management. 2-year associate degree in culinary arts. 2-year associate degree in convention and meeting planning. 2-year associate degree in bakery arts. 3-year associate degree in chef apprentice.

Program Affiliation

American Culinary Federation; American Institute of Baking; American Wine Society; Council on Hotel, Restaurant, and Institutional Education; International Association of Culinary Professionals; International Wine & Food Society; National Restaurant Association; National Restaurant Association Educational Foundation; Research Chefs Association; The Bread Bakers Guild of America; United States Personal Chef Association.

Areas of Study

Baking; beverage management; buffet catering; controlling costs in food service; convenience cookery; culinary skill development; food preparation; food purchasing; food service communication; food service math; garde-manger; international cuisine; introduction to food service; kitchen management; management and human resources; meal planning; meat fabrication; menu and facilities design; nutrition; nutrition and food service; patisserie; restaurant opportunities; sanitation; saucier; seafood processing; soup, stock, sauce, and starch production; wines and spirits.

Facilities

Bake shop; bakery; cafeteria; catering service; 4 classrooms; 2 coffee shops; computer laboratory; demonstration laboratory; food production kitchen; garden; 2 gourmet dining rooms; 2 laboratories; learning resource center; 4 lecture rooms; library; public restaurant; teaching kitchen.

Typical Student Profile

625 total: 325 full-time; 300 part-time. 300 are under 25 years old; 275 are between 25 and 44 years old; 50 are over 44 years old.

Special Programs

Study tour to annual NRA convention in Chicago; participation in local, regional, and national SkillsUSA competition; paid research and development projects for local food manufacturing companies.

Financial Aid

In 2006, 40 scholarships were awarded (average award was $750). Program-specific awards include Omaha Restaurant Association scholarships (up to $1000), Con Agra scholarships ($1000), International Food & Wine Society Scholarship (up to $1000). Employment placement assistance is available. Employment opportunities within the program are available.

Housing

Coed housing available.

Application Information

Students may begin participation in March, June, September, and December. Applications are accepted continuously. In 2006, 985 applied; 710 were accepted. Applicants must submit a formal application.

Contact

Director of Admissions, Institute for the Culinary Arts, PO Box 3777, Omaha, NE 68103-0777. Telephone: 402-457-2510. Fax: 402-457-2984. World Wide Web: http://www.mccneb.edu/culinary.

Southeast Community College, Lincoln Campus

Food Service/Hospitality

Lincoln, Nebraska

General Information

Public, coeducational, two-year college. Urban campus. Founded in 1973. Accredited by North Central Association of Colleges and Schools.

Program Information

Offered since 1973. Accredited by American Culinary Federation Accrediting Commission, American Dietetic Association. National Restaurant Association Educational Foundation ManageFirst certificates available. Program calendar is divided into quarters. 18-month associate degree in lodging. 18-month associate degree in food service management. 18-month associate degree in dietetic technology. 18-month associate degree in culinary arts.

Southeast Community College, Lincoln Campus (continued)

Program Affiliation
American Culinary Federation; American Dietetic Association; Council on Hotel, Restaurant, and Institutional Education; Dietary Managers Association; National Restaurant Association; National Restaurant Association Educational Foundation.

Areas of Study
Baking; beverage management; buffet catering; controlling costs in food service; culinary French; culinary skill development; food preparation; food purchasing; food service math; garde-manger; introduction to food service; kitchen management; management and human resources; meal planning; meat fabrication; menu and facilities design; nutrition; sanitation; saucier; soup, stock, sauce, and starch production.

Facilities
Bakery; cafeteria; catering service; 5 classrooms; computer laboratory; food production kitchen; gourmet dining room; learning resource center; 2 lecture rooms; library; public restaurant; student lounge; teaching kitchen.

Typical Student Profile
125 total: 90 full-time; 35 part-time. 90 are under 25 years old; 31 are between 25 and 44 years old; 4 are over 44 years old.

Special Programs
Trip to the National Restaurant Association show, culinary competitions.

Financial Aid
In 2006, 4 scholarships were awarded (average award was $300). Employment placement assistance is available. Employment opportunities within the program are available.

Application Information
Students may begin participation in January, March, July, and October. Application deadline for fall is September 1. Application deadline for winter is November 23. Application deadline for spring is February 22. Application deadline for summer is May 17. In 2006, 57 applied; 57 were accepted. Applicants must submit a formal application and have high school diploma or GED.

Contact
Director of Admissions, Food Service/Hospitality, 8800 O Street, Southeast Community College, Lincoln, NE 68520. Telephone: 402-437-2465. Fax: 402-437-2404. World Wide Web: http://www.southeast.edu/discover/lincoln.asp.

Nevada

The International Culinary School at The Art Institute of Las Vegas

Henderson, Nevada

General Information
Private, coeducational institution.

Program Information
Associate degree in Culinary Arts. Associate degree in Baking and Pastry. Bachelor's degree in Food and Beverage Management. Bachelor's degree in Culinary Management.

Contact
Office of Admissions, 2350 Corporate Circle, Henderson, NV 89074-7737. Telephone: 702-369-9944. Fax: 702-992-8558. World Wide Web: http://www.artinstitutes.edu/lasvegas/.

See color display following page 332.

Le Cordon Bleu College of Culinary Arts, Las Vegas

Las Vegas, Nevada

General Information
Private, coeducational, culinary institute. Suburban campus. Founded in 2003. Accredited by Accrediting Commission of Career Schools and Colleges of Technology.

Program Information
Offered since 2003. Program calendar is continuous. 15-month associate degree in culinary arts. 9-month certificate in patisserie and baking.

Application Information
Students may begin participation in January, February, April, May, June, August, September, and November.

Contact
Director of Admissions, 1451 Center Crossing Road, Las Vegas, NV 89144.

UNIVERSITY OF NEVADA, LAS VEGAS

Department of Food and Beverage Management

Las Vegas, Nevada

GENERAL INFORMATION
Public, coeducational, university. Urban campus. Founded in 1957. Accredited by Northwest Commission on Colleges and Universities.

PROGRAM INFORMATION
Offered since 1967. Program calendar is divided into semesters. 4-year bachelor's degree in culinary arts management.

PROGRAM AFFILIATION
American Culinary Federation; American Dietetic Association; Council on Hotel, Restaurant, and Institutional Education; International Food Service Executives Association; National Restaurant Association; National Restaurant Association Educational Foundation; Nevada Restaurant Association; Research Chefs Association; Women Chefs and Restaurateurs.

AREAS OF STUDY
Baking; beers; beverage management; buffet catering; controlling costs in food service; culinary skill development; culture and cuisine; food preparation; food purchasing; food science; food service communication; food service math; garde-manger; introduction to food service; kitchen management; management and human resources; meal planning; menu and facilities design; noncommercial food service; nutrition; nutrition and food service; operations management; quantity foods; quick service; restaurant opportunities; sanitation; saucier; soup, stock, sauce, and starch production; wines and spirits.

FACILITIES
Bake shop; catering service; 25 classrooms; computer laboratory; demonstration laboratory; 2 food production kitchens; 3 gourmet dining rooms; 4 laboratories; 25 lecture rooms; library; public restaurant; 2 teaching kitchens; 2 bar/lounges.

TYPICAL STUDENT PROFILE
185 total: 160 full-time; 25 part-time.

SPECIAL PROGRAMS
5-week summer studies in Switzerland and Australia, local and national internships, local and national conferences and trade shows.

FINANCIAL AID
In 2006, 140 scholarships were awarded (average award was $1500). Program-specific awards include Banfi Research Scholarship. Employment placement assistance is available.

HOUSING
Coed housing available.

APPLICATION INFORMATION
Students may begin participation in January, May, and August. Application deadline for fall is February 1. Application deadline for spring is October 1. Application deadline for summer is February 1. Applicants must submit a formal application.

CONTACT
Director of Admissions, Department of Food and Beverage Management, Harrah Hotel College, Office for Student Advising, Las Vegas, NV 89154-6039. Telephone: 702-895-3616. Fax: 702-895-3127. World Wide Web: http://www.unlv.edu/.

NEW HAMPSHIRE

NEW HAMPSHIRE COMMUNITY TECHNICAL COLLEGE

New Hampshire Culinary Institute

Berlin, New Hampshire

GENERAL INFORMATION
Public, coeducational, two-year college. Rural campus. Founded in 1966. Accredited by New England Association of Schools and Colleges.

PROGRAM INFORMATION
Offered since 1965. Program calendar is divided into semesters. 1-year certificate in culinary arts. 1-year diploma in culinary arts (basic). 2-year associate degree in culinary arts. 2-year associate degree in baking.

PROGRAM AFFILIATION
American Culinary Federation; Institute of Food Technologists; National Restaurant Association.

AREAS OF STUDY
Baking; beverage management; buffet catering; confectionery show pieces; controlling costs in food service; culinary skill development; food preparation; food purchasing; food service communication; food service math; garde-manger; international cuisine; introduction to food service; kitchen management; management and human resources; meal planning; meat cutting; meat fabrication; menu and facilities design; nutrition; nutrition and food service; patisserie; restaurant opportunities; sanitation; saucier; seafood processing; soup, stock, sauce, and starch production; wines and spirits.

New Hampshire Community Technical College (continued)

Facilities
Bakery; cafeteria; catering service; 5 computer laboratories; 2 demonstration laboratories; 3 food production kitchens; garden; gourmet dining room; 2 laboratories; learning resource center; 3 lecture rooms; library; public restaurant; snack shop; student lounge; 2 teaching kitchens.

Typical Student Profile
54 total: 48 full-time; 6 part-time. 51 are under 25 years old; 3 are between 25 and 44 years old.

Special Programs
2-course externship at area restaurants, apprenticeship with Balsams Hotel.

Financial Aid
Employment placement assistance is available.

Application Information
Students may begin participation in January and September. Applications are accepted continuously. Applicants must submit a formal application and high school transcript.

Contact
Director of Admissions, New Hampshire Culinary Institute, 2020 Riverside Drive, Berlin, NH 03570-3717. Telephone: 603-752-1113. Fax: 603-752-6335. World Wide Web: http://www.berlin.nhctc.edu/.

Southern New Hampshire University

The School of Professional and Continuing Education

Manchester, New Hampshire

General Information
Private, coeducational, university. Suburban campus. Founded in 1932. Accredited by New England Association of Schools and Colleges.

Program Information
Offered since 1983. Accredited by American Culinary Federation Accrediting Commission. Program calendar is divided into semesters. 2-year associate degree in culinary arts. 2-year associate degree in baking and pastry arts. 2-year master of business administration in hospitality concentration. 4-year bachelor's degree in food and beverage management. 4-year bachelor's degree in culinary arts. 4-year bachelor's degree in hospitality administration. 9-month certificate in culinary arts. 9-month certificate in baking and pastry arts.

Program Affiliation
American Culinary Federation; Council on Hotel, Restaurant, and Institutional Education; International Association of Culinary Professionals; National Restaurant Association; Retailer's Bakery Association; Women Chefs and Restaurateurs.

Areas of Study
Advanced pastry; bakery management; bakeshop; baking; beverage management; buffet catering; classic cuisine; confectionery show pieces; controlling costs in food service; culinary competition; culinary French; culinary skill development; food preparation; food purchasing; food service communication; food service math; garde-manger; holiday baking; international baking; international cuisine; introduction to culinary arts; introduction to food service; kitchen management; meal planning; meat cutting; menu and facilities design; new American cuisine; nutrition; nutrition and food service; patisserie; principles of supervision; regional American cooking; restaurant opportunities; sanitation; saucier; soup, stock, sauce, and starch production; spa cuisine; table service; wines and spirits.

Facilities
2 bake shops; bakery; cafeteria; catering service; 5 classrooms; coffee shop; 2 computer laboratories; 5 demonstration laboratories; 4 food production kitchens; garden; gourmet dining room; 2 laboratories; learning resource center; 9 lecture rooms; library; public restaurant; snack shop; student lounge; 4 teaching kitchens.

Typical Student Profile
107 total: 105 full-time; 2 part-time. 101 are under 25 years old; 5 are between 25 and 44 years old; 1 is over 44 years old.

Special Programs
Internships at various locations in the United States, 12 month paid internship, 3 week culinary tour/class in Spain, culinary competitions, semester abroad in Italy.

Financial Aid
In 2006, 22 scholarships were awarded (average award was $7000). Employment placement assistance is available. Employment opportunities within the program are available.

Housing
Coed, apartment-style, and single-sex housing available.

APPLICATION INFORMATION
Students may begin participation in September. Applications are accepted continuously. In 2006, 159 applied; 121 were accepted. Applicants must submit a formal application, letters of reference, an essay, academic transcripts.

CONTACT
Director of Admissions, The School of Professional and Continuing Education, 2500 North River Road, Manchester, NH 03106-1045. Telephone: 603-645-9611. Fax: 603-645-9693. World Wide Web: http://www.snhu.edu/.

UNIVERSITY OF NEW HAMPSHIRE

Food Services Management

Durham, New Hampshire

GENERAL INFORMATION
Public, coeducational institution. Small-town setting. Founded in 1895. Accredited by New England Association of Schools and Colleges.

PROGRAM INFORMATION
Offered since 1967. Accredited by American Dietetic Association. National Restaurant Association Educational Foundation ManageFirst certificates available. Program calendar is divided into semesters. 2-year associate degree in restaurant management. 2-year associate degree in dietetic technician.

PROGRAM AFFILIATION
American Dietetic Association; Council on Hotel, Restaurant, and Institutional Education; National Restaurant Association; National Restaurant Association Educational Foundation.

AREAS OF STUDY
Baking; beverage management; buffet catering; controlling costs in food service; convenience cookery; culinary skill development; food preparation; food purchasing; food service communication; garde-manger; international cuisine; introduction to food service; kitchen management; management and human resources; meal planning; nutrition; nutrition and food service; restaurant opportunities; sanitation; saucier; soup, stock, sauce, and starch production; wines and spirits.

FACILITIES
3 cafeterias; catering service; 5 classrooms; computer laboratory; 2 demonstration laboratories; 2 food production kitchens; 2 gardens; learning resource center; 3 lecture rooms; library; 3 public restaurants; student lounge; teaching kitchen.

TYPICAL STUDENT PROFILE
450 total: 425 full-time; 25 part-time.

SPECIAL PROGRAMS
3-month paid internship.

FINANCIAL AID
Employment placement assistance is available.

HOUSING
Coed, apartment-style, and single-sex housing available.

APPLICATION INFORMATION
Students may begin participation in January and September. Application deadline for fall (early action) is November 15. Application deadline for fall (regular admission) is February 1. Application deadline for spring is October 15. In 2006, 500 applied; 350 were accepted. Applicants must submit a formal application, letters of reference, an essay, ACT/SAT scores.

CONTACT
Director of Admissions, Food Services Management, Cole Hall, 291 Mast Road, Durham, NH 03824. Telephone: 603-862-3115. Fax: 603-862-2915. World Wide Web: http://www.thompsonschool.unh.edu/.

NEW JERSEY

ATLANTIC CAPE COMMUNITY COLLEGE

Academy of Culinary Arts

Mays Landing, New Jersey

GENERAL INFORMATION
Public, coeducational, two-year college. Small-town setting. Founded in 1964. Accredited by Middle States Association of Colleges and Schools.

PROGRAM INFORMATION
Offered since 1981. Accredited by American Culinary Federation Accrediting Commission. Program calendar is divided into semesters. 2-year associate degree in pastry/baking. 2-year associate degree in food service management. 2-year associate degree in culinary arts. 3-semester certificate in food service management. 3-semester certificate in culinary arts. 3-semester certificate in baking/pastry. 9-month certificate of specialization in pastry/baking. 9-month certificate of specialization in hot foods. 9-month certificate of specialization in food service management. 9-month certificate of specialization in catering.

Atlantic Cape Community College *(continued)*

Program Affiliation
American Culinary Federation; Center for the Advancement of Food Service Education; Foodservice Educators Network International; International Association of Culinary Professionals; National Restaurant Association; National Restaurant Association Educational Foundation; New Jersey Restaurant Association; Retailer's Bakery Association.

Areas of Study
American regional; baking; buffet catering; charcuterie; confectionery show pieces; controlling costs in food service; culinary skill development; food preparation; food purchasing; food service math; garde-manger; international cuisine; introduction to food service; Italian regional and traditional cooking; kitchen management; meal planning; meat cutting; meat fabrication; menu and facilities design; nutrition; patisserie; restaurant operations; sanitation; saucier; soup, stock, sauce, and starch production; vegetarian cooking; wines and spirits.

Facilities
2 bake shops; 4 classrooms; computer laboratory; food production kitchen; gourmet dining room; learning resource center; 4 lecture rooms; library; public restaurant; 5 teaching kitchens; banquet room.

Student Profile
381 total: 317 full-time; 64 part-time. 291 are under 25 years old; 74 are between 25 and 44 years old; 16 are over 44 years old.

Faculty
18 total: 13 full-time; 5 part-time. 18 are industry professionals; 6 are culinary-certified teachers. Prominent faculty: Mary Theresa McCann, CEPC, MS; Philip Cragg, CEC, CCE, AAC; Annmarie Chelius, CCE, CWPC, MS. Faculty-student ratio: 1:20.

Prominent Alumni and Current Affiliation
Michael Schlow, Chef/Owner, Radius, Via Matta, Great Bay, Alta Strada (in Boston); Bill McCarrick, Pastry Chef, Sir Hans Sloane Chocolate & Champagne House of London; Patricia Nash, Executive Pastry Chef, Motor City Casino Hotel, Detroit.

Special Programs
400-hour cooperative education program, culinary competitions, study abroad.

Typical Expenses
Application fee: $35. In-state tuition: $6180 per semester full-time (in district), $1545 per course part-time (in district), $7243 per semester full-time (out-of-district), $1810 per course part-time (out-of-district). Out-of-state

tuition: $9365 per semester full-time, $2341 per course part-time. Program-related fees include $300 for knives and specialty tools; $400 for textbooks; $350 for uniforms.

Financial Aid

In 2007, 121 scholarships were awarded (average award was $1280); 130 loans were granted (average loan was $3766). Program-specific awards include Press of Atlantic City Restaurant Gala Scholarships, New Jersey STARS. Employment placement assistance is available. Employment opportunities within the program are available.

Housing

Average off-campus housing cost per month: $500.

Application Information

Students may begin participation in January and August. Applications are accepted continuously. In 2007, 411 applied; 411 were accepted. Applicants must submit a formal application.

Contact

Linda McLeod, Assistant Director for College Recruitment, Academy of Culinary Arts, 5100 Black Horse Pike, Mays Landing, NJ 08330-2699. Telephone: 609-343-5009. Fax: 609-343-4921. E-mail: accadmit@atlantic.edu. World Wide Web: http://www.atlantic.edu/aca.

Bergen Community College

Hotel/Restaurant/Hospitality

Paramus, New Jersey

General Information

Public, coeducational, two-year college. Suburban campus. Founded in 1965. Accredited by Middle States Association of Colleges and Schools.

Program Information

Offered since 1974. Program calendar is divided into semesters. 1-semester certificate of achievement in professional cooking. 1-year certificate in hospitality management. 1-year certificate in culinary arts. 2-year associate degree in hospitality management. 2-year associate degree in catering/ banquet management.

Program Affiliation

Council on Hotel, Restaurant, and Institutional Education; National Restaurant Association; National Restaurant Association Educational Foundation; New Jersey Restaurant Association.

Areas of Study

Baking; beverage management; buffet catering; controlling costs in food service; culinary skill development; food preparation; food purchasing; garde-manger; international cuisine; introduction to food service; kitchen management; meal planning; nutrition; sanitation; soup, stock, sauce, and starch production; wines and spirits.

Facilities

Cafeteria; 6 classrooms; 2 computer laboratories; 2 food production kitchens; gourmet dining room; learning resource center; library; public restaurant; snack shop; 2 student lounges; teaching kitchen.

Typical Student Profile

230 total: 170 full-time; 60 part-time. 70 are under 25 years old; 100 are between 25 and 44 years old; 60 are over 44 years old.

Special Programs

Co-op work experience.

Financial Aid

Employment placement assistance is available. Employment opportunities within the program are available.

Application Information

Students may begin participation in January, June, July, and September. Application deadline for fall is August 31. Application deadline for spring is January 14. In 2006, 241 applied; 241 were accepted. Applicants must interview; submit a formal application.

Contact

Director of Admissions, Hotel/Restaurant/Hospitality, 400 Paramus Road-E185A, Paramus, NJ 07052-1595. Telephone: 201-447-7192. Fax: 201-612-5240. World Wide Web: http://www.bergen.edu/.

Brookdale Community College

Asbury Park, New Jersey

General Information

Public, coeducational, two-year college. Founded in 1967. Accredited by Middle States Association of Colleges and Schools.

Program Information

Program calendar is divided into semesters. Certificate in culinary arts. 2-year associate degree in food service management. 2-year associate degree in culinary arts.

Facilities

2 bakeries; 5 classrooms; computer laboratory; 3 food production kitchens; learning resource center; 2 public restaurants.

Special Programs

Externships.

Brookdale Community College *(continued)*

Application Information
Applicants must interview; submit a formal application and high school diploma or equivalent, health screen form.

Contact
Director of Admissions, 765 Newman Springs Road, Lincroft, NJ 07738. Telephone: 732-224-2371. World Wide Web: http://www.brookdalecc.edu/fac/culinary.

Burlington County College

Food Service and Hospitality Management

Pemberton, New Jersey

General Information
Public, coeducational, two-year college. Suburban campus. Founded in 1966. Accredited by Middle States Association of Colleges and Schools.

Program Information
Offered since 1997. Program calendar is semester plus 2 summer terms. 1-year certificate in food service and hospitality management. 1.5-year certificate in cooking and baking. 2-year associate degree in food service and hospitality management.

Program Affiliation
National Restaurant Association Educational Foundation.

Areas of Study
Baking; controlling costs in food service; food preparation; food purchasing; food service math; introduction to food service; management and human resources; managing quantity food service; marketing for hospitality; menu and facilities design; nutrition; nutrition and food service; quality service; sanitation.

Facilities
Classroom; food production kitchen; lecture room.

Typical Student Profile
30 total: 10 full-time; 20 part-time. 10 are under 25 years old; 20 are between 25 and 44 years old.

Financial Aid
Employment placement assistance is available. Employment opportunities within the program are available.

Application Information
Students may begin participation in January, May, July, and September. Application deadline for fall is August 25. Application deadline for spring is January 25. Application deadline for summer is May 25. Applicants must submit a formal application.

Contact
Director of Admissions, Food Service and Hospitality Management, Route 530, Pemberton, NJ 08068-1599. Telephone: 609-894-9311 Ext. 2750. Fax: 609-726-0442. World Wide Web: http://staff.bcc.edu/fsm/Index.htm.

Hudson County Community College

Culinary Arts Institute

Jersey City, New Jersey

General Information
Public, coeducational, two-year college. Urban campus. Founded in 1974. Accredited by Middle States Association of Colleges and Schools.

Program Information
Offered since 1983. Accredited by American Culinary Federation Accrediting Commission. National Restaurant Association Educational Foundation ManageFirst certificates available. Program calendar is divided into semesters. 1-semester certificate in hot food production. 1-semester certificate in garde manger. 1-semester certificate in baking. 1-year certificate in hospitality management. 1-year certificate in culinary arts. 2-year associate degree in hospitality management. 2-year associate degree in culinary arts.

Program Affiliation
American Culinary Federation; Council on Hotel, Restaurant, and Institutional Education; International Council on Hotel, Restaurant and Institutional Education; James Beard Foundation, Inc.; National Restaurant Association; National Restaurant Association Educational Foundation.

Areas of Study
Baking; buffet catering; confectionery show pieces; controlling costs in food service; culinary French; culinary skill development; food preparation; food purchasing; garde-manger; international cuisine; introduction to food service; kitchen management; meal planning; menu and facilities design; nutrition; patisserie; sanitation; saucier; soup, stock, sauce, and starch production; wines and spirits.

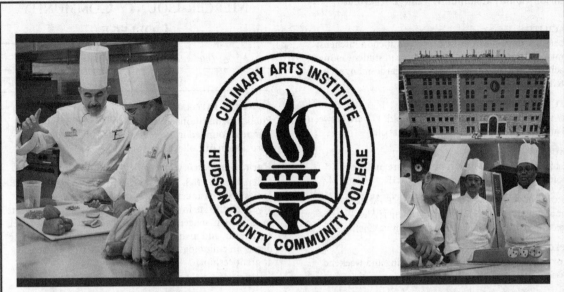

Hudson County Community College *(continued)*

Facilities
2 bake shops; 4 classrooms; 2 food production kitchens; gourmet dining room; public restaurant; student lounge; teaching kitchen; ice carving room; 2 garde-manger kitchens.

Student Profile
417 full-time. 212 are under 25 years old; 117 are between 25 and 44 years old; 84 are over 44 years old.

Faculty
22 total: 8 full-time; 14 part-time. 22 are industry professionals. Faculty-student ratio: 1:15.

Prominent Alumni and Current Affiliation
Omar Giner, La Isla, Hoboken, NJ Owner; Alex Pyka, Executive Chef; Michael Larson, Executive Chef.

Special Programs
Proximity to New York City, day, evening and weekend classes.

Typical Expenses
Application fee: $16. In-state tuition: $15,427 per associate degree; $6499 per certificate full-time (in district), $93 per credit part-time (in district), $21,937 per associate degree; $9528 per certificate full-time (out-of-district), $186 per credit part-time (out-of-district). Out-of-state tuition: $28,447 per associate degree; $12,637 per certificate full-time, $279 per credit part-time. Tuition for international students: $28,447 per associate degree; $12,637 per certificate full-time, $279 per credit part-time. Program-related fees include $240 for knife kit; $260 for uniforms.

Financial Aid
In 2007, 4 scholarships were awarded (average award was $5000). Program-specific awards include Federal and State Financial Aid. Employment placement assistance is available. Employment opportunities within the program are available.

Housing
Average off-campus housing cost per month: $1000.

Application Information
Students may begin participation in January, May, and September. Applications are accepted continuously. In 2007, 627 applied; 627 were accepted. Applicants must submit a formal application and transcripts.

Contact
Janine Nunez, Recruiter, Culinary Arts Institute, 161 Newkirk Street, Jersey City, NJ 07306. Telephone: 201-360-4640. Fax: 201-795-4641. E-mail: cai@hccc.edu or jnunez@hccc.edu. World Wide Web: http://www.hccc.edu/.

See display on page 213.

Mercer County Community College

Hotel and Restaurant Management

Trenton, New Jersey

General Information
Public, coeducational, two-year college. Suburban campus. Founded in 1966. Accredited by Middle States Association of Colleges and Schools.

Program Information
Offered since 1988. Program calendar is divided into semesters. 1-year certificate in professional cooking. 1-year certificate in professional baking. 1-year certificate in catering management. 2-year associate degree in hotel, restaurant, and institution management. 2-year associate degree in culinology. 3-year associate degree in chef apprenticeship.

Application Information
Students may begin participation in January, May, and August. Applications are accepted continuously. Applicants must submit a formal application and high school transcripts or GED, immunization form.

Contact
Director of Admissions, Hotel and Restaurant Management, PO Box B, Trenton, NJ 08690. Telephone: 609-586-4800 Ext. 3447. World Wide Web: http://www.mccc.edu/.

Middlesex County College

Hotel Restaurant and Institution Management

Edison, New Jersey

General Information
Public, coeducational, two-year college. Suburban campus. Founded in 1964. Accredited by Middle States Association of Colleges and Schools.

Program Information
Offered since 1964. Program calendar is divided into semesters. Certificate of achievement in culinary arts. 2-year associate degree in hotel, restaurant, and institution management (with culinary arts option).

Program Affiliation
American Dietetic Association; American Hotel and Lodging Association; Council on Hotel, Restaurant, and Institutional Education; Institute of Food Technologists;

National Association for the Specialty Food Trade, Inc.; National Restaurant Association; National Restaurant Association Educational Foundation.

Areas of Study

Baking; beverage management; controlling costs in food service; culinary skill development; facilities layout and design; food preparation; food purchasing; food service communication; food service math; garde-manger; international cuisine; introduction to food service; kitchen management; management and human resources; meal planning; meat fabrication; menu and facilities design; nutrition; nutrition and food service; restaurant opportunities; sanitation; soup, stock, sauce, and starch production; wines and spirits.

Facilities

Bake shop; cafeteria; catering service; 2 classrooms; computer laboratory; demonstration laboratory; food production kitchen; laboratory; learning resource center; 2 lecture rooms; library; public restaurant; teaching kitchen.

Typical Student Profile

200 total: 125 full-time; 75 part-time.

Special Programs

Externships, cooperative work experiences, Walt Disney World College Program (practicum).

Financial Aid

Employment placement assistance is available. Employment opportunities within the program are available.

Application Information

Students may begin participation in January, May, and August. Application deadline for fall is August 1. Application deadline for spring is December 31. Application deadline for summer is May 1. Applicants must submit a formal application.

Contact

Director of Admissions, Hotel Restaurant and Institution Management, 2600 Woodbridge Avenue, PO Box 3050, Edison, NJ 08818-3050. Telephone: 732-906-2538. Fax: 732-906-7745. World Wide Web: http://www.middlesexcc.edu/.

Technical Institute of Camden County

Culinary Arts

Sicklerville, New Jersey

General Information

Public, coeducational, technical institute. Rural campus. Founded in 1927.

Program Information

Offered since 1927. Accredited by New Jersey Department of Education. Program calendar is divided into semesters. 1-year diploma in culinary arts.

Program Affiliation

National Restaurant Association Educational Foundation.

Areas of Study

Buffet catering; convenience cookery; culinary French; culinary skill development; food preparation; food purchasing; food service communication; food service math; garde-manger; international cuisine; introduction to food service; meal planning; meat cutting; meat fabrication; menu and facilities design; nutrition; nutrition and food service; sanitation; saucier; seafood processing; soup, stock, sauce, and starch production.

Facilities

Cafeteria; 2 classrooms; coffee shop; demonstration laboratory; food production kitchen; gourmet dining room; lecture room; public restaurant; 2 teaching kitchens.

Typical Student Profile

21 full-time. 10 are under 25 years old; 9 are between 25 and 44 years old; 2 are over 44 years old.

Financial Aid

Employment placement assistance is available.

Application Information

Students may begin participation in September. Application deadline for fall is October 15. In 2006, 52 applied; 30 were accepted. Applicants must submit a formal application.

Contact

Director of Admissions, Culinary Arts, 343 Berlin Cross Keys Road, Sicklerville, NJ 08081. Telephone: 856-767-7002. Fax: 856-767-4278. World Wide Web: http://www.ticareers.com/.

THOMAS EDISON STATE COLLEGE

Hospitality Management

Trenton, New Jersey

GENERAL INFORMATION
Public, coeducational, comprehensive institution. Urban campus. Founded in 1972. Accredited by Middle States Association of Colleges and Schools.

PROGRAM INFORMATION
Offered since 1981. Program calendar is continuous. Bachelor's degree in hospitality management.

TYPICAL STUDENT PROFILE
37 part-time.

APPLICATION INFORMATION
Students may begin participation year-round. Applications are accepted continuously. In 2006, 28 applied. Applicants must submit a formal application.

CONTACT
Director of Admissions, Hospitality Management, 101 West State Street, Trenton, NJ 08608. Telephone: 888-442-8372. Fax: 609-984-8447. World Wide Web: http://www.tesc.edu/.

UNION COUNTY COLLEGE

Cranford, New Jersey

GENERAL INFORMATION
Public, coeducational, two-year college. Suburban campus. Founded in 1933. Accredited by Middle States Association of Colleges and Schools.

PROGRAM INFORMATION
Offered since 1996. Program calendar is divided into semesters. 2-year associate degree in restaurant management (offered jointly with Fairleigh Dickinson University). 2-year associate degree in hospitality management.

AREAS OF STUDY
Beverage management; food preparation; food purchasing; food service communication; kitchen management; management and human resources; sanitation.

TYPICAL STUDENT PROFILE
30 total: 21 full-time; 9 part-time. 23 are under 25 years old; 7 are between 25 and 44 years old.

SPECIAL PROGRAMS
Opportunity to transfer to a four-year program in hospitality management.

APPLICATION INFORMATION
Applications are accepted continuously. In 2006, 31 applied; 31 were accepted. Applicants must submit a formal application.

CONTACT
Director of Admissions, 1033 Springfield Avenue, Cranford, NJ 07016. Telephone: 908-709-7596. Fax: 908-709-7131. World Wide Web: http://www.ucc.edu/.

NEW MEXICO

CULINARY BUSINESS ACADEMY

Rio Rancho, New Mexico

GENERAL INFORMATION
Private, coeducational institution. Urban campus. Founded in 1991.

PROGRAM INFORMATION
Offered since 1991. Program calendar is continuous. 100-hour certificate in personal chef (quick start). 100-hour certificate in personal chef (home study). 50-hour certificate in personal chef (mentorship).

PROGRAM AFFILIATION
United States Personal Chef Association.

AREAS OF STUDY
Controlling costs in food service; food purchasing; kitchen management; meal planning; sanitation.

FACILITIES
Classroom; food production kitchen.

TYPICAL STUDENT PROFILE
500 full-time. 25 are under 25 years old; 275 are between 25 and 44 years old; 200 are over 44 years old.

SPECIAL PROGRAMS
USPCA National Conference.

APPLICATION INFORMATION
Students may begin participation year-round. Applications are accepted continuously. In 2006, 500 applied; 500 were accepted. Applicants must have ability to cook.

CONTACT
Director of Admissions, 610 Quantum Road, Rio Rancho, NM 87124. Telephone: 505-994-6392. Fax: 505-994-6399. World Wide Web: http://www.culinarybusiness.com/.

Luna Community College

Culinary Arts Program

Las Vegas, New Mexico

General Information

Public, coeducational, two-year college. Small-town setting. Founded in 1969. Accredited by North Central Association of Colleges and Schools.

Program Information

Offered since 1970. Program calendar is divided into semesters. 18-month certificate in culinary. 2.5-year associate degree in culinary arts. 4-month certificate in NRA ServSafe certification.

Areas of Study

Baking; culinary skill development; nutrition.

Facilities

Bake shop; 7 cafeterias; 5 catering services; 6 computer laboratories; 4 food production kitchens; 7 learning resource centers; 3 lecture rooms; 2 teaching kitchens.

Typical Student Profile

38 total: 15 full-time; 23 part-time. 7 are under 25 years old; 21 are between 25 and 44 years old; 10 are over 44 years old.

Special Programs

Culinary Arts Club monthly activities, Skills USA/VICA competition.

Financial Aid

In 2006, 5 scholarships were awarded (average award was $750); 3 loans were granted (average loan was $1500). Employment placement assistance is available.

Application Information

Students may begin participation in January, June, and August. Applications are accepted continuously. Applicants must submit an application, transcript.

Contact

Director of Admissions, Culinary Arts Program, 366 Luna Drive, Las Vegas, NM 87701. Telephone: 505-454-5346. Fax: 505-454-2588. World Wide Web: http://www.luna.edu/.

New Mexico State University

Hotel, Restaurant, and Tourism Management

Las Cruces, New Mexico

General Information

Public, coeducational, university. Suburban campus. Founded in 1888. Accredited by North Central Association of Colleges and Schools.

Program Information

Offered since 1988. Program calendar is divided into semesters. 4-year bachelor's degree in hotel, restaurant, and tourism management.

Program Affiliation

Council on Hotel, Restaurant, and Institutional Education; National Restaurant Association; National Restaurant Association Educational Foundation.

Areas of Study

Beverage management; controlling costs in food service; culinary skill development; food preparation; food purchasing; food service math; introduction to food service; management and human resources; meal planning; restaurant opportunities; sanitation; soup, stock, sauce, and starch production; wines and spirits.

Facilities

3 classrooms; computer laboratory; demonstration laboratory; food production kitchen.

Typical Student Profile

366 total: 338 full-time; 28 part-time. 305 are under 25 years old; 56 are between 25 and 44 years old; 5 are over 44 years old.

Special Programs

International Hotel Motel Restaurant Show, New York City, NY, National Restaurant Association Restaurant Hotel Motel Show, Chicago, IL, summer internships (paid by industry).

Financial Aid

In 2006, 35 scholarships were awarded (average award was $500). Program-specific awards include industry scholarships outside of university. Employment placement assistance is available. Employment opportunities within the program are available.

Housing

Coed, apartment-style, and single-sex housing available.

Application Information

Students may begin participation in January and August. Applicants must submit a formal application.

New Mexico State University *(continued)*

Contact
Director of Admissions, Hotel, Restaurant, and Tourism Management, PO Box 30001, MSC 3A, Las Cruces, NM 88003-8001. Telephone: 505-646-3121. Fax: 505-646-6330. World Wide Web: http://cahe.nmsu.edu/academics/shrtm/index.html.

The Roswell Job Corps Center

Culinary Arts

Roswell, New Mexico

General Information
Public, coeducational, culinary institute. Rural campus. Founded in 1979. Accredited by North Central Association of Colleges and Schools.

Program Information
Offered since 1979. Program calendar is continuous. 12-month certificate in culinary arts.

Areas of Study
Baking; buffet catering; food preparation; introduction to food service; meal planning; sanitation.

Facilities
12 cafeterias; 8 catering services; 12 classrooms; 12 computer laboratories; 12 food production kitchens; gourmet dining room; student lounge; teaching kitchen.

Typical Student Profile
24 full-time.

Special Programs
Food shows, advanced training at Treasure Island, San Francisco, CA, local and distant catering opportunities.

Financial Aid
In 2006, individual scholarships were awarded at $27,500. Employment placement assistance is available.

Housing
Coed and single-sex housing available.

Application Information
Students may begin participation year-round. Applications are accepted continuously. Applicants must interview; submit a formal application and comprehensive background check; have legal U.S. residence.

Contact
Director of Admissions, Culinary Arts, PO Box 5633, Roswell, NM 88202. Telephone: 505-347-7419. World Wide Web: http://roswell.jobcorps.gov/.

New York

Broome Community College

Hotel Restaurant Management

Binghamton, New York

General Information
Public, coeducational, two-year college. Suburban campus. Founded in 1946. Accredited by Middle States Association of Colleges and Schools.

Program Information
Offered since 1986. Program calendar is divided into semesters. 2-year associate degree in hotel restaurant management.

Program Affiliation
Council on Hotel, Restaurant, and Institutional Education; National Restaurant Association; National Restaurant Association Educational Foundation; New York State Hospitality and Tourism Association.

Areas of Study
Controlling costs in food service; convenience cookery; culinary skill development; food preparation; food service math; management and human resources.

Facilities
3 classrooms; computer laboratory; demonstration laboratory; food production kitchen; laboratory; lecture room; teaching kitchen.

Typical Student Profile
78 total: 63 full-time; 15 part-time. 57 are under 25 years old; 19 are between 25 and 44 years old; 2 are over 44 years old.

Special Programs
American Hotel and Lodging Association and food service trade shows, internship opportunities for credit (one year), study abroad and international internship opportunities.

Financial Aid
Employment placement assistance is available.

Application Information
Students may begin participation in January and September. Applications are accepted continuously. In 2006, 78 applied; 78 were accepted.

Contact
Director of Admissions, Hotel Restaurant Management, PO Box 1017, Binghamton, NY 13902. Telephone: 607-778-5008. World Wide Web: http://www.sunybroome.edu/.

Career Academy of New York

New York, New York

General Information
Founded in 1935. Accredited by Accrediting Commission of Career Schools and Colleges of Technology.

Program Information
Certificate in baking and pastry arts II. Certificate in baking and pastry arts I. 900-hour certificate in hotel and restaurant management. 900-hour certificate in commercial cooking and catering. 900-hour certificate in commercial cooking.

Program Affiliation
American Culinary Federation; American Hotel and Lodging Association; Council on Hotel, Restaurant, and Institutional Education; International Association of Culinary Professionals; National Restaurant Association.

Special Programs
Externship.

Application Information
Applicants must interview; submit a formal application and high school diploma or equivalent.

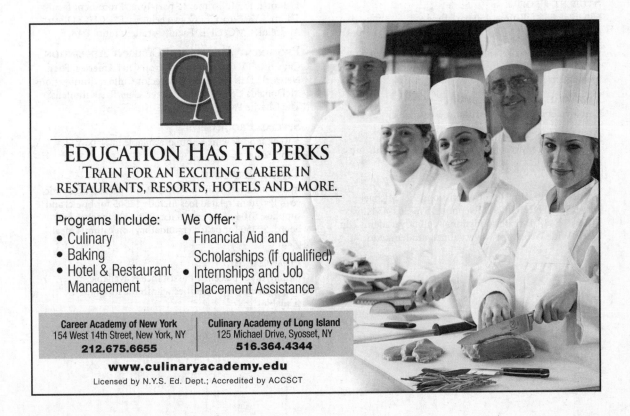

Contact
Director of Student Services, 154 West 14th Street, New York, NY 10011-7307. Telephone: 212-675-6655. World Wide Web: http://www.culinaryacademy.edu/.

Culinary Academy of Long Island

Syosset, New York

General Information
Private, coeducational, culinary institute. Suburban campus. Founded in 1996. Accredited by Accrediting Commission of Career Schools and Colleges of Technology.

Program Information
Offered since 1996. Accredited by American Culinary Federation Accrediting Commission. Program calendar is continuous. 13-session–100 hour certificate in basic baking pastry arts. 13-session–100 hour certificate in advanced baking/pastry arts. 600-hour certificate in professional pastry arts. 600-hour certificate in

Culinary Academy of Long Island *(continued)*

commercial cooking. 900-hour certificate in professional cooking. 900-hour certificate in hotel management (restaurant/management).

Program Affiliation
American Culinary Federation; American Hotel and Lodging Association; Council on Hotel, Restaurant, and Institutional Education; International Association of Culinary Professionals; National Restaurant Association; National Restaurant Association Educational Foundation.

Areas of Study
Baking; buffet catering; controlling costs in food service; culinary skill development; food preparation; food purchasing; food service communication; food service math; garde-manger; international cuisine; kitchen management; management and human resources; meal planning; meat cutting; meat fabrication; menu and facilities design; nutrition; restaurant opportunities; sanitation; saucier; seafood processing; soup, stock, sauce, and starch production.

Facilities
Bake shop; 4 classrooms; computer laboratory; food production kitchen; learning resource center; library; teaching kitchen.

Student Profile
500 total: 350 full-time; 150 part-time.

Typical Expenses
Application fee: $100. Tuition: $11,000–$16,500 per various classes. Program-related fee includes all fees are included in program price.

Financial Aid
Employment placement assistance is available.

Application Information
Applications are accepted continuously. Applicants must interview.

Contact
Derrick Ruffin, Director of Admissions, 125 Michael Drive, Syosset, NY 11791. Telephone: 516-364-4344. Fax: 516-846-8488. E-mail: admissions@culinaryacademy.edu. World Wide Web: http://www.culinaryacademy.edu.

The Culinary Institute of America

Hyde Park, New York

General Information
Private, coeducational, four-year college. Small-town setting. Founded in 1946. Accredited by M, Accrediting Commission of Career Schools and Colleges of Technology.

Program Information
Offered since 1946. Program calendar is continuous. 2-year associate degree in culinary arts. 2-year associate degree in baking and pastry arts. 30-week certificate in culinary arts. 30-week certificate in baking and pastry. 4-year bachelor's degree in culinary arts management. 4-year bachelor's degree in baking and pastry arts management.

Facilities
9 bake shops; library; 5 public restaurants; 32 teaching kitchens.

Student Profile
2823 full-time.

Faculty
178 total: 133 full-time; 45 part-time. Prominent faculty: Thomas Vaccaro, CEPC; Eve Felder, CEC, CHC; Oliver Andreini, CMC, CHE. Faculty-student ratio: 1:18.

Prominent Alumni and Current Affiliation
Cat Cora, TV Celebrity Chef, Iron Chef America, Food Network; Dan Coudreaut, Director Culinary Innovations, McDonalds USA; Charlie Palmer, Chef/Restauranteur, The Charlie Palmer Group.

Special Programs
3-week food & wine seminar available in Napa Valley, CA; Spain & Italy.

Typical Expenses
Application fee: $50. Tuition: $22,330 per full academic year. Program-related fees include $1505 for books and supplies; $1040 for general fee; $10,230 for room and board; $5350 for board (mandatory) on campus meal plan.

Financial Aid
Employment placement assistance is available. Employment opportunities within the program are available.

Housing
Coed housing available.

The Culinary Institute of America *(continued)*

Application Information

In 2007, 1115 applied; 832 were accepted. Applicants must submit a formal application, letters of reference, an essay, academic transcript, interview (for bachelor's degree), assessment test.

Contact

Rachel Birchwood, Director of Admissions, 1946 Campus Drive, Hyde Park, NY 12538. Telephone: 800-CULINARY. Fax: 845-451-1068. E-mail: admissions@culinary.edu. World Wide Web: http://www.ciachef.edu/.

See display on page 221.

Erie Community College, City Campus

Culinary Arts

Buffalo, New York

General Information

Public, coeducational, two-year college. Urban campus. Founded in 1971. Accredited by Middle States Association of Colleges and Schools.

Program Information

Offered since 1984. Program calendar is divided into semesters. 1-year certificate in baking and pastry arts. 2-year associate degree in culinary arts.

Program Affiliation

American Culinary Federation; National Restaurant Association; National Restaurant Association Educational Foundation.

Areas of Study

Baking; beverage management; buffet catering; confectionery show pieces; controlling costs in food service; culinary skill development; food preparation; food purchasing; food service math; garde-manger; international cuisine; introduction to food service; kitchen management; management and human resources; meal planning; menu and facilities design; nutrition; sanitation; soup, stock, sauce, and starch production; wines and spirits.

Facilities

Bake shop; bakery; cafeteria; classroom; coffee shop; computer laboratory; 2 food production kitchens; gourmet dining room; learning resource center; library; 3 teaching kitchens.

Typical Student Profile

83 total: 71 full-time; 12 part-time. 46 are under 25 years old; 31 are between 25 and 44 years old; 6 are over 44 years old.

Financial Aid

In 2006, 50 scholarships were awarded (average award was $700); 40 loans were granted (average loan was $1500). Program-specific awards include Statler Foundation Scholarship. Employment placement assistance is available. Employment opportunities within the program are available.

Application Information

Students may begin participation in January and September. Applications are accepted continuously. In 2006, 126 applied; 92 were accepted. Applicants must submit a formal application.

Contact

Director of Admissions, Culinary Arts, 121 Ellicott Street, Buffalo, NY 14203-2698. Telephone: 716-851-1034. Fax: 716-851-1133. World Wide Web: http://www.ecc.edu/.

Erie Community College, North Campus

Food Service Administration/Restaurant Management

Williamsville, New York

General Information

Public, coeducational, two-year college. Suburban campus. Founded in 1946. Accredited by Middle States Association of Colleges and Schools.

Program Information

Offered since 1953. Accredited by American Dietetic Association, Council on Hotel, Restaurant and Institutional Education, Commission on Accreditation of Hospitality Management Programs. Program calendar is divided into semesters. 2-year associate degree in hotel/restaurant management. 2-year associate degree in food service administration: dietetic technology/nutrition. 2-year associate degree in culinary arts.

Program Affiliation

American Culinary Federation; American Dietetic Association; Confrerie de la Chaine des Rotisseurs; Council on Hotel, Restaurant, and Institutional Education; International Food Service Executives Association; International Foodservice Editorial Council; National Restaurant Association; National Restaurant Association Educational Foundation; New York State Restaurant Association.

Areas of Study

Baking; beverage management; buffet catering; controlling costs in food service; culinary skill development; food preparation; food purchasing; food service communication; food service math; garde-manger; international cuisine; introduction to food service; kitchen management; management and human resources; meal planning; menu and facilities design; nutrition; nutrition and food service; sanitation; soup, stock, sauce, and starch production; wines and spirits.

Facilities

Bake shop; bakery; cafeteria; 2 classrooms; computer laboratory; demonstration laboratory; 3 food production kitchens; gourmet dining room; laboratory; lecture room; library; 2 public restaurants; student lounge; teaching kitchen.

Typical Student Profile

250 total: 201 full-time; 49 part-time. 169 are under 25 years old; 65 are between 25 and 44 years old; 16 are over 44 years old.

Special Programs

8-week off-campus internship, culinary competitions.

Financial Aid

In 2006, 50 scholarships were awarded (average award was $500–$750). Program-specific awards include Erie Community College Foundation scholarships; American Dietetic Association Scholarship, Gertrude Chrymko Memorial Scholarship, Statler Foundation Scholarships, New York State Restaurant Association Scholarships. Employment placement assistance is available. Employment opportunities within the program are available.

Application Information

Students may begin participation in January and September. Applications are accepted continuously. In 2006, 207 applied; 181 were accepted. Applicants must submit a formal application.

Contact

Director of Admissions, Food Service Administration/Restaurant Management, 6205 Main Street, Williamsville, NY 14221. Telephone: 716-851-1391. Fax: 716-851-1429. World Wide Web: http://www.ecc.edu/.

The French Culinary Institute at The International Culinary Center

New York, New York

General Information

Private, coeducational, culinary institute. Urban campus. Founded in 1984. Accredited by Accrediting Commission of Career Schools and Colleges of Technology.

Program Information

Offered since 1984. Accredited by Accrediting Commission of Career Schools and Colleges of Technology. Program calendar is continuous, six-week cycles. 100-hour certificate in Pastry Techniques. 110-hour certificate in Culinary Techniques. 12-hour certificate in Magic Potions: Hydrocolloids. 15-hour certificate in Knife Skills, Deboning, & Filleting. 15-hour certificate in Chocolate Desserts. 15-week certificate in Restaurant Management. 2-month certificate in The Art of International Bread Baking. 25-hour certificate in Fondant & Royal Icing. 25-hour certificate in Breakfast Breads, Pastries, & more. 30-hour certificate in Artisanal Bread Baking. 6-month certificate in Classic Pastry Arts. 6-month certificate in Classic Culinary Arts. 6-week certificate in Food & Wine Pairing. 60-hour certificate in Culinary Techniques 2. 8-week certificate in Fundamentals of Wine. 8-week certificate in Essentials of Fine Cooking.

Program Affiliation

American Institute of Baking; American Institute of Wine & Food; Chefs Collaborative 2000; Council on Hotel, Restaurant, and Institutional Education; Federation of Dining Rooms Professionals; International Association of Culinary Professionals; James Beard Foundation, Inc.; National Restaurant Association; National Restaurant Association Educational Foundation; Slow Food International; The Bread Bakers Guild of America; Women Chefs and Restaurateurs.

Areas of Study

Baking; beverage management; buffet catering; confectionery show pieces; controlling costs in food service; culinary French; culinary skill development; food preparation; food purchasing; food service math; garde-manger; introduction to food service; kitchen management; management and human resources; meal planning; meat cutting; meat fabrication; menu and facilities design; nutrition; nutrition and food service; patisserie; restaurant opportunities; sanitation; saucier; seafood processing; soup, stock, sauce, and starch production; wines and spirits.

The French Culinary Institute at The International Culinary Center ***(continued)***

Facilities
4 classrooms; computer laboratory; demonstration laboratory; food production kitchen; gourmet dining room; 4 lecture rooms; library; public restaurant; student lounge; 13 teaching kitchens.

Student Profile
1,098 total: 463 full-time; 635 part-time. 284 are under 25 years old; 375 are between 25 and 44 years old; 40 are over 44 years old.

Faculty
55 total: 55 full-time. Prominent faculty: Jacques Pépin; André Soltner; Alain Sailhac; Jacques Torres; Alan Richman. Faculty-student ratio: 1:12.

Prominent Alumni and Current Affiliation
Bobby Flay, Mesa Grill, Bolo, Bar Americain; Dan Barber, Blue Hill and Blue Hill of Stone Barns; Wylie Dufresne, wd~50.

Special Programs
Demonstrations in The International Culinary Theater by nightly acclaimed chefs and industry professionals, Internships and on-going Job Placement, Student clubs & Activities: Supper Club, Wine Club, Career Avenues, Forager Club, International Student Club, Real-World Restaurant experience working at The FCI's on-campus highly rated restaurant L' Ecole (available only to students enrolled in classic culinary arts).

Typical Expenses
Application fee: $100. Tuition: Tuition varies by program. Contact school directly for current costs. Program-related fees include $10 for insurance; $40–$700 for books, tools, and uniforms.

Financial Aid
In 2007, 23 scholarships were awarded (average award was $5786). Program-specific awards include Sallie Mae Signature Loan. Employment placement assistance is available. Employment opportunities within the program are available.

Housing
Coed and apartment-style housing available. Average on-campus housing cost per month: $1060. Average off-campus housing cost per month: $2000.

Application Information
Students may begin participation year-round. Applications are accepted continuously. In 2007, 1,990 applied; 1,968 were accepted. Applicants must interview; submit a formal application, an essay, proof of high school graduation or equivalent and resume (career programs only).

Contact
Claudia Ramone, Director of Admission, 462 Broadway, 4th Floor, New York, NY 10013. Telephone: 888-324-CHEF. Fax: 212-431-3065. E-mail: info@frenchculinary.com. World Wide Web: http://www.frenchculinary.com/.

See color display following page 236.

Genesee Community College

Tourism and Hospitality Management

Batavia, New York

General Information
Public, coeducational, two-year college. Small-town setting. Founded in 1967. Accredited by Middle States Association of Colleges and Schools.

Program Information
Offered since 1967. Program calendar is divided into semesters. 2-year associate degree in tourism and hospitality management. 2-year certificate in hospitality management.

Areas of Study
Management and human resources.

Typical Student Profile
17 total: 14 full-time; 3 part-time.

Housing
Coed housing available.

Application Information
Students may begin participation in January and August. In 2006, 42 applied.

Contact
Director of Admissions, Tourism and Hospitality Management, 1 College Road, Batavia, NY 14020. Telephone: 866-CALLGCC. Fax: 585-345-6842. World Wide Web: http://www.genesee.edu/.

The Institute of Culinary Education

Culinary Arts; Pastry and Baking Arts; Culinary Management

New York, New York

General Information
Private, coeducational, culinary institute. Urban campus. Founded in 1975. Accredited by Accrediting Commission of Career Schools and Colleges of Technology.

Program Information
Offered since 1975. Accredited by Accrediting Commission of Career Schools and Colleges of Technology (ACCSCT). Program calendar is continuous. 26-week diploma in full-time career Pastry and Baking Arts. 26-week diploma in full-time career Culinary Management. 28-week diploma in full-time career Culinary Arts. 31-week diploma in part-time career Pastry and Baking Arts. 34-week diploma in part-time career Culinary Arts. 39-week diploma in weekend part-time Culinary Arts. 39-week diploma in weekend part-time career Pastry and Baking Arts.

Program Affiliation
American Institute of Wine & Food; International Association of Culinary Professionals; International Wine & Food Society; James Beard Foundation, Inc.; National Restaurant Association; National Restaurant Association Educational Foundation; Society of Wine Educators; Sommelier Society of America; The Bread Bakers Guild of America; United States Personal Chef Association; Women Chefs and Restaurateurs.

Areas of Study
Baking; beverage management; buffet catering; controlling costs in food service; culinary French; culinary skill development; food preparation; food purchasing; food service communication; food service math; garde-manger; international cuisine; introduction to food service; kitchen management; management and human resources; meal planning; meat cutting; meat fabrication; menu and facilities design; nutrition; nutrition and food service; patisserie; restaurant opportunities; sanitation; seafood processing; soup, stock, sauce, and starch production; wines and spirits.

Facilities
Bake shop; catering service; 3 classrooms; 2 demonstration laboratories; food production kitchen; lecture room; library; 2 student lounges; 12 teaching kitchens.

Student Profile
750 total: 586 full-time; 164 part-time. 101 are under 25 years old; 577 are between 25 and 44 years old; 72 are over 44 years old.

Faculty
32 total: 24 full-time; 8 part-time. Prominent faculty: Nick Malgieri; Toba Garrett; Michael Handel, CCC, CCE; Chris Gesaldi. Faculty-student ratio: 1:14.

Prominent Alumni and Current Affiliation
Marc Murphy, Chef/Owner, Landmarc; Gina DePalma, Executive Pastry Chef, Babbo; Susan Stockton, Vice President of Culinary Production, Food Network,.

Special Programs
210-hours in critically-acclaimed restaurants, hotels, pastry or catering facilities. Sites include: Union Square Café, Le Bernadin, Gramercy Tavern, Daniel, Mesa Grill, and Nobu, 9-day student trip to France including cooking and baking classes, market visits and vineyard tours, elective classes on specialized wine, baking, and cooking topics. Advanced pastry program with visiting masters are available for alumni via ICE's Center for Advance Pastry Studies (CAPS).

Typical Expenses
Tuition: $28,017 for Culinary Arts Diploma program, including supplies; $12,900 for Culinary Management program; $26,334 for Pastry & Baking Arts Diploma program.

Financial Aid
In 2007, 47 scholarships were awarded (average award was $4000); 450 loans were granted (average loan was $27,000). Program-specific awards include career placement services are available.

Application Information
Students may begin participation year-round. Applications are accepted continuously. In 2007, 1,856 applied; 750 were accepted. Applicants must interview; submit a formal application and schedule a personal school tour.

Contact
Brian Aronowitz, Admissions Department, Culinary Arts; Pastry and Baking Arts; Culinary Management, Institute of Culinary Education, 50 West 23rd Street, 5th Floor, New York, NY 10010. Telephone: 888-861-CHEF. E-mail: brian@iceculinary.com. World Wide Web: http://www.ICEculinary.com/.

See color display following page 236.

Julie Sahni's School of Indian Cooking

Brooklyn, New York

General Information
Private, coeducational, culinary institute. Urban campus. Founded in 1974.

Program Information
Offered since 1974. Program calendar is divided into weekends, weekends. 3-day diploma in vegetarian cooking. 3-day diploma in spices and herbs. 3-day diploma in Indian cooking.

Program Affiliation
International Association of Culinary Professionals.

Julie Sahni's School of Indian Cooking *(continued)*

Areas of Study
Indian cooking; international cuisine; spices and herbs.

Application Information
Students may begin participation in January, February, March, April, May, June, September, October, November, and December. Applications are accepted continuously. Applicants must submit a formal application.

Contact
Director of Admissions, PO Box 023792, Brooklyn, NY 11202-3792. Telephone: 718-772-5600. Fax: 718-625-3958.

Mohawk Valley Community College

Hospitality Programs

Rome, New York

General Information
Public, coeducational, two-year college. Urban campus. Founded in 1946. Accredited by Middle States Association of Colleges and Schools.

Program Information
Offered since 1980. Program calendar is divided into semesters. 1-year certificate in chef training. 2-year associate degree in hotel technology: meeting services management. 2-year associate degree in food service administration: restaurant management. 2-year associate degree in culinary arts management.

Program Affiliation
American Culinary Federation; Council on Hotel, Restaurant, and Institutional Education; International Food Service Executives Association; National Restaurant Association; National Restaurant Association Educational Foundation.

Areas of Study
Baking; beverage management; buffet catering; controlling costs in food service; culinary skill development; food preparation; food purchasing; food service math; garde-manger; international cuisine; kitchen management; management and human resources; meal planning; meat cutting; meat fabrication; menu and facilities design; nutrition; patisserie; restaurant opportunities; sanitation; saucier; seafood processing; soup, stock, sauce, and starch production; wines and spirits.

Facilities
Bake shop; catering service; 6 classrooms; computer laboratory; demonstration laboratory; 2 food production kitchens; gourmet dining room; learning resource center; library; public restaurant; snack shop; student lounge; teaching kitchen; banquet room.

Typical Student Profile
120 total: 80 full-time; 40 part-time.

Special Programs
Annual participation in National Restaurant Association and International Hotel and Motel Association shows, semester-long internship/co-op experience.

Financial Aid
Employment placement assistance is available. Employment opportunities within the program are available.

Application Information
Students may begin participation in January, May, and August. Applications are accepted continuously. Applicants must submit a formal application.

Contact
Director of Admissions, Hospitality Programs, 1101 Floyd Avenue, Rome, NY 13440. Telephone: 315-334-7702. World Wide Web: http://www.mvcc.edu/.

Monroe College

Hospitality Management

New Rochelle, New York

General Information
Private, coeducational, four-year college. Suburban campus. Founded in 1933. Accredited by Middle States Association of Colleges and Schools.

Program Information
Offered since 1993. Program calendar is divided into trimesters. 16-month associate degree in hotel/restaurant management. 16-month associate degree in culinary arts. 16-month associate degree in baking and pastry arts. 32-month bachelor's degree in hotel/restaurant management.

Program Affiliation
American Culinary Federation; American Hotel and Lodging Association; Caribbean Tourism Association; Council on Hotel, Restaurant, and Institutional Education; International Association of Culinary Professionals; James Beard Foundation, Inc.; National

Restaurant Association; National Restaurant Association Educational Foundation; Sommelier Society of America; The Bread Bakers Guild of America; Women Chefs and Restaurateurs.

Areas of Study

Baking; confectionery show pieces; culinary skill development; food preparation; food purchasing; food service math; garde-manger; international cuisine; introduction to food service; kitchen management; management and human resources; menu and facilities design; patisserie; restaurant opportunities; sanitation; soup, stock, sauce, and starch production.

Facilities

Bake shop; bakery; 10 classrooms; 6 computer laboratories; demonstration laboratory; 2 food production kitchens; garden; gourmet dining room; 3 laboratories; 2 learning resource centers; 10 lecture rooms; 2 libraries; public restaurant; student lounge; 3 teaching kitchens.

Typical Student Profile

658 total: 644 full-time; 14 part-time.

Special Programs

Paid internships in New York City, semester of study abroad in Italy, residential internships abroad.

Financial Aid

In 2006, 10 scholarships were awarded (average award was $4500). Program-specific awards include industry scholarships, Trades Council (NYC Hotel) scholarship, AH&LA Foundation scholarship. Employment placement assistance is available. Employment opportunities within the program are available.

Housing

Coed, apartment-style, and single-sex housing available.

Application Information

Students may begin participation in January, May, and September. Applications are accepted continuously. In 2006, 613 applied; 179 were accepted. Applicants must interview; submit a formal application, letters of reference, and an essay.

Contact

Director of Admissions, Hospitality Management, 434 Main Street, New Rochelle, NY 10801. Telephone: 914-632-5400. Fax: 914-632-8506. World Wide Web: http://www.monroecollege.edu/.

Monroe Community College

Department of Hospitality Management

Rochester, New York

General Information

Public, coeducational, two-year college. Suburban campus. Founded in 1961. Accredited by Middle States Association of Colleges and Schools.

Program Information

Offered since 1967. National Restaurant Association Educational Foundation ManageFirst certificates available. Program calendar is divided into semesters. 16-month certificate in travel and tourism. 16-month certificate in hotel management. 16-month certificate in food management. 16-month certificate in culinary arts. 2-year associate degree in hospitality management-travel and tourism. 2-year associate degree in hospitality management-physical fitness. 2-year associate degree in hospitality management-hotel. 2-year associate degree in hospitality management-golf management. 2-year associate degree in hospitality management-food service.

Program Affiliation

American Culinary Federation; American Dietetic Association; Council on Hotel, Restaurant, and Institutional Education; International Food Service Executives Association; National Restaurant Association; National Restaurant Association Educational Foundation.

Areas of Study

Baking; beverage management; buffet catering; controlling costs in food service; culinary French; culinary skill development; food preparation; food purchasing; introduction to food service; kitchen management; management and human resources; meal planning; menu and facilities design; nutrition; nutrition and food service; restaurant opportunities; sanitation; soup, stock, sauce, and starch production.

Facilities

2 cafeterias; 2 catering services; coffee shop; 12 computer laboratories; 4 demonstration laboratories; 3 food production kitchens; gourmet dining room; 10 learning resource centers; 2 libraries; public restaurant; snack shop; 2 student lounges; 3 teaching kitchens.

Typical Student Profile

327 total: 247 full-time; 80 part-time. 164 are under 25 years old; 120 are between 25 and 44 years old; 43 are over 44 years old.

Special Programs

Visits to various culinary conventions, culinary tour of Italy-Florence Culinary Institute.

Monroe Community College ***(continued)***

Financial Aid

In 2006, 15 scholarships were awarded (average award was $1000). Employment placement assistance is available. Employment opportunities within the program are available.

Housing

Coed housing available.

Application Information

Students may begin participation in January, May, June, and September. Applications are accepted continuously. In 2006, 445 applied; 311 were accepted. Applicants must submit a formal application.

Contact

Director of Admissions, Department of Hospitality Management, 1000 East Henrietta Road, Rochester, NY 14623. Telephone: 585-292-2580. Fax: 585-292-3826. World Wide Web: http://www.monroecc.edu/.

Nassau Community College

Garden City, New York

General Information

Public, coeducational, two-year college. Suburban campus. Founded in 1959. Accredited by Middle States Association of Colleges and Schools.

Program Information

Offered since 1973. Program calendar is divided into semesters. 1-year certificate in food service technology. 1-year certificate in dietary management. 2-year associate degree in hotel technology administration. 2-year associate degree in food service administration. 2-year associate degree in food and nutrition.

Program Affiliation

American Culinary Federation; American Dietetic Association; Council on Hotel, Restaurant, and Institutional Education; National Restaurant Association; National Restaurant Association Educational Foundation.

Areas of Study

Baking; beverage management; buffet catering; controlling costs in food service; culinary skill development; food preparation; food purchasing; garde-manger; international cuisine; introduction to food service; kitchen management; management and human resources; meal planning; meat cutting; meat fabrication; menu and facilities design; nutrition and food service; restaurant opportunities; sanitation; saucier; soup, stock, sauce, and starch production; wines and spirits.

Facilities

Bake shop; 3 cafeterias; catering service; 3 classrooms; 3 coffee shops; 2 computer laboratories; 3 demonstration laboratories; 4 food production kitchens; 2 laboratories; 5 learning resource centers; 6 lecture rooms; library; 2 snack shops; student lounge; 2 teaching kitchens.

Special Programs

6-month internship at Walt Disney World, 2-week international study abroad (Italy), 4-6 month international work co-op (England).

Financial Aid

In 2006, 3 scholarships were awarded (average award was $500). Employment placement assistance is available. Employment opportunities within the program are available.

Application Information

Students may begin participation in January and September. Applications are accepted continuously.

Contact

Director of Admissions, Hotel/Restaurant Department, Building K, Garden City, NY 11530. Telephone: 516-572-7344. Fax: 516-572-9739. World Wide Web: http://www.sunynassau.edu/.

The Natural Gourmet Institute for Health and Culinary Arts

Chef's Training Program

New York, New York

General Information

Private, coeducational, culinary institute. Urban campus. Founded in 1977. Accredited by Accrediting Council for Continuing Education and Training.

Program Information

Program calendar is continuous. 5-month (full-time), 11 month (part-time) diploma in health-supportive culinary arts.

Program Affiliation

International Association of Culinary Professionals; James Beard Foundation, Inc.

Areas of Study

Baking; business and career skills; controlling costs in food service; culinary skill development; food preparation; food purchasing; food service math; garde-manger; international cooking; international cuisine; living foods; meal planning; nutrition; sanitation;

saucier; seafood processing; soup, stock, sauce, and starch production; teaching a cooking class; theoretical approaches to diet and health.

Facilities

3 food production kitchens; 2 lecture rooms; library; student lounge.

Typical Student Profile

165 total: 100 full-time; 65 part-time. 20 are under 25 years old; 125 are between 25 and 44 years old; 20 are over 44 years old.

Special Programs

Individualized internships, culinary tours of New York City.

Financial Aid

In 2006, 2 scholarships were awarded (average award was $1000). Employment placement assistance is available.

Application Information

Students may begin participation year-round. Applications are accepted continuously. In 2006, 190 applied; 165 were accepted. Applicants must interview; submit a formal application, letters of reference, an essay, documentation of education.

Contact

Director of Admissions, Chef's Training Program, 48 West 21st Street, 2nd Floor, New York, NY 10010. Telephone: 212-645-5170 Ext. 109. Fax: 212-989-1493. World Wide Web: http://www.naturalgourmetschool.com/.

New York City College of Technology of the City University of New York

Hospitality Management

Brooklyn, New York

General Information

Public, coeducational, four-year college. Urban campus. Founded in 1946. Accredited by Middle States Association of Colleges and Schools.

Program Information

Offered since 1947. Accredited by Council on Hotel, Restaurant and Institutional Education, ACPHA-Accrediting Commission for Programs in Hospitality Administration. Program calendar is divided into semesters. 2-year associate degree in hospitality management. 4-year bachelor's degree in hospitality management.

Program Affiliation

American Culinary Federation; American Institute of Wine & Food; Council on Hotel, Restaurant, and Institutional Education; International Association of Culinary Professionals; James Beard Foundation, Inc.; National Restaurant Association; National Restaurant Association Educational Foundation; Women Chefs and Restaurateurs.

Areas of Study

Baking; beverage management; confectionery show pieces; controlling costs in food service; culinary French; food preparation; food purchasing; garde-manger; introduction to food service; management and human resources; meal planning; menu and facilities design; nutrition; patisserie; sanitation; saucier; seafood processing; soup, stock, sauce, and starch production; wines and spirits.

Facilities

2 bake shops; 4 classrooms; 2 computer laboratories; demonstration laboratory; food production kitchen; gourmet dining room; laboratory; learning resource center; 3 lecture rooms; library; teaching kitchen.

Typical Student Profile

740 total: 630 full-time; 110 part-time.

Special Programs

Summer work abroad (hotels and restaurants in France, Germany, Italy, and Spain), study abroad in Paris, Disney internships.

Financial Aid

In 2006, 30 scholarships were awarded (average award was $1500). Employment placement assistance is available.

Application Information

Students may begin participation in February and September. Applications are accepted continuously. Applicants must submit a formal application.

Contact

Director of Admissions, Hospitality Management, 300 Jay Street N220, Brooklyn, NY 11201. Telephone: 718-260-5630. Fax: 718-254-8682. World Wide Web: http://www.citytech.cuny.edu/.

New York Institute of Technology

Center for Hospitality and Culinary Arts

Central Islip, New York

General Information

Private, coeducational, comprehensive institution. Suburban campus. Founded in 1955. Accredited by Middle States Association of Colleges and Schools.

Program Information

Offered since 1985. Accredited by American Culinary Federation Accrediting Commission. Program calendar is divided into semesters. 2-year associate degree in culinary arts. 4-year bachelor's degree in hospitality management. 500-hour certificate in culinary arts. 500-hour certificate in baking and pastry arts.

Program Affiliation

American Culinary Federation; American Institute of Wine & Food; Council on Hotel, Restaurant, and Institutional Education; International Association of Culinary Professionals; National Restaurant Association; National Restaurant Association Educational Foundation; Oldways Preservation and Exchange Trust; Women Chefs and Restaurateurs.

Areas of Study

Allergy specific foods and service; artisanal breads; baking; beverage management; buffet catering; confectionery show pieces; controlling costs in food service; convenience cookery; culinary horticulture; culinary skill development; food preparation; food purchasing; food service communication; food service math; garde-manger; international cuisine; kitchen management; management and human resources; meal planning; meat cutting; meat fabrication; menu and facilities design; nutrition; patisserie; restaurant opportunities; sanitation; saucier; seafood processing; soup, stock, sauce, and starch production; wines and spirits.

Facilities

Bake shop; bakery; 2 cafeterias; catering service; 10 classrooms; coffee shop; 3 computer laboratories; demonstration laboratory; 2 food production kitchens; garden; gourmet dining room; learning resource center; library; public restaurant; snack shop; student lounge; 3 teaching kitchens; sugar and chocolate room; interactive synchronistic lab.

Typical Student Profile

142 total: 127 full-time; 15 part-time. 33 are under 25 years old; 101 are between 25 and 44 years old; 8 are over 44 years old.

Special Programs

Summer program in Switzerland and Italy, 3-month paid externship, culinary competitions.

Financial Aid

Program-specific awards include Whitson's Scholarship ($500), J. King Scholarship ($1000), James Lewis Scholarship ($1000); Scotto Brothers Scholarship. Employment opportunities within the program are available.

Housing

Coed housing available.

Application Information

Students may begin participation in January and September. Application deadline for fall is June 1. Application deadline for spring is December 1. Applicants must submit a formal application, an essay, and have a high school diploma and minimum combined SAT score of 800.

Contact

Director of Admissions, Center for Hospitality and Culinary Arts, PO Box 8000, Old Westbury, NY 11568-8000. Telephone: 800-345-NYIT. Fax: 516-686-7516. World Wide Web: http://iris.nyit.edu/culinary/.

New York University

Steinhardt School of Culture, Education, and Human Development; Department of Nutrition, Food Studies, and Public Health

New York, New York

General Information

Private, coeducational, university. Urban campus. Founded in 1831. Accredited by Middle States Association of Colleges and Schools.

Program Information

Offered since 1926. Accredited by American Dietetic Association, Council on the Education of Public Health (CEPH). Program calendar is divided into semesters. 24-month master's degree in nutrition and dietetics. 24-month master's degree in food studies: food systems. 24-month master's degree in food studies: food culture. 4-year bachelor's degree in nutrition and dietetics. 4-year bachelor's degree in food studies. 4-year bachelor's degree in food and restaurant management. 5-year doctoral degree in nutrition and dietetics. 5-year doctoral degree in food studies and food management.

Program Affiliation

American Dietetic Association; Association for the Study of Food and Society.

Areas of Study
Community public health; food history and culture; food writing; introduction to food service; management and human resources; nutrition; nutrition and food service; public health nutrition.

Facilities
Classroom; computer laboratory; demonstration laboratory; food production kitchen; lecture room; library; teaching kitchen.

Typical Student Profile
501 total: 256 full-time; 245 part-time. 125 are under 25 years old; 313 are between 25 and 44 years old; 63 are over 44 years old.

Special Programs
Internships in every program, summer graduate study in Italy and South Africa, intersession courses.

Financial Aid
In 2006, 200 scholarships were awarded. Program-specific awards include food studies scholarships, graduate assistantships, teaching fellowships. Employment placement assistance is available. Employment opportunities within the program are available.

Housing
Coed, apartment-style, and single-sex housing available.

Application Information
Students may begin participation in January, May, June, July, and September. Application deadline for fall (doctoral) is December 15. Application deadline for fall (bachelor's) is January 15. Application deadline for fall (master's) is February 1. Application deadline for spring (bachelor's and master's) is November 1. In 2006, 314 applied; 233 were accepted. Applicants must submit a formal application, letters of reference, GRE score (MPH and doctoral applicants), MCAT score (alternate for MPH applicants), transcripts.

Contact
Director of Admissions, Steinhardt School of Culture, Education, and Human Development; Department of Nutrition, Food Studies, and Public Health, 35 West 4th Street, Room 1077 I, New York, NY 10012. Telephone: 212-998-5580. Fax: 212-995-4194. World Wide Web: http://www.steinhardt.nyu.edu/.

Niagara County Community College

Culinary Arts Program

Sanborn, New York

General Information
Public, coeducational, two-year college. Founded in 1962. Accredited by Middle States Association of Colleges and Schools.

Program Information
Offered since 1976. Accredited by American Culinary Federation Accrediting Commission. Program calendar is divided into semesters. Associate degree in hospitality operations. 1-year certificate in hospitality operations. 1-year certificate in food service. 1-year certificate in casino operations. 1-year certificate in baking and pastry arts. 2-year associate degree in hospitality management. 2-year associate degree in gaming and casino management. 2-year associate degree in food services. 2-year associate degree in culinary arts. 2-year associate degree in baking and pastry arts.

Program Affiliation
American Culinary Federation; American Dietetic Association; National Restaurant Association.

Areas of Study
Baking; beverage management; casino management; controlling costs in food service; culinary French; food preparation; food purchasing; food service math; garde-manger; hospitality; international cuisine; introduction to food service; management and human resources; meat cutting; menu and facilities design; nutrition; patisserie; sanitation; saucier; soup, stock, sauce, and starch production; wines and spirits.

Facilities
Bake shop; cafeteria; 3 classrooms; coffee shop; computer laboratory; demonstration laboratory; food production kitchen; 3 laboratories; learning resource center; 5 lecture rooms; library; snack shop; 2 food preparation laboratories; baking laboratory.

Typical Student Profile
176 total: 150 full-time; 26 part-time. 85 are under 25 years old; 69 are between 25 and 44 years old; 22 are over 44 years old.

Special Programs
Two 6-month internships/cooperative education, study abroad (Italy and France).

Niagara County Community College *(continued)*

Financial Aid
In 2006, 3 scholarships were awarded (average award was $1000). Program-specific awards include Statler Foundation Scholarship, Antoncci scholarship. Employment placement assistance is available. Employment opportunities within the program are available.

Application Information
Students may begin participation in January, May, and September. Application deadline for fall is August 29. Application deadline for spring is January 16. Application deadline for summer is June 9. In 2006, 200 applied. Applicants must submit a formal application.

Contact
Director of Admissions, Culinary Arts Program, 3111 Saunders Settlement Road, Sanborn, NY 14132-9460. Telephone: 716-614-6201. Fax: 716-614-6820. World Wide Web: http://www.niagaracc.suny.edu/.

Niagara University

College of Hospitality and Tourism Management

Niagara University, New York

General Information
Private, coeducational, comprehensive institution. Suburban campus. Founded in 1856. Accredited by Middle States Association of Colleges and Schools.

Program Information
Offered since 1968. Accredited by Council on Hotel, Restaurant and Institutional Education. Program calendar is divided into semesters. 4-year bachelor's degree in hotel and restaurant management-food service management. 4-year bachelor's degree in hotel and restaurant management-restaurant entrepreneurship. 4-year bachelor's degree in hotel and restaurant management-hotel planning and control.

Program Affiliation
Council on Hotel, Restaurant, and Institutional Education; National Restaurant Association; National Restaurant Association Educational Foundation.

Areas of Study
Beverage management; controlling costs in food service; food preparation; food purchasing; kitchen management; management and human resources; restaurant opportunities.

Facilities
2 cafeterias; catering service; 4 classrooms; 2 coffee shops; 5 computer laboratories; demonstration laboratory; food production kitchen; gourmet dining room; learning resource center; lecture room; library; snack shop; 2 student lounges; teaching kitchen.

Typical Student Profile
460 total: 450 full-time; 10 part-time. 425 are under 25 years old; 30 are between 25 and 44 years old; 5 are over 44 years old.

Special Programs
Work-based program in Como, Italy and co-ops across the country, 60 industry speakers/demonstrations per year, cruise course.

Financial Aid
Program-specific awards include 1-3 Statler Foundation Scholarships of Excellence ($20,000), Statler Scholarships (up to $2000 per year), transfer scholarships. Employment placement assistance is available. Employment opportunities within the program are available.

Housing
Coed, apartment-style, and single-sex housing available.

Application Information
Students may begin participation in January, May, and September. Applications are accepted continuously. In 2006, 450 applied; 200 were accepted. Applicants must submit a formal application, letters of reference, and an essay.

Contact
Director of Admissions, College of Hospitality and Tourism Management, College of Hospitality and Tourism Management, Niagara University, NY 14109-2012. Telephone: 716-286-8272. Fax: 716-286-8277. World Wide Web: http://www.niagara.edu/hospitality.

Onondaga Community College

Food Service Administration/Restaurant Management/Professional Cooking

Syracuse, New York

General Information
Public, coeducational, two-year college. Suburban campus. Founded in 1962. Accredited by Middle States Association of Colleges and Schools.

Program Information
Offered since 1979. Program calendar is divided into semesters. 1-year certificate in professional cooking. 2-year associate degree in hotel technology. 2-year associate degree in food service administration/restaurant management.

Program Affiliation
American Culinary Federation; Council on Hotel, Restaurant, and Institutional Education; International Food Service Executives Association; National Restaurant Association; National Restaurant Association Educational Foundation.

Areas of Study
Buffet catering; controlling costs in food service; food preparation; food purchasing; food service math; international cuisine; management and human resources; meal planning; menu and facilities design; nutrition; nutrition and food service; patisserie; sanitation.

Facilities
Catering service; computer laboratory; 2 food production kitchens; garden; gourmet dining room; 2 laboratories; learning resource center; library; student lounge; 2 teaching kitchens.

Typical Student Profile
100 total: 80 full-time; 20 part-time.

Special Programs
2-day trip to New York City, 5-day tour of restaurants, hotels, and casinos in Las Vegas, Walt Disney World College Program (internship).

Financial Aid
Employment placement assistance is available.

Application Information
Students may begin participation in January and August. Applicants must submit a formal application.

Contact
Director of Admissions, Food Service Administration/ Restaurant Management/Professional Cooking, 4941 Onondaga Road, Syracuse, NY 13215. Telephone: 315-498-2232. Fax: 315-498-2703. World Wide Web: http://www.sunyocc.edu/.

Paul Smith's College

Hotel, Resort and Culinary Management

Paul Smiths, New York

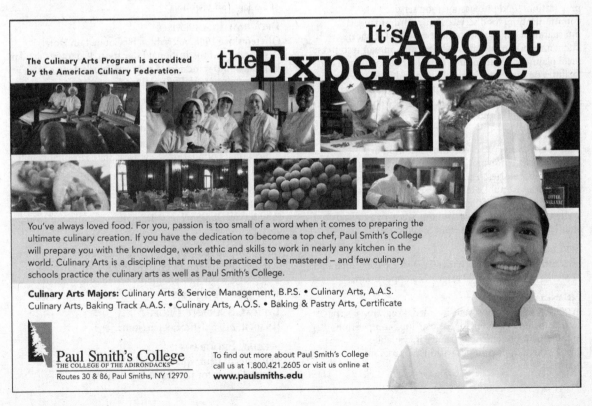

Paul Smith's College *(continued)*

General Information
Private, coeducational, four-year college. Rural campus. Founded in 1937. Accredited by Middle States Association of Colleges and Schools.

Program Information
Offered since 1982. Accredited by American Culinary Federation Accrediting Commission, Council on Hotel, Restaurant and Institutional Education. Program calendar is divided into semesters. 1-year certificate in baking and pastry arts. 2-year associate degree in hotel and restaurant management. 2-year associate degree in culinary arts–baking track. 2-year associate degree in culinary arts. 4-year bachelor's degree in hotel, resort, and tourism management. 4-year bachelor's degree in culinary arts and service management.

Program Affiliation
American Culinary Federation; Council on Hotel, Restaurant, and Institutional Education; National Restaurant Association; National Restaurant Association Educational Foundation; Retailer's Bakery Association.

Areas of Study
Baking; beverage management; buffet catering; confectionery show pieces; controlling costs in food service; culinary French; culinary skill development; food preparation; food purchasing; food service communication; food service math; garde-manger; international cuisine; introduction to food service; kitchen management; management and human resources; meal planning; meat cutting; meat fabrication; menu and facilities design; nutrition; nutrition and food service; patisserie; restaurant opportunities; sanitation; saucier; seafood processing; soup, stock, sauce, and starch production; wines and spirits.

Facilities
Bake shop; bakery; 15 classrooms; 5 computer laboratories; demonstration laboratory; gourmet dining room; 5 laboratories; learning resource center; lecture room; library; 2 public restaurants; snack shop; student lounge; 5 teaching kitchens; on-campus retail bakery; new Wally Ganzi, Jr. Restaurant Training Center (modeled after legendary Palm Restaurant Steakhouse).

Special Programs
International Student Exchange Program, bakery operated 22 weeks a year, over 1100 externship opportunities.

Financial Aid
In 2006, 4 scholarships were awarded. Program-specific awards include Cooking for Scholarships competition. Employment placement assistance is available. Employment opportunities within the program are available.

Housing
Coed and single-sex housing available.

Application Information
Students may begin participation in January and September. Applications are accepted continuously. Applicants must submit a formal application and high school or college transcripts, SAT/ACT scores; letters of recommendation and a personal essay are recommended.

Contact
Director of Admissions, Hotel, Resort and Culinary Management, Routes 86 and 30, PO Box 265, Paul Smiths, NY 12970. Telephone: 800-421-2605. Fax: 518-327-6016. World Wide Web: http://www.paulsmiths.edu/.

Plattsburgh State University of New York

Hotel, Restaurant, and Tourism Management

Plattsburgh, New York

General Information
Public, coeducational, university. Small-town setting. Founded in 1889. Accredited by Middle States Association of Colleges and Schools.

Program Information
Offered since 1988. Accredited by Council on Hotel, Restaurant and Institutional Education. Program calendar is divided into semesters. 4-year bachelor's degree in hotel, restaurant, and tourism management.

Program Affiliation
American Hotel and Lodging Association; Council on Hotel, Restaurant, and Institutional Education; National Restaurant Association; National Restaurant Association Educational Foundation; New York State Hospitality and Tourism Association.

Areas of Study
Beverage management; food preparation; introduction to food service; lodging; restaurant opportunities; tourism.

Facilities
Classroom; coffee shop; computer laboratory; demonstration laboratory; food production kitchen; laboratory; lecture room; public restaurant; student lounge; teaching kitchen.

Typical Student Profile
219 total: 210 full-time; 9 part-time.

Special Programs
800 hours of field work, community-related projects, special dinners for nonprofit organizations.

Financial Aid

In 2006, 15 scholarships were awarded (average award was $883.06); 141 loans were granted (average loan was $4015.30). Program-specific awards include Marriott Corporation Award, Sodexo Award, Restaurants of New York Foundations Awards. Employment opportunities within the program are available.

Housing

Coed housing available.

Application Information

Students may begin participation in January and September. Application deadline for fall is August 1. Application deadline for spring is January 1. In 2006, 91 applied. Applicants must interview; submit a formal application and essay (recommended).

Contact

Director of Admissions, Hotel, Restaurant, and Tourism Management, Kehoe Building, Plattsburgh, NY 12901. Telephone: 518-564-2040. Fax: 518-564-2045. World Wide Web: http://www.plattsburgh.edu/.

Rochester Institute of Technology

School of Hospitality and Service Management

Rochester, New York

General Information

Private, coeducational, comprehensive institution. Suburban campus. Founded in 1829. Accredited by Middle States Association of Colleges and Schools.

Program Information

Offered since 1891. Accredited by American Dietetic Association. Program calendar is divided into quarters. 12-month master's degree in service management. 12-month master's degree in hospitality and tourism management. 4-year bachelor's degree in nutrition management. 4-year bachelor's degree in hospitality and service management.

Program Affiliation

American Dietetic Association; Council on Hotel, Restaurant, and Institutional Education; Institute of Food Technologists; International Food Service Executives Association; National Restaurant Association; National Restaurant Association Educational Foundation.

Areas of Study

Beverage management; controlling costs in food service; food preparation; food purchasing; food service communication; food service math; international cuisine; introduction to food service; kitchen management; management and human resources; meal planning; menu and facilities design; nutrition; nutrition and food service; restaurant opportunities; sanitation; wines and spirits.

Facilities

Bakery; 3 classrooms; computer laboratory; demonstration laboratory; food production kitchen; gourmet dining room; laboratory; learning resource center; lecture room; library; public restaurant; teaching kitchen.

Typical Student Profile

225 total: 200 full-time; 25 part-time.

Special Programs

Required cooperative education plan (provides periods of salaried employment alternated with periods of full-time study), operation of hotel and conference center on campus, international hospitality and food management program in Croatia.

Financial Aid

Program-specific awards include RIT achievement scholarship for hospitality and service management ($5000/year). Employment placement assistance is available. Employment opportunities within the program are available.

Housing

Coed, apartment-style, and single-sex housing available.

Application Information

Students may begin participation in March, June, September, and December. Applications are accepted continuously. In 2006, 177 applied; 119 were accepted. Applicants must submit a formal application and high school and/or college transcripts.

Contact

Director of Admissions, School of Hospitality and Service Management, 60 Lomb Memorial Drive, Rochester, NY 14624. Telephone: 585-475-6631. Fax: 585-475-7428. World Wide Web: http://www.rit.edu/.

St. John's University

Division of Hospitality, Tourism and Sport Management

Queens and Staten Island, New York

General Information

Private, coeducational, university. Urban campus. Founded in 1870. Accredited by Middle States Association of Colleges and Schools.

St. John's University *(continued)*

PROGRAM INFORMATION

Offered since 1997. Accredited by Council on Hotel, Restaurant and Institutional Education, International Society of Travel and Tourism Educators, American Hotel and Lodging Association. Program calendar is divided into semesters. 4-year bachelor's degree in hospitality management.

PROGRAM AFFILIATION

Council on Hotel, Restaurant, and Institutional Education; National Restaurant Association.

AREAS OF STUDY

Beverage management; confectionery show pieces; food purchasing; international cuisine; introduction to food service; management and human resources; menu and facilities design; restaurant opportunities.

FACILITIES

2 cafeterias; catering service; 2 coffee shops; 2 computer laboratories; 2 gardens; learning resource center; lecture room; 2 libraries; student lounge.

TYPICAL STUDENT PROFILE

99 total: 95 full-time; 4 part-time. 89 are under 25 years old; 10 are between 25 and 44 years old.

SPECIAL PROGRAMS

Certificate Program in "Tourism Italy" at Perugia University (5 weeks summer), study abroad program in "Event Management" at Leeds Metropolitan University UK.

HOUSING

Coed housing available.

APPLICATION INFORMATION

Students may begin participation in January, June, and September. Applications are accepted continuously. Applicants must submit a formal application, letters of reference, an essay, SAT or ACT scores, high school transcript.

CONTACT

Director of Admissions, Division of Hospitality, Tourism and Sport Management, 8000 Utopia Parkway, Queens, NY 11439. Telephone: 718-990-2000. Fax: 718-990-5728. World Wide Web: http://www.stjohns.edu/.

STATE UNIVERSITY OF NEW YORK COLLEGE AT COBLESKILL

Culinary Arts, Hospitality, and Tourism

Cobleskill, New York

GENERAL INFORMATION

Public, coeducational, four-year college. Rural campus. Founded in 1916. Accredited by Middle States Association of Colleges and Schools.

PROGRAM INFORMATION

Offered since 1971. Accredited by American Culinary Federation Accrediting Commission. Program calendar is divided into semesters. 1-year certificate in commercial cooking. 2-year associate degree in travel and resort marketing. 2-year associate degree in restaurant management. 2-year associate degree in institutional foods. 2-year associate degree in hotel technology. 2-year associate degree in culinary arts. 4-year bachelor's degree in culinary arts/technology management.

PROGRAM AFFILIATION

American Culinary Federation; American Dietetic Association; Chefs Collaborative 2000; Council on Hotel, Restaurant, and Institutional Education; Institute of Food Technologists; National Restaurant Association; National Restaurant Association Educational Foundation; The Bread Bakers Guild of America; Women Chefs and Restaurateurs.

AREAS OF STUDY

Beverage management; buffet catering; confectionery show pieces; controlling costs in food service; culinary French; culinary skill development; food preparation; food purchasing; food service math; garde-manger; hospitality law; international cuisine; management; management and human resources; marketing; meat cutting; menu and facilities design; nutrition; sanitation; wines and spirits.

FACILITIES

Catering service; 15 classrooms; 4 computer laboratories; demonstration laboratory; food production kitchen; gourmet dining room; learning resource center; 15 lecture rooms; library; public restaurant; 3 teaching kitchens; vineyard.

TYPICAL STUDENT PROFILE

132 total: 120 full-time; 12 part-time.

SPECIAL PROGRAMS

Culinary competitions, student-run restaurant and catering facilities, internship in bachelor's program.

FINANCIAL AID

Program-specific awards include on-campus work-study programs. Employment placement assistance is available.

Housing
Coed and single-sex housing available.

Application Information
Students may begin participation in January and August. Applications are accepted continuously. Applicants must submit a formal application.

Contact
Director of Admissions, Culinary Arts, Hospitality, and Tourism, Knapp Hall, Cobleskill, NY 12043. Telephone: 800-295-8988. Fax: 518-255-6769. World Wide Web: http://www.cobleskill.edu/.

State University of New York College at Oneonta

Food Service and Restaurant Administration

Oneonta, New York

General Information
Public, coeducational, comprehensive institution. Small-town setting. Founded in 1889. Accredited by Middle States Association of Colleges and Schools.

Program Information
Offered since 1974. Accredited by American Association of Family and Consumer Sciences. Program calendar is divided into semesters. 4-year bachelor's degree in food service/restaurant administration.

Program Affiliation
American Dietetic Association; Council on Hotel, Restaurant, and Institutional Education; National Restaurant Association; National Restaurant Association Educational Foundation.

Areas of Study
Buffet catering; controlling costs in food service; food preparation; food purchasing; food service communication; food service math; introduction to food service; kitchen management; management and human resources; meal planning; menu and facilities design; nutrition; nutrition and food service; restaurant opportunities; sanitation; wines and spirits.

Facilities
3 classrooms; computer laboratory; demonstration laboratory; food production kitchen; gourmet dining room; laboratory; learning resource center; 3 lecture rooms; library; student lounge; teaching kitchen.

Typical Student Profile
58 total: 53 full-time; 5 part-time. 57 are under 25 years old; 1 is between 25 and 44 years old.

Special Programs
Food and Nutrition Association, field trips to food shows in the Northeast and speakers from the profession, Nutrition Awareness Week.

Financial Aid
In 2006, 7 scholarships were awarded (average award was $500). Employment placement assistance is available. Employment opportunities within the program are available.

Housing
Coed housing available.

Application Information
Students may begin participation in January and August. Applications are accepted continuously. In 2006, 60 applied; 30 were accepted. Applicants must submit a formal application and an essay.

Contact
Director of Admissions, Food Service and Restaurant Administration, 142 B. Human Ecology Building, Oneonta, NY 13820. Telephone: 607-436-2071. Fax: 607-436-2051. World Wide Web: http://www.oneonta.edu/.

State University of New York College of Agriculture and Technology at Morrisville

Restaurant Management

Morrisville, New York

General Information
Public, coeducational, two-year college. Small-town setting. Founded in 1908. Accredited by Middle States Association of Colleges and Schools.

Program Information
Offered since 1908. Accredited by American Dietetic Association. Program calendar is divided into semesters. 2-year associate degree in restaurant management. 2-year associate degree in food service administration. 4-year bachelor's degree in resort and recreation service management.

Program Affiliation
Council on Hotel, Restaurant, and Institutional Education; International Food Service Executives Association; National Restaurant Association; National Restaurant Association Educational Foundation.

State University of New York College of Agriculture and Technology at Morrisville *(continued)*

Areas of Study
Beverage management; buffet catering; controlling costs in food service; culinary skill development; food preparation; food purchasing; food service math; international cuisine; introduction to food service; kitchen management; management and human resources; meal planning; menu and facilities design; nutrition; nutrition and food service; sanitation; soup, stock, sauce, and starch production.

Facilities
Bake shop; cafeteria; catering service; classroom; computer laboratory; demonstration laboratory; food production kitchen; laboratory; learning resource center; lecture room; library; public restaurant; snack shop; student lounge; teaching kitchen.

Typical Student Profile
125 total: 100 full-time; 25 part-time. 80 are under 25 years old; 30 are between 25 and 44 years old; 15 are over 44 years old.

Special Programs
320-hour paid internship, attendance at International Food Service Executives Association Conference.

Financial Aid
In 2006, 12 scholarships were awarded (average award was $350). Employment placement assistance is available. Employment opportunities within the program are available.

Housing
Coed housing available.

Application Information
Students may begin participation in January and August. Applications are accepted continuously. In 2006, 60 applied; 40 were accepted. Applicants must submit a formal application.

Contact
Director of Admissions, Restaurant Management, Brooks Hall, Morrisville, NY 13408. Telephone: 315-684-6232. Fax: 315-684-6225. World Wide Web: http://www.morrisville.edu/.

State University of New York College of Technology at Alfred

Culinary Arts Program

Wellsville, New York

General Information
Public, coeducational, two-year college. Small-town setting. Founded in 1908. Accredited by Middle States Association of Colleges and Schools.

Program Information
Offered since 1966. Program calendar is divided into semesters. 2-year associate degree in culinary arts. 2-year associate degree in baking and pastry arts.

Program Affiliation
American Culinary Federation; Council on Hotel, Restaurant, and Institutional Education; National Restaurant Association; National Restaurant Association Educational Foundation; New York State Restaurant Association.

Areas of Study
Baking; beverage management; buffet catering; confectionery show pieces; controlling costs in food service; culinary French; culinary skill development; food preparation; food purchasing; food service math; garde-manger; international cuisine; introduction to food service; kitchen management; management and human resources; meal planning; meat cutting; menu and facilities design; nutrition; nutrition and food service; sanitation; seafood processing; soup, stock, sauce, and starch production; wines and spirits.

Facilities
2 bake shops; bakery; cafeteria; catering service; 3 classrooms; coffee shop; computer laboratory; 3 demonstration laboratories; 2 food production kitchens; gourmet dining room; laboratory; learning resource center; 3 lecture rooms; 2 libraries; public restaurant; student lounge; 2 teaching kitchens.

Typical Student Profile
72 full-time. 69 are under 25 years old; 3 are between 25 and 44 years old.

Special Programs
Annual Culinary Arts Food Show, regional ACF Hot Foods and Team Competitions at SUNY Delhi, senior class fine dining excursion and training seminar.

Financial Aid
In 2006, 7 scholarships were awarded (average award was $1700). Employment placement assistance is available.

Housing
Coed housing available.

Application Information
Students may begin participation in August. Applications are accepted continuously. In 2006, 180 applied; 103 were accepted. Applicants must submit a formal application.

Contact
Director of Admissions, Culinary Arts Program, 2530 South Brooklyn Avenue, Wellsville, NY 14895. Telephone: 800-4-ALFRED. Fax: 607-587-3171. World Wide Web: http://www.alfredstate.edu/.

State University of New York College of Technology at Delhi

Hospitality Management

Delhi, New York

General Information
Public, coeducational, two-year college. Rural campus. Founded in 1913. Accredited by Middle States Association of Colleges and Schools.

Program Information
Offered since 1994. Accredited by American Culinary Federation Accrediting Commission. Program calendar is divided into semesters. 2-year associate degree in restaurant management. 2-year associate degree in culinary arts. 4-year bachelor's degree in restaurant management. 4-year bachelor's degree in culinary arts management.

Program Affiliation
American Culinary Federation; Council on Hotel, Restaurant, and Institutional Education; International Food Service Executives Association; International Hotel and Motel Association; National Restaurant Association; New York State Hospitality and Tourism Association; Society of Wine Educators.

Areas of Study
Baking; beverage management; buffet catering; confectionery show pieces; controlling costs in food service; convenience cookery; culinary competition; culinary French; culinary skill development; food preparation; food purchasing; food service communication; food service math; garde-manger; ice carving; international cuisine; introduction to food service; kitchen management; management and human resources; meal planning; meat cutting; meat fabrication; menu and facilities design; nutrition; patisserie; restaurant management; restaurant opportunities; salt carving; sanitation; saucier; seafood processing; soup, stock, sauce, and starch production; wines and spirits.

Facilities
Bakery; catering service; 2 classrooms; computer laboratory; demonstration laboratory; 2 food production kitchens; gourmet dining room; laboratory; learning resource center; 2 lecture rooms; library; public restaurant; 2 teaching kitchens; beverage lounge; charcuterie.

Typical Student Profile
173 full-time. 158 are under 25 years old; 15 are between 25 and 44 years old.

Special Programs
Culinary competitions, organized trips to food shows and businesses.

Financial Aid
In 2006, 6 scholarships were awarded (average award was $300). Employment placement assistance is available. Employment opportunities within the program are available.

Housing
Coed and single-sex housing available.

Application Information
Students may begin participation in January and September. Applications are accepted continuously. In 2006, 334 applied; 218 were accepted. Applicants must submit a formal application.

Contact
Director of Admissions, Hospitality Management, 119 Bush Hall, Main Street, Delhi, NY 13753. Telephone: 607-746-4556. Fax: 607-746-4104. World Wide Web: http://www.delhi.edu/.

Sullivan County Community College

Culinary Arts Division

Loch Sheldrake, New York

General Information
Public, coeducational, two-year college. Rural campus. Founded in 1962. Accredited by Middle States Association of Colleges and Schools.

Program Information
Offered since 1965. Accredited by American Culinary Federation Accrediting Commission. Program calendar is divided into semesters. 1-year certificate in food service.

Sullivan County Community College ***(continued)***

2-year associate degree in professional chef. 2-year associate degree in pastry arts. 2-year associate degree in hospitality management. 2-year associate degree in culinary arts.

Program Affiliation
American Culinary Federation; Council on Hotel, Restaurant, and Institutional Education; National Restaurant Association; National Restaurant Association Educational Foundation; The Bread Bakers Guild of America.

Areas of Study
Baking; beverage management; buffet catering; confectionery show pieces; controlling costs in food service; convenience cookery; culinary French; culinary skill development; food preparation; food purchasing; food service math; garde-manger; international cuisine; introduction to food service; kitchen management; management and human resources; meal planning; meat cutting; meat fabrication; menu and facilities design; nutrition; nutrition and food service; patisserie; restaurant opportunities; sanitation; saucier; seafood processing; soup, stock, sauce, and starch production; wines and spirits.

Facilities
2 bake shops; classroom; 3 demonstration laboratories; 2 food production kitchens; gourmet dining room.

Typical Student Profile
100 total: 75 full-time; 25 part-time. 80 are under 25 years old; 15 are between 25 and 44 years old; 5 are over 44 years old.

Special Programs
Societe Culinaire Philanthropique Salon of Culinary Arts.

Financial Aid
In 2006, 12 scholarships were awarded (average award was $2000). Employment placement assistance is available. Employment opportunities within the program are available.

Housing
Coed housing available.

Application Information
Students may begin participation in January and August. Applications are accepted continuously. Applicants must submit a formal application.

Contact
Director of Admissions, Culinary Arts Division, 112 College Road, Loch Sheldrake, NY 12759. Telephone: 800-577-5243. Fax: 845-434-4806. World Wide Web: http://www.sullivan.suny.edu/.

Syracuse University

Department of Hospitality Management

Syracuse, New York

General Information
Private, coeducational, university. Urban campus. Founded in 1870. Accredited by Middle States Association of Colleges and Schools.

Program Information
Offered since 1986. Accredited by Council on Hotel, Restaurant and Institutional Education. Program calendar is divided into semesters. 4-year bachelor's degree in hospitality management.

Program Affiliation
Council on Hotel, Restaurant, and Institutional Education; National Restaurant Association; National Restaurant Association Educational Foundation.

Areas of Study
Baking; beverage management; buffet catering; controlling costs in food service; culinary skill development; food preparation; food purchasing; introduction to food service; kitchen management; management and human resources; menu and facilities design; nutrition; nutrition and food service; restaurant development; sanitation; wines and spirits.

Facilities
Bake shop; bakery; 8 cafeterias; catering service; 25 classrooms; coffee shop; 5 computer laboratories; 2 demonstration laboratories; 2 food production kitchens; 2 gardens; gourmet dining room; 5 learning resource centers; 12 lecture rooms; 8 libraries; 2 public restaurants; 6 snack shops; 9 student lounges; 2 teaching kitchens.

Typical Student Profile
168 total: 165 full-time; 3 part-time.

Special Programs
ServSafe Program.

Financial Aid
In 2006, 2 scholarships were awarded (average award was $500). Employment placement assistance is available.

Housing
Coed, apartment-style, and single-sex housing available.

Application Information
Students may begin participation in January and August. Application deadline for fall is January 15. Application deadline for spring is November 15. Applicants must submit a formal application and letters of reference.

Contact
Director of Admissions, Department of Hospitality Management, 302 Lyman Hall, Syracuse, NY 13244. Telephone: 315-443-4550. Fax: 315-443-2735. World Wide Web: http://www.syr.edu/.

Tompkins Cortland Community College

Hotel and Restaurant Management

Dryden, New York

General Information
Public, coeducational, two-year college. Small-town setting. Founded in 1969. Accredited by Middle States Association of Colleges and Schools.

Program Information
Offered since 1970. Program calendar is divided into semesters. 2-year associate degree in hotel and restaurant management.

Program Affiliation
Council on Hotel, Restaurant, and Institutional Education; National Restaurant Association.

Areas of Study
Beverage management; food preparation; food purchasing; food service math; introduction to food service; management and human resources; nutrition; sanitation; soup, stock, sauce, and starch production; wines and spirits.

Facilities
5 classrooms; 3 computer laboratories; demonstration laboratory; learning resource center; lecture room.

Typical Student Profile
42 total: 33 full-time; 9 part-time. 28 are under 25 years old; 9 are between 25 and 44 years old; 5 are over 44 years old.

Special Programs
AAS degree program available online.

Financial Aid
Employment placement assistance is available. Employment opportunities within the program are available.

Housing
Apartment-style housing available.

Application Information
Students may begin participation in January and August. Applications are accepted continuously. Applicants must submit a formal application.

Contact
Director of Admissions, Hotel and Restaurant Management, 170 North Street, PO Box 139, Dryden, NY 13053-0139. Telephone: 607-844-6580. Fax: 607-844-6541. World Wide Web: http://www.sunytccc.edu/.

Westchester Community College

Culinary Arts and Management

Valhalla, New York

General Information
Public, coeducational, two-year college. Suburban campus. Founded in 1946. Accredited by Middle States Association of Colleges and Schools.

Program Information
Offered since 1946. National Restaurant Association Educational Foundation ManageFirst certificates available. Program calendar is divided into semesters. 2-year associate degree in food service administration: culinary arts and management.

Program Affiliation
American Dietetic Association; Council on Hotel, Restaurant, and Institutional Education; National Restaurant Association; National Restaurant Association Educational Foundation.

Areas of Study
Baking; beverage management; buffet catering; controlling costs in food service; convenience cookery; culinary French; culinary skill development; food preparation; food purchasing; food service math; garde-manger; international cuisine; introduction to food service; kitchen management; management and human resources; meal planning; menu and facilities design; nutrition; nutrition and food service; patisserie; restaurant opportunities; sanitation; soup, stock, sauce, and starch production; wines and spirits.

Facilities
Catering service; classroom; computer laboratory; demonstration laboratory; 2 food production kitchens; gourmet dining room; 2 laboratories; learning resource center; lecture room; library; public restaurant; student lounge; 2 teaching kitchens.

Typical Student Profile
120 total: 70 full-time; 50 part-time. 60 are under 25 years old; 48 are between 25 and 44 years old; 12 are over 44 years old.

Westchester Community College *(continued)*

Special Programs
Culinary competitions, 3-4 day trip to Chicago in May for NRA Trade Show, industry fund raising events for charity.

Financial Aid
In 2006, 7 scholarships were awarded (average award was $1000). Employment placement assistance is available. Employment opportunities within the program are available.

Application Information
Students may begin participation in January, May, and September. Applications are accepted continuously. Applicants must submit a formal application.

Contact
Director of Admissions, Culinary Arts and Management, 75 Grasslands Road, Valhalla, NY 10595. Telephone: 914-606-6551. Fax: 914-606-7989. World Wide Web: http://www.sunywcc.edu/.

Wilson Technological Center

Culinary Arts

Dix Hills, New York

General Information
Public, coeducational, career school. Suburban campus. Founded in 1948.

Program Information
Offered since 1948. Accredited by American Culinary Federation Accrediting Commission, National Restaurant Association Education Foundation. Program calendar is divided into semesters. 1-year certificate in Culinary Arts II. 1-year certificate in Culinary Arts I.

Program Affiliation
American Culinary Federation; Council on Hotel, Restaurant, and Institutional Education; National Restaurant Association; National Restaurant Association Educational Foundation.

Areas of Study
Baking; buffet catering; confectionery show pieces; controlling costs in food service; culinary skill development; food preparation; food purchasing; food service communication; food service math; garde-manger; international cuisine; introduction to food service; kitchen management; meal planning; meat cutting; meat fabrication; nutrition; nutrition and food service; patisserie; restaurant opportunities; sanitation; saucier; soup, stock, sauce, and starch production.

Facilities
Bake shop; cafeteria; 3 classrooms; computer laboratory; demonstration laboratory; 3 food production kitchens.

Typical Student Profile
185 total: 125 full-time; 60 part-time. 125 are under 25 years old; 40 are between 25 and 44 years old; 20 are over 44 years old.

Special Programs
Individual continuing education courses, Skills USA Food Preparation Assistant Cooking Competition.

Financial Aid
In 2006, 3 scholarships were awarded (average award was $2000). Employment placement assistance is available.

Application Information
Students may begin participation in January and September. Applications are accepted continuously. Applicants must have referral by school district or Continuing Education application.

Contact
Director of Admissions, Culinary Arts, 17 Westminster Avenue, Dix Hills, NY 11746. Telephone: 631-667-6000 Ext. 320. Fax: 631-667-1519. World Wide Web: http://www.wilsontech.org.

North Carolina

Asheville-Buncombe Technical Community College

Culinary Technology

Asheville, North Carolina

General Information
Public, coeducational, two-year college. Urban campus. Founded in 1959. Accredited by Southern Association of Colleges and Schools.

Program Information
Offered since 1967. Accredited by Culinary Technology program accredited by the American Culinary Federation. Program calendar is divided into semesters. 2-year associate degree in hotel and restaurant management. 2-year associate degree in culinary technology. 2-year associate degree in baking and pastry arts.

Program Affiliation
American Culinary Federation; Council on Hotel, Restaurant, and Institutional Education; National Restaurant Association; National Restaurant Association Educational Foundation; Women Chefs and Restaurateurs.

Areas of Study
American regional cuisine; baking; beverage management; classical cuisine; confectionery show pieces; controlling costs in food service; culinary skill development; food preparation; food purchasing; food service math; garde-manger; international cuisine; introduction to food service; management and human resources; meal planning; meat cutting; meat fabrication; menu and facilities design; nutrition; nutrition and food service; patisserie; restaurant opportunities; sanitation; saucier; seafood processing; soup, stock, sauce, and starch production; wines and spirits.

Facilities
Bake shop; 4 classrooms; computer laboratory; demonstration laboratory; food production kitchen; 2 gourmet dining rooms; laboratory; learning resource center; 4 lecture rooms; library; public restaurant; student lounge; 2 teaching kitchens; hotel.

Typical Student Profile
110 total: 70 full-time; 40 part-time.

Special Programs
Culinary competitions, paid internship.

Financial Aid
In 2006, 10 scholarships were awarded (average award was $500). Employment placement assistance is available. Employment opportunities within the program are available.

Application Information
Students may begin participation in January, May, and August. Applications are accepted continuously. In 2006, 120 applied; 60 were accepted. Applicants must submit a formal application and computerized placement test scores.

Contact
Director of Admissions, Culinary Technology, 340 Victoria Road, Asheville, NC 28801. Telephone: 828-254-1921 Ext. 232. Fax: 828-281-9794. World Wide Web: http://www.abtech.edu/.

Central Piedmont Community College

Hospitality Education Division

Charlotte, North Carolina

General Information
Public, coeducational, two-year college. Urban campus. Founded in 1963. Accredited by Southern Association of Colleges and Schools.

Program Information
Offered since 1977. Accredited by American Culinary Federation Accrediting Commission. National Restaurant Association Educational Foundation ManageFirst certificates available. Program calendar is divided into semesters. 1-year certificate in service. 1-year certificate in sales and events. 1-year certificate in restaurant management. 1-year certificate in management skills. 1-year certificate in hotel management. 1-year certificate in hot foods. 1-year certificate in garde manger. 1-year certificate in culinary. 1-year certificate in baking. 1- to 2-year diploma in restaurant management. 1- to 2-year diploma in hotel management. 2-year associate degree in hotel and restaurant management. 2-year associate degree in culinary technology. 2-year associate degree in baking and pastry arts.

Program Affiliation
American Culinary Federation; National Association of Catering Executives; National Restaurant Association; National Restaurant Association Educational Foundation.

Areas of Study
Baking; beverage management; buffet catering; confectionery show pieces; controlling costs in food service; culinary skill development; food preparation; food purchasing; food service communication; garde-manger; international cuisine; introduction to food service; kitchen management; management and human resources; meal planning; meat cutting; nutrition; patisserie; restaurant opportunities; sanitation; soup, stock, sauce, and starch production; wines and spirits.

Facilities
2 bake shops; 4 classrooms; demonstration laboratory; 2 food production kitchens; gourmet dining room; learning resource center; 2 lecture rooms; library; public restaurant.

Typical Student Profile
390 full-time.

Special Programs
Culinary tour of France.

Financial Aid
Employment placement assistance is available.

Central Piedmont Community College ***(continued)***

Application Information
Students may begin participation in January and August. Applications are accepted continuously. Applicants must submit a formal application, have a high school diploma or GED, and take placement test.

Contact
Director of Admissions, Hospitality Education Division, PO Box 35009, Charlotte, NC 28235. Telephone: 704-330-6721. Fax: 704-330-6581. World Wide Web: http://www.cpcc.edu/.

East Carolina University

Department of Hospitality Management

Greenville, North Carolina

General Information
Public, coeducational, university. Small-town setting. Founded in 1907. Accredited by Southern Association of Colleges and Schools.

Program Information
Offered since 1988. Program calendar is divided into semesters. 1- to 2-year master of business administration in hospitality management (concentration). 4-year bachelor's degree in hospitality management (lodging, food and beverage, conventions and special events).

Program Affiliation
American Dietetic Association; American Hotel and Lodging Association; Council on Hotel, Restaurant, and Institutional Education; Culinary Hospitality and Tourism Educators Association of North Carolina; Educational Association of the AH & LA; Hospitality Sales and Marketing Association International; National Restaurant Association; National Restaurant Association Educational Foundation; North Carolina Hotel and Lodging Association; North Carolina Tourism Educational Foundation.

Areas of Study
Food and beverage service; hotel and restaurant management; lodging; Meetings and Conventions; restaurant opportunities.

Facilities
4 classrooms; computer laboratory; demonstration laboratory; food production kitchen; 2 teaching kitchens.

Typical Student Profile
149 total: 133 full-time; 16 part-time. 133 are under 25 years old; 15 are between 25 and 44 years old; 1 is over 44 years old.

Special Programs
Paid internship, international study abroad program, tours of North Carolina wineries, including Biltmore Estates and Childres wineries, attend national professional conferences.

Financial Aid
In 2006, 12 scholarships were awarded (average award was $1500). Program-specific awards include paid internship with Red Lobster, ARAMARK, Biltmore Estates, Pinehurst Resorts, Kingsmill Resort and more. Employment placement assistance is available. Employment opportunities within the program are available.

Housing
Coed, apartment-style, and single-sex housing available.

Application Information
Students may begin participation in January, May, July, and August. Application deadline for summer and fall is March 15. Application deadline for spring is November 1. Application deadline for transfers (summer and fall) is April 15. Applicants must submit a formal application and letters of reference.

Contact
Director of Admissions, Department of Hospitality Management, Rivers Building Room 152, Greenville, NC 27858. Telephone: 252-737-1604. Fax: 252-328-4276. World Wide Web: http://www.ecu.edu/che/hmgt/index.html.

The International Culinary School at The Art Institute of Charlotte

Charlotte, North Carolina

General Information
Private, coeducational institution.

Program Information
Associate degree in Culinary Arts. Bachelor's degree in Culinary Arts Management.

Contact
Office of Admissions, Three Lake Pointe Plaza, 2110 Water Ridge Parkway, Charlotte, NC 28217. Telephone: 704-357-8020. Fax: 704-357-1133. World Wide Web: http://www.artinstitutes.edu/charlotte/.

See color display following page 332.

The International Culinary School at The Art Institute of Raleigh–Durham

Durham, North Carolina

General Information

Private, coeducational institution.

Program Information

Associate degree in Culinary Arts. Bachelor's degree in Culinary Arts Management.

Contact

Office of Admissions, 410 Blackwell Street, Suite 200, Durham, NC 27701. Telephone: 919-317-3050. World Wide Web: http://www.artinstitutes.edu/raleigh-durham.

See color display following page 332.

Johnson & Wales University–Charlotte

College of Culinary Arts

Charlotte, North Carolina

General Information

Private, coeducational, four-year college. Urban campus. Founded in 2004. Accredited by New England Association of Schools and Colleges.

Program Information

Accredited by CADE. Program calendar is divided into quarters. Associate degree in culinary arts. Associate degree in baking and pastry arts. Bachelor's degree in culinary arts and food service management. Bachelor's degree in baking & pastry arts and food service management.

Program Affiliation

American Culinary Federation; American Institute of Wine & Food; Institute of Food Technologists; International Association of Culinary Professionals; National Restaurant Association; National Restaurant Association Educational Foundation; Research Chefs Association; The Bread Bakers Guild of America; Women Chefs and Restaurateurs.

Areas of Study

Baking; beverage management; confectionery show pieces; controlling costs in food service; culinary skill development; food preparation; food purchasing; food service math; garde-manger; international cuisine; introduction to food service; meat cutting; meat fabrication; menu and facilities design; nutrition; patisserie; sanitation; saucier; seafood processing; soup, stock, sauce, and starch production; wines and spirits.

Facilities

6 bake shops; cafeteria; 12 classrooms; 4 computer laboratories; demonstration laboratory; food production kitchen; 3 gourmet dining rooms; learning resource center; lecture room; library; snack shop; 2 student lounges; 11 teaching kitchens; storeroom.

Student Profile

1,304 total: 1272 full-time; 32 part-time. 1140 are under 25 years old; 151 are between 25 and 44 years old; 13 are over 44 years old.

Faculty

37 total: 37 full-time. Prominent faculty: Ed Batten, CEC, CCE, FMP, CCI; Susan Batten, CEC, CCE, FMP, CCI; Frances Burnett, CMB, CEPC; Michael Calenda, CEC. Faculty-student ratio: 1:34.

Prominent Alumni and Current Affiliation

Tuker Florence, Celebrity Chef/Author/Restauranteur; Graham Elliot Bowles, Chef/Owner, Graham Elliot Restaurant; Tom Condron, Corporate Executive Chef-Harpers Restaurant Group.

Special Programs

Summer tour abroad (Germany, France, or Singapore), Inter-Campus Hot Food Competition, International Study and Culinary Competition.

Typical Expenses

Tuition: $21,297 per year. Program-related fees include $1023 for general fee; $265 for orientation fee; $1026 for optional weekend meal plan; $300 for room and board reservation deposit.

Financial Aid

In 2007, 1589 scholarships were awarded (average award was $4115). Employment placement assistance is available.

Housing

Coed housing available. Average on-campus housing cost per month: $988.

Application Information

Students may begin participation in March, September, and December. Applications are accepted continuously. In 2007, 2378 applied; 1636 were accepted. Applicants must submit a formal application and official transcript from high school or college.

Contact

Admissions, College of Culinary Arts, 901 West Trade Street, Charlotte, NC 28202. Telephone: 980-598-1100. Fax: 980-598-1111. E-mail: admissions.clt@jwu.edu. World Wide Web: http://culinary.jwu.edu/.

See color display following page 92.

Southwestern Community College

Culinary Technology

Sylva, North Carolina

General Information
Public, coeducational, two-year college. Small-town setting. Founded in 1964. Accredited by Southern Association of Colleges and Schools.

Program Information
Offered since 1973. Program calendar is divided into semesters. 2-semester certificate in culinary technology. 5-semester associate degree in culinary technology.

Program Affiliation
National Restaurant Association Educational Foundation.

Facilities
Classroom; teaching kitchen.

Typical Student Profile
43 total: 30 full-time; 13 part-time. 26 are under 25 years old; 14 are between 25 and 44 years old; 3 are over 44 years old.

Special Programs
Annual gingerbread house competition at Grove Park Inn.

Financial Aid
Program-specific awards include E.M. Moulton scholarships ($200).

Application Information
Students may begin participation in January, May, and August. Applications are accepted continuously. Applicants must submit a formal application.

Contact
Director of Admissions, Culinary Technology, 447 College Drive, Sylva, NC 28779. Telephone: 828-586-4091 Ext. 217. Fax: 828-586-3129. World Wide Web: http://www.southwesterncc.edu/.

The University of North Carolina at Greensboro

Greensboro, North Carolina

General Information
Public, coeducational, university. Urban campus. Founded in 1891. Accredited by Southern Association of Colleges and Schools.

Program Information
Accredited by American Dietetic Association. Program calendar is divided into semesters. 122-hour bachelor's degree in nutrition. 37- to 40-hour master's degree in nutrition and food service systems. 37- to 40-hour master's degree in nutrition. 4-year bachelor's degree in restaurant and institution management. 63-hour doctoral degree in nutrition.

Program Affiliation
American Dietetic Association.

Areas of Study
Hospitality management; nutrition; nutrition and food service; restaurant opportunities.

Facilities
Classroom; computer laboratory; demonstration laboratory; lecture room; library; student lounge.

Typical Student Profile
207 total: 165 full-time; 42 part-time. 146 are under 25 years old; 55 are between 25 and 44 years old; 6 are over 44 years old.

Special Programs
Dietetic internship.

Housing
Coed, apartment-style, and single-sex housing available.

Application Information
Students may begin participation in January and August. Application deadline for fall is March 1. Application deadline for spring is December 1. Applicants must submit a formal application and SAT or ACT scores.

Contact
Director of Admissions, 1400 Spring Garden Street, PO Box 26170, Greensboro, NC 27402. Telephone: 336-334-5243. Fax: 336-334-4180. World Wide Web: http://www.uncg.edu/.

Wake Technical Community College

Culinary Technology, Hotel/Restaurant Management

Raleigh, North Carolina

General Information
Public, coeducational, two-year college. Suburban campus. Founded in 1958. Accredited by Southern Association of Colleges and Schools.

Program Information
Offered since 1983. Accredited by American Culinary Federation Accrediting Commission. National Restaurant Association Educational Foundation ManageFirst certificates available. Program calendar is divided into semesters. 1-year certificate in restaurant management. 1-year certificate in hotel management. 1-year certificate in culinary technology. 1-year certificate in baking and pastry arts. 2-year associate degree in hotel/restaurant management. 2-year associate degree in culinary technology.

Program Affiliation
American Culinary Federation; American Hotel and Lodging Association; American Institute of Baking; American Institute of Wine & Food; Council on Hotel, Restaurant, and Institutional Education; National Restaurant Association; National Restaurant Association Educational Foundation; North Carolina Culinary, Hospitality, and Tourism Alliance; North Carolina Restaurant and Hotel Management Association; Triangle Area Hotel/Motel Association (TAHMA).

Areas of Study
Baking; beverage management; buffet catering; confectionery show pieces; controlling costs in food service; culinary French; culinary skill development; food preparation; food purchasing; food service communication; food service math; garde-manger; hotel operations; international cuisine; introduction to food service; kitchen management; management and human resources; meal planning; meat cutting; meat fabrication; menu and facilities design; nutrition; nutrition and food service; patisserie; restaurant opportunities; sanitation; saucier; seafood processing; soup, stock, sauce, and starch production; table service; wines and spirits.

Facilities
Bake shop; 2 classrooms; computer laboratory; demonstration laboratory; 4 food production kitchens; gourmet dining room; learning resource center; 2 lecture rooms; library; public restaurant; student lounge; 7 teaching kitchens.

Typical Student Profile
210 total: 160 full-time; 50 part-time. 130 are under 25 years old; 50 are between 25 and 44 years old; 30 are over 44 years old.

Special Programs
3-week work-study in France, American Culinary Federation Hot Food Competition, pastry show and competition.

Financial Aid
In 2006, 4 scholarships were awarded (average award was $1500); 1 loan was granted (loan was $1500). Employment placement assistance is available. Employment opportunities within the program are available.

Application Information
Students may begin participation in January, May, and August. Applications are accepted continuously. In 2006, 125 applied; 90 were accepted. Applicants must submit a formal application and SAT scores or equivalent.

Contact
Director of Admissions, Culinary Technology, Hotel/Restaurant Management, 9101 Fayetteville Road, Raleigh, NC 27603. Telephone: 919-866-5957. World Wide Web: http://www.waketech.edu/.

Wilkes Community College

Culinary Technology and Baking and Pastry Arts

Wilkesboro, North Carolina

General Information
Public, coeducational, two-year college. Rural campus. Founded in 1965. Accredited by Southern Association of Colleges and Schools.

Program Information
Offered since 1997. Program calendar is divided into semesters. 2-year associate degree in culinary technology. 2-year associate degree in baking and pastry arts. 4-month certificate in line cook.

Program Affiliation
Chefs Collaborative 2000.

Areas of Study
Artisanal breads; baking; beverage management; buffet catering; controlling costs in food service; convenience cookery; culinary skill development; food preparation; food purchasing; garde-manger; international cuisine; introduction to food service; kitchen management; nutrition; pastry cooking; sanitation.

Facilities
Bake shop; classroom; food production kitchen; public restaurant; teaching kitchen.

Typical Student Profile
32 total: 22 full-time; 10 part-time. 16 are under 25 years old; 10 are between 25 and 44 years old; 6 are over 44 years old.

Wilkes Community College *(continued)*

Special Programs
Participation in providing food for Merlefest (bluegrass festival), student-run Tory Oak Restaurant on campus, trip to Paris to work in Alain Ducasse, Michael Rostang, and Grand Cascade restaurants.

Financial Aid
In 2006, 10 scholarships were awarded (average award was $1000). Program-specific awards include participation in Ye Host Culinary Club (provides full tuition for up to four semesters). Employment placement assistance is available. Employment opportunities within the program are available.

Application Information
Students may begin participation in January and August. Applications are accepted continuously. In 2006, 20 applied; 20 were accepted. Applicants must submit a formal application.

Contact
Director of Admissions, Culinary Technology and Baking and Pastry Arts, PO Box 120, Wilkesboro, NC 28677. Telephone: 336-838-6141. Fax: 336-838-6547. World Wide Web: http://www.wilkescc.edu/.

North Dakota

North Dakota State College of Science

Culinary Arts

Wahpeton, North Dakota

General Information
Public, coeducational, two-year college. Small-town setting. Founded in 1903. Accredited by North Central Association of Colleges and Schools.

Program Information
Offered since 1971. Program calendar is divided into semesters. 2-year associate degree in restaurant management. 2-year associate degree in chef training and management technology. 2-year diploma in chef training and management technology.

Program Affiliation
American Culinary Federation; National Restaurant Association; North Dakota Hospitality Association.

Areas of Study
Baking; buffet catering; controlling costs in food service; culinary skill development; food preparation; food purchasing; food service math; garde-manger; introduction to food service; kitchen management; management and human resources; meal planning; meat cutting; meat fabrication; menu and facilities design; nutrition and food service; patisserie; sanitation; saucier; seafood processing; soup, stock, sauce, and starch production.

Facilities
Bake shop; bakery; cafeteria; catering service; classroom; coffee shop; 7 computer laboratories; demonstration laboratory; food production kitchen; laboratory; learning resource center; lecture room; 2 libraries; public restaurant; snack shop; 3 student lounges; teaching kitchen.

Typical Student Profile
30 full-time. 25 are under 25 years old; 5 are between 25 and 44 years old.

Special Programs
Cooperative education program (paid internship).

Financial Aid
In 2006, 6 scholarships were awarded (average award was $500). Employment placement assistance is available.

Housing
Coed, apartment-style, and single-sex housing available.

Application Information
Students may begin participation in January and August. Application deadline for fall is August 24. Application deadline for spring is January 8. In 2006, 45 applied; 25 were accepted. Applicants must submit a formal application and ACT scores.

Contact
Director of Admissions, Culinary Arts, 800 North Sixth Street, Wahpeton, ND 58076. Telephone: 701-671-2842. Fax: 701-671-2774. World Wide Web: http://www.ndscs.nodak.edu/departments/culinary-arts/index.jsp.

Ohio

Ashland University

Ashland, Ohio

General Information
Private, coeducational, comprehensive institution. Rural campus. Founded in 1878. Accredited by North Central Association of Colleges and Schools.

Program Information
Accredited by Council on Hotel, Restaurant and Institutional Education. Program calendar is divided into semesters. 4-year bachelor's degree in hotel and restaurant management.

Program Affiliation
American Culinary Federation; Council on Hotel, Restaurant, and Institutional Education; Gold and Silver Plate Society; National Association of College and University Food Service; National Restaurant Association; Ohio Hotel/Motel Association.

Areas of Study
Beverage management; food purchasing; management and human resources.

Facilities
Bakery; cafeteria; catering service; classroom; coffee shop; computer laboratory; demonstration laboratory; food production kitchen; lecture room; public restaurant; snack shop; teaching kitchen.

Typical Student Profile
26 total: 24 full-time; 2 part-time. 24 are under 25 years old; 2 are between 25 and 44 years old.

Special Programs
640-hour internship, semester at Disney (for credit), international internship opportunities, on-campus internships.

Financial Aid
In 2006, 4 scholarships were awarded (average award was $1000); 20 loans were granted (average loan was $2600). Employment placement assistance is available. Employment opportunities within the program are available.

Housing
Coed, apartment-style, and single-sex housing available.

Application Information
Students may begin participation in January and August. Application deadline for fall is August 25. Application deadline for spring is January 15. In 2006, 20 applied; 18 were accepted. Applicants must submit a formal application, an essay, high school transcripts, ACT or SAT score.

Contact
Director of Admissions, 401 College Avenue, Ashland, OH 44805. Telephone: 800-882-1548. Fax: 419-289-5999. World Wide Web: http://www.exploreashland.com/.

Cincinnati State Technical and Community College

Business Division

Cincinnati, Ohio

General Information
Public, coeducational, two-year college. Urban campus. Founded in 1966. Accredited by North Central Association of Colleges and Schools.

Program Information
Offered since 1978. Accredited by American Culinary Federation Accrediting Commission. National Restaurant Association Educational Foundation ManageFirst certificates available. Program calendar is 5 ten-week terms. 1-year certificate in culinary arts. 2-year associate degree in restaurant management. 2-year associate degree in hotel management. 2-year associate degree in culinary arts.

Program Affiliation
American Culinary Federation; Council on Hotel, Restaurant, and Institutional Education; National Restaurant Association; National Restaurant Association Educational Foundation.

Areas of Study
Baking; beverage management; buffet catering; controlling costs in food service; culinary skill development; food preparation; food purchasing; food service math; garde-manger; international cuisine; management and human resources; meat cutting; meat fabrication; nutrition; nutrition and food service; restaurant opportunities; sanitation; seafood processing; soup, stock, sauce, and starch production; wines and spirits.

Facilities
Computer laboratory; demonstration laboratory; food production kitchen; gourmet dining room; 4 lecture rooms; 6 teaching kitchens.

Typical Student Profile
400 total: 300 full-time; 100 part-time.

Special Programs
Cooperative education experience.

Financial Aid
In 2006, 20 scholarships were awarded (average award was $1000). Employment placement assistance is available. Employment opportunities within the program are available.

Cincinnati State Technical and Community College *(continued)*

Application Information

Students may begin participation in February, April, June, September, and November. Applications are accepted continuously. Applicants must submit a formal application and take entrance exam.

Contact

Director of Admissions, Business Division, 3520 Central Parkway, Cincinnati, OH 45223-2690. Telephone: 513-569-1637. Fax: 513-569-1467. World Wide Web: http://www.cincinnatistate.edu/.

Columbus State Community College

Hospitality, Massage Therapy, Sport and Exercise Studies

Columbus, Ohio

General Information

Public, coeducational, two-year college. Urban campus. Founded in 1963. Accredited by North Central Association of Colleges and Schools.

Program Information

Offered since 1966. Accredited by American Culinary Federation Accrediting Commission, American Dietetic Association, Commission on Accreditation of Hospitality Management Programs. National Restaurant Association Educational Foundation ManageFirst certificates available. Program calendar is divided into quarters. 1-year certificate in baking. 2-year associate degree in travel/tourism hotel management. 2-year associate degree in food service/restaurant management. 2-year associate degree in dietetic technician. 3-year associate degree in chef apprenticeship. 9-month certificate in dietary manager.

Program Affiliation

American Dietetic Association; Council on Hotel, Restaurant, and Institutional Education; National Restaurant Association; National Restaurant Association Educational Foundation; Ohio Hotel and Lodging Association; Retailer's Bakery Association.

Areas of Study

Baking; beverage management; catering services; controlling costs in food service; food preparation; food purchasing; food service math; garde-manger; introduction to food service; kitchen management; management and human resources; meal planning; menu and facilities design; nutrition; nutrition and food service; restaurant opportunities; sanitation; soup, stock, sauce, and starch production; wines and spirits.

Facilities

Catering service; 3 classrooms; computer laboratory; demonstration laboratory; 2 food production kitchens; 2 laboratories; learning resource center; 3 lecture rooms; library; 2 teaching kitchens.

Typical Student Profile

450 total: 200 full-time; 250 part-time.

Special Programs

Wine-food pairing competition-2 winners get trip to California wine country, culinary competitions and demonstrations, paid apprenticeship and cooperative work experiences.

Financial Aid

In 2006, 10 scholarships were awarded (average award was $1000). Employment placement assistance is available. Employment opportunities within the program are available.

Application Information

Students may begin participation in January, March, June, and September. Application deadline for fall chef apprenticeships is May 15. Application deadline for spring chef apprenticeships; continuous for other majors is November 15. In 2006, 225 applied; 200 were accepted. Applicants must submit a formal application, 2 letters of reference, and an essay and have an interview (chef apprentice option only).

Contact

Director of Admissions, Hospitality, Massage Therapy, Sport and Exercise Studies, 550 East Spring Street, Columbus, OH 43215. Telephone: 614-287-5126. Fax: 614-287-5973. World Wide Web: http://www.cscc.edu/.

Cuyahoga Community College, Metropolitan Campus

Hospitality Management Department

Cleveland, Ohio

General Information

Public, coeducational, two-year college. Urban campus. Founded in 1963. Accredited by North Central Association of Colleges and Schools.

Program Information

Offered since 1976. Accredited by American Culinary Federation Accrediting Commission, Commission on Accreditation of Hospitality Management Programs.

National Restaurant Association Educational Foundation ManageFirst certificates available. Program calendar is divided into semesters. 1-year certificate in professional baker. 1-year certificate in food and beverage operations. 1-year certificate in culinarian/cook. 2-year associate degree in restaurant/food service management. 2-year associate degree in culinary arts.

Program Affiliation

American Culinary Federation; American Personal Chef Institute & Association; Council on Hotel, Restaurant, and Institutional Education; International Food Service Executives Association; National Restaurant Association; National Restaurant Association Educational Foundation.

Areas of Study

Baking; beverage management; buffet catering; controlling costs in food service; culinary skill development; food preparation; food purchasing; food service math; garde-manger; international cuisine; introduction to food service; kitchen management; management and human resources; meal planning; meat cutting; menu and facilities design; nutrition; nutrition and food service; restaurant opportunities; sanitation; saucier; seafood processing; soup, stock, sauce, and starch production; wines and spirits.

Facilities

Bake shop; 4 classrooms; computer laboratory; demonstration laboratory; 2 food production kitchens; gourmet dining room; learning resource center; lecture room; library; public restaurant; student lounge; 2 teaching kitchens.

Typical Student Profile

150 total: 85 full-time; 65 part-time.

Special Programs

210-hour required practicum and 210-hours management (associate degree), culinary competitions, personal chef, service leaving experience.

Financial Aid

In 2006, 20 scholarships were awarded (average award was $600). Program-specific awards include Chef Boirdee Scholarship, A. LoPresti Scholarship, Hospitality Student Club Scholarship-for books only. Employment placement assistance is available. Employment opportunities within the program are available.

Application Information

Students may begin participation in January, March, May, August, and October. Applications are accepted continuously. In 2006, 231 applied; 231 were accepted. Applicants must interview; submit a formal application and be high school graduate or have GED; take college math and English placements tests.

Contact

Director of Admissions, Hospitality Management Department, Hospitality Management, 2900 Community College Avenue, Cleveland, OH 44115. Telephone: 216-987-4081. Fax: 216-987-4086. World Wide Web: http://www.tri-c.edu/infoaccess.

The International Culinary Arts & Sciences Institute (ICASI)

Chesterland, Ohio

General Information

Private, coeducational, culinary institute. Suburban campus. Founded in 2002.

Program Information

Offered since 2002. Program calendar is divided into quarters. 18-month diploma in pastry arts. 18-month diploma in culinary arts. 6-month certificate in pastry arts. 6-month certificate in culinary arts.

Program Affiliation

American Culinary Federation; American Institute of Wine & Food; International Association of Culinary Professionals.

Areas of Study

Baking; buffet catering; confectionery show pieces; culinary skill development; food preparation; food purchasing; food service math; garde-manger; international cuisine; introduction to food service; kitchen management; meal planning; meat fabrication; menu and facilities design; nutrition; nutrition and food service; patisserie; restaurant opportunities; sanitation; saucier; seafood processing; soup, stock, sauce, and starch production; wines and spirits.

Facilities

Bake shop; classroom; computer laboratory; food production kitchen; garden; lecture room; library; 2 teaching kitchens.

Typical Student Profile

50 are under 25 years old; 46 are between 25 and 44 years old; 8 are over 44 years old.

Special Programs

5-day cooking classes in Italy.

Financial Aid

Employment placement assistance is available. Employment opportunities within the program are available.

The International Culinary Arts & Sciences Institute (ICASI) *(continued)*

Application Information

Students may begin participation in January, April, July, and September. Applications are accepted continuously. In 2006, 90 applied; 90 were accepted. Applicants must interview; submit a formal application, letters of reference, an essay, have high school diploma or GED, and pass entrance exam.

Contact

Director of Admissions, 8700 Mayfield Road, Chesterland, OH 44026. Telephone: 440-729-7340. Fax: 440-729-4546. World Wide Web: http://www.icasi.net/.

The International Culinary School at The Art Institute of Ohio–Cincinnati

Cincinnati, Ohio

General Information

Private, coeducational institution.

Program Information

Associate degree in Culinary Arts. Diploma in Professional Cooking. Diploma in Baking and Pastry.

Contact

Office of Admissions, 8845 Governors Hill Drive, Suite 100, Cincinnati, OH 45249-3317. Telephone: 513-833-2400. World Wide Web: http://www.artinstitutes.edu/cincinnati/.

See color display following page 332.

Owens Community College

Hotel, Restaurant, and Institution Technology

Toledo, Ohio

General Information

Public, coeducational, two-year college. Suburban campus. Founded in 1965. Accredited by North Central Association of Colleges and Schools.

Program Information

Offered since 1968. Program calendar is divided into semesters. 1-year certificate in culinary arts. 2-year associate degree in hospitality management. 2-year associate degree in food service management.

Program Affiliation

National Restaurant Association; Ohio Restaurant Association.

Areas of Study

Advanced food production; baking; beverage management; buffet catering; controlling costs in food service; culinary skill development; food preparation; food purchasing; garde-manger; international cuisine; introduction to food service; management and human resources; meal planning; menu and facilities design; nutrition; restaurant opportunities; sanitation; soup, stock, sauce, and starch production; wines and spirits.

Facilities

Classroom; food production kitchen; public restaurant.

Typical Student Profile

150 total: 50 full-time; 100 part-time. 40 are under 25 years old; 100 are between 25 and 44 years old; 10 are over 44 years old.

Special Programs

Cooperative work experience, department-run Terrace View Café.

Financial Aid

Employment placement assistance is available.

Application Information

Students may begin participation in January, June, and August. Applications are accepted continuously. Applicants must submit a formal application.

Contact

Director of Admissions, Hotel, Restaurant, and Institution Technology, PO Box 10000, Oregon Road, Toledo, OH 43699-1947. Telephone: 567-661-7563. Fax: 567-661-7251. World Wide Web: http://www.owens.edu/academic_dept/health_tech/hri/index.html.

Sinclair Community College

Hospitality Management/Culinary Arts Option

Dayton, Ohio

General Information

Public, coeducational, two-year college. Urban campus. Founded in 1887. Accredited by North Central Association of Colleges and Schools.

Program Information

Offered since 1993. Accredited by American Culinary Federation Accrediting Commission, Commission on Accreditation of Hospitality Management Programs. Program calendar is divided into quarters. 1-year certificate in food service management. 2-year associate degree in tourism. 2-year associate degree in restaurant management. 2-year associate degree in meeting and event planning. 2-year associate degree in hotel lodging. 2-year associate degree in hospitality, management and tourism. 2-year associate degree in hospitality management. 2-year associate degree in culinary arts option.

Program Affiliation

American Culinary Federation; Council on Hotel, Restaurant, and Institutional Education; National Restaurant Association; National Restaurant Association Educational Foundation.

Areas of Study

Baking; beverage management; buffet catering; controlling costs in food service; culinary skill development; food preparation; food purchasing; garde-manger; international cuisine; introduction to food service; management and human resources; meat cutting; meat fabrication; menu and facilities design; nutrition; patisserie; restaurant opportunities; sanitation; saucier; seafood processing; soup, stock, sauce, and starch production; wines and spirits.

Facilities

Catering service; 5 classrooms; 5 computer laboratories; demonstration laboratory; food production kitchen; gourmet dining room; 3 laboratories; learning resource center; library; public restaurant; 3 snack shops; student lounge; 3 teaching kitchens.

Typical Student Profile

400 total: 100 full-time; 300 part-time.

Special Programs

Disney World Internship Program.

Financial Aid

In 2006, 7 scholarships were awarded (average award was $400). Employment placement assistance is available. Employment opportunities within the program are available.

Application Information

Students may begin participation in January, March, June, and September. Applications are accepted continuously. In 2006, 225 applied; 225 were accepted. Applicants must submit a formal application.

Contact

Director of Admissions, Hospitality Management/ Culinary Arts Option, 444 West Third Street, Dayton, OH 45402. Telephone: 937-512-5197. Fax: 937-512-5396. World Wide Web: http://www.sinclair.edu/academics/bps/departments/hmt/.

The University of Akron

Hospitality Management

Akron, Ohio

General Information

Public, coeducational, university. Urban campus. Founded in 1870. Accredited by North Central Association of Colleges and Schools.

Program Information

Offered since 1974. Accredited by ACBSP. Program calendar is divided into semesters. 1-year certificate in restaurant management. 1-year certificate in hotel/motel management. 1-year certificate in culinary arts. 2-year associate degree in restaurant management. 2-year associate degree in hotel/motel management. 2-year associate degree in hospitality marketing and sales. 2-year associate degree in culinary arts.

Program Affiliation

American Culinary Federation; Council on Hotel, Restaurant, and Institutional Education; National Restaurant Association; Ohio Hotel/Motel Association.

Areas of Study

Baking; beverage management; controlling costs in food service; culinary skill development; food preparation; food purchasing; food service communication; food service math; garde-manger; international cuisine; introduction to food service; kitchen management; management and human resources; meal planning; menu and facilities design; nutrition; sanitation; soup, stock, sauce, and starch production; wines and spirits.

Facilities

Food production kitchen; public restaurant.

Typical Student Profile

150 total: 75 full-time; 75 part-time. 90 are under 25 years old; 50 are between 25 and 44 years old; 10 are over 44 years old.

Special Programs

Internships, field trips to local and national professional shows.

Financial Aid

In 2006, 10 scholarships were awarded (average award was $1000). Employment placement assistance is available. Employment opportunities within the program are available.

Housing

Coed, apartment-style, and single-sex housing available.

The University of Akron ***(continued)***

Application Information
Students may begin participation in January and August. Applications are accepted continuously. In 2006, 85 applied; 85 were accepted. Applicants must submit a formal application and have a high school diploma or GED.

Contact
Director of Admissions, Hospitality Management, 302 Buchtel Common, Akron, OH 44325. Telephone: 800-655-4884. World Wide Web: http://www.uakron.edu/.

Zane State College

Culinary Arts Program

Zanesville, Ohio

General Information
Public, coeducational, two-year college. Suburban campus. Founded in 1970. Accredited by North Central Association of Colleges and Schools.

Program Information
Offered since 1993. Accredited by American Culinary Federation Accrediting Commission. Program calendar is divided into quarters. 1-quarter certificate in safety and sanitation. 2-year associate degree in culinary arts.

Program Affiliation
American Culinary Federation; National Restaurant Association; National Restaurant Association Educational Foundation.

Areas of Study
Baking; culinary French; culinary skill development; food preparation; food purchasing; food service math; garde-manger; international cuisine; meat cutting; meat fabrication; menu and facilities design; nutrition and food service; sanitation; soup, stock, sauce, and starch production.

Facilities
Bake shop; cafeteria; classroom; 10 computer laboratories; demonstration laboratory; food production kitchen; learning resource center; lecture room; library; 4 public restaurants; 2 student lounges; teaching kitchen.

Typical Student Profile
30 total: 20 full-time; 10 part-time. 15 are under 25 years old; 10 are between 25 and 44 years old; 5 are over 44 years old.

Financial Aid
Employment placement assistance is available.

Application Information
Students may begin participation in September. Applications are accepted continuously. Applicants must submit a formal application.

Contact
Director of Admissions, Culinary Arts Program, 1555 Newark Road, Zanesville, OH 43701. Telephone: 740-588-1334. Fax: 740-454-0035. World Wide Web: http://www.zanestate.edu/CUL/default.htm.

Oklahoma

Metro Area Vocational Technical School District 22

Oklahoma City, Oklahoma

General Information
Public, coeducational, technical institute. Urban campus. Founded in 1980.

Program Information
Offered since 1980. Program calendar is divided into quarters. 525- to 600-hour certificate in food service production. 525- to 600-hour certificate in food service management/production.

Program Affiliation
American Culinary Federation; National Restaurant Association; National Restaurant Association Educational Foundation; Oklahoma Restaurant Association.

Areas of Study
Baking; buffet catering; controlling costs in food service; food preparation; food purchasing; food service communication; food service math; introduction to food service; kitchen management; meal planning; nutrition; nutrition and food service; sanitation.

Facilities
Bake shop; cafeteria; classroom; demonstration laboratory; food production kitchen; learning resource center; library.

Typical Student Profile
34 total: 1 full-time; 33 part-time. 33 are under 25 years old; 1 is over 44 years old.

Special Programs
400-hour paid internship.

Financial Aid
Employment placement assistance is available. Employment opportunities within the program are available.

Application Information
Students may begin participation in January, February, March, April, May, August, September, October, November, and December. Applications are accepted continuously. Applicants must submit a formal application.

Contact
Director of Admissions, 4901 South Bryant, Oklahoma City, OK 73129. Telephone: 405-605-2206. Fax: 405-671-3410. World Wide Web: http://www.metrotech.org.

Oklahoma State University, Okmulgee

Hospitality Services Department

Okmulgee, Oklahoma

General Information
Public, coeducational, two-year college. Rural campus. Founded in 1946. Accredited by North Central Association of Colleges and Schools.

Program Information
Offered since 1946. Program calendar is divided into trimesters. 90-hour associate degree in culinary arts.

Program Affiliation
Greater Southwest Retail Bakers Association; International Food Service Executives Association; National Restaurant Association; National Restaurant Association Educational Foundation; Oklahoma Restaurant Association; Retailer's Bakery Association.

Areas of Study
Baking; buffet catering; controlling costs in food service; culinary French; culinary skill development; food preparation; food purchasing; garde-manger; international cuisine; introduction to food service; kitchen management; management and human resources; meal planning; meat cutting; meat fabrication; menu and facilities design; nutrition; patisserie; sanitation; saucier; seafood processing; soup, stock, sauce, and starch production; wines and spirits.

Facilities
Cafeteria; 5 classrooms; coffee shop; computer laboratory; demonstration laboratory; 2 food production kitchens; gourmet dining room; learning resource center; library; 2 public restaurants; snack shop; student lounge.

Typical Student Profile
180 total: 175 full-time; 5 part-time.

Special Programs
Class trips to wineries, San Francisco, and fine dining establishments, 8-week paid internships, culinary competitions.

Financial Aid
In 2006, 10 scholarships were awarded (average award was $500); 3 loans were granted (average loan was $2500). Program-specific awards include work-study programs, possible waiver of out-of-state tuition. Employment placement assistance is available. Employment opportunities within the program are available.

Housing
Coed and apartment-style housing available.

Application Information
Students may begin participation in January, April, and August. Application deadline for fall is August 30. Application deadline for spring is January 3. Application deadline for summer is April 25. In 2006, 91 applied; 91 were accepted. Applicants must submit a formal application, ACT scores, and have a high school diploma or GED.

Contact
Director of Admissions, Hospitality Services Department, 1801 East Fourth Street, Okmulgee, OK 74447-3901. Telephone: 918-293-5030. Fax: 918-293-4618. World Wide Web: http://www.osu-okmulgee.edu/.

Oregon

Central Oregon Community College

Cascade Culinary Institute

Bend, Oregon

General Information
Public, coeducational, two-year college. Small-town setting. Founded in 1949. Accredited by Northwest Commission on Colleges and Universities.

Program Information
Offered since 1993. Accredited by American Culinary Federation Accrediting Commission. Program calendar is divided into quarters. 4-term certificate in culinary arts. 6-term associate degree in hospitality/tourism/recreation management. 6-term associate degree in culinary management.

Central Oregon Community College *(continued)*

PROGRAM AFFILIATION
American Culinary Federation; American Dietetic Association; Council on Hotel, Restaurant, and Institutional Education; International Association of Culinary Professionals.

AREAS OF STUDY
Baking; beverage management; controlling costs in food service; culinary skill development; food preparation; food purchasing; food service math; garde-manger; introduction to food service; kitchen management; management and human resources; meal planning; nutrition; nutrition and food service; restaurant opportunities; sanitation; soup, stock, sauce, and starch production; wines and spirits.

FACILITIES
Bake shop; cafeteria; catering service; 2 classrooms; computer laboratory; food production kitchen; 2 lecture rooms; library; public restaurant; snack shop; teaching kitchen.

TYPICAL STUDENT PROFILE
43 full-time.

SPECIAL PROGRAMS
3-day tour of Napa Valley wineries and farm gardens, visit to fisheries on Oregon coast, food and cultural experience in Spain.

FINANCIAL AID
In 2006, 3 scholarships were awarded (average award was $1000); 18 loans were granted (average loan was $2100). Program-specific awards include Pine Tavern Award ($1800). Employment placement assistance is available. Employment opportunities within the program are available.

HOUSING
Coed housing available.

APPLICATION INFORMATION
Students may begin participation in January, March, and September. Application deadline for fall is August 1. Application deadline for winter is November 1. Application deadline for spring is February 1. In 2006, 22 were accepted. Applicants must interview; submit a formal application.

CONTACT
Director of Admissions, Cascade Culinary Institute, 2600 Northwest College Way, Bend, OR 97701-5998. Telephone: 541-383-7715. Fax: 541-383-7508. World Wide Web: http://culinary.cocc.edu/.

CHEMEKETA COMMUNITY COLLEGE

Hospitality and Tourism Management

Salem, Oregon

GENERAL INFORMATION
Public, coeducational, two-year college. Urban campus. Founded in 1955. Accredited by Northwest Commission on Colleges and Universities.

PROGRAM INFORMATION
Offered since 1974. Program calendar is divided into quarters. 1-year certificate in tourism and travel management. 1-year certificate in hospitality management. 1-year certificate in event management. 1-year certificate in destination marketing. 2-year associate degree in tourism and travel management. 2-year associate degree in nutrition and food management with Oregon State University. 2-year associate degree in hotel, restaurant, and resort management. 2-year associate degree in hotel and business management with Washington State University. 2-year associate degree in hospitality management.

PROGRAM AFFILIATION
American Hotel and Lodging Association; Council on Hotel, Restaurant, and Institutional Education; Hospitality Sales and Marketing Association International; National Restaurant Association; National Restaurant Association Educational Foundation; Oregon Lodging Association; Oregon Restaurant Educational Foundation; Portland Oregon Visitors Association.

AREAS OF STUDY
Beverage management; controlling costs in food service; cultural heritage tourism; food purchasing; gaming; introduction to food service; leisure/recreation; lodging; management and human resources; meal planning; meeting and event planning; nature-based tourism; nutrition; nutrition and food service; restaurant opportunities; sanitation; travel and tourism; wines and spirits.

FACILITIES
Classroom; computer laboratory; lecture room; library; vineyard.

TYPICAL STUDENT PROFILE
225 total: 125 full-time; 100 part-time.

SPECIAL PROGRAMS
Online classes (complete degree/certificate are available online), transfer degree to Washington State University School of Hospitality Business Management.

Financial Aid
Employment placement assistance is available. Employment opportunities within the program are available.

Application Information
Students may begin participation in January, March, June, and September. Applications are accepted continuously. Applicants must submit a formal application and have high school diploma or GED, and take placement test.

Contact
Director of Admissions, Hospitality and Tourism Management, 4000 Lancaster Drive NE, Salem, OR 97305. Telephone: 503-399-5296. Fax: 503-365-4770. World Wide Web: http://www.hsm.org.

Culinary Awakenings

Portland, Oregon

General Information
Private, coeducational institution. Urban campus. Founded in 1993.

Program Information
Offered since 1993. Program calendar is custom programs all year. 1—20 day certificate in vegan culinary arts.

Program Affiliation
American Vegan Society; Bioneers; Chefs Collaborative 2000; International Vegetarian Union; North American Vegetarian Society; Northwest VEG; Vegetarian Resource Group.

Areas of Study
Baking; culinary skill development; food preparation; introduction to food service; meal planning; menu and facilities design; sanitation.

Facilities
Garden; lecture room; teaching kitchen.

Typical Student Profile
30 part-time.

Special Programs
20 day vegan culinary arts program, kitchen and pantry transformation, outing days to local vegan businesses, business consultations, public speaking services, workshops and training programs.

Financial Aid
Program-specific awards include sous chef discounts. Employment placement assistance is available.

Application Information
Applications are accepted continuously. In 2006, 30 applied; 30 were accepted. Applicants must phone interview, client contact form.

Contact
Director of Admissions, 4110 SE Hawthorne Boulevard #173, Portland, OR 97214. Telephone: 503-752-2588. World Wide Web: http://www.chefal.org.

International School of Baking

Bend, Oregon

General Information
Private, coeducational, culinary institute. Urban campus. Founded in 1986.

Program Information
Offered since 1986. Program calendar is customized to meet student needs. 1-month certificate in start-up bakery course. 2-week certificate in European pastries. 2-week certificate in artisan breads. 3-day certificate in individualized specialization. 6-week certificate in start-up bakery course including wedding cakes.

Program Affiliation
American Culinary Federation; International Association of Culinary Professionals; James Beard Foundation, Inc.; Retailer's Bakery Association; The Bread Bakers Guild of America.

Areas of Study
Bakery start-up; baking; custom designed studies; kitchen management; menu and facilities design; patisserie; sanitation.

Facilities
Bakery; classroom; demonstration laboratory; food production kitchen; garden; learning resource center; library; teaching kitchen.

Typical Student Profile
21 total: 5 full-time; 16 part-time.

Special Programs
6-month unpaid internship, 1-year unpaid internship.

Financial Aid
Employment placement assistance is available.

Application Information
Students may begin participation year-round. Applications are accepted continuously. Application deadline for each course is 2 months prior to start date. In 2006, 24 applied; 21 were accepted. Applicants must submit a formal application.

International School of Baking *(continued)*

Contact

Director of Admissions, 1971 NW Juniper Street, Bend, OR 97701. Telephone: 541-389-8553. Fax: 541-389-3736. World Wide Web: http://www.schoolofbaking.com/.

Lane Community College

Culinary Arts and Hospitality Management

Eugene, Oregon

General Information

Public, coeducational, two-year college. Suburban campus. Founded in 1964. Accredited by Northwest Commission on Colleges and Universities.

Program Information

Offered since 1979. Accredited by American Culinary Federation. Program calendar is divided into quarters. 1-year certificate of completion in hospitality management. 2-year associate degree in hospitality management. 2-year associate degree in culinary arts.

Program Affiliation

Council on Hotel, Restaurant, and Institutional Education; Educational Institute-American Hotel and Motel Association; National Restaurant Association; National Restaurant Association Educational Foundation.

Areas of Study

Baking; beverage management; buffet catering; controlling costs in food service; culinary skill development; food preparation; food purchasing; food service math; garde-manger; international cuisine; introduction to food service; management and human resources; menu and facilities design; nutrition; sanitation; soup, stock, sauce, and starch production.

Facilities

3 classrooms; 3 demonstration laboratories; 2 food production kitchens; gourmet dining room; learning resource center; 3 lecture rooms; library; public restaurant; 3 teaching kitchens.

Typical Student Profile

105 total: 85 full-time; 20 part-time.

Special Programs

Culinary competition.

Financial Aid

Employment placement assistance is available. Employment opportunities within the program are available.

Application Information

Students may begin participation in January, April, and September. Application deadline for fall is June 30. Applicants must interview; submit a formal application, letters of reference, test scores.

Contact

Director of Admissions, Culinary Arts and Hospitality Management, 4000 East 30th Avenue, Building 19 Room 202, Eugene, OR 97405. Telephone: 541-463-3510 Ext. 3510. Fax: 541-463-4738. World Wide Web: http://www.lanecc.edu/.

Linn-Benton Community College

Culinary Arts/Restaurant Management

Albany, Oregon

General Information

Public, coeducational, two-year college. Rural campus. Founded in 1966. Accredited by Northwest Commission on Colleges and Universities.

Program Information

Offered since 1969. Program calendar is divided into quarters. 2-year associate degree in wine and food dynamics. 2-year associate degree in pre-restaurant management. 2-year associate degree in chef training.

Program Affiliation

American Culinary Federation; Council on Hotel, Restaurant, and Institutional Education; National Restaurant Association; Women Chefs and Restaurateurs.

Areas of Study

Baking; beverage management; buffet catering; confectionery show pieces; controlling costs in food service; culinary French; culinary skill development; food preparation; food purchasing; food service math; garde-manger; international cuisine; introduction to food service; kitchen management; management and human resources; meal planning; meat cutting; meat fabrication; menu and facilities design; nutrition; patisserie; sanitation; saucier; seafood processing; soup, stock, sauce, and starch production; wine and food; wines and spirits.

Facilities

Bake shop; bakery; cafeteria; catering service; classroom; coffee shop; computer laboratory; food production kitchen; garden; gourmet dining room; laboratory; learning resource center; lecture room; library; public restaurant; snack shop; student lounge.

Typical Student Profile
45 full-time. 15 are under 25 years old; 25 are between 25 and 44 years old; 5 are over 44 years old.

Financial Aid
In 2006, 7 scholarships were awarded (average award was $500). Program-specific awards include 36 credits of tuition waiver per year for program club officers. Employment placement assistance is available.

Application Information
Students may begin participation in September. Applications are accepted continuously. In 2006, 45 applied; 45 were accepted. Applicants must submit a formal application.

Contact
Director of Admissions, Culinary Arts/Restaurant Management, 6500 Southwest Pacific Boulevard, Albany, OR 97321. Telephone: 541-917-4388. Fax: 541-917-4395. World Wide Web: http://www.linnbenton.edu/.

Oregon Coast Culinary Institute

Coos Bay, Oregon

General Information
Public, coeducational, culinary institute. Small-town setting. Founded in 2000. Accredited by Northwest Commission on Colleges and Universities.

Program Information
Offered since 2000. Accredited by American Culinary Federation Accrediting Commission. Program calendar is divided into quarters. 15-month associate degree in culinary arts. 15-month associate degree in baking and pastry arts.

Program Affiliation
American Culinary Federation; National Restaurant Association.

Areas of Study
Baking; beverage management; buffet catering; confectionery show pieces; controlling costs in food service; culinary skill development; food preparation; food purchasing; food service communication; food service math; garde-manger; international cuisine; introduction to food service; kitchen management; management and human resources; meal planning; meat cutting; meat fabrication; menu and facilities design; Northwest cuisine; nutrition; nutrition and food service; patisserie; restaurant opportunities; sanitation; saucier; seafood processing; soup, stock, sauce, and starch production; wines and spirits.

Facilities
Bakery; cafeteria; catering service; 3 classrooms; computer laboratory; demonstration laboratory; food production kitchen; gourmet dining room; learning resource center; 3 lecture rooms; library; snack shop; student lounge; 2 teaching kitchens.

Student Profile
60 full-time. 40 are under 25 years old; 20 are between 25 and 44 years old.

Faculty
8 total: 3 full-time; 5 part-time. 3 are industry professionals; 1 is a master baker; 2 are culinary-certified teachers. Prominent faculty: Shawn Hanlin, CEC; Tom Roberts, CEC, CCE; Nilda Dovale, CCC, CCE; Tina Powers, CMB. Faculty-student ratio: 1:20.

Special Programs
Externships, culinary competition, including team events.

Typical Expenses
Application fee: $30. In-state tuition: $19,500 per 15-month program (includes textbooks, knife set, 2 sets of chef uniforms). Out-of-state tuition: $19,500 per 15-month program (includes textbooks, knife set, 2 sets of chef uniforms). Program-related fee includes $250 for deposit reserves place in program and goes toward tuition.

Financial Aid
In 2007, 15 scholarships were awarded (average award was $2470); 72 loans were granted (average loan was $6782). Program-specific awards include ProStart certificate scholarship, GPA tuition discount. Employment placement assistance is available. Employment opportunities within the program are available.

Housing
Coed and apartment-style housing available. Average on-campus housing cost per month: $400–$600. Average off-campus housing cost per month: $500.

Application Information
Students may begin participation in September. Applications are accepted continuously. In 2007, 105 applied; 60 were accepted. Applicants must submit a formal application.

Contact
Jamie Cook, Student Services Representative, 1988 Newmark Avenue, Coos Bay, OR 97420. Telephone: 877-895-CHEF. Fax: 541-888-7195. E-mail: jcook@socc.edu. World Wide Web: http://www.occi.net/.

See display on page 260.

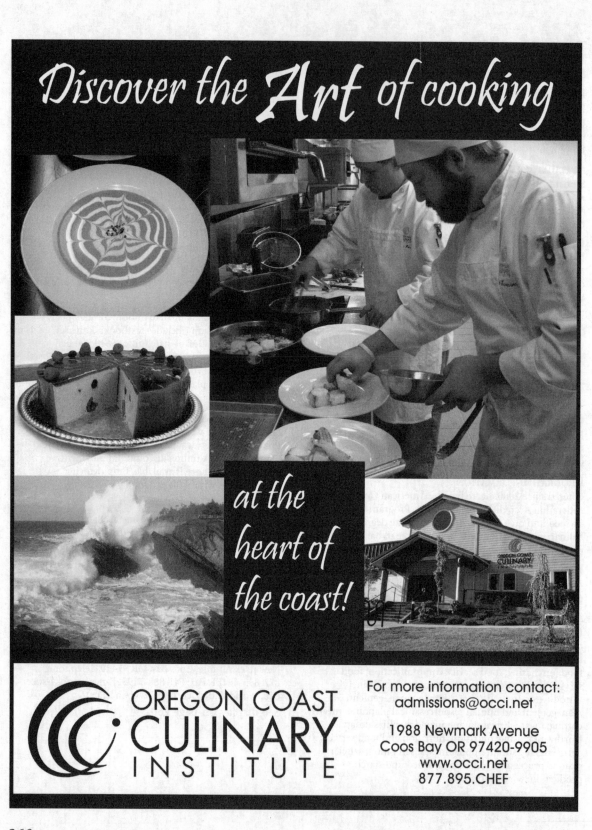

Oregon Culinary Institute

Portland, Oregon

General Information
Private, coeducational, culinary institute. Founded in 2006. Accredited by Accrediting Council for Independent Colleges and Schools.

Program Information
Program calendar is continuous. Associate degree in culinary arts. Certificate in baking and pastry. Diploma in culinary arts.

Facilities
Computer laboratory; 3 food production kitchens; gourmet dining room.

Financial Aid
Employment placement assistance is available. Employment opportunities within the program are available.

Application Information
Applications are accepted continuously. Applicants must interview; submit a formal application and high school diploma or GED, ACT Career Programs Assessment or one year post-secondary education (minimum 2.5 GPA).

Contact
Director of Admissions, 1717 SW Madison Street, Portland, OR 97205. Telephone: 888-OCI-CHEF. Fax: 503-961-6240. World Wide Web: http://www.oregonculinaryinstitute.com/.

Southern Oregon University

Hospitality and Tourism Management

Ashland, Oregon

General Information
Public, coeducational, four-year college. Small-town setting. Founded in 1926. Accredited by Northwest Commission on Colleges and Universities.

Program Information
Offered since 1992. Program calendar is divided into quarters. 4-year bachelor's degree in business administration (hospitality and tourism management).

Areas of Study
Beverage management; controlling costs in food service; food purchasing; food service communication; food service math; introduction to food service; management and human resources; restaurant opportunities; wines and spirits.

Facilities
Cafeteria; catering service; 10 classrooms; coffee shop; 2 computer laboratories; food production kitchen; learning resource center; lecture room; library; public restaurant; student lounge; vineyard.

Typical Student Profile
40 full-time.

Special Programs
Internships with industry leaders, hands on event planning and execution.

Financial Aid
Employment placement assistance is available. Employment opportunities within the program are available.

Housing
Coed housing available.

Application Information
Students may begin participation in January, April, June, and September. Applications are accepted continuously. In 2006, 40 applied; 40 were accepted. Applicants must submit a formal application.

Contact
Director of Admissions, Hospitality and Tourism Management, 1250 Siskiyou Boulevard, Ashland, OR 97520. Telephone: 541-552-6483. World Wide Web: http://www.sou.edu/business.

Western Culinary Institute

Le Cordon Bleu Programs at Western Culinary Institute

Portland, Oregon

General Information
Private, coeducational, culinary institute. Urban campus. Founded in 1983. Accredited by Accrediting Commission of Career Schools and Colleges of Technology.

Program Information
Offered since 1983. Accredited by American Culinary Federation Accrediting Commission. Program calendar is divided into six-week cycles. 15-month associate degree in patisserie and baking. 15-month associate degree in hospitality and restaurant management. 15-month associate degree in culinary arts. 9-month diploma in patisserie and baking. 9-month diploma in culinary arts.

Program Affiliation
American Culinary Federation; California Restaurant Association; International Sommelier Guild; James Beard Foundation, Inc.; National Restaurant Association;

Western Culinary Institute ***(continued)***

National Restaurant Association Educational Foundation; Ontario Restaurant Association; Washington Restaurant Association; Women Chefs and Restaurateurs.

Areas of Study

Baking; beverage management; buffet catering; confectionery show pieces; controlling costs in food service; convenience cookery; culinary French; culinary skill development; food preparation; food purchasing; food service communication; food service math; garde-manger; international cuisine; introduction to food service; kitchen management; management and human resources; meal planning; meat cutting; meat fabrication; menu and facilities design; nutrition; nutrition and food service; patisserie; restaurant opportunities; sanitation; saucier; soup, stock, sauce, and starch production; wines and spirits.

Facilities

Bake shop; bakery; cafeteria; catering service; 7 classrooms; coffee shop; 3 computer laboratories; 2 demonstration laboratories; 13 food production kitchens; gourmet dining room; learning resource center; 7 lecture rooms; library; 2 public restaurants; 2 student lounges; bakery/delicatessen.

Typical Student Profile

950 full-time.

Special Programs

6 to 12 week internship required at U.S. or international location, culinary competitions.

Financial Aid

In 2006, 93 scholarships were awarded. Employment placement assistance is available. Employment opportunities within the program are available.

Application Information

Students may begin participation in January, February, April, May, July, August, October, and November. Applications are accepted continuously. Applicants must submit a formal application and have a high school diploma.

Contact

Director of Admissions, Le Cordon Bleu Programs at Western Culinary Institute, 921 SW Morrison Street, Suite 400, Portland, OR 97205. Telephone: 888-848-3202. Fax: 503-223-5554. World Wide Web: http://www.wci.edu/.

Pennsylvania

Bucks County Community College

Business Department

Newtown, Pennsylvania

General Information

Public, coeducational, two-year college. Suburban campus. Founded in 1964. Accredited by Middle States Association of Colleges and Schools.

Program Information

Offered since 1967. Program calendar is divided into semesters. 1-year associate degree in travel and event planning. 1-year certificate in travel and event planning. 1-year certificate in hospitality/restaurant/institutional supervision. 1-year certificate in culinary/pastry and catering arts. 2-year associate degree in tourism/hospitality/restaurant management. 3-year associate degree in chef apprenticeship-pastry emphasis. 3-year associate degree in chef apprenticeship-foods emphasis.

Program Affiliation

American Culinary Federation; Confrerie de la Chaine des Rotisseurs; International Association of Culinary Professionals; International Food Service Executives Association; National Restaurant Association; National Restaurant Association Educational Foundation.

Areas of Study

Baking; buffet catering; confectionery show pieces; controlling costs in food service; culinary skill development; food preparation; food purchasing; food service communication; food service math; garde-manger; introduction to food service; kitchen management; management and human resources; meal planning; meat cutting; meat fabrication; menu and facilities design; nutrition; nutrition and food service; patisserie; restaurant opportunities; sanitation; saucier; seafood processing; soup, stock, sauce, and starch production.

Facilities

Cafeteria; 5 classrooms; computer laboratory; demonstration laboratory; 2 food production kitchens; gourmet dining room; laboratory; learning resource center; library; snack shop; student lounge; teaching kitchen; greenhouse.

Special Programs

Required paid cooperative education and paid summer internship in management.

Financial Aid
Employment placement assistance is available. Employment opportunities within the program are available.

Application Information
Students may begin participation in January and August. Applicants must submit a formal application and an essay.

Contact
Director of Admissions, Business Department, 275 Swamp Road, Newton, PA 18901-4106. Telephone: 215-968-8241. Fax: 215-504-8509. World Wide Web: http://www.bucks.edu/.

Butler County Community College

Hospitality Management/Dietary Management

Butler, Pennsylvania

General Information
Public, coeducational, two-year college. Small-town setting. Founded in 1965. Accredited by Middle States Association of Colleges and Schools.

Program Information
Offered since 1988. Program calendar is divided into semesters. 1-year certificate in hospitality management. 2-year associate degree in hospitality management/dietary manager. 2-year associate degree in hospitality management.

Program Affiliation
Dietary Managers Association; National Restaurant Association Educational Foundation.

Areas of Study
Buffet catering; controlling costs in food service; diet therapy; food preparation; food purchasing; food service communication; food service math; international cuisine; kitchen management; lodging; management and human resources; meal planning; nutrition; nutrition and food service; sanitation; travel and tourism.

Facilities
Cafeteria; classroom; 2 computer laboratories; demonstration laboratory; food production kitchen; laboratory; learning resource center; lecture room; library.

Typical Student Profile
34 total: 24 full-time; 10 part-time.

Special Programs
Attendance at NRA show and local food shows.

Financial Aid
Program-specific awards include National Restaurant Association scholarships ($2000), Hoss's Steak House scholarship ($500). Employment placement assistance is available. Employment opportunities within the program are available.

Application Information
Students may begin participation in January, May, and August. Applications are accepted continuously. In 2006, 22 were accepted. Applicants must submit a formal application and have a high school transcript.

Contact
Director of Admissions, Hospitality Management/Dietary Management, PO Box 1203, Butler, PA 16003-1203. Telephone: 724-287-8711 Ext. 388. Fax: 724-285-6047. World Wide Web: http://bc3.cc.pa.us/.

Cheyney University of Pennsylvania

Hotel and Restaurant Management

Cheyney, Pennsylvania

General Information
Public, coeducational, comprehensive institution. Rural campus. Founded in 1837. Accredited by Middle States Association of Colleges and Schools.

Program Information
Offered since 1976. Program calendar is divided into 4-1-4. 4-year bachelor's degree in hotel and restaurant management.

Program Affiliation
Council on Hotel, Restaurant, and Institutional Education; National Restaurant Association; National Restaurant Association Educational Foundation; Pennsylvania Travel Council.

Areas of Study
Beverage management; buffet catering; controlling costs in food service; culinary skill development; food preparation; food purchasing; food service math; international cuisine; kitchen management; management and human resources; menu and facilities design; nutrition; sanitation.

Facilities
Cafeteria; catering service; 4 classrooms; computer laboratory; demonstration laboratory; food production kitchen; laboratory; learning resource center; 4 lecture rooms; library; 2 teaching kitchens.

Cheyney University of Pennsylvania ***(continued)***

Typical Student Profile
40 total: 37 full-time; 3 part-time. 35 are under 25 years old; 3 are between 25 and 44 years old; 2 are over 44 years old.

Special Programs
One-year internship, student-operated dining facility.

Financial Aid
In 2006, 1 scholarship was awarded. Program-specific awards include Walt Disney Scholarship Endowment. Employment placement assistance is available.

Housing
Coed and single-sex housing available.

Application Information
Students may begin participation in January and September. Applications are accepted continuously. Applicants must interview; submit a formal application, letters of reference, an essay, academic transcript.

Contact
Director of Admissions, Hotel and Restaurant Management, 1837 University Circle, PO Box 200, Cheyney, PA 19319. Telephone: 610-399-2275. Fax: 610-399-2099. World Wide Web: http://www.cheyney.edu/.

Commonwealth Technical Institute

Culinary Arts Program

Johnstown, Pennsylvania

General Information
Private, coeducational, technical institute. Suburban campus. Founded in 1959. Accredited by Accrediting Commission of Career Schools and Colleges of Technology.

Program Information
Offered since 1974. Program calendar is divided into trimesters. 16-month associate degree in culinary arts. 8-month diploma in kitchen helper.

Program Affiliation
Council on Hotel, Restaurant, and Institutional Education.

Areas of Study
Baking; controlling costs in food service; food preparation; food purchasing; food service math; introduction to food service; management and human resources; meal planning; menu and facilities design; nutrition; sanitation; soup, stock, sauce, and starch production.

Facilities
Bake shop; cafeteria; 3 classrooms; 2 computer laboratories; food production kitchen; 2 laboratories; learning resource center; library; snack shop; teaching kitchen.

Typical Student Profile
74 full-time. 66 are under 25 years old; 8 are between 25 and 44 years old.

Financial Aid
Employment placement assistance is available.

Housing
Single-sex housing available.

Application Information
Students may begin participation in January, May, and September. Applications are accepted continuously. In 2006, 39 applied; 35 were accepted. Applicants must submit a formal application.

Contact
Director of Admissions, Culinary Arts Program, 727 Goucher Street, Johnstown, PA 15905. Telephone: 814-255-8256. World Wide Web: http://www.hgac.org.

Delaware Valley College

Food Science and Management

Doylestown, Pennsylvania

General Information
Private, coeducational, four-year college. Suburban campus. Founded in 1896. Accredited by Middle States Association of Colleges and Schools.

Program Information
Offered since 1961. Program calendar is divided into semesters. 2-year associate degree in culinary arts. 4-year bachelor's degree in food management.

Program Affiliation
American Institute of Wine & Food; American Wine Society; Institute of Food Technologists; National Restaurant Association Educational Foundation; Slow Food International; Society of Wine Educators; United States Personal Chef Association.

Areas of Study
Baking; beverage management; confectionery show pieces; controlling costs in food service; convenience cookery; culinary skill development; food preparation; food purchasing; food service communication; garde-manger; international cuisine; introduction to food service; kitchen management; management and human resources; meal planning; meat cutting; meat fabrication; menu and facilities design; nutrition; nutrition and food service; patisserie; restaurant opportunities; sanitation; saucier; soup, stock, sauce, and starch production; wines and spirits.

Facilities
Bake shop; bakery; cafeteria; classroom; computer laboratory; demonstration laboratory; food production kitchen; garden; gourmet dining room; laboratory; learning resource center; lecture room; library; student lounge; teaching kitchen.

Typical Student Profile
30 total: 23 full-time; 7 part-time.

Special Programs
Tour of International Experiences, access to 500-acre operating farm, access to beef on the dairy farm.

Housing
Coed housing available.

Application Information
Students may begin participation in January and September. Applications are accepted continuously. In 2006, 9 applied; 2 were accepted. Applicants must submit a formal application and an essay.

Contact
Director of Admissions, Food Science and Management, 700 East Butler Avenue, Doylestown, PA 18901. Telephone: 800-2DELVAL. Fax: 215-230-2968.

Drexel University

Hospitality Management, Culinary Arts, Culinary Science and Food Science

Philadelphia, Pennsylvania

General Information
Private, coeducational, university. Urban campus. Founded in 1891. Accredited by Middle States Association of Colleges and Schools.

Program Information
Offered since 1988. Accredited by Council on Hotel, Restaurant and Institutional Education, Commission on Accreditation of Hospitality Management Programs. Program calendar is divided into quarters. 4-year bachelor's degree in culinary science. 4-year bachelor's degree in hospitality management. 4-year bachelor's degree in culinary arts.

Program Affiliation
American Culinary Federation; American Dietetic Association; American Institute of Wine & Food; American Vegan Society; American Wine Society; Confrerie de la Chaine des Rotisseurs; Council on Hotel, Restaurant, and Institutional Education; International Association of Culinary Professionals; International Wine & Food Society; James Beard Foundation, Inc.; National Restaurant Association; National Restaurant Association Educational Foundation; Society of Wine Educators; Women Chefs and Restaurateurs.

Areas of Study
Baking; beverage management; buffet catering; confectionery show pieces; controlling costs in food service; convenience cookery; culinary French; culinary skill development; food preparation; food purchasing; food service communication; garde-manger; international cuisine; kitchen management; management and human resources; meal planning; meat cutting; meat fabrication; menu and facilities design; nutrition; nutrition and food service; patisserie; restaurant opportunities; sanitation; saucier; seafood processing; soup, stock, sauce, and starch production; wines and spirits.

Facilities
Bake shop; bakery; catering service; 10 classrooms; coffee shop; 7 computer laboratories; demonstration laboratory; 3 food production kitchens; garden; 2 gourmet dining rooms; 4 laboratories; learning resource center; 2 lecture rooms; 2 libraries; public restaurant; snack shop; student lounge; 2 teaching kitchens.

Typical Student Profile
156 total: 127 full-time; 29 part-time. 146 are under 25 years old; 10 are between 25 and 44 years old.

Special Programs
Study abroad in London, cooperative employment experience.

Financial Aid
In 2006, 10 scholarships were awarded (average award was $4000). Employment placement assistance is available. Employment opportunities within the program are available.

Housing
Coed and apartment-style housing available.

Application Information
Students may begin participation in January, April, June, and September. Application deadline for fall is March 1. In 2006, 353 applied; 173 were accepted. Applicants must submit a formal application, letters of reference, and an essay.

Drexel University *(continued)*

Contact
Director of Admissions, Hospitality Management, Culinary Arts, Culinary Science and Food Science, 33rd and Arch Street, Suite 110, Philadelphia, PA 19104. Telephone: 215-895-2836. Fax: 215-895-2426. World Wide Web: http://www.drexel.edu/.

East Stroudsburg University of Pennsylvania

Hotel, Restaurant and Tourism Management

East Stroudsburg, Pennsylvania

General Information
Public, coeducational, four-year college. Founded in 1893. Accredited by Middle States Association of Colleges and Schools.

Program Information
Offered since 1980. Program calendar is divided into semesters. 4-year bachelor's degree in tourism management. 4-year bachelor's degree in restaurant management. 4-year bachelor's degree in hotel management.

Program Affiliation
Council on Hotel, Restaurant, and Institutional Education; International Special Events Society; Meeting Professionals International; National Restaurant Association; National Restaurant Association Educational Foundation; National Tour Association; Society of Travel and Tourism Educators.

Areas of Study
Controlling costs in food service; food preparation; food purchasing; food service communication; international cuisine; introduction to food service; kitchen management; management and human resources; marketing; meal planning; menu and facilities design; restaurant opportunities; sanitation.

Facilities
3 classrooms; computer laboratory; demonstration laboratory; 2 food production kitchens; gourmet dining room; laboratory; 2 lecture rooms; library; public restaurant; teaching kitchen.

Typical Student Profile
216 total: 208 full-time; 8 part-time. 208 are under 25 years old; 8 are between 25 and 44 years old.

Special Programs
2 day casino tour focusing on food and beverage management, 12-15 week internship.

Financial Aid
In 2006, 13 scholarships were awarded (average award was $1500). Employment placement assistance is available. Employment opportunities within the program are available.

Housing
Coed housing available.

Application Information
Students may begin participation in January and August. Application deadline for fall is April 1. Application deadline for spring is November 15. In 2006, 120 applied; 84 were accepted. Applicants must submit a formal application.

Contact
Director of Admissions, Hotel, Restaurant and Tourism Management, East Stroudsburg University, East Stroudsburg, PA 18301. Telephone: 877-230-5547. Fax: 570-422-3933. World Wide Web: http://www.esu.edu/hrtm.

Greater Altoona Career and Technology Center

Altoona, Pennsylvania

General Information
Public, coeducational, adult vocational school. Founded in 1970. Accredited by Council on Occupational Education, Middle States Association of Colleges and Schools.

Program Information
Offered since 2000. National Restaurant Association Educational Foundation ManageFirst certificates available. Program calendar is divided into semesters. 9-month diploma in culinary arts. 9-month diploma in baker/pastry cook.

Program Affiliation
American Culinary Federation.

Areas of Study
Baking; culinary skill development.

Facilities
Bake shop; bakery; 2 classrooms; computer laboratory; food production kitchen; public restaurant; teaching kitchen.

Typical Student Profile
6 full-time. 5 are under 25 years old; 1 is between 25 and 44 years old.

Financial Aid
Employment placement assistance is available. Employment opportunities within the program are available.

Application Information
Students may begin participation in August. Application deadline for fall is August 25. In 2006, 6 applied; 6 were accepted. Applicants must interview; submit a formal application and take Test of Adult Basic Education.

Contact
Director of Admissions, 1500 Fourth Avenue, Altoona, PA 16602. Telephone: 814-946-8469. Fax: 814-941-4690. World Wide Web: http://www.gactc.com/cont-ed.

Harrisburg Area Community College

Hospitality, Restaurant, and Institutional Management Department

Harrisburg, Pennsylvania

General Information
Public, coeducational, two-year college. Suburban campus. Founded in 1964. Accredited by Middle States Association of Colleges and Schools.

Program Information
Offered since 1989. National Restaurant Association Educational Foundation ManageFirst certificates available. Program calendar is divided into semesters. 1-year diploma in institutional food service. 1-year diploma in culinary arts/catering. 10-month diploma in dietary manager. 12-month certificate in baking and pastry arts. 16-month certificate in restaurant food service management. 17-month certificate in culinary arts. 21-month associate degree in restaurant food service management. 21-month associate degree in hotel and motel management. 21-month associate degree in health care food service. 21-month associate degree in culinary arts.

Program Affiliation
American Culinary Federation; American Dietetic Association; College Restaurant Hospitality Institute Educators; Council on Hotel, Restaurant, and Institutional Education; National Restaurant Association; National Restaurant Association Educational Foundation.

Areas of Study
Baking; controlling costs in food service; culinary skill development; food preparation; food purchasing; introduction to hospitality; kitchen management; management and human resources; meal planning; meat cutting; menu and facilities design; nutrition; sanitation; soup, stock, sauce, and starch production.

Facilities
Bake shop; classroom; computer laboratory; demonstration laboratory; food production kitchen; gourmet dining room; learning resource center; lecture room; library; public restaurant; teaching kitchen; herb garden; public meat and artisan cheese shop.

Typical Student Profile
150 total: 75 full-time; 75 part-time. 83 are under 25 years old; 45 are between 25 and 44 years old; 22 are over 44 years old.

Special Programs
4-month paid internship, culinary competitions, participation in community charity events.

Financial Aid
In 2006, 4 scholarships were awarded (average award was $1200). Employment placement assistance is available.

Application Information
Students may begin participation in January, May, and August. Application deadline for fall is May 1. Application deadline for spring is November 1. In 2006, 175 applied; 50 were accepted. Applicants must interview; submit a formal application, an essay, letters of reference, and have a health certificate.

Contact
Director of Admissions, Hospitality, Restaurant, and Institutional Management Department, 125-E One HACC Drive, Harrisburg, PA 17110-2999. Telephone: 717-780-2674. Fax: 717-780-1130. World Wide Web: http://www.hacc.edu/.

Indiana University of Pennsylvania

Academy of Culinary Arts

Punxsutawney, Pennsylvania

General Information
Public, coeducational, university. Rural campus. Founded in 1875. Accredited by Middle States Association of Colleges and Schools.

Program Information
Offered since 1989. Accredited by American Culinary Federation Accrediting Commission. Program calendar is divided into semesters. 12-month certificate in baking and pastry arts. 16-month certificate in culinary arts. 2-year

Indiana University of Pennsylvania *(continued)*

certificate in culinary arts and baking and pastry arts. 4-year bachelor's degree in food and nutrition. 4-year bachelor's degree in hotel, restaurant, and institutional management.

Program Affiliation

American Culinary Federation; American Dietetic Association; Confrerie de la Chaine des Rotisseurs; Council on Hotel, Restaurant, and Institutional Education; International Association of Culinary Professionals; National Restaurant Association; National Restaurant Association Educational Foundation.

Areas of Study

Baking; beverage management; buffet catering; confectionery show pieces; controlling costs in food service; convenience cookery; culinary French; culinary skill development; food preparation; food purchasing; food service communication; food service math; garde-manger; international cuisine; introduction to food service; kitchen management; management and human resources; meal planning; meat cutting; meat fabrication; menu and facilities design; nutrition; nutrition and food service; patisserie; restaurant opportunities; sanitation; saucier; seafood processing; soup, stock, sauce, and starch production; wines and spirits.

Facilities

Bake shop; cafeteria; 6 classrooms; computer laboratory; 2 demonstration laboratories; food production kitchen; garden; gourmet dining room; learning resource center; lecture room; library; student lounge; 2 teaching kitchens.

Typical Student Profile

127 full-time. 115 are under 25 years old; 11 are between 25 and 44 years old; 1 is over 44 years old.

Special Programs

International externship option, international study tours, advanced baking and pastry arts instruction.

Financial Aid

In 2006, 16 scholarships were awarded (average award was $2300). Program-specific awards include private scholarship support for program students. Employment placement assistance is available. Employment opportunities within the program are available.

Housing

Coed, apartment-style, and single-sex housing available.

Application Information

Students may begin participation in September. Applications are accepted continuously. In 2006, 294 applied; 176 were accepted. Applicants must submit a formal application, letters of reference, an essay, official high school transcript or GED certificate, and visit school.

Contact

Director of Admissions, Academy of Culinary Arts, 1012 Winslow Street, Punxsutawney, PA 15767. Telephone: 800-438-6424. Fax: 814-938-1158. World Wide Web: http://www.iup.edu/culinary.

The International Culinary School at The Art Institute of Philadelphia

Philadelphia, Pennsylvania

General Information

Private, coeducational institution.

Program Information

Accredited by American Culinary Federation (Associate in Culinary Arts program). Associate degree in Culinary Arts. Bachelor's degree in Culinary Management. Diploma in Culinary Arts. Diploma in Baking and Pastry.

Contact

Office of Admissions, 1622 Chestnut Street, Philadelphia, PA 19103-5119. Telephone: 215-567-7080. World Wide Web: http://www.artinstitutes.edu/philadelphia/.

See color display following page 332.

The International Culinary School at The Art Institute of Pittsburgh

Pittsburgh, Pennsylvania

General Information

Private, coeducational institution.

Program Information

Accredited by Accrediting Commission of The American Culinary Federation (Associate in Culinary Arts program). Associate degree in Culinary Arts. Bachelor's degree in Hotel and Restaurant Management. Bachelor's degree in Culinary Management. Diploma in The Art of Cooking.

Contact

Office of Admissions, 420 Boulevard of the Allies, Pittsburgh, PA 15219. Telephone: 800-275-2470. Fax: 412-263-6667. World Wide Web: http://www.artinstitutes.edu/pittsburgh/.

See color display following page 332.

The International Culinary School at The Art Institute of Pittsburgh—Online Division

Pittsburgh, Pennsylvania

General Information
Private, coeducational institution.

Program Information
Bachelor's degree in Hotel and Restaurant Management. Bachelor's degree in Culinary Management.

Contact
Office of Admissions, 1400 Penn Avenue, Pittsburgh, PA 15222-4332. Telephone: 877-872-8869. World Wide Web: http://www.aionline.edu.

See color display following page 332.

JNA Institute of Culinary Arts

Culinary Arts Restaurant Management

Philadelphia, Pennsylvania

General Information
Private, coeducational, culinary institute. Urban campus. Founded in 1988. Accredited by Accrediting Commission of Career Schools and Colleges of Technology.

Program Information
Offered since 1988. Program calendar is divided into quarters, ten-week cycles. 30-week diploma in specialized food service management. 30-week diploma in food service training/professional cooking. 60-week associate degree in culinary arts/restaurant management.

Program Affiliation
American Culinary Federation; Foodservice Educators Network International; International Food Service Executives Association; National Restaurant Association; National Restaurant Association Educational Foundation.

Areas of Study
Baking; beverage management; buffet catering; controlling costs in food service; culinary French; culinary skill development; food preparation; food purchasing; food service communication; food service math; garde-manger; international cuisine; introduction to food service; kitchen management; management and human resources; meal planning; meat cutting; menu and facilities design;

JNA Institute of Culinary Arts *(continued)*

nutrition; nutrition and food service; patisserie; restaurant opportunities; sanitation; saucier; seafood processing; soup, stock, sauce, and starch production; wines and spirits.

Facilities
Bake shop; cafeteria; catering service; 4 classrooms; computer laboratory; demonstration laboratory; food production kitchen; learning resource center; lecture room; library; public restaurant; student lounge; teaching kitchen.

Student Profile
71 total: 68 full-time; 3 part-time.

Faculty
10 total: 7 full-time; 3 part-time. 10 are industry professionals. Prominent faculty: Joseph DiGironimo, CFE, FMP; Michael DeLuca, FMP; Roland Pasche; Michael Gilletto, MCFE, FMP. Faculty-student ratio: 1:12.

Special Programs
Paid externships, student clubs (wine club, culinary club), culinary competitions.

Typical Expenses
Tuition: $8500 per diploma; $17,000 per degree full-time, $188 per credit part-time. Program-related fees include $75 for registration; $150 for knives.

Financial Aid
In 2007, 4 scholarships were awarded (average award was $8500); 51 loans were granted (average loan was $3000). Employment placement assistance is available. Employment opportunities within the program are available.

Housing
Average off-campus housing cost per month: $650.

Application Information
Students may begin participation in January, March, April, June, July, September, October, and December. Applications are accepted continuously. In 2007, 103 applied; 75 were accepted. Applicants must submit a formal application and schedule an interview or provide letters of reference.

Contact
John English, Admissions Department, Culinary Arts Restaurant Management, 1212 South Broad Street, Philadelphia, PA 19146. Telephone: 215-468-8800. Fax: 215-468-8838. E-mail: admissions@culinaryarts.com. World Wide Web: http://www.culinaryarts.com/.

Keystone Technical Institute

Harrisburg, Pennsylvania

General Information
Private, coeducational, culinary institute. Suburban campus. Founded in 1980. Accredited by Accrediting Commission of Career Schools and Colleges of Technology.

Program Information
Program calendar is continuous. 15-month degree in culinary arts.

Program Affiliation
American Culinary Federation.

Areas of Study
Baking; buffet catering; controlling costs in food service; culinary skill development; food preparation; food purchasing; food service communication; food service math; garde-manger; introduction to food service; kitchen management; meal planning; meat cutting; menu and facilities design; nutrition; nutrition and food service; sanitation; saucier; seafood processing; soup, stock, sauce, and starch production.

Facilities
10 classrooms; 3 computer laboratories; learning resource center; library; snack shop; student lounge; teaching kitchen.

Typical Student Profile
15 full-time.

Financial Aid
In 2006, 2 scholarships were awarded (average award was $12,000). Employment placement assistance is available.

Application Information
Applications are accepted continuously. Applicants must interview; submit a formal application.

Contact
Director of Admissions, 2301 Academy Drive, Harrisburg, PA 17112. Telephone: 717-545-4747. Fax: 717-901-9090. World Wide Web: http://www.kti.edu/.

Lehigh Carbon Community College

Hotel/Restaurant Management–Foodservice Management

Schnecksville, Pennsylvania

General Information
Public, coeducational, two-year college. Suburban campus. Founded in 1967. Accredited by Middle States Association of Colleges and Schools.

Program Information
Offered since 1986. National Restaurant Association Educational Foundation ManageFirst certificates available. Program calendar is divided into semesters. 2-year associate degree in hotel/resort management. 2-year associate degree in foodservice management.

Program Affiliation
American Culinary Federation; Council on Hotel, Restaurant, and Institutional Education; National Restaurant Association; National Restaurant Association Educational Foundation.

Areas of Study
Baking; beverage management; controlling costs in food service; culinary skill development; dining room operation; food preparation; food purchasing; food service math; international cuisine; introduction to food service; management and human resources; meal planning; menu and facilities design; nutrition; nutrition and food service; sanitation; soup, stock, sauce, and starch production.

Facilities
Classroom; computer laboratory; lecture room; student lounge; teaching kitchen.

Typical Student Profile
116 total: 31 full-time; 85 part-time. 78 are under 25 years old; 31 are between 25 and 44 years old; 7 are over 44 years old.

Special Programs
Paid internships in all degree programs, for-credit participation in Walt Disney World College program.

Financial Aid
Employment placement assistance is available.

Application Information
Students may begin participation in January and August. Applications are accepted continuously. In 2006, 77 applied. Applicants must submit a formal application.

Contact
Director of Admissions, Hotel/Restaurant Management–Foodservice Management, 4525 Education Park Drive, Schnecksville, PA 18078. Telephone: 610-794-1852. World Wide Web: http://www.lccc.edu/.

Mercyhurst College

The Culinary and Wine Institute of Mercyhurst North East

North East, Pennsylvania

General Information
Private, coeducational, comprehensive institution. Small-town setting. Founded in 1926. Accredited by Middle States Association of Colleges and Schools.

Program Information
Offered since 1995. Accredited by Accreditation Commission for Programs in Hospitality Administration (ACPHA). Program calendar is term 4-3-3. 2-year associate degree in hospitality management. 2-year associate degree in culinary arts. 4-year bachelor's degree in hotel, restaurant, and institutional management (culinary arts concentration).

Program Affiliation
American Culinary Federation; Council on Hotel, Restaurant, and Institutional Education; National Restaurant Association.

Areas of Study
Baking; beverage management; buffet catering; controlling costs in food service; culinary skill development; food preparation; food purchasing; food service communication; food service math; garde-manger; international cuisine; introduction to food service; kitchen management; management and human resources; meal planning; meat cutting; meat fabrication; menu and facilities design; nutrition; nutrition and food service; patisserie; restaurant opportunities; sanitation; saucier; seafood processing; soup, stock, sauce, and starch production; wine making; wines and spirits.

Facilities
Bake shop; cafeteria; 4 classrooms; 2 computer laboratories; 3 demonstration laboratories; 3 food production kitchens; garden; gourmet dining room; learning resource center; 2 lecture rooms; library; student lounge; 2 teaching kitchens; vineyard.

Typical Student Profile
55 total: 53 full-time; 2 part-time. 44 are under 25 years old; 10 are between 25 and 44 years old; 1 is over 44 years old.

Mercyhurst College *(continued)*

Special Programs
400-hour culinary externship, 120 hour culinar service hour component, food distribution/food show participant.

Financial Aid
Program-specific awards include institution grants. Employment placement assistance is available.

Housing
Coed, apartment-style, and single-sex housing available.

Application Information
Students may begin participation in March, September, and November. Applications are accepted continuously. In 2006, 116 applied; 112 were accepted. Applicants must submit a formal application and high school diploma or GED.

Contact
Director of Admissions, The Culinary and Wine Institute of Mercyhurst North East, 16 West Division Street, North East, PA 16428. Telephone: 814-725-6144. Fax: 814-725-6251. World Wide Web: http://northeast.mercyhurst.edu/.

Northampton County Area Community College

Culinary Arts

Bethlehem, Pennsylvania

General Information
Public, coeducational, two-year college. Suburban campus. Founded in 1967. Accredited by Middle States Association of Colleges and Schools.

Program Information
Offered since 1993. National Restaurant Association Educational Foundation ManageFirst certificates available. Program calendar is divided into semesters. 2-year associate degree in restaurant/hotel management. 2-year associate degree in culinary arts. 45-week diploma in culinary arts.

Areas of Study
Baking; beverage management; controlling costs in food service; culinary skill development; food preparation; food purchasing; garde-manger; introduction to food service; meat cutting; meat fabrication; nutrition; restaurant opportunities; sanitation; seafood processing; soup, stock, sauce, and starch production; wines and spirits.

Facilities
Bakery; cafeteria; catering service; 10 computer laboratories; food production kitchen; gourmet dining room; learning resource center; lecture room; library; public restaurant; snack shop; student lounge; teaching kitchen.

Typical Student Profile
60 full-time.

Financial Aid
In 2006, 1 scholarship was awarded (award was $250); 10 loans were granted (average loan was $2000). Employment placement assistance is available.

Housing
Coed and apartment-style housing available.

Application Information
Students may begin participation in March and September. Applications are accepted continuously. In 2006, 100 applied; 56 were accepted. Applicants must submit a formal application.

Contact
Director of Admissions, Culinary Arts, 3835 Green Pond Road, Bethlehem, PA 18020. Telephone: 610-861-5593. Fax: 610-861-5487. World Wide Web: http://www.northampton.edu/academics/departments/culinary/.

Pennsylvania College of Technology

School of Hospitality

Williamsport, Pennsylvania

General Information
Public, coeducational, two-year college. Small-town setting. Founded in 1965. Accredited by Middle States Association of Colleges and Schools.

Program Information
Offered since 1965. Accredited by American Culinary Federation Accrediting Commission, Commission on Accreditation of Hospitality Management Programs. National Restaurant Association Educational Foundation certificates available in cost control, revenue management, and operations management. Program calendar is divided into semesters. 2-year associate degree in Hospitality Management, Baking & Pastry Arts, and Culinary Arts Technology. 4-year bachelor's degree in Culinary Arts & Systems. 8-month competency credential in Professional Cooking, Professional Baking, and Dining Room Service.

Program Affiliation
American Culinary Federation; American Institute of Baking; Council on Hotel, Restaurant, and Institutional Education; National Restaurant Association; Pennsylvania Travel Council; Retailer's Bakery Association; Sommelier Society of America; The Bread Bakers Guild of America; Women Chefs and Restaurateurs.

Areas of Study
Baking; beverage management; catering; confectionery show pieces; controlling costs in food service; culinary French; culinary skill development; food preparation; food purchasing; garde-manger; international cuisine; introduction to food service; kitchen management; management and human resources; meal planning; meat cutting; meat fabrication; menu and facilities design; nutrition; nutrition and food service; patisserie; restaurant opportunities; sanitation; seafood processing; wines and spirits.

Facilities
Catering service; 3 classrooms; computer laboratory; 4 food production kitchens; garden; gourmet dining room; learning resource center; lecture room; library; public restaurant; teaching kitchen; conference center; performing arts center; culinary, baking, and pastry skills lab.

Student Profile
215 total: 201 full-time; 14 part-time. 200 are under 25 years old; 14 are between 25 and 44 years old; 1 is over 44 years old.

Faculty
22 total: 9 full-time; 13 part-time. 18 are industry professionals; 2 are culinary-certified teachers; 1 is a certified hospitality educator. Prominent faculty: Paul Mach, CHE; Mike Ditchfield, CEC, CCE; Judith Shimp, CEC, CCE. Faculty-student ratio: 1:24 lecture; 1:12 lab.

Prominent Alumni and Current Affiliation
James Parker, veggyart.com.

Special Programs
Semi-annual Visiting Chefs Series, Hunt County Vineyards; Finger Lakes Harvest Festival, Kentucky Derby Experience.

Typical Expenses
Application fee: $50. In-state tuition: $11,790 per year full-time (in district), $393 per credit part-time. Out-of-state tuition: $14,820 per year full-time, $494 per credit part-time. Program-related fees include $190 for knife kit; $215 for uniforms; $250 for tools.

Financial Aid
In 2007, 15 scholarships were awarded (average award was $1950). Program-specific awards include D.L. Stroehmann Culinary Scholarship, Hector Boiardi Scholarship, Penn College Visiting Chef Scholarship, David B. Person Memorial Scholarship, Ann Miglio Scholarship, Louis A. Miele Sr. Memorial Scholarship, Labels by Pulizzi Scholarship, Girio Family Scholarship, Burger King Scholarship. Employment placement assistance is available. Employment opportunities within the program are available.

Housing
Coed housing available. Average off-campus housing cost per month: $300.

Application Information
Students may begin participation in January, May, and August. In 2007, 195 applied; 176 were accepted. Applicants must submit a formal application and Penn College operates under a rolling admission practice. As applications become complete, they are reviewed. With limited enrollments for these majors, applicants are encouraged to apply early to enhance their opportunity of gaining admission.

Contact
Chester D. Schuman, Director of Admissions, School of Hospitality, One College Avenue, Williamsport, PA 17701. Telephone: 800-367-9222. Fax: 570-321-5551. E-mail: pctinfo@pct.edu. World Wide Web: http://www.pct.edu/peter.

See color display following page 284.

Pennsylvania Culinary Institute

Le Cordon Bleu Culinary Arts

Pittsburgh, Pennsylvania

General Information
Private, coeducational, culinary institute. Urban campus. Founded in 1986. Accredited by Accrediting Commission of Career Schools and Colleges of Technology.

Program Information
Offered since 1986. Associate degree in Le Cordon Bleu Patisserie and Baking. Associate degree in Le Cordon Bleu Hospitality and Restaurant Management. Associate degree in Le Cordon Bleu culinary arts. Diploma in Le Cordon Bleu culinary techniques.

Special Programs
Externships, culinary competitions.

Housing
Coed and apartment-style housing available.

Application Information
Applications are accepted continuously. Applicants must interview; submit a formal application and high school diploma/GED.

Pennsylvania Culinary Institute *(continued)*

Contact

Director of Admissions, Le Cordon Bleu Culinary Arts, 717 Liberty Avenue, Pittsburgh, PA 15222-3500. Telephone: 888-314-8222. World Wide Web: http://www.pci.edu/.

The Pennsylvania State University–University Park Campus

School of Hospitality Management

University Park, Pennsylvania

General Information

Public, coeducational, university. Small-town setting. Founded in 1855. Accredited by Middle States Association of Colleges and Schools.

Program Information

Offered since 1937. Program calendar is divided into semesters. 18-month master's degree in hospitality management. 2-year associate degree in hospitality management. 4-year bachelor's degree in hospitality management. 4-year doctoral degree in hospitality management.

Program Affiliation

Council on Hotel, Restaurant, and Institutional Education; National Restaurant Association; National Restaurant Association Educational Foundation.

Facilities

Cafeteria; 4 classrooms; 2 computer laboratories; demonstration laboratory; food production kitchen; gourmet dining room; learning resource center; lecture room; public restaurant; teaching kitchen.

Typical Student Profile

800 total: 740 full-time; 60 part-time.

Special Programs

Spring break trips to Italy, Greece, Spain, culinary program in Lyon, France, 6-week trip to Switzerland.

Financial Aid

In 2006, individual scholarships were awarded at $180. Employment placement assistance is available.

Housing

Coed and apartment-style housing available.

Application Information

Students may begin participation in January and August. Applicants must submit a formal application.

Contact

Director of Admissions, School of Hospitality Management, 201 Mateer Building, University Park, PA 16802. Telephone: 814-865-7033. Fax: 814-863-4257. World Wide Web: http://www.hhdev.psu.edu/shm.

The Restaurant School at Walnut Hill College

School of Hospitality Management/School of Culinary and Pastry Arts

Philadelphia, Pennsylvania

General Information

Private, coeducational, four-year college. Urban campus. Founded in 1974. Accredited by Accrediting Commission of Career Schools and Colleges of Technology.

Program Information

Program calendar is divided into semesters. 18-month associate degree in restaurant management. 18-month associate degree in pastry arts. 18-month associate degree in hotel management. 18-month associate degree in culinary arts. 36-month bachelor's degree in restaurant management. 36-month bachelor's degree in pastry arts. 36-month bachelor's degree in hotel management. 36-month bachelor's degree in culinary arts.

Program Affiliation

American Culinary Federation; American Institute of Wine & Food; Council on Hotel, Restaurant, and Institutional Education; International Association of Culinary Professionals; National Restaurant Association; National Restaurant Association Educational Foundation.

Special Programs

8-day gastronomic tour of France (culinary students), 8-day Florida and Bahamas cruise and resort tour (management students), culinary competitions.

Financial Aid

Employment placement assistance is available. Employment opportunities within the program are available.

Housing

Coed and apartment-style housing available.

Application Information

Students may begin participation in January, May, September, and November. Applications are accepted continuously. Applicants must interview; submit a formal application, letters of reference, and an essay.

CONTACT
Director of Admissions, School of Hospitality Management/School of Culinary and Pastry Arts, 4207 Walnut Street, Philadelphia, PA 19104-3518. Telephone: 215-222-4200 Ext. 3011. Fax: 215-222-2811. World Wide Web: http://www.walnuthillcollege.edu/.

SETON HILL UNIVERSITY

Hospitality and Tourism; Dietetics

Greensburg, Pennsylvania

GENERAL INFORMATION
Private, coeducational, comprehensive institution. Small-town setting. Founded in 1883. Accredited by Middle States Association of Colleges and Schools.

PROGRAM INFORMATION
Accredited by American Dietetic Association. Program calendar is divided into semesters. 4-year bachelor's degree in hospitality and tourism. 4-year bachelor's degree in dietetics.

PROGRAM AFFILIATION
American Dietetic Association; Council on Hotel, Restaurant, and Institutional Education; National Restaurant Association; National Restaurant Association Educational Foundation.

AREAS OF STUDY
Controlling costs in food service; food preparation; food purchasing; food service math; introduction to food service; management and human resources; meal planning; menu and facilities design; nutrition; nutrition and food service; sanitation.

FACILITIES
Computer laboratory; demonstration laboratory; food production kitchen; 2 laboratories; learning resource center; teaching kitchen.

TYPICAL STUDENT PROFILE
50 full-time. 48 are under 25 years old; 2 are between 25 and 44 years old.

SPECIAL PROGRAMS
Internship (required), coordinated supervised practice.

FINANCIAL AID
Program-specific awards include dedicated scholarship for dietetics students. Employment placement assistance is available.

Seton Hill University *(continued)*

Housing
Coed and single-sex housing available.

Application Information
Students may begin participation in January and August. Application deadline for spring is December 1. Application deadline for fall is August 1. In 2006, 42 applied; 31 were accepted. Applicants must submit letters of reference, an essay, transcripts, SAT or ACT scores.

Contact
Director of Admissions, Hospitality and Tourism; Dietetics, Seton Hill Drive, Greensburg, PA 15601. Telephone: 724-838-4255. Fax: 724-830-1294. World Wide Web: http://www.setonhill.edu/.

Westmoreland County Community College

Hospitality Programs Department

Youngwood, Pennsylvania

General Information
Public, coeducational, two-year college. Rural campus. Founded in 1970. Accredited by Middle States Association of Colleges and Schools.

Program Information
Offered since 1980. Accredited by American Culinary Federation Accrediting Commission, American Dietetic Association. Program calendar is divided into semesters. 16-month associate degree in culinary arts-nonapprenticeship. 2-year associate degree in travel and tourism. 2-year associate degree in restaurant and culinary management. 2-year associate degree in hotel/motel management. 2-year associate degree in dietetic technician. 2-year associate degree in culinary-nonapprenticeship. 2-year associate degree in baking and pastry nonapprenticeship. 3-year associate degree in culinary arts-apprenticeship. 3-year associate degree in baking and pastry apprenticeship. 5-month certificate in hotel/motel management. 5-month certificate in dining room management. 5-month certificate in culinary arts. 5-month certificate in baking and pastry.

Program Affiliation
American Culinary Federation; American Dietetic Association; Council on Hotel, Restaurant, and Institutional Education; National Restaurant Association.

Areas of Study
Baking; beverage management; buffet catering; confectionery show pieces; controlling costs in food service; convenience cookery; culinary French; culinary skill development; food preparation; food purchasing; food service communication; food service math; garde-manger; international cuisine; introduction to food service; kitchen management; management and human resources; meal planning; menu and facilities design; nutrition; nutrition and food service; patisserie; restaurant opportunities; sanitation; saucier; seafood processing; soup, stock, sauce, and starch production; wines and spirits.

Facilities
2 bake shops; cafeteria; 10 classrooms; 4 computer laboratories; demonstration laboratory; food production kitchen; gourmet dining room; laboratory; learning resource center; lecture room; library; 2 student lounges; teaching kitchen.

Typical Student Profile
201 total: 131 full-time; 70 part-time. 135 are under 25 years old; 42 are between 25 and 44 years old; 24 are over 44 years old.

Special Programs
10-day hospitality study tour of Italy, culinary competition, paid apprenticeship.

Financial Aid
Employment placement assistance is available. Employment opportunities within the program are available.

Application Information
Students may begin participation in January, May, and August. Applications are accepted continuously. Applicants must submit a formal application and take a physical exam.

Contact
Director of Admissions, Hospitality Programs Department, 400 Armbrust Road, Youngwood, PA 15697. Telephone: 724-925-4123. Fax: 724-925-5802. World Wide Web: http://wccc.edu/ac/programpages/culinary/index.html.

Widener University

School of Hospitality Management

Chester, Pennsylvania

General Information
Private, coeducational, university. Suburban campus. Founded in 1821. Accredited by Middle States Association of Colleges and Schools.

Program Information
Offered since 1981. Accredited by Council on Hotel, Restaurant and Institutional Education, Accreditation Commission for Programs in Hospitality Administration (ACPHA). Program calendar is divided into semesters. 2-year master's degree in hospitality management. 4-year bachelor's degree in hospitality management.

Program Affiliation
American Dietetic Association; Council on Hotel, Restaurant, and Institutional Education; International Food Service Executives Association; National Restaurant Association; National Restaurant Association Educational Foundation; Society for Foodservice Management.

Areas of Study
Beverage management; club management; contract services management; controlling costs in food service; food preparation; food purchasing; gaming and racing management; hotel management; introduction to food service; kitchen management; management and human resources; menu and facilities design; nutrition; nutrition and food service; resort management; restaurant opportunities; sanitation; wines and spirits.

Facilities
5 classrooms; computer laboratory; demonstration laboratory; food production kitchen; gourmet dining room; laboratory; lecture room; library; public restaurant; student lounge; teaching kitchen; hotel technology laboratory.

Typical Student Profile
180 total: 175 full-time; 5 part-time.

Special Programs
2 paid summer internships, paid cooperative education semester, study abroad program.

Financial Aid
In 2006, 6 scholarships were awarded (average award was $1000). Employment placement assistance is available. Employment opportunities within the program are available.

Housing
Coed, apartment-style, and single-sex housing available.

Application Information
Students may begin participation in January and September. Applications are accepted continuously. In 2006, 125 applied; 82 were accepted. Applicants must submit a formal application, an essay, SAT or ACT scores, and high school transcripts.

Contact
Director of Admissions, School of Hospitality Management, Widener University, One University Place, Chester, PA 19013. Telephone: 610-499-4126. Fax: 610-499-4676. World Wide Web: http://www.widener.edu/shm/.

Winner Institute of Arts & Sciences Culinary Education

Culinary Arts Program

Transfer, Pennsylvania

General Information
Private, coeducational, culinary institute. Rural campus. Founded in 1997. Accredited by Council on Occupational Education.

Program Information
Accredited by American Culinary Federation Accrediting Commission. 15-month associate degree in culinary arts.

Program Affiliation
American Culinary Federation.

Housing
Apartment-style housing available.

Application Information
Students may begin participation in January, April, July, and October. Applications are accepted continuously. Applicants must interview; submit a formal application and take an entrance exam.

Contact
Director of Admissions, Culinary Arts Program, One Winner Place, Transfer, PA 16154. Telephone: 724-646-2433. Fax: 724-646-0218. World Wide Web: http://www.winner-institute.edu/.

Yorktowne Business Institute

School of Culinary Arts

York, Pennsylvania

General Information
Private, coeducational, two-year college. Founded in 1976. Accredited by Accrediting Council for Independent Colleges and Schools.

Program Information
Offered since 1998. 12-month diploma in professional baking and pastry. 12-month diploma in food service. 16-month associate degree in culinary arts. 5-week certificate in professional bartending.

Special Programs
6-week externship (including European locations), culinary competitions, participation in student-run restaurant.

Financial Aid
Employment placement assistance is available. Employment opportunities within the program are available.

Application Information
Applicants must interview; submit a formal application and take entrance exam.

Contact
Director of Admissions, School of Culinary Arts, West 7th Avenue, York, PA 17404. Telephone: 800-840-1004. Fax: 717-848-4584. World Wide Web: http://www.yorkchef.com/.

YTI Career Institute

Lancaster, Pennsylvania

General Information
Private, coeducational, two-year college. Suburban campus. Founded in 1967. Accredited by Accrediting Commission of Career Schools and Colleges of Technology.

Program Information
Offered since 1999. Program calendar is continuous. 12-month diploma in pastry arts. 21-month associate degree in culinary arts/restaurant management.

Program Affiliation
American Culinary Federation; National Restaurant Association Educational Foundation; Pennsylvania Restaurant Association.

Areas of Study
Baking; beverage management; buffet catering; confectionery show pieces; controlling costs in food service; culinary skill development; food preparation; food purchasing; food service communication; food service math; garde-manger; international cuisine; introduction to food service; kitchen management; management and human resources; meal planning; meat fabrication; menu and facilities design; nutrition; patisserie; restaurant opportunities; sanitation; saucier; seafood processing; soup, stock, sauce, and starch production; wines and spirits.

Facilities
Bakery; 7 classrooms; computer laboratory; demonstration laboratory; 4 food production kitchens; gourmet dining room; learning resource center; 7 lecture rooms; library; student lounge.

Typical Student Profile
200 full-time.

Financial Aid
Employment placement assistance is available. Employment opportunities within the program are available.

Application Information
Students may begin participation in January, July, and October. Applications are accepted continuously. Applicants must interview; submit a formal application and transcript.

Contact
Director of Admissions, Lancaster Campus, 3050 Hempland Road, Lancaster, PA 17601. Telephone: 866-984-4723. Fax: 717-295-1135. World Wide Web: http://cuisine.yti.edu/.

Rhode Island

Johnson & Wales University

College of Culinary Arts

Providence, Rhode Island

General Information
Private, coeducational, comprehensive institution. Urban campus. Founded in 1914. Accredited by New England Association of Schools and Colleges.

Program Information
Offered since 1973. Accredited by American Dietetic Association. Program calendar is divided into quarters. Associate degree in culinary arts. Associate degree in baking and pastry arts. Bachelor's degree in food service entrepreneurship. Bachelor's degree in food marketing. Bachelor's degree in culinary nutrition. Bachelor's degree in culinary arts and food service management. Bachelor's degree in baking and pastry arts. Bachelor's degree in baking & pastry arts and food service management.

Program Affiliation
American Culinary Federation; American Dietetic Association; American Institute of Baking; American Institute of Wine & Food; Confrerie de la Chaine des Rotisseurs; Council on Hotel, Restaurant, and Institutional Education; Institute of Food Technologists; International Association of Culinary Professionals; International Food Service Executives Association; International Foodservice Editorial Council; James Beard Foundation, Inc.; National Restaurant Association; National Restaurant Association Educational Foundation; Oldways Preservation and Exchange Trust; Society of Wine Educators; The Bread Bakers Guild of America; Women Chefs and Restaurateurs.

Areas of Study
Baking; beverage management; buffet catering; confectionery show pieces; controlling costs in food service; convenience cookery; culinary French; culinary skill development; food preparation; food purchasing; food service communication; food service math; garde-manger; international cuisine; introduction to food service; kitchen management; management and human resources; meal planning; meat cutting; meat fabrication; menu and facilities design; nutrition; nutrition and food service; patisserie; sanitation; saucier; seafood processing; soup, stock, sauce, and starch production; wines and spirits.

Facilities
4 bake shops; bakery; 4 cafeterias; catering service; 22 classrooms; coffee shop; 4 computer laboratories; demonstration laboratory; 21 food production kitchens; 2 gardens; 4 gourmet dining rooms; 4 laboratories; learning resource center; 22 lecture rooms; 2 libraries; 10 public restaurants; snack shop; student lounge.

Student Profile
2,568 total: 2416 full-time; 152 part-time. 2301 are under 25 years old; 222 are between 25 and 44 years old; 45 are over 44 years old.

Faculty
80 total: 80 full-time. Prominent faculty: Frank Terranova, CEC, CCE; Robert Lucier, CEC; George O'Palenick, CEC, CCE, AAC; Stephen Scaife, CEC, CCE, CFE. Faculty-student ratio: 1:32.

Johnson & Wales University *(continued)*

Prominent Alumni and Current Affiliation
Emeril Lagasse, Celebrity Chef/Author Restaurateur; Darryl 'Chip' Wade, Senior VP-Darden Restaurants; Gerry Fernandez, Founder/President, Multicultural/Food Service and Hospitality Alliance.

Special Programs
Customized corporate and commercial training programs, every culinary student gets a real life, career-building work experience through internship/co-op, ACF certification and 1-year membership for all completing associates degree.

Typical Expenses
Tuition: $21,297 per year. Program-related fees include $1023 for general fee; $265 for orientation; $1026 for optional weekend meal plan; $300 for room and board reservation deposit.

Financial Aid
In 2007, 3154 scholarships were awarded (average award was $4361). Employment placement assistance is available. Employment opportunities within the program are available.

Housing
Coed housing available. Average on-campus housing cost per month: $988.

Application Information
Students may begin participation in March, June, September, and December. Applications are accepted continuously. In 2007, 3623 applied; 2731 were accepted. Applicants must submit a formal application and high school and/or college transcripts.

Contact
Amy Podbelski, Assistant Director of Admissions, College of Culinary Arts, 8 Abbott Park Place, Providence, RI 02903-3703. Telephone: 800-342-5598 Ext. 2370. Fax: 401-598-2948. E-mail: admissions.prd@jwu.edu. World Wide Web: http://culinary.jwu.edu//.

See color display following page 92.

South Carolina

The Culinary Institute of Charleston

The Culinary Institute of Charleston at Trident Technical College

Charleston, South Carolina

General Information
Public, coeducational, two-year college. Urban campus. Founded in 1964. Accredited by Southern Association of Colleges and Schools.

Program Information
Offered since 1988. Accredited by American Culinary Federation Accrediting Commission, Council on Hotel, Restaurant and Institutional Education, Commission on Accreditation of Hospitality Management Programs. National Restaurant Association Educational Foundation ManageFirst certificates available. Program calendar is divided into semesters. 1-year advanced certificate in hotel operations. 1-year advanced certificate in event management. 1-year advanced certificate in culinary arts. 1-year advanced certificate in advanced culinary arts. 1-year advanced certificate in advanced baking and pastry. 1-year certificate in hospitality industry service. 1-year certificate in baking and pastry. 2-year associate degree in hospitality and tourism management. 2-year associate degree in culinary arts technology.

Program Affiliation
American Culinary Federation; Council on Hotel, Restaurant, and Institutional Education; Federation of Dining Rooms Professionals; International Association of Culinary Professionals; Les Dames d'Escoffier; National Association of Catering Executives; National Restaurant Association; National Restaurant Association Educational Foundation; Serve Safe Sanitation National Certification Association; Southeast Council in Hotel, Restaurant and Institutional Education.

Areas of Study
Baking; beverage management; buffet catering; controlling costs in food service; convenience cookery; culinary skill development; food preparation; food purchasing; food service math; garde-manger; ice carving; international cuisine; introduction to food service; kitchen management; management and human resources; meal planning; meat cutting; meat fabrication; menu and facilities design; nutrition; nutrition and food service; patisserie; restaurant opportunities; sanitation; saucier; seafood processing; soup, stock, sauce, and starch production; wines and spirits.

Facilities
3 bake shops; catering service; 14 classrooms; computer laboratory; 5 demonstration laboratories; 2 food production kitchens; garden; 2 gourmet dining rooms; learning resource center; 6 lecture rooms; library; 2 public restaurants; student lounge; 4 teaching kitchens; 2 broadcast kitchen amphitheaters.

Student Profile
688 total: 319 full-time; 369 part-time. 370 are under 25 years old; 165 are between 25 and 44 years old; 44 are over 44 years old.

Faculty
26 total: 14 full-time; 12 part-time. 12 are industry professionals; 2 are master bakers; 7 are culinary-certified teachers. Prominent faculty: Michael Carmel, CEC, CCE; Benjamin Black, CCC; Berndt Gronert, CMPC; Ward Morgan, CWC, CCE. Faculty-student ratio: 1:16.

Prominent Alumni and Current Affiliation
Garret Hutchson, Cypress Restaurant; John Whisenan, The Fat Hen; Kelly Franz, Magnolias Restaurant.

Special Programs
Participation in Annual Chef's Fest Benefit for Lowcountry Food Bank for 900 guests, participation in formal, black tie Vintners Dinner for 600 guests, participation in annual Wine Expo with 1800 guests and 40 vintners, participation in annual Charleston Food & Wine Festival weekend.

Typical Expenses
Application fee: $25. In-state tuition: $1665 per semester full-time (in district), $135 per credit hour part-time (in district), $1848 per semester full-time (out-of-district), $150 per credit hour part-time (out-of-district). Out-of-state tuition: $3154 per semester full-time, $259 per credit hour part-time. Program-related fees include $98.60 for uniforms culinary; $271 for knife kit; $176 for pastry kit; $138.10 for uniforms (dining room).

Financial Aid
In 2007, 5 scholarships were awarded (average award was $1000). Program-specific awards include Hotel and Restaurant Association scholarships, Wine Savvy Women scholarship, Franz Meier scholarship, scholarships sponsored by College Foundation, NACE scholarship, Concierge Association of Charleston scholarship, Hospitality Education Fund. Employment placement assistance is available. Employment opportunities within the program are available.

Housing
Average off-campus housing cost per month: $775.

Application Information
Students may begin participation in January, May, and August. Application deadline for Maymestor is May 1. Application deadline for summer is May 15. Applicants must submit a formal application and placement tests, high school diploma or GED.

Contact
Chef Michael Carmel, Culinary Department Chair, The Culinary Institute of Charleston at Trident Technical College, PO Box 118067, HT-M, Charleston, SC 29423-8067. Telephone: 843-820-5096. Fax: 843-820-5060. E-mail: cicinfo@tridenttech.edu. World Wide Web: http://www.culinaryinstituteofcharleston.com/.

See color display following page 284.

Greenville Technical College

Culinary Arts/Hospitality Education

Greenville, South Carolina

General Information
Public, coeducational, two-year college. Suburban campus. Founded in 1962. Accredited by Southern Association of Colleges and Schools.

Program Information
Accredited by American Culinary Federation Accrediting Commission, American Dietetic Association, Association of Collegiate Business Schools and Programs. Program calendar is divided into semesters. 1-year certificate in sales/catering and events management. 1-year certificate in hospitality management. 1-year certificate in culinary education. 1-year certificate in catering. 1-year certificate in baking and pastry arts. 2-year associate degree in culinary arts/food service management.

Program Affiliation
American Culinary Federation; American Dietetic Association; Council on Hotel, Restaurant, and Institutional Education; National Restaurant Association; South Carolina Hospitality Association.

Areas of Study
Baking; beverage management; buffet catering; confectionery show pieces; controlling costs in food service; convenience cookery; culinary skill development; food preparation; food purchasing; food service communication; food service math; garde-manger; international cuisine; introduction to food service; kitchen management; management and human resources; meal planning; meat cutting; meat fabrication; menu and facilities design; nutrition; nutrition and food service; sanitation; saucier; seafood processing; soup, stock, sauce, and starch production.

Greenville Technical College *(continued)*

Facilities
Bake shop; 3 classrooms; computer laboratory; 5 demonstration laboratories; 2 food production kitchens; garden; gourmet dining room; 5 laboratories; learning resource center; 3 lecture rooms; library; student lounge; 5 teaching kitchens.

Financial Aid
Employment placement assistance is available.

Housing
Apartment-style and single-sex housing available.

Application Information
Students may begin participation in January, May, and August. Applications are accepted continuously. Applicants must submit a formal application.

Contact
Director of Admissions, Culinary Arts/Hospitality Education, PO Box 5616, Greenville, SC 29606-5616. Telephone: 864-250-8404. Fax: 864-250-8455. World Wide Web: http://www.culinaryartsatgtc.com/.

Horry-Georgetown Technical College

Culinary Arts Department

Conway, South Carolina

General Information
Public, coeducational, two-year college. Suburban campus. Founded in 1965. Accredited by Southern Association of Colleges and Schools.

Program Information
Offered since 1987. Accredited by American Culinary Federation Accrediting Commission. Program calendar is divided into semesters. 1-semester certificate in culinary arts certification. 2-semester certificate in baking and pastry arts. 5-semester associate degree in culinary arts technology-business major.

Program Affiliation
American Culinary Federation; Council on Hotel, Restaurant, and Institutional Education; National Restaurant Association Educational Foundation.

Areas of Study
Baking; beverage management; buffet catering; controlling costs in food service; culinary French; food preparation; food purchasing; food service communication; food service math; garde-manger; international cuisine; introduction to food service; kitchen management; management and human resources; meat fabrication; menu and facilities design; nutrition; sanitation; saucier; seafood processing; soup, stock, sauce, and starch production.

Facilities
2 bake shops; cafeteria; 3 classrooms; computer laboratory; 2 demonstration laboratories; 4 food production kitchens; garden; 3 gourmet dining rooms; 2 learning resource centers; 2 lecture rooms; 2 libraries; 2 public restaurants; 2 student lounges; teaching kitchen.

Typical Student Profile
140 full-time.

Special Programs
Student exchange program with Bahamas Hotel Training College, Nassau, Bahamas.

Financial Aid
In 2006, 50 scholarships were awarded (average award was $680); 3 loans were granted (average loan was $300). Employment placement assistance is available.

Application Information
Students may begin participation in January, May, and August. Applications are accepted continuously. In 2006, 70 applied. Applicants must submit a formal application and SAT, CPT, or ACT scores.

Contact
Director of Admissions, Culinary Arts Department, 2050 Hwy 501 East, Conway, SC 29526. Telephone: 843-349-5333. Fax: 843-349-7577. World Wide Web: http://www.hgtc.edu/.

The International Culinary School at The Art Institute of Charleston

A Branch of the Art Institute of Atlanta, GA

Charleston, South Carolina

General Information
Private, coeducational institution.

Program Information
Associate degree in Culinary Arts with a concentration in Baking and Pastry. Associate degree in Culinary Arts. Bachelor's degree in Culinary Arts Management. Certificate in Culinary Arts: Skills.

Special Programs
"The Art Institute of Charleston is licensed by the South Carolina Commission on Higher Education, 1333 Main St., Suite 200, Columbia, SC 29201, 803-737-2260,

www.che.sc.gov., Licensure indicates only that minimum standards have been met; it is not an endorsement or guarantee of quality".

Contact
Office of Admissions, A Branch of the Art Institute of Atlanta, GA, 24 North Market Street, Charleston, SC 29401-2623. Telephone: 843-727-3500. World Wide Web: http://www.artinstitutes.edu/charleston/.

See color display following page 332.

South Dakota

Mitchell Technical Institute

Culinary Arts Program

Mitchell, South Dakota

General Information
Coeducational, two-year college. Rural campus. Founded in 1968. Accredited by North Central Association of Colleges and Schools.

Program Information
Offered since 1968. Program calendar is divided into semesters. 1-year diploma in culinary arts. 2-year associate degree in culinary arts.

Special Programs
Paid internship.

Financial Aid
Employment placement assistance is available.

Application Information
Students may begin participation in January and August. Applications are accepted continuously. Applicants must submit a formal application, high school/college transcripts.

Contact
Director of Admissions, Culinary Arts Program, 821 North Capital Street, Mitchell, SD 57301. Telephone: 605-995-3025. World Wide Web: http://www.mitchelltech.com/.

South Dakota State University

Hotel and Foodservice Management

Brookings, South Dakota

General Information
Public, coeducational, university. Small-town setting. Founded in 1881. Accredited by North Central Association of Colleges and Schools.

Program Information
Program calendar is divided into semesters. 30-month master's degree in nutrition and food science. 4-year bachelor's degree in nutrition and food science/nutritional sciences specialization. 4-year bachelor's degree in nutrition and food science/food science specialization. 4-year bachelor's degree in nutrition and food science/dietetics specialization. 4-year bachelor's degree in hotel and foodservice management/hotel and hospitality management specialization. 4-year bachelor's degree in hotel and foodservice management/foodservice management specialization. 48-month doctoral degree in nutrition and food science.

Financial Aid
Employment placement assistance is available.

Housing
Coed and apartment-style housing available.

Application Information
Students may begin participation in January and September. Applications are accepted continuously. Applicants must submit a formal application and high school transcript.

Contact
Director of Admissions, Hotel and Foodservice Management, Box 2201, Brookings, SD 57007. Telephone: 800-952-3541. Fax: 605-688-6891. World Wide Web: http://www3.sdstate.edu/.

Tennessee

The International Culinary School at The Art Institute of Tennessee–Nashville

A Branch of the Art Institute of Atlanta, GA

Nashville, Tennessee

General Information
Private, coeducational institution.

The International Culinary School at The Art Institute of Tennessee–Nashville *(continued)*

Program Information

Accredited by The Art Institute of Tennessee–Nashville is authorized for operation as a post-secondary educational institution by the Tennessee Higher Education Commission. Associate degree in Culinary Arts. Bachelor's degree in Culinary Arts Management. Diploma in Culinary Arts–Culinary Skills. Diploma in Culinary Arts–Baking and Pastry.

Contact

Office of Admissions, A Branch of the Art Institute of Atlanta, GA, 100 Centerview Drive, Suite 250, Nashville, TN 37214. Telephone: 866-747-5770. World Wide Web: http://www.artinstitutes.edu/nashville/.

See color display following page 332.

Nashville State Technical Community College

Culinary Arts

Nashville, Tennessee

General Information

Public, coeducational, two-year college. Suburban campus. Founded in 1970. Accredited by Southern Association of Colleges and Schools.

Program Information

Offered since 1996. Program calendar is divided into semesters. 1-year technical certificate in culinary arts. 2-year associate degree in culinary arts.

Areas of Study

Baking; beverage management; buffet catering; culinary French; culinary skill development; food preparation; food purchasing; food service communication; food service math; garde-manger; international cuisine; kitchen management; management and human resources; meal planning; meat cutting; menu and facilities design; nutrition; patisserie; sanitation; saucier; soup, stock, sauce, and starch production.

Facilities

Demonstration laboratory; food production kitchen; learning resource center; library; teaching kitchen.

Typical Student Profile

120 total: 70 full-time; 50 part-time.

Special Programs

Paid internship.

Financial Aid

Employment placement assistance is available.

Application Information

Students may begin participation in January and August. Applications are accepted continuously. Applicants must submit a formal application.

Contact

Director of Admissions, Culinary Arts, 120 White Bridge Road, Nashville, TN 37209. Telephone: 615-353-3419. Fax: 615-353-3428. World Wide Web: http://www.nscc.edu/.

Pellissippi State Technical Community College

Hospitality and Tourism

Knoxville, Tennessee

General Information

Public, coeducational, two-year college. Suburban campus. Founded in 1974. Accredited by Southern Association of Colleges and Schools.

Program Information

Offered since 1998. Accredited by Council on Hotel, Restaurant and Institutional Education, Association of Collegiate Business Schools and Programs. Program calendar is divided into semesters. 12-month certificate in travel and tourism. 12-month certificate in lodging. 12-month certificate in food and beverage. 2-year associate degree in hospitality.

Program Affiliation

Council on Hotel, Restaurant, and Institutional Education.

Areas of Study

Beverage management; buffet catering; controlling costs in food service; food preparation; food purchasing; introduction to food service; wines and spirits.

Facilities

2 cafeterias; 10 computer laboratories; demonstration laboratory; food production kitchen; laboratory; 4 learning resource centers; library; 3 snack shops; 4 student lounges; teaching kitchen.

Typical Student Profile

84 total: 63 full-time; 21 part-time.

Special Programs

600-hour paid internship, Knoxville Tourism Alliance student membership.

Financial Aid
In 2006, 4 scholarships were awarded (average award was $500). Employment placement assistance is available.

Application Information
Students may begin participation in January and August. Application deadline for fall is August 20. Application deadline for spring is January 10. In 2006, 42 applied; 42 were accepted. Applicants must submit a formal application.

Contact
Director of Admissions, Hospitality and Tourism, PO Box 22990, Knoxville, TN 37933-0990. Telephone: 865-694-6572. Fax: 865-539-7217. World Wide Web: http://www.pstcc.edu/.

Walters State Community College

Hospitality Business/Rel Maples Institute for Culinary Arts

Sevierville, Tennessee

General Information
Public, coeducational, two-year college. Small-town setting. Founded in 1970. Accredited by Southern Association of Colleges and Schools.

Program Information
Offered since 1997. Accredited by American Culinary Federation Accrediting Commission. Program calendar is divided into semesters. 1-year certificate in culinary arts. 2-year associate degree in hotel/restaurant management. 2-year associate degree in culinary arts.

Program Affiliation
American Culinary Federation; National Restaurant Association; Sevier County Hospitality Association; Tennessee Restaurant Association.

Areas of Study
Baking; beverage management; buffet catering; confectionery show pieces; controlling costs in food service; culinary French; culinary skill development; food preparation; food purchasing; food service communication; food service math; garde-manger; international cuisine; introduction to food service; kitchen management; management and human resources; meal planning; meat cutting; meat fabrication; menu and facilities design; nutrition; nutrition and food service; patisserie; restaurant opportunities; sanitation; saucier; seafood processing; soup, stock, sauce, and starch production.

Facilities
Bake shop; cafeteria; catering service; 4 classrooms; 2 computer laboratories; demonstration laboratory; food production kitchen; garden; gourmet dining room; learning resource center; lecture room; library; student lounge; teaching kitchen; herb garden.

Typical Student Profile
115 total: 75 full-time; 40 part-time. 67 are under 25 years old; 30 are between 25 and 44 years old; 18 are over 44 years old.

Special Programs
Culinary Competition Team, annual visit to National Restaurant Show (Chicago), biennial trips emphasizing the culinary industry.

Financial Aid
In 2006, 6 scholarships were awarded (average award was $500). Program-specific awards include state and local tourism association scholarships. Employment placement assistance is available. Employment opportunities within the program are available.

Application Information
Students may begin participation in January and August. Applications are accepted continuously. In 2006, 50 applied; 45 were accepted. Applicants must submit a formal application.

Contact
Director of Admissions, Hospitality Business/Rel Maples Institute for Culinary Arts, 500 South Davy Crockett Parkway, Morristown, TN 37813. Telephone: 423-585-2691. Fax: 423-585-6786. World Wide Web: http://www.ws.edu/.

Texas

Aims Academy

Carrollton, Texas

General Information
Private, coeducational, culinary institute. Suburban campus. Founded in 1987. Accredited by Council on Occupational Education.

Program Information
Offered since 1987. Accredited by Council On Occupation Education. Program calendar is continuous. 9-month diploma in culinary.

Aims Academy *(continued)*

AREAS OF STUDY
Baking; food preparation; food purchasing; introduction to food service; meat fabrication; nutrition; nutrition and food service; restaurant opportunities; sanitation; seafood processing; soup, stock, sauce, and starch production.

FACILITIES
3 classrooms; food production kitchen; 2 lecture rooms; library; 2 public restaurants; snack shop; student lounge; teaching kitchen.

TYPICAL STUDENT PROFILE
81 full-time. 14 are under 25 years old; 59 are between 25 and 44 years old; 8 are over 44 years old.

SPECIAL PROGRAMS
Certified Food Protection Certificate, TABC certifications.

FINANCIAL AID
Program-specific awards include Title Four Funding. Employment placement assistance is available.

APPLICATION INFORMATION
Students may begin participation in January, February, March, April, May, June, July, August, September, October, and November. Applications are accepted continuously. In 2006, 109 applied; 81 were accepted. Applicants must interview, and high school diploma or GED.

CONTACT
Director of Admissions, 1711 I35 East, Carrollton, TX 75006. Telephone: 972-323-6333.

AIMS ACADEMY SCHOOL OF CULINARY ARTS

School of Culinary Arts/School of Professional Bartending

Dallas, Texas

GENERAL INFORMATION
Private, coeducational, culinary institute. Urban campus. Founded in 1987.

PROGRAM INFORMATION
Offered since 1987. Program calendar is continuous. 14-day diploma in professional bartending. 9-month diploma in culinary arts.

FINANCIAL AID
Employment placement assistance is available.

APPLICATION INFORMATION
Applications are accepted continuously. Applicants must interview; submit a formal application and have a high school diploma or GED.

CONTACT
Director of Admissions, School of Culinary Arts/School of Professional Bartending, SMU 6116, North Central Expressway, Suite 140, Dallas, TX 75206. Telephone: 972-988-3202. World Wide Web: http://aimsacademy.com/.

AUSTIN COMMUNITY COLLEGE

Culinary Arts

Austin, Texas

GENERAL INFORMATION
Public, coeducational, two-year college. Urban campus. Founded in 1972. Accredited by Southern Association of Colleges and Schools.

PROGRAM INFORMATION
Accredited by American Culinary Federation Accrediting Commission. Program calendar is divided into semesters. 1-year certificate in hospitality management. 12-month certificate in culinary arts. 2-year associate degree in hospitality management. 2-year associate degree in culinary arts.

PROGRAM AFFILIATION
American Culinary Federation; American Institute of Baking; Council on Hotel, Restaurant, and Institutional Education; International Association of Culinary Professionals; International Foodservice Editorial Council; International Sommelier Guild; National Restaurant Association; National Restaurant Association Educational Foundation; Society of Wine Educators; The Bread Bakers Guild of America; Women Chefs and Restaurateurs.

AREAS OF STUDY
Beverage management; controlling costs in food service; culinary skill development; food service math; international cuisine; kitchen management; management and human resources; meat cutting; meat fabrication; nutrition; restaurant opportunities; sanitation; wines and spirits.

FACILITIES
10 classrooms; 4 computer laboratories; demonstration laboratory; food production kitchen; gourmet dining room; learning resource center; library; snack shop; student lounge.

TYPICAL STUDENT PROFILE
150 total: 50 full-time; 100 part-time.

Special Programs
School trips (Napa Valley, New York), culinary competitions, internships/practicums.

Financial Aid
In 2006, 5 scholarships were awarded (average award was $425). Employment opportunities within the program are available.

Application Information
Students may begin participation in January, May, and August. Applications are accepted continuously. In 2006, 60 applied; 45 were accepted.

Contact
Director of Admissions, Culinary Arts, 3401 Webberville Road, Austin, TX 78702. Telephone: 512-223-5173. Fax: 512-223-5125. World Wide Web: http://www2.austincc.edu/hospmgmt.

Central Texas College

Hospitality Management/Culinary Arts

Killeen, Texas

General Information
Public, coeducational, two-year college. Small-town setting. Founded in 1965. Accredited by Southern Association of Colleges and Schools.

Program Information
Offered since 1970. Program calendar is divided into semesters. 16-month certificate in institutional food service operations. 16-month certificate in culinary arts. 2-year associate degree in restaurant and culinary management. 2-year associate degree in food service management. 2-year associate degree in food and beverage management. 9-month certificate in restaurant skills. 9-month certificate in food and beverage management.

Program Affiliation
American Culinary Federation; American Hotel and Lodging Association; Council on Hotel, Restaurant, and Institutional Education; Institute of Food Technologists; National Restaurant Association; National Restaurant Association Educational Foundation; Texas Restaurant Association; Texas State Food Servers Association.

Areas of Study
Baking; beverage management; buffet catering; confectionery show pieces; controlling costs in food service; culinary French; culinary skill development; food preparation; food purchasing; food service math; garde-manger; international cuisine; introduction to food service; kitchen management; management and human resources; meal planning; meat cutting; menu and facilities design; nutrition; nutrition and food service; restaurant opportunities; sanitation; saucier; seafood processing; soup, stock, sauce, and starch production; wines and spirits.

Facilities
Bake shop; bakery; cafeteria; catering service; 6 classrooms; 2 computer laboratories; demonstration laboratory; food production kitchen; gourmet dining room; laboratory; learning resource center; lecture room; library; snack shop; student lounge; teaching kitchen.

Typical Student Profile
300 total: 100 full-time; 200 part-time. 120 are under 25 years old; 120 are between 25 and 44 years old; 60 are over 44 years old.

Special Programs
Dual credit program for high school students.

Financial Aid
In 2006, 8 scholarships were awarded (average award was $500). Program-specific awards include Charles Leopard Scholarship.

Housing
Coed housing available.

Application Information
Students may begin participation in January, May, and August. Applications are accepted continuously. In 2006, 300 applied. Applicants must interview; submit a formal application.

Contact
Director of Admissions, Hospitality Management/Culinary Arts, PO Box 1800, Killeen, TX 76540-1800. Telephone: 800-792-3348 Ext. 1539. Fax: 254-526-1841. World Wide Web: http://www.ctcd.edu/.

Culinary Academy of Austin, Inc.

Austin, Texas

General Information
Private, coeducational, culinary institute. Urban campus. Founded in 1998. Accredited by Council on Occupational Education.

Program Information
Offered since 1998. Program calendar is divided into quarters. 15-month diploma in professional culinary arts. 6-month diploma in professional pastry arts.

Culinary Academy of Austin, Inc. *(continued)*

Program Affiliation
American Culinary Federation; Foodservice Educators Network International; National Restaurant Association; Texas Restaurant Association; The Bread Bakers Guild of America.

Areas of Study
Baking; buffet catering; controlling costs in food service; convenience cookery; culinary skill development; food history and culture; food preparation; food service math; garde-manger; international cuisine; introduction to food service; kitchen management; meal planning; meat cutting; menu and facilities design; nutrition; nutrition and food service; patisserie; restaurant opportunities; sanitation; saucier; seafood processing; soup, stock, sauce, and starch production; wines and spirits.

Facilities
Bake shop; catering service; 2 classrooms; computer laboratory; food production kitchen; learning resource center; library.

Typical Student Profile
15 are under 25 years old; 12 are between 25 and 44 years old; 7 are over 44 years old.

Special Programs
International culinary programs in Italy, culinary competitions, food and drink symposium.

Financial Aid
In 2006, 2 scholarships were awarded (average award was $1000); 2 loans were granted (average loan was $2200). Program-specific awards include work-study with professional catering company. Employment placement assistance is available. Employment opportunities within the program are available.

Application Information
Students may begin participation in January, April, July, and October. Applications are accepted continuously. In 2006, 48 applied; 42 were accepted. Applicants must interview; submit a formal application, letters of reference, an essay, high school diploma.

Contact
Director of Admissions, 6020 B. Dillard Circle, Austin, TX 78752. Telephone: 512-451-5743. Fax: 512-467-9120. World Wide Web: http://www.culinaryacademyofaustin.com/.

Culinary Institute Alain and Marie LeNôtre

Houston, Texas

General Information
Private, coeducational, culinary institute. Urban campus. Founded in 1998. Accredited by Accrediting Commission of Career Schools and Colleges of Technology.

Program Information
Offered since 1998. Accredited by Accrediting Commission of Career Schools and Colleges of Technology (ACCSCT). Endorsed for quality education by the American Culinary Federation Foundation. National Restaurant Association Educational Foundation ManageFirst certificates available. Program calendar is continuous, with a new cycle every 10 weeks. 20- to 40-week diploma in sous-chef patissier. 20- to 40-week diploma in sous-chef de cuisine. 30- to 60-week diploma in culinary arts: specialty in cooking and catering. 30- to 60-week diploma in culinary arts: specialty in baking and pastry. 60- to 100-week associate degree in culinary arts. 60- to 100-week associate degree in baking and pastry arts.

Program Affiliation
American Culinary Federation; Houston Professional Chef Association; National Restaurant Association; Texas Chefs Association; Texas Restaurant Association.

Areas of Study
Bakery Operations; baking; beverage management; buffet catering; cakes; Career Exploration and Planning; chocolate candy making; chocolate décor; confectionery show pieces; controlling costs in food service; croissant; culinary French; culinary skill development; danishes; Dining Room service; Food and Beverage Control; food and beverage management; food preparation; food purchasing; food service math; garde-manger; Hospitality Marketing/Sales; human resource management; ice cream and sorbet; international cuisine; introduction to hospitality; Italian, Sushi, Regional American and French Cuisine; kitchen management; management and human resources; meat cutting; menu and facilities design; Menu Management; nutrition; nutrition and food service; Nutrition for Food Service Professionals; pastry; patisserie; pies; purchasing; rotisserie; sanitation; Sanitation and Safety; saucier; seafood; seafood processing; soup; soup, stock, sauce, and starch production; stock & sauce; tarts; wines and spirits.

Facilities
Classroom; computer laboratory; gourmet dining room; learning resource center; library; student lounge; 6 teaching kitchens.

Typical Student Profile
156 total: 94 full-time; 62 part-time. 68 are under 25 years old; 70 are between 25 and 44 years old; 18 are over 44 years old.

Special Programs
Culinary internships in France, externships in US, team building, culinary competitions, summer camp for teenagers and adults, monthly Chef Club cooking classes, alumni workshops, etc.

Financial Aid
Program-specific awards include many in-house and outside scholarships for those who qualify. Employment placement assistance is available. Employment opportunities within the program are available.

Application Information
Students may begin participation year-round. Applications are accepted continuously. In 2006, 174 applied; 156 were accepted. Applicants must submit a formal application, an essay, and have a high school diploma or GED; essay for scholarship consideration for those who qualify.

Contact
Director of Admissions, 7070 Allensby, Houston, TX 77022. Telephone: 713-692-0077. Fax: 713-692-7399. World Wide Web: http://www.ciaml.com/.

Del Mar College

Department of Hospitality Management

Corpus Christi, Texas

General Information
Public, coeducational, two-year college. Urban campus. Founded in 1935. Accredited by Southern Association of Colleges and Schools.

Program Information
Offered since 1963. Accredited by American Culinary Federation Accrediting Commission. Program calendar is divided into semesters. 1-year certificate in restaurant supervisor. 1-year certificate in kitchen supervisor. 2-year associate degree in restaurant management specialization. 2-year associate degree in culinary arts. 2-year associate degree in baking pastry specialization. 9-month certificate in cook/baker.

Program Affiliation
American Culinary Federation; Coastal Bend Hotel Motel Condominium Association; Coastal Bend Restaurant Association; Council on Hotel, Restaurant, and Institutional Education; National Restaurant Association; Texas Chefs Association; Texas Restaurant Association.

Areas of Study
Baking; beverage management; buffet catering; confectionery show pieces; controlling costs in food service; culinary skill development; food preparation; food purchasing; garde-manger; international cuisine; introduction to food service; kitchen management; management and human resources; menu and facilities design; nutrition; nutrition and food service; patisserie; restaurant opportunities; sanitation; saucier; soup, stock, sauce, and starch production.

Facilities
Bake shop; cafeteria; catering service; 4 classrooms; computer laboratory; 2 demonstration laboratories; 2 food production kitchens; gourmet dining room; 2 laboratories; learning resource center; 4 lecture rooms; 2 libraries; public restaurant; 2 teaching kitchens; herb garden; ice carving room.

Typical Student Profile
120 total: 24 full-time; 96 part-time. 24 are under 25 years old; 84 are between 25 and 44 years old; 12 are over 44 years old.

Special Programs
Paid internships in local restaurants, hotels, and clubs, annual pastry and garde manger competition.

Financial Aid
Employment placement assistance is available. Employment opportunities within the program are available.

Application Information
Students may begin participation in January, June, and September. Application deadline for fall is August 18. Application deadline for spring is January 15. Application deadline for summer is May 25. Applicants must submit a formal application, academic transcripts, and test scores.

Contact
Director of Admissions, Department of Hospitality Management, 101 Baldwin Boulevard, Corpus Christi, TX 78404-3897. Telephone: 361-698-1734. Fax: 361-698-1829. World Wide Web: http://www.delmar.edu/hospmgmt.

El Paso Community College

Culinary Arts and Related Sciences

El Paso, Texas

General Information
Public, coeducational, two-year college. Urban campus. Founded in 1969. Accredited by Southern Association of Colleges and Schools.

El Paso Community College *(continued)*

Program Information

Offered since 1989. National Restaurant Association Educational Foundation ManageFirst certificates available. Program calendar is divided into semesters. 1-year certificate of completion in restaurant/food service management. 1-year certificate of completion in pastry. 1-year certificate of completion in culinary arts. 2-year associate degree in restaurant/food service management. 2-year associate degree in pastry. 2-year associate degree in culinary arts.

Program Affiliation

American Culinary Federation; American Hotel and Lodging Association Educational Institute; Council on Hotel, Restaurant, and Institutional Education; National Restaurant Association Educational Foundation.

Areas of Study

Baking; beverage management; buffet catering; confectionery show pieces; controlling costs in food service; culinary French; culinary skill development; food and beverage management; food and beverage service; food preparation; food purchasing; garde-manger; international cuisine; introduction to food service; kitchen management; management and human resources; meal planning; meat cutting; menu and facilities design; nutrition; patisserie; sanitation; saucier; soup, stock, sauce, and starch production.

Facilities

Bake shop; 3 classrooms; computer laboratory; 2 food production kitchens; 2 gardens; gourmet dining room; 6 lecture rooms; library; teaching kitchen.

Typical Student Profile

218 total: 176 full-time; 42 part-time. 34 are under 25 years old; 148 are between 25 and 44 years old; 36 are over 44 years old.

Financial Aid

In 2006, 6 scholarships were awarded (average award was $1000). Employment placement assistance is available. Employment opportunities within the program are available.

Application Information

Students may begin participation in January, June, and September. Application deadline for fall is July 22. Application deadline for spring is November 18. Application deadline for summer is May 4. Applicants must submit a formal application and have a high school diploma or GED.

Contact

Director of Admissions, Culinary Arts and Related Sciences, 9570 Gateway North, El Paso, TX 79924. Telephone: 915-831-5148. Fax: 915-831-5017. World Wide Web: http://www.epcc.edu/.

Galveston College

Culinary Arts Academy

Galveston, Texas

General Information

Public, coeducational, two-year college. Urban campus. Founded in 1967. Accredited by Southern Association of Colleges and Schools.

Program Information

Offered since 1987. National Restaurant Association Educational Foundation ManageFirst certificates available. Program calendar is divided into semesters. 1-year certificate in culinary/hospitality management. 1-year certificate in culinary arts. 2-year associate degree in culinary arts/hospitality.

Program Affiliation

American Culinary Federation; Confrerie de la Chaine des Rotisseurs; International Association of Culinary Professionals; National Restaurant Association; National Restaurant Association Educational Foundation; Texas Chefs Association; Texas Restaurant Association.

Areas of Study

Baking; beverage management; culinary skill development; food preparation; food purchasing; garde-manger; international cuisine; kitchen management; menu and facilities design; nutrition; sanitation; soup, stock, sauce, and starch production.

Facilities

Bake shop; 3 classrooms; 2 computer laboratories; food production kitchen; learning resource center; library; snack shop; student lounge; teaching kitchen.

Typical Student Profile

40 total: 25 full-time; 15 part-time.

Special Programs

320-hour paid internships, ServSafe certification.

Financial Aid

In 2006, 2 scholarships were awarded (average award was $500); 15 loans were granted (average loan was $750). Employment placement assistance is available.

Application Information
Students may begin participation in January, February, March, April, May, June, July, August, September, October, and November. Applications are accepted continuously. In 2006, 40 applied; 40 were accepted. Applicants must submit a formal application.

Contact
Director of Admissions, Culinary Arts Academy, 4015 Avenue Q, Galveston, TX 77550. Telephone: 409-944-1304. Fax: 409-944-1511. World Wide Web: http://www.gc.edu/gc/Culinary_Arts.asp?SnID=1069165685.

Houston Community College System

Culinary Services and Hospitality Services

Houston, Texas

General Information
Public, coeducational, two-year college. Urban campus. Founded in 1972. Accredited by Southern Association of Colleges and Schools.

Program Information
Offered since 1980. National Restaurant Association Educational Foundation ManageFirst certificates available. Program calendar is divided into semesters. 1-semester certificate in travel and tourism. 2-semester certificate in restaurant management. 2-semester certificate in hotel management. 3-semester certificate in pastry arts. 3-semester certificate in culinary arts. 4-semester associate degree in travel and tourism. 4-semester associate degree in pastry arts. 4-semester associate degree in hotel and restaurant management. 4-semester associate degree in culinary arts.

Program Affiliation
American Institute of Baking; Council on Hotel, Restaurant, and Institutional Education; Foodservice Educators Network International; Les Dames d'Escoffier; National Restaurant Association.

Areas of Study
Baking; beverage management; breads; confectionery show pieces; controlling costs in food service; croissant, Danish, and puff pastry; culinary skill development; food preparation; food purchasing; food service math; garde-manger; international cuisine; introduction to food service; kitchen management; management and human resources; nutrition; patisserie; restaurant opportunities; sanitation; saucier; soup, stock, sauce, and starch production.

Facilities
2 bake shops; cafeteria; 5 classrooms; 2 computer laboratories; demonstration laboratory; 2 food production kitchens; gourmet dining room; learning resource center; 2 lecture rooms; library; public restaurant; student lounge.

Typical Student Profile
700 total: 350 full-time; 350 part-time. 150 are under 25 years old; 400 are between 25 and 44 years old; 150 are over 44 years old.

Special Programs
5-day classes with Lenôtre in France
-day classes with Lenôtre in France, 7-8 day European trips, marketable skills courses for individuals working in the industry who want to upgrade their skills.

Financial Aid
In 2006, 2 scholarships were awarded (average award was $5000). Employment placement assistance is available. Employment opportunities within the program are available.

Application Information
Students may begin participation in January, May, and August. Applications are accepted continuously. Applicants must take Test of Adult Basic Education.

Contact
Director of Admissions, Culinary Services and Hospitality Services, 1300 Holman, Room 302-A, Houston, TX 77004. Telephone: 713-718-6072. Fax: 713-718-6044. World Wide Web: http://www.hccs.edu/.

The International Culinary School at The Art Institute of Dallas

Dallas, Texas

General Information
Private, coeducational institution.

Program Information
Accredited by American Culinary Federation (Associate in Culinary Arts program & Art of Cooking certificate program). Associate degree in Restaurant and Catering Management. Associate degree in Culinary Arts. Bachelor's degree in Culinary Management. Certificate in Art of Cooking.

The International Culinary School at The Art Institute of Dallas *(continued)*

Contact
Office of Admissions, 8080 Park Lane, Suite 100, Dallas, TX 75231-5993. Telephone: 214-692-8080. World Wide Web: http://www.artinstitutes.edu/dallas/.

See color display following page 332.

The International Culinary School at The Art Institute of Houston

Houston, Texas

General Information
Private, coeducational institution.

Program Information
Accredited by American Culinary Federation (Associate in Culinary Arts program). Associate degree in Restaurant and Catering Management. Associate degree in Culinary Arts. Associate degree in Baking and Pastry. Bachelor's degree in Culinary Management. Diploma in Culinary Arts.

Contact
Office of Admissions, 1900 Yorktown Street, Houston, TX 77056. Telephone: 713-623-2040. World Wide Web: http://www.artinstitutes.edu/houston/.

See color display following page 332.

Lamar University

Family and Consumer Sciences–Hospitality Management

Beaumont, Texas

General Information
Public, coeducational, university. Urban campus. Founded in 1923. Accredited by Southern Association of Colleges and Schools.

Program Information
Offered since 1986. Accredited by American Culinary Federation Accrediting Commission, American Dietetic Association. Program calendar is divided into semesters. 2-year certificate in restaurant management. 2-year certificate in lodging. 2-year certificate in culinary arts. 2-year master's degree in family and consumer sciences. 4-year bachelor's degree in hospitality management.

Program Affiliation
American Dietetic Association; American Hotel and Lodging Association; Confrerie de la Chaine des Rotisseurs; Council on Hotel, Restaurant, and Institutional Education; International Food Service Executives Association; National Restaurant Association; National Restaurant Association Educational Foundation.

Areas of Study
Baking; beverage management; buffet catering; controlling costs in food service; culinary French; culinary skill development; food preparation; food purchasing; food service math; garde-manger; introduction to food service; kitchen management; management and human resources; meal planning; meat cutting; menu and facilities design; nutrition; nutrition and food service; patisserie; restaurant opportunities; sanitation; saucier; soup, stock, sauce, and starch production; wines and spirits.

Facilities
2 cafeterias; catering service; 6 classrooms; 2 computer laboratories; demonstration laboratory; food production kitchen; laboratory; 2 learning resource centers; 6 lecture rooms; library; teaching kitchen.

Typical Student Profile
70 total: 50 full-time; 20 part-time.

Special Programs
Culinary competitions, paid internships with local properties.

Financial Aid
Employment placement assistance is available. Employment opportunities within the program are available.

Housing
Coed housing available.

Application Information
Students may begin participation in January and August. Applications are accepted continuously. Applicants must submit a formal application and an essay.

Contact
Director of Admissions, Family and Consumer Sciences-Hospitality Management, 211 Redbird Lane, Box 10035, Beaumont, TX 77710. Telephone: 409-880-1744. Fax: 409-880-8666. World Wide Web: http://www.lamar.edu/.

Le Cordon Bleu Institute of Culinary Arts

Dallas, Texas

General Information
Coeducational, culinary institute. Founded in 1999.

Program Information
15-month diploma in Le Cordon Bleu Culinary Arts.

Special Programs
3-month externship.

Financial Aid
Employment placement assistance is available.

Application Information
Applications are accepted continuously.

Contact
Director of Admissions, 11830 Webb Chapel Road, Dallas, TX 75234. Telephone: 888-495-5222. World Wide Web: http://www.dallasculinary.com/programs.

Northwood University, Texas Campus

Hotel, Restaurant, and Resort Management

Cedar Hill, Texas

General Information
Private, coeducational, four-year college. Suburban campus. Founded in 1965. Accredited by North Central Association of Colleges and Schools.

Program Information
Offered since 1966. National Restaurant Association Educational Foundation ManageFirst certificates available. Program calendar is divided into quarters. 2-year associate degree in hotel, restaurant, resort management. 4-year bachelor's degree in hotel, restaurant, resort management.

Program Affiliation
Council on Hotel, Restaurant, and Institutional Education; Institute of Food Technologists; National Restaurant Association; National Restaurant Association Educational Foundation.

Areas of Study
Beverage management; food preparation; food purchasing; food service communication; food service math; introduction to food service; kitchen management; management and human resources; meal planning; menu and facilities design; nutrition; nutrition and food service; restaurant opportunities; sanitation.

Facilities
Classroom; demonstration laboratory; lecture room.

Typical Student Profile
32 total: 31 full-time; 1 part-time. 31 are under 25 years old; 1 is between 25 and 44 years old.

Special Programs
Trip to NRA trade show in Chicago.

Financial Aid
In 2006, 1 scholarship was awarded (award was $1250). Employment placement assistance is available. Employment opportunities within the program are available.

Housing
Single-sex housing available.

Application Information
Students may begin participation in March, September, and December. Applications are accepted continuously. In 2006, 49 applied; 21 were accepted. Applicants must submit a formal application and an essay.

Contact
Director of Admissions, Hotel, Restaurant, and Resort Management, 1114 West FM 1382, Cedar Hill, TX 75104. Telephone: 800-927-9663. Fax: 972-291-3824. World Wide Web: http://www.northwood.edu/.

Remington College–Dallas Campus

Dallas Culinary Arts Program

Garland, Texas

General Information
Private, two-year college. Founded in 1987. Accredited by Accrediting Council for Independent Colleges and Schools.

Program Information
Associate degree in culinary arts.

Application Information
Applicants must high school diploma or equivalent.

Contact
Director of Admissions, Dallas Culinary Arts Program, 1800 Eastgate Drive, Garland, TX 75041-5513. Telephone: 800-725-1327.

San Jacinto College–Central Campus

Culinary Arts/Restaurant Management/ Dietetic Technology

Pasadena, Texas

General Information
Public, coeducational, two-year college. Suburban campus. Founded in 1961. Accredited by Southern Association of Colleges and Schools.

Program Information
Accredited by American Dietetic Association. Program calendar is divided into semesters. 1-year certificate in restaurant management. 1-year certificate in dietetic technology. 1-year certificate in culinary arts. 2-year associate degree in restaurant management. 2-year associate degree in dietetic technology. 2-year associate degree in culinary arts.

Program Affiliation
National Restaurant Association; Texas Restaurant Association.

Areas of Study
Baking; beverage management; buffet catering; confectionery show pieces; controlling costs in food service; convenience cookery; culinary French; culinary skill development; food preparation; food purchasing; food service communication; food service math; garde-manger; international cuisine; introduction to food service; kitchen management; management and human resources; meal planning; meat cutting; meat fabrication; menu and facilities design; nutrition; nutrition and food service; patisserie; restaurant opportunities; sanitation; saucier; seafood processing; soup, stock, sauce, and starch production; wines and spirits.

Facilities
Cafeteria; catering service; 4 classrooms; food production kitchen; learning resource center; lecture room; library; public restaurant; snack shop; student lounge.

Typical Student Profile
110 total: 50 full-time; 60 part-time.

Special Programs
Paid internships.

Financial Aid
Employment placement assistance is available.

Application Information
Students may begin participation in January, June, and September. Applications are accepted continuously. Applicants must interview, submit a formal application and take the Texas Academic Skills Program test.

Contact
Director of Admissions, Culinary Arts/Restaurant Management/Dietetic Technology, 8060 Spencer Highway, Pasadena, TX 77505. Telephone: 281-542-2099. Fax: 281-478-2790. World Wide Web: http://www.sjcd.edu/.

Texas Culinary Academy

Le Cordon Bleu Program

Austin, Texas

General Information
Private, coeducational, culinary institute. Urban campus. Founded in 1981. Accredited by Accrediting Council for Independent Colleges and Schools.

Program Information
Program calendar is continuous. Associate degree in Le Cordon Bleu Culinary Arts. Certificate in Le Cordon Bleu Patisserie and Baking.

Special Programs
Externships, culinary competitions.

Application Information
Applications are accepted continuously. Applicants must interview; submit a formal application and have a high school diploma or GED.

Contact
Director of Admissions, Le Cordon Bleu Program, 11400 Burnet Road, Suite 2100, Austin, TX 78758. Telephone: 888-559-7222. World Wide Web: http://www.tca.com/.

University of Houston

Conrad N. Hilton College of Hotel and Restaurant Management

Houston, Texas

General Information
Public, coeducational, university. Urban campus. Founded in 1927. Accredited by Southern Association of Colleges and Schools.

Program Information
Offered since 1969. Accredited by Council on Hotel, Restaurant and Institutional Education. Program calendar is divided into semesters. 1- to 2-year master's degree in hospitality management. 4-year bachelor's degree in hotel and restaurant management.

Program Affiliation
American Hotel and Lodging Association; Confrerie de la Chaine des Rotisseurs; Council on Hotel, Restaurant, and Institutional Education; Greater Houston Restaurant Association; International Food Service Executives Association; International Hotel and Restaurant Association; National Restaurant Association; National Restaurant Association Educational Foundation; Society of Wine Educators; Texas Restaurant Association.

Areas of Study
Beverage management; buffet catering; catering (management); controlling costs in food service; culinary skill development; facilities layout and design; food and beverage management; food and beverage of gaming operation; food and beverage service; food preparation; food purchasing; food service communication; food service math; hotel food and beverage management; international cuisine; introduction to food service; kitchen management; management and human resources; meal planning; menu and facilities design; nutrition and food service; restaurant development; restaurant management; restaurant opportunities; sanitation; wines and spirits.

Facilities
Bake shop; cafeteria; catering service; 6 classrooms; coffee shop; 4 computer laboratories; 2 demonstration laboratories; 8 food production kitchens; gourmet dining room; 2 laboratories; learning resource center; library; 2 public restaurants; snack shop; student lounge; 2 teaching kitchens.

Typical Student Profile
841 total: 681 full-time; 160 part-time. 676 are under 25 years old; 158 are between 25 and 44 years old; 7 are over 44 years old.

Special Programs
Paid internships, international programs in France, Mexico and Hong Kong, domestic programs in casino operations in Nevada, New Jersey, and Mississippi, wine program in California, marking programs in New York and Chicago.

Financial Aid
In 2006, 139 scholarships were awarded (average award was $2500). Program-specific awards include Conrad N. Hilton College Scholarships, teaching and research assistantships for graduate students. Employment placement assistance is available. Employment opportunities within the program are available.

Housing
Coed and apartment-style housing available.

Application Information
Students may begin participation in January, May, and August. Application deadline for summer/fall is May 1. Application deadline for spring is December 1. In 2006, 302 applied; 247 were accepted. Applicants must submit a formal application and letters of reference and essay (for master's program only).

Contact
Director of Admissions, Conrad N. Hilton College of Hotel and Restaurant Management, 229 C. N. Hilton Hotel-College, Houston, TX 77204-3028. Telephone: 713-743-2446. Fax: 713-743-2581. World Wide Web: http://www.hrm.uh.edu/.

University of North Texas

Hospitality Management

Denton, Texas

General Information
Public, coeducational, university. Urban campus. Founded in 1890. Accredited by Southern Association of Colleges and Schools.

Program Information
Offered since 1985. Accredited by Council on Hotel, Restaurant and Institutional Education. Program calendar is divided into semesters. 2-year master's degree in hospitality management. 4-year bachelor's degree in hospitality management.

Program Affiliation
American Dietetic Association; American Hotel and Lodging Association; Council on Hotel, Restaurant, and Institutional Education; International Wine & Food Society; National Restaurant Association; National Restaurant Association Educational Foundation.

Areas of Study
Controlling costs in food service; food preparation; food purchasing; international cuisine; introduction to food service; kitchen management; management and human resources; menu and facilities design; nutrition; nutrition and food service; restaurant opportunities; sanitation; wines and spirits.

Facilities
4 classrooms; 6 computer laboratories; 2 demonstration laboratories; 2 food production kitchens; gourmet dining room; 2 laboratories; learning resource center; 4 lecture rooms; 2 libraries; public restaurant; 2 teaching kitchens.

Typical Student Profile
450 full-time.

University of North Texas *(continued)*

Special Programs
Faculty-supervised internships, student-operated laboratory restaurant.

Financial Aid
Employment placement assistance is available.

Housing
Coed and apartment-style housing available.

Application Information
Students may begin participation in January, May, June, July, and August. Applications are accepted continuously. Applicants must submit a formal application.

Contact
Director of Admissions, Hospitality Management, PO Box 311100, Denton, TX 75057. Telephone: 940-565-2436. Fax: 940-565-4348. World Wide Web: http://www.smhm.unt.edu/.

Utah

The International Culinary School at The Art Institute of Salt Lake City

Draper, Utah

General Information
Private, coeducational institution.

Program Information
Associate degree in Culinary Arts. Associate degree in Baking and Pastry. Bachelor's degree in Culinary Management. Diploma in The Art of Cooking. Diploma in Baking and Pastry.

Contact
Office of Admissions, 121 West Election Road, Suite 100, Draper, UT 84020-9492. Telephone: 801-601-4700. World Wide Web: http://www.artinstitutes.edu/saltlakecity/.

See color display following page 332.

Utah Valley State College

Culinary Arts Institute

Orem, Utah

General Information
Public, coeducational, four-year college. Urban campus. Founded in 1941. Accredited by Northwest Commission on Colleges and Universities.

Program Information
Offered since 1990. Program calendar is divided into semesters. Associate degree in culinary arts.

Program Affiliation
American Culinary Federation; National Restaurant Association; National Restaurant Association Educational Foundation.

Areas of Study
Baking; beverage management; buffet catering; controlling costs in food service; culinary skill development; food preparation; food purchasing; garde-manger; international cuisine; introduction to food service; meal planning; menu and facilities design; nutrition and food service; patisserie; restaurant opportunities; sanitation; saucier; seafood processing; soup, stock, sauce, and starch production; wines and spirits.

Facilities
Bake shop; cafeteria; catering service; classroom; computer laboratory; demonstration laboratory; food production kitchen; gourmet dining room; public restaurant; teaching kitchen.

Special Programs
Culinary competitions, international internships, large group catering.

Financial Aid
In 2006, individual scholarships were awarded at $800. Program-specific awards include privately funded scholarships, Culinary Arts program scholarships. Employment placement assistance is available. Employment opportunities within the program are available.

Application Information
Students may begin participation in January and August. Application deadline for fall semester is August 1. Application deadline for spring semester is February 1. In 2006, 168 applied; 20 were accepted. Applicants must submit a formal application and have pre-requisite courses (2) and college level math; English and reading skills determined by ACT scores or Compass exam.

Contact
Director of Admissions, Culinary Arts Institute, 800 West University Parkway, Orem, UT 84058. Telephone: 801-863-8914. Fax: 801-863-6103. World Wide Web: http://www.uvsc.edu/.

Vermont

Champlain College

Hospitality Industry Management

Burlington, Vermont

General Information
Private, coeducational, four-year college. Urban campus. Founded in 1878. Accredited by New England Association of Schools and Colleges.

Program Information
Offered since 1979. Program calendar is divided into semesters. 1-year certificate in hotel/restaurant management. 1-year certificate in event management. 4-year bachelor's degree in event management. 4-year bachelor's degree in hotel/restaurant management.

Program Affiliation
American Culinary Federation; American Hotel and Lodging Association; Council on Hotel, Restaurant, and Institutional Education; National Restaurant Association; National Restaurant Association Educational Foundation; Vermont Lodging and Restaurant Association.

Areas of Study
Controlling costs in food service; culinary skill development; food preparation; food purchasing; food service math; introduction to food service; kitchen management; management and human resources; nutrition; nutrition and food service; restaurant opportunities; sanitation; soup, stock, sauce, and starch production.

Facilities
5 classrooms; 2 computer laboratories; 2 demonstration laboratories; food production kitchen; gourmet dining room; 2 laboratories; learning resource center; lecture room; library; public restaurant; snack shop; student lounge; teaching kitchen; bistro.

Typical Student Profile
90 total: 80 full-time; 10 part-time. 84 are under 25 years old; 6 are between 25 and 44 years old.

Special Programs
10-day spring break European tour, paid internship, resort management apprenticeship (during senior year).

Financial Aid
In 2006, 3 scholarships were awarded (average award was $1000). Employment placement assistance is available. Employment opportunities within the program are available.

Housing
Coed, apartment-style, and single-sex housing available.

Application Information
Students may begin participation in January and September. Application deadline for fall is January 31. Applicants must submit a formal application, letters of reference, an essay, SAT or ACT scores, TOEFL score for international applicants.

Contact
Director of Admissions, Hospitality Industry Management, 163 South Willard Street, Burlington, VT 05401. Telephone: 802-860-2727. Fax: 802-860-2767. World Wide Web: http://www.champlain.edu/.

Johnson State College

Hospitality and Tourism Management

Johnson, Vermont

General Information
Public, coeducational, four-year college. Rural campus. Founded in 1828. Accredited by New England Association of Schools and Colleges.

Program Information
Offered since 1986. Program calendar is divided into semesters. 4-year bachelor's degree in tourism management. 4-year bachelor's degree in lodging management. 4-year bachelor's degree in food service management.

Program Affiliation
American Hotel and Lodging Association; Council on Hotel, Restaurant, and Institutional Education; National Restaurant Association; National Restaurant Association Educational Foundation; Vermont Lodging and Restaurant Association.

Areas of Study
Beverage management; controlling costs in food service; dining room management; food preparation; food purchasing; introduction to food service; kitchen management; management and human resources; menu and facilities design; menu explosion analysis; restaurant opportunities; sanitation; wines and spirits.

Johnson State College ***(continued)***

Facilities

Cafeteria; catering service; 6 classrooms; coffee shop; 3 computer laboratories; food production kitchen; learning resource center; 2 lecture rooms; library; snack shop; student lounge.

Typical Student Profile

71 full-time. 58 are under 25 years old; 13 are between 25 and 44 years old.

Special Programs

Paid internships and General Manager Mentorship Program, trip to the New York Hotel Show, 4-day tour of hotel and restaurant facilities in Canada.

Financial Aid

Employment placement assistance is available.

Housing

Coed, apartment-style, and single-sex housing available.

Application Information

Students may begin participation in January and August. Applications are accepted continuously. Applicants must submit a formal application, letters of reference, an essay, interview (recommended).

Contact

Director of Admissions, Hospitality and Tourism Management, 337 College Hill, Johnson, VT 05656. Telephone: 802-635-1219. Fax: 802-635-1230. World Wide Web: http://www.jsc.vsc.edu/.

New England Culinary Institute

Montpelier and Essex Junction, Vermont

General Information

Private, coeducational, culinary institute. Founded in 1980. Accredited by Accrediting Commission of Career Schools and Colleges of Technology.

Program Information

Offered since 1980. Accredited by Accrediting Commission of Career Schools and Colleges of Technology. Program calendar is divided into quarters. 10-month certificate in professional pastry. 10-month certificate in professional cooking. 10-month certificate in professional baking. 15-month associate degree in hospitality and restaurant management. 18-month bachelor's degree in hospitality and restaurant management (must have 60 prior credits). 2-year associate degree in culinary arts. 2-year associate degree in baking and pastry arts. 39-month bachelor's degree in culinary arts.

Program Affiliation

American Culinary Federation; American Institute of Wine & Food; Council on Hotel, Restaurant, and Institutional Education; International Association of Culinary Professionals; James Beard Foundation, Inc.; National Restaurant Association; National Restaurant Association Educational Foundation; Vermont Fresh Network; Women Chefs and Restaurateurs.

Areas of Study

Baking; beverage management; buffet catering; controlling costs in food service; culinary skill development; financial analysis; food preparation; food purchasing; food service communication; food service math; garde-manger; introduction to food service; kitchen knife skills management; management and human resources; meal planning; meat cutting; meat fabrication; menu and facilities design; non-commercial preparation; nutrition; patisserie; restaurant service and operations management; sanitation; saucier; seafood processing; soup, stock, sauce, and starch production; sustainability in food service; technology applications; wines and spirits.

Facilities

2 bake shops; bakery; 3 cafeterias; 2 catering services; 20 classrooms; 2 computer laboratories; 12 food production kitchens; 2 gardens; 2 gourmet dining rooms; 2 laboratories; 2 learning resource centers; 2 libraries; 5 public restaurants; student lounge; non-commercial food kitchen; wireless dorms.

Student Profile

500 full-time.

Faculty

69 total: 51 full-time; 18 part-time. Faculty-student ratio: 1:10 production classes.

Prominent Alumni and Current Affiliation

Alton Brown, Food Network; Gavin Kaysen, Chef de Cuisine Cafè Boulud; Steve Jackson, Personal Chef, Chicago Bulls.

Special Programs

6-month paid internship following 6-month residency in culinary arts or baking and pastry arts, 6-month paid internship following calendar year in residency in hospitality and restaurant management, 6-month paid internship following 15-week residency in basic cooking or baking and pastry arts, 9-month paid internship following an additional 6-month residency for BA in Culinary Arts.

New England Culinary Institute *(continued)*

Typical Expenses
Tuition: $21,165–$35,358 per year for associates and bachelors; $8108–$12,000 for certificate programs. Program-related fees include $650 for books (culinary arts); $893 for knives (culinary arts and basic cooking); $750 for books (hospitality and restaurant management); $275 for books (certificate programs); $447 for knives (hospitality and restaurant management).

Financial Aid
Program-specific awards include more than 95% of NECI students receive financial aid in the form of scholarships, grants, loans, and Federal work-study. Employment placement assistance is available.

Housing
Coed, apartment-style, and single-sex housing available.

Application Information
Students may begin participation in January, March, June, July, September, and December. Applications are accepted continuously. In 2007, 840 applied; 588 were accepted. Applicants must interview; submit a formal application, letters of reference, an essay, high school transcripts or GED.

Contact
Ted Wiechman, Director of Admissions, 56 College Street, Montpelier, VT 05602-3115. Telephone: 802-225-3219. Fax: 802-225-3280. E-mail: ted.wiechman@neci.edu. World Wide Web: http://www.neci.edu/home.html.

See display on page 299.

Virginia

The International Culinary School at The Art Institute of Washington

A Branch of the Art Institute of Atlanta, GA

Arlington, Virginia

General Information
Private, coeducational institution.

Program Information
Accredited by American Culinary Federation (Associate in Culinary Arts program). Associate degree in Wines, Spirits and Beverage Management. Associate degree in Culinary Arts. Bachelor's degree in Food and Beverage Management. Bachelor's degree in Culinary Arts Management. Diploma in Culinary Arts–Culinary Skills. Diploma in Culinary Arts–Baking and Pastry.

Application Information
Applicants participation in the Wines, Spirits & Beverage Management program for those under 21 years of age will be conducted in accord with state law regarding the possession and consumption of alcoholic beverages.

Contact
Office of Admissions, A Branch of the Art Institute of Atlanta, GA, 1820 North Fort Myer Drive, Arlington, VA 22209. Telephone: 877-303-3771. World Wide Web: http://www.artinstitutes.edu/arlington/.

See color display following page 332.

James Madison University

Hospitality and Tourism Management

Harrisonburg, Virginia

General Information
Public, coeducational, comprehensive institution. Small-town setting. Founded in 1908. Accredited by Southern Association of Colleges and Schools.

Program Information
Offered since 1974. Accredited by Council on Hotel, Restaurant and Institutional Education, The Association to Advance Collegiate Schools of Business. Program calendar is divided into semesters. 4-year bachelor's degree in meeting planning. 4-year bachelor's degree in food and beverage management. 4-year bachelor's degree in entertainment. 4-year bachelor's degree in hospitality and tourism management. 4-year bachelor's degree in club and resort management.

Program Affiliation
Club Managers Association of America; Council on Hotel, Restaurant, and Institutional Education; National Restaurant Association; National Restaurant Association Educational Foundation.

Areas of Study
Beverage management; buffet catering; culinary skill development; food preparation; food purchasing; gastronomy; introduction to food service; management and human resources; restaurant opportunities.

Facilities
Classroom; computer laboratory; demonstration laboratory; lecture room; snack shop.

Typical Student Profile
350 total: 340 full-time; 10 part-time. 340 are under 25 years old; 10 are between 25 and 44 years old.

Special Programs
Six-day tour of California wineries, culinary project with The Greenbrier, paid internships.

Financial Aid
In 2006, 7 scholarships were awarded (average award was $1000). Employment placement assistance is available. Employment opportunities within the program are available.

Housing
Coed and single-sex housing available.

Application Information
Students may begin participation in January, May, and August. Application deadline for fall is March 1. Application deadline for spring is October 15. In 2006, 100 applied; 70 were accepted. Applicants must submit a formal application, an essay, SAT/ACT scores.

Contact
Director of Admissions, Hospitality and Tourism Management, James Madison University, MSC 0202, Harrisonburg, VA 22807. Telephone: 540-568-3037. Fax: 540-568-3273. World Wide Web: http://www.jmu.edu/hospitality.

J. Sargeant Reynolds Community College

School of Culinary Arts, Tourism, and Hospitality

Richmond, Virginia

General Information
Public, coeducational, two-year college. Urban campus. Founded in 1972. Accredited by Southern Association of Colleges and Schools.

Program Information
Offered since 1973. Accredited by American Culinary Federation Accrediting Commission. Program calendar is divided into semesters. 2-semester certificate in pastry arts. 2-year associate degree in hospitality management. 2-year associate degree in culinary arts.

Program Affiliation
American Culinary Federation; Confrerie de la Chaine des Rotisseurs; Council on Hotel, Restaurant, and Institutional Education; Foodservice Educators Network International; International Society of Travel and Tourism Educators; National Restaurant Association; National Restaurant Association Educational Foundation; Society of Wine Educators.

Areas of Study
Baking; beverage management; buffet catering; controlling costs in food service; culinary skill development; food and beverage service management; food preparation; food purchasing; garde-manger; international cuisine; introduction to food service; kitchen management; management and human resources; meat cutting; meat fabrication; menu and facilities design; nutrition; nutrition and food service; patisserie; restaurant opportunities; sanitation; saucier; seafood processing; soup, stock, sauce, and starch production; total quality management for hospitality; wines and spirits.

Facilities
Bake shop; bakery; cafeteria; catering service; 5 classrooms; 4 computer laboratories; demonstration laboratory; food production kitchen; laboratory; 3 learning resource centers; 3 lecture rooms; 3 libraries; snack shop; student lounge; 2 teaching kitchens.

Typical Student Profile
143 total: 55 full-time; 88 part-time. 80 are under 25 years old; 41 are between 25 and 44 years old; 22 are over 44 years old.

Special Programs
Semi-annual "President's Dinner" (multi-course, white glove gastronomic event), mentorship with Virginia Chefs Association professional chefs, advanced placement for previous experience.

Financial Aid
In 2006, 6 scholarships were awarded (average award was $500); 60 loans were granted (average loan was $2000). Program-specific awards include Virginia Hospitality and Travel Association Scholarship, American Hotel Foundation Scholarship. Employment placement assistance is available.

Application Information
Students may begin participation in January, May, and August. Applications are accepted continuously. In 2006, 57 applied; 57 were accepted. Applicants must interview; submit a formal application and academic transcripts.

Contact
Director of Admissions, School of Culinary Arts, Tourism, and Hospitality, 701 East Jackson Street, Richmond, VA 23219. Telephone: 804-523-5069. Fax: 804-786-5465. World Wide Web: http://www.reynolds.edu/hospitality.

Northern Virginia Community College

Hospitality Management/Culinary Arts

Annandale, Virginia

General Information

Public, coeducational, two-year college. Suburban campus. Founded in 1965. Accredited by Southern Association of Colleges and Schools.

Program Information

Offered since 1965. Accredited by American Culinary Federation Accrediting Commission. Program calendar is divided into semesters. 1-year certificate in hotel management. 1-year certificate in food service management. 1-year certificate in culinary arts. 2-year associate degree in nutrition management. 2-year associate degree in hotel management. 2-year associate degree in hospitality management. 2-year associate degree in food service management.

Program Affiliation

American Culinary Federation; American Dietetic Association; Council on Hotel, Restaurant, and Institutional Education; National Restaurant Association.

Areas of Study

Baking; buffet catering; controlling costs in food service; food preparation; food purchasing; food service communication; food service math; garde-manger; introduction to food service; management and human resources; meal planning; menu and facilities design; nutrition; nutrition and food service; patisserie; restaurant opportunities; sanitation.

Facilities

Cafeteria; 3 classrooms; 2 computer laboratories; demonstration laboratory; food production kitchen; garden; gourmet dining room; learning resource center; 3 lecture rooms; library; student lounge; teaching kitchen.

Typical Student Profile

350 total: 125 full-time; 225 part-time. 75 are under 25 years old; 225 are between 25 and 44 years old; 50 are over 44 years old.

Special Programs

ACF apprenticeship program, ACF regional student hot food competitions, New York international hotel/ restaurant show and tour.

Financial Aid

In 2006, 4 scholarships were awarded (average award was $6000). Program-specific awards include industry internships (paid). Employment placement assistance is available.

Application Information

Students may begin participation in January, May, and August. Application deadline for spring is January 15. Application deadline for fall is August 15. Application deadline for summer is May 15. In 2006, 87 applied; 87 were accepted. Applicants must submit a formal application.

Contact

Director of Admissions, Hospitality Management/ Culinary Arts, 8333 Little River Turnpike, Annandale, VA 22003. Telephone: 703-323-3458. Fax: 703-323-3509. World Wide Web: http://www.nvcc.edu/.

Stratford University

School of Culinary Arts and Hospitality Management

Falls Church, Virginia

General Information

Private, coeducational, four-year college. Suburban campus. Founded in 1976. Accredited by Accrediting Council for Independent Colleges and Schools.

Program Information

Offered since 1991. Accredited by American Culinary Federation Foundation Accrediting Commission. Program calendar is continuous. 12-month diploma in culinary arts. 15-month associate degree in hotel and restaurant management. 15-month associate degree in culinary arts. 15-month associate degree in baking and pastry arts. 30-month bachelor's degree in hospitality management.

Program Affiliation

American Culinary Federation; American Dietetic Association; American Institute of Wine & Food; Council on Hotel, Restaurant, and Institutional Education; International Association of Culinary Professionals; National Restaurant Association.

Areas of Study

Baking; culinary skill development; introduction to food service; management and human resources.

Facilities

Bake shop; 10 classrooms; 4 computer laboratories; 4 food production kitchens; gourmet dining room; lecture room; library; public restaurant; snack shop; 3 student lounges; 5 teaching kitchens.

Typical Student Profile

290 total: 200 full-time; 90 part-time. 90 are under 25 years old; 150 are between 25 and 44 years old; 50 are over 44 years old.

School of Culinary Arts & Hospitality

At Stratford University, not only are you able to graduate with a 4 year Culinary degree in 2 ½ years, you can be placed in a fast past work environment on day one.

- Hospitality Management BA Degree
- Hotel and Restaurant Management AAS Degree
- Baking and Pastry Arts AAS Degree
- Advanced Culinary Arts AAS Degree
- Advanced Culinary Arts Professional Diploma

The Career University for the Future
Falls Church, Virginia

Give us a quick call today to get your career on the fast track!
Accredited Member, American Culinary Federation (ACF)

1-800-444-0804 · www.stratford.edu

Certified by SCHEV to operate campuses in Virginia. Accredited Member, Accrediting Council of Independent Colleges and Schools (ACICS)

Stratford University *(continued)*

Special Programs
Paid externships, culinary competitions, AH&LA certification.

Financial Aid
In 2006, 5 scholarships were awarded (average award was $1000); 5 loans were granted (average loan was $3500). Program-specific awards include ACG Grant, Smart Grant. Employment placement assistance is available.

Housing
Apartment-style housing available.

Application Information
Students may begin participation in January, February, March, April, May, June, July, August, September, October, and November. Applications are accepted continuously. In 2006, 500 applied; 495 were accepted. Applicants must interview; submit a formal application and written essay for scholarships (HS senior only).

Contact
Director of Admissions, School of Culinary Arts and Hospitality Management, 7777 Leesburg Pike, Falls Church, VA 22043. Telephone: 703-734-5326. Fax: 703-734-5336. World Wide Web: http://www.stratford.edu/.

See display on page 303.

Tidewater Community College

Culinary Arts

Norfolk, Virginia

General Information
Public, coeducational, two-year college. Urban campus. Founded in 1968. Accredited by Southern Association of Colleges and Schools.

Program Information
Offered since 1997. Program calendar is divided into semesters. 1-year certificate in kitchen management. 1-year certificate in classical cooking. 1-year certificate in catering. 2-year associate degree in lodging management. 2-year associate degree in hospitality management culinary arts specialization. 2-year associate degree in food and beverage management.

Program Affiliation
American Culinary Federation; National Restaurant Association; National Restaurant Association Educational Foundation.

Areas of Study
Baking; buffet catering; controlling costs in food service; culinary French; culinary skill development; food purchasing; garde-manger; international cuisine; meat cutting; meat fabrication; nutrition; sanitation; seafood processing; soup, stock, sauce, and starch production; wines and spirits.

Facilities
2 classrooms; 2 food production kitchens; gourmet dining room; library.

Typical Student Profile
307 total: 162 full-time; 145 part-time.

Special Programs
Culinary competitions, cooperative education (apprenticeship).

Financial Aid
In 2006, 2 scholarships were awarded (average award was $1500). Employment placement assistance is available. Employment opportunities within the program are available.

Application Information
Students may begin participation in January, May, and August. Applications are accepted continuously. Applicants must submit a formal application.

Contact
Director of Admissions, Culinary Arts, 300 Granby Street, Norfolk, VA 23510-9956. Telephone: 757-822-1122. Fax: 757-822-1060. World Wide Web: http://www.tcc.edu/.

Virginia State University

Hospitality Management

Petersburg, Virginia

General Information
Public, coeducational, four-year college. Small-town setting. Founded in 1882. Accredited by Southern Association of Colleges and Schools.

Program Information
Offered since 1981. Accredited by Council on Hotel, Restaurant and Institutional Education, Accreditation Commission for Programs in Hospitality Administration (ACPHA). Program calendar is divided into semesters. 4-year bachelor's degree in hospitality management.

Program Affiliation
American Hotel and Lodging Association; Council on Hotel, Restaurant, and Institutional Education; International Food Service Executives Association; Multicultural Hospitality and Foodservice Alliance;

Virginia State University *(continued)*

National Association of Black Hotel Owners and Operators; National Coalition of Black Meeting Managers; National Restaurant Association Educational Foundation; National Society for Minorities in Hospitality; Virginia Hospitality Tourism Association.

Areas of Study

Food and beverage management; food preparation; food purchasing; lodging operations management; meal planning; meeting and event planning; nutrition and food service; restaurant management and culinary.

Facilities

Computer laboratory; food production kitchen; gourmet dining room; lecture room; public restaurant; snack shop; teaching kitchen; lodging labs; automated front desk.

Student Profile

70 total: 65 full-time; 5 part-time.

Faculty

5 total: 3 full-time; 2 part-time. 1 is a culinary-certified teacher. Prominent faculty: Deanne Williams, EdD, CHE. Faculty-student ratio: 1:15.

Special Programs

Paid internships, conferences relating to the hospitality industry, professional development seminars, international study tour, annual food show and exhibition.

Typical Expenses

In-state tuition: $2827 per semester. Out-of-state tuition: $6653 per semester.

Financial Aid

Program-specific awards include Presidential and Provost scholarships (to qualified students), various industry scholarships, program-specific awards include assistance with trip cost, industry sponsorships. Employment opportunities within the program are available.

Housing

Coed and apartment-style housing available.

Application Information

Students may begin participation in January and August. Applications are accepted continuously. Applicants must submit a formal application, letters of reference, and an essay.

Contact

Dr. Deanne Williams, Program Director, Hospitality Management, PO Box 9211, Petersburg, VA 23806. Telephone: 804-524-6753. Fax: 804-524-6843. E-mail: dwilliam@vsu.edu. World Wide Web: http://www.vsu.edu/pages/751.asp.

See display on page 305.

Washington

Bellingham Technical College

Culinary Arts

Bellingham, Washington

General Information

Public, coeducational, two-year college. Small-town setting. Founded in 1957. Accredited by Northwest Commission on Colleges and Universities.

Program Information

Offered since 1957. Accredited by American Culinary Federation Accrediting Commission. Program calendar is divided into quarters. 1-quarter certificate in pastry. 1-year certificate in culinary arts. 2-year associate degree in culinary arts.

Program Affiliation

American Culinary Federation; National Restaurant Association Educational Foundation; Sustainable Connections.

Areas of Study

Baking; management and human resources; nutrition and food service; sanitation.

Facilities

Bake shop; bakery; cafeteria; catering service; classroom; coffee shop; computer laboratory; demonstration laboratory; food production kitchen; garden; gourmet dining room; learning resource center; lecture room; library; public restaurant; snack shop; student lounge.

Typical Student Profile

50 full-time.

Special Programs

ACF culinary competitions, 6-week internship.

Financial Aid

In 2006, 8 scholarships were awarded (average award was $750); 11 loans were granted (average loan was $4500). Program-specific awards include work-study. Employment placement assistance is available. Employment opportunities within the program are available.

Application Information

Students may begin participation in April and September. Application deadline for fall is September 5. Application deadline for spring is April 1. In 2006, 50 applied; 50 were accepted. Applicants must submit a formal application, be at least 16 years of age, and complete an entrance exam.

Contact

Director of Admissions, Culinary Arts, 3028 Lindbergh Avenue, Bellingham, WA 98225. Telephone: 360-752-8400. Fax: 360-752-7400.

The International Culinary School at The Art Institute of Seattle

Seattle, Washington

General Information

Private, coeducational institution.

Program Information

Accredited by American Culinary Federation (Associate in Culinary Arts program). Associate degree in Baking and Pastry. Bachelor's degree in Culinary Arts Management. 1-year diploma in The Art of Cooking. 1-year diploma in Baking and Pastry. 2-year associate degree in Culinary Arts.

Contact

Office of Admissions, 2323 Elliott Avenue, Seattle, WA 98121. Telephone: 206-448-0900. World Wide Web: http://www.artinstitutes.edu/seattle/.

See color display following page 332.

Olympic College

Culinary Arts and Hospitality Management

Bremerton, Washington

General Information

Public, coeducational, two-year college. Suburban campus. Founded in 1946. Accredited by Northwest Commission on Colleges and Universities.

Program Information

Offered since 1978. Program calendar is divided into quarters. 12-month associate degree in sous chef. 12-month associate degree in hospitality management. 3-month certificate in cook's helper. 6-month certificate of completion in prep cook. 6-month certificate of completion in hospitality supervisor. 9-month certificate of specialization in lead cook. 9-month certificate of specialization in hospitality operations.

Program Affiliation

American Culinary Federation; Council on Hotel, Restaurant, and Institutional Education; National Association of College Services; National Restaurant Association; National Restaurant Association Educational Foundation; United States Personal Chef Association; Washington State Chefs Association.

Areas of Study

Baking; beverage management; buffet catering; controlling costs in food service; convenience cookery; culinary French; culinary skill development; food preparation; food purchasing; food service communication; food service math; garde-manger; international cuisine; introduction to food service; kitchen management; management and human resources; meal planning; meat cutting; meat fabrication; menu and facilities design; nutrition; nutrition and food service; sanitation; saucier; seafood processing; soup, stock, sauce, and starch production.

Facilities

Cafeteria; catering service; classroom; food production kitchen; gourmet dining room; learning resource center; lecture room; library; public restaurant; snack shop; student lounge; teaching kitchen; banquet hall.

Typical Student Profile

54 total: 37 full-time; 17 part-time.

Special Programs

5-day gourmet cooking class, specialty training in specific cuisine areas, 6-week internships.

Financial Aid

In 2006, 4 scholarships were awarded (average award was $500); 33 loans were granted (average loan was $5000). Program-specific awards include afternoon employment opportunities in food service. Employment placement assistance is available. Employment opportunities within the program are available.

Application Information

Students may begin participation in January, April, and September. Application deadline for fall is September 20. Application deadline for winter is December 30. Application deadline for spring is March 28. In 2006, 75 applied; 60 were accepted. Applicants must interview, and take pre-admission test.

Contact

Director of Admissions, Culinary Arts and Hospitality Management, 1600 Chester Avenue, Bremerton, WA 98337-1699. Telephone: 360-475-7571. Fax: 360-475-7575. World Wide Web: http://www.oc.ctc.edu/~oc/.

Seattle Central Community College

Seattle Culinary Academy

Seattle, Washington

General Information

Public, coeducational, two-year college. Urban campus. Founded in 1941. Accredited by Northwest Commission on Colleges and Universities.

Program Information

Offered since 1941. Accredited by American Culinary Federation Accrediting Commission. Program calendar is divided into quarters. 5-quarter certificate of completion in specialty desserts and breads. 6-quarter associate degree in specialty desserts and breads. 6-quarter certificate of completion in culinary arts. 7-quarter associate degree in culinary arts.

Program Affiliation

American Culinary Federation; Council on Hotel, Restaurant, and Institutional Education; National Restaurant Association Educational Foundation; Slow Food International; The Bread Bakers Guild of America; Washington Restaurant Association; Women Chefs and Restaurateurs.

Areas of Study

Baking; buffet catering; confectionery show pieces; controlling costs in food service; culinary skill development; food preparation; food purchasing; food service math; garde-manger; international cuisine; introduction to food service; management and human resources; menu design; nutrition; nutrition and food service; patisserie; restaurant opportunities; sanitation; saucier; soup, stock, sauce, and starch production; wines and spirits.

Facilities

Bake shop; bakery; cafeteria; catering service; 5 classrooms; computer laboratory; demonstration laboratory; 5 food production kitchens; garden; gourmet dining room; 3 lecture rooms; library; 2 public restaurants; snack shop; student lounge; teaching kitchen; student activity center.

Typical Student Profile

150 full-time. 40 are under 25 years old; 90 are between 25 and 44 years old; 20 are over 44 years old.

Special Programs

Chef-of-the-Day (students create a menu and oversee its production for the restaurant), newly developed sustainable course, 20-hour externship and culinary competitions.

Financial Aid

In 2006, 9 scholarships were awarded (average award was $300–$800). Program-specific awards include Les Dames D'Escoffier scholarship (full-tuition), 2-3 food-related scholarships ($700), Quillisasau Farm School Scholarships.

Application Information

Students may begin participation in January, April, and September. Applications are accepted continuously. In 2006, 180 applied; 150 were accepted. Applicants must submit a formal application, an essay, COMPASS scores or college transcripts that reflect the students level of math and English.

Contact

Director of Admissions, Seattle Culinary Academy, Mailstop 2BE2120, 1701 Broadway, Seattle, WA 98122. Telephone: 206-587-5424. Fax: 206-344-4323. World Wide Web: http://seattlecentral.edu/seattleculinary/.

South Puget Sound Community College

Food and Hospitality Services

Olympia, Washington

General Information

Public, coeducational, two-year college. Suburban campus. Founded in 1970. Accredited by Northwest Commission on Colleges and Universities.

Program Information

Offered since 1990. Program calendar is divided into quarters. Associate degree in culinary arts. 1-year certificate in culinary arts.

Program Affiliation

American Culinary Federation.

Typical Student Profile

46 total: 35 full-time; 11 part-time.

Financial Aid

In 2006, 10 scholarships were awarded (average award was $500); 3 loans were granted (average loan was $2000). Program-specific awards include scholarships from endowment. Employment placement assistance is available. Employment opportunities within the program are available.

Application Information

Students may begin participation in January, April, and September. Applications are accepted continuously. Applicants must submit a formal application.

Contact
Director of Admissions, Food and Hospitality Services, 2011 Mottman Road, SW, Olympia, WA 98512-6292. Telephone: 360-754-7711 Ext. 5347. World Wide Web: http://www.spscc.ctc.edu/.

West Virginia

West Virginia Northern Community College

Culinary Arts Department

Wheeling, West Virginia

General Information
Public, coeducational, two-year college. Small-town setting. Founded in 1972. Accredited by North Central Association of Colleges and Schools.

Program Information
Offered since 1974. Accredited by American Culinary Federation Accrediting Commission. Program calendar is divided into semesters. 1-year certificate in culinary arts. 2-year associate degree in culinary arts.

Program Affiliation
American Culinary Federation; National Restaurant Association; National Restaurant Association Educational Foundation.

Areas of Study
Baking; confectionery show pieces; controlling costs in food service; culinary skill development; food preparation; food purchasing; garde-manger; international cuisine; management and human resources; meal planning; menu and facilities design; nutrition; patisserie; sanitation; saucier; seafood processing; soup, stock, sauce, and starch production; wines and spirits.

Facilities
Bake shop; 3 classrooms; 4 computer laboratories; 3 demonstration laboratories; 3 food production kitchens; gourmet dining room; 3 laboratories; 3 learning resource centers; 3 lecture rooms; 3 libraries; public restaurant; 3 student lounges; teaching kitchen.

Typical Student Profile
57 total: 45 full-time; 12 part-time.

Financial Aid
Employment placement assistance is available. Employment opportunities within the program are available.

Application Information
Students may begin participation in January and August. Applications are accepted continuously. In 2006, 40 applied; 40 were accepted. Applicants must submit a formal application.

Contact
Director of Admissions, Culinary Arts Department, 1704 Market Street, Wheeling, WV 26003. Telephone: 304-233-5900 Ext. 4243. World Wide Web: http://www.wvnorthern.edu/programs/cartsprog/index.cfm?.

Wisconsin

Blackhawk Technical College

Culinary Arts Program

Janesville, Wisconsin

General Information
Public, coeducational, two-year college. Rural campus. Founded in 1968. Accredited by North Central Association of Colleges and Schools.

Program Information
Offered since 1980. Accredited by American Culinary Federation Accrediting Commission, American Culinary Federation. Program calendar is divided into semesters. 2-year associate degree in culinary arts. 4-month certificate in quantity production. 4-month certificate in baking.

Program Affiliation
American Culinary Federation; National Restaurant Association.

Areas of Study
Baking; beverage management; buffet catering; confectionery show pieces; controlling costs in food service; culinary French; culinary skill development; food preparation; food purchasing; food service math; garde-manger; international cuisine; introduction to food service; kitchen management; management and human resources; meal planning; meat cutting; menu and facilities design; nutrition; restaurant opportunities; sanitation; saucier; seafood processing; soup, stock, sauce, and starch production; wines and spirits.

Facilities
Bake shop; bakery; cafeteria; 2 classrooms; computer laboratory; demonstration laboratory; food production kitchen; gourmet dining room; laboratory; learning resource center; lecture room; library; public restaurant; teaching kitchen.

Blackhawk Technical College *(continued)*

Typical Student Profile
83 total: 62 full-time; 21 part-time. 60 are under 25 years old; 15 are between 25 and 44 years old; 8 are over 44 years old.

Special Programs
Culinary competitions, externships, National Restaurant Association show in Chicago.

Financial Aid
Employment placement assistance is available.

Application Information
Students may begin participation in January and August. Application deadline for fall is August 25. Application deadline for spring is January 6. Applicants must submit a formal application.

Contact
Director of Admissions, Culinary Arts Program, 6004 Prairie Road, Jamesville, WI 53547. Telephone: 608-757-7696. Fax: 608-743-4407. World Wide Web: http://www.blackhawk.edu/programs/associates/culinary_arts.htm.

Fox Valley Technical College

Culinary Arts and Hospitality Department

Appleton, Wisconsin

General Information
Public, coeducational, two-year college. Urban campus. Founded in 1913. Accredited by North Central Association of Colleges and Schools.

Program Information
Offered since 1973. Accredited by American Culinary Federation Accrediting Commission. Program calendar is divided into semesters. 1-year certificate in hospitality supervisor. 1-year certificate in advanced baking. 1-year diploma in food service production. 2-year associate degree in hotel and restaurant management. 2-year associate degree in culinary arts.

Program Affiliation
American Culinary Federation; Fox Cities Lodging and Hospitality Association; Fox Valley Culinary Association; International Food Service Executives Association; National Restaurant Association; National Restaurant Association Educational Foundation; Wisconsin Restaurant Association.

Areas of Study
Baking; beverage management; buffet catering; confectionery show pieces; controlling costs in food service; convenience cookery; culinary French; culinary skill development; food preparation; food purchasing; food service communication; food service math; garde-manger; international cuisine; introduction to food service; kitchen management; management and human resources; meal planning; meat cutting; meat fabrication; menu and facilities design; nutrition; nutrition and food service; patisserie; restaurant opportunities; sanitation; saucier; seafood processing; soup, stock, sauce, and starch production; wines and spirits.

Facilities
Bake shop; bakery; cafeteria; catering service; 2 classrooms; 2 computer laboratories; demonstration laboratory; 4 food production kitchens; garden; gourmet dining room; learning resource center; lecture room; library; public restaurant; snack shop; student lounge; teaching kitchen.

Typical Student Profile
240 total: 120 full-time; 120 part-time. 140 are under 25 years old; 50 are between 25 and 44 years old; 50 are over 44 years old.

Special Programs
Culinary and ice carving competitions, annual 7-day culinary tour (locations vary), National Restaurant Association show in Chicago.

Financial Aid
In 2006, 32 scholarships were awarded (average award was $500). Employment placement assistance is available. Employment opportunities within the program are available.

Application Information
Students may begin participation in January, June, and August. Applications are accepted continuously. In 2006, 120 applied; 120 were accepted. Applicants must submit a formal application.

Contact
Director of Admissions, Culinary Arts and Hospitality Department, 1825 North Bluemound, PO Box 2277, Appleton, WI 54912-2277. Telephone: 920-735-5643. Fax: 920-735-5655. World Wide Web: http://www.fvtc.edu/.

Madison Area Technical College

Culinary Trades Department

Madison, Wisconsin

General Information
Public, coeducational, two-year college. Urban campus. Founded in 1911. Accredited by North Central Association of Colleges and Schools.

Program Information
Offered since 1960. Accredited by American Culinary Federation Accrediting Commission. Program calendar is divided into semesters. 1-year diploma in food service production. 1-year diploma in baking/pastry arts. 2-year associate degree in culinary arts.

Program Affiliation
American Culinary Federation; International Food Service Executives Association; National Restaurant Association; National Restaurant Association Educational Foundation; Retailer's Bakery Association; The Bread Bakers Guild of America.

Areas of Study
Baking; buffet catering; controlling costs in food service; culinary French; culinary skill development; food preparation; food purchasing; food service communication; food service math; garde-manger; international cuisine; introduction to food service; management and human resources; meal planning; meat cutting; menu and facilities design; nutrition; sanitation; soup, stock, sauce, and starch production; wines and spirits.

Facilities
Bake shop; bakery; 2 cafeterias; catering service; computer laboratory; demonstration laboratory; 2 food production kitchens; gourmet dining room; learning resource center; lecture room; library; snack shop; student lounge; 2 teaching kitchens.

Typical Student Profile
105 total: 80 full-time; 25 part-time. 63 are under 25 years old; 21 are between 25 and 44 years old; 21 are over 44 years old.

Special Programs
2-credit internship, field experiences (domestic and international), culinary competitions.

Financial Aid
Employment placement assistance is available. Employment opportunities within the program are available.

Application Information
Students may begin participation in August. Application deadline for fall is July 1. Applicants must submit a formal application and academic transcripts.

Contact
Director of Admissions, Culinary Trades Department, 3550 Anderson Street, Madison, WI 53704-2599. Telephone: 608-246-6368. Fax: 608-246-6316. World Wide Web: http://matcmadison.edu/.

Milwaukee Area Technical College

Culinary Arts

Milwaukee, Wisconsin

General Information
Public, coeducational, two-year college. Urban campus. Founded in 1912. Accredited by North Central Association of Colleges and Schools.

Program Information
Offered since 1954. Accredited by American Culinary Federation. Program calendar is divided into semesters. 1-year technical diploma in food service technical diploma. 1-year technical diploma in baking production technical diploma. 2-year associate degree in culinary arts.

Program Affiliation
American Culinary Federation; Council on Hotel, Restaurant, and Institutional Education; National Restaurant Association Educational Foundation; Wisconsin Restaurant Association.

Areas of Study
Baking; beverage management; buffet catering; confectionery show pieces; controlling costs in food service; culinary skill development; food preparation; food purchasing; food service math; garde-manger; international cuisine; introduction to food service; management and human resources; meal planning; menu and facilities design; nutrition; patisserie; restaurant opportunities; sanitation; soup, stock, sauce, and starch production.

Facilities
Bake shop; bakery; cafeteria; 3 classrooms; computer laboratory; demonstration laboratory; 2 food production kitchens; gourmet dining room; library; 2 teaching kitchens.

Typical Student Profile
100 total: 65 full-time; 35 part-time. 25 are under 25 years old; 60 are between 25 and 44 years old; 15 are over 44 years old.

Special Programs
Culinary competition.

Financial Aid
Program-specific awards include Five Star Culinary Endowment Grant. Employment placement assistance is available. Employment opportunities within the program are available.

Milwaukee Area Technical College *(continued)*

Application Information

Students may begin participation in January and August. Application deadline for first day of class each semester. Applicants must submit a formal application and math and reading placement tests.

Contact

Director of Admissions, Culinary Arts, 700 West State Street, Milwaukee, WI 53233. Telephone: 414-297-7897. Fax: 414-297-7990. World Wide Web: http://www.matc.edu/documents/catalog/culinary_arts_aas_degree.html.

Moraine Park Technical College

Culinary Arts/Food Service Production

Fond du Lac, Wisconsin

General Information

Public, coeducational, two-year college. Small-town setting. Founded in 1967. Accredited by North Central Association of Colleges and Schools.

Program Information

Offered since 1976. Accredited by American Culinary Federation Accrediting Commission. Program calendar is divided into semesters. 1-semester certificate in food production. 1-semester certificate in bakery/deli. 1-year certificate in specialty baking. 1-year certificate in school food service. 1-year certificate in culinary basics. 1-year technical diploma in food service production. 2-year associate degree in culinary arts.

Program Affiliation

American Culinary Federation; National Restaurant Association; Wisconsin Restaurant Association.

Areas of Study

Baking; beverage management; buffet catering; controlling costs in food service; convenience cookery; culinary skill development; food preparation; food purchasing; food service communication; food service math; garde-manger; international cuisine; introduction to food service; kitchen management; meal planning; meat cutting; menu and facilities design; nutrition; nutrition and food service; restaurant opportunities; sales and service; sanitation; saucier; seafood processing; soup, stock, sauce, and starch production.

Facilities

Bake shop; bakery; cafeteria; catering service; 2 classrooms; 3 computer laboratories; demonstration laboratory; 2 food production kitchens; gourmet dining room; learning resource center; 2 lecture rooms; library; public restaurant; snack shop; teaching kitchen.

Typical Student Profile

85 total: 70 full-time; 15 part-time.

Special Programs

Culinary competitions, National Restaurant Association Convention, attendance at Wisconsin Restaurant Association and Inn Keepers Convention.

Financial Aid

In 2006, 9 scholarships were awarded (average award was $570); 29 loans were granted (average loan was $2735). Program-specific awards include paid internships. Employment placement assistance is available.

Application Information

Students may begin participation in January, March, August, and October. Applications are accepted continuously. In 2006, 45 applied; 41 were accepted. Applicants must interview; submit a formal application.

Contact

Director of Admissions, Culinary Arts/Food Service Production, 235 North National Avenue, PO Box 1940, Fond du Lac, WI 54936-1940. Telephone: 920-924-3333. Fax: 920-924-6356. World Wide Web: http://www.morainepark.edu/.

Nicolet Area Technical College

Culinary Arts

Rhinelander, Wisconsin

General Information

Public, coeducational, two-year college. Rural campus. Founded in 1968. Accredited by North Central Association of Colleges and Schools.

Program Information

National Restaurant Association Educational Foundation ManageFirst certificates available. Program calendar is divided into semesters. 1-year technical diploma in food service production. 13-credit certificate in catering. 14-credit certificate in baking. 2-year associate degree in culinary arts. 8-course certificate in food service management.

Program Affiliation
American Culinary Federation; National Restaurant Association; National Restaurant Association Educational Foundation; Wisconsin Restaurant Association.

Areas of Study
Baking; beverage management; buffet catering; controlling costs in food service; culinary skill development; food practicum; food preparation; food purchasing; food service math; garde-manger; international cuisine; introduction to food service; management and human resources; meal planning; menu and facilities design; nutrition; nutrition and food service; restaurant opportunities; restaurant practicum; sanitation; saucier; soup, stock, sauce, and starch production; wines and spirits.

Facilities
Cafeteria; classroom; demonstration laboratory; food production kitchen; gourmet dining room; learning resource center; lecture room; library; student lounge; teaching kitchen.

Typical Student Profile
40 total: 20 full-time; 20 part-time. 28 are under 25 years old; 12 are between 25 and 44 years old.

Special Programs
Internship in culinary arts (2 credits), attendance at the Central Regional ACF conference, culinary competition at the Wisconsin Restaurant Association Show.

Financial Aid
In 2006, 8 scholarships were awarded (average award was $500). Program-specific awards include Wisconsin Restaurant Association scholarships, NRA Education Foundation scholarships, NICA Manage First Program scholarships. Employment placement assistance is available. Employment opportunities within the program are available.

Application Information
Students may begin participation in January and August. Application deadline for fall is August 15. Application deadline for spring is January 15. In 2006, 30 applied; 18 were accepted. Applicants must submit a formal application, academic transcripts, and complete an Accuplacer test.

Contact
Director of Admissions, Culinary Arts, Nicolet College, Box 518, Rhinelander, WI 54501. Telephone: 715-365-4451. Fax: 715-365-4411. World Wide Web: http://www.nicoletcollege.edu/.

Southwest Wisconsin Technical College

Culinary Management

Fennimore, Wisconsin

General Information
Public, coeducational, two-year college. Small-town setting. Founded in 1967. Accredited by North Central Association of Colleges and Schools.

Program Information
Offered since 1994. Accredited by American Dietetic Association. Program calendar is divided into semesters. 1-year technical diploma in catering. 2-year associate degree in culinary management.

Program Affiliation
Catersource; National Restaurant Association.

Areas of Study
Baking; buffet catering; controlling costs in food service; culinary skill development; food preparation; food purchasing; food service communication; food service math; garde-manger; introduction to food service; kitchen management; management and human resources; meat cutting; meat fabrication; menu and facilities design; nutrition; sanitation; soup, stock, sauce, and starch production; wines and spirits.

Facilities
Bake shop; classroom; computer laboratory; food production kitchen; gourmet dining room; laboratory; learning resource center; library.

Typical Student Profile
20 full-time. 16 are under 25 years old; 3 are between 25 and 44 years old; 1 is over 44 years old.

Financial Aid
In 2006, 3 scholarships were awarded (average award was $333). Employment placement assistance is available. Employment opportunities within the program are available.

Housing
Apartment-style housing available.

Application Information
Students may begin participation in August. Application deadline for fall is August 15. In 2006, 18 applied; 18 were accepted. Applicants must interview, submit a formal application and take an entrance test.

Contact
Director of Admissions, Culinary Management, 1800 Bronson Boulevard, Fennimore, WI 53809. Telephone: 608-822-3262. World Wide Web: http://www.swtc.edu/.

University of Wisconsin–Stout

Department of Hospitality and Tourism

Menomonie, Wisconsin

General Information

Public, coeducational, comprehensive institution. Small-town setting. Founded in 1891. Accredited by North Central Association of Colleges and Schools.

Program Information

Offered since 1969. Program calendar is divided into semesters. 2-year master's degree in hospitality and tourism. 4-year bachelor's degree in hotel, restaurant, and tourism management.

Program Affiliation

American Dietetic Association; Council on Hotel, Restaurant, and Institutional Education; National Restaurant Association; National Restaurant Association Educational Foundation.

Areas of Study

Beverage management; buffet catering; controlling costs in food service; food preparation; food purchasing; introduction to food service; kitchen management; management and human resources; meal planning; menu and facilities design; nutrition; nutrition and food service; restaurant opportunities; sanitation; soup, stock, sauce, and starch production; wines and spirits.

Facilities

Bake shop; cafeteria; catering service; 10 classrooms; computer laboratory; 2 food production kitchens; gourmet dining room; learning resource center; 5 lecture rooms; library; 2 public restaurants; 2 teaching kitchens.

Typical Student Profile

625 total: 550 full-time; 75 part-time. 605 are under 25 years old; 20 are between 25 and 44 years old.

Special Programs

3-week wine and food pairing course in Palmade Mallorca (Spain) and Australia, catering opportunities, culinary competitions.

Financial Aid

In 2006, 40 scholarships were awarded (average award was $500). Employment placement assistance is available. Employment opportunities within the program are available.

Housing

Coed housing available.

Application Information

Students may begin participation in January and August. Applications are accepted continuously. In 2006, 230 applied; 180 were accepted. Applicants must submit a formal application and letters of reference.

Contact

Director of Admissions, Department of Hospitality and Tourism, 432 Home Economics Building, Menomonie, WI 54751. Telephone: 715-232-2532. Fax: 715-232-2588. World Wide Web: http://www.uwstout.edu/.

Wyoming

Sheridan College

Hospitality Management/Culinary Arts

Sheridan, Wyoming

General Information

Public, coeducational, two-year college. Small-town setting. Founded in 1948. Accredited by North Central Association of Colleges and Schools.

Program Information

Offered since 1994. Accredited by American Culinary Federation Accrediting Commission. National Restaurant Association Educational Foundation ManageFirst certificates available. Program calendar is divided into semesters. 1-year certificate in hospitality management. 1-year certificate in culinary arts. 2-year associate degree in hospitality management. 2-year associate degree in culinary arts.

Program Affiliation

American Culinary Federation; American Hotel and Lodging Association; National Restaurant Association; National Restaurant Association Educational Foundation; Wyoming Lodging and Restaurant Association; Wyoming State-Wide Consortium for Hospitality Management; Wyoming Travel Industry Coalition.

Areas of Study

Baking; beverage management; confectionery show pieces; controlling costs in food service; culinary French; culinary skill development; food preparation; food purchasing; food service math; front office operations; garde-manger; international cuisine; introduction to food service; kitchen management; law; management and human resources; marketing; meal planning; meat cutting; meat fabrication; menu and facilities design; nutrition; nutrition and food service; patisserie; restaurant opportunities; sanitation; security and loss; soup, stock, sauce, and starch production; wines and spirits.

Facilities
Catering service; 3 classrooms; 2 computer laboratories; demonstration laboratory; food production kitchen; garden; gourmet dining room; learning resource center; lecture room; library; public restaurant; 3 student lounges; 2 teaching kitchens; compress video classroom.

Typical Student Profile
35 total: 30 full-time; 5 part-time. 25 are under 25 years old; 10 are between 25 and 44 years old.

Special Programs
Attendance at Wyoming Governor's Conference on Travel and Tourism, internships (paid only), tours of hotels, restaurants, guest ranches, ski resorts.

Financial Aid
In 2006, 15 scholarships were awarded (average award was $500). Program-specific awards include Sheridan County Liquor Dealers Association Scholarship ($750), ProMgmt. Scholarship ($850), National Tourism Foundation Scholarship-Wyoming ($500). Employment placement assistance is available. Employment opportunities within the program are available.

Housing
Coed and single-sex housing available.

Application Information
Students may begin participation in January and August. Applications are accepted continuously. In 2006, 24 applied; 24 were accepted. Applicants must interview; submit a formal application.

Contact
Director of Admissions, Hospitality Management/ Culinary Arts, Box 1500, Sheridan, WY 82801. Telephone: 307-674-6446 Ext. 3508. Fax: 307-672-2103. World Wide Web: http://www.sheridan.edu/.

U.S. Territory - Virgin Islands

University of the Virgin Islands

Hotel and Restaurant Management Program

St. Thomas, Virgin Islands

General Information
Public, coeducational, comprehensive institution. Small-town setting. Founded in 1962. Accredited by Middle States Association of Colleges and Schools.

Program Information
Offered since 1962. Program calendar is divided into semesters. 2-year associate degree in hotel and restaurant management.

Program Affiliation
Educational Institute American Hotel and Motel Association.

Areas of Study
Food and beverage management; rooms division management.

Typical Student Profile
6 total: 4 full-time; 2 part-time. 5 are under 25 years old; 1 is between 25 and 44 years old.

Financial Aid
Employment placement assistance is available.

Housing
Single-sex housing available.

Application Information
Students may begin participation in January and August. Application deadline for fall is April 30. Application deadline for spring is October 30. In 2006, 5 applied; 3 were accepted. Applicants must submit a formal application and an essay.

Contact
Director of Admissions, Hotel and Restaurant Management Program, 2 John Brewers Bay, St. Thomas, VI 00802. Telephone: 340-693-1152. Fax: 340-693-1227. World Wide Web: http://www.uvi.edu/.

Canadore College of Applied Arts & Technology

School of Hospitality and Tourism

North Bay, Ontario, Canada

General Information

Public, coeducational, technical college. Rural campus. Founded in 1967.

Program Information

Offered since 1967. Program calendar is divided into semesters. 1-year certificate in culinary skills/chef training. 2-year diploma in hotel, restaurant, resort management. 2-year diploma in culinary management. 3-year diploma in hotel, restaurant, resort administration. 3-year diploma in culinary administration.

Program Affiliation

American Culinary Federation; Canadian Federation of Chefs and Cooks; Canadian Restaurant Association; Council on Hotel, Restaurant, and Institutional Education.

Areas of Study

Baking; beverage management; buffet catering; confectionery show pieces; controlling costs in food service; convenience cookery; culinary French; culinary skill development; food preparation; food purchasing; food service communication; food service math; garde-manger; international cuisine; introduction to food service; kitchen management; management and human resources; meal planning; meat fabrication; menu and facilities design; nutrition; nutrition and food service; patisserie; restaurant opportunities; sanitation; saucier; seafood processing; soup, stock, sauce, and starch production; wines and spirits.

Facilities

Bake shop; bakery; cafeteria; 4 classrooms; 2 computer laboratories; demonstration laboratory; food production kitchen; gourmet dining room; learning resource center; lecture room; library; public restaurant; student lounge; teaching kitchen; experimental food lab.

Typical Student Profile

95 total: 90 full-time; 5 part-time. 76 are under 25 years old; 16 are between 25 and 44 years old; 3 are over 44 years old.

Special Programs

Tour of culinary sites in the Caribbean region, provincial and international student competitions.

Financial Aid

In 2006, 15 scholarships were awarded (average award was Can$250). Employment placement assistance is available. Employment opportunities within the program are available.

Housing

Single-sex housing available.

Application Information

Students may begin participation in September. Application deadline for fall is May 15. In 2006, 211 applied; 65 were accepted. Applicants must submit a formal application.

Contact

Director of Admissions, School of Hospitality and Tourism, 100 College Drive, North Bay, ON P1B 8K9, Canada. Telephone: 705-474-7600 Ext. 5218. Fax: 705-474-2384. World Wide Web: http://www.canadorec.on.ca.

Culinary Institute of Vancouver Island at Vancouver Island University

Nanaimo, British Columbia, Canada

General Information

Public, coeducational, culinary institute. Small-town setting. Founded in 1968. Accredited by Association of Universities and Colleges of Canada.

Program Information

Offered since 1968. Accredited by Industry Training Authority (ITA) of British Columbia. Program calendar is continuous. 1-year certificate in professional baking. 1-year certificate in culinary arts. 2-year diploma in hospitality management. 2-year diploma in culinary arts. 4-year degree in hospitality management.

Program Affiliation

Baking Association of Canada; British Columbia Restaurant and Foodservices Association; Canadian Culinary Federation; Canadian Restaurant Association; Confrerie de la Chaine des Rotisseurs; Island Chefs Collaborative; Slow Food International.

Areas of Study
Baking; beverage management; buffet catering; confectionery show pieces; controlling costs in food service; convenience cookery; culinary French; culinary skill development; food preparation; food purchasing; food service communication; food service math; garde-manger; international cuisine; introduction to food service; kitchen management; management and human resources; meal planning; meat cutting; meat fabrication; menu and facilities design; nutrition; nutrition and food service; patisserie; restaurant opportunities; sanitation; saucier; seafood processing; soup, stock, sauce, and starch production; wines and spirits.

Facilities
Bake shop; 2 bakeries; 2 cafeterias; catering service; 4 classrooms; computer laboratory; demonstration laboratory; 2 food production kitchens; garden; gourmet dining room; laboratory; learning resource center; 2 lecture rooms; library; 2 public restaurants; student lounge; 2 teaching kitchens; herb garden.

Student Profile
200 total: 140 full-time; 60 part-time.

Faculty
15 total: 12 full-time; 3 part-time. 12 are industry professionals; 1 is a master baker; 12 are culinary-certified teachers. Prominent faculty: Michael Pelletier, CCC, past Culinary Team Canada member; Ken Harper, past Culinary Team Canada member; Bill Clay, Baking Team Canada member. Faculty-student ratio: 1:18.

Prominent Alumni and Current Affiliation
Derek Poivier, Valrohna, Paris; David Wong, Executive Chef, Fairmont, Edmonton/Bocuse D'Or 2009; Simon Lazarus, Executive Chef, Westin Bear Mountain; Corporate Food and Beverage Director, Hilton International, Dubai, UAE.

Special Programs
Paid co-op/experiential learning, BC Hot Competition, Salon Culinaire Vancouver and Victoria, Feast of Fields celebration of locally produced food, apprenticeship.

Typical Expenses
Application fee: Can$200. Tuition: Can$5000 per year full-time (in district), Can$360 per month part-time. Tuition for international students: Can$15,000 per year. Program-related fees include Can$900 for books and knives, partial uniform; Can$600 for co-op (domestic) or Can$1300 international.

Culinary Institute of Vancouver Island at Vancouver Island University *(continued)*

Financial Aid
In 2007, 15 scholarships were awarded (average award was Can$250); individual loans were awarded at Can$10,581. Program-specific awards include $500 entrance scholarship (essay mapping career), students are often hired by the Campus Caterers for various events. Employment placement assistance is available. Employment opportunities within the program are available.

Housing
Coed and apartment-style housing available. Average on-campus housing cost per month: Can$350.

Application Information
Students may begin participation in January and August. Applications are accepted continuously. In 2007, 196 applied; 86 were accepted. Applicants must interview; submit a formal application, an essay; complete grade 12 or provincial equivalent; and take entrance examination.

Contact
Debbie Shore, Department Chair, 900 5th Street, Nanaimo, BC V9R 555, Canada. Telephone: 250-740-6137. Fax: 250-740-6441. E-mail: debbie.shore@viu.ca. World Wide Web: http://www.viu.ca/culinary/index.asp.

George Brown College

Centre for Hospitality and Culinary Arts/George Brown Chef School

Toronto, Ontario, Canada

General Information
Public, coeducational, two-year college. Urban campus. Founded in 1960.

Program Information
Offered since 1967. Accredited by American Culinary Federation Accrediting Commission, Council on Hotel, Restaurant and Institutional Education. Program calendar is divided into trimesters. 1-year certificate in culinary skills. 1-year certificate in baking and pastry arts. 1-year post diploma in culinary arts (Italian). 1-year post diploma in culinary arts (Indian). 1-year post diploma in culinary arts (French). 1-year post diploma in advanced food and beverage management. 14-week certificate in Chinese cuisine. 18-week certificate in basic food preparation. 2-year diploma in hotel management. 2-year diploma in food and beverage management. 2-year diploma in culinary management. 2-year diploma in baking and pastry arts management. 3-year certificate in apprentice cook. 3-year diploma in patissier-apprentice baker.

Program Affiliation
American Culinary Federation; Council on Hotel, Restaurant, and Institutional Education; Institute of Food Technologists; National Restaurant Association; National Restaurant Association Educational Foundation; Society of Wine Educators; Sommelier Guild of Canada.

Areas of Study
Baking; beverage management; buffet catering; confectionery show pieces; controlling costs in food service; culinary French; culinary skill development; food preparation; food purchasing; food service communication; food service math; French cuisine; garde-manger; Indian Cuisine; international cuisine; introduction to food service; Italian cuisine; kitchen management; management and human resources; meat cutting; menu and facilities design; nutrition; nutrition and food service; patisserie; restaurant operations; sanitation; saucier; sommelier; soup, stock, sauce, and starch production; wines and spirits.

Facilities
4 bake shops; bakery; cafeteria; catering service; 40 classrooms; 2 computer laboratories; 4 demonstration laboratories; 12 food production kitchens; gourmet dining room; 8 laboratories; learning resource center; 8 lecture rooms; library; public restaurant; student lounge; 16 teaching kitchens; beverage mixology classroom; wine & beverage lab.

Typical Student Profile
8,500 total: 2500 full-time; 6000 part-time.

Special Programs
Culinary Arts Italian (includes 3-month internship in Italy), French Cuisine (includes international field-trip to Bocuse Institute).

Financial Aid
In 2006, 600 scholarships were awarded (average award was Can$500). Employment placement assistance is available. Employment opportunities within the program are available.

Application Information
Students may begin participation in January, May, and October. Application deadline for fall is March 1. Application deadline for January semester is June 1. Application deadline for summer semester is January 1. In 2006, 7000 applied; 1000 were accepted. Applicants must submit a formal application and have a grade 12 high school diploma.

Contact
Director of Admissions, Centre for Hospitality and Culinary Arts/George Brown Chef School, 300 Adelaide Street East, Toronto, ON M5A 1N1, Canada. Telephone: 416-415-5000. Fax: 416-415-2501. World Wide Web: http://www.georgebrown.ca.

Georgian College of Applied Arts and Technology

Culinary Management Program

Barrie, Ontario, Canada

General Information
Public, coeducational institution. Small-town setting. Founded in 1967. Accredited by Ontario Ministry of Education and Training.

Program Information
Offered since 1984. Program calendar is divided into semesters. 2-year diploma in culinary arts.

Program Affiliation
Muskoka & District Chefs Association.

Areas of Study
Baking; beverage management; buffet catering; controlling costs in food service; convenience cookery; culinary French; culinary skill development; food preparation; food purchasing; food service communication; food service math; garde-manger; international cuisine; introduction to food service; kitchen management; management and human resources; meal planning; meat fabrication; menu and facilities design; nutrition; patisserie; restaurant opportunities; sanitation; saucier; seafood processing; soup, stock, sauce, and starch production; wines and spirits.

Facilities
Bake shop; 2 computer laboratories; food production kitchen; gourmet dining room; 2 laboratories; learning resource center.

Typical Student Profile
50 full-time. 42 are under 25 years old; 8 are between 25 and 44 years old.

Financial Aid
In 2006, 8 scholarships were awarded (average award was Can$400); 30 loans were granted (average loan was Can$400). Program-specific awards include Entry Scholarship (Can$500).

Housing
Coed and apartment-style housing available.

Application Information
Students may begin participation in September. Application deadline for fall is March 1. In 2006, 158 applied; 146 were accepted. Applicants must submit a formal application.

Contact
Director of Admissions, Culinary Management Program, 370 Speedvale Avenue West, PO Box 810, Guelph, ON N1H 6M4, Canada. Telephone: 519-763-4725. World Wide Web: http://www.georgianc.on.ca.

Holland College

Culinary Institute of Canada

Charlottetown, Prince Edward Island, Canada

General Information
Public, coeducational, culinary institute. Urban campus. Founded in 1983.

Program Information
Offered since 1983. Program calendar is divided into trimesters. 1-year certificate in pastry arts. 2-year diploma in hotel restaurant management. 2-year diploma in culinary arts. 4-year applied degree in culinary operations.

Program Affiliation
Canadian Federation of Chefs and Cooks; Confrerie de la Chaine des Rotisseurs; Council on Hotel, Restaurant, and Institutional Education; International Association of Culinary Professionals.

Areas of Study
Baking; beverage management; buffet catering; confectionery show pieces; controlling costs in food service; convenience cookery; culinary French; culinary skill development; food preparation; food purchasing; food service communication; food service math; garde-manger; international cuisine; introduction to food service; kitchen management; management and human resources; meal planning; meat cutting; meat fabrication; menu and facilities design; nutrition; nutrition and food service; patisserie; restaurant opportunities; sanitation; saucier; seafood processing; soup, stock, sauce, and starch production; wines and spirits.

Facilities
Bake shop; bakery; cafeteria; 5 catering services; 14 classrooms; 3 computer laboratories; demonstration laboratory; 7 food production kitchens; gourmet dining room; learning resource center; lecture room; 2 public restaurants; snack shop; 2 student lounges; 6 teaching kitchens.

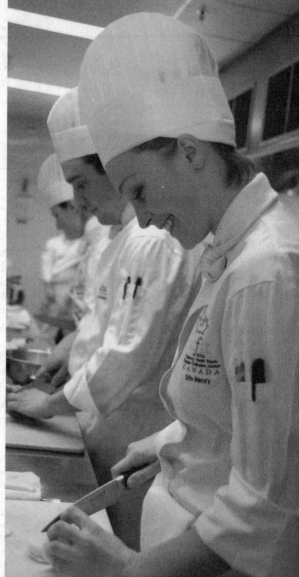

Student Profile
215 full-time.

Faculty
28 total: 19 full-time; 9 part-time. 8 are industry professionals; 10 are culinary-certified teachers. Faculty-student ratio: 1:18.

Special Programs
5-month paid internship, culinary competitions.

Typical Expenses
Application fee: Can$40. Tuition: Can$6450 per year. Program-related fees include Can$505 for book (for 2 years); Can$300 for knives; Can$1700 for lab fees (for 2 years); Can$1935 for uniforms and laundry (for 2 years); Can$490 for student union fee and health insurance fee (for 2 years).

Financial Aid
In 2007, 20 scholarships were awarded (average award was Can$1000). Employment placement assistance is available.

Housing
Coed and apartment-style housing available. Average on-campus housing cost per month: Can$500. Average off-campus housing cost per month: Can$400.

Application Information
Students may begin participation in March and September. Application deadline for spring is January 5. Application deadline for fall is February 25. Applicants must submit a formal application and resume.

Contact
Austin Clement, Culinary Programs Manager, Culinary Institute of Canada, 4 Sydney Street, Charlottetown, PE C1A 1E9, Canada. Telephone: 902-894-6805. Fax: 902-894-6835. E-mail: aclement@hollandcollege.com. World Wide Web: http://www.hollandcollege.com/.

See display on page 320.

Humber Institute of Technology and Advanced Learning

School of Hospitality, Recreation, and Tourism

Toronto, Ontario, Canada

General Information
Public, coeducational, comprehensive institution. Urban campus. Founded in 1967.

Program Information
Offered since 1982. Program calendar is divided into semesters. 1-year certificate in food and beverage. 1-year certificate in culinary skills. 2-year diploma in hospitality management/hotel and restaurant. 2-year diploma in culinary management.

Program Affiliation
American Vegan Society.

Areas of Study
Baking; confectionery show pieces; controlling costs in food service; culinary French; culinary skill development; food preparation; food purchasing; food service communication; food service math; garde-manger; international cuisine; introduction to food service; kitchen management; meal planning; meat cutting; meat fabrication; menu and facilities design; nutrition; patisserie; sanitation; saucier; seafood processing; soup, stock, sauce, and starch production; wines and spirits.

Facilities
Bake shop; bakery; 3 cafeterias; 2 catering services; 12 classrooms; 2 coffee shops; 6 computer laboratories; demonstration laboratory; 4 food production kitchens; 4 gardens; gourmet dining room; learning resource center; lecture room; library; 2 public restaurants; 2 snack shops; 3 student lounges; teaching kitchen.

Typical Student Profile
485 total: 400 full-time; 85 part-time.

Special Programs
Study abroad opportunities, university articulation agreements, internship.

Financial Aid
In 2006, 1 scholarship was awarded (award was Can$3500); individual loans were awarded at Can$750. Employment placement assistance is available. Employment opportunities within the program are available.

Housing
Coed, apartment-style, and single-sex housing available.

Application Information
Students may begin participation in January and September. Application deadline for fall is August 1. Application deadline for winter/spring is December 1. In 2006, 2000 applied; 240 were accepted. Applicants must submit a formal application.

Contact
Director of Admissions, School of Hospitality, Recreation, and Tourism, 205 Humber College Boulevard, Toronto, ON M9W 5L7, Canada. Telephone: 416-675-6622 Ext. 5276. Fax: 416-675-3062. World Wide Web: http://www.humber.ca.

The International Culinary School at The Art Institute of Vancouver

Vancouver, British Columbia, Canada

Program Information

Advanced diploma in Culinary Arts and Restaurant Ownership. Certificate in Culinary Arts (Levels 1 and 2). Certificate in Baking and Pastry Arts (Levels 1 and 2). Diploma in Hospitality and Restaurant Business Management. Diploma in Entrepreneurship and Restaurant Ownership. Diploma in Culinary Arts. Diploma in Baking and Pastry Arts.

Contact

Office of Admissions, The Canaccord Tower-Pacific Centre, 300-609 Granville Street, Vancouver, BC V7Y 1G5, Canada. World Wide Web: http://www.artinstitutes.edu/vancouver/.

See color display following page 332.

Le Cordon Bleu, Ottawa Culinary Arts Institute

The Classic Cycle

Ottawa, Ontario, Canada

General Information

Private, coeducational, culinary institute. Urban campus. Founded in 1988. Accredited by Ministry of Training, Colleges and Universities.

Program Information

Offered since 1988. Program calendar is divided into quarters. 10-to 12-week certificate in superior pastry. 10-to 12-week certificate in superior cuisine. 10-to 12-week certificate in intermediate pastry. 10-to 12-week certificate in intermediate cuisine. 10-to 12-week certificate in basic pastry. 10-to 12-week certificate in basic cuisine. 4-week certificate in introduction to catering. 9-month diploma in patisserie arts. 9-month diploma in culinary arts. 9-month grand diploma in culinary and patisserie arts.

Program Affiliation

American Institute of Wine & Food; Canadian Federation of Chefs and Cooks; Canadian Restaurant and Food Services Association; Confrerie de la Chaine des Rotisseurs; Council on Hotel, Restaurant, and Institutional Education; International Association of Culinary Professionals; James Beard Foundation, Inc.; Women Chefs and Restaurateurs; World Association of Cooks Societies.

Areas of Study

Baking; buffet catering; confectionery show pieces; culinary French; culinary skill development; food preparation; garde-manger; introduction to food service; meat cutting; meat fabrication; patisserie; sanitation; saucier; soup, stock, sauce, and starch production; wines and spirits.

Facilities

2 demonstration laboratories; food production kitchen; gourmet dining room; learning resource center; lecture room; library; public restaurant; student lounge; 4 teaching kitchens.

Student Profile

360 full-time. 144 are under 25 years old; 189 are between 25 and 44 years old; 27 are over 44 years old.

Faculty

12 total: 12 full-time. 12 are master chefs. Prominent faculty: Chef Philippe Guiet; Chef Christian Faure; Chef Armando Baisas; Chef Hervé Chabert. Faculty-student ratio: 1:15.

Prominent Alumni and Current Affiliation

Joshua Drache, former chef to Prime Minister; Matthew Dobry, Marriott, Toronto.

Special Programs

1-week programs in cuisine and pastry topics of general interest, short workshops in boulangerie, chocolate, sugar work, and creative cakes, introduction to catering.

Typical Expenses

Application fee: Can$500. Tuition: Can$7000–$42,000 per 10 weeks to 9 months. Program-related fees include Can$1215 for uniform and equipment; Can$100 for student activities fee.

Financial Aid

In 2007, 2 scholarships were awarded (average award was Can$6000). Program-specific awards include Canadian Federation of Chefs and Cooks Awards (Can$5500), International Association of Culinary Professionals awards (Can$5500), The Culinary Trust. Employment placement assistance is available.

Housing

Average off-campus housing cost per month: Can$550.

Application Information

Students may begin participation in January, April, June, September, and November. Applications are accepted continuously. In 2007, 375 applied; 360 were accepted. Applicants must submit a formal application, an essay, secondary school transcript.

CONTACT

Peter Baumgart, Sales and Recruitment Coordinator, The Classic Cycle, 453 Laurier Avenue East, Ottawa, ON K1N 6R4, Canada. Telephone: 613-236-2433. Fax: 613-236-2460. E-mail: ottawa@cordonbleu.edu. World Wide Web: http://www.lcbottawa.com/.

See color displays following pages 92 and 332.

LIAISON COLLEGE

Culinary Arts

Hamilton, Ontario, Canada

GENERAL INFORMATION

Private, coeducational, culinary institute. Urban campus. Founded in 1996. Accredited by Ontario's Ministry of Education & Training and Apprenticeship Board.

PROGRAM INFORMATION

Offered since 1996. Accredited by Ministry of Colleges and Universities. Program calendar is continuous. 300-hour diploma in cook (basic). 300-hour diploma in cook (advanced). 400-hour diploma in hospitality administration. 80-hour diploma in personal chef.

PROGRAM AFFILIATION

Canadian Association of Food Service Professionals; Canadian Chef Educators; Canadian Federation of Chefs and Cooks; Canadian Restaurant and Food Services Association; Cuisine Canada; Personal Chef Association; Women in Food Industry Management.

AREAS OF STUDY

Baking; buffet catering; controlling costs in food service; convenience cookery; culinary French; culinary skill development; food preparation; food purchasing; food service communication; food service math; garde-manger; international cuisine; introduction to food service; kitchen management; management and human resources; meal planning; menu and facilities design; nutrition; nutrition and food service; patisserie; restaurant opportunities; sanitation; saucier; seafood processing; soup, stock, sauce, and starch production.

FACILITIES

Bake shop; classroom; gourmet dining room; lecture room; teaching kitchen.

STUDENT PROFILE

800 total: 600 full-time; 200 part-time. 300 are under 25 years old; 375 are between 25 and 44 years old; 125 are over 44 years old.

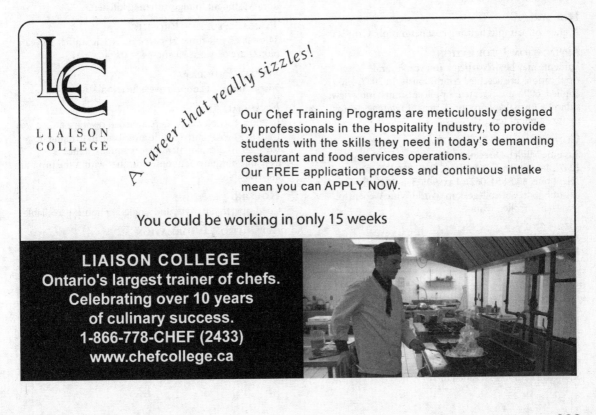

Liaison College *(continued)*

Faculty
30 total: 20 full-time; 10 part-time. 10 are industry professionals; 8 are master chefs; 22 are culinary-certified teachers. Prominent faculty: Michael Elliott, CCC; Gary Gingras; Steve Hepting; Shawn Whalen, CCC. Faculty-student ratio: 1:15.

Prominent Alumni and Current Affiliation
Felix Sano, Club Links; Trevor Cadera, Casino Rama; Greg Guthrie, Springwater Golf Club.

Special Programs
Culinary competitions, day trips to culinary interest spots, co-op (optional).

Typical Expenses
Application fee: Can$495. Tuition: Can$6495 per 300 hours (4 months) full-time, Can$6495 per 300 hours (10 months) part-time. Program-related fees include Can$500 for utensil/tool kit; Can$245 for uniform; Can$150 for text; Can$70 for fees/dues.

Financial Aid
In 2007, 4 scholarships were awarded (average award was Can$800). Program-specific awards include full-payment discounts, tuition financing OAC. Employment placement assistance is available. Employment opportunities within the program are available.

Housing
Average off-campus housing cost per month: Can$500.

Application Information
Students may begin participation year-round. Applications are accepted continuously. In 2007, 1400 applied; 600 were accepted. Applicants must interview; submit a formal application, letters of reference; show mature student testing.

Contact
Susanne Mikler, Director of Admissions, Culinary Arts, 1047 Main Street E, Hamilton, ON L8M IN5, Canada. Telephone: 800-854-0621. Fax: 905-545-1010. E-mail: liaisonhq@liaisoncollege.com. World Wide Web: http://www.liaisoncollege.com/.

Mount Saint Vincent University

Business Administration and Tourism and Hospitality Management

Halifax, Nova Scotia, Canada

General Information
Public, coeducational, comprehensive institution. Suburban campus. Founded in 1873.

Program Information
Offered since 1986. Accredited by Canadian Association for Cooperative Education. Program calendar is divided into semesters. 2-year certificate in tourism and hospitality management. 3-year diploma in tourism and hospitality management. 4-year bachelor's degree in tourism and hospitality management.

Program Affiliation
Canadian Food Service Executives Association; Council on Hotel, Restaurant, and Institutional Education; Nova Scotia Restaurant and Food Service Association; Sommelier Guild of Canada; Tourism Industry Association of Canada; Tourism Industry Association of Nova Scotia; Travel and Tourism Research Association.

Areas of Study
Beverage management; controlling costs in food service; culinary skill development; food preparation; food purchasing; food service communication; food service math; international cuisine; introduction to food service; kitchen management; management and human resources; meal planning; menu and facilities design; nutrition and food service; sanitation; wines and spirits.

Facilities
Classroom; computer laboratory; demonstration laboratory; food production kitchen; gourmet dining room; laboratory; learning resource center; lecture room; library; student lounge; teaching kitchen.

Typical Student Profile
84 total: 63 full-time; 21 part-time. 63 are under 25 years old; 21 are between 25 and 44 years old.

Special Programs
3 work terms of cooperative education, study tour.

Financial Aid
In 2006, 4 scholarships were awarded (average award was Can$875). Program-specific awards include mandatory work terms. Employment placement assistance is available. Employment opportunities within the program are available.

Housing
Coed, apartment-style, and single-sex housing available.

Application Information
Students may begin participation in January and September. Applications are accepted continuously. In 2006, 92 applied; 49 were accepted. Applicants must submit a formal application.

Contact
Director of Admissions, Business Administration and Tourism and Hospitality Management, 166 Bedford Highway, Halifax, NS B3M 2J6, Canada. Telephone: 902-457-6117. Fax: 902-457-6498. World Wide Web: http://www.msvu.ca.

Niagara College Canada

Niagara Culinary Institute

Niagara-on-the-Lake, Ontario, Canada

General Information

Public, coeducational, two-year college. Small-town setting. Founded in 1967.

Program Information

Program calendar is divided into semesters. 1-year certificate in culinary skills-chef training. 1-year graduate certificate in hospitality and tourism management systems. 1-year graduate certificate in event management. 2-year diploma in tourism management-business development. 2-year diploma in hospitality management-hotel and restaurant. 2-year diploma in culinary management. 4-year bachelor's degree in applied business-hospitality operations.

Areas of Study

Baking; culinary skill development; kitchen management; patisserie; restaurant opportunities.

Facilities

Bake shop; catering service; 3 computer laboratories; demonstration laboratory; food production kitchen; garden; gourmet dining room; learning resource center; 30 lecture rooms; library; public restaurant; 3 teaching kitchens; vineyard; wine laboratory.

Typical Student Profile

1000 full-time. 800 are under 25 years old; 150 are between 25 and 44 years old; 50 are over 44 years old.

Special Programs

4-month apprenticeship programs (cook 1 & 2, baker 1 & 2).

Housing

Coed housing available.

Application Information

Students may begin participation in January and September. Application deadline for fall is February 1. Application deadline for winter is October 1. Applicants must submit a formal application.

Contact

Director of Admissions, Niagara Culinary Institute, 300 Woodlawn Road, Welland, ON L3C 7L3, Canada. Telephone: 905-641-2252 Ext. 7558. World Wide Web: http://www.niagarac.on.ca/study/programs/fulltime/mmc0435/career.html.

Northern Alberta Institute of Technology

School of Hospitality and Culinary Arts

Edmonton, Alberta, Canada

General Information

Public, coeducational, two-year college. Urban campus. Founded in 1963. Accredited by Advanced Education and Technology.

Program Information

Offered since 1965. Program calendar is divided into semesters. 1-semester certificate in retail meat cutting. 1-year certificate in hospitality management. 1-year certificate in culinary arts. 1-year certificate in baking. 2-year diploma in hospitality management. 2-year diploma in culinary arts. 3-year journeyman's certificate in cooking or baking.

Program Affiliation

American Institute of Baking; Canadian Culinary Federation; Confrerie de la Chaine des Rotisseurs; Council on Hotel, Restaurant, and Institutional Education; Cuisine Canada; International Association of Culinary Professionals; International Sommelier Guild; International Wine & Food Society; The Bread Bakers Guild of America.

Areas of Study

Baking; beverage management; buffet catering; confectionery show pieces; controlling costs in food service; convenience cookery; culinary French; culinary skill development; food preparation; food purchasing; food service communication; food service math; garde-manger; gastronomy; international cuisine; introduction to food service; kitchen management; management and human resources; meat cutting; meat fabrication; menu and facilities design; nutrition; patisserie; sanitation; saucier; seafood processing; soup, stock, sauce, and starch production; wines and spirits.

Facilities

Bake shop; bakery; 2 cafeterias; catering service; 3 classrooms; 2 computer laboratories; demonstration laboratory; food production kitchen; gourmet dining room; 2 learning resource centers; lecture room; library; public restaurant; snack shop; 3 student lounges; 10 teaching kitchens; mixology laboratory.

Typical Student Profile

600 total: 380 full-time; 220 part-time. 460 are under 25 years old; 110 are between 25 and 44 years old; 30 are over 44 years old.

Northern Alberta Institute of Technology *(continued)*

Special Programs

Culinary Team for competitions, study tours, international student exchange.

Financial Aid

In 2006, 20–25 scholarships were awarded (average award was Can$750). Employment placement assistance is available. Employment opportunities within the program are available.

Application Information

Students may begin participation in January and September. Applications are accepted continuously. In 2006, 600 applied; 360 were accepted. Applicants must submit a formal application, an essay, transcripts from secondary-level school.

Contact

Director of Admissions, School of Hospitality and Culinary Arts, 11762-106 Street, Edmonton, AB T5G 2R1, Canada. Telephone: 780-471-8679. Fax: 780-471-8914. World Wide Web: http://www.nait.ca/schoolofhospitality.

Northwest Culinary Academy of Vancouver

Vancouver, British Columbia, Canada

General Information

Private, coeducational, culinary institute. Urban campus. Founded in 2003. Accredited by Private Career Training Institutions Agency.

Program Information

Offered since 2003. Accredited by Private Career Training Institutions Agency of BC "PCTIA". Program calendar is continuous. 15-week diploma in professional pastry and bread. 15-week diploma in professional culinary. 42-week diploma in professional culinary and pastry/bread.

Program Affiliation

British Columbia Chefs' Association; British Columbia Restaurant and Foodservices Association.

Areas of Study

Baking; buffet catering; confectionery show pieces; controlling costs in food service; culinary French; culinary skill development; food preparation; food service math; garde-manger; international cuisine; kitchen management; meal planning; meat cutting; menu and

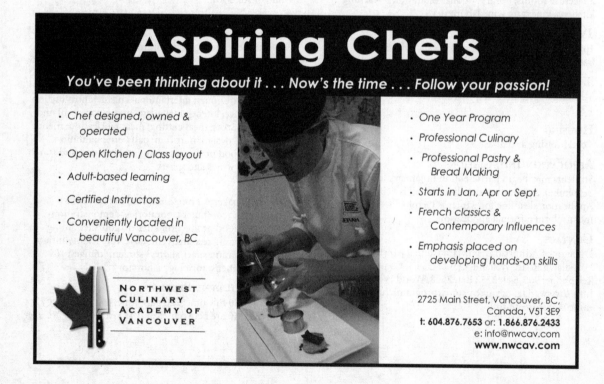

facilities design; nutrition; nutrition and food service; patisserie; sanitation; saucier; seafood processing; soup, stock, sauce, and starch production; wines and spirits.

Facilities

Bake shop; classroom; demonstration laboratory; food production kitchen; learning resource center; library; teaching kitchen; chef's demo station; kitchen lab; chef's table and pastry shop.

Faculty

5 total: 4 full-time; 1 part-time. 3 are industry professionals; 3 are culinary-certified teachers; 1 is a pastry chef instructor. Prominent faculty: Tony Minichiello; Christophe Kwiatkowsky; Ian Lai; Timothy Muehlbauer. Faculty-student ratio: 1:12.

Prominent Alumni and Current Affiliation

Dan Creyke, Raincity Grill; Alessandro Vianello, Fairmont Hotel; Kimberley Slobodian, Rouxbe.com.

Special Programs

Culinary competitions, work experience in catering setting: work experience ("stage") in restaurant, hotel, bakery, etc., TerraNova schoolyard project.

Typical Expenses

Application fee: Can$50–$100. Tuition: Professional culinary & pastry/bread (42 week program) Can$12,900 (Canadians) & Can$14,900 (international); professional culinary or professional pastry/bread (15 week programs) Can$6950 (Canadians) & Can$7950 (international) per program. Program-related fees include Can$476 for culinary tool kit; Can$428 for chef's uniform; Can$140 for culinary text book; Can$148 for pastry text book; Can$554 for pastry tool kit & Can$151 pastry supplemental tool kit.

Financial Aid

In 2007, 5 scholarships were awarded (average award was Can$3000). Program-specific awards include tuition installment plan is available to qualifying students. Employment placement assistance is available.

Housing

Average off-campus housing cost per month: Can$700.

Application Information

Students may begin participation in January, April, and September. Applications are accepted continuously. Applicants must interview; submit a formal application, letters of reference, an essay; have English fluency, good health (confirmed by doctor).

Contact

Tony Minichiello or Christophe Kwiatkowsky, Chef Instructors, Owners, 2725 Main Street, Vancouver, BC V5T 3E9, Canada. Telephone: 604-876-7653. Fax: 604-876-7023. E-mail: chefs@nwcav.com. World Wide Web: http://www.nwcav.com/.

Pacific Institute of Culinary Arts

Culinary Arts and Baking and Pastry Arts

Vancouver, British Columbia, Canada

General Information

Private, coeducational, culinary institute. Urban campus. Founded in 1996.

Program Information

Offered since 1996. Accredited by Private Career Training Institutions Agency of British Columbia. Program calendar is divided into quarters. Certificate in restaurant management. 6-month diploma in culinary arts. 6-month diploma in baking and pastry arts.

Program Affiliation

British Columbia Chefs' Association; British Columbia Restaurant and Foodservices Association; International Association of Culinary Professionals; National Career Colleges Association.

Areas of Study

Baking; beverage management; buffet catering; confectionery show pieces; controlling costs in food service; culinary French; culinary skill development; food preparation; food purchasing; garde-manger; international cuisine; introduction to food service; kitchen management; meal planning; meat cutting; nutrition; patisserie; restaurant opportunities; sanitation; saucier; soup, stock, sauce, and starch production; wines and spirits.

Facilities

Bake shop; bakery; catering service; 2 classrooms; coffee shop; computer laboratory; 4 food production kitchens; gourmet dining room; learning resource center; 3 lecture rooms; library; public restaurant; student lounge; 4 teaching kitchens; chocolate studio; cake-decorating studio.

Student Profile

175 full-time. 81 are under 25 years old; 77 are between 25 and 44 years old; 17 are over 44 years old.

Faculty

12 total: 12 full-time. 3 are industry professionals; 1 is a master baker; 8 are culinary-certified teachers. Prominent faculty: Julian Bond, Executive Chef.

Prominent Alumni and Current Affiliation

Mark Perrier, Cin Cin; James Schenk, Destino; Cheryl Wakerhauser, Pix Patisserie.

Special Programs

Industry field days at local farms, fisheries, etc., guest chef speakers, culinary competitions.

Pacific Institute of Culinary Arts *(continued)*

Typical Expenses

Application fee: Can$100. Tuition: Can$13,375 per diploma. Program-related fees include Can$550 for uniforms and shoes; Can$140 for textbooks; Can$995 for knives.

Financial Aid

In 2007, 3 scholarships were awarded (average award was Can$500). Employment placement assistance is available. Employment opportunities within the program are available.

Housing

Average off-campus housing cost per month: Can$600.

Application Information

Students may begin participation in January, April, June, and September. Applications are accepted continuously. In 2007, 225 applied; 200 were accepted. Applicants must interview; submit a formal application, letters of reference, and an essay.

Contact

Bali Mann, Director of Admissions, Culinary Arts and Baking and Pastry Arts, 1505 West 2nd Avenue, Vancouver, BC V6H 3Y4, Canada. Telephone: 800-416-4040. Fax: 604-734-4408. E-mail: info@picachef.com. World Wide Web: http://www.picachef.com/.

St. Clair College of Applied Arts and Technology

Hospitality

Windsor, Ontario, Canada

General Information

Public, coeducational, two-year college. Urban campus. Founded in 1967.

Program Information

Offered since 1994. Program calendar is divided into semesters. 1-year certificate in chef training. 2-year diploma in hotel and restaurant management. 2-year diploma in culinary management.

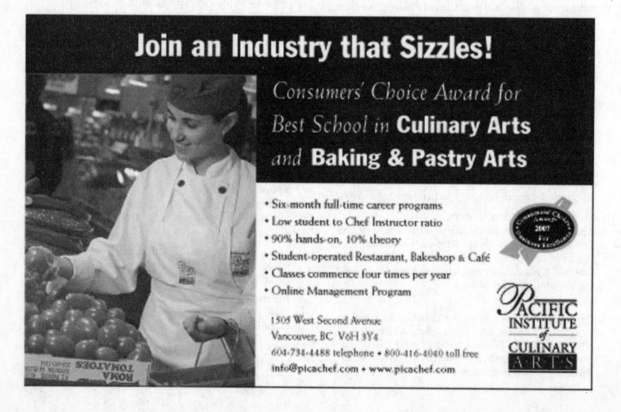

PROGRAM AFFILIATION
Council on Hotel, Restaurant, and Institutional Education; Ontario Restaurant, Hotel & Motel Association; Ontario Tourism Education Corporation; Windsor/Essex County Tourism and Convention Bureau.

AREAS OF STUDY
Baking; beverage management; buffet catering; confectionery show pieces; controlling costs in food service; culinary French; culinary skill development; customer service; food preparation; food purchasing; food service communication; food service math; garde-manger; hospitality marketing; international cuisine; introduction to food service; kitchen management; management and human resources; meal planning; menu and facilities design; nutrition; nutrition and food service; patisserie; restaurant opportunities; sanitation; saucier; soup, stock, sauce, and starch production; wines and spirits.

FACILITIES
Cafeteria; catering service; 2 classrooms; coffee shop; 4 computer laboratories; 2 demonstration laboratories; 2 food production kitchens; 2 gardens; gourmet dining room; learning resource center; 2 lecture rooms; library; public restaurant; 2 snack shops; student lounge; 2 teaching kitchens.

TYPICAL STUDENT PROFILE
265 total: 220 full-time; 45 part-time. 172 are under 25 years old; 53 are between 25 and 44 years old; 40 are over 44 years old.

SPECIAL PROGRAMS
Guest lecture and tours of local casinos, banquet facilities, and wineries, domestic internship opportunity, regional culinary competition (annual).

FINANCIAL AID
Program-specific awards include South Western Ontario Vintners Association bursary. Employment placement assistance is available. Employment opportunities within the program are available.

HOUSING
Apartment-style housing available.

APPLICATION INFORMATION
Students may begin participation in September. Application deadline for fall is March 1. Applicants must submit a formal application.

CONTACT
Director of Admissions, Hospitality, 2000 Talbot Road West, Windsor, ON N9A 6S4, Canada. Telephone: 519-972-2727 Ext. 4140. Fax: 519-972-2748. World Wide Web: http://www.stclaircollege.ca.

SAIT-POLYTECHNIC SCHOOL OF HOSPITALITY AND TOURISM

Professional Cooking, Baking and Pastry Arts, Hospitality Management, Travel and Tourism, Meat Operations and Management

Calgary, Alberta, Canada

GENERAL INFORMATION
Public, coeducational, two-year college. Urban campus. Founded in 1916.

PROGRAM INFORMATION
Offered since 1948. Accredited by Alberta Advanced Education. Program calendar is divided into semesters. 2-year diploma in travel and tourism. 2-year diploma in hospitality management. 2-year diploma in baking and pastry arts. 56-week diploma in professional cooking. 6-month certificate in meat operations and management.

PROGRAM AFFILIATION
Canadian Federation of Chefs and Cooks; Canadian Restaurant Association; Confrerie de la Chaine des Rotisseurs; Council on Hotel, Restaurant, and Institutional Education; World Association of Chefs and Cooks.

AREAS OF STUDY
Baking; beverage management; confectionery show pieces; controlling costs in food service; culinary French; culinary skill development; food preparation; food purchasing; food service communication; food service math; garde-manger; ice carving/fat sculpture; international cuisine; introduction to food service; kitchen management; management and human resources; meal planning; meat cutting; meat fabrication; menu and facilities design; nutrition; nutrition and food service; patisserie; restaurant opportunities; sanitation; saucier; seafood processing; soup, stock, sauce, and starch production; wines and spirits.

FACILITIES
2 bakeries; 3 cafeterias; catering service; 5 classrooms; 2 coffee shops; 2 computer laboratories; 3 demonstration laboratories; 4 food production kitchens; gourmet dining room; 2 laboratories; learning resource center; 3 lecture rooms; library; 2 public restaurants; 6 snack shops; student lounge; 2 teaching kitchens; test kitchen; bakery merchandizing classroom; retail shop.

TYPICAL STUDENT PROFILE
205 full-time. 123 are under 25 years old; 62 are between 25 and 44 years old; 20 are over 44 years old.

SAIT-Polytechnic School of Hospitality and Tourism *(continued)*

Special Programs
5-day study tours to food processing and manufacturing sites, 1-month exchange programs in Scotland, Austria, Australia, 5-day study tour to selected wine areas and 14-day study tour to Thailand, Australia, and Napa Valley, France, Spain, Canada's Niagara Region, Chile.

Financial Aid
In 2006, 46 scholarships were awarded (average award was Can$400); 45 loans were granted. Program-specific awards include tuition paid-guaranteed employment in industry meat operations and management. Employment placement assistance is available. Employment opportunities within the program are available.

Housing
Apartment-style housing available.

Application Information
Students may begin participation in January and September. Applications are accepted continuously. In 2006, 350 applied; 221 were accepted. Applicants must submit a formal application and academic transcripts.

Contact
Director of Admissions, Professional Cooking, Baking and Pastry Arts, Hospitality Management, Travel and Tourism, Meat Operations and Management, 1301-16 Avenue NW, Calgary, AB T2M 0L4, Canada. Telephone: 403-210-4015. Fax: 403-284-7034. World Wide Web: http://www.sait.ca/hospitalityandtourism.

Stratford Chefs School

Stratford, Ontario, Canada

General Information
Private, coeducational, culinary institute. Small-town setting. Founded in 1983. Accredited by Ontario Ministry of Education and Training.

Program Information
Offered since 1983. Accredited by Ontario Ministry of Training Colleges and Universities-Apprenticeship Branch. Program calendar is divided into trimesters. 2-year diploma in professional cookery.

Program Affiliation
Canadian Restaurant and Food Services Association; Ontario Hostelry Association; Slow Food International; Women's Culinary Network.

Areas of Study
Baking; controlling costs in food service; culinary French; culinary skill development; food preparation; food purchasing; food service communication; food service math; garde-manger; international cuisine; introduction to food service; kitchen management; management and human resources; meal planning; meat cutting; menu and facilities design; nutrition; nutrition and food service; patisserie; restaurant opportunities; sanitation; saucier; seafood processing; soup, stock, sauce, and starch production; wines and spirits.

Facilities
3 classrooms; computer laboratory; 3 demonstration laboratories; 3 food production kitchens; gourmet dining room; lecture room; library; 3 teaching kitchens.

Typical Student Profile
70 full-time. 20 are under 25 years old; 48 are between 25 and 44 years old; 2 are over 44 years old.

Special Programs
Apprenticeship program, international guest chefs.

Financial Aid
In 2006, 9 scholarships were awarded (average award was Can$625). Employment placement assistance is available.

Application Information
Students may begin participation in November. Applications are accepted continuously. In 2006, 123 applied; 36 were accepted. Applicants must interview; submit a formal application, an essay; kitchen interview; letters of reference for students who cannot attend; personal interview.

Contact
Director of Admissions, 68 Nilest, Stratford, ON N5A 4C5, Canada. Telephone: 519-271-1414. Fax: 519-271-5679. World Wide Web: http://www.stratfordchef.on.ca.

University of Guelph

School of Hospitality and Tourism Management

Guelph, Ontario, Canada

General Information
Public, coeducational, university. Suburban campus. Founded in 1964. Accredited by Association of Universities and Colleges of Canada.

Program Information
Offered since 1969. Program calendar is divided into trimesters. 1-year master of business administration in hospitality and tourism. 4-year bachelor of commerce in hotel and food administration.

Program Affiliation
American Dietetic Association; Canadian Food Service Executives Association; Council on Hotel, Restaurant, and Institutional Education.

Areas of Study
Foodservice management; hotel management; tourism management.

Facilities
6 cafeterias; catering service; coffee shop; 4 computer laboratories; 2 demonstration laboratories; food production kitchen; gourmet dining room; 2 laboratories; learning resource center; library; public restaurant; snack shop; student lounge; teaching kitchen.

Typical Student Profile
650 total: 600 full-time; 50 part-time. 550 are under 25 years old; 100 are between 25 and 44 years old.

Special Programs
Fall study abroad semester in France, semester exchange programs in Mexico, England, and Australia, Austria, Hong Kong, Finland, co-operative education program in Hotel and Food Administration.

Financial Aid
In 2006, 35 scholarships were awarded (average award was Can$900). Employment placement assistance is available. Employment opportunities within the program are available.

Housing
Coed, apartment-style, and single-sex housing available.

Application Information
Students may begin participation in September. Application deadline for fall is April 1. In 2006, 800 applied; 170 were accepted. Applicants must submit a formal application and background information sheet describing previous hospitality-related work experience and reasons for applying.

Contact
Director of Admissions, School of Hospitality and Tourism Management, 50 Stone Road East, Guelph, ON W1G 2WI, Canada. Telephone: 519-824-4120. Fax: 519-823-5512. World Wide Web: http://www.htm.uoguelph.ca.

University of New Brunswick, Saint John Campus

Faculty of Business, Applied Management (Hospitality and Tourism)

Saint John, New Brunswick, Canada

General Information
Public, coeducational, university. Suburban campus. Founded in 1964.

Program Information
Offered since 1998. Program calendar is divided into semesters, Canadian standard year. 4-year bachelor's degree in hospitality and tourism.

Program Affiliation
Council on Hotel, Restaurant, and Institutional Education; Travel and Tourism Research Association.

Areas of Study
Culinary skill development; culinary tourism; international tourism; travel and tourism.

Facilities
Cafeteria; 26 classrooms; coffee shop; 6 computer laboratories; learning resource center; 10 lecture rooms; library; 3 student lounges.

Typical Student Profile
57 total: 50 full-time; 7 part-time. 32 are under 25 years old; 25 are between 25 and 44 years old.

Special Programs
Study abroad, optional co-op program (paid), Program is articulated with New Brunswick Community College. Culinary training is completed at New Brunswick Community College while other courses are completed on-site.

Financial Aid
In 2006, 7 scholarships were awarded (average award was Can$1000). Program-specific awards include on-campus student work grants. Employment placement assistance is available. Employment opportunities within the program are available.

Housing
Coed and apartment-style housing available.

Application Information
Students may begin participation in January, May, and September. Applications are accepted continuously. In 2006, 63 applied; 41 were accepted. Applicants must submit a formal application and transcripts, course outlines (in some cases).

University of New Brunswick, Saint John Campus *(continued)*

Contact

Director of Admissions, Faculty of Business, Applied Management (Hospitality and Tourism), University of New Brunswick, Saint John, PO Box 5050, Saint John, NB E2L 4L5, Canada. Telephone: 506-648-5670. Fax: 506-648-5691. World Wide Web: http://www.unbsj.ca/business.

Australia

Le Cordon Bleu Australia

Regency Park, SA, Australia

General Information

Private, coeducational, culinary institute. Suburban campus. Founded in 1998.

Program Information

Offered since 1998. Program calendar is divided into semesters. 18-month master's degree in gastronomy. 2-year advanced diploma in restaurant and catering management. 2-year diploma in professional culinary management. 2-year master's degree in International hospitality and restaurant management. 2.5-year bachelor's degree in international hotel management. 2.5-year bachelor's degree in international restaurant management. 9-month certificate in pastry. 9-month certificate in commercial cooking.

Program Affiliation

American Culinary Federation; American Institute of Wine & Food; Confrerie de la Chaine des Rotisseurs; Council on Hotel, Restaurant, and Institutional Education; International Association of Culinary Professionals; James Beard Foundation, Inc.

Areas of Study

Accounting; beverage management; business plan development; controlling costs in food service; culinary skill development; finance; food and wine philosophy; food preparation; food purchasing; human resources; information technology; international cuisine; kitchen management; legal aspects of food service management; management and human resources; marketing; menu and facilities design; nutrition; restaurant opportunities; sanitation; soup, stock, sauce, and starch production; wines and spirits.

Facilities

Bakery; cafeteria; classroom; coffee shop; computer laboratory; demonstration laboratory; garden; gourmet dining room; learning resource center; lecture room; library; public restaurant; student lounge; auditorium; butchery; winery; food science laboratory.

Student Profile

520 total: 500 full-time; 20 part-time.

Faculty

40 total: 40 full-time. 40 are industry professionals. Prominent faculty: Paul Reynolds; Stan Szczypiorski; Brian Lawes. Faculty-student ratio: 1:15.

Special Programs

1-year paid internship for bachelor and advanced diploma programs, 6-month paid internship for diploma program.

Typical Expenses

Application fee: A$500. Tuition: A$59,400 per 2–5 years for bachelor; A$39,600 for 2 years for advanced diploma. Program-related fee includes A$1980 for professional culinary tool kit.

Financial Aid

In 2007, 25 scholarships were awarded (average award was A$10,000). Program-specific awards include required paid internship within Australia (up to 1 year). Employment opportunities within the program are available.

Housing

Apartment-style housing available. Average on-campus housing cost per month: A$950. Average off-campus housing cost per month: A$800.

Application Information

Students may begin participation in January and July. Application deadline for January/February intake is November 30. Application deadline for July intake is May 31. Applicants must submit a formal application, letters of reference, 2 passport photos, evidence of English fluency (if English not first language), evidence of satisfactory completion of year 12 or equivalent.

Contact

Nina Lucas, Manager, Client Services, Days Road, Regency Park, South Australia, 5010, Australia. Telephone: 61-8-83463700. Fax: 61-8-83463755. E-mail: australia@cordonbleu.edu. World Wide Web: http://www.lecordonbleu.com.au.

See color displays following pages 92 and 332.

Le Cordon Bleu Sydney Culinary Arts Institute

Sydney, Australia

General Information

Private, coeducational, culinary institute. Suburban campus. Founded in 1996.

Le Cordon Bleu Sydney Culinary Arts Institute ***(continued)***

Program Information

Offered since 1996. Accredited by Training and Skills Commission South Australia. Program calendar is divided into quarters. 10-week certificate I in basic patisserie. 10-week certificate I in basic cuisine. 2-year diploma in professional culinary management. 22-week certificate II in intermediate patisserie. 22-week certificate II in intermediate cuisine. 36-week certificate lll in superior patisserie. 36-week certificate lll in superior cuisine.

Program Affiliation

Council on Hotel, Restaurant, and Institutional Education; International Association of Culinary Professionals; James Beard Foundation, Inc.

Areas of Study

Australian cuisine; baking; buffet catering; confectionery show pieces; controlling costs in food service; culinary French; culinary skill development; food preparation; food purchasing; food service math; French cuisine; garde-manger; international cuisine; kitchen management; management and human resources; meal planning; meat cutting; menu and facilities design; nutrition and food service; patisserie; sanitation; saucier; seafood processing; soup, stock, sauce, and starch production.

Facilities

Cafeteria; classroom; demonstration laboratory; food production kitchen; garden; gourmet dining room; learning resource center; lecture room; library; public restaurant; snack shop; student lounge; teaching kitchen.

Student Profile

600 full-time. 350 are under 25 years old; 200 are between 25 and 44 years old; 50 are over 44 years old.

Faculty

15 total: 15 full-time. 8 are industry professionals; 10 are master chefs; 6 are master bakers; 12 are culinary-certified teachers. Prominent faculty: Lynley Houghton; Patrick Harris; Herve Boutin. Faculty-student ratio: 1:12.

Special Programs

Post graduate opportunities through Le Cordon Bleu in Adelaide, opportunity to mix and match course components in different world-wide locations.

Typical Expenses

Application fee: A$500. Tuition: A$7500–A$9500 per 10 weeks per certificates level course. Program-related fee includes A$1980 for uniforms and equipment tool kit.

Application Information

Students may begin participation in January, April, July, and October. Applications are accepted continuously. In 2007, 1,000 applied; 600 were accepted. Applicants must submit a formal application and proof of English language proficiency (if English not first language), evidence of completion of year 11 in high school.

Contact

Admissions Manager, Culinary Arts Program, Days Road, Regency Park, 5010, Australia. Telephone: 61-8-83463700. Fax: 61-8-83463755. E-mail: australia@cordonbleu.edu. World Wide Web: http://www.lecordonbleu.com.au.

See color displays following pages 92 and 332.

Finland

Haaga-Helia University of Applied Sciences

Hotel, Restaurant, and Tourism Management

Helsinki, Finland

General Information

Public, coeducational institution. Suburban campus. Founded in 1969.

Program Information

Offered since 1993. Accredited by Council on Hotel, Restaurant and Institutional Education, Leading Hotel Schools of the World. Program calendar is divided into terms. 1.5-year master's degree in tourism (in English). 1.5-year master's degree in hotel, restaurant and tourism management (in Finnish). 3.5-year bachelor's degree in tourism management (in Finnish). 3.5-year bachelor's degree in hotel and restaurant management (in Finnish). 3.5-year bachelor's degree in food production management (in Finnish). 3.5-year bachelor's degree in hotel, restaurant, and tourism management (in English). 3.5-year bachelor's degree in experience and wellness management (in English).

Program Affiliation

Council on Hotel, Restaurant, and Institutional Education; Hotel and Catering International Management Association; International Association of Hotel School; World Tourism Organization.

Areas of Study

Beverage management; controlling costs in food service; culinary French; food preparation; food purchasing; food service communication; food service math; international cuisine; introduction to food service; kitchen management; management and human resources; meal planning; menu and facilities design; nutrition; nutrition and food service; restaurant opportunities; sanitation; wines and spirits.

Facilities
Cafeteria; 25 classrooms; 3 computer laboratories; demonstration laboratory; food production kitchen; gourmet dining room; learning resource center; 2 lecture rooms; library; public restaurant; student lounge; teaching kitchen; wine cellar; 2 demonstration hotel rooms.

Typical Student Profile
1,300 total: 900 full-time; 400 part-time. 900 are under 25 years old; 350 are between 25 and 44 years old; 50 are over 44 years old.

Special Programs
Specialization modules abroad (e.g. Aviation Management in Germany), paid internships in Finland and abroad, exchange semester abroad.

Financial Aid
Employment placement assistance is available. Employment opportunities within the program are available.

Housing
Single-sex housing available.

Application Information
Students may begin participation in August. Application deadline for spring is January 7. In 2006, 3,000 applied; 260 were accepted. Applicants must submit a formal application, an essay, written exam, and TOEFL scores.

Contact
Director of Admissions, Hotel, Restaurant, and Tourism Management, PO Box 8, Helsinki, 00321, Finland. Telephone: 358-9-22966326. World Wide Web: http://www.haaga-helia.fi.

France

Ecole des Arts Culinaires et de l'Hôtellerie de Lyon

Hotel, Restaurant and Culinary Arts

Lyon-Ecully, Cedex, France

General Information
Private, coeducational, culinary institute. Small-town setting. Founded in 1990.

Program Information
Offered since 1990. Program calendar is divided into semesters. 2.5- to 5-year diploma in management and culinary arts. 3-month certificate in cuisine and culture. 3-year bachelor's degree in hotel and restaurant management. 3-year bachelor's degree in culinary arts. 3-year diploma in hotel management. 5-year master's degree in administration in hotel and foodservice.

Program Affiliation
Council on Hotel, Restaurant, and Institutional Education.

Areas of Study
Baking; beverage management; buffet catering; confectionery show pieces; controlling costs in food service; culinary French; culinary skill development; food preparation; food purchasing; food service math; garde-manger; introduction to food service; kitchen management; management and human resources; meal planning; meat cutting; meat fabrication; menu and facilities design; nutrition and food service; patisserie; sanitation; saucier; soup, stock, sauce, and starch production; wines and spirits.

Facilities
Bakery; cafeteria; catering service; 11 classrooms; computer laboratory; 6 demonstration laboratories; 2 food production kitchens; garden; gourmet dining room; library; public restaurant; student lounge; teaching kitchen; vineyard.

Typical Student Profile
240 full-time. 210 are under 25 years old; 30 are between 25 and 44 years old.

Special Programs
Visits to area surrounding Lyons, 4-month internship each year France or abroad.

Financial Aid
Employment placement assistance is available. Employment opportunities within the program are available.

Housing
Coed housing available.

Application Information
Students may begin participation in January, April, May, and October. Applications are accepted continuously. In 2006, 300 applied; 100 were accepted. Applicants must interview; submit an essay and submit a formal application.

Contact
Director of Admissions, Hotel, Restaurant and Culinary Arts, Château du Viner, Ecully, 69130, France. Telephone: 33-472-18-02-20. Fax: 33-478-43-33-51. World Wide Web: http://www.each-lyon.com/.

ECOLE SUPÉRIEURE DE CUISINE FRANÇAISE GROUPE FERRANDI

Professional Bilingual Culinary, Pastry, and Bread Baking Programs

Paris, France

GENERAL INFORMATION
Coeducational, culinary institute. Urban campus. Founded in 1932.

PROGRAM INFORMATION
Offered since 1986. Accredited by United States Department of Education. Program calendar is divided into semesters. 5-month certificate in culinary arts (plus 3-month internship). 5-month certificate in classic French pastry and bread baking (plus 3-month internship).

AREAS OF STUDY
Baking; buffet catering; confectionery show pieces; controlling costs in food service; culinary French; culinary skill development; food preparation; French cuisine; garde-manger; meat cutting; patisserie; restaurant opportunities; sanitation; saucier; soup, stock, sauce, and starch production; wines and spirits.

FACILITIES
Bakery; cafeteria; catering service; 10 classrooms; 3 computer laboratories; demonstration laboratory; 4 food production kitchens; gourmet dining room; laboratory; learning resource center; 4 lecture rooms; library; public restaurant; 10 teaching kitchens.

TYPICAL STUDENT PROFILE
24 full-time. 8 are under 25 years old; 16 are between 25 and 44 years old.

SPECIAL PROGRAMS
Excursions to French wine regions, 1 end-of-year gastronomic excursion, 3-month apprenticeship program after completion of 5-month program.

FINANCIAL AID
Employment opportunities within the program are available.

APPLICATION INFORMATION
Students may begin participation in February and September. Application deadline for fall is May 1. Application deadline for spring is September 15. Applicants must interview; submit a formal application, letters of reference, and an essay.

CONTACT
Director of Admissions, Professional Bilingual Culinary, Pastry, and Bread Baking Programs, 10 rue Poussin, Paris, 75016, France. Telephone: 33-1-45270909. World Wide Web: http://www.escf.ccip.fr.

LE CORDON BLEU

The Grand Diplôme, The Diploma and Certificate Program

Paris, France

GENERAL INFORMATION
Private, coeducational, culinary institute. Urban campus. Founded in 1895.

PROGRAM INFORMATION
Offered since 1895. Program calendar is divided into trimesters, terms. 1-trimester certificate in basic, intermediate, and superior pastry. 1-trimester certificate in basic, intermediate, and superior cuisine. 1-year diploma in Le Grand Diplôme-cuisine and pastry. 1-year diploma in basic, intermediate, and superior pastry. 1-year diploma in basic, intermediate, and superior cuisine. 4-day certificate in French pastry technique (bread baking). 4-day certificate in French culinary technique (regional). 4-week certificate in professional in pastry. 5-week certificate in professional in cuisine.

PROGRAM AFFILIATION
American Institute of Wine & Food; Confrerie de la Chaine des Rotisseurs; Council on Hotel, Restaurant, and Institutional Education; International Association of Culinary Professionals; James Beard Foundation, Inc.; National Association for the Specialty Food Trade, Inc.; National Restaurant Association.

AREAS OF STUDY
Baking; cheese; confectionery show pieces; culinary French; culinary skill development; food preparation; garde-manger; meal planning; meat cutting; patisserie; saucier; soup, stock, sauce, and starch production; wines and spirits.

FACILITIES
2 demonstration laboratories; food production kitchen; student lounge; 4 teaching kitchens; boutique; showroom.

STUDENT PROFILE
380 full-time. 300 are under 25 years old; 80 are between 25 and 44 years old.

FACULTY
12 total: 12 full-time. 10 are master chefs. Prominent faculty: Patrick Terrien; Jean Francois Degrignet. Faculty-student ratio: 1:12.

PROMINENT ALUMNI AND CURRENT AFFILIATION
Gastón Acurio, Ashid & Gaston; Bomberg Brothers, Blue Ribbon.

Special Programs
4-day program in French culinary technique, Mediterranean flavors, French regional cuisine and bread baking, 1-2 day vineyard and cultural excursions, professional internships, guest chefs.

Typical Expenses
Application fee: 500–1500 euros. Tuition: 35,955 euros per Grand Diplôme; 21,900 euros per cuisine diploma; 16,055 euros per pastry diploma full-time, 5700 euros–7750 euros for 1 trimester part-time. Program-related fees include uniform package (included in tuition); equipment package (included in tuition).

Financial Aid
In 2007, 15 scholarships were awarded (average award was 10,000 euros). Program-specific awards include work-study program. Employment placement assistance is available.

Housing
Average off-campus housing cost per month: 800 euros.

Application Information
Students may begin participation in January, March, June, September, and November. Applications are accepted continuously. In 2007, 420 applied. Applicants must submit a formal application, an essay, application fee.

Contact
Christel Hernandez, Admissions Director, The Grand Diplôme, The Diploma and Certificate Program, 8 rue Léon Delhomme, Paris, France. Telephone: 33-1-53682250. Fax: 33-1-48560396. E-mail: paris@cordonbleu.edu. World Wide Web: http://www.cordonbleu.edu/.

See color displays following pages 92 and 332.

Ritz–Escoffier Paris

Paris Cedex 01, France

General Information
Private, coeducational, culinary institute. Urban campus. Founded in 1988.

Program Information
Offered since 1988. Program calendar is divided into trimesters. 1-week certificate in intermediate cuisine and pastry. 1-week certificate in baking and breakfast pastry. 1- to 2-year master of business administration in hospitality business. 12-week diploma in intermediate and advanced pastry. 12-week diploma in advanced cuisine and pastry. 2-week diploma in advanced professional course. 6-week diploma in intermediate cuisine and pastry.

Program Affiliation
American Institute of Wine & Food; International Association of Culinary Professionals.

Areas of Study
Art de vivre; baking; cours de cocktails; culinary French; culinary skill development; flower arranging; food preparation; garde-manger; meat cutting; patisserie; sanitation; saucier; soup, stock, sauce, and starch production; wines and spirits.

Facilities
Bakery; cafeteria; food production kitchen; lecture room; library; public restaurant; teaching kitchen.

Typical Student Profile
3,000 total: 1600 full-time; 1400 part-time.

Special Programs
6-week internship for the 12-week diplomas, Saturday workshops, wines and food pairing evening classes.

Financial Aid
Employment placement assistance is available.

Application Information
Students may begin participation year-round. Application deadline for admission is 6 months in advance of program start date. Applicants must submit a formal application, medical certificate, and portfolio.

Contact
Director of Admissions, 15, place Vendôme, Paris, 75041, France. Telephone: 33-1-43163050. Fax: 33-1-43163150. World Wide Web: http://www.ritzescoffier.fr/com/jp.

Italy

APICIUS International School of Hospitality

Florence, Italy

General Information
Private, coeducational, culinary institute. Urban campus. Founded in 1996.

Program Information
Offered since 1996. Program calendar is divided into semesters. 1–4-semester certificate in culinary arts. 2-semester certificate in wine studies and enology. 2-semester certificate in master in Italian cuisine. 2-semester certificate in Italian baking and pastry. 2-semester certificate in hospitality management. 2-semester certificate in food communications and publishing.

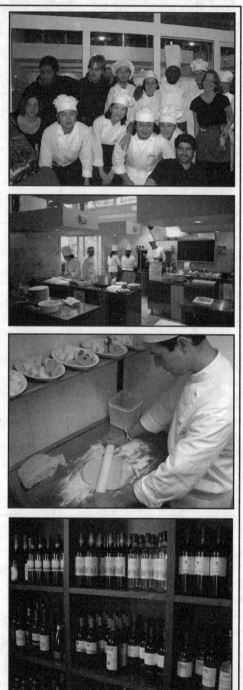

Program Affiliation
Association of Professional Italian Chefs; International Association of Culinary Professionals.

Areas of Study
Baking; culinary skill development; food preparation; international cuisine; meal planning; meat cutting; patisserie; restaurant opportunities; soup, stock, sauce, and starch production; wines and spirits.

Facilities
6 classrooms; computer laboratory; 3 demonstration laboratories; 2 food production kitchens; garden; 2 lecture rooms; library; public restaurant; 3 student lounges; 6 teaching kitchens; state of the art wine appreciation room.

Student Profile
100 full-time. 70 are under 25 years old; 15 are between 25 and 44 years old; 15 are over 44 years old.

Faculty
13 total: 10 full-time; 3 part-time. 5 are master chefs; 1 is a master baker; 7 are culinary-certified teachers. Prominent faculty: Marcella Ansaldo; Duccio Bagnoli; Andrea Trapani; Diletta Frescobaldi. Faculty-student ratio: 1:8.

Special Programs
Internships in local restaurants/hotels/wineries, 10-day tours of Tuscany, private customized cooking classes.

Typical Expenses
Application fee: $75. Tuition: $7300 per semester full-time, $3200 per monthly part-time. Program-related fee includes $950 for student service fee.

Financial Aid
In 2007, 4 scholarships were awarded (average award was $2000). Employment placement assistance is available.

Housing
Apartment-style housing available. Average on-campus housing cost per month: $1000.

Application Information
Students may begin participation in January, June, July, and September. Application deadline for spring is November 1. Application deadline for fall is July 1. Application deadline for summer is April 1. In 2007, 80 applied; 80 were accepted. Applicants must submit a formal application and curriculum vitae/resume for advanced-level applicants.

Contact
Marilyn Etchell, Admissions Officer, 7151 Wilton Avenue, Suite 202, Sebastopol, CA 95472. Telephone: 707-824-8965. Fax: 707-824-0198. E-mail: mae@studyabroaditaly.com. World Wide Web: http://www.ApiciusinFlorence.com/.

See display on page 338.

The International Cooking School of Italian Food and Wine

Bologna, Italy

General Information
Private, coeducational, culinary institute. Urban campus. Founded in 1987.

Program Information
Offered since 1987. Program calendar is divided into weeks, weeks. 1-week certificate in foundation of Italian cooking.

Program Affiliation
International Association of Culinary Professionals; James Beard Foundation, Inc.; New York Association of Cooking Teachers; Women Chefs and Restaurateurs.

Areas of Study
Italian cuisine.

Facilities
Food production kitchen; 3 gourmet dining rooms; 3 public restaurants; teaching kitchen; 2 vineyards; pasta production kitchen; pizza production kitchen.

Typical Student Profile
10 full-time.

Special Programs
Private tours and tastings in Emilia-Romagna and Piedmont regions.

Financial Aid
In 2006, 2 scholarships were awarded (average award was $3000).

Application Information
Students may begin participation in May, June, September, and October. Applications are accepted continuously. Applicants must submit a formal application.

Contact
Director of Admissions, 201 East 28th Street, Suite 15B, New York, NY 10016-8538. Telephone: 212-779-1921. Fax: 212-779-3248. World Wide Web: http://www.internationalcookingschool.com/.

Italian Culinary Institute for Foreigners–USA

Costigliole d'Asti, Italy

General Information

Private, coeducational, culinary institute. Small-town setting. Founded in 1991.

Program Information

Program calendar is continuous. 3-month certificate in master-culinary arts-Italian. 6-month diploma in master-culinary arts-Italian.

Special Programs

Visits to wineries and food producers, externships.

Housing

Coed and apartment-style housing available.

Application Information

Applications are accepted continuously. Applicants must submit a formal application, letters of reference, and an essay.

Contact

Director of Admissions, 126 Second Place, Brooklyn, NY 11231. Telephone: 718-875-0547. Fax: 718-875-5856. World Wide Web: http://www.icif.com/.

Italian Food Artisans, LLC

various regions of Italy, Italy

General Information

Private, coeducational institution. Small-town setting. Founded in 1993.

Program Information

Offered since 1993. Accredited by IACP. Program calendar is divided into weeks. 1-week certificate of completion in Italian regional cuisine.

Program Affiliation

American Institute of Wine & Food; International Association of Culinary Professionals; Oldways Preservation and Exchange Trust; Roundtable for Women in Foodservice; Slow Food International.

Areas of Study

Baking; culinary skill development; food preparation; food purchasing; international cuisine; Italian cuisine; Italian regional cuisine (truffles, risotto); wines and spirits.

Facilities

Garden; gourmet dining room; teaching kitchen; vineyard; farmhouse kitchen.

Typical Student Profile

150 part-time. 30 are under 25 years old; 50 are between 25 and 44 years old; 70 are over 44 years old.

Special Programs

1 week olive harvest and olive oil production in Tuscany, 1-week cheese-making workshop (pecorino, mozzarella, ricotta), 1 week grape harvest and wine-making workshop in Tuscany.

Housing

Coed and apartment-style housing available.

Application Information

Students may begin participation in March, April, May, June, July, August, September, October, and November. Applications are accepted continuously.

Contact

Director of Admissions, 27 West Anapamu Street #427, Santa Barbara, CA 93101. Telephone: 805-963-7289. World Wide Web: http://www.foodartisans.com/.

Italian Institute for Advanced Culinary and Pastry Arts

Satriano, Italy

General Information

Private, coeducational, culinary institute. Suburban campus. Founded in 1997. Accredited by Accrediting Commission of Career Schools and Colleges of Technology.

Program Information

Accredited by Selected Chef and Culinary Federations. 3-month certificate in regional Italian cuisine.

Program Affiliation

American Culinary Federation; Confrerie de la Chaine des Rotisseurs; International Association of Culinary Professionals; National Restaurant Association.

Areas of Study

Baking; buffet catering; confectionery show pieces; controlling costs in food service; convenience cookery; culinary skill development; food preparation; food purchasing; food service math; garde-manger; international cuisine; introduction to food service; kitchen management; meal planning; meat cutting; menu and facilities design; patisserie; sanitation; saucier; soup, stock, sauce, and starch production; wines and spirits.

Facilities

Bake shop; cafeteria; 2 classrooms; coffee shop; demonstration laboratory; food production kitchen; 3 gardens; 2 laboratories; 2 lecture rooms; public restaurant; student lounge; teaching kitchen; 2 vineyards.

Typical Student Profile
1,100 total: 550 full-time; 550 part-time.

Special Programs
Tour of artisan food makers in Italy, participation in international culinary competitions, 3-6 month internships in Italy.

Financial Aid
In 2006, 4 scholarships were awarded. Program-specific awards include sponsorship for selected participants to compete in international events. Employment placement assistance is available. Employment opportunities within the program are available.

Application Information
Students may begin participation in January, February, April, May, June, September, and October. Applications are accepted continuously. In 2006, 2000 applied; 550 were accepted. Applicants must submit a formal application and an essay.

Contact
Director of Admissions, Via T. Campanella, 37, Satriano, CZ, 88060, Italy. Telephone: 39-334-333-2554. Fax: 39-096-721-189. World Wide Web: http://www.italianculinary.it.

Japan

Le Cordon Bleu Japan

Classic Cycle Program & Culinary Management Program

Tokyo, Japan

General Information
Private, coeducational, culinary institute. Urban campus. Founded in 1991.

Program Information
Offered since 1991. Program calendar is divided into trimesters. 3-month certificate in superior pastry. 3-month certificate in superior cuisine. 3-month certificate in intermediate cuisine. 3-month certificate in basic pastry. 3-month certificate in basic cuisine. 3-month certificate in basic bakery. 3-month certificate in advanced pastry. 3-month certificate in advanced cuisine. 3-month certificate in advanced bakery. 6-month certificate in culinary management-restaurant quality system. 6-month certificate in culinary management-restaurant operation system. 6-month certificate in culinary management-restaurant marketing. 6-month certificate in culinary management-restaurant finances management. 6-month certificate in culinary management-menu engineering. 6-month certificate in culinary management-human resources management.

Program Affiliation
Confrerie de la Chaine des Rotisseurs; James Beard Foundation, Inc.

Areas of Study
Baking; buffet catering; culinary French; patisserie; wines and spirits.

Facilities
2 demonstration laboratories; 3 lecture rooms; student lounge; 4 teaching kitchens.

Student Profile
1200 full-time.

Faculty
19 total: 13 full-time; 6 part-time. 6 are industry professionals; 13 are master chefs. Prominent faculty: Patrick Lemesle; Olivier Oddos; Bruno Le Derf; Dominique Gros.

Special Programs
Introduction to cuisine, pâtisserie, and boulangerie, wines and spirits courses, cheese courses.

Typical Expenses
Application fee: 50,000 yen. Tuition: 574,000 yen–728,000 yen (classic courses) for 3 months full-time, 200,000 yen (Culinary Management program) for 3 months part-time. Program-related fee includes 36,500 yen–90,500 yen for uniforms, knives set, pastry/cuisine tools.

Housing
Average off-campus housing cost per month: 100,000 yen.

Application Information
Students may begin participation in January, April, July, and October. Application deadline for winter is December 15. Application deadline for spring is March 15. Application deadline for summer is June 15. Application deadline for fall is September 15. In 2007, 1200 applied; 1200 were accepted. Applicants must submit a formal application.

Contact
Aiko Kurokawa, Student Service and Sales Manager, Classic Cycle Program & Culinary Management Program, ROOB-1, 28-13 Sarugaku-cho, Shibuya-ku, Tokyo, 150-0033, Japan. Telephone: 81-3-54890141. Fax: 81-3-54890145. E-mail: tokyo@cordonbleu.edu. World Wide Web: http://www.cordonbleu.co.jp.

See color displays following pages 92 and 332.

Le Cordon Bleu Kobe

Classic Cycle Program

Kobe, Japan

General Information

Private, coeducational, culinary institute. Urban campus. Founded in 2004.

Program Information

Offered since 2004. Program calendar is divided into trimesters. 3-month certificate in superior pastry. 3-month certificate in superior cuisine. 3-month certificate in intermediate pastry. 3-month certificate in intermediate cuisine. 3-month certificate in initiation cuisine. 3-month certificate in basic pastry. 3-month certificate in basic cuisine. 3-month certificate in basic bakery. 3-month certificate in advanced bakery.

Program Affiliation

Confrerie de la Chaine des Rotisseurs; James Beard Foundation, Inc.

Areas of Study

Baking; buffet catering; culinary French; patisserie; wines and spirits.

Facilities

2 demonstration laboratories; 2 teaching kitchens.

Typical Student Profile

500 full-time.

Special Programs

Introduction to cuisine, patisserie, and boulangerie, wine and spirits courses, cheese courses.

Application Information

Students may begin participation in January, April, July, and October. Application deadline for winter is December 15. Application deadline for spring is March 15. Application deadline for summer is June 15. Application deadline for fall is September 15. In 2006, 500 applied; 500 were accepted. Applicants must submit a formal application.

Contact

Director of Admissions, Classic Cycle Program, The 45th, 6/7 Floor, 45 Harima-machi, Chou-ku, Kobe-city, Hyogo, 650-0036, Japan. Telephone: 81-78-393-8221. Fax: 81-78-393-8222. World Wide Web: http://www.cordonbleu.co.jp.

See color displays following pages 92 and 332.

Lebanon

Le Cordon Bleu Liban

Culinary Arts

Jounieh, Lebanon

General Information

Private, culinary institute.

Contact

Director of Admissions, Culinary Arts, Rectorat B.P. 446, USEK University-Kaslik, Jounieh, Lebanon. Telephone: 961-9640664. Fax: 961-9642333.

See color displays following pages 92 and 332.

Mexico

Le Cordon Bleu Mexico

Mexico City, Mexico

General Information

Culinary institute.

Program Information

Certificate in superior patisserie (North campus). Certificate in superior cuisine (North campus). Certificate in intermediate patisserie (North campus). Certificate in intermediate cuisine (South campus). Certificate in intermediate cuisine (North campus). Certificate in basic patisserie (South campus). Certificate in basic patisserie (North campus). Certificate in basic cuisine (South campus). Certificate in basic cuisine (North campus). Diploma in patisserie diplome (North campus). Diploma in Le Grand Diplome (North campus). Diploma in cuisine diplome (North campus).

Contact

Director of Admissions, Universidad Anahuac, Av. Lomas Anahuac, s/n. Lomos Anahuac, Mexico, C.P., 52760, Mexico. Telephone: 52-55-5627-0210 Ext. 7132. Fax: 52-55- 5627-0210 Ext. 8724. World Wide Web: http://www.lcbmexico.com/.

See color displays following pages 92 and 332.

Le Cordon Bleu Mexico

Mexico City, Mexico

General Information
Culinary institute.

Contact
Admissions Office, Universidad Anáhuac del Sur, Avenida de las Torres # 131, Col. Olivar de los Padres, C.P. 01780, Del. Álvaro Obregón, Mexico. Telephone: 52-55-5628-8800. Fax: 52-55-5628-8837. E-mail: mexico@cordonbleu.edu.

See color displays following pages 92 and 332.

Netherlands

Le Cordon Bleu Amsterdam

Amsterdam, Netherlands

General Information
Private, coeducational, culinary institute.

Contact
Admissions Office, Herengracht 314, 1016 CD, Amsterdam, Netherlands. Telephone: 31-20-627-87-25. Fax: 31-20-620-34-91. E-mail: amsterdam@cordonbleu.edu.

See color displays following pages 92 and 332.

New Zealand

New Zealand School of Food and Wine

Foundation Cookery Skills

Christchurch, New Zealand

General Information
Private, coeducational, culinary institute. Urban campus. Founded in 1994.

Program Information
Offered since 1995. Accredited by New Zealand Qualifications Authority. Program calendar is divided into trimesters. 12-week certificate in professional wine knowledge (sommelier). 15-week certificate in cookery and hospitality (introduction). 16-week certificate in cookery.

Program Affiliation
Restaurant Association of New Zealand.

Areas of Study
Baking; beverage management; controlling costs in food service; culinary French; culinary skill development; food preparation; food service math; garde-manger; international cuisine; management and human resources; meal planning; meat cutting; menu and facilities design; nutrition; patisserie; sanitation; saucier; seafood processing; soup, stock, sauce, and starch production; wines and spirits.

Facilities
2 classrooms; computer laboratory; demonstration laboratory; food production kitchen; library; public restaurant; teaching kitchen.

Typical Student Profile
80 full-time. 20 are under 25 years old; 50 are between 25 and 44 years old; 10 are over 44 years old.

Special Programs
Local vineyard tours, trips to relevant conferences, certification in wine.

Application Information
Students may begin participation in January, May, July, August, and September. Applications are accepted continuously. In 2006, 100 applied; 100 were accepted. Applicants must interview; submit a formal application and letters of reference.

Contact
Director of Admissions, Foundation Cookery Skills, PO Box 25217, Christchurch, 8144, New Zealand. Telephone: 064-3-3797501. Fax: 064-3-3662302. World Wide Web: http://www.foodandwine.co.nz.

Peru

Le Cordon Bleu Peru

Lima, Peru

General Information
Private, coeducational, culinary institute. Urban campus. Founded in 1994. Accredited by Accrediting Commission of Career Schools and Colleges of Technology.

Program Information
Offered since 1994. Accredited by Council on Hotel, Restaurant and Institutional Education. Program calendar is continuous. 18-month certificate in administration of hotels and restaurants. 2-year certificate in pastry. 2-year certificate in cuisine. 2-year certificate in bar and cocktails.

Le Cordon Bleu Peru *(continued)*

3-year certificate in gastronomy and culinary arts. 3-year certificate in alimentary industries. 4-year certificate in hotel and restaurant administration.

Program Affiliation
Organizacion Mundial del Turismo; World Association of Cooks Societies.

Areas of Study
Beverage management; buffet catering; culinary French; culinary skill development; international cuisine; kitchen management; menu and facilities design; nutrition; patisserie; restaurant opportunities; sanitation; wines and spirits.

Facilities
Cafeteria; 16 classrooms; coffee shop; computer laboratory; 2 demonstration laboratories; food production kitchen; 10 laboratories; lecture room; library; public restaurant; 6 teaching kitchens; dairy processing plant.

Student Profile
1,022 total: 822 full-time; 200 part-time. 690 are under 25 years old; 121 are between 25 and 44 years old; 11 are over 44 years old.

Faculty
120 total: 20 full-time; 100 part-time. Prominent faculty: Dr. Sixtilio Dalmau Castañon, Director; Sra. Patricia Dalmau de Galfré, Administrative Assistant.

Prominent Alumni and Current Affiliation
Rafael Piaveras, Fusion Restaurant; Hajime Kasuga, Hanzo Restaurant; Christian Bravo, Bravo Restobar.

Special Programs
Practical opportunities, culinary and bar competitions, job opportunities.

Typical Expenses
Tuition: $25,400 per 3 years full-time, $3000 per 18 months part-time. Program-related fee includes $1200 for uniforms, cutlery, books, and insurance (accidental).

Financial Aid
Employment placement assistance is available.

Housing
Average off-campus housing cost per month: $300.

Application Information
Students may begin participation in March and August. Application deadline for fall is February 1. Application deadline for winter is June 1. In 2007, 320 applied; 225 were accepted. Applicants must submit a formal application.

Contact
Maria Laura Bentin, Admission, Av. Nunez de Balboa 530, Miraflores, Lima, 18, Peru. Telephone: 51-1-2428222. Fax: 51-1-2429209. E-mail: admision@cordonbleuperu.edu.pe. World Wide Web: http://www.cordonbleuperu.edu.pe.

See color displays following pages 92 and 332.

Philippines

Center for Culinary Arts, Manila

Quezon City, Philippines

General Information
Private, coeducational, culinary institute. Urban campus. Founded in 1996.

Program Information
Offered since 1996. Program calendar is divided into terms. 1-year certificate in culinary arts. 1-year certificate in baking and pastry arts. 2-year diploma in culinary arts and technology management. 2-year diploma in baking, pastry arts and technology management.

Program Affiliation
International Association of Culinary Professionals; National Restaurant Association.

Special Programs
Continuing education program, culinary competitions, apprenticeships.

Financial Aid
Employment placement assistance is available. Employment opportunities within the program are available.

Application Information
Students may begin participation in January, June, August, and October. Applicants must interview; submit a formal application, letters of reference, an essay, academic transcripts, and results of medical examination.

Contact
Director of Admissions, Katipunan Avenue, Loyola Heights, Quezon City, 1108, Philippines. Telephone: 63-2-426-4840. Fax: 63-2-426-4836. World Wide Web: http://www.cca-manila.com/.

Republic of Korea

Le Cordon Bleu Korea

Seoul, Republic of Korea

General Information
Private, coeducational, culinary institute. Urban campus. Founded in 2002.

Program Information
Offered since 2002. Program calendar is divided into quarters. 1-year diploma in culinary arts. 10- to 20-week certificate in culinary arts. 2-year master of business administration in hospitality management. 4-year bachelor's degree in restaurant management.

Areas of Study
Baking; culinary French; patisserie.

Facilities
3 classrooms; demonstration laboratory; food production kitchen; library; student lounge; 5 teaching kitchens.

Typical Student Profile
500 full-time. 300 are under 25 years old; 200 are between 25 and 44 years old.

Special Programs
Workshops for gourmet enthusiasts.

Financial Aid
Employment placement assistance is available.

Application Information
Students may begin participation in February, May, September, and November. Applications are accepted continuously. In 2006, 520 applied; 480 were accepted. Applicants must submit a formal application, an essay, resume.

Contact
Director of Admissions, Le Cordon Bleu Korea, 7th Floor, Social Education Building 53-12, Chungpadong 2K, Yongsan-ku, Seoul, 140-742, Republic of Korea. Telephone: 82-2-719-6961. Fax: 82-2-719-7569. World Wide Web: http://www.cordonbleu.co.kr.

See color displays following pages 92 and 332.

Singapore

At-Sunrice GlobalChef Academy

Singapore

General Information
Private, coeducational, culinary institute. Urban campus. Founded in 2000.

Program Information
Accredited by American Culinary Federation Accrediting Commission, Singapore Workforce Development Agency, Singapore Workforce Skills Qualification. Program calendar is divided into quarters. 15-month diploma in Pastry and Baking Arts. 15-month diploma in Culinary Craft and Service Excellence. 2-week certificate in Continuing Modules (Western & Asian Cuisine). 24-month diploma in Advanced Culinary Placement. 8-week certificate in Personal and Leisure Chef.

Program Affiliation
American Culinary Federation; International Association of Culinary Professionals; Restaurant Association of Singapore; Singapore Chefs Association; Singapore Pastry Association.

Areas of Study
Eastern and Western Cuisines; herb and spices; Old and New World Techniques; study and work rotation.

Facilities
Library; seminar room; kitchen labs; Wine Academy; professional Western kitchen; professional Asian kitchen; professional Pastry kitchen; private luxury kitchen.

Student Profile
6,716 total: 216 full-time; 6,500 part-time. 1,192 are under 25 years old; 5,280 are between 25 and 44 years old; 244 are over 44 years old.

Faculty
36 total: 16 full-time; 20 part-time. 26 are industry professionals; 1 is a master chef; 34 are culinary-certified teachers; 3 are Executive chefs. Prominent faculty: Christophe Megel; Mizuho Hara; Frederic Deshayes; Sony Haq. Faculty-student ratio: 1:18 full time; 1:25 part time.

Prominent Alumni and Current Affiliation
Aaron Goh, Daniel Boulud Group-Bistro Moderne (United States); Satish Kumar, Cullen Winery (Australia); K. Sundharapandiyan, The Setai (United States).

Global Chefs Made in Singapore!

Singapore, the small vibrant nation houses a culinary academy dedicated to the culinary arts and cultures of the east and west, with students from 25 countries and outstanding graduate placements in properties around the world.

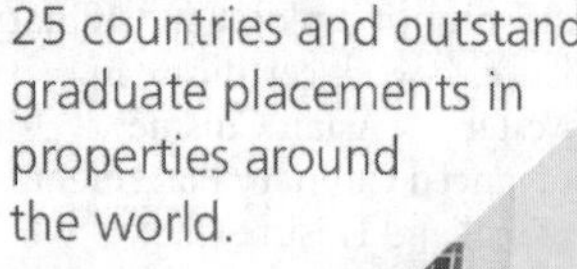

Study & Work in Singapore

Guaranteed Paid On-the-Job Training

Apply online: www.at-sunrice.com

At-Sunrice GlobalChef Academy
Fort Canning Centre, Fort Canning Park, Singapore 179618
Tel: (65) 6336 3307 Fax: (65) 6336 9353
Email: academy@at-sunrice.com

Join the world of food & food service profession!

Business Registration No. 52912482C

Special Programs
TalentMatch graduate placements, 15-24 month paid on-the-job-training, culinary competitions including World Gourmet Summit and Food & Hotel Asia, special catering to VIP's, monthly homecoming with special guest from industry, product knowledge seminars, and field trips.

Typical Expenses
Tuition: Singapore $39,000 (24-month culinary arts diploma program); Singapore $23,400 (15-month culinary diploma). Program-related fees include Singapore $500–$800 application fee; Singapore $580 onwards for knife set; Singapore $160 for uniform (2 sets).

Financial Aid
Program-specific awards include 250 scholarships valued at Singapore $4,360,000 for Singapore citizens & permanent residents. Employment placement assistance is available. Employment opportunities within the program are available.

Housing
Average off-campus housing cost per month: Singapore $300–$500.

Application Information
Students may begin participation in January, February, April, May, June, July, August, September, October, November, and December. Applications are accepted continuously. In 2007, 500 applied; 216 were accepted. Applicants must interview; submit a formal application, letters of reference, an essay, IELTS 5.5/TOEFL 500.

Contact
Ms. Heng Wai Leng, Recruitment and Leisure Sales Manager, Fort Canning Centre, Fort Canning Park, 179618, Singapore. Telephone: 65-6877-6989. Fax: 65-6336-9353. E-mail: academy@at-sunrice.com. World Wide Web: http://www.at-sunrice.com.

See display on page 346.

South Africa

Christina Martin School of Food and Wine

Durban, South Africa

General Information
Private, coeducational, culinary institute. Urban campus. Founded in 1973. Accredited by Accrediting Council for Independent Colleges and Schools.

Program Information
Offered since 1973. Accredited by American Culinary Federation Accrediting Commission. Program calendar is continuous. 1-year diploma in patisseurier. 1-year diploma in food preparation and culinary art. 6-month certificate in patisseurier. 6-month certificate in food preparation and culinary arts.

Program Affiliation
Confrerie de la Chaine des Rotisseurs; Council on Hotel, Restaurant, and Institutional Education; International Association of Culinary Professionals; International Wine & Food Society; Women Chefs and Restaurateurs.

Areas of Study
Baking; beverage management; buffet catering; confectionery show pieces; controlling costs in food service; convenience cookery; culinary French; culinary skill development; food preparation; food purchasing; food service communication; food service math; garde-manger; international cuisine; introduction to food service; kitchen management; management and human resources; meal planning; meat cutting; menu and facilities design; nutrition; nutrition and food service; patisserie; restaurant opportunities; sanitation; saucier; seafood processing; soup, stock, sauce, and starch production; wines and spirits.

Facilities
Bake shop; 2 bakeries; cafeteria; 3 catering services; 3 classrooms; coffee shop; computer laboratory; 2 demonstration laboratories; 3 food production kitchens; garden; gourmet dining room; learning resource center; lecture room; library; public restaurant; snack shop; student lounge; 5 teaching kitchens.

Typical Student Profile
100 total: 60 full-time; 40 part-time.

Special Programs
Lindt chocolate and sugar course, culinary competitions.

Financial Aid
Employment placement assistance is available. Employment opportunities within the program are available.

Application Information
Students may begin participation in January. Application deadline for spring is October 1. Application deadline for summer is November 1. Application deadline for winter is July 1. Application deadline for autumn is September 1. In 2006, 60 applied. Applicants must interview; submit a formal application and letters of reference.

Contact
Director of Admissions, PO Box 4601, Durban, 4000, South Africa. Telephone: 031-3032111. Fax: 031-3123342.

SPAIN

LE CORDON BLEU MADRID

Culinary Arts

Madrid, Spain

GENERAL INFORMATION

Private, culinary institute.

CONTACT

Admissions, Culinary Arts, Univerisdad Francisco de Vitoria, Ctra. Pozuelo-Majadahonda, Km. 1,800 Pozuelo de Alarcón, Madrid, 28223, Spain. Telephone: 34-91-351-0303. Fax: 34-91-351-1555. E-mail: madrid@cordonbleu.edu.

See color displays following pages 92 and 332.

SWITZERLAND

DCT HOTEL AND CULINARY ARTS SCHOOL, SWITZERLAND

European Culinary Center

Vitznau, Switzerland

GENERAL INFORMATION

Private, coeducational, two-year college. Small-town setting. Founded in 1992. Accredited by New England Association of Schools and Colleges.

PROGRAM INFORMATION

Offered since 1997. Accredited by American Culinary Federation Accrediting Commission, Swiss Hotel Schools Association, ACFFAC Exemplary Status. Program calendar is divided into quarters. 11-week certificate in foundation in European cuisine. 11-week certificate in European pastry and chocolate. 11-week certificate in European gourmet cuisine. 11-week certificate in European food and beverage service. 12–18-month advanced diploma in European culinary management.

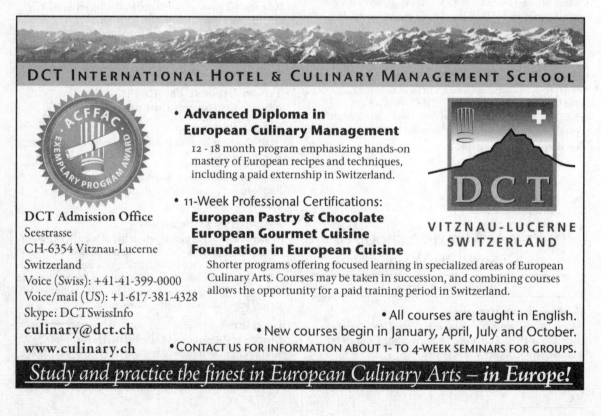

Program Affiliation

American Culinary Federation; Council on Hotel, Restaurant, and Institutional Education; International Hotel and Restaurant Association; National Restaurant Association; Swiss Chef Association; World Association of Cooks Societies.

Areas of Study

Baking; beverage management; chocolate; confectionery show pieces; controlling costs in food service; culinary skill development; European pastries; food preparation; food purchasing; food service communication; garde-manger; international cuisine; introduction to food service; kitchen management; management and human resources; menu and facilities design; nutrition; nutrition and food service; patisserie; sanitation; saucier; soup, stock, sauce, and starch production; wines and spirits.

Facilities

Bakery; cafeteria; 7 classrooms; computer laboratory; food production kitchen; laboratory; learning resource center; library; student lounge; 2 teaching kitchens.

Student Profile

45 full-time. 40 are under 25 years old; 4 are between 25 and 44 years old; 1 is over 44 years old.

Faculty

9 total: 3 full-time; 6 part-time. 4 are industry professionals; 2 are master chefs; 1 is a master baker; 2 are culinary-certified teachers. Prominent faculty: Dr. Birgit Black, Dean; Swiss Master Chef Patrick Diethelm; Swiss Master Chef Urs Meichtry; Chef Stacy Black, CEC. Faculty-student ratio: 1:8.

Special Programs

6-9 month paid internship in Switzerland, tours of wineries and chocolate factories, study European cuisine in Europe.

Typical Expenses

Application fee: 100 Sw Fr. Tuition: 11,500 Sw Fr per 3-month term (includes room and board). Program-related fee includes 1200 Sw Fr for required medical and liability insurance, uniforms, texts and classroom supplies, field trips.

Financial Aid

Program-specific awards include paid Swiss internships in top-ranked restaurants. Employment placement assistance is available. Employment opportunities within the program are available.

Housing

Coed housing available. Average off-campus housing cost per month: 600–$800 Sw Fr.

Application Information

Students may begin participation in January, April, July, and October. Applications are accepted continuously. In 2007, 75 applied; 50 were accepted. Applicants must submit a formal application and transcripts, prior diplomas, TOEFL score or equivalent, proof of high school graduation or professional experience.

Contact

Mrs. Sharon Spaltenstein, Director of Marketing and Admission, European Culinary Center, Seestrasse, Vitznau, 6354, Switzerland. Telephone: 41-413990000. Fax: 41-413990101. E-mail: culinary@dct.ch. World Wide Web: http://www.culinary.ch.

IMI University Centre

International Culinary Management Institute Switzerland

Lucerne/Kastanienbaum, Switzerland

General Information

Private, coeducational, culinary institute. Suburban campus. Founded in 1991.

Program Information

Offered since 2005. Accredited by Manchester Metropolitan University UK. Program calendar is divided into semesters. 6-month bachelor's degree in European Culinary Management. 6-month Higher Diploma in European Culinary Management.

Program Affiliation

Cercle des Chefs de Cuisine; Craft Guild of Chefs; Swiss Chefs Society; World Association of Chefs Society (WACS).

Areas of Study

Baking; beverage management; buffet catering; controlling costs in food service; convenience cookery; culinary French; culinary skill development; food preparation; food purchasing; food service communication; food service math; garde-manger; international cuisine; introduction to food service; kitchen management; management and human resources; meal planning; meat cutting; menu and facilities design; nutrition; patisserie; restaurant opportunities; sanitation; saucier; seafood processing; soup, stock, sauce, and starch production; wines and spirits.

Facilities

Cafeteria; classroom; computer laboratory; demonstration laboratory; food production kitchen; garden; gourmet dining room; learning resource center; lecture room; library; public restaurant; snack shop; student lounge; teaching kitchen.

IMI University Centre *(continued)*

Student Profile

30 full-time. 20 are under 25 years old; 10 are between 25 and 44 years old.

Faculty

15 total: 7 full-time; 8 part-time. 3 are industry professionals; 1 is a master chef; 3 are culinary-certified teachers. Prominent faculty: Shaun Leonard, Senior Head Chef; Yong Chul–Krauer; Dawei Sun; Stephan Hachler. Faculty-student ratio: 1:5.

Prominent Alumni and Current Affiliation

Andy Choy, Hilton Dubai Creek UAI Demi Chef de Partie in Verre by Gordan Ramsays; Haresh Sambnani, Spice Concepts in Singapore.

Special Programs

Swiss customs and food, cheese making, wine production, schnapps distilling, kitchen artistry (carving), industry fieldtrips (chocolates).

Typical Expenses

Application fee: 2800 Sw Fr. Tuition for international students: 25,000–27,000 Sw Fr per 6 months all inclusive.

Financial Aid

Program-specific awards include Kitchen scholarship of 1200 Sw Fr. Employment placement assistance is available. Employment opportunities within the program are available.

Housing

Apartment-style housing available.

Application Information

Students may begin participation in January and June. Application deadline for January/February is August 30. Application deadline for June/July is March 30. In 2007, 34 applied; 30 were accepted. Applicants must submit a formal application; be 18 years of age; must have a high school certificate or equivalent, proficiency in English, 500 TOEFL (paper-based), 173 TOEFL (computer-based), 5.0 IELTS scores or equivalent.

Contact

Lukas Ritzel, Head of Marketing Switzerland, International Culinary Management Institute Switzerland, IMI University Centre, Seeacherstr 1, Kastanienbaum, Lucerne, 6047, Switzerland. Telephone: 41-41-349-64-00. Fax: 41-41-349-64-44. E-mail: L.Ritzel@imi-luzern.com. World Wide Web: http://www.ici-luzern.com.

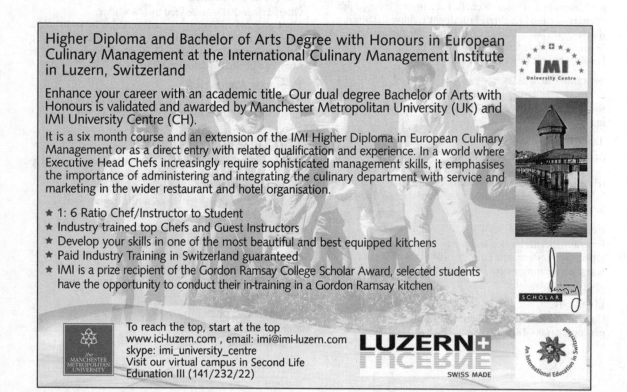

THAILAND

LE CORDON BLEU DUSIT CULINARY SCHOOL

Bangkok, Thailand

GENERAL INFORMATION

Private, coeducational, culinary institute. Urban campus. Founded in 2007.

PROGRAM INFORMATION

Offered since 2007. Accredited by Thailand Ministry of Education. Program calendar is divided into quarters. 3-month certificate in Intermediate Course-English Language for Culinary and Hospitality. 3-month certificate in Certificat de Patisserie Supérieure. 3-month certificate in Certificat de Patisserie Intermédiaire. 3-month certificate in Certificat de Patisserie de Base. 3-month certificate in Certificat de Cuisine Supérieure. 3-month certificate in Certificat de Cuisine Intermédiaire. 3-month certificate in Certificat de Cuisine de Base. 3-month certificate in Basic Course-English Language for Culinary and Hospitality. 3-month certificate in Advanced Course-English Language for Culinary and Hospitality. 6-month certificate in Certificat de Chef de Partie. 6-month diploma in Diplôme de Direction de Cuisine. 9-month diploma in Diplôme de Patisserie. 9-month diploma in Diplôme de Cuisine. 9-month grand diploma in Grand Diplôme.

AREAS OF STUDY

Culinary English; culinary French; management.

FACILITIES

2 classrooms; 2 demonstration laboratories; 4 food production kitchens; library; public restaurant; 5 teaching kitchens.

TYPICAL STUDENT PROFILE

81 full-time. 10 are under 25 years old; 66 are between 25 and 44 years old; 5 are over 44 years old.

SPECIAL PROGRAMS

Industry placement after the completion of Superior Level-Culinary Arts Program, industry placement after the completion of Certificat de Chef de Partie.

FINANCIAL AID

Program-specific awards include installment payments.

APPLICATION INFORMATION

Students may begin participation in January, April, July, and October. Applications are accepted continuously. In 2006, 81 applied; 81 were accepted. Applicants must submit a formal application and copy of educational certificate/diploma, TOEFL/IELTS for non-Thai and non-English native speakers, copy of ID/passport and 4 1-inch photos.

CONTACT

Director of Admissions, 946 The Dusit Thani Building, Rama IV Road, Silom, Bangrak, Bangkok, 10500, Thailand. Telephone: 66-2-237-8877. Fax: 66-2-237-8878. World Wide Web: http://www.cordonbleudusit.com/.

See color displays following pages 92 and 332.

UNITED KINGDOM

COOKERY AT THE GRANGE

The Essential Cookery Course

Near Frome, Somerset, United Kingdom

GENERAL INFORMATION

Private, coeducational, culinary institute. Rural campus. Founded in 1981.

PROGRAM INFORMATION

Offered since 1981. Program calendar is divided into four-week cycles, four-week cycles. 1-month certificate in cookery.

AREAS OF STUDY

Baking; culinary skill development; food preparation; general cookery; meal planning; meat cutting; menu and facilities design; soup, stock, sauce, and starch production; wines and spirits.

FACILITIES

Garden; student lounge; teaching kitchen.

TYPICAL STUDENT PROFILE

24 full-time.

HOUSING

Coed housing available.

APPLICATION INFORMATION

Students may begin participation in January, February, May, June, July, August, September, October, and November. Applicants must submit a formal application.

CONTACT

Director of Admissions, The Essential Cookery Course, The Grange, Whatley, Near Frome, Somerset, BA11 3JU, United Kingdom. Telephone: 44-1373836579. Fax: 44-1373836579. World Wide Web: http://www.cookeryatthegrange.co.uk.

Le Cordon Bleu–London Culinary Institute

Le Cordon Bleu Classic Cycle Programme

London, United Kingdom

General Information
Private, coeducational, culinary institute. Urban campus. Founded in 1895.

Program Information
Offered since 1933. Accredited by American Culinary Federation Accrediting Commission. Program calendar is divided into quarters. 10-week certificate in superior patisserie. 10-week certificate in superior cuisine. 10-week certificate in intermediate patisserie. 10-week certificate in intermediate cuisine. 10-week certificate in basic patisserie. 10-week certificate in basic cuisine. 30-week diploma in patisserie. 30-week diploma in grand diplome. 30-week diploma in cuisine.

Program Affiliation
American Institute of Wine & Food; Confrerie de la Chaine des Rotisseurs; Council on Hotel, Restaurant, and Institutional Education; International Association of Culinary Professionals; James Beard Foundation, Inc.

Areas of Study
Baking; buffet catering; cheese; confectionery show pieces; controlling costs in food service; culinary French; culinary skill development; food preparation; food purchasing; international cuisine; introduction to food service; kitchen management; meal planning; nutrition; nutrition and food service; patisserie; sanitation; table service; wines and spirits.

Facilities
2 bakeries; 2 demonstration laboratories; food production kitchen; student lounge; 4 teaching kitchens.

Student Profile
460 full-time.

Faculty
9 total: 9 full-time. 9 are industry professionals; 6 are master chefs; 3 are master bakers. Prominent faculty: Chef Yann Barraud, Head Chef; Chef Julie Walsh, Head Patisserie Chef. Faculty-student ratio: 1:10.

Special Programs
Restaurant market tours and hotel visits, exchanges between Le Cordon Bleu Schools worldwide, culinary competitions.

Typical Expenses
Tuition: £3390-£29,475 for 10 weeks–9 months.

Financial Aid
In 2007, 10 scholarships were awarded (average award was £2230). Program-specific awards include International Association of Culinary Professionals scholarship, James Beard Foundation scholarship. Employment opportunities within the program are available.

Housing
Average off-campus housing cost per month: £1400.

Application Information
Students may begin participation in January, March, June, and October. Applications are accepted continuously. In 2007, 431 applied. Applicants must submit a formal application, curriculum vitae, and letter of motivation.

Contact
Ms. Yoko Uchiyama, Admissions Officer, Le Cordon Bleu Classic Cycle Programme, 114 Marylebone Lane, London, W1U 2HH, United Kingdom. Telephone: 44-20-79353503. Fax: 44-20-79357621. E-mail: london@cordonbleu.edu. World Wide Web: http://www.cordonbleu.edu/.

See color displays following pages 92 and 332.

Leith's School of Food and Wine

London, United Kingdom

General Information
Private, coeducational, culinary institute. Urban campus. Founded in 1975.

Program Information
Offered since 1975. Program calendar is divided into trimesters. 1-month certificate of completion in cookery (beginners/advanced). 1-month certificate in practical cookery. 1-term certificate in food and wine (intermediate). 1-term certificate in food and wine (beginners). 1-term certificate in food and wine (advanced). 1-week certificate of completion in easy dinner parties. 1-week certificate of completion in beginners' skills. 1-week certificate of completion in advanced skills. 1-year diploma in food and wine. 10-class (evenings) certificate of completion in intermediate skills. 10-class (evenings) certificate of completion in beginners' skills. 2-term diploma in food and wine. 5-class certificate in wine.

Areas of Study
Baking; buffet catering; chocolate; confectionery show pieces; controlling costs in food service; culinary French; culinary skill development; easy dinner party; fish cookery; food preparation; food purchasing; game; healthy eating; international cuisine; introduction to food service; Italian; kitchen management; meal planning; meat

cutting; menu and facilities design; nutrition; nutrition and food service; patisserie; restaurant opportunities; sanitation; saucier; seafood processing; soup, stock, sauce, and starch production; wines and spirits.

Facilities
Demonstration laboratory; food production kitchen; lecture room; library; student lounge; 3 teaching kitchens.

Typical Student Profile
546 total: 96 full-time; 450 part-time.

Special Programs
Excursions to Billingsgate and Smithfield markets, recipe writing competition, restaurant work placements.

Financial Aid
Employment placement assistance is available. Employment opportunities within the program are available.

Application Information
Students may begin participation in January, March, April, July, August, September, and December. Applications are accepted continuously. Applicants must interview (if possible); submit a formal application and letters of reference.

Contact
Director of Admissions, 21 St Alban's Grove, London, W8 5BP, United Kingdom. Telephone: 44-20-72290177. Fax: 44-20-79375257. World Wide Web: http://www.leiths.com/.

Rosie Davies

Courses for Cooks

Frome, Somerset, United Kingdom

General Information
Private, coeducational institution. Rural campus. Founded in 1996.

Program Information
Offered since 1996. Program calendar is divided into months, months. 1-month certificate in basic cooking on yachts. 1-month certificate in basic cooking in chalets. 1-month certificate in basic cooking.

Areas of Study
Baking; beverage management; buffet catering; controlling costs in food service; convenience cookery; culinary French; culinary skill development; food preparation; food purchasing; food service communication; food service math; international cuisine; introduction to food service; kitchen management; meal planning; meat cutting; menu and facilities design; nutrition; nutrition and food service; patisserie; sanitation; saucier; seafood processing; soup, stock, sauce, and starch production; wines and spirits.

Facilities
Food production kitchen; garden; gourmet dining room; library; student lounge; teaching kitchen.

Typical Student Profile
35 full-time. 15 are under 25 years old; 14 are between 25 and 44 years old; 6 are over 44 years old.

Housing
Coed housing available.

Application Information
Students may begin participation in January, February, April, July, September, October, and November. Applications are accepted continuously. In 2006, 100 applied; 35 were accepted. Applicants must submit a formal application.

Contact
Director of Admissions, Courses for Cooks, Penny's Mill, Horn Street, Nunney, Frome, SO BA11 4NP, United Kingdom. Telephone: 44-1373836210. Fax: 44-1373836018. World Wide Web: http://www.rosiedavies.co.uk.

Tante Marie School of Cookery

Woking, Surrey, United Kingdom

General Information
Private, coeducational, culinary institute. Urban campus. Founded in 1954. Accredited by Accrediting Council for Independent Colleges and Schools.

Program Information
Offered since 1954. Accredited by British Accreditation Council for Independent Further and Higher Education and The Year Out Group. Program calendar is divided into trimesters. 3-month certificate in Cordon Bleu cookery. 6-month intensive diploma in Cordon Bleu cookery. 9-month diploma in Cordon Bleu cookery.

Areas of Study
Baking; buffet catering; confectionery show pieces; controlling costs in food service; convenience cookery; culinary French; culinary skill development; food preparation; food purchasing; garde-manger; international cuisine; introduction to food service; kitchen management; meal planning; meat cutting; meat fabrication; menu and facilities design; nutrition;

Tante Marie School of Cookery *(continued)*

nutrition and food service; patisserie; restaurant opportunities; sanitation; saucier; seafood processing; soup, stock, sauce, and starch production; wines and spirits.

Facilities

Garden; lecture room; library; student lounge; 5 teaching kitchens; vineyard; demonstration theatre.

Typical Student Profile

206 total: 98 full-time; 108 part-time.

Special Programs

3-day course on wines and spirits, 1-day course on food safety and hygiene, visits to Smithfield Market, herb farm and vegetable growers.

Financial Aid

In 2006, 5 scholarships were awarded (average award was £2000). Employment placement assistance is available. Employment opportunities within the program are available.

Application Information

Students may begin participation in January, April, July, September, October, and November. Applications are accepted continuously. In 2006, 232 applied; 232 were accepted. Applicants must submit a formal application.

Contact

Director of Admissions, Woodham House, Carlton Road, Woking, SU GU21 4HF, United Kingdom. Telephone: 44-1483726957. Fax: 44-1483724173. World Wide Web: http://www.tantemarie.co.uk/press.html.

PROFILES OF APPRENTICESHIP PROGRAMS

Alabama

ACF Greater Montgomery Chapter

Montgomery, Alabama

Program Information
Approved by the American Culinary Federation. Academic requirements are met through a chef-taught curriculum and at Trenholm State Technical College (degree available). Special apprenticeships available in baking and pastries and catering; hospitality management.

Placement Information
Participants are placed in 1 of 32 locations, including full-service restaurants, hotels, private clubs, fine dining restaurants, and catering businesses. Most popular placement locations are Wyn Lakes Country Club, City Grill, and Embassy Suites.

Typical Apprentice Profile
Applicants must interview; submit a formal application, an essay, and letters of reference (recommended).

Contact
Director of Apprenticeship Program, 1225 Airbase Boulevard, Montgomery, AL 36108. Telephone: 334-420-4495. Fax: 334-420-4491. World Wide Web: http://www.acfchefs.org/Content/presidents_portal/ACFChapter.cfm?ChapterChoice=AL032.

Arizona

Chefs Association of Southern Arizona, Tucson

Tucson, Arizona

Program Information
Approved by the American Culinary Federation. Academic requirements are met at Pima Community College (degree available). Special apprenticeships available in pastry.

Placement Information
Participants are placed in 1 of 9 locations, including hotels, country clubs, restaurants, and casinos. Most popular placement locations are Hilton El Conquistador, Desert Diamond Casino, and Accacia Restaurant.

Typical Apprentice Profile
Applicants must submit a formal application.

Contact
Director of Apprenticeship Program, 3438 E Bellevue Street, Tucson, AZ 85716-3910. Telephone: 520-318-3448. World Wide Web: http://www.acfchefs.org/presidents_portal/ACFChapter.cfm?ChapterChoice=AZ023.

California

Barona Valley Ranch Resort & Casino

Lakeside, California

Program Information
Approved by the American Culinary Federation. Academic requirements are met through a chef-taught curriculum at Grossmont College (degree available).

Placement Information
Participants are placed in Barona Valley Ranch (resort, hotel, and casino).

Typical Apprentice Profile
Applicants must interview; submit an essay and obtain a culinary position/Barona Gaming License.

Contact
Director of Apprenticeship Program, 1932 Wildcat Canyon Road, Lakeside, CA 92040. Telephone: 619-328-3524. Fax: 619-443-2418. World Wide Web: http://www.barona.com/.

San Francisco Culinary/Pastry Program

San Francisco, California

Program Information
Academic requirements are met through a chef-taught curriculum and at City College of San Francisco. Special apprenticeships available in pastry (4000 hours).

Placement Information
Participants are placed in hotels/clubs/restaurants. Most popular placement locations are the Palace Hotel, the Hilton Hotel, and Michael Mina Restaurant.

Typical Apprentice Profile
Applicants must interview; submit a formal application and letters of reference; have a high school diploma or GED.

Contact
Director of Apprenticeship Program, 760 Market Street, Suite 1066, San Francisco, CA 94102. Telephone: 415-989-8726. Fax: 415-989-2920.

Colorado

ACF Colorado Chefs Association

Denver, Colorado

Program Information
Approved by the American Culinary Federation. Academic requirements are met through a chef-taught curriculum.

Placement Information
Participants are placed in 1 of 30 locations, including hotels, restaurants, country clubs, assisted living, and universities.

Typical Apprentice Profile
Applicants must submit a formal application, letters of reference, an essay, have a high school diploma or GED; must be 17 years of age.

Contact
Director of Apprenticeship Program, Johnson&Wales University, 7150 Montview Boulevard, Denver, CO 80220. Telephone: 303-264-3005. Fax: 303-264-3007. World Wide Web: http://www.acfcoloradochefs.org.

Colorado Mountain College

Edwards, Colorado

Program Information
Approved by the American Culinary Federation. Academic requirements are met through a chef-taught curriculum and at Colorado Mountain College (degree available).

Placement Information
Participants are placed in 1 of 11 locations, including restaurants. Most popular placement locations are Beano's Cabin, Toscanini, and Zach's Cabin.

Typical Apprentice Profile
Applicants must interview; submit a formal application, letters of reference, and an essay.

Contact
Director of Apprenticeship Program, Colorado Mountain College, Culinary Apprenticeship Program, 831 Grand Avenue, Glenwood Springs, CO 81601. Telephone: 800-621-8559. Fax: 970-947-8324. World Wide Web: http://www.coloradomtn.edu/culinary.

Florida

ACF Treasure Coast Chapter

Fort Pierce, Florida

Program Information
Approved by the American Culinary Federation. Academic requirements are met at Indian River Community College (degree available). Special apprenticeships available in pastry and cook's apprentice.

Placement Information
Participants are placed in 1 of 90 locations, including restaurants, hotels, country clubs, and institutional settings. Most popular placement locations are Bent Pines Golf Club, Ian's Tropical Grill, and Indian River Plantation-Marriott.

Typical Apprentice Profile
Applicants must interview; submit a formal application; have a high school diploma or GED; must be 18 years of age.

Contact
Director of Apprenticeship Program, 3209 Virginia Avenue, Ft. Pierce, FL 34981-5596. Telephone: 772-462-7641. Fax: 772-462-4796. World Wide Web: http://www.acfchefs.org/content/chapter/fl121.html.

Fort Lauderdale ACF Inc.

Coconut Creek, Florida

Program Information
Approved by the American Culinary Federation. Academic requirements are met through a chef-taught curriculum and at Atlantic Technical Center.

Placement Information
Participants are placed in 1 of 20 locations, including hotel and resorts, restaurants, hospitals and retirement homes, retail bakeries, and country clubs. Most popular placement locations are Westin Diplomat Hotel and Resort, Radisson Bridge Resort Hotel (Carmens), and Marriott Hotel and Resort.

Typical Apprentice Profile
Applicants must interview; submit a formal application.

Contact
Director of Apprenticeship Program, Atlantic Technical Center, 4700 NW Coconut Creek Parkway, Coconut Creek, FL 33063. Telephone: 954-309-3591.

Indian River Community College

Fort Pierce, Florida

Program Information
Approved by the American Culinary Federation. Academic requirements are met through a chef-taught curriculum and at Indian River Community College (degree available).

Placement Information
Participants are placed in country club, institutions, and hotels. Most popular placement locations are Orchid Isle Country Club, Disney Reports, and Bent Pines Gold Club.

Typical Apprentice Profile
Applicants must interview; submit a formal application.

Contact
Director of Apprenticeship Program, 3209 Virginia Avenue, Ft. Pierce, FL 34981. Telephone: 772-462-7641.

Kansas

Johnson County Community College

Overland Park, Kansas

Program Information
Approved by the American Culinary Federation. Academic requirements are met at Johnson County Community College (degree available).

Placement Information
Participants are placed in 1 of 60 locations, including hotels, restaurants, country clubs, casinos, and health-care facilities. Most popular placement locations are the Westin Crown Center Hotel, Hyatt Regency Hotel, and Mission Hills Country Club.

Typical Apprentice Profile
Applicants must interview; submit a formal application.

Contact
Director of Apprenticeship Program, Johnson County Community College, 12345 College Boulevard, Overland Park, KS 66210. Telephone: 913-469-8500 Ext. 3250. Fax: 913-469-2560.

Louisiana

Delgado Community College

New Orleans, Louisiana

Program Information
Approved by the American Culinary Federation. Academic requirements are met through a chef-taught curriculum and at Delgado Community College (degree available).

Placement Information
Participants are placed in 1 of 80 locations, including restaurants, hotels, hospitals, and convention centers. Most popular placement locations are Ritz-Carlton Hotel, Hilton Hotel, and Brennan's Family Restaurants.

Typical Apprentice Profile
Applicants must submit a formal application, letters of reference, ACT scores; have a high school diploma or GED.

Contact
Director of Apprenticeship Program, Delgado Community College, 615 City Park Avenue, New Orleans, LA 70119. Telephone: 504-671-6199. Fax: 504-483-4893. World Wide Web: http://www.dcc.edu/.

Michigan

ACF Blue Water Chefs Association

Clinton Township, Michigan

Program Information
Approved by the American Culinary Federation. Academic requirements are met through a chef-taught curriculum and at Macomb Community College (degree available).

Placement Information
Participants are placed in restaurants and hotels.

Typical Apprentice Profile
Applicants must interview; submit a formal application, letters of reference, and an essay.

Contact
Director of Apprenticeship Program, 44575 Garfield Road, Room K-124-1, Clinton Township, MI 48038. Telephone: 586-286-2088. Fax: 586-226-4725. World Wide Web: http://www.macomb.edu/.

ACF Michigan Chefs de Cuisine Association

Farmington Hills, Michigan

Program Information
Approved by the American Culinary Federation. Academic requirements are met through a chef-taught curriculum and at Oakland Community College (degree available).

Placement Information
Participants are placed in 1 of 60 locations, including restaurants, clubs, and hotels. Most popular placement locations are the Detroit Athletic Club, the Palace of Auburn Hills, and the Bloomfield Hills Country Club.

Typical Apprentice Profile
Applicants must interview; submit a formal application, letters of reference, and an essay.

Contact
Director of Apprenticeship Program, 27055 Orchard Lake Road, Farmington Hills, MI 48334. Telephone: 248-522-3710. Fax: 248-522-3706. World Wide Web: http://www.acfchefs.org/Content/presidents_portal/ACFChapter.cfm?ChapterChoice=MI012.

Missouri

Chefs de Cuisine of St. Louis Association

St. Louis, Missouri

Program Information
Approved by the American Culinary Federation. Academic requirements are met at St. Louis Community College at Forest Park (degree available). Special apprenticeships available in baking and pastry.

Placement Information
Participants are placed in 1 of 42 locations, including country clubs, hotels, fine dining restaurants, and casinos. Most popular placement locations are Old Warson Country Club, Westwood Country Club, and Bellerive Country Club.

Typical Apprentice Profile
Applicants must interview; submit a formal application, an essay, and letters of reference; complete one semester of studies.

Contact
Director of Apprenticeship Program, Gatesworth 1 McKnight Place, St. Louis, MO 63124. Telephone: 314-993-0111. World Wide Web: http://www.stlcc.edu/.

Columbia Missouri Chapter ACF

Columbia, Missouri

Program Information
Approved by the American Culinary Federation. Academic requirements are met through a chef-taught curriculum and at Johnson County Community College (degree available).

Placement Information
Participants are placed in 1 of 2 locations, including private clubs, hotels, and restaurants. Most popular placement locations are University Club and Capital Plaza Hotel.

Columbia Missouri Chapter ACF *(continued)*

Typical Apprentice Profile
Applicants must interview; submit a formal application and letters of reference.

Contact
Director of Apprenticeship Program, University Club of Missouri, 107 Donald W. Reynolds Alumni Center, Columbia, MO 65211. Telephone: 573-882-2433. Fax: 573-884-2063. World Wide Web: http://acfchefs.missouri.org.

Nebraska

ACF Professional Chefs and Culinarians of the Heartland

Omaha, Nebraska

Program Information
Approved by the American Culinary Federation. Academic requirements are met at Metropolitan Community College (degree available).

Placement Information
Participants are placed in 1 of 21 locations, including country clubs, hotels, restaurants, and casinos. Most popular placement locations are the Happy Hollow Country Club, Doubletree Hotel, and Ameristar.

Typical Apprentice Profile
Applicants must submit a formal application.

Contact
Director of Apprenticeship Program, PO Box 3777, Omaha, NE 68103. Telephone: 402-457-2510. Fax: 402-457-2833. World Wide Web: http://www.acfchefs.org/content/chapter/ne032.html.

Ohio

ACF Columbus Chapter

Columbus, Ohio

Program Information
Approved by the American Culinary Federation. Academic requirements are met at Columbus State Community College (degree available).

Placement Information
Participants are placed in 1 of 55 locations, including hotels, catering firms, clubs, and restaurants. Most popular placement locations are Cameron Mitchell Restaurants, all Country Clubs in the Central Ohio area, and Hyatt Regency-Hyatt on Capital Square.

Typical Apprentice Profile
Applicants must interview; submit a formal application, an essay, letters of reference, and academic transcripts.

Contact
Director of Apprenticeship Program, Columbus State Community College, 550 East Spring Street, Columbus, OH 43215. Telephone: 614-287-5061. Fax: 614-287-5973. World Wide Web: http://www.acfcolumbus.org.

Pennsylvania

ACF Laurel Highlands Chapter

Youngwood, Pennsylvania

Program Information
Approved by the American Culinary Federation. Academic requirements are met through a chef-taught curriculum and at Westmoreland County Community College (degree available). Special apprenticeships available in culinary arts and baking and pastry.

Placement Information
Participants are placed in 1 of 100 locations, including clubs, resorts, hotels, fine dining facilities, and institutional feeding sites.

Typical Apprentice Profile
Applicants must submit a formal application and take a physical exam.

Contact
Director of Apprenticeship Program, Westmoreland County Community College, Youngwood, PA 15697-1898. Telephone: 724-925-4123. Fax: 724-925-5802. World Wide Web: http://chefpertise.com/Content/presidents_portal/ACFChapter.cfm?ChapterChoice=PA021.

Bucks County Community College

Newtown, Pennsylvania

Program Information

Academic requirements are met through a chef-taught curriculum and at Bucks County Community College (degree available).

Placement Information

Participants are placed in 1 of 120 locations, including hotels, restaurants and country clubs, contract food services, extended-care facilities, and supermarkets.

Typical Apprentice Profile

Applicants must interview; submit a formal application and an essay.

Contact

Director of Apprenticeship Program, 275 Swamp Road, Newtown, PA 18940. Telephone: 215-968-8241. Fax: 215-504-8509. World Wide Web: http://www.bucks.edu/.

Wisconsin

Chefs of Milwaukee

Germantown, Wisconsin

Program Information

Approved by the American Culinary Federation. Academic requirements are met at Milwaukee Area Technical College (degree available).

Placement Information

Participants are placed in 1 of 37 locations, including restaurants, hotels/resorts, caterers, private clubs, and institutional food service. Most popular placement locations are Hilton Milwaukee City Center, Coquette Café/Sanford Restaurant, and The American Club.

Typical Apprentice Profile

Applicants must interview.

Contact

Director of Apprenticeship Program, 700 West State Street, Milwaukee, WI 53233. Telephone: 414-297-6861. Fax: 414-297-7990. World Wide Web: http://www.acfchefsofmilwaukee.com/.

INDEXES

Certificate and Diploma Programs

U.S.

Alabama

Alaska

Arizona

Arkansas

California

Colorado

Connecticut

Delaware

Florida

Nebraska

Nevada

New Hampshire

New Jersey

New Mexico

New York

North Carolina

North Dakota

Ohio

Oklahoma

Oregon

Pennsylvania

South Carolina

South Dakota

Tennessee

Texas

United Kingdom

Associate Degree Programs

U.S.

Alabama

Alaska

Arizona

Arkansas

California

Colorado

Connecticut

Delaware

Florida

Georgia

New Hampshire

New Jersey

New Mexico

New York

North Carolina

North Dakota

Ohio

Oklahoma

Oregon

Pennsylvania

Rhode Island

South Carolina

South Dakota

Tennessee

Texas

Utah

Vermont

Virginia

Washington

West Virginia

Wisconsin

Wyoming

U.S. Territory - Virgin Islands

Bachelor's Degree Programs

U.S.

Alabama

Alaska

Arizona

Arkansas

California

Colorado

Delaware

District of Columbia

Florida

Master's Degree Programs

Doctoral Degree Programs

ALPHABETICAL LISTING OF SCHOOLS AND PROGRAMS

(A) = Apprenticeship Programs (P) = Professional Programs

D

E

F

G

H

I

(A) = Apprenticeship Programs (P) = Professional Programs

J

K

L

M

(A) = *Apprenticeship Programs* (P) = *Professional Programs*

NOTES